The Last Great Frenchman

The Last Great Frenchman

A LIFE OF GENERAL DE GAULLE

Charles Williams

John Wiley & Sons, Inc.
New York • Chichester • Brisbane • Toronto • Singapore

Library of Congress Cataloging-in-Publication Data:

Williams, Charles, 1933–
    The last great Frenchman : a life of General de Gaulle / Charles
Williams.
        p.   cm.
    Includes bibliographical references and index.
    ISBN 0-471-11711-0 (alk. paper)
    1. Gaulle, Charles de, 1890-1970.   2. Presidents—France—
Biography.   3. Generals—France—Biography   4. France. Armée—
Biography.   5. Authors, French—20th century—Biography.
6. France—Politics and government—20th century.   7. France—
Foreign relations—20th century.   I. Title.
DC420.W535   1995
944.83′6′092—dc20
[B]   94-42881

Printed in the United States of America.

10 9 8 7 6 5 4 3 2 1

For Jane

CONTENTS

LIST OF ILLUSTRATIONS

To France, to Notre Dame la France,
this and this only have we to say today:
that nothing is of moment to us, nothing of concern to us,
except to serve her.
Of her we have nothing to ask, save perhaps this:
that on the Day of Deliverance
she find it in her heart to open to us a mother's arms
and let us weep there:
and on the day when death will come to take us
she shroud us in her kind and holy earth.

Charles de Gaulle
Tunis 27 June 1943

PREFACE

I suppose that, in the end, it was a sense of the romance of it, in the classical meaning of the word, that moved me to write the story of General de Gaulle. The more I looked at it, the more I felt in my imagination that the story could easily have been narrated, in an earlier time and in a different context, by a medieval balladeer: the humble origins, the early setbacks, the fiery determination to meet a great challenge, the rejection by his own kind, the passage in the wilderness and then the triumphant return to power – the whole poem shot through with a deep feeling for history and the use of language.

Be that as it may, my adventure was, I admit, presumptuous. At the latest count, some 1400 books or articles have been written about de Gaulle, analysing in scholarly detail almost every aspect of a long life. There have been many biographies, the prince of which is the fine three-volume work by Jean Lacouture. Others preceded him, and others have followed. All in all, the furrow that I was proposing to plough had already been well and truly ploughed by many, I have to confess, much better qualified than myself.

Nevertheless, the story – and in this book I treat it as such – bears repeating and elaborating. Furthermore, the 100th anniversary of de Gaulle's birth in 1990 brought an effusion of new material about the man, his origins, his upbringing, his military career and his family life, material which has not to date found its way into coherent form in a biography. We now know much more about this extraordinary and contradictory personality than we did a few years ago.

Perhaps more important, the resurgence of interest in de Gaulle, not least because of the political developments in Europe – the greater Europe – over the last few years, seemed to me to justify retelling the de

Gaulle story, particularly in English and in terms that those brought up in the whole cultural complex of the English language, or 'Anglo-Saxons' as the General would have called us, can understand.

My initial diffidence was overcome by the encouragement of a number of friends, colleagues and acquaintances whom I consulted about the project. First and foremost, Admiral Philippe de Gaulle gave me what I would describe as a friendly *nil obstat*. In turn, Michael Palliser, Roy Jenkins, Denis Greenhill, Max Beloff, Gladwyn Jebb, Nicholas Henderson and Ted Willis – if I may use for the moment their names as friends, rather than their formal titles – all added their authoritative voices to what became a chorus that, in all vanity, I found impossible to resist. I am beyond measure grateful to them, since without them, or even without their unanimity of support, I believe that my courage would have failed me.

Once embarked on the project, I found that there was a wider groundswell of enthusiasm to help which gave further encouragement. Almost everybody whom I approached, as well as those who came to me of their own accord, wanted to talk about de Gaulle. Each had his or her own de Gaulle anecdote and was only too anxious to relate it to me. In truth, some of these were apocryphal, and some simply repeated others previously heard; but I mention the fact only to show that the memory of the General, good or bad according to the experience of individuals, is still very much alive.

Inevitably, the book relies heavily on secondary sources. I have tried to list in the bibliography all those that have been useful. Nevertheless I have had the great benefit of discussion with many who knew de Gaulle personally, and I can only thank them most warmly for the time and trouble they took to help me in my work. On the British side, if I may use that expression, I am deeply indebted to Lady Soames, Lord Gladwyn, the Earl of Bessborough, Lord Sherfield (formerly Roger Makins), Baroness Warnock ('Roo' in Elisabeth de Gaulle's letters) and Neal Ascherson, who was with de Gaulle on his visit to Poland in 1967. I mention them in particular, but there were many others who helped, even by references in casual conversation. All of them have added to my perception of the General's character. On the French side, to use an expression of equivalent inaccuracy, I am particularly grateful to M. Bernard Tricot, M. Pierre Messmer and M. Pierre Lefranc for their kindness in seeing me and giving me the benefit of their personal experiences of a man they so obviously loved and honoured. There are also many French friends, dating particularly from the three and a half years I spent in Paris at the end of de Gaulle's last period in power, who will recognise their contribution – even in the smallest phrase – to the book.

Even though secondary sources may be reliable, there is still a matter of probing, interpreting and sometimes expanding the information that they report. There, too, I have had invaluable help. Professor Bernard Smith has devoured books on my behalf, with a facility to extract relevant information at what turned out to be an alarming speed. He was also the main compiler of the short biographical footnotes. Philip Bell, of the University of Liverpool, patiently read through each chapter as it appeared in draft and corrected the many errors each contained, as well as pointing me to sources of which – with his great knowledge of, and insight into, modern Franco-British relations – he was aware and which I had missed. I think that I can truly say that without them this book could not have seen the light of any reasonable day. Of all those who helped me I have to give both of them the joint ultimate accolade.

In relation to particular specialities, Lord Carver advised on tank warfare, and Lord McColl of Dulwich on certain intricacies of medicine. Christopher Wade, historian supreme of Hampstead, gave me information on the Frognal period, and George Ball was kind enough to correspond with me on the de Gaulle–Roosevelt relationship. Baroness Warnock gave me sight of the letters to her from Elisabeth de Gaulle over a number of years in the 1940s. Lord Sherfield dug into his memory and his archives to help me with his recollections of life in Algiers in 1943–44 and allowed me to quote excerpts from the letters he wrote to his wife at the time. Lady Soames was particularly helpful in her accounts of meetings with the General, from the war period right through to her life as the wife of the British ambassador to Paris in the 1960s. Seamus McConville, of *The Kerryman* in Tralee, County Kerry, produced some fascinating material on de Gaulle's stay in Ireland at the end of his life. I am grateful to all of them.

Nevertheless, libraries have been all-important, and I have everywhere received efficient and courteous help. My special thanks go to Steven Sowards, Humanities Librarian at the McCabe Library, Swarthmore College, Pennsylvania, and to Mme Françoise Lafon, Information Officer (Education) of the British Council in Paris. Thanks also to the staffs of the Bibliothèque Nationale in Paris; the Bodleian Library, Oxford; the National Library of Wales, Aberystwyth; the Hugh Owen Library, University College, Aberystwyth; and the Public Record Office at Kew.

Pride of place, however, must go to the House of Lords Library, and in particular to Isolde Victory, Anne Kelly (before she left to get married), Celia Adams and Parthenope Ward, all of whom put up uncomplainingly with the usual tantrums of an author and launched themselves into tracking down improbable sources without so much as a half-raised eyebrow. Following not far behind in honour is the Institut Charles de Gaulle in Paris, and in particular M. Bruno Leroux, always unfailingly willing and helpful.

Finally, I thank those who were asked, and willingly volunteered, for the penance of reading my final draft: Sir Michael Palliser, Lord Willis (now, alas, dead), Godfrey Hodgson and Bernard Tricot. It was a daunting task, but undertaken without hesitation, and the result of their efforts has been a very much improved final product. Martin Gilbert very kindly helped with the proofs; and Alan Samson and Helga Houghton of Little, Brown have been indefatigable in bringing the ship safely to port. In spite of all this expert help, I realise the result is far from perfect, and I hope that it goes without saying that I alone am responsible for the errors and flaws that remain.

This book is dedicated to my wife in gratitude for her support in everything I do, and in particular for her constructive criticism of my first literary endeavour. Without her love and encouragement, none of this could possibly have happened.

Pant-y-Rhiw
April 1993

Colombey

COLOMBEY

C'est ma demeure.[*]

On the morning of Sunday 14 September 1958 both men were nervous. Konrad Adenauer, Chancellor of the Federal Republic of Germany was nervous at the very idea of visiting France at all, let alone visiting the new French Prime Minister in his own home. As the convoy of three lumbering Mercedes-Benz limousines, with their four motorcycle outriders, drove through village after village – each with its own carefully tended cemetery where lay buried the French soldiers who had died at German hands – his nervousness increased. France was hostile; the new man was said to be autocratic and offensive. Perhaps, he thought, the whole project had been a bad error of judgement.

The Prime Minister of France, on the other hand, General Charles de Gaulle, was nervous for a different reason. The Germans, quite unexpectedly, were late. They had stopped by mistake at Colombey-les-Belles, and had wasted valuable time. There was nothing to be done but wait. The problem was that lunch, carefully prepared under the strict instructions of Mme de Gaulle, who had never wanted the Germans in her home in the first place, would undoubtedly be spoiled.

When they finally arrived, Adenauer's car had to manoeuvre its way carefully through the narrow gateway into the property marked 'Private'. It was followed, equally carefully, by the second car; and then the iron gates were shut against further intrusion. Guards with sub-machine-guns protected the entrance. The two cars moved slowly down the drive, and turned on the gravelled space in front of the house. De Gaulle was waiting in the doorway, just out of sight.

[*] 'It's my home.' Charles de Gaulle, *Mémoires de Guerre*, vol.3, page 288; Plon, Paris, 1959.

As Adenauer got out of his car – slowly, because he was feeling his eighty-two years – he was met by the tall figure striding out to shake him warmly with both hands, speaking volubly in German. Adenauer's ADC and interpreter were introduced and, almost before he knew what was happening, the Chancellor was ushered into the house. Such was the speed of the event that the old Adenauer missed his footing on the second step leading up to the doorway and had to put out a steadying hand to stop himself falling over.

It was not the most auspicious start for the great Franco–German post-war reconciliation. But the villagers who, on that fine morning of late summer, had come out from Mass and lined the roads in silent astonishment at seeing Germans come in peace – some with disapproval, soon walking off pointedly with their noses in the air, others staying just to stand and look, but most going quietly home to their long Sunday lunch – had all witnessed a most remarkable event. For the first and last time in his life, Charles de Gaulle had invited another statesman – and a German at that – to share the intimacy of his own, very private, home.

Colombey-les-Deux-Eglises lies in the gently undulating landscape of eastern France, not far from the meeting of the frontiers of Champagne, Burgundy and Lorraine. It is a pleasant enough village, like its neighbours in Champagne Ardenne, and indeed like a thousand others up and down the length and breadth of France. It has seen, too, its fair share of history. The main route from Paris to Basel in Switzerland passed this way, and brought with it much traffic – soldiers of fortune, businessmen and, of course, refugees. Voltaire, for instance, spent thirteen years at nearby Cirey-sur-Blaise, avoiding Louis XV's spies and whiling away the time translating Newton's *Principia Mathematica* into French. The Revolutionaries came from Paris, and burnt the Cluniac priory which had given the village its second church. Napoleon rampaged through in his hectic rearguard campaign against Blücher and Schwarzenberg just before his abdication, and the German armies twice overran the village, in 1870 and 1940. But none of these events was peculiar to Colombey; other villages had just as full a story to tell. What is Colombey's own is that in 1970 it became the holy shrine of Gaullism.

The visitor is given early warning by the sight at long distance of a gigantic Croix de Lorraine standing on the little hill above the village. It is an awesome monument, some 160 feet high, weighing 1500 tons and containing 130 cubic yards of pink granite, staring bleakly towards

Germany, as though defying a future army to invade. Down in the village, at a more homely level, there are souvenir shops, cafés, restaurants and the usual evidence of a thriving tourist trade.

None of this, however, has affected La Boisserie, the house where de Gaulle lived for over thirty years, and where he died. The atmosphere here is quite different. There is no tourist trade – no junk souvenirs, no high-flown monument. There is only a modest property, albeit with a largish garden, situated just outside the village and away from the road, with fields and woods stretching away as far as the eye can see. Built at the beginning of the nineteenth century, the house had hardly changed over the years before the de Gaulles bought it in 1933. The furnishings are sparse and without elegance. The desk where de Gaulle worked is equally simple in taste, and the main feature of his study is not rows of books or of photographs but the view out towards the valley of the river Aube. The pictures in the library which is connected directly to his study are either of ancestors or – one which he particularly favoured – an indifferent oil painting of the Revolutionary Army in full cry. The dining room is equally devoid of decoration, and the hall outside has only some African mementoes, a few assegais and a two-handed sword hung over the door. In short, it is the type of interior that would suit a military man from the provinces – no frippery or unnecessary luxury – a soldier's house, in which a soldier's wife might sit knitting as he read his books or played patience. The contrast with the official residences that he had occupied, particularly the Elysée Palace, could not possibly be more marked.

De Gaulle died at about 7.25 p.m. on 9 November 1970, a few days before his eightieth birthday. Death, when it came, was quick. At about seven o'clock he was sitting quietly in his chair in the library, having just closed the shutters against the cold November night, when he suffered a rupture of the lower aorta which led to massive bleeding into the abdominal cavity and consequent intense pain in the spinal area. The loss of blood to the brain, together with the acute pain, sent him into unconsciousness almost immediately, and by the time the doctor arrived, having left another patient's bedside to attend to the General, it was too late for anything to be done.

The funeral arrangements, at his own wish, were as simple as his house. The coffin was transported from La Boisserie to the parish church of Our Lady of the Assumption in the middle of the village by an armoured car. The ceremony was attended by his family, some old friends from the days of the Free French, and the villagers; and the body was buried in an unadorned grave in Colombey churchyard. As in life, however, so in death: there was on the same day as the modest funeral in Colombey a solemn Requiem Mass in the Cathedral of Notre-Dame in Paris, celebrated by the Cardinal Archbishop of Paris in great splendour and style. The world demanded no less.

There is no reason to believe that de Gaulle himself would have disapproved of these arrangements. He of all people understood that there had to be a certain grandeur in public life, but he insisted on privacy in his personal life. Whether he would have liked the subsequent efforts of his followers to celebrate his memory, however well intentioned they may have been, is another matter. Perhaps he would have recognised that he was, as it were, public property, and that it would have been impossible for him just to fade away like other old soldiers. Yet his name, like that of other great men, has been used to support some very dubious causes and, public property or not, he would have drawn the line at some of them. He seems to have foreseen the growth of the myth, but there is no evidence that he liked it. Apotheosis, however superficially attractive, has its disadvantages.

As the years have gone by, the potency of the myth may be starting to recede. In his life, de Gaulle inspired both great hatred and great devotion, and these two emotions need time to work themselves out. But the apparent indifference shown by the youth of today's France in 1990 to the celebrations to mark the centenary of his birth, particularly when they were confronted by an outsize replica of a 1940s wireless set in the Place de la Concorde, complete with disembodied voice intoning the 'Appel' of 18 June 1940 – is in a way encouraging. It means that it may just be possible, at long last, for those who never knew de Gaulle, or who were never directly affected by the power of his personality, to start to put into historical perspective the life and career of the man, and to leave the legend behind. If this is so, it can only be to the good, since the man himself is great enough to hold his own in history without the false support of the legend.

De Gaulle was a product of northern French provincial society of the nineteenth century: austere, Catholic, monarchist and nationalist. He himself wrote in later life that as a child nothing moved him more than the story of French misfortunes, of the weakness and the mistakes, of the surrender to the British at Fashoda, the Dreyfus affair, social conflicts and religious strife. The genteel poverty of his family excluded many careers both for the father and the sons, and out of a limited number of options the army was de Gaulle's choice. It was a choice that affected all that he did in later life, his dislike of parliamentary politics, his romantic identification with his own perception of France, his authoritarian view of government, his distrust of supra-nationality, even his frequent use of barrack-room language.

For most of his first fifty years, de Gaulle was a professional soldier. Whether he was a good soldier or a bad soldier is a matter for discussion; whether his intellectual brilliance, combined with his conviction that he was always right, made for the sort of virtues that a military leader requires, or whether the indiscipline that resulted from his individualism was compatible with the management of a modern army, are questions which are open for argument. What is beyond doubt is that, had the aeroplane carrying him to England in June 1940 crashed into the sea, his life would have been no more than a footnote in the long history of the French army. He would no doubt have been remembered as a brilliant staff officer and the source of some interesting ideas, but at forty-nine no more than a temporary brigadier-general with a career of mainly staff posts behind him and comparatively little active service.

De Gaulle's achievement in the Second World War was to rescue the dignity of France. The military contribution to the war effort of the forces under his command was peripheral: the European war would have been won in any event by the Western Allies and the Soviet Union, with or without French help, and the Far Eastern war was a matter for the United States and the British Empire. Yet, by refusing all blandishments from his compatriots to create a force that would work within the British command structure, like the Poles, the Czechs, the Dutch and the Belgians, by insisting that France was still alive and fighting in her own right, and by pursuing that course with infuriating obstinacy, he succeeded, in some measure at least, in redressing the contempt that many had felt for France after the collapse in 1940, and in restoring his country to her full post-war position as one of the world's Big Five nations.

In the last phase of his extraordinary career, from 1958 onwards, his achievement was equally striking. At the age of sixty-eight, he took on the running of France, almost certainly saved the country from civil war, gave her a constitution which has lasted longer than any since the Revolution with the exception of that of the Third Republic, and in addition assumed an international role that carried with it a prestige that would have been quite unthinkable for a French head of state in the previous decade.

Yet France after the de Gaulle era found a revived enthusiasm for the new Europe. Integration into the European Community has now passed the point of return. All de Gaulle's successors, even the Gaullists, have been men of Europe: Pompidou, Giscard d'Estaing and Mitterrand. They have accepted the logic of de Gaulle's opponents who argued, as consistently as de Gaulle argued in the opposite direction, that the only way to contain Germany in the future was to bring her into partnership under a common European superstructure. The alternative logic, the Gaullist *Europe des états*★, in which France would control Germany by superior political and diplomatic skill, was a hangover from the nineteenth century, finally shown to be mistaken by the reunification of Germany in 1990. If there is one way, the current argument goes, to ensure the domination of Europe, economic and political, by a newly resurgent Germany, especially when the process of reunification is finally complete, it is to allow her to flex her muscles in a loose association of sovereign nation-states.

De Gaulle saved France's honour in 1940, and saved France itself in 1958. Ironically, though, his legacy has been a France strong enough to be a viable partner in an integrated Europe but not strong enough to stand on its own against Germany in a more loosely constructed Europe. It might have been done had de Gaulle called in aid the one European power which instinctively shared, and probably still shares, his suspicion of supra-nationality – the United Kingdom. But the psychological footprint of Fashoda was too marked, and when he finally came round to it the accumulated bitternesses, and personal enmities, were too strong for the ground that had been lost to be made up.

In the end, de Gaulle may have lost the argument, although the embers of the nationalism which he represented are certainly far from cold. The tantalisingly close result of the referendum of September 1992 on the Maastricht Treaty and the unambiguous defeat of the pro-European Socialists in the Assembly elections of March 1993 provide ample proof of that. But there would have been no argument at all had there been no France, and there would have been no France if there had been no de Gaulle. His successors have felt and will continue to feel, with varying degrees of enthusiasm and sometimes perhaps only by the force of economic circumstance, that their home is with France in Europe. De Gaulle was in no doubt that, whatever the circumstance, his home was at Colombey, in France. There will be others who may

---

★ 'Europe of States' (de Gaulle's own expression; '*Europe des Patries*' was Michel Debré's invention).

prove to be as great and they may well be French. But it is in his single-minded devotion to his country, and in his skill and strength in its service, that Charles de Gaulle can justly be called the last great Frenchman.

PART ONE

CHILD

1

A PARISIAN BOY FROM LILLE

Mon père n'a pas eu une enfance drôle.★

Custom had it in the nineteenth century that the daughters of Lille returned to their parental home to give birth to their children, and Jeanne de Gaulle, née Maillot-Delannoy, dutifully obeyed the convention. She had, after all, done so in the cases of her first two children, a boy and a girl, and there was no reason to break the tradition in the case of the third. In any case, she was not the sort of wife or daughter who would wish to break tradition. This third, a boy, was therefore born between three and four in the morning of 22 November 1890 at his grandparents' home, a house of some, but not too much, substance in what was then a prosperous bourgeois street in old Lille.

The child was christened the following morning in the cavernous baroque church of St André, the church of the parish in which he was born. The given names were Charles André Joseph Marie, and his godparents were his aunt, Lucie Maillot, and his uncle, Gustave de Corbie, a professor at the Catholic Institute of Lille.

This family ritual completed, Jeanne and her husband, Henri, returned after a few weeks to their home in Paris. Yet for them it had not been an empty ritual. Both the de Gaulles and the Maillots had their origins in Lille, or at least in the wide plain of northern France of which Lille was the capital. Henri and Jeanne were first cousins, and the closeness of the two families and the influence of northern France were to be important elements in the upbringing of the new baby.

On the father's side, the de Gaulles were of the minor aristocracy. An ancestor had fought at Agincourt, another had been speaker of the

★ 'My father did not have an amusing childhood.' Philippe de Gaulle, in an interview with *Le Figaro, L'Actualité*, 12 April 1990.

Paris Parlement in the early eighteenth century. Yet another was caught up in the Revolution, but managed to escape the guillotine and subsequently served with some distinction in Napoleon's *Grande Armée*. Their descendants, by then settled in Paris, were generally well educated and able to occupy useful but minor posts, as clerks, civil servants, writers or secretaries at the law courts. As befits the lesser nobility, there was an undercurrent of mild and harmless eccentricity in the family. Charles's grandfather, Julien-Philippe, was a geographer, publishing in 1841 his *Histoire de Paris et ses Environs* – a book of inordinate size; his grandmother, Josephine (née Maillot), wrote romantic novels in the style, as she thought, of the English writers of the same period, as well as lengthy biographies of Chateaubriand and O'Connell. The two uncles, Charles and Jules, were specialists in their field, the one in Breton literature – the high point of his studies being a tract in Gaelic entitled *Appel aux Celtes* – the other in the study of insects, enumerating in his *Catalogue systématique et biologique* no fewer than 5000 types of hymenoptera to be found in France alone.

On the mother's side, the Maillots were more down to earth, concerned with the business side of life. Lille was a rich city, the capital of French Flanders, lying just north of a major coal basin, and it was in Lille that the Maillots had been settled for many generations. They were hard-nosed, Catholic, puritan and monarchist. They were in favour of the fleur-de-lys – the symbol of the legitimacy of France which had been destroyed by the Revolution – and, more immediately, of the instant recovery of Alsace-Lorraine, which France had lost under the settlement at the end of the Franco-Prussian war in 1871; and recovery, too, by the intervention of the glorious French army. As is often the way, the fact that the glorious French army no longer existed, if indeed it ever had since 1815, or the fact that the Roman Catholic church in France was dissolute and venal, did not affect the Maillot beliefs; indeed, if the facts themselves were admitted, which on the whole they were not, they were disregarded as some form of left-wing propaganda.

Henri de Gaulle was in many ways what would now be called an unsatisfactory character, and he quite clearly felt it. His effort to establish the genealogy of his family, to prove his ancestry, is not the work of a man confident in himself. He had fought in the 1870 war and had wanted to continue a military career, but he was too poor and was forced to become a teacher. A pupil of the Jesuits, he was deeply, perhaps neurotically, Catholic, a fervent monarchist, 'out of his time',[1] as he himself put it, and intensely patriotic.

As a teacher, Henri tended to deliver lectures to a silent audience rather than elicit comment from his students. He stood on a rostrum in front of his class, a white wall and a solitary crucifix behind him, to expound what he believed to be the ultimate truths. He spoke of France, of her history and destiny, of the monarchy. 'I am a legitimist',[2] he used to declare, striding up and down, his hands crossed behind the tails of his frock-coat. From time to time, he would take out a small white handkerchief and clean his steel-rimmed pince-nez, which he then used to gesticulate to his audience in support of the point that he was making.

His lectures were far from the impartial assessments familiar to modern teachers. The revolution of 1789 was condemned outright, as was 1848 and the whole Orléans dynasty. Napoleon was a 'usurper', Louis Napoleon 'a new Caesar' whose Empire had started the process which had led to social disorder: 'You can see proof of it every day.' Universal suffrage was a disaster, giving the same weight to votes of 'charwomen' as it did to the votes of the élite. The defeat of 1870 at the hands of the Prussian army obsessed him, and he was reassured by only one hope: that a restored king would save France.

Even by the standards of the day this was heady stuff. But Henri's views were to be reinforced by the launch, in 1898, of *Action Française*, a creation of the young Charles Maurras, which stood for all the values that Henri de Gaulle had espoused: order, tradition, the monarchy, Catholicism and patriotism. Those views were to maintain a powerful influence for nearly half a century – not least, apart from devotion to the monarchy, on the future General de Gaulle. It was this Henri – deeply introspective, fanatical for France, a failed soldier – who, at the age of nearly forty, had sought in marriage, and won, the hand of his first cousin, Jeanne Maillot.

Jeanne held similar views to her new husband, but was altogether a much tougher character. Physically small, but with attractive dark eyes, she was a serious girl whose only concession to diversion was sketching. As a wife, she continually reproached her husband for being too complimentary to people. 'How could you say such nice things about such an ugly baby?'[3] she said to him when he was miserably trying to be kind to some fond mother. She was equally fierce towards the outside world. There was to be no dancing in her home, and the theatre was the invention of the devil – views which she had inherited from her own mother in Lille. When a friend congratulated her on the success of her four sons, while they were still at school, she replied that they caused her much anguish. Asked why, she said with a heavy sigh: 'They are republicans.'[4]

Henri and Jeanne de Gaulle had five children: Xavier, born in 1887, Marie-Agnès in 1889, Charles in 1890, Jacques in 1893 and Pierre in 1897. As the children grew they learnt to look to their parents as models. But the family life of the de Gaulles was, by present-day standards, and arguably by any standards, somewhat bizarre. At meals, after grace, there were short extempore speeches in Latin, the theme being that day's soup. There were weekly visits to the Invalides, to meditate at the tomb of 'the usurper' Napoleon, or to the Arc de Triomphe. Sometimes they went to Stains, where Henri had been wounded in a sortie from the besieged Paris in 1871. There were endless readings in the evening from Rostand or Seneca, or some other improving author. Nor were the children allowed by their mother to forget their Lille inheritance. Instead of receiving their presents at Christmas, like any ordinary Parisian child, the young de Gaulles would receive theirs on 6 December, the feast of St Nicolas. It had always been so in Lille, and so it was in the de Gaulle household in Paris. If that made for an uncomfortable Christmas for the children, so be it.

There were also intense discussions of contemporary political events, and the children were treated to lectures from their father on the dreadful significance of these, not least on the evidence they provided of the continuing and accelerating decadence of France. The two most memorable events of this nature in Charles's childhood were the Franco-British confrontation at Fashoda in the Sudan and what came to be known as the Dreyfus affair. Such was the emotion that both topics aroused in the de Gaulle household that the impression of them, and the lessons supposedly to be drawn from them, remained with the child for the rest of his life.

The facts of the incident at Fashoda are reasonably straightforward. In the scramble for African colonies at the end of the nineteenth century, France and Britain disputed much of the territory of north and central Africa. As might be imagined, the dispute was fragmented and confused, but in the end the French established a hold over large tracts of west Africa, while the British concentrated on Egypt and the Sudan. This state of affairs had been more or less formalised in the Anglo-French agreement of August 1890 which defined the different countries' 'spheres of influence'. Agreements of this nature, however, had limited value on either side in those buccaneering days, and it was not long before this one broke down.

By the end of 1895, the French Government had endorsed a plan, put forward by a certain Commandant Jean-Baptiste Marchand, to mount an expedition to cross Africa from the Congo to the Nile – in order, it was said, to allow France the right to participate in any future conference on 'spheres of influence' in the Sudan and the territory of the Upper Nile. It was to be an expedition of 'civilians', ready to make sensible arrangements with any native tribes they encountered – in particular with the Mahdists, a fanatical group whose main achievement had been to overcome in 1885 a British force in Khartoum and to kill, in what the British regarded as particularly outrageous fashion, its leader General Gordon.

In reality, Marchand had designed his expedition, with the connivance of officials in the French ministry of colonies, to occupy a key point on the White Nile, with the objective of placing a barrier between the British in Egypt and the British further south in Uganda. A French presence there would ensure that the British project of a rail link between the south and the north, and consequent dominance over the eastern side of the continent, could not succeed.

It was the British decision in January 1896 to instruct the commanding general, Herbert Kitchener, to advance from Egypt across the frontier up the Nile and into the Sudan that prompted Paris to give the final approval for Marchand's expedition to assume openly its true military character. At the same time, two further French expeditions were put in train from the French settlements on the Red Sea in the east, to meet up with Marchand coming across Africa from the west. The meeting point was to be on the White Nile, some 700 miles south of Khartoum, where the river finally turns northwards after being joined by its tributaries, the Sobat from the east and the Bahr al-Ghazal from the west. It can hardly be said that the point held much attraction in itself: there was a ruined Egyptian fort, a few mud huts, some palm trees and armies of mosquitoes – not to mention fleets of crocodiles waiting for anyone unfortunate enough to fall into the river. But there it was; and the name of the little settlement, if indeed it can even be called a settlement, was Fashoda.

Marchand took two years to complete his journey. At first, the going had been relatively easy. He had started, with a handful of French officers and some 200 Senegalese troops and boatmen, up the Congo river to the point where the river turned south. He then had to confront the traverse of 300 miles of watershed between the Congo and the Nile. From then on, the going became much rougher. It was not just a question of crossing the unexplored bush, or of placating the Yakoma or Karari tribes that stood in his way, or even of resisting the elephant charges that came suddenly and terrifyingly out of the tall grass. Marchand had set himself another problem. At the outset, he had commandeered an eighty-foot postal steam launch, to give him the big naval support he thought he would need when he reached the Nile.

The *Faidherbe*, as the launch was renamed – after the French general who had led 200,000 French troops to destroy an Algerian revolt in the 1840s and had gone on to enforce French rule in Senegal in the 1850s and 1860s – was not made for such a journey. To go overland, she had to be taken to bits, piece by piece, and carried on the backs of slave porters. Her brass boilers could not be carried, but were dragged – for 300 miles across the bush. The boat was then reassembled, astonishingly without a piece missing and ready to sail.

Marchand had to wait for six months on the Nile side of the watershed, waiting for the rains which would allow him to move down towards the great river itself. By June 1898 they had come in sufficient quantity for his light boats to move, although there was not enough water for the reconstituted *Faidherbe*, which had to wait behind for deeper water. With great courage and endurance, the depleted force managed to struggle through the swamp that separated them from the Bahr al-Ghazal, join the White Nile and arrive at Fashoda on 10 July. The Tricolor was formally raised – although in the excitement the rope broke and the whole ceremony had to be started again. Bottles of champagne, which had apparently survived the dreadful journey, were broken open. It was a famous moment for France.

No sooner had the ceremony been performed than the French had to face a challenge from the Mahdists, who arrived on 25 August with two gunboats captured from Gordon thirteen years earlier at Khartoum. The attack was repulsed, and the gunboats severely damaged – not without Dr Emily, the anglophile French doctor to the Marchand expedition, remarking that General Gordon would have been surprised to learn that it had been the French who had avenged his defeat.

The Mahdists obviously intended to return and this time to settle the matter. But the next visitors were in fact British. After the battle of Omdurman, and with Khartoum recovered, Kitchener had been ordered to move up the Upper Nile and ensure that British claims were absolute. So it was that Kitchener sailed southwards with five gunboats and a small infantry contingent – and on 17 September arrived at Fashoda.

The negotiations that followed between Kitchener and Marchand were delicate in the extreme. Letters were exchanged – written in French. Marchand visited Kitchener on his flagship, the *Dal*, and was entertained with whisky and soda. Kitchener had also brought the latest French newspapers. Later in the day, the hospitality was returned by Marchand with champagne. There was a good deal of convivial discussion about how many Africans each had killed.

The upshot of the talks was that the matter would have to be referred to Paris and London for resolution. In passing, Marchand's soldiers told the British of their relief when they had seen that the five gunboats were British rather than Mahdist. With the irony of history, it had been the French who had avenged Gordon's defeat at Khartoum and the British who had protected Marchand's force at Fashoda from what would have been a brutal destruction at the hands of the Mahdists.

When the request for instructions reached Paris, it was soon clear that there was only one thing to do. Reinforcements were out of the question, and military defeat was certain, if only through the force of numbers. The Government in Paris instructed Marchand to retreat, and so he did. There was uproar in the French press, and talk of general mobilisation against England. In the end, wiser counsels prevailed, but the temperature remained high and the talk, not least in the de Gaulle household, was feverish. Thus did the name of Fashoda print itself on the young Charles's mind as a supreme example at one and the same time of French political impotence and of deep British treachery.

The French Government's impotence over Fashoda, or realism as it might more properly be called, was all the more understandable in that they were embroiled in another affair, this time on their own doorstep. The two weeks prior to Marchand's request for orders had seen riots on the streets of Paris, a strike of some 20,000 building workers and no fewer than 60,000 soldiers camped in the streets. The cause had been renewed agitation over the fate of one Captain Dreyfus; indeed, it was on the day after instructions had been given to Marchand to retreat from Fashoda that the French cabinet agreed to reopen the Dreyfus case.

The Dreyfus affair had started some four years earlier. In September 1894 a list of French military documents had been collected by a minor French agent doing daily duty emptying the wastepaper basket in the German embassy in Paris. The counter-espionage service of the army, operating as it did under the strange title of the 'Statistical Section', mounted an inquiry, and quickly arrived at the conclusion, on the slenderest evidence conceivable, that a traitor was operating in the French War Office, specifically Captain Alfred Dreyfus, a Jew from Alsace who had taken French nationality after his homeland had been annexed by the Germans in the 1871 settlement.

Dreyfus was tried in a secret court-martial, found guilty and, because he failed to do the honourable thing and commit suicide, was sentenced, after a humiliating public ceremony at which his sword was broken and his officer's insignia were torn off his uniform, to solitary confinement on the French penal settlement of Devil's Island off the coast of French Guiana. There the unfortunate man remained for the next four years.

There the matter rested, and might have rested for ever but for the persistence of Dreyfus's family and the intervention of the novelist Emile Zola, who in January 1898 published an open letter to the president of the republic – the now famous *J'accuse* – in which he claimed that the War Office had been guilty of a judicial crime. Uproar followed. The Catholic establishment, which included the officer corps but whose mouthpiece was the Archbishop of Paris, formed what became known as the Laborum League. The question, it was said, was not whether a wretched individual was guilty or innocent, it was whether the Jews and the Protestants were, or were not, the masters of the country. On the other side, the anti-clericals, the Protestants, intellectuals and most of the press fulminated in the Dreyfusard cause. They formed the League for the Defence of the Rights of Man, countered by the Catholics with the formation of the Ligue de la Patrie Française. Tracts were written and demonstrations held. The most influential of the anti-Dreyfusard writers, Maurice Barrès,★ managed to convey the impression that what was at stake was the integrity of the nation. In the midst of all this political confusion, the general staff, backed by the War Ministry, had only one objective: to protect the army from what they saw as a slur on its honour and the consequent danger to national security. To that purpose, further forged evidence was produced to demonstrate Dreyfus's guilt.

By the autumn of 1898 the affair was the central topic of conversation in almost every household, at least in Paris, and of hot disagreement

---

★ Maurice Barrès (1862–1923): Writer and politician. Uncompromisingly right-wing and anti-semitic, the intellectual mentor of the pre-1914 Nationalist movement; Deputy for Nancy, then for Paris up to 1914; brash but effective oratorical style.

within families, at times to the point of violence. The de Gaulle household was no exception. Henri himself, contrary to the current views of
his church, was a convinced supporter of Dreyfus's innocence; Jeanne's
opinion, perhaps wisely, is not recorded. But, whatever the outcome of
those discussions, the affair, and the revelation of fierce internal conflicts
within France, remained in the memory of the young de Gaulle, and
found its place, like Fashoda, on the first page of his later memoirs.

If the atmosphere in the Parisian home was highly charged, holidays
were rather easier. The family usually went to the seaside, to a villa rented by grandmother Maillot at Wimille near Wimereux, two or three
miles inland and within easy distance of Boulogne-sur-Mer, where she
kept open house for the de Gaulles and their Maillot cousins. The
regime was somewhat freer there, not least because grandparents were
there to spoil their grandchildren. There was croquet and tug-of-war,
and other games with brothers and cousins. Alternatively, and more frequently as adolescence approached, there were country holidays at La
Ligerie, a property near Bergerac in the Lower Dordogne that Henri de
Gaulle had bought for a small sum shortly before 1900. The house was
of a good size, and was able to accommodate the family, without, apparently, being able to contain the horde of cousins from the north. It was
for that reason, perhaps, a wise purchase, but if nothing else it took the
de Gaulle children away from the harshness of the north and showed
them the gentler, wider, more fertile France.

Even in the wider France, the family kept themselves to themselves.
The truth is that the de Gaulle family lived in its own world, the world
of the de Gaulles and the Maillots, the world of a large and bourgeois
family in northern France. That was the sum of the universe in which
the young Charles grew up. And yet it was not for lack of opportunity
that they failed to participate in a wider world. The Paris of the day was
sparkling with glamour and wit. If survival is a test of political success in
France, the Third Republic had passed that test. By 1914, it had out-
lived all previous regimes since 1789, and even in 1993 still held the
record for longevity. Culturally, it was the world described by its most
famous son, Marcel Proust; the social scene glittered in the Faubourg St
Germain, led by the real-life equivalents of the Duchesse de
Guermantes; painting was enriched by the real-life Elstirs – Manet,
Monet, Pissarro, Sisley, and many others; music by the real-life Vinteuils
– Debussy, Fauré, Dukas and Ravel; history was being written by Taine
and Renan, and Sarah Bernhardt dominated the stage.

None of this touched the de Gaulles. Apart from one visit to the theatre with his father – as a treat for his tenth birthday – to see Bernhardt in Rostand's *L'Aiglon*, Charles de Gaulle was subjected to an upbringing which, given the variety of the Paris of the day, was severely limited. Above all, it was dominated by the discipline of northern Catholicism.

Against all the intricacies of his family background, it is not easy to disentangle the real effect of the different strands that made up his childhood on the complex adult that de Gaulle became. There are, of course, the stories, the anecdotes that with the hindsight of history showed miraculous powers, exceptional prowess or uncannily predictive behaviour, and these can be easily discounted. On a realistic view, he competed, as any second son is bound to, for the attention of his mother; he is said by his sister to have been an unruly child who only accepted the authority of his father. As for his brothers, they were in the future hardly to be mentioned other than as tangential to his own childhood; and de Gaulle himself, writing more than fifty years later, was certainly more concerned with his mystical relationship with France – with Fashoda and the Dreyfus affair – than he was with mundane family relationships, apart from one.

A few days before his death, de Gaulle confided to his elder sister, Marie-Agnès: 'What has often reassured me . . . is the conviction that Mama would have been behind me always and in everything.'[5] Therein perhaps lies a clue to the secret of the personality of the adult de Gaulle.

2

THE STEPS OF ST IGNATIUS

Praeceptorem tuum amabis et observabis ut parentem. *

Given the unrelenting piety of the de Gaulle parents, it is little wonder that the children's schooling carried a heavy and rather lugubrious religious bias. French schools at the turn of the century were not in any event centres of frivolity, any more than were British schools of the same period. Discipline was often harsh and learning by rote. But there is no doubt that the education in church schools, particularly those of the Jesuits, was among the best to be had; and the best was what Mme de Gaulle, at least, wanted for her second son.

Charles's first school, which he joined in October 1895, when not quite five years old, was run by a relatively obscure religious order called the Brothers of the Christian Schools of St Thomas Aquinas. A lay, male order, it was founded by one Jean de la Salle, originally for working-class children. He laid down that his teachers should receive no gifts from parents or pupils, and that all children were to be treated equally, regardless of ability or personal qualities. Members of the order wore habits with four sleeves – hence their nickname 'Four Arms' – but little is known about the curriculum they practised or their teaching method, although it would be fair to assume that neither was particularly sophisticated.

No record of de Gaulle's activities, scholastic or otherwise, survives from the five years he spent at his first school. He achieved enough, however, to follow his cleverer elder brother, Xavier, as a pupil at the great Jesuit College of the Immaculate Conception in the rue de

---

* 'You shall love and obey your teacher as a parent.' From the rules pertaining to Jesuit students in the *Ratio Studiorum* of 1599. Allan Farrell, *The Jesuit Code of Liberal Education*; Bruce Publishing, Milwaukee, 1938.

Vaugirard. The de Gaulles had by then settled at the rue de Staël, just around the corner, and since, at the age of nearly ten, it was time for Charles to start learning Latin in a serious manner, Vaugirard must have seemed the obvious place.

Jesuit education has had, and still has, an aura of somewhat sinister controversy. By the end of the nineteenth century, that controversy had not abated at all. The Jesuits themselves were regarded with deepest hostility by the anti-clerical governments of the Third Republic. They were held, with some truth, to owe their allegiance not just to the Pope in Rome, which was bad enough, but – much, much worse – to the cause of the restoration of the French monarchy. The consequence was continued official attack, culminating in the attempted suppression of the Jesuit schools by law in 1880 and the final restriction on church ownership of property in the 1905 Law of Separation. It was no wonder that the Jesuits responded defensively and suspiciously, and this siege mentality communicated itself to their pupils.

In the late 1870s Vaugirard was the largest Jesuit college in France, with no fewer than 681 pupils, 552 of them boarders and 129 dayboys, and 42 Jesuit fathers to teach them. In 1880 it had only escaped extinction by a ruse. The education laws of the anti-clerical minister Jules Ferry provided not just generally for secularisation of the educational system but specifically for the prohibition on anyone belonging to a 'non-authorised religious congregation' from teaching at all. The prohibition was aimed directly at the Jesuits. In the event, after much public outcry, the Senate narrowly rejected the specific prohibition, but the Government replied robustly with a decree dissolving the Jesuit order in France, citing as authority pre-revolutionary edicts and two revolutionary laws of 1790 and 1792.

It was a shabby enough manoeuvre, which received the response it deserved. More than 400 magistrates resigned rather than enforce the decrees, and a further protest was made by nearly 2000 lawyers. The police were sent in by the Government to break down the doors of Jesuit residences, while the Society turned its collective mind to how it could maintain its educational function while remaining within the letter of the law. The response at Vaugirard was typical of the Society's ingenuity: the decree had not expropriated property, and Vaugirard was able to turn itself into a private company with trust status and a sympathetic layman as president. A further company was set up to lease the college property and to run it at a profit; all the directors of that company were equally sympathetic laymen. A superior was found, one

Monsignor de Forges, a former auxiliary bishop of Rennes, and Jesuit priests were engaged individually by the new company as principal, assistant principal and teachers. It was, so to speak, business as usual.

By the time the young Charles de Gaulle arrived, in October 1900, these harrowing events were in the past, but the memory of them was very much alive, and Vaugirard had only seven more years of existence before the same forces of political anti-clericalism were to finish it for ever. Yet the Society of Jesus made no apparent effort to compromise with the opposition. It owed allegiance to the Pope, as it had ever since its foundation at the height of the counter-reformation, and to the universal Catholic church. Compromise was therefore out of the question. As for modernisation, this too was subject to the overriding objective of preparing pupils to become devout followers of Christ according to the teaching of the Holy See. For instance, when a group of businessmen proposed a commercial course in the college at Bordeaux, it was turned down flat on the grounds that it was 'not in accord with our teaching apostolate'.[1] Nevertheless, and within these constraints, there is little doubt that Jesuit education was at least equal to the best available in France at the time.

The curriculum in the Jesuit colleges of those days reflects the traditional attitudes. Admittedly, there had been a revision of the *Ratio Studiorum* in 1832, and pupils were no longer required to converse with their teachers in Latin, but the basic subjects had not changed to any great degree: Latin, Greek, French, bible and church history, French history, geography and arithmetic. The day started at 8 a.m., with recitation for half an hour from memory and continued with instruction on the various basic subjects through the morning until the break at 10.30 a.m. (for a quarter of an hour). Then there was study and written assignments, lunch at midday (during which an edifying book was read while pupils munched in silence), more written assignments and correction of them in public and more recitation, perhaps of the rules of Greek grammar or of some vernacular author. This was followed by more study of the basic subjects until the rosary at 4.30 p.m. and spiritual reading until supper at 7.15. All in all, it was a very hard day.

On first arrival, at the age of ten, de Gaulle would have concentrated on obtaining a perfect knowledge of the rudiments of Latin grammar and the beginnings of Greek. Two years on, he would have been expected to know the whole of Latin grammar, and to be able to recite passages of Cicero, Caesar and Quintus Curtius, as well as the easier of Ovid's poems, Aesop and selected and expurgated works of Lucian. By

the age of fourteen, he would have had as his target a complete knowledge of Latin idiom, and be reading Sallust, Livy and Virgil. In Greek,
he would have been studying Xenophon, St John Chrysostom, Plutarch
and, especially, St Basil's treatise *On the reading of pagan authors*. Side by
side, he would have been taking the course in rhetoric, the object of
which was to train pupils to 'perfect eloquence'; Cicero, Demosthenes
and St John Chrysostom were the models. Then there was history,
with stress on Joan of Arc and the mission of France. Finally there was
philosophy and the catechism, to which everything else was ultimately
directed.

It had to be so, and so it was. Religion, after all, held pride of place
and all other studies were seen as just one facet of the only one that really mattered. An encyclical letter of 1860 was clear on the matter: Jesuit
colleges existed 'to make of the young men confided to us Christians as
to their religious duties and solidly grounded in the practice of virtue,
to make of them men deeply instructed and capable of filling with distinction the positions to which they are destined'.[2] There was therefore
daily attendance at Mass, a daily rosary and periods of prayer in the
morning and afternoon. There was a formal retreat of three or four days
at the beginning of each academic year. The formula, prescribed by St
Ignatius, consisted of meditations on the Creation and the Last
Judgement, on sin and death and hell, on penitence and damnation – all
in the lurid colours of the Spanish counter-reformation.

Furthermore, there was a special characteristic in the piety of Jesuit
colleges that did not apply to other Roman Catholic establishments. St
Ignatius had been a soldier-saint, and the role of the Society as the
'Militia of the Pope' was impressed on the young pupils of the colleges.
In at least one college of the period, students were given military ranks,
and their graduation from one rank to another depended not simply on
their conduct in the classroom but on the nature, content and enthusiasm of their prayers and sacrifices offered in support of the Holy Father
in his struggles to maintain the purity of the faith.

The first high point of a pupil's spiritual career was his acceptance as
a full participating member of the universal and apostolic church: his
first Communion. For Charles de Gaulle the great day was 16 May
1901. May was the customary month for first Communions in Jesuit
colleges, and Charles, along with some thirty of his schoolfellows,
would have followed special catechism courses for the previous six
months to prepare him for the event. When the day came there was a
Mass of particular solemnity, to which his parents, brothers and sister,

aunts and uncles were all invited. In later life that day seemed to de Gaulle to mark the end of his childhood.

Charles's life at Vaugirard was complicated by the presence of his father on the teaching staff. There is a revealing photograph, taken in 1906, of the rhetoric class in Latin and Greek. Sixteen-year-old Charles, already sporting a watchchain looped through the correct buttonhole in his waistcoat and a handkerchief in his top jacket pocket, stands in attempted insouciance with his left hand resting on the back of a chair in the front row; and Henri, his father, tightly buttoned up in a black frock coat, his hair close-cropped, his moustache emphasising the unsmiling mouth, sits in the middle of the front row staring straight in front of him. It was a situation, as Charles's son was later to remark, that was not appreciated with enthusiasm.

The situation, such as it was, must have been made the more difficult by the disciplinary regime of the college. The Jesuits of the day were, as might be expected, suspicious of what they regarded as the lax moral attitudes of the time. Paris was obviously a prime target for their displeasure. Their answer was not simply to rely on the uncertain benefits of a life of prayer, the results of which might not be evident until the pupil arrived in the next world, but to supplement these by the more visible results that came from imposing an exacting discipline. A whole series of punishments were imposed on pupils guilty of minor infractions of the rules: they could be required to stand in one place, kneel at the foot of their beds or miss one dish at a meal. More serious transgressions were punished by requiring the pupil to kneel in public or to fast for a full day.

Nevertheless, there was a degree of humanity in these punishments which was missing from contemporary educational establishments in Britain. Corporal punishment was not permitted under any circumstances; even touching a pupil was prohibited. Where pupils were made to kneel, it was a rule that this should never be for more than fifteen minutes. The object was to demonstrate to the transgressor that his sin had been noted but that there was always the possibility of redemption for the sinner. Punishment was never inflicted as a cover for official sadism.

Life was not all drudgery. Every day, there was a period reserved for organised games. These games were devised by the priest known as the *surveillant*, or overseer, and were designed to occupy the maximum number of pupils in a type of physical exercise that would also improve their spiritual life. There were races, tugs-of-war, volleyball, skating and a curious kind of football played on stilts. The games could become quite rough, to the point where on one recorded occasion, though not at Vaugirard, a nervous visiting officer of the French army, watching his son playing one of these games, had to be reproved by one of the fathers: 'General, we are not raising little girls.'[3]

Then there were the theatrical productions. These had started in the colleges as simple declamations on improving themes, but they gradually became more elaborate – so much so that the Society's attitude to them became somewhat ambiguous. The themes had not changed: tragedy, religious and historical subjects were still predominant. What was worrying was the tendency of those involved in productions to concentrate on entertainment rather than instruction. At Vaugirard, this tendency is illustrated by a production in 1903 of an historical drama, no doubt written, as was the custom in the colleges, by a Jesuit father, in which de Gaulle played a starring role as the king of France. The costumes were finely made, the banner of the fleur-de-lys proudly displayed, the attitudes of the actors struck with haughty disdain. There is no sense of gravity in this event; it is a straightforward exhibition of exuberance in a setting of adolescent fantasy. It is hardly surprising that the fathers, while always wishing to encourage their young charges, felt that such productions were on the outer edge of what could be regarded as religiously respectable.

The future General's scholastic record was at first by no means impressive. He was rather lazy and, according to his father, lacked good sense. It was only when he was berated by Henri and after he had decided, in 1905, on a military career, that Charles applied his undoubted intelligence to his studies at school. As a result he won six first prizes in July 1906, among them French composition, mathematics, history and geography.

Vaugirard was closed down at the end of the 1906 academic year. The fall-out from the Dreyfus affair brought a new government and another piece of legislation on Church–state relations: the Law of Separation, finally passed in December 1905, which effectively removed the state from the responsibilities it had assumed under the Napoleonic Concordat. In particular, religious bodies were to be allowed to keep their property only on condition that they formed recognised associations to do so. Rome was outraged, and the result of the subsequent bad-tempered exchange between the Vatican and the French Government was, *inter alia*, the closure of Vaugirard.

For the last period of his studies before starting the year required to learn the subjects set in the examination for entry into St Cyr, Charles de Gaulle was sent to the Jesuit college of the Sacred Heart at Antoing, in Belgium, close to the French frontier. The curriculum, language and discipline were the same; only the sport was better, and the future General distinguished himself as an aggressive full-back in the Antoing first team. But the point was that Antoing was in Belgium. Instead of accepting a legitimate political decision, Henri de Gaulle and his son had preferred to look outside France for the remaining year of Charles's formal education. Rome was stronger than Paris.

Once he had made the decision to make a career in the army, the pattern of the young de Gaulle's education settled down. He had to study history, natural history and above all, German. There were extra classes on Wednesdays and Sundays, at which pupils who enrolled were required to recite in German, without recourse to a dictionary, the fables of La Fontaine. Charles attended these without fail. But he spent a summer holiday – apparently by himself – first at Rieden, near Baden-Baden, and then wandering in the Black Forest, practising his German on anybody he happened to meet and noting the names on the memorials to the German dead in the Franco-Prussian war of 1870.

The return to Paris in October 1908 was to a lay college, the Stanislas College in the rue Notre-Dame-des-Champs. By now, the objective was clear: to win entry to St Cyr. Again, the academic record was spotty, and was better in class than in examination. But in the end Charles de Gaulle was good enough to come 119th out of 221 in the entrance examination to St Cyr; mediocre, but just enough. On the threshold of adulthood, he had achieved the first object of his ambition. It was not to be the Church, which he had earlier toyed with, but the French army. But times were far from trouble-free, and the army he had chosen to join was as much given to self-doubt as was the Third Republic itself.

PART TWO

SOLDIER

1

THE ARMY OF THE REPUBLIC

*Mon premier colonel, Pétain, me démontra ce que valent le don et l'art
de commander.*★

The Third Republic, which rose from the ashes of the Franco-Prussian
war of 1870 and the consequent collapse of the Second Empire, had
been remarkably successful. Economic recovery had been swift, and
although national morale had suffered a devastating blow the political
system had generally held together. In large measure this was due to the
army of the time. It was, as it were, the great common denominator in
a divided country, and consequently reaped a reward in terms of its popularity. Whoever else was blamed for the fiasco of 1870 – Louis
Napoleon for interfering too much, the high command for incompetence, the Government for frivolity – nobody blamed the army.

Indeed, by its stand for established order against the *communards* of
Paris in 1871, the army had emerged with enhanced prestige. The
politicians of the new republic allowed it greater autonomy within the
secular state. The officer corps of the Second Empire was retained,
conscription was introduced and new weaponry brought into service.
The number of candidates for the officer corps, and the intellectual level
of the graduates, improved markedly; and military expenditure was
substantially increased.

Nevertheless, the relationship between army and republic was a continuing source of difficulty throughout the whole period up to 1914. As
time went by, and the republic became less self-confident, the army
became more assertive; and the republic in turn became more suspicious. On the one hand, politicians believed that they had democratised
the army by the introduction of conscription; on the other, they were

★ 'My first colonel, Pétain, showed me the worth of the gift and the art of command.'
Charles de Gaulle, *Mémoires de Guerre*, vol.1, page 2; Plon, Paris, 1959.

continually wary of the officer corps, which was suspected of monarchist tendencies and a willingness to use its political and social power to wield authority as a state within a state.

By the 1890s the revanchist patriotism, and the determination to recover Alsace-Lorraine, that had followed the 1870 defeat had started to decline, at least in Parisian society and among intellectuals. 'Personally,' commented one writer, 'I would not give the little finger of my left hand in exchange for those forgotten lands. I need it to shake the ash off my cigarette.'[1] It was perhaps the most extreme and cutting statement of the anti-war view, but it found an echo in popular opinion. Even in the army morale was low. The officers themselves were trapped by the familiar problems of a peacetime military force: boredom, slow promotion, low motivation. A series of anti-militarist novels appeared in the late 1880s and early 1890s, and the sudden arrival of forty-three socialists in the Assembly after the 1893 elections introduced a loud pacifist and internationalist voice into its deliberations. The army was accused of being aristocratic and Jesuit-dominated, ready to overthrow the republic on the smallest pretext.

It was therefore small wonder that after 1890 the quality of those choosing the army as a career started to decline, and after 1900 both the quality and the quantity of officer candidates fell drastically. It took the purge of the high command by Marshal Joffre in 1914 to reveal how bad they really were. Yet although the army may have been declining in quality by the turn of the century, there is no evidence that it was deeply anti-republican. In fact, if anything it became less anti-republican as the years went by and 1871 became a memory of a previous generation. The truth was that the army maintained the old tradition that it had held on to before, and again after, the Napoleonic era, that of disciplined service to any regime, however unattractive, that was capable of giving coherent orders.

The Dreyfus affair, with its strident anti-semitism and the suggestion of a protective conspiracy in the high command, raised again, in acute form, the problem of the relations between the army and the republic. Indeed, at one point in late 1898 it looked in Paris as though the country might be slipping perilously towards civil war. That this was avoided was not due to the weakness of the passions aroused, but to the indifference of most of France outside Paris to the political impact of the affair. In the past, major conflagrations in France had resulted from a combination of Parisian political emotion and provincial administrative dissatisfaction. This had been true of 1789, 1830 and 1848. At the end of the nineteenth century, however, France was generally well run and reasonably prosperous. There was no reason for the provinces to complain – at least not to the point of revolution.

Nevertheless, the affair had considerable political fall-out. The climax came in June 1899, soon after an appeal court in Rennes had heard the case again and, after listening to senior army officers quite clearly perjuring themselves for the army's honour, had sentenced the unfortunate Captain Dreyfus to a further ten years' detention. At the spring meeting at Auteuil, a racecourse on the edge of Paris, a young royalist baron approached the President of the Republic and knocked off his hat with a sweep of his cane. This was, as all admitted, going too far. The coalition of the moderate right that had run France for most of the decade collapsed, to be replaced by a left-leaning coalition under a new Prime Minister. A new Cabinet was formed on an platform of military reform and anti-clericalism, the latter now reinforced by secular revulsion against the Catholic Church's appeal to violence and anti-semitism almost throughout the whole unpleasant crisis.

By the early 1900s the affair, as a political event, was receding into the background, although Captain Dreyfus himself, having been brought back, a broken man whose hair had turned prematurely white and whose skin was wrinkled and grey, had to wait for a Presidential pardon before he was free; and for a subsequent hearing in the appeal court in 1906, seven years after the Rennes verdict, for an official admission that the whole thing had been a most regrettable miscarriage of justice.

The affair had destroyed a Government and changed the political complexion of France. The Radicals were in the ascendant again and there was even a Socialist in the new Cabinet. By the time new elections were held, in May 1902, the Government had consolidated its position and secured a substantial majority in the Assembly, albeit with only a small plurality in the popular vote. Reinforced by its new majority, the Government introduced not only the Law of Separation, which effectively forced the closure of Vaugirard, but also the requirement that entrants to the officer corps should spend a year in the ranks. The campaign to reassert political supremacy over the Church and the army had begun in earnest.

This was the climate in which the future General de Gaulle joined the army; but little of it seemed to have registered with the new recruit. When he joined the army, he was to say, it was one of the greatest things in the world. Beneath the criticisms and the insults that had been heaped on it, the army was, he said, 'feeling with serenity and even silent hope the approach of the days when everything would depend on it'.[2]

It was certainly an idealistic view; but it was in that mood, in this period of great uncertainty, and at the humblest possible level, that Charles de Gaulle joined, in October 1909, the 33rd Regiment of Infantry. Its barracks were at Arras, in northern France, almost midway between Lille and Paris, midway between his birthplace and the home of his adolescence, and it was there that he signed on, took the oath and spent the first year of his military service.

It was not a year that he enjoyed. Shy, intellectual, now six foot five inches in height, he was an obvious target for the ribaldry of his fellow soldiers. They laughed at him, roughed him up and generally contrived to make his life a misery. They taught the fastidious Jesuit schoolboy the scatological and sub-sexual language of the fighting man. There were forced marches, parades, inspections, exercises, mock battles and all the usual paraphernalia of a peacetime standing army. Although he was made a corporal in April 1910, de Gaulle did not win the rank of sergeant, which would have been the normal grade – at least it was achieved by most of his officer-cadet contemporaries – probably because he found it difficult to hide his dislike and contempt for the whole process. The year passed slowly, but it passed. By October it was finished, and the future General was thoroughly glad to be out of it.

He had now arrived at the first object of his ambition, the Ecole Spéciale Militaire, which trained all aspiring senior officers of the French army. It was named after one of the youngest saints in the Christian calendar, St Cyr – martyred in the fourth century at the age of three. The school had been built next door to the royal palace at Versailles by Mme de Maintenon, the official mistress of Louis XIV, to educate the daughters of impoverished nobility. Oddly enough, the hymn which was composed by Lully to be sung when Mme de Maintenon entered a classroom to view the results of her generosity was the precursor, later suitably arranged by Dr Arne, of what is now the national anthem of the United Kingdom. Be that as it may, the school was abolished at the Revolution, and the building – still bearing the name of the infant martyr saint – taken over and reinstated by Napoleon as a military academy to replace a much less imposing officer training unit at Fontainebleau. It was into this by then rather gloomy establishment that Officer Cadet Designate Charles de Gaulle marched, in pouring rain, on 14 October 1910. He may have thought that he had arrived at a haven, but the teasing and the bullying he had experienced at Arras did not stop at St Cyr. His physical characteristics were accentuated by the shaved head, common to all cadets; the nose and the ears just stuck out all the more. He was called 'the Great Asparagus' or 'Turkey Cock' and made to lie down to measure the width of a courtyard in 'melon-kilometres', which meant in the length of his own body.

At St Cyr, réveillé was at 5.30 a.m. and breakfast at 6.00. This was followed by study until 7.00 and two hours of gymnastics, fencing and instruction in horsemanship. Then came study again until midday, lunch, military lessons until 4.30 and study until 7.30. After dinner there was free time until the roll-call at 9.00, and lights out at 10.00. As at the Jesuit college of Vaugirard, it was a very full day.

There does not appear in his first year to have been much time for relaxation or diversion. There were long walks with his fellow cadets and discussions about strategy, the future of the army or of the likelihood of renewed hostilities with Germany over Alsace-Lorraine. But it was only on Sundays that de Gaulle was allowed out and able to make the journey into Paris to see his parents. On one occasion he played an elaborate – but in many ways significant – joke. A message was sent ahead to announce the visit of an important military visitor, of the highest rank. The de Gaulle parents prepared themselves accordingly. In due course there came a knock at their front door. A visiting card was sent in: 'General Faidherbe' was awaiting their permission to enter.

Of course, it was all a silly adolescent prank. 'Faidherbe' was in reality Officer Cadet Designate Charles de Gaulle. But the fact that he had chosen to be 'Faidherbe' rather than any other general is clear indication not just of his admiration for the hero of North Africa but of the retention in his memory, even perhaps subconsciously, of the name of the postal launch that had travelled across Africa with Marchand to Fashoda.

Things became a little easier at the end of the first year, when the title of Officer Cadet was formally awarded, and accepted, and the previous year's intake formed itself into an officially recognised group. In July 1911, Officer Cadet de Gaulle joined his contemporaries in the 'Promotion Fez', named, it appears, after the occupation of the Moroccan capital in that same year by French forces. The studies, however, did not vary, nor did the timetable. What did change, as in all such establishments, was the opportunity to look down contemptuously on juniors, and greater freedom and confidence to organise more elaborate entertainments. Thus there were pantomimes, plays and dances. There is even an invitation, still preserved, to the ball given by his Promotion in 1912.

De Gaulle left St Cyr in September 1912 with the rank of second lieutenant and with good reports in all subjects except rifle shooting, horsemanship and fencing. He was a particularly bad rifle shot, but made up for it in his overall classification by particular distinction in practical fieldwork, 'moral education' and 'resistance to tiredness'. His final grade, though not excellent, was good enough for him to be able to choose the regiment to which he wished to be posted. Given his northern background, and in spite of his previous rather less than happy experience with them, he chose to return as a commissioned officer to the regiment he had served in as an infantryman, the 33rd Infantry, still stationed, as might be expected, at Arras.

Apart from his sentimental attachment to the north of France, his decision was probably influenced by the knowledge that the new commanding officer of the regiment was one Philippe Pétain,* a former instructor at the Ecole Supérieure de Guerre, the staff college of the day, and himself of peasant origin – in this case from Picardy – and not at all the aristocrat. Pétain, apart from his reputation as an outstanding instructor, had been noted for his persistent view, held wholly in opposition to that of the contemporary high command, that what mattered in modern warfare was not who held the initiative by taking the offensive, but who could assemble the greater concentration of fire power. As if this was not enough, he showed little respect for the generally accepted conventions of the army, once replying to a ministerial enquiry about how many of his officers went to Mass: 'Sitting as I do in the first row of the faithful, I am not accustomed to turn my head to look behind me during the ceremony.'[3]

Pétain was by then fifty-six and would normally have been coming to the end of his career. Yet he was still full of energy, with piercing blue eyes set in a taut face, nearly bald and with the rest of his hair close-cropped, and still obviously attractive to women, to judge from the reports that circulated freely in Arras. He greeted his new second lieutenant tersely, in the Schramm barracks in Arras, welcoming him to 'the army' – as though nothing that had happened to him earlier in his military career constituted the army in any serious sense.

Second lieutenant de Gaulle was given charge of a platoon of the

---

* Philippe Pétain (1856–1951): Soldier and politician. Peasant origin; undistinguished career in army, apart from controversial lectures at Ecole Supérieure de Guerre, until First World War; 'victor of Verdun' 1916; Marshal of France 1918; Vice President Supreme War Council 1919 onwards; Minister for War 1934; Ambassador, Madrid 1939; Head of Vichy Government 1940–4; tried and convicted for treason 1945; sentence commuted by de Gaulle to life imprisonment on Isle d'Yeu.

same kind of soldier that he had earlier served with on terms of equality, both heavy and rather morose, as he himself was later to say, and at once set about giving them lectures on their duties and obligations. It was the usual lecture from a new platoon commander, and must have provoked the usual reaction of boredom. The only difference in this case was that the platoon commander, unlike many platoon commanders then and now, had researched and remembered every detail of his soldiers' lives – much, presumably, to their consternation.

Each year the army engaged in 'manoeuvres'. It was not easy to see the point of these, other than the need to keep young men occupied. Certainly, there was no question of maintaining secrecy; indeed, the one serious casualty of the 1913 manoeuvres was the German military attaché, Colonel von Winterfeld, whose car went off the road while he was on his way to observe events. Nor was it easy to see how such staged performances would train the participants to perform better if war ever did break out. But it was part of the established routine, and as such was not open to discussion.

The high point of the autumn manoeuvres of 1913 was the deployment in mock warfare of virtually the whole French army in the south-west, in the flat countryside around Toulouse. It was felt that, by holding them there, the irritation created by the incident in Germany would be minimised. There was a dignified and disciplined representation of total war, with umpires declaring platoons wiped out and gun batteries blown to pieces. The German Emperor was very pleased that the exercise had gone so well, and wrote as much to the President of France. It was, as a matter of fact, only a few hours later that he told the King of the Belgians, who was visiting Berlin at the time, that he was tired of the French and determined to finish them off 'by a necessary and inevitable war'.[4] The uncomfortable message eventually found its way back to Paris, and the French Government at last realised that the peace of Europe was under serious threat.

Certainly, the climate of opinion was no longer pacifist. The effect on public opinion of the Dreyfus affair had worn itself out by 1910, and there was a strong and identifiable move back to patriotism, which came to be known as the *réveil national*. The Radicals had been disappointing in government and were trying to retrieve their fortunes by recognising the virtues of patriotic and even militaristic sentiments. It was even possible for a Radical deputy to say in 1911, 'When the guns begin to speak, it is best that the politicians keep quiet.'[5] A succession of crises in Morocco kept the temperature high, and the appointment in the same year of Joffre as chief of the general staff at the age of fifty-nine was a sign that new ideas were needed.

One regiment where these new ideas had already taken hold, thanks to the influence of its commanding officer Pétain, was the 33rd at Arras. Discipline had been tightened and training brought up to date; morale was correspondingly high. By the end of 1913, when Pétain left the regiment to command a brigade, the officers of the 33rd knew that war was coming, and they felt ready for it. The how and the why were still unclear; through the winter, and then the spring and summer of 1914, the only sensible course of action was to sit and wait. There was really nothing else to do.

Pétain's departure had left the 33rd poorer in terms of its command, but he had left his mark on the young de Gaulle, who had been promoted to full lieutenant in September 1913. Pétain himself felt that his career was coming to an end. He had been a troublemaker, consistently complaining, fiercely and publicly, about the stupidity of the high command in their unthinking advocacy of total offensive at any cost. On his promotion to the command of a brigade, he had heard that a high official at the Ministry of War had said that there was no question of his becoming a full general. He had even prepared for his retirement by buying a small house near St Omer in the Pas de Calais.

Events, of course, were to change the course of Pétain's career. But if Lieutenant de Gaulle was deeply impressed by his battalion commander – 'Pétain is a great man,' he declared[6] – it is less clear why Pétain should have been impressed by the young lieutenant. The answer is probably that, more than de Gaulle would admit in later life, the two men shared characteristics that were uncommon in the officer corps of the day. Both had their roots in the north, Pétain in Picardy and de Gaulle in Flanders. They had both been Catholic educated, Pétain by the Dominicans, de Gaulle by the Jesuits. Above all, Pétain recognised in de Gaulle a proud fellow rebel, irritated by the mediocrity which surrounded him.

The two men did not meet, as far as is known, between late 1913 and 1921 – almost eight years during which the world was convulsed by the First World War and its aftermath. Even after that length of time, and even after their widely different experiences during the war, Pétain, by then a Marshal of France, went out of his way to promote the post-war career of Captain de Gaulle, former prisoner-of-war – implying that relations between the two in Arras in 1913 must have been much closer than history has yet recorded. It is by no means the least intriguing part of their long relationship.

2

A War to End Wars

*Ce prince était né général; l'art de la guerre semblait en
lui un instinct naturel.* ★

The order for general mobilisation of the French army was issued on 1
August 1914, and news of it arrived in Arras at the headquarters of the
33rd Infantry Regiment at about 4.30 that afternoon. Hectic activity
followed. The reservists arrived, some deserters tried to rejoin, orders
were issued to all companies to be prepared to leave barracks for the
front. On 3 August, Germany declared war. On 5 August, the 33rd
Infantry Regiment left Arras for Hirson on the Belgian frontier with
orders to join 1st Army Corps in moving into Belgium to take up
positions at Dinant defending the bridge, and hence the line of the river
Meuse, against the German right hook through Belgium into France.
There had been a cheerful farewell dinner and the send-off from Arras
was unrestrained in its enthusiasm. The young Lieutenant de Gaulle
shared in this enthusiasm, as did so many other young men who set off
for that terrible war. Letters home to his mother and sister reflected the
tragic innocence of 1914: 'The troops are absolutely splendid . . .we are
full of confidence.'[1]

   The first dose of reality came almost immediately after the 1st Army
Corps, shadowed by a German spotter plane, had crossed the frontier
into Belgium on 13 August. A night march had seen the French troops
cover the best part of 50 miles to reach Dinant before it was occupied
by the enemy. Just as the exhausted soldiers, having achieved their
objective, were settling down to rest, the German artillery opened up.
It was six o'clock in the morning.

★ 'This prince was born a general; the art of war seemed to be a natural instinct in him.'
  Voltaire on the Duc d'Enghien; quoted by Charles de Gaulle to his platoon on the
  eve of the engagement at Dinant Bridge.

German machine-gunners and riflemen, firing downwards from the citadel of Dinant on the other side of the river, started to pick off the French infantry at will. The carnage was dreadful. The French artillery were late in arriving; the 33rd were without cover; de Gaulle's platoon took what shelter it could on either side of a level crossing. Then, as the point platoon of 11th Company, they were ordered on to the bridge to prevent the enemy advancing across.

It was not, to say the least, a sensible manoeuvre. But de Gaulle roused his platoon and ran towards the bridge. Just as he reached it he was hit in the knee by a bullet. He fell – and his platoon sergeant fell dead on top of him. As he lay there, de Gaulle noted 'the dull thud of bullets entering the bodies of the dead and the wounded that lay about'.[2] Finally, with much effort, he managed to drag himself away and, along with the pitiful remnants of 11th Company, find refuge in friendly houses in Dinant. At that point, far too late, the French artillery started to open fire.

Dinant Bridge was not a glorious episode in French military history. Were it not for the terrible bloodshed, which presaged worse to come, it might easily be written off as just another wartime fiasco. But it amply demonstrated, only eleven days after war had been declared, how ill prepared the French army had been for the confrontation, and how empty and vain was the enthusiasm with which the war had been greeted, not least by Lieutenant de Gaulle.

In spite of his bravado, de Gaulle had, under Pétain's influence, sensed that the French army of 1914 – apart, that is, from the 33rd Regiment of Infantry – was far from ready for the German challenge. But Dinant Bridge had told him things about himself that he had not previously known. He had recognised two seconds of intense fear at the first early morning German artillery barrage; he had also noted that being under fire held no terrors which he could not master; finally, his military conclusion was that of Pétain, that in modern warfare fire power deter-mined the outcome. On the other hand, although he said later that the noise of bullets thudding into corpses was one that he would never for-get, what he did not appear to acknowledge at all was his own lack of interest in the fate of his fellow officers or his men as people. His description of the deaths of his company adjutant and his platoon sergeant might just as well be descriptions of the deaths of puppets.

The wounded from Dinant were taken first to Charleroi, to a transit hospital behind the lines. From there, de Gaulle himself was transferred to the Saint-Joseph hospital in Paris, where an operation was performed

to clean up the bullet wound and to alleviate the partial paralysis in his
right leg which it had caused. Convalescence was at a hospital in Lyons;
although not particularly painful, it was long and tedious. Apart from
'electrical' treatment, of uncertain nature, to restore sensation to a dead
sciatic nerve, it was a question of waiting in patience.

He occupied himself by writing a military analysis of the battle of
Dinant Bridge, including a complaint that the 'English' troops arrived
too late (without identifying the British contingent allegedly at fault),
and possibly – though not certainly at this time – writing a bizarre
romantic story about a young lieutenant who fell in love with the wife
of his company commander, was wounded at the same time as his commander was himself killed, and subsequently renounced his love of the
widow in terms which outdo those of any romantic novelist of the current generation. An episode describing the widow's visit to the young
lieutenant in hospital relates that 'she wanted to take the young man's
hand, but he seized hers and kissed them with the tenderness of
farewell.'[3] It was certainly strong stuff, and some have tried to read an
autobiographical theme into the story of the young lieutenant. But, perhaps disappointingly, a more likely hypothesis is that it was the result of
post-operative tension and the romantic fantasies of a Jesuit-educated
and sexually mature young man.

After a further period of physiotherapy and convalescence at Cognac
in the Charente, de Gaulle rejoined the 33rd Infantry Regiment in
mid-October 1914 on the front near Rheims. He had missed the first
battle of the Marne, fought in September 1914 while he had been in
hospital; but he noted ruefully that the French Government had not yet,
in October, returned to Paris from Bordeaux, where it had taken refuge
when the capital had been threatened by the German advance.

By the time de Gaulle rejoined his regiment, the war on the ground
had started to assume the characteristics of tactical stalemate that were
later to develop into the horrors of trench warfare. But life in the early
days was not too hard; on 22 October and 1 November there were
champagne dinners in the French lines – for officers, of course – on the
latter date with Sauternes to follow. Besides, precipitate action was dis-
couraged by the authorities. When the Germans dug a trench into the
French positions and the eager young lieutenant organised a raiding
party to flush them out, he was told not to do that sort of thing again,
since it would lead to 'conflagrations'. When his platoon took charge of
two new mortars, he was advised not to use them, since to do so would
provoke reprisals from the German artillery, which, if left alone, would

remain quiescent. In the end, he did fire one of the mortars – and his company was relieved the very next day by a unit with more accommodating officers.

In December 1914, Lieutenant de Gaulle was appointed regimental adjutant at the headquarters of the 33rd, reporting directly to the colonel. Almost immediately, the regiment moved southwards to take up position near Châlons-sur-Marne. Promotion to temporary captain came soon, in February 1915, as did a mention in dispatches and the Croix de Guerre. Away from the front, the new captain found himself in a period of comparative calm.

That calm was not to last for long. The battles between the opposing trenches were becoming steadily more ferocious and more costly. During the period 10 February to 10 March 1915, the regiment lost 19 officers – 4 killed, 13 wounded, and 2 missing presumed dead – and 700 other ranks. Among the injured officers was the newly promoted Captain de Gaulle. A shrapnel wound in the left hand, probably sustained on or around 10 March, became infected. The wound was, by the standards of the day, barely more than superficial, but it was enough to send him back to hospital.

Pronounced fit once more, de Gaulle returned to the 33rd in June 1915, by which time they had moved northwards to the front on the river Aisne. The promotion to captain had been confirmed, but the task was the same: by now it was prolonged, bloody trench warfare. From June 1915 to January 1916 the 33rd was either in the line or in reserve. As the weeks went by, Captain de Gaulle's anger against the politicians who were directing the war grew more intense. 'Parliament becomes more and more hateful and stupid,' he wrote furiously.[4]

In mid-February 1916, the Germans launched their major offensive on the weakest point of the French front, where it hinged southwards at the salient of Verdun. There followed a ten-month battle, which is recorded in the history of warfare as one of the bloodiest of all time. The whole area, to the north-east of the city of Verdun, is even today scarred for mile upon mile. The slaughter was seemingly endless, but time after time both sides mounted hopeless and suicidal attacks to gain no more than a few yards of ground. The fort at Douaumont, for instance, was captured by the Germans in March 1916 and recaptured by the French in October 1916. Throughout those months the fighting around the fort had been relentless, and the casualties were such that trenches could not be dug because corpses lay in layers on the spot.

The 33rd were allotted the battle sector around the church of the village of Douaumont, half a mile from the fort. On 2 March, at 6.30 a.m., the German bombardment started. The earth, according to contemporary witnesses, shook as though there were an earthquake. The German infantry attacked around midday, amid smoke and confusion. Casualties on both sides were dreadful, but at one point a French position was overrun, and, as men fought hand to hand with bayonets, a group of French soldiers was isolated from other units and forced to surrender. At the head of that group was Captain de Gaulle, who himself had been wounded by a bayonet thrust through his left thigh. At that point it seems most likely that de Gaulle was either unconscious or semi-conscious, possibly from the effects of an explosion or from the pain of the bayonet wound.

By then, the 33rd Infantry Regiment had virtually ceased to exist. In three days of fighting over 60 per cent of its original complement of men had been put out of action – either killed or seriously wounded – defending a minor road from the village of Fleury to the church at Douaumont. Wounded prisoners, de Gaulle among them, were taken from the battlefield to the German military hospital at Mainz. There he was treated for his wound, then – apparently fully recovered after no more than ten days – he was moved to a transit camp at Neisse. The camp at Osnabrück was the next stop, then back to Neisse for transport to a prison further away from the Western Front.

Not surprisingly, once his wound was healed, Captain de Gaulle was anxious to return to active warfare, and at Neisse his first escape attempt was hatched: a hare-brained scheme which involved sailing down the Danube to the Black Sea. Perhaps fortunately, the plot was discovered easily enough and the plotters were sent off to a punishment camp in an old sawmill at Szczucin in Lithuania. It was a long and unpleasant journey, and it was May 1916 before they arrived.

Szczucin camp was a miserable place. Some fifty French officers lived side by side with a hundred Russians in poor conditions and a harsh climate. It was enlivened, however, by the presence of one Lieutenant-Colonel Tardiù, an officer in the French army of Indochinese origin, whose prewar career had been spent in Tonkin. His insolence towards his captors was such that by the time of his release in 1918 he had accumulated a hundred years of detention by way of punishment. He was always planning ingenious escapes, and by August de Gaulle had decided to dig a tunnel with him and another French officer, Lieutenant Roederer, who, apart from being a tunnelling expert, had a passing knowledge of Russian. However, the entrance to the tunnel was quickly discovered, and further punishment followed, this time in the form of a transfer for the three of them to the highest security prison of them all: Fort IX at Ingolstadt.

Ingolstadt itself lies in central Bavaria, straddling the Danube about 100 miles north of Munich. The countryside around is flat and uninteresting, and the climate harsher than its latitude would normally suggest. At the time, Ingolstadt was a town of about 40,000 inhabitants, with no particular distinctive feature other than an attractive church in the southern German Baroque style. Fort IX was five miles due south of the town, an oblong mound some 350 yards long and 60 feet high. Within an encircling rampart was a moat 15 yards wide and 4 to 6 feet deep, which protected the main building. Beyond the moat was a heavy iron and wire gate, the entrance to the main courtyard; on the other side of that was the main prison building, with walls of brick and dug into the heart of the hill; a massive iron door led to all appearances straight into the hill itself. Apart from a brief episode of freedom after another escape attempt, this would be de Gaulle's home for the next year.

In the early days of the war Fort IX had been a quiet, well-behaved sort of place, but in 1916 the Germans decided to strengthen its defences, and to reserve it for those prisoners-of-war who had made attempts to escape from other camps. By the time of de Gaulle's arrival, there were about 150 officer prisoners in the camp, French, British and Russian. The commandant was a full general, with responsibility for all prison camps in the Ingolstadt area, whose predecessor is said to have been driven to such distraction by the inmates of Fort IX that he ended his days in a lunatic asylum. The general, Peters by name, was not much liked; indeed, his very appearance told against him – short, thickset, with a large drooping moustache and pince-nez for reading. He was described as resembling an amiable shopkeeper cursed with occasional fits of violent temper. Although General Peters was the commanding officer, in practice three non-commissioned officers ran Fort IX, with forty or so soldiers under their command. Since at any one time at least three-quarters of its inmates were planning escape by one means or another, this was not an easy task.

The prisoners' food was very poor: one loaf of bread, one bowl of cabbage soup, one potato and a cup of acorn coffee with a lump of sugar per day. There was meat every ten days or so, and occasionally some fish, which, it was said, only the Russians managed to eat. The bread was made of rye, potato and sawdust, but made a useful missile as it hardened with age, and if rolled in the mud, could be used as a rugby ball. The diet was supplemented by parcels which were sent by the prisoners' friends and relatives, and although they examined them with great suspicion the German guards were conscientious about their distribution. Deliveries were irregular, and there were times when twenty or thirty parcels would arrive simultaneously for the six officers who shared a cell. The guards helped out by making shelves in the parcel office so that not all parcels had to be opened immediately but could be claimed as required.

Prison routine was inevitably boring, but the camaraderie between officers of all nationalities, and the persistent planning of escape attempts, served to alleviate it. There were three *Appels*, or roll-calls, mostly indoors but sometimes out of doors when the commandant had something of importance to say, at regular times each day. In between these were morning lessons in languages or history, sports in the afternoon, and bridge, reading or lectures in the evening. Sometimes there were entertainments, such as fancy-dress balls; and the French officers were particularly ingenious in their dress, the greatest success, needless to say, being reserved for those who got themselves up as ladies of easy virtue.

But planning escape was the main occupation, and Captain de Gaulle applied himself to the task with energy and determination. He discovered that the prison hospital was an annexe to the main garrison hospital and situated outside the walls of the fort. Together with one Captain Ducret, he accumulated from parcels and from other inmates, and even perhaps from one or two of the guards, the necessities for escape – food, papers, civilian clothes, and so on.

The method finally chosen was bold. De Gaulle's mother used to send him an ointment to help with his chilblains. Swallowing it – as he did – induced alarming symptoms of advanced jaundice: yellow eyes, blotched skin and clouded urine. Seeing these, the fort doctor sent him straight to the prison hospital, where he found Ducret. The problem now was how to get out of the prison annexe and into the main hospital itself. A German officer was suborned and, once implicated, was obliged not only to buy a helmet and a map for the fugitives, but finally, indignity of indignities, to surrender his trousers. Ducret, dressed as a German male nurse, then solemnly escorted Captain de Gaulle out of captivity. The two officers, having made their escape, headed for the Swiss frontier at Schaffhausen, some 190 miles away. There followed eight days of freedom, mostly in pouring rain, until they were recaptured just south of

Ulm, only 60 miles from the frontier. It was back to Fort IX.

The attempt having failed, and suitable punishment meted out, it was time for reflection. From November 1916 to July 1917, Captain de Gaulle decided that discretion was most definitely the better part of valour. But he was far from idle. He set about participating in the activities of the prison. He resumed his study of German, taught French to a future Russian Marshal, Tukhachevsky, worked in the library, and above all gave a series of lectures to his fellow prisoners, later to form the basis of his book *La Discorde chez l'Ennemi*.

By the middle of 1917, however, discretion had lost its charm, and it was time to attempt another escape. Instead of a breakout, de Gaulle sought transfer to a less secure camp. After seven months of good behaviour, the transfer had apparently been earned, and de Gaulle, together with three other French officers, was moved to the strikingly theatrical fortress of Rosenberg in Franconia, the 'Little Switzerland' of Germany. Within four months the four officers had escaped.

Again the destination was Schaffhausen, but after ten days on the run the four took refuge in a dovecote. It was not a wise decision – the resulting noise led to their recapture. Back in Rosenberg, de Gaulle and one of the original four tried again. By sawing through a bar in their window, they managed to get out, down the steep cliff and then, disguised not just in civilian clothes but with false moustaches and spectacles, they sped off into the darkness. It was too improbable to succeed, and at Lichtenfels, the nearest station, they were arrested while trying to take the train to Aachen and the Dutch frontier.

By then the German authorities had had enough and the insubordinate captain was sent back to Fort IX at Ingolstadt. He had to suffer the appropriate punishment for his repeated attempts to escape: two months in solitary confinement, with shutters across the windows, no artificial light, nothing to read and nothing to write with or on, a specially harsh diet, and only half an hour's exercise a day in the courtyard. After that, there was nothing to do but wait.

By the time de Gaulle left Ingolstadt, in April 1918, the tension between prisoners and prison guards in Fort IX had snapped. A French officer had been shot while escaping, and the German NCOs had panicked, threatening to shoot at random. A charge was preferred by several officers, both French and British, against the senior NCO of 'instigating his men to murder'. There was no doubt about the evidence and, such were the gentlemanly conventions of the times, a serious scandal resulted. It was made worse by the fact that those who had been threatened were commissioned officers and those who had issued the threat were not.

The captive officers won their case and Fort IX was shut down by the German authorities at the end of the month. De Gaulle was moved, together with some of his fellow prisoners, first to a fort at Prinz Karl, and then to a rather stronger fortress at Wülzburg, situated on a hill some three miles east of the town of Weissenburg in central Bavaria. There was, needless to say, another escape attempt, similar to that first tried at Ingolstadt. A German uniform was procured, this time by theft, and de Gaulle was solemnly led to the gate of the prison by an 'escort'. In addition, the French chaplain at Wülzburg, one Abbé Michel, tagged along, as far as the gate, to allay the guards' suspicions.

Another success, another failure. The two were picked up after one night and one day, having completed only half the journey to Nuremberg, where they had hoped to take a train to Frankfurt. Returned to Wülzburg, de Gaulle planned his next effort – by means of concealment in a laundry basket. Again, the initial plan worked, and he reached Nuremberg, bought a ticket to Frankfurt and boarded a train. This time, however, it was illness that defeated him, in the form of a severe bout of gastric influenza. Bad luck indeed, but the result was the same, and he found himself quickly back in Wülzburg, serving the customary punishment.

It was de Gaulle's last effort to escape; and he then gave up hope of being able to return to France before the end of the war. As hostilities drew to a close, he was moved to Passau, then to a transit camp at Magdeburg, then to Ludwigshafen, from where, three weeks after the armistice on 11 November 1918, he crossed the Swiss frontier – to arrive, via Geneva, Lyons and Paris, at La Ligerie in the early days of December. His father had assembled the family to greet him. It was nothing less than a miracle that all four of his sons had survived the war, and Henri de Gaulle was duly thankful. But he must have recognised that Charles had been extraordinarily lucky. If he had not been taken prisoner at Verdun, the statistical likelihood, given the mortality rate among French officers in the two years up to the armistice, was that he would not have come back alive.

Towards the end of the war, Captain de Gaulle had started to assess his own situation. It was not a promising one. A professional soldier, he had in one way or another missed most of the greatest military adventure the world had ever seen. His record under fire had been courageous, perhaps even foolhardy, but lacking in any great distinction.

Writing to his mother from prison in September 1918, he showed signs of despair. He talked of leaving the army, on the grounds that he had not been able to observe at first hand the changes that had taken place in the way warfare was conducted, and of doubts whether he had any career in front of him.

Nevertheless, as a prisoner-of-war the future General had developed characteristics that were to be of great significance in later life. Courage he had demonstrated in full measure; ingenuity, too, and the ability to take punishment without too much complaint. But, more important, he had, in the boring confines of prison, thought deeply about the nature of war and of leadership. His lectures to his fellow prisoners show the same perception and intellectual rigour as his future lectures and writings. They were regarded with awe, and listened to with fascination. In that sense, prison was his university, where he learnt to think – and think profoundly. The callow cadet of St Cyr, and the foolhardy platoon commander of Dinant Bridge, were left behind. De Gaulle's intellect was able to focus, in those two years of inaction, on the adult problems that were to be the stuff of his future career.

Along with the growing intellectual intensity, there developed, according to reports of his fellow prisoners, the aloofness that was later to become such a marked feature of the man. 'Do you know that I am really a very shy person?'[5] he asked one of them; certainly there was amazement at Wülzburg that all the young captains spoke to each other using the familiar '*tu*' – all, that is, except for Captain de Gaulle; it was considered astonishing that with forty officers sharing the same shower room, which had no partitions, everybody washed without inhibition in front of one another except the prudish Captain de Gaulle, whom nobody ever saw naked. It was noted, too, that when he spoke, either in a formal lecture or in impromptu conversation in the prison courtyard, he was listened to with something bordering on reverence.

Nobody comes out of the experience of war, especially a war as terrible as the First World War, without either a personality breakdown or a toughened character. Captain de Gaulle's character had certainly been toughened. The question now uppermost in his mind was not how he had managed to survive but how he could possibly make up for the lost years. For a peacetime officer in a ravaged army, it was not an easy question to answer.

3

POLISH INTERLUDE

Tanks, Comrade Corps Commander! How can
one sabre them when they are made of steel?★

The map of Europe at the end of the First World War was in greater
confusion than it had been at any time since the end of the Napoleonic
wars just over a century earlier. Not only had eastern Europe, the first
cockpit of the war, to be reconstructed, but all the victorious participants, having suffered enormous losses both in men and in resources,
felt they were each entitled to their own particular pound of flesh,
whatever – and wherever – that might be.

It was not easy for the United States to define her pound of flesh,
since her entry into the war, albeit decisive, had been late, and the
United States had no territorial ambitions on the European continent.
Yet even the United States had political imperatives, and one of these
was to respond to the complaints of the immigrant Polish community,
whose 'motherland' – however that term might be defined, given
Poland's constantly shifting frontiers – had been 'trampled on' by the
belligerents in eastern Europe, Germany, Austria-Hungary and Russia.
It was domestic political pressures that obliged President Woodrow
Wilson to proclaim, as a condition of the Americans' agreeing to the
peace, that Poland should be re-established as 'a united, independent
and autonomous' nation.

The eastern European political scene was, however, much more
complicated than that. The revolution in Russia, now Soviet Russia,
had not only taken one major belligerent out of the war in late 1917 but
had also introduced a political system whose methods and behaviour

★ A Cossack trooper, reported in General Ghai's memoirs, *Na Varshavu*; Moscow,
1928. Quoted in Norman Davies, *White Eagle, Red Star*, page 148; Orbis, London,
1983.

were as yet unknown quantities to the western powers. Both Austria and Germany had collapsed politically at the end of the war. As a result the worst possible situation had ensued, a political vacuum with hundreds of thousands, perhaps millions, of battle-hardened soldiers scattered around, uncertain where their loyalties lay.

Not only did the Americans insist on the reconstitution of an independent Poland, but they actively encouraged an army of Polish volunteers from the United States and elsewhere to assemble in France, under a certain General Józef Haller, with a view to moving across Europe and forming the nucleus of an army of the new Poland. It was an idea that was conceived so many thousands of miles from the scene of its application that it inevitably carried an air of impracticality, but so powerful was its emotional appeal that by the end of 1918 the army amounted to no fewer than six divisions, made up of Poles from all over the world. This motley force was to be transported, according to the plan, through Germany to Poland to join up with other troops who had fought in the war, and who were simultaneously assembling in Poland. It was not, of course, nearly as easy as that. Those who had fought had done so on different sides and against a variety of opponents. Some had fought for the Germans against the Russian enemy; others had fought for Russia against the Prussian enemy; still others had fought for various separatist groups against the Austrian enemy; all of them fighting with similar passion and enthusiasm.

Other Polish units were summoned from various points of the compass at about the same time as Haller's army. A Polish division came, after a three-month march, from Odessa, where it had been fighting alongside the White Russians against the Soviets. A detachment arrived from Murmansk, and another from Vladivostok. The Poznán regiments in the German army took up the Polish cause as well. The result of this diversified effort was that some Poles had learnt the German language and Prussian or Austrian military methods, while others had learnt Russian and Russian military methods. All that was needed to complete the cocktail was another Polish contingent which had learnt French and French military methods. This is precisely what happened when the Haller army arrived in Poland in May 1919.

Among the 2000 or so French officers who accompanied Haller and who were under the command of the French General Henrys was Captain Charles de Gaulle. It had been clear for some time that some unifying discipline was necessary, and since by then the Americans had washed their hands of the whole affair and the British were no longer interested in continental adventures, the burden was conveniently allocated to France.

From de Gaulle's point of view, it was a blessing. Having been out of the war for all the last period, he had had to go on a refresher course, to learn what developments in military strategy and tactics had taken place during his period of captivity. The fact that this course, at the Ecole de St Maixent, lasted no more than two and a half months perhaps indicated the intellectual poverty of such developments in the latter stages of the war. Even while there, de Gaulle saw that the only way to make up the ground he had lost was to get back into military action. Hence his application for secondment to the Polish army as an adviser – which was all that Polish national pride would allow a French officer to become.

The application approved, de Gaulle signed a renewable one-year engagement on 4 April 1919, joined the 5th Chasseurs Polonais in May and set off with Haller's army on a miserable train journey across Germany, which, given the dislocation of transport at the time, they were lucky to complete in one week. Haller's last act in France was to pray at the tomb of Stanislas Leszcynski, the last King of Poland, in Nancy Cathedral. The act was perhaps symbolic of the somewhat operatic nature of the whole endeavour.

On arrival in Poland, the first task was to set up proper training facilities for Polish officers, which was done at Rembertow, twelve miles or so north of Warsaw. De Gaulle – who, like all the other French officers, had been temporarily moved up a rank to commandant – found the whole exercise depressing. For a start, he was just teaching soldiering rather than being a soldier himself. Then he found that he had been assigned, as servant and factotum, a Polish soldier who had not only fought for Germany in the war but had actually fought in the lines opposite de Gaulle himself on the Western Front in 1915. The officers he was meant to train were of poor quality; not only that, but they themselves could not see any defect in their attitude or performance. Added to those burdens, de Gaulle commented in a rare burst of anti-semitism, there were countless numbers of 'those', who had done very well out of the war.[1]

The Allies' objective was to create a Polish army capable of defending itself against on the one hand the Soviets to the east and on the other – though this was less often said – against the possible revival of Germany to the west. But whatever the intentions of the Allies they had reckoned without the ambitions of Marshal Józef Klemens Ginet-Pilsudski.

Pilsudski had emerged from a German prison to become the leader of the new Poland. Born into the minor Polish aristocracy, educated under the Tsars, he had dedicated himself in romantic fashion to Poland herself. He ate little, wore a plain uniform, was tall, pallid and infinitely resolute. Those who met him were struck by the intensity of his grey-blue eyes. He was not a man to forget, and Captain de Gaulle, for his part, never forgot him.

Pilsudski immediately recognised that although the Allies had sanctioned the existence of an independent Poland they had failed to be precise about its frontiers. The way was open for an expansionary move against the old enemy Russia, which was still convulsed in the civil war that had followed the 1917 Revolution. Pilsudski could not resist the temptation, and during 1919, in a series of sorties, moved the whole Polish front some 150 miles to the north and 100 miles to the east. By the end of August he had captured Minsk, and the way lay open to Smolensk and the river Dnieper. But at this point he had called a halt, knowing that the winter was coming and mindful of the fate of Napoleon's army in the Russian winter. Besides, the Allies were getting restive; they were prepared to help Poland defend herself against Germany if necessary – but not to encourage her to engage in wholesale self-aggrandisement.

Pilsudski, however, was not to be held on a short rein. Hostilities resumed in April 1920, when he launched his newly reinforced army eastwards into the Ukraine. Their progress was little short of spectacular. On 17 May the Poles occupied Kiev and were within striking distance of Odessa. Pilsudski allowed himself to declare the aim of establishing Greater Poland, stretching from the Baltic to the Black Sea.

He had, of course, like others before and after him, neglected the resilience of Mother Russia. Even under an alien regime, the motherland was still to be defended, and Trotsky, the organiser of the Red Army, had gone a long way to re-establishing the discipline that had broken down in 1917. Above all, the Russian spirit was up, and although it was a ragged crowd that assembled to defy the Polish army just outside Kiev, it was full of fight.

The main battle unit was the First Cavalry Army – known as the Konarmiya – made up of former Cossacks and partisans from the steppes, which, under the command of General Budyenny, had adopted Cossack tactics: the charge was with the sabre, and there were to be no prisoners. Nor were civilians to be spared. Before the final charge they trotted eight abreast, their brown cloaks and black astrakhan hats fearsomely identifiable even at a distance; but when they drew their sabres and held them high as they moved into a gallop, they seemed like the reincarnation of Genghis Khan and his Tatar hordes.

The counter-offensive started at the end of May. The Konarmiya's charges proved too much for the Poles. After ten days' resistance, on 5 June they simply broke and fled. 'We ran all the way to Kiev,' said one, 'and we ran all the way back.'[2] But they could not run fast enough. Cossacks could advance for three days across the flat terrain without stopping for food or rest, and after a day's respite push on for another three days. They lived off the land; all resistance was overcome by the indiscriminate use of the sabre. The carefully trained officers of the Polish army had no answer to this onslaught. In one month the Ukraine was back in Soviet hands.

The battle for the Ukraine had been one of dash and movement. But at the same time the Soviets were establishing more solid positions to the north. On 28 April 1920 a new Soviet general had been given command of the whole western front. It was none other than Mikhail Nikolayevich Tukhachevsky, de Gaulle's fellow prisoner – and French pupil – at Fort IX at Ingolstadt. He was only twenty-seven, a son of the nobility but a convinced Marxist. When he left Ingolstadt, it was said that he had boasted: 'I shall be a general by the time I'm twenty-five, or else they will have me shot.'[3] In the event he was not far off the mark. His record in the Russian civil war in 1918 and 1919 had earned him the highest distinction, that of Marshal of the Red Army, and in the 1930s he was shot in the Stalinist purge.

Under Tukhachevsky's command, the Red Army broke the Polish line in the north in early July. Again, the spearhead had been the Caucasian cavalry corps, led by the Armenian General Ghai. Their only setback occurred on 19 July, when they encountered a group of Polish officer cadets advancing in the shelter of four Renault tanks. Two brigades of horse cavalry were halted and forced to retreat. But the Poles had a mere thirty tanks, and fifteen of them were stuck in a marshalling yard, able to fire only at targets in range of the railway station. Of the other fifteen, most broke down or ran out of petrol. Only two survived anything like intact. 'An armoured tank,' General Ghai concluded, 'is nothing to frighten a skilled cavalryman.'[4] By the end of the month the combined Soviet forces were encamped on a broad front along the river Vistula, their closest unit being within two days' march of Warsaw. Whatever the western Allies might say, by early August 1920 it looked as though Poland was doomed.

In Warsaw there was, as might be expected, panic. The Poles

requested help from the Allies. None replied except France. In response to pleas for troops, guns, matériel, ammunition, indeed almost anything, the French answered by sending General Maxime Weygand* to give further advice. 'Believe me,' Marshal Foch said to the Polish Prime Minister, Wladyslaw Grabski, 'he is worth ten divisions.'[5] It was perhaps an exaggeration, but at least Weygand had been Foch's chief of staff in the last year of the war – for what that was worth.

When Weygand arrived in Poland and set up his headquarters in a train in a siding at Warsaw station, he sent for Pilsudski, who immediately asked him how many divisions he had brought with him. 'None, *monsieur le Maréchal*,' came the solemn reply.[6] After that, Weygand was ignored and Pilsudski went on as before. None of this was known in France and, on his return to Paris, Weygand – admittedly somewhat to his surprise – was fêted as the real victor of the battle of Warsaw.

At the same time, the Russians announced their war aim: it was quite simply to reduce Poland to the status of a Soviet satellite under a newly formed 'provisional Polish revolutionary committee'. This uncompromising attitude might have been expected to harden the resolve of the Allies to come to the help of the Poland that they had created only a year earlier, but they were tired of war, and the Allied governments remained unmoved.

Temporary Commandant de Gaulle, recently returned to Poland after a month's leave and a month's detachment to the office of decorations in the War Ministry in Paris, noticed a decisive change in Polish spirit and morale. Now that the existence of their country was threatened, Poles of all classes and ages rallied to the flag. Solemn Masses were sung to invoke the aid of God against the heathen, and perhaps also against the Lutheran God, in the event of the Prussians taking advantage of the Polish plight to attack from the rear. De Gaulle was deeply impressed by the transformation in Polish morale, and he was even more pleased when he, together with his fellow officers, was authorised by the French Government to join the Polish fighting forces – still, of course, as adviser. Rembertow had been closed down for some time now and the French officers there had been reduced to mere observers of events.

---

* Maxime Weygand (1867–1965): Soldier. Of uncertain parentage and origin. Military career in cavalry (horse); Chief of Staff to Marshal Foch 1914–23; honorary British knighthood 1918; C.-in-C. French army 1931–5; Commander French Forces Near East 1940; C.-in-C. all French forces 19 May 1940 until the armistice in June 1940; Vichy Gov.-Gen. in French Africa 1941: imprisoned by Germans 1942–5, by French 1945–6.

Pilsudski's battle plan was to contain the Soviet thrust to Warsaw in the north, to hold the line on that front, and then immediately thereafter to launch a right hook from the south into the Russian left flank. To achieve this, a strike force had to be assembled to the south, and there were tense moments while the Poles moved their troops into the new formation. Had Tukhachevsky attacked then, he would have caught the Poles in disarray; but either he failed to spot the manoeuvre or his forces were unprepared, and the moment passed.

It was on 16 August 1920, the day after the feast of the Assumption of the Blessed Virgin Mary, that the battle of Warsaw − or the Miracle of the Vistula, as it is sometimes known − finally began. It was to be the last set piece confrontation between two large armies until the Second World War. The Red Army totalled about 200,000 fighting troops with, it is said, a further 800,000 camp followers. The Polish army was somewhat smaller, perhaps about 150,000 fighting troops. The Soviets attacked, as expected, on a direct line to Warsaw in the north. Their assault was held, and the Polish flanking manoeuvre from the south was brilliantly executed. By the evening of 17 August the battle was effectively over and Tukhachevsky gave the order to retreat.

Defeat turned into a rout, which ended in a further battle at the Niemen, in which the Red Army was conclusively broken. Apart from the casualties, which were heavy, the Russians left 70,000 prisoners in Polish hands and a further 100,000 escaped across the border into eastern Prussia. The campaign − and the war − had ended in total Soviet failure. Poland was safe for a generation − but only, as it turned out, for one generation.

De Gaulle's operational activity in Poland was now at an end and he settled down to write his reports and draw his own conclusions. In spite of the popularity in Warsaw of the French officers, he avoided the liberal social life of the Polish *haut monde,* except for the salon of Countess Strumilla, where he was frequently to be seen − to the point where the curious assumed that he was drawn by a romantic liaison with the Countess herself. The curious may have been right, since later in life he showed an attachment for Poland that can only be described as sentimental − a rare emotion for the General, as he then was. He also went for long walks by himself, apparently only stopping every so often to indulge at Chez Blikle his weakness for patisseries. He made an odd sight, this tall gangling French officer, either sitting by himself at a table on the pavement or, odder still, taking away a pastry or two, which he held by the thread of its wrapping on the end of the finger of one hand, by now protected by the white gloves which he had started to affect.

In those days, de Gaulle took little trouble to be friendly to his fellow countrymen. A year earlier, at Rembertow, he had been reported by the Polish officer Medwecki, his adjutant, as being distant towards his colleagues, never going to their mess or joining in their jokes. Besides, he had no money. Soon after his arrival in Poland, he had had to ask his mother for a loan to re-equip himself after his quarters were burgled and he was left with only what he stood up in.

Released from the final months of his Polish engagement in January 1921, de Gaulle, now returned to his permanent rank of captain, went back to Paris. Already the lessons of his Polish experience were becoming clear and were to be reflected in a series of lectures and writings over the next two decades. He had realised that it was possible, after all, to fight a war of movement, and that the secret of mobility was not, obviously, the Cossack charge, which was incompatible with a sustained preparatory artillery barrage, but the modern combination of the two: in other words, the tank. Fundamental to this tactic was that the armoured force must not be dispersed but concentrated. Then there was the importance of morale. First the Russians and then the Poles had been so inspired in the defence of their country that they each in turn had become capable of acts well beyond what might normally be expected of them. Lastly, he was so impressed by the Poles that, in a final lecture to French officers before leaving Warsaw, he said specifically: 'To watch Germany . . .we need a continental ally on whom we can always count. Poland will be that ally.'[7] It was a sentiment that many Frenchmen echoed in the heady days of victory at the river Vistula in front of Warsaw. It was also a sentiment that was to bring a heavy obligation in 1939.

Countess Strumilla and the pastries of Chez Blikle had now to be forgotten, since de Gaulle's return to Paris marked another turning point in his life. In November 1920, on a visit to Paris, de Gaulle had become engaged to Yvonne Vendroux, and they were married on 7 April 1921. Everybody agreed that it was a very suitable match. Indeed so unanimous was the verdict, and so encouraging the behaviour of both families in the period leading up to the engagement and the wedding, that it is difficult to avoid the conclusion that this was very much an arranged marriage – not, to be sure, an unusual event at the time.

The Vendroux were an eminently respectable family, Dutch by origin but claiming an ancestress who was the illegitimate daughter of a

Pope. They had settled in Calais at the turn of the eighteenth century, and had been prominent in the business and social life of the city ever since, most recently in the manufacture of biscuits. Yvonne herself was pretty without being beautiful. She had inherited from her mother a rather small and stocky figure, but she had large black eyes, an oval face and a high forehead when her mass of black hair was swept back. She was full of character and charm, tempered by a certain puritan severity of character. But the character, and the looks, certainly pleased the tall and clumsy captain, and after a period of courtship involving a spillage of tea (or punch, depending on the version) over her dress, and then a ball at St Cyr, the matter was concluded with speed and decorum.

The wedding took place at Calais, on 6 April in the office of the mayor, and then, on the 7th – the true marriage in the eyes of the couple – in the brooding fortified church of Notre-Dame-de-Calais, in the presence of all who mattered in Calais society. There was a large lunch, followed by the usual waltz, led by the tall bridegroom and the stocky bride, and joined, no doubt with varying degrees of athleticism, by the assembled company of notables. It was not until seven o'clock that the newly-weds were able to make their escape, taking the train to Paris and then on to Lake Maggiore for the honeymoon.

Even while planning his marriage, de Gaulle had not neglected his military career. There were two ways forward in the peacetime army: a detachment to a colonial army, with the possibility of seeing action, or a staff posting within France. De Gaulle chose the latter, in the knowledge that in order to succeed he had to acquire an outstanding record as a theoretician, and also to have passed successfully through the French staff college, the Ecole Supérieure de Guerre. On his return from Poland he therefore applied for, and obtained in open competition, the post of assistant professor of history at St Cyr. The job suited him perfectly. He could live in Paris with his new wife, cultivating useful acquaintances and renewing those that had lapsed. He was also able to cultivate the qualities of rhetoric that he had been taught by the Jesuits and had started to practise in Ingolstadt and at Rembertow. A note of theatricality entered his presentation and delivery, the most notable sign of which was wearing his white gloves even when he was lecturing.

White gloves or no white gloves, his lectures were by all accounts immensely successful and made military history come alive for the otherwise bored officer cadets. Yet it was quite an easy life in terms of workload. He was required at the school for only a few hours a week and was otherwise free to spend time with his new wife and at his writing.

One of the acquaintances that was most important to renew was with his old commanding officer, Marshal Pétain. Pétain had emerged from the war as France's hero. As a Marshal of France, he enjoyed the highest prestige; but as a former battalion commander of the 33rd Regiment he had developed an unusual relationship with his former subordinate officer and now seemed, after all those years, resolved to give the captain what assistance he could. Whatever else may be said against Pétain, he had never been afraid of new ideas. After all, it was he who had argued with the general staff before the war, insisting on the importance of superior firepower, and he was still willing to encourage those who challenged accepted belief. The young captain was, in his view, one of those.

Fortunately, or by design, the de Gaulles had found an apartment in the Boulevard de Grenelle, just around the corner from the Ecole Militaire and the home of Pétain in the Place de Latour-Maubourg. The de Gaulles did not live in luxury; the Métro passed almost above their heads on to what is now the Pont Bir Hakeim. Nevertheless, the location served its purpose – that of promoting the career of the ambitious young captain.

Even at this stage, the relationship with Pétain was not without its difficulties. Although the two men admired each other greatly, the social arrangements were far from easy. Pétain had married, in September 1920 at the age of sixty-four, a divorced lady who went by the name of Nini. It had not been considered a wise move either by society or by the military authorities of the day. Nobody could quite understand why the Marshal had wished to set the seal of legal approval on this liaison, particularly since the problems of protocol that the marriage raised were extremely grave. After all, no respectable lady could sit down at table with a remarried divorcée, be she or be she not Mme la Maréchale. There was therefore no question of Mme de Gaulle accompanying her husband to dinner with the Marshal if Nini was to be present. The Marshal, however, had a simple answer: he installed Nini, not in his own apartment, but in a neighbouring one, with a communicating door which was only opened when the happy couple were by themselves. When there were visitors, it was kept firmly shut and Nini was excluded from the general company. On those occasions where a hostess was required, the Marshal used to make his selection for the honour from among the wives of his guests. There is unfortunately no record of what Nini thought of these arrangements.

It was obvious to the military world, which followed these events with intense interest, that Captain de Gaulle was now under the special protection of the Marshal of France, and that it would only be a matter of time before he entered the Ecole Supérieure de Guerre. On the birth of their first child, a son, in December 1921, the de Gaulles had to move to more commodious lodgings, further away from the Marshal and Nini. It is also true that there was the matter of an entry examination to the college. Neither of these was a serious hindrance. Pétain, although excluded by his marital status from being a godfather, adopted an avuncular attitude to the young boy, whose name, by pure coincidence of course, was Philippe like his own; and the examination was a test not of imagination or good sense but purely academic ability and good memory. For a former pupil of the Jesuits that posed no problem at all.

The list of the 129 successful candidates of the 44th *Promotion* to the Ecole Supérieure de Guerre was published on 2 May 1922, and it was no surprise to find the name of Captain de Gaulle on it. It had now become clear, even if there had been any doubt previously, that de Gaulle had been recognised as the disciple, and the favoured disciple at that, of the most powerful man in the French army. It was a relationship that was to last nearly six years, but was to finish in bitterness and, at the very end, was to culminate in tragedy.

4

PÉTAIN'S CHICKEN

Le Maréchal Pétain était un grand homme: il
est mort en 1925.★

To be so obviously under the protection of a great man is not an
unmixed blessing. De Gaulle was immediately perceived by his colleagues at the Ecole Supérieure de Guerre as '*le poulain préféré*' of Pétain.[1]
It was also clear that he was already much better qualified, for instance in
military history, than many of his tutors. Furthermore, he was extremely intelligent, which is in truth more than can be said either for the staff
or indeed for the generality of the pupils. There was therefore some justification for the advice of contemporaries at the time of his arrival in the
Champ-de-Mars, in November 1922 – after short periods of training
with a tank regiment, an artillery battery and an aviation squadron – that
he would do well to remember that he was entering as a pupil not as a
teacher.

That advice was hardly heeded in his first year, and not at all in his
second. It was in that year, the second of his two-year course, that
some of the less attractive sides of the character of the thirty-three-year-
old captain started to show through very clearly. Now that he was
under the protection of Pétain, he needed no longer to pretend that the
proper attitude was to hide his light under a bushel. The white gloves of
St Cyr became the conceit of the Ecole Supérieure de Guerre. The
inability to make friends among his contemporaries, the refusal to listen
to the opinions of others, the insolence towards his superiors, and his
general attitude suggested that of a 'king in exile', as one report on his
progress puts it.[2] Some of his colleagues at first reacted with hostility.
'He walked very straight, stiff and solemn,' commented one, 'strutting

★ 'Marshal Pétain was a great man; he died in 1925.' Charles de Gaulle, quoted in J.-R.
Tournoux, *Pétain et de Gaulle*; Plon, Paris, 1964.

as though he were moving his own statue.' But they were gradually won over, partly by his obvious ability, partly by 'his intense inner life', in which 'his gaze was firmly fixed on things rather than people', but, perhaps most important, by his 'fund of gaiety' which in spite of his reserve led him, for instance, 'to join his somewhat sepulchral voice to ours when we sang in chorus during a journey'.[3]

Admittedly, the studies at the Ecole were very boring. The selection process ensured that successful candidates were much more likely to become medium-rank staff officers than leaders, and the method of teaching was to expound the current military theories of the day *ex cathedra* without leaving the pupils any opportunity to dispute them. Since those theories were essentially of the crucial importance of defence over offence, views that had been formulated out of the experience of Verdun and the trench warfare of 1917–18, they took no account of the alternative that de Gaulle had seen on the Vistula, the war of movement. In short, in the words of one commentator, 'The army contemplated itself in the mirror of the last war and found itself beautiful. There was total admiration for what our outstanding officers and their heroic troops had achieved.'[4] This was not an attitude calculated to appeal to de Gaulle, who had spent most of that war in a prison camp. Worse still, in order to preserve the purity of the mirror, the War Ministry had prohibited anybody who had taken part in the war from writing about it without its express authorisation. Too many unpalatable truths might have come to light.

The result was a sterile curriculum based on a manual written in October 1920. Four years later the manual had not been revised. It explained, in great detail, how to organise a static war on the basis of the supremacy of fire power; in other words the machine-gun, since the infantry was still regarded as the queen of the battlefield. It was not so much that de Gaulle disagreed with these views. After all, he was at the time working on a study of the role of the fortress in French military history, published the following year. What distressed him and others was that the high command was concerned to train pupils to perfection in only one form of warfare and not to admit, or even to hold discussions about, possible alternatives.

As far as the staff at the Ecole went, de Gaulle became more and more of a nuisance, not least in the way he persisted in correcting his teachers. He was also considered to be rather detached in his work, and outrageously self-satisfied. Finally, in a great affront to authority, he had published, in March 1924, before even receiving his final certificate from the Ecole, his first book, *La Discorde chez l'Ennemi*, which dealt with the themes of war and peace which he was supposed to have been learning about at the Ecole Supérieure de Guerre.

All this posed severe problems when it came to the process of final classification. It was clear that de Gaulle was no ordinary pupil. By any standards, he was an outstanding officer, and only in horsemanship was his record below average. But his attitude was generally perceived to be one of arrogant indiscipline, and the examining board had to take that into account. However brilliant an officer, so it was said, a professional army cannot function unless there is precise discipline in all ranks, and an officer cannot expect to impose discipline on his subordinates unless he is capable of accepting, and working to, the same discipline himself.

The dilemma was clear. There were three possible grades, other than failure, which was out of the question for a protégé of Pétain: *'assez bien'*, the equivalent of a mere pass; *'bien'*, which was neither good nor bad, but the usual category for worthy souls who had worked hard but failed to make any impact; and *'très bien'*, reserved for those who would, in the view of the examiners, go on to occupy the highest positions in the French army. Some of the staff were in favour of awarding de Gaulle simply *'assez bien'*, which would have been more than insulting. After intervention from Pétain, who had heard of the discussions, and at the insistence of the new commandant, General Dufieux, he was finally placed in the ranks of the mediocre: *'bien'* it was.

De Gaulle exploded. He swore that he would never again set foot in the place other than to take charge of it himself. The language he used to describe the instructors was much richer. There was no question of it being a fair verdict. They were idiots – to paraphrase an obscenity – and that was the end of the matter.

Whatever the real or supposed injustice of the case, de Gaulle's grade at the Ecole Supérieure de Guerre had an immediate effect on his future. He had been hoping for a lectureship at the college, but there was no chance of such a post being awarded to any officer who had not passed out with the accolade *'très bien'*. As with all graduates, he was posted to a staff position – not, as happened to those who came in the highest class, to a prominent position with the general staff of the army, but to a job as officer in charge of kitchen equipment and refrigerated food storage at army headquarters. Then, after a few months, he was moved to the staff of the French army of the Rhine, whose headquarters were in Mainz, with the same general area of responsibility for supplies and rations. It was the French military equivalent of Siberia. His wife and family, which now included a new baby daughter, Elisabeth, dutifully went with him.

It was not until July 1925, nine months after leaving the Ecole Supérieure de Guerre, that he was finally rescued, again by Pétain, who had him posted to his own personal staff at his offices in the Boulevard des Invalides. This position was much more to de Gaulle's liking. He obviously enjoyed his work, and could frequently be seen striding across the gardens of the Champ-de-Mars on his way to the office, his height increased by a bowler hat, looking preoccupied and waving his cane as though writing in the air. It was, no doubt, a sign of contentment, since once at the office he worked efficiently and hard.

Pétain's working methods were not always easy to adapt to. He wrote very little himself, and never a first draft, but would choose which of his officers he thought most suitable for the task in hand. He would then outline the idea that he wanted developed into a text and go on to pre-scribe the method: paragraphs few in number and in length proportionate to the point they were making; the simplest possible lan-guage; no adjectives – adjectives were 'ridiculous, like the silk sashes worn by army officers in operettas';[5] never any superlatives, and very few adverbs – and then only when exactly to the point. It was never easy for his staff to follow these instructions, but it was particularly dif-ficult for Captain de Gaulle, whose literary style was quite different.

Nevertheless, de Gaulle seems to have profited from his period with Pétain, working very personally, and in a small group, usually of five officers under the command of a colonel, directly responsible to the Marshal himself. He was particularly fortunate in that Pétain assigned him the special task of studying problems of the longer-term future, a task for which he was eminently well qualified. It was in considering the general problems of military philosophy that he came to articulate, and start to draft, some of the thoughts that formed the basis of his book *Le Fil de l'Epée* (*The Edge of the Sword*).

The truth was that Pétain had considered the class awarded to de Gaulle by the Ecole as almost an insult to himself. He had always mis-trusted the college as being too dogmatic and conservative, and this mistrust was deepened by what seemed to be vindictiveness towards his protégé. By 1926, he was still saying, this time to the new commandant, General Hering, that the more he thought about it, the more he thought that the business was as monstrous as a miscarriage of justice. In 1927 he hit on an idea to revenge himself and his protégé on the stuffed-shirts of the Ecole. The idea was brilliant: he would use his authority as a Marshal of France to insist that Captain de Gaulle be invited to deliver a series of lectures on a subject of his choosing, at the college, with the Marshal himself presiding. There was no precedent for such action, but at least it ensured that the whole college staff would be present to hear, uninterrupted, the words of their rejected pupil.

The first lecture took place on 7 April 1927. The hall was packed. As everybody moved aside to let Pétain through, he pushed de Gaulle forward in front of him, on the grounds that, as he said, it was the lecturer's privilege to lead the way, and, furthermore, that once he had entered the hall he was entitled to teach what he wished. It was an occasion, not least in its theatricality, that was ideally suited to de Gaulle's character, and he made the most of it. In full-dress uniform, with his captain's braid on his arms and his medals on his chest, he mounted the platform. He took off his képi, put his sword down beside it, drew off his white gloves and, on Pétain's brief invitation, delivered himself of a lecture the like of which the assembled company had never heard before.

The subject was military leadership, but those present could have been forgiven for thinking that he was referring as well to political leadership, and indeed, for those who had understood the young captain's ambition, to himself. 'Powerful personalities,' he proclaimed, 'organised for conflict, crises, great events, do not always possess the easy manners and superficially attractive qualities which go down well in ordinary life. They are usually blunt and uncompromising, without social graces. Although deep down the masses may obscurely do them justice, recognising their superiority, they are rarely loved and in consequence rarely find an easy way to the top. Selection boards are inclined to go more on personal charm than merit.'[6] And so it went on.

The audience sat through the speech in mounting indignation. When de Gaulle quoted by heart passages from Plato, Lucretius, Caesar, Frederick the Great, Scharnhorst, Tolstoy, Goethe and Bergson, they were all amazed, but nothing could remove the impression of brilliant arrogance that the captain projected. As most of them said when they filed out of the hall in a state of intellectual shock, this man had never so much as commanded a company, and yet here he was giving them lectures on military leadership. They were insulted at having been required by the Marshal to listen to such impertinence.

The next broadside came a week later. On this occasion, the subject was 'character', and there was an excoriating critique of French military leaders since 1815. Frequently staring at his hero Pétain, de Gaulle went on to describe the real and lasting foundations of a true man of

character. He left little doubt that, as on the first occasion, he was referring to the qualities that he saw firstly in Pétain and then in himself. He
quoted Admiral Fisher's judgement on Admiral Jellicoe after his failure
to rout the German Grand Fleet at Jutland in 1916: 'He has all Nelson's
qualities except one; he does not know how to disobey.'[7]

Once more the staff of the college were stunned, but by this time
they were becoming used to the experience, and by the time the third
lecture was delivered, a further week later, they listened in virtual indifference to a long discursus on the nature of prestige. Most of it went
way above their heads, but the brilliance of delivery had held their
attention, and afterwards no longer could anybody say that the young
captain was someone of no account. The most hostile comment, but an
interesting one, was that he was only a 'pale imitation of Pétain'.[8]

It was now time to leave Pétain's staff, but before he did so de Gaulle
received permission to repeat his three lectures again to a civilian audience at the Sorbonne. The event was sponsored by *Action Française*,
which in itself was enough to provoke some left-wing attempts to have
the whole thing stopped, but otherwise the lectures created little stir.
The public turned out to be rather bored. But the affair of the lectures
had at least established de Gaulle's claim to be a potential future leader,
after his performance and grading at the Ecole de Guerre had virtually
destroyed it. It also shows how far Pétain was prepared to go in defending and promoting de Gaulle's career.

Pétain has been the object of almost universal obloquy since 1940,
and remains under a historical cloud. His record as an almost half-wit-
ted old man, however, in leading France down the path of surrender
and collaboration should not diminish his achievements or detract from
the brilliance of his prime, from his military genius, his courage, his personal charm, or, indeed – and this is singular in a great public figure –
from the efforts he made, without regard to his own interest, to encourage and succour someone whom he believed would make a worthy
successor, not because he liked him, but because of the qualities that he
saw. On the other side, there is no doubt that de Gaulle felt more
admiration for Pétain than he did for any other living man. He recognised this himself, as the dedicatory note to *The Edge of the Sword*,
published finally in 1932 and based mainly on the three lectures of
1927, amply demonstrates. 'This work,' de Gaulle wrote, 'could only be
dedicated to you, *Monsieur le Maréchal*, since nothing demonstrates better than your glory what virtue can be brought to action through the
illumination of pure thought.'[9]

It was in this context that de Gaulle, now promoted major and battalion commander, sought his first command. General Matter, at the time director of infantry in the general staff, and responsible for senior postings, was aware from gossip that he was placing a future commander-in-chief. The position he chose for the Marshal's protégé was that of commander of the 19th Battalion of Alpine Rifles, stationed at Trier in Germany. De Gaulle assumed his command in December 1927, and started to train his battalion to the peak of fitness and morale. Discipline was strict, but the commanding officer also exercised a paternalistic surveillance over the welfare of his men and, thanks to his Jesuit-trained memory, was able to remember their family histories and circumstances without the need for notes.

As a battalion commander, however, Major de Gaulle's record was not without blemish. 'He stood out,' reported one of his officers later, 'not so much because of his size but because of his ego, which shone from afar.'[10] There were too, as might be imagined, difficulties with superior officers, from whom de Gaulle took orders only with reluctance and from whom he rarely accepted criticism. When General Putois, the garrison commander at Trier, reproved de Gaulle's battalion in public for sloppy conduct during manoeuvres, for instance, the battalion commander turned to his troops and shouted to them that the 19th had done well, and that there would be one day off.

De Gaulle even tangled with ministers. The training regime was so fierce that some of his troops asked for a transfer. Through the good offices of a member of the National Assembly, one succeeded. The unfortunate man was immediately thrown into the cells. Further protest followed, prompting a journey to Paris by de Gaulle to seek the intercession of Pétain. Pétain resolved the matter by decisive – and by any standards improper – intervention with the Minister of War in de Gaulle's favour.

Outside barracks, de Gaulle's life was uneventful – apart from the birth of his third child. He and his wife lived in a modest house on the opposite bank of the Mosel from the barracks. He used to walk across the bridge – at a brisk light-infantry pace – to work each morning and back across to his home each evening, lunching alone in the officers' mess at midday. But Trier was always to be a sad place for him and Yvonne, since it was there that their Down's syndrome daughter, Anne, was born. Sad as the event was, the new daughter immediately gained a place in her father's heart, and was to bring out quite unsuspected tenderness in both parents during her stunted life, which lasted altogether some twenty years. But nothing could lift the shadow from her birth-place at Trier on the Mosel.

Almost simultaneously, and perhaps as a consequence, de Gaulle's relationship with his protector became somewhat tetchy. He was disappointed, at the end of his term as battalion commander in Germany, not to be reappointed to Pétain's staff. Marshal Foch had died, and Pétain had been elected to his place in that most distinguished of bodies, the Académie Française. The election of a new academician was always celebrated by an important address, which would be widely read and consequently influential in the right quarters. Everybody knew that Pétain would never draft his own speech, and it was assumed that the task would fall to Major de Gaulle, particularly since he had been keeping his hand in, as it were, by addressing audiences at the French army of the Rhine while still fulfilling his functions as a battalion commander. Furthermore, de Gaulle was believed to be sympathetic with Pétain's critique of Foch, which, it was generally assumed, would be set out in detail in his inaugural address to the Académie. The critique was simple: Pétain held that in signing the 1918 armistice Foch had let the Germans off the hook. He had 'laid down his sword before the enemy was destroyed', had 'spared the proud German army a humiliating disaster', and had allowed it 'to go back across the Rhine unmolested'.[11]

The speech indeed reflected those beliefs, but it was not drafted by de Gaulle, who had been posted to Beirut to the staff of the general officer commanding the French troops in the Levant, General de Bigault du Grandrut. The 'Levant' is not an expression much in use nowadays, but at the time, and indeed up until the end of the Second World War, it was a generic term embracing those territories at the eastern end of the Mediterranean that had been provinces of the Ottoman Empire for some four hundred years, and were now, as the result of the collapse of the Empire in the years leading up to the First World War, and during the war itself, emerging as ethnic groups in their own right. The League of Nations had given France a mandate to administer what are now Syria and the Lebanon, and it was in fulfilment of that mandate that French troops were stationed there to keep the peace. This was not as much of a formality as it might seem; the French had a force of nearly 30,000 men in place in 1929, and between 1917 and 1929 the army had lost more than 9,000 officers and men. It was a sacrifice not lost on the newly arrived major.

The de Gaulles, husband, wife and three children, arrived in Beirut in November 1929 and installed themselves in a spacious house in the

Druze quarter of the city. Their son, Philippe, was enrolled in the Jesuit school, and their daughter, Elisabeth, started her schooling there, at the ancient Convent of the Women of Nazareth. De Gaulle himself used to get up early and, as in Trier, would walk to his office. Strangely enough, the headquarters of the French army in the Levant were located in a large building that had previously housed the harem of the local bey. At least staff officers were assured of comfortable offices, and the new major, whatever his private views, presumably overlooked the unfortunate history of the place.

Social life in Beirut, as in Trier, was uneventful. The de Gaulles hardly went out and entertained little – indeed Mme de Gaulle was hardly seen, preoccupied as she was with little Anne. They had one holiday together, spending two weeks in what they described as 'the Holy Land' in late 1930. Otherwise de Gaulle travelled by himself, or with officer colleagues, particularly in the summer, when the family went to the hills above Beirut to escape the heat. He was able to visit Aleppo, travel beyond the Euphrates, inspect French outposts on the Turkish frontier. The short frontier between Syria and Turkey offered the most military excitement. There was action at Bec du Canard in July 1930, when a Turkish incursion was repelled; and there were other skirmishes. But these were minor events, and de Gaulle, in writing to his father after Bec du Canard, was far more concerned with the French evacuation of the Rhineland, the news of which had arrived in the Levant at the same time.

Meanwhile, de Gaulle continued work on his 1927 lectures, to bring them into a form that could be published as a book. This was his main preoccupation, but he could not help noting the history and circumstances of the French involvement in the Levant, and he joined a Major Yvon in compiling a history of the subject. The work has vanished almost without trace, but it included an elaborate attempt to establish the legitimacy of the French presence, both military and political, in the area by an extended historical analysis, with particular reference to the medieval Crusades. The argument is not, perhaps, wholly convincing, but the important point is that the effort was made. This inquiry, and a recognition of the casualties that France had suffered in keeping the peace in that region, were powerful influences on de Gaulle's future attitudes, not least towards British action in Syria and the Lebanon in the Second World War.

In November 1931, Major de Gaulle had completed his two-year assignment in the Levant and was due for a new job. He was posted, again perhaps on Pétain's initiative, to the Secretariat of National Defence, a body created by the Marshal to review the state of national preparedness in the event of war. It was intellectual work, and de Gaulle responded as an intellectual, writing an assessment of the French military strength in the Levant, a long article on the economics of mobilisation and an extensive discussion document for a national defence plan. *The Edge of the Sword* was finally published in July 1932, just two months after the death of his father Henri. These, again, were difficult moments. He had lost his father. Now aged forty-two, with a record of eventful, but not wholly distinguished, military service behind him, he was about to lose conclusively the protection of the man who had done more than any other to further, against many obstacles, his professional career. In spite of all the courtesies, the Pétain era was now over.

A TOE IN POLITICAL WATERS

Qu'as-tu fait, ô toi que voilà
pleurant sans cesse,
Dis, qu'as-tu fait, toi que voilà,
de ta jeunesse?★

Marshal Pétain was able, by the very weight of his authority as the 'victor of Verdun', to imbue disputes over military doctrine with the flavour of theological controversy. It was not done without purpose. Disputes on both military doctrine and theology have in common that they are disputes about unknown future events; but that only serves to enhance the status of the high priest whose opinion is the more respected. Pétain was very comfortable in the role of high priest. Furthermore, disputes about military doctrine and theology generate an inordinate amount of intellectual heat, and no little bitterness. Pétain was used to that as well.

It was therefore not surprising that the manual of warfare taught at the Ecole Supérieure de Guerre, drafted as it was by the Ecole's commandant, General Debeney, under the guidance of a commission of thirteen senior officers headed by Marshal Pétain and published with the title *Provisional Instruction on the Tactical Employment of Large Units*, became known as the 'Bible'. Based on a distillation of the common experience of the First World War, it set out the elements of strategy for a future war. It advocated a doctrine based primarily on defence, replacing that of the manual of 1913, in which the doctrine of the offensive had been supreme.

The reasons for this change were obvious: France had lost in the war no fewer than 1.3 million men, or 27 per cent of males between the ages of 18 and 27, a casualty rate higher than any other major participant. The strategy for the next war – and nobody doubted that there

---

★ 'What have you done, you, here, who are endlessly weeping; tell me what you have done – you, here – with your youth?' Paul Verlaine, quoted by Charles de Gaulle at the end of the First World War.

would be a next war – could not envisage the repetition of such slaughter. The conclusion was that the proper course of action was to rely on a combination of powerful fire power in defence – 'the preponderant factor of combat', as the document called it[1] – and subsequent offence only when the enemy had been broken. This strategy had allowed Pétain to hold Verdun in 1916, and was to be the pattern for the future.

Just as the consensus in favour of the offensive à l'outrance had been accepted before the war – not least by Lieutenant de Gaulle, both in his addresses to the troops at Arras in 1913 and in his actions when in command of his platoon at Dinant Bridge in 1914 – so the consensus in favour of defence followed by counter-attack was also accepted after the war. But, in spite of the apparent preparedness of the commission to accept modifications to its general thesis as armament technology progressed, the teaching of the doctrine had become ossified as 'defence and nothing but defence'.

Later it was realised that the French army could not simply sit on a defensive line along the Franco-German frontier, and plans were developed for an offensive incursion into Belgium and Holland – to counter the expected German repetition of the Schlieffen Plan invasion through the Low Countries – as well as for an expedition to, of all places, Romania. Experimentation in the latest forms of weaponry was also pursued with vigour. Such was the impression given of strength and vitality that on the eve of the Second World War the French army was considered by many, including Winston Churchill, to be the strongest in Europe, although he warned in 1938 that the balance was swiftly changing in favour of Germany.

It was not a correct impression, as subsequent events were to show. By the end of 1935, the French army was short of men and equipment. The drop in the birth rate during the First World War was making itself felt. About one-fifth of the military budget in 1936 was allocated to building defensive forts, at the expense of re-equipping the fighting troops. The taxis of the Marne and the voie sacrée to supply food to Verdun were forgotten, and military transport regressed to rely on railways and horses. Other armies were trying out radio; the French depended on the telephone. The new rifle was not introduced until 1936, and the numbers issued by 1939 fell well short of the million required.

Above all, the French general staff had failed to make a serious analysis of how far the arrival of the tank had changed the nature of modern warfare. In particular, there was no consideration of whether by proper deployment, not as a support for infantry but as an armament in its own right, the tank could create the sort of war of movement exemplified by the Cossacks who had recreated it in the Ukraine counter-attack against the Poles in 1920. Arguments against the broad consensus in favour of defensive firepower were gradually submerged under the weight of Pétain's prestige.

It was not as though the arguments had never been made. Generals Estienne and Buat, Colonels Allehaut, Chedeville and Doumenc had all either written or spoken in the 1920s and early 1930s in favour of tactical mobility and the importance of the striking power of tanks in their own right. In 1935 Colonel Allehaut even took up the cause of air power, something that most others, except the German high command, had ignored. In Britain, it was the era of 'Boney' Fuller and Basil Liddell Hart. Fuller was a senior officer in the British army who had grasped the problem with enthusiasm and issued a Plan 1919, which described a force employing some 5,000 tanks with support from the air which would strike deep into enemy, that is German, territory. Liddell Hart was also a former British army officer who recognised the decisive change in the conduct of war as the result of the development of the tank, and who had the radical notion in 1925 of a new sort of army, based on the tank, which would operate independently of the normal means of transport such as roads and railways.

The dissidents were never more than a minority, and by 1935 the Pétainist view had decisively won the day. Buat had died, to be succeeded as chief of the general staff by Debeney; Estienne had retired, and others found promotion blocked. The doctrine of static defence had found its most visible memorial in the construction between 1930 and 1935 of a succession of fixed, interlinked and permanently garrisoned fortifications stretching from the Swiss frontier to Luxembourg, named the Maginot Line after André Maginot, the Minister of Defence who piloted the law through in 1930.

Major de Gaulle had noted these developments, and did not like them. His first protest was in muted but, as it turned out, effective form. Soon after the war, Pétain had conceived the idea of writing a book or, to be more accurate, of getting other people to write a book that would appear under his name. It would be a detailed history of the soldier from earliest times to the present day.

By the time de Gaulle was posted to his personal staff, Pétain's project was well advanced. Each of the officers on the staff were allocated a section to draft. De Gaulle was entrusted with, among others, a section dealing with the First World War. He wrote seven chapters which, apart from three anodyne opening chapters on the state of the French army in 1914, were generally critical of the French performance. Since this performance had been based, apart from the disastrous Nivelle offensive of 1917, on Pétain's doctrine of the supremacy of defensive firepower, it was clear that the real target for de Gaulle's draft was precisely the current strategy that Pétain was so strongly advocating.

Colonel Audet, de Gaulle's successor on Pétain's personal staff, was asked to continue work on this section, but in a completely different vein, Pétain having, for instance, described one of de Gaulle's chapters as 'uniformly catastrophic'.[2] Indeed, Pétain's belief that de Gaulle would in time make a worthy successor to him was sharply modified to an attitude of indifference tending towards hostility. In the event, Pétain's magnum opus never saw the light of day. De Gaulle's contribution, on the other hand, did, in the form of a long section of *La France et son Armée,* published in 1938, much, as might be imagined, to the annoyance of Marshal Pétain. The row between the two men that accompanied the drafting of that book's dedication to the Marshal has reverberated ever since.

Audet had, at de Gaulle's request, kept him informed of the Marshal's opinion of the offending chapters, and the fact that de Gaulle was not brought back to Pétain's staff in 1929 told its own story. De Gaulle was now officially out of favour. But the demotion from the position of favourite son had one clear advantage: it meant that de Gaulle could be more forthright in championing views opposed to the Marshal's military doctrine. Once back from the Levant at the Secretariat of National Defence, this is what he started to do.

De Gaulle's task during his long period at the Secretariat, from November 1931 to July 1937, was to study and refine the plans already made to cope with an outbreak of war. Logistical difficulties, problems of national mobilisation and the balance of military resources in Europe all required scrutiny. It was an invaluable preparation for the future General. He was able to dig deep into politics and their relationship to the military problems of the day, to learn to understand the nature of manoeuvre, of keeping options open, of always having a reserve plan in case the preferred tactic failed, of the nature and fallibility of human decisions, and of the springs of ambition. They were all lessons that prepared him for the career that at that point he only dimly perceived for himself but which was to come in its due time. What occupied a great deal of his time, however, was not the pursuit of duties set by the Pétainist agenda, but the study of the alternative agenda that had been set by Buat, Estienne, Liddell Hart and others. He was so persuaded by their arguments that he drafted a pamphlet advocating the cause of a self-sufficient motorised force, which would move wherever it wished and attack the enemy at the most opportune moment.

Vers l'Armée de Métier was published in early 1934, just after de Gaulle had been promoted lieutenant-colonel. There had, in fact, been a preview of the book in the *Revue politique et parlementaire* in May 1933, not that anybody noticed it. The book itself was hardly a best-seller; some 750 copies were sold in France, although it was said that more were sold abroad. By itself, the book is little more than an elegant rewriting of old ideas, and failed, in its first version (amended by de Gaulle after the Second World War) to recognise, as the Germans were starting to recognise, that the successful blitzkrieg could only be conducted by a combination of armoured power and air power working together.

In some respects the timing of publication could not have been better. A disarmament conference had recently been held in Geneva; a new French Government had been sworn in (not that that was anything other than a regular event); Hitler had come to power in Germany on a nationalist and revanchist platform; and there were voices in Britain urging France to reduce the size of its standing army. The idea of a smaller, professional, more expert army was well timed. In another sense, however, the timing could not have been worse. The French Government were investing vast sums of money in the Maginot Line, and Pétain had become Minister of War. The publication of the book, written by a serving officer, became in itself a political event.

At this point, de Gaulle, aged forty-four and making slow progress up the military career ladder. was obviously prepared to take risks. Pétain's protection had been lost, for good or ill, and he had to make his own way. As a serving officer, without power or even much influence, there was little he could do to promote what he believed to be right. There were lectures, certainly, but these were of limited use in rousing informed opinion. In the defence debate in the Chamber of Deputies in June 1934, the radical Edouard Daladier,* the 'bull of Vaucluse', tore the opposition apart in defending the strategy of the Maginot Line, and

* Edouard Daladier (1884–1970): Politician. Radical Mayor of Carpentras (Vaucluse) 1912–58; Prime Minister 1933–4 and 1938–40; signed Munich agreement 1938 (for which British awarded him the Grand Cross of the Order of St Michael and St George); arrested by Vichy, held in custody in Germany 1943–5, including some months in Buchenwald; opposed de Gaulle in 1958, lost his seat and faded from sight.

three months later Léon Blum,* the socialist leader, had declared his opposition to the concept of a professional standing army in an article in *Le Populaire*. But at least the argument was now near the top of the political agenda, and that was to the advantage of those such as de Gaulle who were trying to make the French Government change course before, as they saw it, it was too late.

It was, of course, much too late. The army high command had prepared its defences. From the time of the publication of de Gaulle's book until 1940, the ideas contained in it were systematically attacked by every military leader. There was a good deal in the book, quite apart from its lack of originality, that could reasonably be attacked. The soldiers in the army that de Gaulle advocated appeared to be very close to a master race, as Blum pointed out; the army itself was supposed to live off the land – shades of the 1920 Cossacks – even to the point of being able to bake its own bread; fuel supply was not envisaged as a problem. The whole picture, perhaps rather too romantic to sound real, was open to ridicule.

It was not the detail of what was proposed that was important, however, but the principle. Lieutenant-Colonel de Gaulle was now entering the world of politics, and he quickly realised that in politics it does not matter what is said as much as who says it. It so happened that there was a politician of stature willing to champion his cause. Paul Reynaud,[†] a former Finance Minister, politically right-wing but not an extremist, had understood the principle, and sought expert advice. Reynaud wished to consult a serving officer on the practical problems of the new military doctrine. De Gaulle was the obvious person.

But it was not enough to consult only one man. Reynaud was lucky enough to find not just de Gaulle – controversial, arrogant, perhaps too conceited – but a group of officers, and civilians interested in the military future, who generally shared his opinions. The formation of this group had been a strange affair. Some time in the late 1920s, while he

---

* Léon Blum (1872–1950): Politician and writer. Socialist; wrote for *L'Humanité* 1904–14 (described by de Gaulle's mother as 'agent of Satan'); Deputy 1919–1940 and post war; Prime Minister 1936–7 and 1938; arrested by Vichy 1940, deported to Germany 1943; Prime Minister again 1946–7.

[†] Paul Reynaud (1878–1966): Lawyer and politician. Barrister at Paris Court of Appeal; Deputy for Basses-Alpes 1919, for Paris 1928, 1932, 1936: Minister for Colonies, Justice (twice), Finance (thrice), Foreign Affairs in 1930s; Prime Minister 20 March–16 June 1940; imprisoned 1940–5; Deputy Prime Minister 1953; Delegate to Council of Europe 1949–52.

was still officially attached to Marshal Pétain, de Gaulle had started to meet, and not just to meet but to meet for serious purposes, a number of friends – all, it should be said, male. From the early 1930s onwards, particularly when de Gaulle returned from the Lebanon, they had been meeting regularly in a brasserie in Montparnasse for discussion, and indeed out of friendship. It was in the disputation of this group that de Gaulle was to test the military theories that he now espoused, and in which Paul Reynaud had come to be interested.

The leading figures in this group, which never numbered more than eight or ten, were Lieutenant-Colonel Emile Mayer and Captain Lucien Nachin. Their names are not themselves significant but for the fact that de Gaulle was not, and never would be, given to close male friendships and these men were probably the closest friends he ever had in his whole life.

Mayer was already an old man, born in 1851 of a Jewish family in Angoulême, and subsequently drifting into the army for lack of anything better, but nevertheless writing some rather contentious articles about military affairs, always against the grain of the opinion of the times. Although he had been for a time under the protection of Foch, he was unpopular with the military authorities, and had to wait seventeen years to be promoted from the rank of captain. A spiky character in his seventies, he attached himself to de Gaulle. So too did Nachin, Mayer's friend and more than thirty years his junior. Here was a real acolyte, such as de Gaulle attracted throughout his life. He was the son of a policeman and, like de Gaulle, had his origins in northern France. Also like de Gaulle, he had spent most of the First World War as a prisoner, but had never wished to stay in the army, instead pursuing a career as an official of the Paris Métro.

It was in this group, and in the Montparnasse brasserie, that de Gaulle came to know Paul Reynaud – who, although an admirer of de Gaulle, was certainly no acolyte. He came from a quite different background and had quite different tastes. Of farming stock in southern France, he had become a successful lawyer and also, as it happened, an expert on Chinese art. He was small in stature, but pugnacious and courageous. His eyebrows had a habit of jerking upwards when he spoke, making it difficult to take what he said altogether seriously. He was aggressive in debate, however, making no concessions to his opponents either in style or in content.

In 1934 Reynaud's objective was similar to that of Winston Churchill: to draw attention to the reality of what was going on in

Germany – and he pursued it with the same single-mindedness in France as Churchill did in Britain. Indeed, the two men kept in touch with one another and exchanged ideas. In neither country did their efforts meet with much success. For Churchill, the political climate in Britain was unfavourable, and for Reynaud in France the parliamentary debates of 1934 and 1935 achieved nothing apart from fine speeches; and while the speeches were being made, Europe can be seen, with hindsight, as moving inexorably towards war.

In January 1935 a plebiscite in the Saarland returned the province to Germany. On 7 March 1936 Hitler remilitarised the Rhineland. On 16 March conscription was reintroduced in Germany. France, who two years previously had told the disarmament conference that she would 'henceforth guarantee her security by her own means',[3] did nothing. General Gamelin, the new commander-in-chief, had said that any action would involve a general mobilisation. It was unthinkable; after all, a general election was only a few weeks away. So nothing was done. Hitler's first and greatest gamble succeeded, and it was only a matter of time before France herself paid the price.

Throughout the early 1930s, and indeed up until the Second World War, the political atmosphere in France was nothing if not feverish. Governments came and went, tempers ran high, and political fragmentation seemed, as in other countries, to be the dominant theme of the moment. *Action Française* – now proscribed by the Vatican and therefore officially off de Gaulle's reading list – proclaimed, 'We must bring Pétain to power, and he will restore the king.'[4] There was a series of right-wing conspiracies, such as the one involving three generals in a 'secret committee for revolutionary action', whose mission seems to have been to counter the alarming prospect of squadrons of Soviet aeroplanes taking off from Spanish airfields and occupying French bases.

Then there were the financial scandals. In 1928, a former Finance Minister, Klotz, had been arrested on a charge of issuing bogus cheques. In 1930, a certain Oustric had managed to build up a large banking establishment, financed somehow by the Banque de France, whose assets turned out to be illusory. But the major scandal was provided by Serge Stavisky in 1933. The son of a Russian-Jewish dentist, Stavisky became a society financier who used his connections to deal in securities to the advantage of himself and his friends. In late 1933, however, he overreached himself by arranging for the issue of a sizeable volume of bonds on the Paris market, the proceeds of which were apparently to be used to finance a small municipal pawnshop in Bayonne. The bonds, thanks to Stavisky's network of contacts, were fully subscribed, but the destination of the funds was not as advertised. In short, the destination was to be Stavisky's own pocket. When this came to light, Stavisky himself tried to escape to Switzerland, but, on being cornered by the French police, shot himself.

The Radical government of the day tried to hush up the matter, but the right wing claimed that Stavisky had been murdered to prevent him from revealing the identities of influential politicians who had benefited financially from his activities. There was talk of a Jewish conspiracy, combined, odd as it may seem, with a Radical freemason plot. There was even suspicion, perhaps unjustified, that the police had been less hasty in the performance of their duties than they might have been. The police officer charged with the investigation was later found dead on a railway line, tied up and full of poison. Again, the right-wing press assumed that he had been silenced.

All in all, it was an unhappy story, and the end of it was that the current Prime Minister, Camille Chautemps, whose own conduct was not beyond suspicion, was forced to resign. This, in turn, led to riots in front of the Chamber of Deputies in February 1934. There were 40,000 demonstrators, and in the confusion the police opened fire, killing 16 and wounding more than 600. Over 600 policemen were injured. The Government resigned, to be replaced by a new 'national' Government, with Pétain as Minister of War. At the same time, the Socialists under Blum and the Communists under Maurice Thorez reached agreement on a Popular Front against fascism. It took until October 1935 for the Radicals to throw in their lot too, and then another six months before a general election swept the Popular Front into power. The enthusiasm for the new order was intense. On 24 May 1936, 400,000 marched through the centre of Paris shouting '*Vive la Commune!*' – a reminder of the Commune of 1871. The Popular Front was now well and truly in office.

De Gaulle watched these events with a sense of helpless fear, which turned to fury when he found that he had been left off the list for promotion to colonel in 1936, on the instructions of General Maurin, who had replaced Pétain as Minister of War but was thoroughly Pétainist in military doctrine. It was an obvious rebuke for his efforts at political lobbying and his suspected association with the right wing. The gesture was petty, but that was the climate of the times. In any case, after an approach to Daladier, de Gaulle's name was put back on the list, and in November 1937, as a full colonel, he was given command of the 507th Regiment of Fighter Tanks stationed at Metz. As de Gaulle left for his posting, Maurin said, 'You have given us enough trouble with your paper tanks. Let us see what you make of the metal sort.'[5]

By this time de Gaulle had become almost obsessed with the theory of tank warfare, to the point where, even in manoeuvres, he was prepared to disobey orders to demonstrate his point. The fact that his army corps commander was General Giraud was to add spice for the future, not least because Giraud referred to him as '*mon petit de Gaulle*',[6] which was descriptively inaccurate as well as being deliberately offensive. By that time, anyway, it was all too late. The Rhineland had been remilitarised by Hitler without any French intervention. The Popular Front had come and gone. There was Munich, then Poland, and then war. The ultimate test of French military doctrine, like the ultimate test of theological theory, had arrived. Colonel de Gaulle, sitting as he was in the shadow of the Maginot Line, viewed the prospect with the most profound pessimism.

6

THE CUT OF THE SICKLE

Schwarzbraun ist die Haselnuss;
Schwarzbraun bin ich auch – ja ich;
Schwarzbraun muss mein Mädel sein,
Gerade so wie ich. *

It was generally agreed that the summer season of 1939 was one of the most brilliant that Paris had seen for many years. The omens, after all, were favourable. The Popular Front, which according to some had threatened the imminent arrival of full-scale communism – the cry 'Rather Hitler than Blum' had been frequently heard – had collapsed; civil war had been averted; Munich had brought peace with Hitler; the defence of the country, if peace failed, was in the capable hands of Daladier and that clever General Gamelin. All was therefore for the best, and Le Tout Paris, indulging in one of its periodic bouts of self-indulgence, was determined to have a good time.

Apart from the 14 July parade, which was, as always, the climax of the season – with its procession of cuirassiers in their polished breastplates, troops from the African empire, cavalry on prancing horses, and so on – there was one social event which it was considered the worst fortune to have missed. The annual party at the Polish embassy in early July was undoubtedly the place to be and to be seen. It was in the grandest possible style. In passing, it was perhaps noted that too many of the distinguished guests were anxious to pay court to the suave and ever-popular Herr Otto Abetz from the German embassy and his delightful French wife. In their turn, of course, they were particularly assiduous in explaining, in careful asides, how the interests of France and Germany marched in common. Apart from that slightly sinister undercurrent, the whole event was a quite splendid occasion, culminating in the Polish

---

* 'The hazelnut is dark brown; I too am dark brown; my girl must be dark brown, exactly like me.' Marching song of the German infantry in May 1940. Henri de Wailly, *De Gaulle sous le casque*, page 30; Perrin, Paris, 1990.

ambassador leading his staff, barefoot and at three o'clock in the morning, in a polonaise across the embassy lawn.

Ten weeks later, although the Polish embassy still stood, Poland herself had been removed from the map by the German blitzkrieg and the cynical territorial ambition of the Germans' new ally the Soviet Union. The season was well and truly over. Indeed, a polonaise of such style was never to be danced again.

To be fair to the revellers, they had had no inkling of what to expect. This was the first time that the world had seen the German military machine in full action. There had been dress rehearsals, during the Spanish Civil War and, in a small way, in Czechoslovakia, but nobody had seen the real thing.

The blitzkrieg – 'lightning war' – was a combination of three different and well-developed techniques. First, there was the panzer spearhead: massed armour supported by motorised infantry, motorcycle troops who buzzed like wasps around the armoured columns eliminating stray pockets of resistance. Second, there was the true infantry, the real Wehrmacht, marching at times many miles behind the panzers but in the end catching them and occupying the ground across which the armour had rampaged. Third – and this was the new element that neither Liddell Hart, nor de Gaulle, nor even the German tank expert Heinz Guderian had foreseen in the 1920s and 1930s – supporting these ground troops was the Luftwaffe, the air arm. The Luftwaffe supplied both the attacking barrage needed to soften up the enemy before the panzer charge and the air cover to protect the supporting infantry from the enemy's aviation counter-attack. Principally, this air arm consisted of three types of aircraft: the Ju-87 dive-bomber, the Sturzkampfflugzeug, 'Stuka' for short; the Ju-52 transport plane, which could land on almost any flat piece of ground and bring up supplies to keep the Stukas in action at the front; and the fighter, the Me-109, which was the most manoeuvrable aeroplane in the air at the time, and faster than all except the British Spitfire.

The Stukas were particularly frightening. Although their accuracy in bombing was no better than mediocre, they dived almost vertically and were equipped with a howling siren, the sound of which once heard, it was said, was never forgotten. Each soldier below felt that the Stuka was heading directly for him, and that there was no escape. Immediately after such a battering, to have to resist the onrush of the tanks was more than man could take. At least it proved so in the case of Poland, which succumbed after a spirited, often heroic but ultimately fruitless resistance.

All this was noted by Colonel de Gaulle. For him, 1938 and the first half of 1939 was a period of almost constant depression, and the 507th Tank Regiment bore the brunt of his bad humour. By strict discipline he brought the regiment to a high standard of efficiency, and this, among other things, was reported by de Gaulle to Reynaud, with whom he maintained a regular correspondence; to Blum, who although ostracised in Paris because of his leadership of the Popular Front, was more and more convinced of the ideas that de Gaulle was articulating; and to many others. At this time too, de Gaulle's gloom was intensified, not only by the death of his friend Emile Mayer, but also by his growing belief that the Third Republic itself was dying. He joined a mildly rebellious Catholic group which supported an anti-fascist pamphlet *Temps Présent*, whose views, although not as extreme as the monarchism of Maurras, were nevertheless authoritarian and anti-parliament; and he continued to press on anybody who would listen the necessity of a total reorganisation of the French defence effort.

The main concern was whether France would learn the lessons of Poland. The portents were bad. Immediately after the invasion de Gaulle was back in Paris awaiting appointment to a new post and lobbying for support. He noted the debates in the Assembly over the declaration of war. They make absurd reading: there was ludicrous talk of invoking the mediation of Mussolini and irrelevant questions about whether Frenchmen were prepared to die for Danzig. None of this impressed de Gaulle, who, after a short period in Paris, talking to anybody who would talk to him – Reynaud, Blum, Edouard Herriot* and others – left to take up his new appointment as staff colonel coordinating the tank units of the French 5th Army, tucked in behind the Maginot Line in Alsace. What 'coordinating' meant was not at all clear, but what was clear was that the French armour, instead of being concentrated, was again being dispersed. Even the 507th Tank Regiment was split up. Far from learning the lessons of Poland, Gamelin seemed determined to ignore them.

The phoney war, as it became known, lasted from September 1939 to May 1940. The French army simply sat and waited, partly behind the Maginot Line, and partly along the northern frontier, ready to move

---

* Edouard Herriot (1872–1957): Politician. Called himself 'Socialist-Radical' but sometimes difficult to pin down politically. Mayor of Lyon 1905; Minister for Transport during First World War; Prime Minister 1924–5, 1926 and 1932; imprisoned by Vichy and then Germans 1942–45; President of National Assembly 1947–53. Académie Française.

swiftly into Belgium once the Germans attacked – as Gamelin, ensconced in his gloomy headquarters at the Château de Vincennes, was sure they would do – along the same line as they had in 1914. The British Expeditionary Force (BEF) under Lord Gort came alongside, ready at the French command to join in the move that Gamelin had planned. It was all to be quite simple. The Germans would repeat the Schlieffen Plan of 1914, breaking through into Belgium north of the Ardennes – the Ardennes themselves having been declared 'impassable' by the French high command on Pétain's advice, although Pétain had added 'provided certain measures are taken'[1] – and then would swing down through Flanders to encircle Paris. To combat this manoeuvre, the Armée du Nord, consisting of the 1st, 2nd, 7th and 9th French armies under Generals Blanchard, Huntziger, Giraud and Corap respectively, and the BEF under General Gort, with Marshal Gaston Billotte in overall command, would move rapidly to positions in Holland and Belgium, to be known as the Breda–Dyle line, thereby totally frustrating the enemy. The war would then have been won, as it was won in 1918.

It all made perfectly good sense, and turned out to be quite wrong. What the French had not understood was the power of the blitzkrieg, or the tactical brilliance of the German generals who were in charge of it. It had all been in a French military intelligence analysis at the beginning of 1940, but the high command believed that there were special conditions in Poland which made a blitzkrieg suitable there, while those conditions did not obtain on the Western Front. De Gaulle took a different view, which he expressed with some force to those who could be induced to listen, not least a group of British MPs visiting the front in February 1940. One of them reported later that he had had to stand for two hours in the snow, wearing only an ordinary London suit and overcoat, 'watching his [de Gaulle's] beastly tanks going up and down a hill', while de Gaulle had a leather overcoat and high boots.[2] They were then treated to a lecture by the colonel, who informed them crisply that 'this war is lost; we must now prepare to win the next – with machines'.[3]

This message was the nub of a memorandum that the colonel had written a week or so before, when he had seen the intelligence analysis of the Polish campaign. Although not preserved in the original, and reproduced only in a shortened version, it shows clearly that de Gaulle had fully understood the nature of the German military threat, although neither he nor anyone else could predict the exact direction it would take. The memorandum was sent to eighty prominent people, both civilian and military; as he himself later remarked, in a rare outburst of modesty, it 'produced no shock'.[4]

November 1939 saw the invasion of Finland by some remarkably inefficient elements of the Red Army – the opposition to which was seized on by the western press, in default of anything more interesting in the real war, as the defence of civilisation against the assault of the Russian bear. Resistance duly petered out in mid-March 1940, but the episode had the surprising effect, owing to the heroic postures that had been struck at the beginning and the subsequent inaction throughout the conflict, of bringing down the Daladier Government on 19 March. President Lebrun called on Reynaud to form a government, and for the first time de Gaulle saw hope both for France and for himself. He was not slow to make his views felt to his old friend; indeed, he volunteered himself for ministerial office – an offer which Reynaud would have accepted, but that his majority in the Assembly (one vote) made him dependent on Daladier's support, and Daladier would not have de Gaulle anywhere near the Government at any price.

Worse still, Reynaud went on to appoint Paul Baudouin, a known defeatist, to the post that he had earmarked for de Gaulle. In disgust, de Gaulle asked to go back to his military command and to his tanks. Two things, however, assuaged his disappointment: first, the news that the Reynaud Government was to sign a binding commitment with the British Government, still under Neville Chamberlain, that neither would sign a separate peace agreement without the other; and, second, the informal advice he received that an armoured division, the fourth of a series, was planned, and that he would be given its command. It was not much consolation, but it was all that there was.

There was an immediate surprise in store for Reynaud and, indeed, for the world. Within a few hours on 8 April 1940 the Germans over-ran Denmark, and on the next day occupied all the main ports in Norway, effectively sealing off Scandinavia from the Allies. The British Government tried to organise a military response, but it was half-heart-ed and inefficient, and ended in retreat, albeit after some heroic moments. As a result, Hitler had now secured access to the iron-ore supplies which his armies needed, and the British had been shown up in the eyes of the world, and particularly of the United States, as bum-bling incompetents, unable to carry through any successful military operation. The lesson was not lost on the House of Commons, which in debates of 7 and 8 May made clear their disapproval of the

Chamberlain Government. Chamberlain resigned and, after much discussion, Winston Churchill became leader of a Coalition Government.

Colonel de Gaulle had been appointed to command the 4th Armoured Division on 7 May, the first day of the Commons debate in London. The division, of course, did not as yet exist. Units were still being assembled, and the staff work would take time. Furthermore, there was a major crisis in the new Reynaud Government. The Prime Minister declared himself in total opposition to his own Minister of Defence, Daladier, and delivered a damning assessment of the commander-in-chief, General Gamelin. It threatened another government collapse, but in the event was of no consequence, because all discussion was overtaken by the next surprise, the launch, at first light on 10 May 1940, of Operation Sichelschnitt.

Sichelschnitt, 'the cut of the sickle', was the codename for the long-awaited German offensive against France (Belgium and Holland being attacked simultaneously). It was one of the most brilliant military plans in the history of warfare. The original intention of the German high command had been to repeat the Schlieffen Plan, as Gamelin had expected them to do; but as the months went by and Hitler was denied the attack that he had badly wanted before the end of 1939, the plan was modified, and modified again and again. Its final version was mostly the concept of Erich von Manstein, a Polish–German general who had changed his name from Lewinski and worked his way up the German ranks to become chief of staff of Marshal von Rundstedt's Army Group 'A', which was to launch the attack on the ground.

The plan was, like all good plans, very simple. The main attack, or *Schwerpunkt*, would be at the weakest part of the French defences, where the Maginot Line petered out and where Gamelin thought he was protected by the Ardennes. It was precisely through the Ardennes, which in fact formed perfect cover for tank movements, that the panzer group under General von Kleist, and more particularly XIX Panzer Corps under Guderian, would move to attack Sedan. A secondary attack would be launched into Belgium to cross the river Meuse at Dinant further north; this would be led by 7 Panzer Division under General Rommel.

In spite of last-minute scares and leaks (which the French did not believe), Sichelschnitt achieved total surprise. Some 2000 tanks were manoeuvred into battle positions, most of them through the Ardennes, without being spotted by Allied reconnaissance. The lines of the supporting infantry on the march stretched back across the north German plain, equally unnoticed. The assault took place as planned, and on the fifth day Guderian had crossed the Meuse and captured Sedan. Within the next few hours, he, and Rommel to the north, broke westwards in strength. The battle was, to all intents and purposes, over. France was lost.

It was part of the beauty of Sichelschnitt, not fully appreciated even by the Germans at the time, that it allowed so many options once the panzers had broken through. The Germans could make a right turn and hit the allied Armée du Nord in its southern flank; they could make a left turn and roll up the Maginot Line from the rear; they could head directly for Paris to the south-west; or, finally, they could drive for the Channel ports, cutting off the Armée du Nord and, with luck, preventing the BEF from returning to England. The last option was the most dangerous, since it would expose their southern and northern flanks to counter-attack at the same time, precisely during the difficult period when the infantry was still a long way behind the armour and unable to occupy securely the territory in the panzers' rear. Such was the Germans' confidence, however, that they had little hesitation in choosing the last option. The race to the Channel was on.

Gamelin was taken completely by surprise. On 10 May the Armée du Nord had duly moved into Belgium and Holland, and the first reports had been encouraging. The German attack had been expected there, and was being countered; Rommel was held up – for a day or two. But the full extent of Guderian's assault on Sedan had not been appreciated. De Gaulle was convinced that the northern attack was not the main one, but even he thought that the main attack would be delayed. Five days later, after Guderian's capture of Sedan, the situation had changed completely. The French 2nd Army under Huntziger and 9th Army under Corap had been broken by the German onslaught; the 7th Army under Giraud was stranded north of Antwerp; and the British were obviously starting to look for a way home. In all the confusion the only real question was which of their options the Germans would take. The French, not unnaturally, thought that they would head for Paris.

Gamelin, and his subordinate General Georges, the operational commander on the Northern Front, decided to move the French 6th Army under General Touchon from behind the shelter of the Maginot Line, where they had been waiting for the German attack that never came, to the line of the river Aisne, to block the expected advance of the enemy on Paris. As this manoeuvre would take time, the 4th Armoured Division – de Gaulle's division – was ordered to engage the enemy in the area of Laon, to give a breathing space for the 6th Army to settle into its new positions.

For the first time, Colonel de Gaulle was in command of a tank force of the kind that he had been advocating for many years. Admittedly, the 4th Division was far from complete, and on his way to the combat area de Gaulle had to recruit a number of stragglers, dispersed units of light tanks, armoured cars and artillery – which he did by the simple expedient of shouting at them in a loud voice that they were under his orders, a statement which they were obviously too surprised to contest. What became progressively clear to him on 16 May, the day after he had set up his operational headquarters, was that the enemy were not making for Paris at all, as Gamelin and Georges had supposed, but for the west, St Quentin, the Somme – and the sea. The realisation that the French generals had been duped was bad enough, but the final insult was the spectacle of lines of French soldiers trooping sullenly southwards, caught by the panzer drive and told to throw down their arms and march to the south so as not to block the roads along which the German tanks were advancing. 'We haven't got time,' the Germans yelled as they passed, 'to take you prisoner.'[5]

The explosion of de Gaulle's rage is audible even fifty years after the event and thirty-five years after he expressed it in his memoirs. This was the point, he wrote, at which he had decided that, whatever the cost, he personally would fight on until this enemy was defeated. There is no reason on this occasion to doubt his own version; nor is there any reason to doubt his unwavering commitment in that moment to whatever was to follow, a commitment which was certainly to be severely tested in the years to come.

Meanwhile, there was work to be done. Even if the panzers were making for the Channel, there was no reason not to harry them as they went, and there was always the chance of a concerted move between the northern and southern armies which would cut in two the panzer corridor, as it became known, and so turn the tables on the attackers.

By 17 May, Guderian had been forced to accept a halt in the panzer drive. Vehicles badly needed maintenance; men needed rest; the infantry needed time to catch up; permanent communications had to be established, forward airfields consolidated, and so on. It was time for a twenty-four-hour pause, the first real day of rest since the beginning of the campaign a week earlier. As luck would have it, 17 May was also the day chosen by General Georges for a series of incursions into the corridor from the north and the south. The 4th Armoured Division was set to make one of these incursions, and de Gaulle decided, after reconnaissance, that he would try to cut into Guderian's supply line by occupying the road junction of Montcornet, some 20 miles north-east of Laon and 30 miles due north of Rheims.

By dawn on 17 May, de Gaulle had only four battalions of tanks, of which two comprised light Renault R-35s mounted with the obsolete 37mm gun, another R-35s with an updated gun, and the fourth heavier tanks with the powerful 75mm gun, which had undergone only one practice shoot. He was soon joined by a company of D-2 light tanks, armed with the powerful 47mm gun, but there was no air support. All in all, it was not much of an armoured division. Nevertheless, de Gaulle gave the order to advance, and the division rolled up the road from Laon to Montcornet, overrunning a motorcycle detachment as they went, destroying a few armoured cars that happened to be in their way, cleaning up three villages and a group of German lorries, and finally arriving at the outskirts of Montcornet at three o'clock in the afternoon.

De Gaulle had selected a good target, not just because of the road junction but because Montcornet, or rather Lislet, a small village just across the river, turned out to be the command post of 1st Panzer Division at the time. General Kirchner, the divisional commander, had been the victim of an accident two days before, when a truck had run over his knee while he was asleep. Apoplectic with rage and pain, he had refused to leave his post, and sat glowering in front of the operations map, relying on others to be his eyes and ears. The news that they brought at 3.30 that afternoon was so improbable as to provoke total disbelief: it was simply not possible that French tanks could be so close. Besides, all the German tanks were either in the workshops or parked, their crews resting.

But it was true. French tanks were already entering Lislet. Barriers were hastily erected, and there was a quick evacuation of the divisional command post. A staff officer, Kielmansegg, drove at speed back to Guderian's headquarters at Soize, a village three miles to the west, to warn the corps commander. On his way he saw a few tanks coming out of the workshops and ordered them into action immediately. At the same time a battery of 88mm anti-aircraft guns opened up from the hill behind Lislet and knocked out several of the light tanks. When Kielmansegg returned to Lislet, the village was on fire and burned out French tanks littered the street. The lighter Renaults had retired, to be replaced a little later by the heavier B1-bis tanks, but these were not able to withstand the gunfire aimed at their tracks and, after seeing the leading tank blown up with the squadron commander in it, they soon turned about and headed back.

By now the Germans were fully alert. The 88mm guns stopped another column of French tanks and the German armour itself was now joining in the skirmish. 'Lost children thirty kilometres in advance of the Aisne,' de Gaulle later wrote. 'We had to put an end to a situation that was risky, to say the least.'[6] Bombed mercilessly by Stukas on their way back, the French tanks struggled to safety. Captain Idée, the commander of a squadron of Renaults, thought, 'We shall never get out of this; I am blinded by sweat; I wipe myself with my sleeve – and the medallion of Ste Thérèse which I carry on my wrist smiles at me; I kiss it.'[7]

The whole affair was over in a day. It had achieved little beyond showing the Germans that there were still some Frenchmen who were prepared to fight. De Gaulle's own account in his memoirs makes the most, and more than the most, of the engagement, but his official report, that it was an 'offensive reconnaissance', is nearer the mark. The 4th Armoured Division lost 23 tanks out of 90 that started the day, and there is no record of a single German tank being put out of action.

Nothing daunted, however, de Gaulle attacked again two days later. This time, his objective was to take the bridges across the Serre at Crécy-sur-Serre, and so to cut into Guderian's line of advance. The division, reinforced by a regiment of artillery and two squadrons of medium tanks, and now consisting of about 150 tanks, started moving northwards at dawn on 19 May. At first the going was easy, but Crécy was heavily defended, and when they arrived there the French tanks came under heavy anti-tank fire. The advance halted, it was the turn of the Stukas, which came screaming down vertically out of a clear blue sky. De Gaulle made a desperate plea for French air support, which should have been there already but for a muddle between the two commands over the timing of the attack, but it was too late, and he was forced to pull back. He later commented that a properly organised and supported mechanised force could have easily broken right through, joined up with the northern army, cut off most of the panzers to the west and turned to face the German infantry, which was still laboriously trying to catch up in the east.

That chance had been lost. The infantry arrived to fill the vacuum left by the speed of the panzer advance. As Churchill remarked: 'The tortoise has protruded its head very far from its shell',[8] but it was more than the Allies could do to cut its head off. Gamelin was sacked but replaced by, of all people, the seventy-three-year-old Weygand, who had been brought back out of retirement to command the French forces in Syria, where he had been since the beginning of the war, dreaming up complex schemes for launching attacks on the Balkans or bombing the Baku oilfields. Weygand's first analysis showed that the German corridor was now 100 miles wide; a coordinated pincer movement was out of the question, even if there had been any reserves to throw in, which there were not. Defeatism was now in the air.

Weygand's answer was to form a line along the Somme and the Aisne, and defend it, leaving the Armée du Nord to fend for itself. Orders were therefore issued to regroup along that line. The 4th Armoured Division, still commanded by de Gaulle but now with the temporary rank of brigadier-general, moved westwards to take up position just south of Abbeville at the mouth of the Somme. By the time the division arrived, the German infantry had crossed the Somme at Abbeville and formed a bridgehead, with the aim of securing and holding the river crossings while the panzers turned north to deal with the Allied forces trapped to the north and the British making their way in haste towards the evacuation point at Dunkirk.

The battle of Abbeville aroused controversy which has lasted to this day. At the time, although it was an engagement involving major forces, it was wholly overshadowed by the Dunkirk evacuation. De Gaulle's own account, which reflects great credit on himself, is far from trustworthy. However, some facts are not in doubt – for instance, that de Gaulle was ordered to attack and eliminate the German bridgehead, and that he failed to do so, as had the British before him. A force of more than 160 French tanks, of which 33 were the heavy B1-bis, was held by two German infantry battalions and two artillery groups. The French gained about 4½ miles of territory and took some 250 prisoners, but by the end of the battle had only 24 tanks in working order. The true victor of the battle, if there was a true victor, was Lieutenant-Colonel Wolf, the German commander of the 88mm gun batteries in the bridgehead. The French armour, even the B1-bis, could not withstand the power of the 88mm, and repeated tank charges into the teeth of the artillery served the French as badly as had repeated charges against the English archers on the same field at Crécy-en-Ponthieu 600 years earlier.

De Gaulle gave a much rosier account of the engagement, not just in his memoirs but in a telephone call to Reynaud after the battle. He was subsequently summoned to Paris, and it seems likely that Reynaud at this time raised the possibility of his joining the Government. He reported in person to Weygand, who was justifiably irritated when he found out that de Gaulle had already been in direct contact with Reynaud to report on events at Abbeville. De Gaulle's proposal that the specialist armoured divisions should be brought together in a corps under his own command met with a frosty answer from the commander-in-chief. De Gaulle retorted by writing Reynaud a blistering letter attacking him for abandoning France to 'men of yesteryear' – an obvious reference to Pétain and Weygand – who were blocking all progress, and exhorting him to stand up and play the man.

Two days later, on 5 June 1940, General de Gaulle was invited to join Reynaud's Government as Under-Secretary of State for War. The soldier was about to become a politician. Perhaps, almost subconsciously, the transition had already begun, throughout the 1930s and into 1940. The army by itself was no longer able to save France. Strong government was required, and de Gaulle already believed that he was the man to provide it.

7

IS HE A NEW NAPOLEON?

There is, apparently, a young French General called de Gaulle,
of whom Winston thinks a great deal. *

Reynaud's Council of Ministers of June 1940 could hardly be described
as a determined and united body of men. There had been no question
of a repeat of the *union sacrée* of the First World War, when political parties had sunk their differences in the common patriotic cause and
President Poincaré (albeit reluctantly and then not until late 1917) had
agreed to serve alongside Clemenceau for the good of France. For a
start, the head of state, President Albert Lebrun, who might have been
able to give a lead, was old and weak, perhaps even verging on senility.
He was unable to remember names, dates or even simple facts. Political
rivalries were anyway too entrenched. Daladier had earlier tried to
bring the big names together into his Government, but Edouard
Herriot, when asked to become Foreign Minister, had replied 'What
for?'; and the old Marshal Pétain had said that he would join the
Government only if Herriot were excluded. With his one-vote majority in the Assembly, Reynaud could not afford experiments and had to
put up with what he could get.

What he got was a mixture of abilities and attitudes. In the jargon of
the day, Reynaud himself was a 'hard' and was supported by a number
of like-minded ministers, such as Georges Mandel,† but he was forced
into accepting others, such as Baudouin, who were distinctly 'soft'.
There was therefore no unified sense of purpose in the conduct of
the war. Above all, there was the general problem of Daladier, whose

* Sir John Colville, *The Fringes of Power*, page 153; Hodder and Stoughton, London,
1958. Diary entry, 12 June 1940.

† Georges Mandel (1885–1944): Politician. Clemenceau's aide in 1917; Minister for
Posts and Telecommunications 1934–6, Colonies 1938; tried to escape to North
Africa 1940; imprisoned by Vichy, later murdered by French Milice.

support Reynaud needed but whom he could not personally abide, a feeling which was amply reciprocated. Not only was the personal dislike of the two men intense, but it also spread to their respective mistresses. Daladier's close relationship was with the Marquise de Crussol, a good-looking blonde lady whose family had important interests in sardine canning, while Reynaud's affections were concentrated on the Comtesse de Portes. The two women could not stand one another.

Hélène de Portes was something of an enigma. First of all, nobody could quite make out why Reynaud was so taken with her. She was not physically very attractive, with a sallow complexion, a big mouth, untidy in dress, and she talked a lot. In short she was, in the words of one observer, 'a dark, homely, talkative little woman . . . she had many friends and a lot of notions about everything.'[1] But she made Reynaud, a small man physically, feel 'tall, grand and powerful', and that was probably her hold over him. 'Had Reynaud been three inches taller,' it was later said, 'the history of the world might have been changed.'[2] What was certainly true was that she was very anti-British, was a close friend of Otto Abetz, and that she had a powerful and at times sinister influence over Reynaud, which she did not hesitate to exercise. She would not hesitate to ring him on his private line in the middle of a ministerial meeting; she would interfere in his decisions about appointments; she would read his confidential correspondence behind his back; she would even purloin documents, as on the occasion when a secret telegram from the French embassy in London could not be found for several hours, until an embarrassed private secretary revealed that it had turned up 'in Mme de Portes's bed'.[3]

General de Gaulle, as might be imagined, did not take to the Comtesse de Portes, to the point where, some say, his view of the lady affected his whole future attitude to women in politics. But he was busy setting up his office, and had not much time to spare for the social niceties that would have endeared him to her and perhaps her to him. Equally, he was somewhat abrupt with Reynaud's staff, marching into one office and telling the occupant how happy he was at having the man under his orders, to which the other replied with spirit that he was in no way under orders to anybody other than the Prime Minister.

Part of the trouble was that de Gaulle's brief was not clear. At their first ministerial meeting on 6 June, Reynaud asked him to look after what was going on behind the front lines and to keep the British happy. The new minister was not satisfied. He went immediately to see Weygand, the commander-in-chief, who showed all the signs of a defeated man;

then he advised Reynaud to sack Weygand and appoint Huntziger in his stead. It was an odd suggestion, since Huntziger was one of the two generals who had been humiliated by Guderian at Sedan, and Reynaud quite properly told de Gaulle that, whatever Huntziger's military virtues, such an appointment would be political nonsense. De Gaulle went away to ponder the idea of a general retreat to a fortified redoubt in Brittany – an idea which attracted him for a time until he was persuaded that it was wholly unrealistic and that he should study the more practical alternative: the continuance of the war from North Africa.

It was the British part of his brief that was clearest, and on 9 June the Minister, accompanied by two young diplomats, Geoffroy de Courcel[*] and Roland de Margerie,[†] flew from Paris to London for his first meeting with Winston Churchill. The circumstances were not propitious, since Churchill had heard that Italy was preparing to enter the war on the following day, and when the three Frenchmen arrived they found a Prime Minister striding up and down, cursing the Italians and snapping everybody's head off. De Gaulle finally managed to ask him to send more British aircraft to France. The answer was a flat negative, since the field of battle on the ground was getting further and further away from Britain and the entire Royal Air Force would soon be needed for the battle that was certain to come.

De Gaulle's mission was a failure, but the interview itself had gone reasonably well. The new and relatively junior minister had been far from overawed by his first meeting with the British Prime Minister. Admittedly, he had been helped by the diplomatic skills of his two French colleagues, but it was none the less a remarkable exhibition of self-confidence.

Furthermore, de Gaulle had shown a refreshing sense of realism that had escaped other French ministers. Churchill reported to that evening's War Cabinet that de Gaulle had given him 'a more favourable impression of French morale and determination', and that when he had explained that Britain could not engage the whole of her air force in

---

[*] Geoffroy de Courcel (1912–1992): Diplomat. Elegant anglophile (sent one of his sons to Eton). French Foreign Office 1937–40; ADC and Principal Private Secretary to de Gaulle 1940; fought in Egypt and North Africa 1941–2; official in Algiers 1943; Permanent French Ambassador to NATO 1948; Ambassador, London 1962–72.

[†] Roland de Margerie (1899–1990): Diplomat. Anglophile; followed family tradition in Foreign Service. Brilliant, but sometimes found intimidating, perhaps because of his fearsome spectacles. 1933–9 Counsellor in London; Private Sec. to Reynaud in 1940; Chargé d'Affaires, Peking 1940–6; Ambassador to Vatican, then Madrid, then Bonn.

the battle for France, de Gaulle had replied that 'speaking for himself, he agreed with our policy'.[4]

By the time de Gaulle returned to France, the Government had left Paris, declaring it – against his advice – an open city. Churchill had tried to intervene, responding to a request from Reynaud to fly to France to bolster the morale of his Government. But, just as he was about to leave for Hendon aerodrome, a message came through that Paris was about to be abandoned, and his trip had to be cancelled since 'there was no perch on which he could alight'.[5]

The upshot was that ministries were dispersed – in considerable confusion – in the region of Tours, taking over many of the Loire châteaux for their purposes. To try to salvage what he could from the chaos, Reynaud convened a meeting of the Council of Ministers for the evening of 11 June at the Château de Muguet near Briare, which developed into a meeting of the Supreme Allied War Council with the arrival – finally – of Churchill, accompanied by Generals Dill, Ismay and Spears.

It did not go well. The French generals, Weygand and Georges, said that they had no reserves left; Pétain talked of the suffering of the French people; only Reynaud seemed to want to fight on. De Gaulle then spoke, his first ever intervention at an Allied meeting. His proposal was to amalgamate the British armoured division then in France with the French armoured forces. Combining the heavier French tanks with the lighter British reconnaisance vehicles, which the French lacked, would create 'a much higher effectiveness'. Churchill, impressed, said that this would be 'examined at once'.[6] At dinner that evening, de Gaulle sat next to Churchill, and each commented later on the sense of resolution that he found in the other.

The following morning, 12 June, de Gaulle went to Rennes to talk about the feasibility of the 'Breton redoubt' with the general commanding forces in the area, Altmeyer. He then returned to his own offices in Beauvais to discuss a possible retreat to North Africa with the chief of staff of the Armée de Terre, General Colson. By the time he had finished those discussions, unsatisfactory as they turned out, he was due for a further meeting with Reynaud at Château Chissay, the Prime Minister's headquarters. Reynaud was still smouldering from a meeting of the Council of Ministers, held earlier in the day at Cangé, at which Pétain and Weygand had finally come out into the open and asked for a rapid armistice. His resolve stiffened by de Gaulle, Reynaud wrote an instruction to Weygand to hold fast in the Massif Central and Brittany while the struggle was being organised in the empire.

Reynaud's resolution did not last long. Just after midnight he rang Churchill to request another meeting, but the line was so bad that it was left to the private secretaries to carry on the conversation, with the two principals shouting agitatedly in the background. Churchill was asked to go back to France later that day, for a meeting at the Préfecture at Tours at 2.45 p.m. Such was the tension that Reynaud, much to Churchill's fury, since he was sure the Germans were listening in – specified times of arrival and meetings on the open telephone line.

By this time, Reynaud was exhausted, continually harried by his colleagues and his mistress. 'You don't know,' he had sighed to a friend, 'what a man who has been hard at work all day will put up with to make sure of an evening's peace.'[7] He intended to ask Churchill for a release from the agreement binding France not to accept a peace without Great Britain. Since he knew that de Gaulle would argue against him, Reynaud had decided to exclude him from the meeting. De Gaulle, although he had seen Reynaud again that morning at Chissay, when it was decided to move the government from Tours to Bordeaux, was told about the meeting by Margerie only after his return to Beauvais. He rushed back to Tours. He was only one hour late for the start of the meeting, but during that hour the damage had been done: France was already on the road to suing for peace.

Churchill, Halifax,[*] Ismay, Spears and Cadogan[†] had arrived at Tours soon after noon, borrowed a car and drove into the city to the Préfecture. Reynaud arrived late, looking tired and depressed. He immediately outlined the desperate position that France was in and asked whether Britain would release her from her promise not to make a separate peace. Churchill made a long speech about the acknowledged sufferings of France but refused to release France from the agreement on a separate peace. However, the expression 'I fully understand what France is still suffering',[8] was enough for the defeatists, and during a break in which Churchill and his colleagues retired to consider the situation, Baudouin interpreted to the French, including de Gaulle, who

---

[*] Edward Lindley Wood, 1st Earl Halifax (1881–1959): Politician. Born with atrophied left arm without a hand. Of great intellectual brilliance and deep religious faith. MP for Ripon 1910–25; created Baron Irwin, Viceroy of India 1926–31; succeeded as Viscount Halifax 1934; Leader of House of Lords 1935–8; Sec. of State for Foreign Affairs 1938–40; Ambassador, Washington 1941–6.

[†] Sir Alexander Cadogan (1884–1968): Diplomat. Educated Eton and Oxford; Minister and Ambassador, Peking 1933–6; Permanent Under-Secretary for Foreign Affairs 1938–46; UK Permanent Representative to UN 1946–50; Chairman of Governors of BBC 1952–7; noted for gentlemanly calmness but kept surprisingly vituperative diaries.

had just arrived, that Churchill's 'understanding' was tantamount to permission. De Gaulle's account of what followed makes it clear that he accepted Baudouin's interpretation, and that he thought that Churchill was acquiescing in a separate peace. It was the first, but by no means the last, of de Gaulle's misunderstandings of Churchill's intentions.

De Gaulle recorded that, when the conference resumed, the British moved on to discuss the position of the French fleet in the event of an armistice. Churchill 'became very precise and very rigorous. It was plain that the British Government was so afraid of seeing the French fleet handed over to the Germans that it was disposed, while there was still time, to barter its renunciation of the agreement of 28 March against guarantees about the fate of our ships.'[9]

In fact, nothing of the sort took place at Tours. Churchill did not bring up the problem of the French fleet, and de Gaulle's account of the meeting is – untypically – inaccurate. This was perhaps no more than a pertinent example of the tricks that memory can play. Yet it also illustrates de Gaulle's evident and long-lasting mistrust of the British position – a mistrust that was at least partially justified. The British were terrified that the French fleet, which was the fourth largest in the world and had been brought by Admiral François Darlan to a high state of efficiency, would be used against Britain. The only two major assets that Britain now still had were its control of the seas of the eastern Atlantic and its control of the air over south-eastern England and the Channel. Were either of these two assets to be lost, Britain's position would become almost hopeless. The French and German fleets, if combined, would be more than a match for the Royal Navy, and at least one of the vital assets would be lost. The greater the British pessimism about the outcome of the land battle in France, the more intense were the worries about the French fleet. It was the scent of that pessimism that de Gaulle had picked up.

Furthermore, if, by any chance remark, not recorded but enough to register with the suspicious General, the British, after their huddle – in the garden – came back and seemed to have placed the matter of the future of the French fleet on the table, this in itself would have been highly significant. It would have shown that the British had taken the step of allowing themselves to consider the possibility of a separate French armistice. As de Gaulle repeatedly pointed out, the only certain way to keep the French fleet out of German hands was to keep France at war, even if it meant a seat of government in North Africa, London or elsewhere. As long as the legitimacy of government was maintained, and the government remained in the war, the fleet would remain loyal.

To de Gaulle's sensitive ears, any suspicion that the British might be abandoning support for this position could easily sound like perfidy.

In fact, there was some way to go before the future of the French fleet became an open negotiating point. The way included an appeal to President Roosevelt to intervene to save France, an appeal which, although it showed no understanding of American politics or the United States constitution, seemed to revive the glimmer of hope in Reynaud. But there was no doubt that the atmosphere had changed and that there was justification for the view expressed by de Gaulle to the Canadian Prime Minister just over four years later: 'It was . . .at that time that I had formed the impression that Britain was ready to let France go if the necessity arose to save herself.'[10]

The meeting at Tours finished inconclusively at about half-past five in the afternoon. Churchill went back to London, telling Colville on his return, 'They were very nearly gone.'[11] On his way out, he had seen de Gaulle 'standing stolid and expressionless at the doorway. Greeting him, I said in a low tone, in French: "*l'homme du destin*". He remained impassive.'[12] It was all very dramatic, but de Gaulle remained impassive for the simple reason that he had not heard the great man's remark.

De Gaulle immediately tackled Reynaud, asking him point blank whether he was contemplating the prospect of France asking for an armistice. 'Certainly not' came the reply.[13] But de Gaulle knew that it was untrue. As he went back to Beauvais, leaving Reynaud to report to the Council of Ministers, he concluded that it would not now be long before France gave up the struggle. Whatever Reynaud might say, the will to fight on was no longer there. De Gaulle thought very seriously about resigning and was about to draft a letter to the Prime Minister, when the Minister for the Interior, Georges Mandel, arrived, having been alerted by de Gaulle's private secretary that resignation was in the air. Mandel pointed out that what was happening was only the beginning of a world war, and that de Gaulle, with his record untarnished by the politics of defeatism, was in the best position to play a crucial role, but that this possibility would be thrown away if he resigned office. It was, as much as anything, an appeal to personal ambition, but Mandel had read his man well. De Gaulle abandoned the idea forthwith.

On the morning of 14 June, with the German tanks entering Paris, the French Government transferred to Bordeaux. Again, the junior minister harangued the Prime Minister about continuing the battle from North Africa, and yet again Reynaud's resistance to defeat was rekindled. He sent for Darlan to discuss the logistics of moving to North Africa, and

ordered de Gaulle to London to request British assistance in the move.
While waiting for arrangements to be made for an aeroplane to take him
to London, de Gaulle went for a quiet dinner at the Hôtel Splendide. At
the table next to his was sitting the old Marshal Pétain himself. When he
had finished dinner, de Gaulle went over to Pétain's table and shook his
hand without a word. They were never to see each other again.

In the event, there was no aeroplane. A car was hastily found, and de
Gaulle set out northwards to Brittany, accompanied by Courcel. They
drove through the night in silence, reaching Rennes in the early morning. After a short meeting with General Altmeyer, they went on to
Paimpont, where de Gaulle's mother lay dying. He said his last, hurried
farewells, and then made for Carantec, the place of refuge of his wife
and two daughters. Again, a quick greeting, instructions on what to do
if the worst came to the worst, and he drove on to Brest. After a brief
and unfriendly meeting with the Admiral in command of the Atlantic
fleet, Laborde, he boarded the destroyer *Milan* and set out for Plymouth.

De Gaulle was quite clearly preparing himself for the worst and decid-
ing on his own course of action in the event of a complete collapse. It
was not just a question of giving a warning to his family to be ready to
move at a moment's notice, but also at each stage taking decisions that led
him inexorably to the action that he finally took. On arrival in London
on the morning of Sunday, 16 June, he gave orders, on his own authority, for the merchant ship *Pasteur*, en route for France with a large
shipment of arms and ammunition, to make for a British port. It was an
action which lay quite outside his powers, as his ministerial colleagues in
Bordeaux were not slow to point out; if things had turned out differently,
it would almost certainly have led to dismissal if not to a court martial.

There was, however, to be one last throw before admitting defeat.
While de Gaulle was shaving in his room at the Hyde Park Hotel, Jean
Monnet* and the French ambassador, Charles Corbin, burst in. Monnet
had been working on a scheme. It had been discussed with Desmond
Morton,† one of Churchill's close advisers, and, the previous day, with

---

*Jean Monnet (1888–1979): Businessman and civil servant. Known by some as the
'Father of Europe', but never stood for elective office. Family business in brandy
(Cognac); Deputy Secretary-General League of Nations 1918; Chairman, Franco-
British Economic Co-ordinating Committee 1939–40; Washington 1940–3; sent by
Roosevelt to Algiers 1943; created French Planning Authority 1946; President
European Coal and Steel Community 1952–5; Chairman, Action Committee for the
United States of Europe 1956–75.

† Desmond Morton (1891–1971): Soldier. Shot through the heart in First World War,

the Foreign Secretary, Lord Halifax, and his Chief Diplomatic Adviser, Sir Robert Vansittart. It was nothing less than a proposed union between the United Kingdom and France. There was to be a federal constitution, one parliament, one government and common citizenship.

It was, to say the least, an ambitious plan, and it was a measure of the desperation that had taken hold that it could even be entertained. Everybody knew that its realisation would take time and effort, but at the time it did not seem wholly impracticable, and was the only way to keep France in the war. It was the first, but by no means the last, of the ideas for supra-nationality that flowed from Monnet's fertile mind, and it was the only one that de Gaulle agreed with. But agree with it he did, and not only that, but he undertook to use his best efforts to bring Churchill round to the scheme.

De Gaulle had been due to have lunch with Churchill at Chequers with Anthony Eden and General Sir John Dill in attendance, but the news from France was bad enough for Churchill to call a War Cabinet meeting in London. Reynaud was still pressing for a British view on a separate armistice. Finally, the Cabinet agreed to allow France to explore possible terms for an armistice – without agreeing to one – provided that the French fleet was sailed into British ports. It was not at all satisfactory, and was tantamount to agreeing to an armistice, but it might hold the position for a while. The fleet was very much on Churchill's mind when lunch finally took place at the Carlton Club. The Monnet plan was hardly discussed, until it became clear that it was in practice the only way to keep France, and hence the French fleet, in the war against Germany. Churchill agreed, summoned the Cabinet again for 3 p.m. and gave orders for the telegrams to the French Government drafted earlier to be held up. Churchill then asked de Gaulle to help draft the proclamation to be submitted to the War Cabinet.

The excitement became intense. Cabinet ministers were told that 'something stupendous' was in the air, that Chamberlain was 'in on it' as well as others, and that de Gaulle was one of its most ardent supporters. 'De Gaulle is a magnificent crook,' said Morton, 'another Max Beaverbrook, just what we want!'[14] The Cabinet was formally presented with the idea, which by then had caught Churchill's imagination. De Gaulle and

---

but somehow survived. Pale and unhealthy, never married. ADC to Field Marshal Earl Haig 1917–18; seconded Foreign Office 1919; War Office (Intelligence) 1919–30; Dir. Industrial Intelligence Centre 1930–9, fed Churchill with politically useful information; Personal Asst. to PM 1940–6; PM's Special Liaison Officer with the Intelligence Services 1940-5; knighted 1946.

Corbin waited in Morton's room, next door to the Cabinet Room. The Cabinet Secretary, Edward Bridges, came out of the meeting and dictated a text of a declaration of union to the most senior of Churchill's personal secretaries, Mrs Hill. The Cabinet was told that de Gaulle had called Reynaud to alert him to the plan – although they were not told that de Gaulle had held out to Reynaud the possibility of his becoming head of a Franco-British War Cabinet. Reynaud jumped at the idea, but said that time was now of the essence. He gave de Gaulle half an hour to be more specific. After that, his own Council of Ministers would be meeting.

In fact, the Cabinet discussed Bridges's draft for two hours, with ministers coming out, from time to time, to clear points with the French. Differences were resolved and Churchill emerged, followed by other ministers, shouting, '*Nous sommes d'accord!*' At that point, the meeting started to degenerate. According to Colville's report, de Gaulle 'has been strutting about in the Cabinet room, with Corbin too; the Cabinet turned into a sort of promenade, Winston beginning a speech in the Cabinet room, and finishing it in some other room; and everybody has been slapping de Gaulle on the back and telling him he shall be Commander-in-Chief (Winston muttering: "*je l'arrangerai*"). Is he a new Napoleon? From what I hear, it seems that a lot of people think so. He treats Reynaud (whom he called "*ce poisson gelé*") like dirt . . .'[15] So far, so good; but it was still necessary to convince the French Council of Ministers.

De Gaulle was given the job of briefing Reynaud on the British decision, and at 4.40 p.m. he rang Bordeaux. At first he could only get Margerie, who later claimed that de Gaulle had told him to pass the message to Reynaud that the British were agreed on the plan for union, and that he, Reynaud, could if he wished become Prime Minister of the two countries after federation. It sounds an unlikely story, particularly with Churchill standing next to him at the time, but, whatever the truth, de Gaulle was certainly doing his best to stiffen Reynaud's resolve. The call was cut off, then resumed, and Churchill himself grabbed the telephone and confirmed the news. A further meeting of the Supreme Allied War Council was agreed for the next day, at Concarneau. Such was the excitement that it was only then remembered that nobody had told King George VI that his empire was about to be disposed of.

Reynaud was transfigured, as Spears noted, and immediately summoned his Council of Ministers. At five o'clock they were assembled, twenty-four in all, to hear the British proposal. Two hours later it was all over. There had been no vote, but as the discussion had developed it had become clear that the waverers were moving against the plan and in favour of armistice. The 'softs' had won. Reynaud accepted that there was no majority on his side, but that there was a majority for a proposal to ask the Germans, without commitment, to set out their terms for an armistice. He resigned. Three hours later, President Lebrun had asked Marshal Pétain to form a new government.

General de Gaulle had left for France at 6.30 p.m., to be present for the French approval of the unity plan and to prepare the following day's meeting at Concarneau. Before he left, he had had one more meeting with Churchill to try to persuade him to send more British aircraft to France for 'the decisive battle'. He was supported by Monnet, who did almost all the talking, but Churchill was adamant. As the Frenchmen went out, according to Churchill, de Gaulle turned round, took two or three steps back, and said, in English: 'I think you are quite right.' 'Under an impassive, imperturbable demeanour,' Churchill goes on, 'he seemed to me to have a remarkable capacity for feeling pain. I preserved the impression, in contact with this very tall, phlegmatic man: "Here is the Constable of France." '[16]

De Gaulle arrived at Mérignac airport just outside Bordeaux at about 10 p.m. He was met by Colonel Humbert, one of his trusted supporters, who told him of Reynaud's resignation. He went straight to see Reynaud, who was under no illusions about the outcome. De Gaulle said that he would return to England, and, in a last gesture, Reynaud drew 100,000 francs from secret government funds and sent them privately by messenger to London. At the residence of the British ambassador, Ronald Campbell, de Gaulle told him and Spears about his plans. The following morning, de Gaulle, Courcel and Spears left Bordeaux in the same aircraft in which they had arrived. The destination was London.

De Gaulle's return to London was the mark of his rejection of defeat. At first, he believed that his protest could be limited to a military objection to surrender. When he replied to Mme Monnet, who asked on the evening of 17 June what mission he was on, 'Madame, I am not on a mission. I am here to save the honour of France,'[17] he was, however pompous the words, making a protest against the military humiliation of France. After all, it had taken the Germans only six weeks to submerge the once-proud French army. Not only had the French been out-generalled but, with one or two valiant exceptions, their leaders had been craven and cowardly. De Gaulle had seen it for himself and was ashamed.

It was this rejection of French military defeat that so heartened Churchill. Time and again, Churchill was to refer to those days in June

1940, when Britain stood alone and when the only ally which came with her was 'undefeated France'. On that day, 17 June, undefeated France was represented by the tall, thin, gangling two-star French general who stood before him early in the afternoon as he sat in the garden of 10 Downing Street enjoying the sunshine. It was no wonder that, when Churchill got up to greet his guest, 'his smile of welcome was very warm and friendly'.[18] Long afterwards, the memory of that moment would bring tears to Churchill's eyes.

General de Gaulle ceased being an active soldier and became a politician – and, incidentally, a traitor – when he flew back to London with Courcel and Spears on the morning of 17 June 1940. But it was only in the ensuing two or three days that the consequences of his action became apparent, perhaps even to himself. The fact was that he was raising the standard of revolt against the legal government of France. It was a long way from the role of Joan of Arc. She, after all, had fought for the established legal authority, however unsatisfactory that turned out to be, and had never renounced allegiance. De Gaulle was doing just that, and, although he would have denied it with horror at the time, had by doing so assumed the mantle not of Joan of Arc but of Robespierre. Once the legal authority is defied, and its elimination envisaged, it becomes necessary to devise something to put in its place. By refusing to accept defeat, the very defeat that had been accepted by the properly constituted government, de Gaulle had put himself in that position. Thus did the soldier become not just a politician, but a Jacobin rebel to boot.

The dilemma might have been less acute had he been prepared to serve in the British army, as many of his compatriots were to do. Jean Monnet, among others, was to advocate this course of action, with the idea that, once victory had been achieved, the government of the Third Republic would be realigned and France would continue constitutionally as before. But Fashoda, his parents, the Jesuits, the military oath, all that had hitherto gone to make the man, made it impossible for him to accept a role of subordination to the British. When he was crossing the Channel in the destroyer *Milan* on the night of 15 June, after having said a final goodbye to his mother, he asked the captain, 'Would you be prepared to fight under British colours?'[19] The captain replied in the negative, but it is clear that the questioner was not interested in a reply. He was thinking only about his own position; and he came to the same conclusion.

As an active soldier, de Gaulle's record was mixed. He had not done particularly well at St Cyr, had missed a great deal of the First World War, and had presented himself as an intellectual – and somewhat affected – staff officer in the inter-war period, prone to tell others what to do in the conviction that he was always right. On the other hand, he had shown great courage in the field, on the bridge at Dinant, at Douaumont, Montcornet and Abbeville. Above all, he had no physical fear that he could not conquer.

Nevertheless, as a field commander de Gaulle had not been a success. The character traits that were so valuable later on were destructive in combat: single-mindedness, impatience of human failings, intolerance of others' opinions, and the occasional furious rage when crossed. All of these traits were on show at Abbeville – he told one unfortunate tank squadron commander if he came back alive from this battle he would have him shot – to the point where 4th Armoured Division officers were so disillusioned with their divisional commander that none of them later joined the Free French. It is a sad commentary. De Gaulle, as Pétain was to remark, 'had no friends in the army. He was heartless.'[20]

But if as a field commander he achieved no great distinction, he was certainly outstanding as a staff officer and tactician. Thanks to his experience in Poland after the First World War, he rediscovered the war of movement well before his French contemporaries, and was unabashed in pursuing his crusade, even over the heads of his military superiors, for a force of massed tank formations. It was not that his thoughts were particularly original, or that they were read outside France. Others had preceded him in the theory, and others were to be in advance of him in the practice. What was remarkable was his persistence in the pursuit of modern ideas, even to the point of putting his own promotion prospects at risk, in the face of the confident self-satisfaction that characterised the French high command at the time.

In his active service as a soldier, the best that can be said is that the newly promoted General de Gaulle had made the most of his courage and intellectual strength in what had been, after all, an unsuccessful military environment. But the legacy from the first fifty years of his life that he carried with him into his new, self-ordained career was absolute: total respect for the military virtues – discipline, courage, loyalty and energy. If these virtues came with the comparable vices – intolerance to argument, blind respect for authority and contempt for weakness – so be it. That was the price of being a soldier – and in his character the General, whatever the other roles he learned to play during the rest of his life, was always, first and foremost, a soldier.

PART THREE

EXILE

1

LAYING THE CORNER STONE

'Tis better using France than trusting France. ★

To all outward appearance, Major-General Sir Edward Louis Spears, Bt, KBE, CB, MC, was the quintessence of an English military gentleman. Educated privately, he had been gazetted first into the 8th Hussars, subsequently to transfer to the 11th Hussars, two regiments of the highest social tone. Of medium height, his hair cut short – but not too short – over a receding hairline, a square jaw, a moustache clipped in the manner of the time, a long straight nose ending, it seemed, in the extension of the pipe which he smoked without pause, he looked like any other member of the British officer class of his day. Only the elongated eyebrows and the slightly hooded eyes would have indicated that neither his character nor his intellect were those of an ordinary career soldier.

His record in the First World War was as distinguished as any: mentioned in dispatches five times in addition to his Military Cross; cited in French army orders three times; Croix de Guerre with three palms and Commander of the Légion d'Honneur; Grand Cross of the White Eagle of Serbia; head of the British military mission to the French high command in 1917, with special commendation from the victor of Verdun himself, Marshal Pétain. He went on to be elected to the House of Commons, first as a National Liberal and then as a Unionist, and sat as a member of the House until 1943. He was appointed Churchill's personal representative with Paul Reynaud as Prime Minister of France in May 1940, and subsequently head of the British mission to General de Gaulle in June 1940. He was also Churchill's friend. Mrs Churchill, on the other hand, never liked him, believing him given to deceit and fantasy. As it turned out, her judgement was perhaps wiser than her

---

★ Lord Hastings, in Shakespeare, *Henry VI, Part 2,* Act IV, Scene 1.

husband's. Others, too, regarded him as conceited and bombastic. Moreover, Spears's admittedly elegant version of events does not, to put it politely, always accord with the reality. But he was, for all that, a true friend of France by his own standards, and it is a sad echo of the bitter rows towards the end of the Second World War, when Spears turned against de Gaulle, that he now occupies a very special place in Gaullist demonology.

How all this came about is, almost in itself, the story of the General's struggle for a French independent identity as the war progressed, and the conflicts and misunderstandings that ensued. At the beginning, Spears's relationship with de Gaulle was very close. It was Spears, after all, who had helped him and Courcel in their last-minute flight from Bordeaux, who had bought de Gaulle a cup of coffee in the canteen at Jersey airport where the plane stopped to refuel, which de Gaulle mistook for tea – 'his first introduction,' Spears wrote, 'to the tepid liquid which in England passes for either one or the other'.[1] He later took de Gaulle to a small flat in what is now Curzon Place which was to be his temporary home, on to lunch at the Royal Automobile Club and then to the meeting with Churchill in the afternoon.

By that time it was evident that Pétain would sue for peace – although it was not until later that evening that the old Marshal's feeble voice could be heard on Bordeaux radio: 'It is with a broken heart that I tell you today that it is necessary to stop fighting.'[2] Churchill and de Gaulle wasted no time in regrets over the collapse of France. De Gaulle immediately set about persuading Churchill to allow him to use the only weapon that would be effective at that time – the BBC. Churchill's agreement was swift and decisive; he asked de Gaulle to wait only for definite news of Pétain's decision and for the approval of the War Cabinet. That evening de Gaulle started drafting. Meanwhile Courcel had telephoned one of the secretaries at a French economic mission which happened to be in London at the time and whom he had known previously, to be ready on the following day to type 'an important text'. Thus Elisabeth de Méribel became the first, honoured recruit to the Free French.

The following day, the 125th anniversary of the battle of Waterloo as it happened, the text was ready, typed and, although de Gaulle later denied the fact, submitted to the War Cabinet meeting by Duff Cooper,★ the Minister for Information. Churchill was absent and the meeting was taken by Neville Chamberlain. To Duff Cooper's surprise

★ Alfred Duff Cooper (1890–1954): Politician and diplomat. Fought in First World

and annoyance, the Cabinet turned the whole idea down flat, on the grounds that de Gaulle's text, although not technically disloyal to the Pétain Government, was certainly so in practice since it was a direct appeal to the French armed forces. This was not the time, they opined, to offend Pétain; the broadcast was therefore vetoed.

Duff Cooper reported the decision to Spears, who rushed off to the House of Commons, where Churchill had just finished speaking. Spears pleaded with Churchill, claiming to have new evidence showing why it was essential that de Gaulle should do his broadcast. There were many aircraft at Bordeaux, he said, which could still be saved if an appeal were made to their pilots. Churchill told Spears that he could only agree to the broadcast if the rest of the War Cabinet agreed, and Spears, 'looking miserable and hot', as Colville reported,[3] set off on his tour of conversion.

Formidable as it was, the Cabinet decision was not the only obstacle. The Foreign Office had hatched a plan to send a high-level delegation to Bordeaux, partly to impress on the new Pétain Government the strength of the British Government's views, but partly, if all else failed, to win over senior French ministers to the idea of breaking with Pétain and continuing a government in exile. The plan obviously ruled out the de Gaulle broadcast. Sir Robert Vansittart and Morton arrived in Downing Street demanding to see Churchill and explain all this to him. But by this time Churchill, who had just returned from making an exhausting speech and was himself to broadcast that evening, had taken to his bed. The blinds of his bedroom were drawn; disturbance was, to say the least, unwelcome.

Vansittart and Morton insisted, however, and Churchill was woken up. When he emerged from under the bedclothes and after he had removed the velvet blindfold – 'bandage' as he called it – with which he habitually covered his eyes to keep out the light, and in no good humour, he listened to the arguments and took a decision: both the Foreign Office scheme and the de Gaulle broadcast (if approved by the members of the War Cabinet) should go ahead.

By that time, Spears and Duff Cooper had secured the agreement of each member of the War Cabinet individually to de Gaulle's broadcast.

War; MP for Oldham 1924–9, Westminster 1931–45; Financial Secretary War Office 1928–9, Treasury 1934–5; Sec. of State for War 1937–8; resigned in protest at Munich agreement; Minister for Information 1940–1; Govt. Rep. to French National Committee, Algiers 1943–4; UK Ambassador, Paris 1944–7. Created Viscount Norwich.

So it was that the General appeared at the BBC studios in Langham Place, in full military uniform with shining top-boots, to deliver what is now known as '*l'Appel du 18 Juin*'. It went on the air at 8.15 p.m. London time, but it had been within a hair's breadth of not going on the air at all.

The text of the 'Appel' itself amply rewards close study. De Gaulle had been in a dilemma about its drafting, which, although the broadcast was over in four minutes, had taken him several hours. He could, of course, have declared outright treason, rejecting the actions of the Government of which he had until recently been a member; but that would have led to severe difficulties with the British Government, which had not given up hope of a continuing relationship with the Pétain Government. Alternatively, he could simply have invited any French survivors from the débâcle to join him in London and form a group – like the Poles, Czechs, Belgians and others had done – to fight under British command; but to do that would have negated his whole purpose of constituting a separate, undefeated France, sovereign in its own right. Furthermore, he had to remember that he was only a temporary brigadier-general, without any authority to speak for anyone.

The result was a masterly compromise; the General was quite clearly learning the politician's trade at astonishing speed. He starts off with the simple statement that French military leaders have formed a Government, and that Government has made contact with the enemy for the purpose of cessation of hostilities. Reynaud and his Government is thereby exonerated, and the whole blame for the armistice is laid on Pétain and Weygand. De Gaulle goes on to acknowledge the French military defeat, although he cannot resist a sideswipe at the tactics of the French generals in their use of armour and air power. There then follow two broad assertions: first, that the French Empire stands behind France, and can make common cause with the British Empire; second, that France can, like Britain, make use without limit of the vast industrial resources of the United States.

The first assertion was factually true, although the extent of the French Empire's allegiance to the Pétain Government remained to be tested, and in the event turned out to be stronger than de Gaulle had perhaps expected. Nevertheless, he could argue that if a new government were formed to replace the defeatist one, the Empire would stand behind it, and that it was perfectly proper for any politician, particularly a former minister, to call for a change of government. The second assertion was no more than partially true, and equally dubious in practice. The United States was in no mood to abandon its support for the Pétain Government and would not be for many months to come. The condition for American industrial help was a French government that was not only recognised as legitimate but was also prepared to continue the war, and no such government existed or was even on the horizon.

The purpose of these two dubious assertions was clear. De Gaulle wished to give the impression that only a government led by him, or by a leader of whom he approved, would enjoy the support of the Empire and the United States, but without actually saying so. This in turn enabled him to identify himself – '*Moi, Général de Gaulle*'[4] – which he had to do since nobody outside a very restricted circle had any idea who he was, and to 'invite', not 'call on', members of the French armed forces who were, or who might in the future find themselves, on British soil, to make contact with him.

All in all, it was a superb piece of craftmanship, full of Jesuitical subtlety and cunning. Without overstepping the mark either of legality or of offence to his British hosts, he succeeded in giving the impression of a roar of defiance. He also succeeded in slipping in at the end a promise that he would be speaking again on the BBC the following day. This was a complete surprise to the BBC producers, who were not aware that they had invited him to do so. But de Gaulle, as one of them later remarked, was a law unto himself.

As it happened, the 'Appel' was not widely heard. The French survivors from Norway and Dunkirk, who numbered some tens of thousands, did not listen to the BBC, and the main media attention was on the broadcast that Churchill made on the same day. Not only that, but all available recording equipment had been used for Churchill's speech rather than de Gaulle's, so that the 'Appel' went unrecorded. As might be imagined, the General was far from pleased when he found out.

The next day, although grey and dull, brought some good news. The register that had been opened in Curzon Place now contained a few names of those who wished to join him; the response was no more than a trickle, and the list included nobody of great distinction, but it was a start. The next piece of good news was that his wife and two daughters had succeeded in crossing the Channel to England. Their escape had been, in itself, a dramatic and frightening adventure. Following the instructions that de Gaulle had left with them when they had met three days before, they made contact with the British consul in Brest, secured their passage aboard a Polish freighter bound for Plymouth and, just as the German tanks moved into the Breton peninsula, heading straight towards them, took flight. But the car taking them from Carantec to Brest broke down, and by the time it was repaired and they arrived in Brest, the ship had sailed. They were lost, with the prospect of being interned by the enemy and never seeing their husband and father again. In the event, and as luck would have it, they were doubly blessed; first, there was a second ship about to leave, just as they arrived at Brest harbour, a British tramp ship which was the last ship out that night; and secondly, the Polish freighter they were to have taken was sunk in mid-Channel by German torpedo boats with the loss of all hands. God was indeed on their side. On her arrival at Plymouth, Yvonne telephoned her husband to announce her safe arrival. He seemed unperturbed by her adventure. 'Ah,' he replied, 'it's you? I am in London. I am waiting for you.'[5]

It was perhaps the safe arrival of his wife and daughters that moved de Gaulle, in his broadcast of 19 June, to run up his true colours, no longer hiding behind the constitutional niceties. The tone was quite different from that of the day before. He proclaimed that he was now speaking in the name of France. In the name of France, he went on, 'I announce formally the following: any Frenchman who still has weapons has the absolute duty to continue the resistance; to lay down arms, to abandon a military position, to accept the surrender of any piece of French land to the enemy, would be crimes against the nation.'[6] He went on to instruct the resident generals in the French Empire, ignoring their superiority to him in rank, on their duty to refuse to obey any instructions coming from the enemy. In short, it was an astounding, and wholly typical, piece of cheek.

The British Foreign Office was aghast. The expedition that had gone to Bordeaux to make contact with senior politicians was reporting some progress, and the last thing that the diplomats wanted was an inflammatory broadcast on the official British radio. There was hope that Reynaud and Mandel would come over, but both in the end refused, strangely enough for the same reason: they were too attached to their respective mistresses, Mme de Portes and Mme Bretty. But as Jean Monnet, who was part of the London team, remarked, the flying-boat that was returning to England was quite big enough to carry both of them, even the ample Mme Bretty.

The decision did neither of them much good. Only a week later Reynaud was driving in southern France when his car ran off the road and hit a tree. A suitcase in the back of the car careered forward and struck Hélène de Portes in the back of the neck, killing her instantly. Reynaud himself was taken to hospital unconscious, but recovered well enough, only to find himself arrested. He spent the rest of the war in German prisons.

Mandel fared no better. He decided to make for North Africa and, along with several other former ministers, including Daladier, sailed on the armed auxiliary cruiser *Massilia* on 21 June. Three days later they arrived at Casablanca but were arrested by the Resident General and forbidden to leave the ship. Duff Cooper was dispatched from London to negotiate their release, but the French authorities were adamant and he returned empty handed. The prisoners were sent back to France under arrest and imprisoned. Mandel himself was killed later in the war by the Vichy para-military police.

The *Massilia* episode marked the end of any serious attempt by Britain to bring over 'big game', as Churchill called them, and the British made up their minds, somewhat reluctantly in the case of the Foreign Office, that they would have to make do with de Gaulle. Overruling the last objections from the Foreign Office, which still wanted to maintain relations with the Pétain Government, Churchill decided that enough was enough, and on the morning of 28 June he issued the following communiqué: 'His Majesty's Government recognises General de Gaulle as leader of all Free Frenchmen, wherever they may be, who rally to him in support of the Allied cause.'[7] In spite of all the setbacks, the danger and the hostility, the General had succeeded in his first task: to establish a legal basis for the 'Free French'.

De Gaulle now had to set up an office, find staff and arrange funds, and generally establish a firm base. Again, Spears came to the rescue, letting the Free French have the third floor of St Stephen's House, a rather gloomy building on the Embankment opposite Big Ben and overlooking the river, where Spears himself had his offices. In the meantime, Yvonne had decided to move out of London to the suburbs, where it would be quieter for little Anne, and she found, and immediately rented, a house of negligible architectural distinction, in the style known as mock-Tudor, at Petts Wood in Kent. The head of the Free French was thus obliged to become a commuter to Victoria Station.

Recruitment continued, slowly and unspectacularly. Few of the French survivors of Norway and Dunkirk decided to throw in their lot with the unknown new organisation; many had opted to go home to France. Of the major French figures in London, Monnet was the most hostile. He objected to the principle of setting up a separate French political authority outside France. His objective was to detach certain members of the Pétain Government to North Africa, and to continue the fight from there. De Gaulle's initiative in London could only be at best irrelevant, at worst a serious impediment. Besides, Monnet thought that de Gaulle was being 'too dramatic' and 'too personal'.[8] Monnet's closest colleague, René Pleven,* on the other hand, took the opposite view, and quickly joined the de Gaulle camp. Margerie also thought that de Gaulle had chosen the wrong route, but others – Christian Fouchet, Maurice Schumann, René Cassin and Gaston Palewski[†] – were won over.

They were none of them very big fish. Fouchet was a young army lieutenant who had got out of Bordeaux just before the final débâcle; Cassin was an elderly lawyer who had jumped on a British ship at St Jean-de-Luz; Schumann was a journalist working with an advertising agency; and Palewski was on active service in a bomber squadron in Tunis. But whatever their quality, the names continued to mount: Koenig, Dewavrin (later to be known as 'Passy'), Tissier; these were officers whose troops had chosen to return to France. It was perhaps not much, but it was a start, and meant, among other things, a move to larger offices than those of General Spears in St Stephen's House.

Before that happened, however, there occurred the first major incident to disrupt the now almost honeymoon relationship between the Free French and the British Government. The armistice between France and Germany had been signed on 22 June, at Rethondes in the forest of Compiègne – in the same place, and in the same railway carriage, as the Germans had been forced to sign their own surrender in 1918. It was humiliating, and designed to be so. The terms of the armistice were onerous, but the point that concerned the British was the destiny of the French fleet. The Pétain Government had repeatedly assured the British that the fleet would never fall into Hitler's hands, but there were doubts, at least, about the worth of such promises.

---

* René Pleven (1901–1993): Breton businessman and politician. In business until 1940; joined Free French in 1940; Commissioner for Finance in Algiers 1943–4; presided conference at Brazzaville July 1944; Minister for Finance 1944; Prime Minister 1950–1 and 1951–2; Minister for Justice 1972.

† Gaston Palewski (1901–1984): Polish origin. Flamboyant (known to at least one of his mistresses as 'The Colonel'), but from 1940 loyal de Gaulle supporter. Director, Free French political affairs 1940; Principal Private Secretary to de Gaulle 1942–6; founder member of RPF; Ambassador, Rome 1957–62.

In the event the doubts were justified. Article 8 of the armistice provided for the disarming of the fleet 'under German or Italian control', with a German assurance that the ships would not be used for their own purposes while the war lasted. From the British point of view, this clearly pointed to disaster. They therefore conceived, and proceeded to execute, Operation Catapult, which was designed to take out of action, in one way or another, those elements of the French fleet which were not in the shelter of ports controlled by the Germans or Italians.

It so happened that most of the fleet lay outside metropolitan French ports. Darlan had envisaged stationing the bulk of it at Dakar, in French West Africa, and at Martinique, in the Caribbean, to pursue the war, but on becoming Minister of Marine in Pétain's Government, he had felt unable to give the order to sail. As a result, the fleet was scattered around various stations in the North Sea and the Mediterranean, without any clear idea of what it was supposed to do,

Two ships decided that they had had enough. One, the submarine *Narval*, slipped her moorings at Sousse in Tunisia at 11 p.m. on 24 June and headed for Malta. At 8 a.m. on 26 June she was sighted, on the surface in choppy seas, by the British destroyer HMS *Diamond*, which came up astern at high speed. It was a close call. The *Diamond* almost blew the *Narval* out of the water, thinking her to be an Italian submarine, but an officer on the bridge fortunately recognised the out-of-date code that the *Narval* was using and realised that she was French. After identification, the *Diamond* asked the *Narval* her purpose. The reply came back: 'French submarine *Narval* making for Valletta to join the Royal Navy.' The shout of elation that went up from the British destroyer's bridge could, it was said, 'have been heard in Sicily'.[9]

The other, the minelaying submarine *Rubis*, which had been sowing mines in the Norwegian fjords, was caught at the armistice in operations with the British North Sea Fleet. The officers were unclear what to do, so they put the matter of their future allegiance to democratic vote. Forty-two out of a crew of forty-four voted to join the Free French. The next day the *Rubis* sailed serenely into Dundee.

These, however, were the exceptions. Others, including the main battle fleet, stayed where they were, waiting for instructions about what to do next. Apart from the ships still in Toulon, Cherbourg and Brest, there was a sizeable flotilla at Alexandria, and others at Sousse, Bizerta and Algiers. A few units were in British ports or in Dakar, and some in the West Indies. The major capital ships, however, were concentrated with their escorts at Mers el-Kébir.

Mers el-Kébir is situated just to the west of Oran in Algeria, and is a natural strategic point from which to command access to the straits of Gibraltar. It was an obvious place for the French Fleet to anchor. But such had been the indolence of inter-war French governments that the construction of jetties necessary to harbour a major capital fleet had been started only in 1935. By 1940, only one section of a jetty had been completed to the point where large ships could berth with sterns moored to the jetty and bows riding on offshore anchors. So it was that the fleet commanded by Vice-Admiral Marcel Gensoul in late June 1940 found itself awkwardly moored against an unfinished jetty.

The four battleships, the *Dunkerque* and the *Strasbourg* built in 1937–38 and the older *Provence* and *Bretagne* built in 1915–16, were berthed within 150 yards of one another. Clustered around were six destroyers, *Mogador*, *Volta*, *Terrible*, *Kersaint*, *Tigre* and *Lynx*, twelve torpedo boats, six submarines, and other supporting ships. They were all, in reality, sitting ducks.

Operation Catapult was accomplished without bloodshed at all ports except Mers el-Kébir, apart from a minor incident on the mammoth submarine *Surcouf* at Plymouth. In total, some 130 French ships in British ports, including two battleships, two light cruisers, eight destroyers and five submarines were quietly acquired. At Alexandria, a long and elegant correspondence between the two opposing admirals led to the peaceful immobilisation of the French ships. The *Rubis* in Dundee was no problem. On the whole, it had been a very smooth operation.

But it had been far from smooth at Mers el-Kébir. Expecting trouble, the British had assembled 'Force H', consisting of the battleships *Resolution* and *Valiant*, the battlecruiser *Hood*, the aircraft-carrier *Ark Royal*, two cruisers and eight destroyers, under the command of Vice-Admiral Somerville. Somerville was perhaps not by nature a subtle man, and there was no subtlety about the operation. Nor possibly could there have been. If the French ships of the line had been allowed to get up steam, they could have deployed their heavy armaments, and the British might have sustained a level of casualty, both in men and equipment, which would have been intolerable.

Somerville's approach was direct. At 8.05 a.m. on 3 July the destroyer *Foxhound* entered the harbour with a message for the French. It was an ultimatum: either you come with us, or you give your ships over to us, or you sail under our escort to ports in the West Indies or the United States. If the French refused all these options, they were to scuttle their ships. Failing that, the message went on, we will use whatever force is necessary to stop your ships from falling into enemy hands.

Gensoul was completely taken aback, not least because he and all his subordinates desired nothing more than to continue the fight against the Germans alongside their British allies. He could only play for time. There followed a gentlemanly exchange of views between the two naval negotiators. The British ultimatum was rejected, but Captain Holland, Somerville's negotiator, assured Gensoul – 'as officer to officer' – that if he had been in Gensoul's place his response would have been no different.

The truth was that no effort had been made by the British to understand the predicament of French naval officers, unlike at Alexandria, where the matter was settled, and the French flotilla immobilised, without bloodshed. But the French Admiralty was now alerted to the situation at Mers el-Kébir, and although Holland had started what seemed like a genuine negotiation, the two Admiralties moved, almost simultaneously and certainly coincidentally, to ensure the worst possible solution. The French, although, or perhaps because, the Government was at that moment moving from Bordeaux to Vichy, announced by radio, *en clair*, that cruisers from Toulon were moving to Gensoul's assistance, and the British Admiralty instructed Somerville to get it all over with before nightfall. Time had run out.

The British opened fire on the stationary French ships at 5.56 p.m. The action lasted nine minutes. The *Dunkerque* ran aground, the *Bretagne* blew up, the *Provence* was beached, and many of the minor ships were, in one way or another, immobilised. Only the *Strasbourg*, with a destroyer escort, managed to escape the orgy of destruction and limped away to Toulon. In all, 1297 French officers and men were killed, and a further 351 wounded. There were no British casualties. As General Dill said on hearing the news, the two nations who were fighting for civilisation had turned and rent each other while the barbarians sat back and laughed.

Such was the dislike of Pétainist France in London at the time, and such was the desire for action of any sort – whomever it was against – that when Churchill announced the news of the engagement in the House of Commons on the following day he was listened to in enthralled amazement, and when he sat down Members rose, waved their order papers and cheered him to the echo. It was not a reception that Churchill enjoyed, since, for him, the decision to proceed with Catapult had been for him exceptionally painful.

De Gaulle's reaction was, as might be imagined, quite different. To start with, it was a difficult time for him. Five days earlier he had been served notice by the Vichy authorities that he was under arrest and that he should present himself in Toulouse for court-martial. The judgement of the court – conviction and a four-year prison sentence – was announced on the day that Churchill made his statement to the Commons about Mers el-Kébir. Even then, he knew perfectly well that that was not the end. The judges in the case were deemed by the Vichy authorities to have been too lenient, and a further hearing at Clermont-Ferrand resulted in his being condemned to loss of citizenship, confiscation of all assets and, finally, to death.

It is no wonder, then, that de Gaulle's initial reactions to Mers el-Kébir were tempestuous. It was not just the unfortunate moment, nor even the gratuitous loss of French lives; it was the realisation that Vichy would make the most of the affair in the propaganda war to discredit the Free French. As indeed they did. It was therefore with trepidation that Spears went round to see him on the following day. By that time, however, de Gaulle had calmed down, and had recognised that the operation, however painful, had been inevitable. But he was depressed about the longer-term effects, and thought that he might give up the struggle and retire to private life in Canada.

It was the first time that de Gaulle had become profoundly disheartened, and there were three days of tense reflection before he felt able to broadcast again. But when he did so it was in terms which satisfied the British without any reservations. He preferred, he said, to know that even the *Dunkerque* – their dear, magnificent, powerful *Dunkerque* – was stranded off Mers el-Kébir, rather than to learn one day that she was manned by Germans and used to shell British ports. From the British point of view, the broadcast could not have been better, and it was an act of great dignity and courage, but there was also some shrewd calculation behind it. After all, Vichy had broken off diplomatic relations with London after Mers el-Kébir, and there was no reason why de Gaulle should not profit from that.

Nevertheless, it is difficult to resist the thought that de Gaulle was very strongly influenced by the response that he had evoked from the British public. It was not just the press; wherever he went, he met friendliness and warmth from the man in the street. Of course, his gigantic figure made him unmistakeable; but even beyond the desire to touch celebrity there was, in the British public at large, a feeling that he, alone among Frenchmen, had shown the courage that they had expected from France – the courage, indeed, that they themselves were going to have to show over the next weeks, months and years, now that Britain was on her own.

So it was that, when de Gaulle took the salute at the Bastille Day Parade on 14 July 1940 in Grosvenor Gardens, in front of the statue of Marshal Foch, there may have been only two or three hundred Free French marching past, but there were hundreds, perhaps thousands, of Londoners there. Their rendition of the 'Marseillaise', however inaccurate and out of tune, was sufficient to show conclusively to de Gaulle both that he had the support of the British people, and that the British people would hold out to the end. Retirement to private life in Canada was no longer an option.

2

AFRIC'S SUNNY FOUNTAINS

They are the Wild Geese of this century, these men of de Gaulle's. ★

'I think he felt the dishonour of France as few men can feel anything, and that he had literally taken on himself the national dishonour, as Christ according to the Christian faith took on himself the sins of the world. I think he was like a man, during those days, who had been skinned alive, and that the slightest contact with friendly, well-meaning people got him on the raw to such an extent that he wanted to bite, as a dog that has been run over will bite any would-be friend who comes to its rescue.'[1] So wrote Mary Borden, Spears's American novelist wife, about the de Gaulle of July 1940.

Spears and de Gaulle were, of course, in constant contact. It was part of Spears's task to introduce de Gaulle to those in London who might be of help to him, and there were select dinner parties once or twice a week, at the RAC or the Connaught, or in private homes. They would be parties of five or six, all male, except when Spears's wife came up from Aldershot, where she was running a hospital for the Free French. Mme de Gaulle was not invited, except to dinners *en famille* with the Spears, where she appeared as a 'gentle, charming, slight, timid figure'.[2]

Apart from these deliberately promotional dinner parties, there was no lack of social life. The Free French were taken up by many of London's society lionesses. Committees of enthusiastic supporters were formed, such as the Amis des Volontaires Français; Lady Peel even turned her substantial house into a hostel for the Free French; a little club was started in St James's Place, the Petit Club Français; ladies vied with each other to extend hospitality to their gallant French allies, even

★ From a letter by Helen Waddell. Quoted in D. Felicitas Corrigan, *Helen Waddell, A Biography*; Gollancz, London, 1986.

to the point where such hospitality exceeded the normal social conventions. Gaston Palewski's long relationship with the author Nancy Mitford is only one example.

On the other hand, official relations, following the Mers el-Kébir episode, were still very tense. There was constant sniping from the Foreign Office about de Gaulle's self-proclaimed political role; and Churchill himself at one point pronounced that de Gaulle should now act as a 'Scarlet Pimpernel', to establish an 'underground railway' that would bring Frenchmen who wanted to continue the fight into the welcoming arms of British command. Even this was too much for the British chiefs of staff; General Dill was so contemptuous of the French military performance of May 1940 that he, for one, did not want anything more to do with them. They should all go home, he told the War Cabinet, as soon as possible.

Not surprisingly, recruitment to the Free French from the British internment camps dropped to a trickle. Even before Mers el-Kébir, de Gaulle's visits to the camps, where some 21,000 French troops led life as best they could, had been difficult. The War Office representatives who accompanied him seemed to set themselves the task of undoing all his efforts to rally his compatriots to his standard, by slipping around in de Gaulle's wake and telling internees that if they joined him they would be acting at 'their own risk and peril' and liable to be considered traitors in their own country.

After Mers el-Kébir, even this blocking action was unnecessary. Anti-British feeling in the camps did its own work; morale and discipline collapsed, and it was a relief on all sides, except for the Free French, when the large majority opted to go home and were repatriated. The relief turned to bitterness when the merchant ship *Meknes,* sailing to Brest to repatriate 1100 French naval officers and men, was sunk by a German E-boat in the Channel on 24 July, with the loss of 400 men drowned.

Nevertheless, in those gloomy days, made gloomier for de Gaulle by the news of his mother's death on 16 July, there were some shafts of light. After all, for the Free French the failure of British efforts to maintain any sort of relationship with the Vichy Government could only be considered hopeful. Then, somewhat surprisingly, at Desmond Morton's suggestion the British had gone so far as to appoint a publicity agent, one Richmond Temple, to promote de Gaulle's image with the public and with British embassies and missions abroad. De Gaulle was presented as 'the man of destiny', but it was suggested that his 'sincere modesty' would prevent him from claiming such a role for himself. The language was rich, and the image not immediately identifiable to those who knew their man well. De Gaulle himself was predictably scathing: 'Churchill wants to promote me like a bar of soap.'[3] But at least the British were trying.

There was also the recruitment of Vice-Admiral Emile Muselier,* the first senior officer to join the Free French. Although his reputation was not without blemish – in fact, he was known to be something of a rogue – he was a big enough name to merit immediately the post of commander of the Free French naval forces. His relationship with de Gaulle could never be said to have been easy; where de Gaulle was formal, Muselier gesticulated; where de Gaulle was solemnly dedicated to the cause of France, Muselier was jovial and salacious; where de Gaulle was aloof, Muselier was all Mediterranean charm.

Nevertheless, Muselier was a sailor of undoubted courage and dash, and he was the only one among fifty French admirals who had chosen to continue the fight against Germany. When he arrived in a flying boat from Gibraltar on 30 June, having persuaded the officers and men of an armed merchant ship to follow him in due course, he had no idea who de Gaulle was; and when they met, it was de Gaulle's ungainly physique that struck Muselier immediately: his great height, his rather small head and low forehead. 'His small grey eyes did not look squarely into one's own, but always turned away when he was answering a precise question. The chin, of a very peculiar shape, did not suggest a strong will. The pronunciation was slow, as if he were listening to himself speaking; and his mouth, neither large nor small, sometimes opened in a complete circle over his irregular teeth. The nose was powerful, almost Bourbon. The ears, badly formed, stuck out widely.'[4] But the General's powers of persuasion were up to the task, and Muselier signed on. Not only did he sign on, but, on his appointment as naval commander, he insisted on an emblem that his ships could wear to distinguish them from Vichy ships. That emblem, which he chose out of respect for his mother's origins, was the Croix de Lorraine. Thus did Muselier's legacy, whatever happened afterwards, find its place in history.

* Emile Muselier (1882–1965): Sailor. Marseillais by origin, Mediterranean by temperament. Educated at naval school; Captain 1914; Vice-Admiral 1939; Commander Marseilles port 1939; C.-in-C. Free French Naval Forces 1941; assistant to Gen. Giraud Algiers 1943, then active service until 1946: dabbled unsuccessfully in post-war politics 1946–7.

Then there was General Georges Catroux,★ the Governor-General of Indo-China. This was a big catch: a four-star general of impeccable social and military credentials, who had never concealed his dislike of the armistice, and who had been sacked by Vichy in consequence. Not only that, but he had known de Gaulle as a fellow prisoner in Fort IX at Ingolstadt during the First World War, and had given him advice, at de Gaulle's own request, on the situation in the Levant on his posting there in 1929.

The British Foreign Office took a great deal of trouble over Catroux, not least because they saw him as a possible leader of the Free French in place of Churchill's troublesome protégé. He was shepherded carefully to London, on the assumption, as the Foreign Office informed the British consul-general in Saigon, that 'de Gaulle would make no difficulty about deferring to Catroux'.[5] Not for the first time, the Foreign Office read the situation wrongly. When he arrived in London, Catroux told Churchill quietly but firmly that he was not prepared to take the leadership of the Free French, and that he had already placed himself at the disposal of General de Gaulle.

By mid-August, the Free French army comprised some 2250 officers and men: insignificant by any standards, but it was a beginning. The new offices into which the Free French moved on 2 July, elegant premises at No. 4 Carlton Gardens, were further evidence of British support. Best of all, British agents had discovered a cache of French francs, worth some £13 million, in the courtyard of a French bank in occupied France, and had made off with them. The money was to be used to finance de Gaulle. 'So the Secret Service,' remarked Colville, 'are not entirely useless.'[6]

It was from this beginning that de Gaulle concluded that it was time to break out. Free France in the summer of 1940 was of no great consequence, depending entirely on the British, with only a small London base, generally ignored or distrusted by the French themselves. Four months later, much to everybody's surprise — including, perhaps, de Gaulle's — Free France represented thousands of square miles of territory and armed forces of 17,500 men. The story of how that happened is one of blunders and brilliance, of good and bad luck, of improbable

★ Georges Catroux (1877–1969): Soldier. Aristocratic in origin and bearing. After St Cyr, fought in First World War, wounded, imprisoned with de Gaulle at Ingolstadt; divisional army then corps commander between wars; Gov.-Gen. Indo-China 1939–40; Free French Commander Near East 1940–1; Gov.-Gen. Algeria 1944; Ambassador, Moscow 1945–8.

coincidences, and of courage and tenacity; and the theatre for the drama was the French Empire in Africa.

Africa had been a problem ever since the armistice. In the north, the French governors in Morocco, Algeria and Tunisia had been assiduously wooed by the British and the Free French, but in the end had failed to make the break with Vichy. In Central and Equatorial Africa, there were large tracts of territory, mostly either desert or rain forest, which were nominally in the Empire or under French mandate but which, because of geography, climate and sparse and scattered indigenous populations, tended to be, at best, uncertain quantities. Yet the strategic importance of the African Empire after the fall of France suddenly became evident. North Africa commanded the access from the Atlantic to the Mediterranean, and thence to the Suez Canal and India, while Central and Equatorial Africa, if in friendly hands, would provide a safe air route from the Gold Coast across the continent to Egypt and the Middle East.

As early as 28 June, after Duff Cooper, the Minister for Information, had reported on the failure of the mission to secure the release of the passengers on the *Massilia*, the War Cabinet had agreed a plan to land a joint British–Free French expeditionary force at Casablanca in Morocco, a plan which came to be known as Operation Susan. The chiefs of staff were not impressed, and reported on 1 July that it would be most unwise to strip the defences of Britain of troops at that time, and in such a hazardous enterprise. Besides, Operation Catapult was then imminent.

After Catapult, and particularly Mers el-Kébir, there could be no question of an invasion of Morocco. The French authorities and servicemen throughout North Africa had been so incensed by the slaughter that any thought of such an invasion receiving a friendly welcome was now quite obviously absurd. But the idea survived. Only the target changed; and the target became Dakar.

Dakar lies at the southern end of the peninsula of Cap Vert, which is itself the westernmost point of the African continent. It is an agreeable place, the north-east wind bringing cool, dry weather from the Sahara in the winter, while the summer south-westerly brings heat and humidity, but rarely to the point of the discomfort that is felt frequently further south. The city was built in French colonial style, after its occupation by the French in 1857, and such was its growth, both in size and style, that it soon became known as the 'Paris of Africa'. Its strategic importance lay in the fact that Cap Vert provided the largest sheltered anchorage on the coast of West Africa, and was therefore a natural base from which submarines or surface raiders could harass shipping in the Atlantic. It made obvious sense, both from the British and from the Free French point of view, that it should be in Allied hands.

As it turned out, the Dakar expedition of September 1940 was a fiasco from start to finish. To start with, the basic intelligence was faulty. De Gaulle's original plan, worked out together with Spears and Morton, was to land at Konakry in the French colony of Guinea, some 500 miles to the south, and to march northwards to Dakar. As they went north, the forces of Free France, in de Gaulle's view, would 'grow by contagion'.[7] This view was supported by French agents in Dakar, who had assured him that 70 per cent of the garrison supported Free France, 20 per cent were neutral and only 10 per cent pro-Vichy. The British assessment was of a 'majority of junior officers, garrison troops and population in sympathy with General de Gaulle'.[8]

Nothing could have been further from the truth. Mers el-Kébir had already turned opinion in Dakar away from the British and de Gaulle, and anti-British feelings were further inflamed by the subsequent torpedo attack by British aircraft on the battleship *Richelieu,* which had damaged her so severely that she was now laid up in Dakar harbour under extensive repair, her officers and crew seething with rage. The result was that, on the eve of the operation, the population was said by one French officer to be only 20 per cent favourable to de Gaulle, comprising mainly those with a vested interest, 'merchants or producers of peanuts who wanted at any cost to sell their produce'. Of the rest, it was said that half of them wished to be left in peace and a further third or so were prepared to resist to the end.

The plan itself went through several versions. Following the General's request for a British military and naval commitment, a series of meetings was held, out of which there emerged a scheme for an operation considerably larger than that of de Gaulle's original plan. The scheme came with a guarded but definite recommendation from the chiefs of staff, their main reservation being political – that there was a conflict between the policy of improving relations with Vichy and encouraging elements in the French colonies to continue the war against Germany, and that to support de Gaulle might lead to war with Vichy. In the ensuing discussion, Churchill put his authority behind de Gaulle. After a long discussion, it was decided to go ahead, but it was agreed that the only effective place to land de Gaulle's force was Dakar itself. Furthermore, the expedition would be under British command.

The trouble was that it was still unclear, and indeed never became clear, whether the operation was to be one of friendly persuasion of a cooperative population or to be one of armed attack; and it ended up as an uneasy mixture of the two. Nor did the Dakar operation, now codenamed Menace – since the original codename 'Scipio', however classically elegant, suffered from the obvious giveaway that the Roman general's title was Africanus – have any luck. It became muddled up with a quite separate Free French initiative in Africa, which in turn provoked a Vichy reaction that nearly spiked Menace altogether.

On 6 August, three days before the new plan for Menace was agreed by Churchill, de Gaulle decided to send Pleven, Jean Parant and Claude Hettier de Boislambert, three of his closest followers, and subsequently Leclerc,[*] to Equatorial Africa to try to detach Chad, the French Congo and Cameroon from Vichy. This was in response to a telegram from Félix Eboué, the Governor of Chad and himself a proconsul of considerable flamboyance, that he intended to bring Chad into the Free French camp. As it turned out, the mission was spectacularly successful. Between 26 and 28 August, Chad duly declared for de Gaulle; Leclerc and Boislambert took the town of Duala, and with it Cameroon, after landing by night in the pouring rain with some twenty men from three native canoes; and the enterprising Colonel de Larminat[†] crossed the Congo river to Brazzaville, took over the city, and declared French Congo for de Gaulle – and himself head of government in Free French Africa.

'Les Trois Glorieuses', as the 'rallying' of Chad, Congo and Cameroon came to be called, sounded the alarm in Vichy, and Darlan decided to send a squadron of six ships, three heavy and three light cruisers, to reinforce existing garrisons to prevent further haemorrhage and, if possible, to recover the countries that had defected. Once the German naval command had approved its departure, Force Y sailed from Toulon on 9 September, heading for the Straits of Gibraltar at its

---

[*] Philippe-Marie de Hautecloque Leclerc (1902–1947): Soldier. Served in Somaliland 1940, then joining Free French; commanded expeditions in Africa 1941; commanded division in Normandy 1944; liberation of Paris 1944; captured near Strasbourg November 1944; posted to Indo-China 1945; killed in aircrash on way to posting in North Africa.

[†] Edgard de Larminat (1895–1962): Soldier. Levant in 1940; posted to Central Africa by Vichy; High Commissioner for Free French Africa 1940–1; served under Leclerc in Fighting French forces in North Africa 1942–3; under Juin Italy 1944, and in southern France 1944. Supported de Gaulle in 1958; committed suicide in 1962.

full speed of 25 knots, and aiming to slip through at dawn on the 11th.

The story of how they succeeded is one of unalleviated British incompetence. Six hours after Force Y's departure from Toulon, the British consul-general in Tangiers signalled Gibraltar that he had reliable information that a French squadron was to try to run the Straits within seventy-two hours. The signal was passed immediately to London, but such was the chaos there, chaos compounded by the daily and nightly German bombing raids, that it took four days to reach the Admiralty. Furthermore, on 10 September the British naval attaché in Madrid was told 'officially' by his Vichy opposite number that Force Y would be going through the following morning, and he immediately alerted the Admiralty. Nothing was done. Finally, Force Y was spotted by a British destroyer before dawn on the 11th, sailing at high speed 50 miles east of the Straits.

Admiral Somerville, commanding the British Force H in harbour at Gibraltar, put the the battlecruiser *Renown* on one hour's notice to sail and waited for instructions. Well before he heard back from London, Force Y had not only passed the Straits but had identified themselves to the Port War Signal Station at Gibraltar, were presumed to be friendly, and had been wished '*bon voyage*'. By the time Somerville received his instructions, and the *Renown* was ready with a destroyer escort to give chase, he was told that aircraft from Gibraltar shadowing the French squadron had seen them entering the port of Casablanca. When he was given the Admiralty's signal to intercept Force Y, Somerville turned to his flag lieutenant and said that they must be mad.

Meanwhile, a fortnight earlier, on 30 August, the Franco–British force had finally sailed from Liverpool. The event was perhaps the least well kept secret in the history of the war. Assault landing craft had rolled into Liverpool 'like the Durham ox, to the wonder and consternation of the countryside';[9] the dockers knew exactly where their cargo was bound. A British officer had walked into a London map shop and had asked openly for a map of Dakar; de Gaulle himself had visited Simpson's in Piccadilly and ordered tropical outfits, explaining that he was going to 'West Africa'; both in London and in Liverpool, Free French officers had held farewell dinners at which the toast was '*à Dakar*'. Most farcically of all, just as the military train was about to pull out of Euston, a porter rushed up with a large case on a barrow; the case fell off, burst open and revealed quantities of leaflets headed '*Aux Habitants de Dakar*', which blew about the platform until hastily collected. Finally, the crowd of well-wishers at Euston was so dense that the train had difficulty leaving. 'I have never seen,' wrote Spears, 'so many people from VIPs, civil and military, to wives and girl-friends gathered together to see off the heads of an ultra-secret expedition.'[10]

Fortunately, Vichy intelligence was just as, perhaps even more, incompetent. When all this was duly reported to them through the Spanish embassy network, they inquired further and finally swallowed a story put out by British agents that indeed there was an expedition, but that its true purpose was to sail round the Cape and deposit de Gaulle in Egypt. The British and Free French by no means had a monopoly in stupidity.

When Menace finally got under way, the landing force consisted of four Royal Marine battalions, two independent marine companies, with support services, and two Free French battalions; while the naval force consisted of two battleships, an aircraft carrier, three cruisers, nine destroyers and three Free French sloops, two armed trawlers and four cargo boats. In addition, there were two Dutch liners, in one of which, the 16,000-ton *Westernland,* de Gaulle decided to set up his headquarters. He could not possibly, he pointed out, be associated with any attack on fellow Frenchmen, and therefore could not set up a joint command. The long-suffering General Spears was to sail with him. The British commanders, Admiral Cunningham and General Irwin, set up their headquarters in the battleship *Barham.* Given the inevitable wireless silence, communication between the two command centres was almost impossible.

De Gaulle was supremely optimistic about the expedition. He had left a letter for Catroux, due to arrive soon in London: 'When you receive this letter, I shall have left for Dakar with troops, ships, aircraft and . . .the support of the British. I have full confidence in final victory.'[11] He even wore his Chasseurs Alpins beret on the bridge of the *Westernland,* pulled over his head, as usual, to make him look like an oversize doll. One dyspeptic British officer, on the other hand, took a different view. In his opinion, it was 'an ill-omened expedition, sponsored on us by the PM in spite of bitter opposition from the Service Chiefs. It is part of the price we pay for having Winston as PM.'[12]

The expedition lumbered southwards, making a wide detour out into the Atlantic and taking seventeen days to reach Freetown, the British port some 500 miles south of Dakar and the jumping-off point for the final approach. Just before they got there, however, the whole enterprise was abruptly, without warning, cancelled by the War Cabinet.

There was consternation. The new orders from London were

received with disbelief: de Gaulle and his troops were to go straight on to Equatorial Africa, to consolidate his position there; the ships were to stay in Freetown and await further orders. The reason for this volte-face quickly became plain. The news of the arrival of the French Force Y in Dakar had reached London, and the War Cabinet had concluded that the naval balance had been thereby seriously altered. The risk was therefore too great. Yet even the new orders were tentative, ending with the words 'unless de Gaulle has any strong objections'. De Gaulle certainly did have strong objections, which were made clear by Spears in an explosive personal signal to Churchill. The change in policy was 'heartbreaking . . .impossible to understand'.[13] The Vichy ships were lying helpless in harbour under awnings. If de Gaulle was left to 'vegetate', his ability to rally any other part of the French Empire was gone for ever.

In the face of this verbal onslaught, which was supported by Menace's British commanders, the War Cabinet changed tack again and allowed Menace to continue. It was not exactly an example of decisive government, but de Gaulle had got what he wanted, and he was encouraged when it was discovered that the three heavy cruisers of Force Y had been spotted leaving Dakar, making southwards, directly towards the British fleet. Pierre Boisson, the Governor-General of French West Africa, had instructed Admiral Bourragué to move at all speed to shore up the Vichy position in Gabon. He was not to know that he was sending them straight into the enemy's jaws.

The first contact between French and British units took place the following day. HMS *Cornwall* pulled across the bows of the heavy cruiser *Primaguet,* and a message was delivered from de Gaulle's representative, Commandant d'Argenlieu,* inviting Bourragué either to join Free France immediately or to sail to Casablanca. This stern message was accompanied by a soothing letter from *Cornwall's* captain to the French captain Goybet, recalling nostalgically the jollity in Shanghai in the summer of 1939 when the crews of the two ships had entertained one another. After a tense five hours, the tactic achieved at least a partial success. Bourragué did not decide to join the Free French forthwith, but did order the *Primaguet* back to Casablanca; he himself managed in the pouring rain to slip away in his own flagship, the *Georges Leygues,* and

* Thierry d'Argenlieu (1889–1984): Sailor and monk. Fought in navy in First World War; joined monastic order of Discalced Carmelites; rejoined service in 1939, taken prisoner in 1940, but escaped to London; wounded at Dakar 1940; Admiral by 1945 but returned to the cloister in 1947.

make it back to Dakar. The third cruiser, the *Gloire,* developed engine trouble and was escorted by the British into Casablanca. When he returned to Dakar, Bourragué was promptly sacked by Darlan, who reaffirmed his order that all British ships which came within 20 miles of French territory should be fired on. But by that time the Dakar reinforcements had been reduced to only four ships.

This was not the only result. The real success lay in removing the Vichy threat to Equatorial Africa. De Gaulle could now go on to consolidate his position there and move later against Dakar. But there was still a problem. The naval action, such as it was, had been entirely British. There had been no Free French success to use as good propaganda and, although strategically it would have been sensible to call off the Dakar operation at that point, politically de Gaulle needed his own success. Menace therefore went ahead as planned.

It all went wrong from the start. Arriving off Dakar at dawn on 23 September, the fleet found dense fog – almost unknown in that season. De Gaulle's two small aircraft, in French colours and with pilots wearing French uniforms, took off from the British aircraft carrier and landed at Ouakam airfield, expecting a friendly reception. They were immediately put under arrest. Then two launches sporting the Tricolor, with d'Argenlieu on board, gingerly entered the harbour; after a short shouting bout with onshore French sailors, they were fired on by heavy machine-guns and fled. De Gaulle's message to Boisson, appealing him to allow the entry of Free French ships into port, was met with furious rejection and the full mobilisation of the defences, including the *Richelieu.* Shots were exchanged between the shore batteries and the British ships, which had been groping their way shoreward through the mist. De Gaulle tried in late afternoon to land Free French troops on a beach just to the north. They were repelled, with casualties on both sides. All in all, it had been a bad day.

If the first day was bad, the second was no better. Just before midnight the British commanders had sent an ultimatum to Boisson claiming that his attitude gave them 'every reason to believe' that Dakar might 'at any moment' be handed over by him to the Germans,[14] and stating that unless they complied with de Gaulle's requirements the British force would attack at six o'clock the following morning. The drafting was astonishingly clumsy. There were no Germans around, and the French in Dakar had no intention of handing the city over to them even if there were. They just did not want de Gaulle and the British. The ultimatum was simply yet another irritant.

In the morning the engagement started on time, as advertised, in conditions which were little better than those of the previous day. The battleships and shore batteries engaged each other at a range of 4 miles. Some 400 15-inch rounds were fired by the British, with nothing to show for them. The French were more accurate, damaging the *Barham* with heavy shells. Otherwise, the only victor was the fog.

At this point, de Gaulle came to terms with the reality, which was quite simply that Dakar was not for the taking. He wanted to call the whole thing off. Cunningham and Irwin, however, decided on one last throw. Accordingly, on the third morning, the battleships engaged the shore batteries at very long range, in much improved visibility. The result was no different. The French resistance was skilful and brave, and after twenty-five minutes a French submarine succeeded in a direct torpedo strike on the battleship *Resolution*, causing serious damage. It was time to call it a day, and the British commanders finally accepted de Gaulle's view that the whole endeavour had been a failure.

It was generally agreed that de Gaulle himself had behaved impeccably in the face of this disaster. As General Irwin wrote, 'De Gaulle's bearing was remarkable for its brave acceptance of a great disappointment . . .both Vice-Admiral Cunningham and I felt the greatest admiration for a man with such quiet courage and with so cool and clear a brain.'[15] Churchill defended de Gaulle robustly in the House of Commons. But the British press was not impressed. In the *Daily Mirror* of 28 September, Cassandra wrote: 'The Dakar debacle is worse than appeasement. It has the unmistakeable imprint of weak and frightened men. It's going to be hard to convince us that Mr Churchill has feet of clay; but we can't stand much more of this.'[16] The American press was even more outspoken. All in all, reactions were predictably gloomy. 'This may be the end of de Gaulle' was a typical comment heard among the Prime Minister's circle in London.[17]

The effect on General de Gaulle was to throw him into the deepest depression. For him Dakar had been the start of the climb back from the shame of May 1940 – and it had ended in expensive and humiliating farce. The Free French, in his eyes, had made fools of themselves the first time they went into battle, and he felt himself the biggest fool of them all. Again he wondered whether it was worthwhile going on, but this time it would not have been a matter of retiring honourably to Canada and private life, but of withdrawing dishonourably and in failure, with his pride permanently bruised. Indeed, he was so depressed that, as he himself was to write, he actually contemplated suicide.

But if Dakar was the low point of de Gaulle and the Free French, it was not, as it turned out, by any means the end. The General and his troops were escorted by the British ships to Duala, where they arrived on 8 October – to be greeted as heroes. The next two months were something like a royal progress. Wherever they went, there were crowds and Free French flags. When he asked de Larminat: 'Well, shall we go on?' there was no hesitation about the positive reply. He went on a tour of the Chad deserts and the Congo rainforests. It was, as de Larminat reported, a veritable cleansing of the soul. Spears, who had been dragged around with him – he and de Gaulle had had a bad row over Dakar – was more cautious, noting that the only disadvantage of the trip was a revival of de Gaulle's previous tendency to assume the role of an 'absolute monarch'.

The last operation to secure the Free French African base was the capture of Gabon. In early November, in spite of British doubts, two columns moved in overland, led by de Larminat from Cameroon and Parant from Congo, and a seaborne attack was mounted by Leclerc. It was vigorous, and efficient and quick. Within a fortnight the whole episode was over, and the Vichy Governor of Gabon had hanged himself.

De Gaulle's procession through Equatorial Africa amply illustrated Spears's difficulty. Now that he had the major provinces at his back, even before the 'liberation' of Gabon, de Gaulle had moved to establish his credentials as an independent power to be reckoned with. In London he had been a minor figure, wholly under the protection of the British. Now he controlled a large slice of the French Empire, and he could, and would, speak for it.

At Brazzaville, on 27 October, there were issued a manifesto, two ordinances and an 'organic declaration' which constituted nothing more or less than a charter for government. The manifesto declared that the Vichy Government was wholly 'unconstitutional' and that de Gaulle would assume 'the sacred duty' of directing the French war effort. Furthermore, he went on, 'I shall exercise my powers in the name of France and solely in order to defend her and I solemnly undertake to render an account of my actions to the representatives of the French people as soon as it shall have been possible for it to designate such freely.'[18] The ordinances announced the formation of an Empire Defence Council, while, naturally, making it clear that de Gaulle himself held the power of decision 'after consulting, if need be, the Defence Council'. The organic declaration justified these measures, in true

Jesuitical fashion, by reference to various laws from 1872 onwards on the role of general councils in times of national emergency.

Needless to say, these pronouncements were read in London with dismay. The British still had high hopes of Vichy, even to the point of thinking that some of their leaders might possibly be lured back into the war with Germany. Weygand, for instance, had recently been appointed delegate-general in North Africa, and approaches were being made to him. In October, Pétain had sent Professor Louis Rougier to London on a secret mission to negotiate a *modus vivendi* between the two Governments. These various discussions were continuing, and the last thing the British wanted was for de Gaulle to undermine them.

De Gaulle returned to London on 12 November, at the time when London was still being heavily bombed. Yvonne had moved from Petts Wood. She had been offered, and had accepted, a larger house at Dudleston Heath in Shropshire, known as Gadlas Hall. It is now a home for the elderly, with every modern convenience, but in 1940 it had no electricity, no mains water or indoor sanitation. Communications, too, were poor. A telephone had to be put in, and the cobbled drive had to be patched up to allow cars to drive up to the house. But at least 'little Anne' was less frightened away from the bombs, although she was in a fractious mood at times, and Yvonne could be by herself, looking after Anne with only daily help from the nearby village. The house was pleasant enough – the wistaria and a little duck pond were features – but the countryside was flat and bleak, and Yvonne was nervous about talking to strangers. She kept herself to herself, and was known to refuse to answer the doorbell if neighbours came calling.

The General could not live in Shropshire and work in London – there was five hours' hard driving between the two, and he could only make the trip once a month at best. He therefore had to find somewhere to stay in London, and decided to make his home first at the Connaught Hotel, even then one of the most elegant hotels in Mayfair, and then at a small flat he rented at 15 Grosvenor Square – just round the corner from the Connaught, where he continued to have his meals. It was a comfortable and convenient arrangement, and he was within walking distance of his office, by way of Berkeley Square and St James's. In spite of the blitz, which seems not to have bothered him at all, it was a good time for de Gaulle to be in London. He had to take charge again at Carlton Gardens, where rivalries among his subordinates had broken out in his absence and, at the end of 1940, he could see that the British negotiations with Vichy were not going well. Although his efforts to persuade them to drop the negotiations altogether were not as yet successful, he was sure, from his repeated visits to Chequers – where the two leaders ranged widely in their conversation over history and philosophy as well as the conduct of the war – that Churchill was on his side and would not abandon him. It was also the time of some of Churchill's greatest speeches, and the General was overcome with admiration, not just at their content but at Churchill's oratorical technique. '*Quel grand artiste!*' he said again and again. '*Quel grand artiste!*'

3

WHO IS FIGHTING WHOM?

Vers l'Orient compliqué, je volais avec des idées simples. ★

'I am France,' General de Gaulle informed the British Foreign Secretary, Lord Halifax, soon after his return from Africa.[1] Although the assertion met at best with embarrassed titters, and often hostile sneers, from his British protectors, it was no longer an idle boast. He had indeed changed the political balance, although it would take many months for the British, and years for the Americans, to recognise the fact.

It is not hard to see why. 1941 was a year of ambiguous and constantly shifting relations between Vichy, Britain and Free France; and it was often difficult at any one time and in any one place to know who was fighting whom, and to what purpose. To be sure, everybody knew that the common problem was how to deal with Germany, but beyond that the political landscape was misty and uncertain. It was this uncertainty that caused near-breakdown in de Gaulle's relations with the British Government in the first of a series of rows over the Levant, rows which were to rumble on right throughout the war and into the peace. They were not, of course, just rows about who was entitled to administer which piece of territory in the Near East. The dispute went much deeper than that.

The major difficulty was the relationship of the Free French with Britain on the one hand and with Vichy on the other. After de Gaulle's successes in Africa, confrontation between Free France and Vichy now appeared to be head-on. Frenchman had fired on Frenchman, and there had been bloodshed. However much de Gaulle had tried to avoid it, it had happened. His only possible justification was that he represented the

★ 'To the complicated East, I flew with simple ideas.' Charles de Gaulle, *Mémoires de Guerre*, vol.1, page 145; Plon, Paris, 1959.

legitimate, the true France, and Vichy was the renegade, in complicity with the enemy of France. That was precisely what he asserted when claiming to be France in his conversations with Halifax and others. The British, on the other hand, were determined to keep Vichy – and its remaining fleet – out of the war; they were therefore much softer in their approach, and continued to keep a diplomatic line open.

As it happened, de Gaulle's claim had been helped by events in Vichy itself. As early as July 1940, the Third Republic no longer existed; it had been voted into extinction by resolutions of the very Assembly that had originally been elected in 1936 and had spawned the Popular Front. Pétain had been proclaimed chief of state, with powers in many ways greater than those enjoyed by the kings of the *ancien régime*. The three men who were his closest lieutenants, Darlan, Weygand and, most sinister of all, Pierre Laval,★ exercised their functions by appointment only. There was no longer any pretence of democracy. Furthermore, the three lieutenants agreed on hardly anything, and the direction of government – if indeed there was any direction other than unquestioning obedience to the Marshal – was totally confused. Personal intrigue had taken the place of ordered authority.

Pétain's favourite, Admiral Darlan, came from an old naval family whose pride, as he was fond of recalling, was the death of his great-grandfather at Trafalgar; but he was, in the words of one, 'a pushy little Gascon', with a nose for political skulduggery, cold and self-absorbed, coarse in manner and tone, and 'without the halo of nobility which characterised the Marshal'.[2] Viciously anti-British – he wrote of Dunkirk that 'the prospect of getting out suddenly made the British grow wings'[3] – he was the author of the collaboration agreements of May 1941 which even his Vichy colleagues found too much to swallow. Furthermore, he had no reputation as a sailor, only as an administrator; indeed, he was one of the few officers in French naval history to have reached the office of commander-in-chief without ever having been in command of a ship.

Weygand, on the other hand, was the least collaborationist of the three. Of doubtful parentage – some said he was Belgian, from a Polish mother, others said he was the son of the Emperor Maximilian and a

---

★ Pierre Laval (1883–1945): Politician. Brilliant speaker, performance enhanced by habit of always wearing distinctive white necktie. Socialist Deputy 1914–19, Independent 1924–7; Minister for Justice 1926, Labour 1930, Foreign Affairs 1936; Chief Minister Vichy 1940 and 1942–4. Arrested by Gestapo 1944 and interned. Tried in Paris for treason and executed, October 1945.

Mexican woman – small, with the face of a fox, he reminded one Englishman of an 'aged jockey'[4] – he was generally agreed to be a very political general. Certainly his record in Poland, Lebanon and, ultimately, France was not impressive in any military sense. He, too, had never commanded troops in action when he took over from Gamelin in May 1940, and the whole thing had been too much for him. He was old and tired, and had no stomach for Vichy intrigue.

Pierre Laval was a much more complex character. A politician by career and by temperament, he fitted uneasily into the Pétain scheme of things. Weygand described him as 'Pétain's evil genius',[5] and it is true that he was much in favour of collaboration with the Germans – probably because he thought that they were certain to win the war. Nonetheless, his back-slapping charm endeared him to the man in the Vichy street and, to his credit, he was opposed to the blacklisting of harmless individuals purely on the grounds that they were anti-clerical or freemasons. But Pétain despised him, and found him a difficult subordinate; besides, he had a way of blowing cigarette smoke up the Marshal's nose that Pétain could not stand.

When Weygand was bounced out to North Africa as Governor-General in October 1940, the field was left to Darlan and Laval. Of the two, Laval was much closer to the Germans: he had met Hitler personally, and accompanied Pétain to a meeting with Hitler on the railway platform at Montoire on 24 October (although he had no idea that Pétain had sent Professor Rougier on his mission to London at exactly the same time to explore whether the British blockade imposed at the time of the armistice could be lifted and, if so, under what conditions). It was Laval who had been most sympathetic when Otto Abetz, now German ambassador to Vichy, had summoned General Huntziger, the commander-in-chief of the army, to dinner on 28 November to discuss the basis for Vichy's entry into the war against Britain.

But Darlan was closer to Pétain; and finally, when he and Pétain found Laval's pro-German machinations too much to bear, they got rid of him by a trick – requesting the resignation of the entire Council of Ministers in order to form a new government and promptly reinstating all but Laval – and put him under arrest. The Germans immediately ordered Pétain to release Laval and take him back into the Government; when Pétain showed unexpected stubbornness, Abetz himself arrived with SS outriders and simply took his protégé back with him to Paris. So much for the sovereignty of unoccupied France.

The upheavals at Vichy quickly became known in London. Darlan was now the undisputed crown prince and was viewed with the deepest suspicion by de Gaulle. His behaviour over the French fleet at the time of the armistice had been pusillanimous and deceitful, and now that he was in charge at Vichy it was quite possible, in de Gaulle's view, that he would use the French fleet against the Free French. Force Y, after all, had been intended for precisely that purpose.

On the other hand, de Gaulle's attitude to Vichy had to be carefully balanced. Clearly, he had to substantiate his claim to represent the true France, and that meant total hostility to Vichy. But it was not as easy as that. De Gaulle knew that Pétain was still popular and that he could badly damage his cause by provoking military engagements which involved Frenchmen opening fire on fellow Frenchmen. Furthermore, there was still at least a possibility of detaching at least a part of the French Empire still under Vichy control, and the Dakar adventure had shown him how difficult that could be unless circumstances were wholly propitious. Finally, he was fully aware that the British had by no means given up hope of reaching some sort of accommodation with Pétain, and he still needed their support.

It was not any longer, however, total dependence. After Africa, de Gaulle felt instinctively that he could speak to Churchill as an equal. He started to resent the frequent presence of Spears, who had tended to regard Free France as a rather unruly nephew, given to occasional bouts of youthful folly but accepting the subsequent avuncular admonition and guidance. There were arguments. De Gaulle was not somebody who was easily patronised, and the British were patronising. To be sure, they had other things on their mind than the teasingly intricate problem of the exact relative status of Free France and Vichy. After all, late 1940 and early 1941 were, in retrospect, the most difficult months of the war for Britain. The bombing of London continued; Greece was lost; the desert war in Libya was going wrong; Japan was threatening, and America was ambivalent; the invasion of Britain still seemed imminent. These were moments of great fear and anxiety.

For de Gaulle, there was another front which he had to guard. Tension was not confined to his relations with Vichy and the British Government. His staff in Carlton Gardens were in a state of constant intrigue against one another. Their backgrounds, and their political views, were so diverse that there was bound to be trouble. Supporters of the pre-war Popular Front lived cheek-by-jowl with fascists; each accused the other of being a Vichy spy. Some of them adopted false names: Antoine, a manufacturer, suddenly became Major Fontaine; Dewavrin became Colonel Passy. It was these two, both of them anti-republicans, who had provoked the first trouble, while de Gaulle was in Africa.

With de Gaulle away, Fontaine decided to sack a former Socialist Deputy, André Labarthe. Muselier protested, but de Gaulle backed Fontaine, and Labarthe left, taking with him several supporters to found a magazine, published in London, which was both anti-German and anti-de Gaulle. That was an irritant, but worse was to come. Passy, in charge of intelligence for the Free French, had had suspicions about some of his colleagues. Security, he said, had to be improved. He therefore appointed a certain Meffre to head a new security organisation. It was not a happy appointment. Meffre, who took the pseudonym 'Howard', introduced a stringent regime. There was 'vetting'; papers in the office were secretly searched; blotting paper was removed and its imprints scrutinised; movements were watched.

When de Gaulle returned from Africa, Admiral Muselier told him of Howard's activities and the effect they were having on morale among the Free French. At first, de Gaulle was reluctant to take action, but Muselier persisted. Finally, after a good deal of argument, it was agreed that Howard must go and he was given notice. Before he had worked it out, however, he passed to British intelligence four letters purporting to be from the Vichy General Rozoy, and apparently sent from London to Vichy through the Brazilian embassy. The letters revealed that Muselier had told Vichy all about the Dakar operation, that he had planned to send the submarine *Surcouf* back to a Vichy-controlled port, and that he had been bribed to dissuade French sailors from signing up with Free France.

British intelligence, already suspicious of the Free French in general and Passy in particular, reported the matter directly to Churchill. Churchill, without further ado, ordered the immediate arrest of everybody mentioned in the letters. De Gaulle was to be informed by special messenger. It was easier said than done. Muselier was in Portsmouth celebrating the New Year and could not be found, while de Gaulle was with his family in Shropshire. It took the police twenty-four hours to catch up with the Admiral, who was finally arrested on his return to London early on 2 January and unceremoniously locked up, first in Scotland Yard and then in Pentonville prison. They then went on to arrest two other Free French officers and two French ladies, one of whom was found in bed with a doctor attached to the Free French, while in the other's house was found, stark naked, the second secretary of the Brazilian embassy. It was all very exciting.

De Gaulle, on the other hand, was neither excited nor amused. Anthony Eden, the new Foreign Secretary, had been given the delicate task of breaking the news to the General, which he did on the morning of 2 January. De Gaulle, knowing of the intrigues in his office, was immediately suspicious, and left for London to sort out the mess. The whole thing was, of course, a great deal of nonsense. The letters had been forged by one Collin, whom Howard had employed for the purpose. One moment's serious scrutiny would have shown that. Three days later, de Gaulle was able to produce a complete refutation of the charges against Muselier. Howard and Collin confessed, and the Admiral was released, to the accompaniment of a chorus of apology from the British, including a personal retraction by Churchill and culminating in an audience for de Gaulle with the King. As far as the British were concerned, in spite of the embarrassment, the matter was thus decently closed.

The matter was far from closed for either Muselier or de Gaulle. Muselier was convinced that de Gaulle was behind the whole business, and remained so, while de Gaulle suspected that Howard and Collin had been planted by MI5. 'This lamentable incident . . .,' he later wrote, 'did not fail to influence my philosophy of what our relations with the British State really ought to be.'[6] He immediately ordered all Britons working in Carlton Gardens, even the tea-lady, to be sacked forthwith, and was only persuaded to rescind the order after much difficult negotiation.

It was not a good start to 1941. In other ways, however, life became somewhat easier. Mme de Gaulle moved with little Anne from Gadlas Hall to a house at Ashridge Park, just outside Berkhamsted; Elisabeth was preparing to leave the nuns of Our Lady of Sion in Shropshire to go up to Oxford as an undergraduate at Lady Margaret Hall; and Philippe was away serving in the Free French navy. Passy moved with his intelligence service to Duke Street, and Muselier took the marine and air headquarters to Westminster House. There was less opportunity for intrigue. Furthermore, Spears, whose relations with de Gaulle were becoming more and more difficult as Free France asserted its independence, was replaced as head of the British mission to the Free French by a much less colourful civil servant by the name of Somerville-Smith.

Yet although life in London was easier, de Gaulle was not making the progress he wanted elsewhere. He needed to get the Free French back into the fight against Germany, and this he was having difficulty in doing. He offered to send a contingent to help in the defence of Greece, but the chiefs of staff thought that it was all too much trouble and declined. He wrote to Weygand urging him to unite the French North African army with the Free French, and come back into the war, but Weygand showed no interest.

There were more satisfactory developments in Africa. Colonel Colonna d'Ornano, resplendent in Tuareg dress and black eyeglass, had in December led a detachment from Chad across several hundred miles of desert and attacked an Italian outpost at Murzuq in south-western Libya. Now de Gaulle ordered Leclerc to mount a similar operation against the oasis of Kufra, a refuelling station at the south-eastern end of the Libyan desert and on the main line of communication between the Mediterranean ports and the Italian forces in Ethiopia. The operation was wholly successful. After a journey of 600 miles, Leclerc laid siege to Kufra for a month and took 300 Italians prisoner when the oasis finally fell. Churchill had special praise for the operation when he reported it to the House of Commons.

Free French units also fought with British forces under General Wavell in North Africa, and two battalions formed the Brigade d'Orient under Colonel Monclar, fighting alongside British and Indian troops in Eritrea. French Somaliland, on the other hand, had failed to follow General Legentilhomme, the former commander of the French troops in Djibouti, who had come over to de Gaulle. Apart from that exception, however, Free France was showing life on the battlefield – enough life, indeed, for de Gaulle to have posted Catroux to Cairo to supervise operations. But the desert sideshows, however glamorous, were not important enough to require Catroux's presence. The big target was not in Africa; it was the eastern Mediterranean, the Levant, which was now, after the fall of Greece in late April and the simultaneous offensive by Rommel in Libya, taking on the highest strategic significance. It would also be the theatre for de Gaulle's first serious confrontation, not just with Vichy but with the British Government itself.

The lands on the eastern shore of the Mediterranean have been fought over almost since man first settled in the Mesopotamian delta. Over two millennia, armies from Egypt did battle there with Hittites, Assyrians, Persians and Alexander the Great; the Greeks came, and then the Romans, followed in turn by the Arabs and the Turks. The Levant is the cockpit in which three great religions, Judaism, Christianity and Islam, have struggled for supremacy for over a thousand years. There was wealth, too; the ports of the Levant were the outlet for the silks and spices which had been brought along the great trading routes from the east. It was no wonder that, with the gradual break-up of the Ottoman Empire in the nineteenth century, the Great Powers – in particular Britain and France – became intensely interested in capturing for themselves the Turkish imperial inheritance.

As a result of the final collapse of Turkey at the end of the 1914–18 War, Syria and the Lebanon were, at the beginning of the Second World War, administered by France under League of Nations mandate, while Palestine and Transjordan were administered by Britain; but for all practical purposes mandated territories were regarded as colonies. When the armistice came in France, the French high commissioner had declared for the Free French, and, in spite of rapidly changing his mind, had been promptly replaced by one of Pétain's most faithful supporters, General Dentz.

Dentz was an Alsatian whose father had emigrated to France in 1871 to prevent his two sons becoming German citizens, and his relations with the British were excellent. The British consul-general in Beirut had a French wife and was frequently entertained by the high commissioner. Officially, the general blockade on Vichy was supposed to operate in the Levant, but it was not enforced, on the grounds, as the protesting de Gaulle was told by the British in Cairo, that it would 'adversely affect Arab opinion towards us'.[7] Besides, General Wavell was now having to prepare for a German offensive towards Cairo and resources were limited. De Gaulle could only wonder, as he did out loud, whether the British were at all serious in their proclaimed intention to recover the Levant for the Allies.

General Dentz was not altogether pleased to receive a signal from Darlan in early February 1941 instructing him to cooperate with two German intelligence agents, von Hintig and Rosen, who arrived disguised as commercial travellers. Their activities were far from commercial. They were there to make contact with German sympathisers and to survey the possibilities for German use of Syrian airfields.

News of this visit reached London soon afterwards. De Gaulle immediately requested, and was granted, facilities to travel to Cairo. When he arrived, after an exhausting journey involving a detour through Khartoum, Catroux gave him a depressing analysis. His agents in Beirut had told him that, if the Free French appeared in force, there would only be token resistance to them, but if they appeared in small numbers there would be serious fighting and, since Dentz had 30,000 troops at his disposal, certain defeat. But the Free French, Catroux went on, had fewer than 6,000 men in an incomplete division under General

Legentilhomme, with only ten tanks, eight artillery field-pieces and twenty-four planes. Any attack would be suicide unless – and this was the major point – it was supported in strength by the British. And the British quite plainly were not prepared to move.

De Gaulle did his best to shift Wavell at a meeting in Cairo in mid-April. It was essential, he argued, to mount an immediate operation to secure Syria for the Allies, but this could not be done without British tanks and aircraft. Spears, who had accompanied de Gaulle at Churchill's personal request, in spite of the deteriorating personal relationship, spoke up in support. But Wavell would have none of it. His forces were badly stretched and the German threat to Cairo and the Suez Canal was his major preoccupation. De Gaulle and Spears then appealed to Eden, who referred the matter to the British chiefs of staff. The reply was categoric: 'Any Free French coup against the Syrian administration must be ruled out absolutely',[8] on the grounds that Wavell had better use for the resources at his disposal. It must, they said, be settled by diplomacy.

All this was too much for de Gaulle, who retreated to Brazzaville in a fever of anti-British exasperation. The Muselier affair was still fresh in his mind, and he was deeply suspicious already of British ambiguity. All the old prejudices came to the surface. Tired and very depressed, he told the British consul-general in Brazzaville, in a long tirade, that Britain attached no value to the moral side of his movement, that he was weakened by British complaisance towards Vichy, and that he could not understand the British attitude towards Pétain and Weygand, 'whose self-seeking, treason, mental decay and moral untrustworthiness are . . . so notorious as to be beyond discussion'.[9] De Gaulle then instructed Catroux to leave Cairo and to make it clear that he was leaving as a mark of displeasure.

As it happened, the British were forced into action by a series of unexpected events. On 2 May the Prime Minister of Iraq, Rashid Ali, after prolonged German wooing, staged an anti-British coup d'état in Baghdad and laid siege to the British base at Habbaniya airport. The overland route to India, as well as a major source of oil, was threatened. Then, on 11 May, Hitler told Darlan that the Germans needed to use the French airbases in Syria. It was now clear that Germany meant to support the Iraqi coup by using Syria as a staging-post for its forces. Their eyes were on the oil and India.

Churchill took personal control of the crisis. 'It is no use General Wavell being vexed at this disturbance on his eastern flanks,' he wrote to

General Ismay on 8 May. 'We ought to help in every way without minding what happens at Vichy.'[10] Instructions were issued to the chiefs of staff to do their best, and in turn to Wavell to 'improvise the largest force that he could provide without prejudice to the security of the Western desert' and to 'prepare himself to move into Syria at the earliest possible date'.[11] A telegram was sent at the same time to de Gaulle in Brazzaville requesting him not to remove Catroux from his post, with a 'cordial' invitation to de Gaulle himself to go to Cairo.

De Gaulle's response to this new initiative was immediate, and personal to Churchill. He wrote, for the first and last time, in English. The message was simple: '1) Thank you. 2) Catroux remains in Palestine. 3) I shall go to Cairo soon. 4) You will win the war.'[12]

From that point onwards, and in spite of Wavell's protests, the Syrian operation moved to the stage of serious military planning. It was always, of course, going to be extremely difficult. Wavell had, indeed, complained that it was impossible, to the point of suggesting his own resignation, but he had retreated in the face of a fierce signal from Churchill – concluding that, should he find himself unwilling to give effect to the Prime Minister's decision, arrangements would be made to meet any wish he might express to be relieved of his command.

The command of the British forces in the Syrian expedition was entrusted to General Henry Maitland Wilson, nicknamed 'Jumbo'. From the Free French point of view, it was an unfortunate choice. 'He was an enormous, bald man,' Spears wrote, 'active for his size, unexpectedly so, like an outsize child's balloon rising into space at the lightest touch.' In character, he was not easy: he showed total loyalty – to the point of partiality in making appointments – to his old regiment, the Rifle Brigade, and Spears for one found him too caustic. 'I never located the benevolence his wide paunch seemed to proclaim,'[13] he went on. The French found Maitland Wilson even less sympathetic. He disliked and distrusted them, and they him. It was difficult to imagine a worse climate in which to launch a joint operation.

By mid-May German aeroplanes were using Syrian airfields quite openly. Dentz claimed that the landings were 'forced', and that in conformity with the conditions of the armistice the French authorities were moving the planes out as quickly as possible, but nobody believed him, particularly as the number of German planes involved was not 15, as he claimed, but 106.

By the time de Gaulle returned to Cairo, on 25 May, he had become convinced that the real reason for British procrastination was that their ultimate ambition was to take over from France as the controlling power in the Levant. Underneath a cold, and even friendly, exterior, he was furious and he told Spears as much, and went on to add that if the British decided to advance into Syria they could not do so without his, de Gaulle's, permission. That remark – combined with the 'exasperating' Cairo flies – was too much for Spears, who reported that he told de Gaulle that 'such an attitude on his part would one day finally snap the thread of good will towards himself which he seemed determined to wear very thin'.[14] Their relationship took another turn for the worse.

In fact, there were no grounds for de Gaulle's general suspicions of British intentions, nor have any come to light since. They were simply too busy elsewhere to give the Levant much thought. But there was reason for complaint. Just before the General arrived in Cairo, it was learned that a Colonel Collet was about to come over from Syria to the Free French with a number of troops. The news was leaked, de Gaulle assumed by the British, and broadcast on Brazzaville radio. Collet managed to evade the consequent Vichy order of immediate arrest, and appeared without his troops. Worse still, a French pilot, Lieutenant Labas, had gone the other way; he deserted to the Vichy forces in Syria, taking with him a precious modern fighter. De Gaulle by that time was in such a rage that he spoilt his case by saying to Air Marshal Tedder, at that time Air Officer Commanding-in-Chief, Middle East, that not only Vichy pilots would receive summary justice but that Frenchmen who had joined the RAF and wore British uniform were deserters and would be shot if they landed in territories controlled by him. It was not, to say the least, a helpful contribution.

The background to the Syrian expedition was thus far from satisfactory. It was made worse by the British insistence, as a condition of their support for the Free French, that Syria and the Lebanon should be promised independence. De Gaulle agreed to this, but there was no timetable, and he rejected outright the idea of a British guarantee of the promise, on the grounds that it offended French sovereignty.

The campaign, such as it was, opened on 8 June. At 2 a.m. a motley army of British, Australian and Free French forces crossed the southern borders of the Lebanon and Syria. They amounted to two divisions, supported by some sixty aircraft. The Australians moved up the coast road towards Beirut, the British headed into western Syria, and the Free French, under Legentilhomme, went straight for Damascus. Needless to say, as soon as Dentz discovered the puny size of the expedition, he ordered total resistance. The Australians were quickly stopped; a British battalion was overrun by French tanks; Legentilhomme was wounded, and in spite of the tactic adopted by the Free French of playing the 'Marseillaise' in front of them as they advanced, the Vichy French were not impressed. Indeed, on the Free French side, one battalion of the Foreign Legion refused to fire on their Vichy opponents and had to be withdrawn. The confusion was compounded by lack of communication between the various units, since telephone lines were primitive and constantly cut, and the terrain of high and abrupt ravines covered in thorn-bush was of no help to runners.

Fortunately, Rashid Ali's rebellion collapsed towards the end of June, when the Allied forces were held up on all fronts, although the Free French had succeeded in capturing Damascus. Wavell was able to send reinforcements to Syria, and in the first week of July two columns of British troops moved into the Syrian desert from the east and south-east. At that point, Dentz had had enough, and sued for peace.

The armistice negotiations that followed were mishandled by the British from the beginning. Wavell had just been replaced by General Claude Auchinleck, who was, as far as de Gaulle was concerned, an unknown quantity. Worse, Maitland Wilson's relations with Catroux had deteriorated, under the pressure of the campaign and Catroux's irritating punctiliousness, to the point where they were hardly on speaking terms. Furthermore, there emerged a powerful lobby of influential British in the area – such as 'Glubb Pasha' in Jordan, whose Frontier Force had played a part in the campaign – whose ambition for some time had been to see the French excluded entirely from the region. Finally, the legal basis for any agreement was, to say the least, very doubtful; in 1936 France had concluded treaties with the Syrians and Lebanese, ending the League of Nations mandate and granting them independence, but the treaties had not been ratified by the French parliament.

The clash was obvious. The British were determined that Syria and the Lebanon should be offered independence there and then, in line with the 1936 treaties, while de Gaulle was set on asserting Free French sovereignty in the two countries. De Gaulle, with characteristic foresight, had seen all this coming. He had, even by 19 June, drawn up terms of a peace that would be acceptable to him; they were unacceptable to the British because they included a British guarantee that French interests in the Levant would be maintained. The text was amended in London and a different version sent back, without any British guarantee. Then, when Damascus fell to the Free French on 21 June, de

Gaulle immediately flew there and appointed Catroux 'delegate-general and plenipotentiary in the Levant'. Realising how much this would irritate the British, whose troops had, after all, fought and died in the Syrian campaign, de Gaulle flew off to Brazzaville, in order, as he himself put it, 'to gain space and height, to reach some cloud and from there swoop down upon a convention which would not bind me and which, as far as I was able, I would tear up'.[15]

'Jumbo' Wilson and the Vichy General Verdilhac signed the armistice on 14 July in a mess tent at Acre, a Crusader city on what is now the Israeli coast just north of Haifa. The negotiations had not been without incident. Catroux, whom de Gaulle had insisted must be present, had left his gold-leafed képi on the back seat of his car and it been stolen by an Australian soldier collecting souvenirs. He was hatless throughout the talks and felt the indignity deeply. Then, as dusk fell, all the lights in the tent had gone out, and negotiations had continued in darkness until an Australian officer installed a motorcycle under the flap of the tent, which produced a blinding light but also a thundering noise, since the engine had to be kept going to stop the battery running down.

The final terms of the armistice confirmed de Gaulle's worst suspicions. Verdilhac surrendered to the British, and only to the British. His troops were allowed to return to France with full military honours and his supplies and matériel were to be handed over to the British. Any Frenchman who wished to come over to the 'Allied' cause could do so, but in a secret protocol between the two generals it was agreed that the Free French were not to be allowed to canvass for recruits. Nowhere in the twenty-three clauses of the document was there any reference to the Free French. Spears called the terms quite preposterous.

It was humiliating, as presumably it was designed to be. Catroux was touchy and weak, doing nothing to prevent the British imposition of this shabby arrangement. De Gaulle, on the other hand, when he heard the news in Brazzaville, immediately repudiated the armistice terms and left for Cairo to see the new resident British minister of state, Oliver Lyttelton. At each staging point on his journey he delivered a broadside to the most senior British official he could find: the Governor-General of the Sudan at Khartoum; the Governor at Kampala; the manager of the club at Wadi Halfa. The object was to make sure that he was preceded by 'alarming telegrams'.[16] By the time he arrived in Cairo, Lyttelton was to know what to expect.

Lyttelton was anyway unhappy about the armistice. As the telegrams came in reporting de Gaulle's fiery progress across Africa, he became, as

Spears wrote, 'perturbed at the prospect of having to face de Gaulle on such a bad wicket'.[17] He was right to be. The onslaught, when it came, was ferocious. The General launched into the most violent complaint against the British. Their conduct in the whole affair, he claimed, had been incompatible with the honour and interests of France. Finally, he handed Lyttelton a memorandum announcing the withdrawal of all Free French forces in the Levant from British command. Lyttelton was completely taken aback, protesting that this was an ultimatum; to this the General replied rudely that if Lyttelton wanted to regard it as an ultimatum he could do so. At any rate, he, de Gaulle, no longer had any confidence in the British high command, which had conducted the campaign in an unskilful and dilatory way. At this point, as Lyttelton later wrote, 'There was nothing for it but what women call a "scene", and a scene we certainly had.'[18]

Later the same day the two men met again, both in a calmer frame of mind, and proceeded in effect to rewrite the terms of the armistice. The 'interpretative agreement' worked out the next day provided for access by the Free French to all French troops; retention by the Free French of war supplies previously in Vichy hands; integration of the Syrian and Lebanese levies into the Free French rather than the British army; non-intervention by the British in Syrian political and administrative affairs; and protection for the historical interests of the French in Syria.

It was a clean sweep. Lyttelton had conceded every point of substance, and de Gaulle was able to write to his colleagues in London that evening that, in all, the British change of direction had been favourable; that the crisis had been hot, and indeed was not entirely over. It certainly was not over, but de Gaulle had scored a victory, perhaps the first in what was to be the long-drawn-out Free French struggle against Britain for independence and sovereignty. It was a struggle of words and threats, with no physical violence, conducted within the norms of civilised behaviour that both cultures recognised. Churchill, in a moment of intemperate anger, called it 'psychological warfare'. Perhaps so; but it was a warfare between Allies. Nevertheless, as in a family, such warfare is sometimes the most bitter.

4

THE EAGLE AND THE BEAR
JOIN THE PARTY

Over there, over there,
Send the word, send the word over there,
That the Yanks are coming, the Yanks are coming,
The drums rum-tumming everywhere. ★

'Is de Gaulle still a general, or has he become a politician?' Churchill asked René Cassin, legal adviser to the Free French, in July 1941.[1] It was an odd question, since the answer should have been obvious. But the fact that it was asked in mid-1941 showed how difficult it was for the Prime Minister and his colleagues to come to terms with de Gaulle's spreading political ambitions.

It was not that these ambitions were kept secret. De Gaulle had always said that France was special and should be treated as such. The other governments-in-exile in London were legitimate governments who had moved residence, as Reynaud should have done, to continue the war; but France, the betrayed France, had in her indignity sought an armistice, which the 'real' France – Free France – had rejected. All this was known, and heroic, and in earlier days, in the dark days of June 1940, had been easy to accept. Times then were difficult and anxious, and anyway de Gaulle himself had been quite content to serve the 'real' France as a soldier if senior French political leaders had come over to London, and in close cooperation with the British, too. He had shown that at Dakar.

But no one came; and when no one came de Gaulle made it quite clear that he regarded the mantle as having fallen on him. The stronger Free France became, the more believable was his claim, and the more uncomfortable the position for the British. However much they might have wished to put the clock back to the honeymoon of 1940, the British could not ignore the realities of a year later. The public and the

★ Marching song, written by George M. Cohan, of the US Expeditionary Force in 1917, and revived by US troops in 1942.

press still found the Free French bold and romantic, but the organisation was much tougher in its official dealings. It was also painfully obvious that, in defence of his new position, de Gaulle was far from gentle; on the contrary, he was single-minded and, if necessary, brutal. It was in his make-up; if battle there was to be, it would be fought fiercely, and, at times, with venom.

All wars, even psychological wars, have their casualties, and this one was no exception. Among the first was General Spears. De Gaulle's treatment of Lyttelton in Cairo had deeply shocked him. Recalling the Cairo episode, Spears wrote, 'He appeared much of the time to be little better than a raving lunatic [on whom] the perfect manners of Lyttelton could take no hold.'[2] De Gaulle's assaults were 'insane', his temper 'ugly'. When he told Spears that he was interested not in England's winning the war but only in France's victory, and that they were not at all the same thing, it was going too far. 'I do not think,' wrote Spears ruefully, 'I ever forgot the mutilated France we were trying to succour; but, in the last resort, was de Gaulle likely to be less impossible to work with than our avowed enemies such as Darlan?'[3]

De Gaulle had expressed his true feelings, as Spears was intelligent enough to recognise. True, he had not smashed the ornaments on the mantelpiece of Shepheard's Hotel, as had happened before, but he had done enough to break the back of Spears's friendship. It had been just over a year since the two men had flown together out of Bordeaux, and they were now to work against one another. It was not merely a sad turn of events; de Gaulle was not affected by that sort of sentimentality. Nor was it particularly Spears's fault, since he had been set an impossible task – to reconcile the interests of Britain and Free France in the area, difficult enough given France's traditional position and de Gaulle's insistence on maintaining it when the British armed forces were the only obvious protection against a German incursion – and also to contain the growing nationalist movements in the area. But the break with Spears was to cause de Gaulle a great deal of trouble in the future, since Spears's energy was formidable whichever side he was on. Besides, he was Churchill's friend.

The casualties were not all on one side. The General had also given his colleagues in London a dreadful fright. They even asked him to calm down a bit. They should have known better. 'I measured, better than anyone else,' reported de Gaulle from Brazzaville, 'the grave national and international consequences that could have resulted from a rupture between France and England . . . I invite you to close ranks and to permit no suggestion that my conduct does not follow our policies exactly. Our grandeur and our force consist uniquely in the intransigence we show in defending the rights of France. We will need that intransigence until we cross the Rhine.'[4]

The dispute over the Levant rumbled on, even after the 'interpretative agreement' of Cairo. In July and August de Gaulle bombarded both Churchill and Eden with long, complaining telegrams; he sent Cassin to see Eden on 1 August to point out that 'meddling by England was leading us to the gravest complications';[5] and finally went back to Syria and the Lebanon with Catroux to ensure personally that the agreement was being properly implemented.

Needless to say, 'Jumbo' Wilson was hardly bothering to implement it at all. Indeed, he was threatening to declare martial law and take over all power, both military and administrative. Again, de Gaulle countered with the threat of an immediate break between Free France and 'England'. It nearly came to outright hostilities. When the Free French arrived to take control of the Maison de France in Soueida, the capital of the Druze country in the Lebanon, they found the Union Jack flying over it. The British commander refused to leave, whereupon de Gaulle wrote to Wilson, 'I do not suppose I can conquer the British Empire, but if you do not leave Soueida we shall fire.'[6] Not surprisingly, the British withdrew. There was a similar story at Jezireh; on that occasion de Gaulle stood and harangued a crowd that had appeared, until the British got tired of it and moved out.

Churchill had no time to spend on what he called the 'hateful difficulties' with the Free French in the Levant. He was far too preoccupied with the military situation in the Western Desert, and the change in the balance of the war after the German invasion of the Soviet Union and the consequent entry of Russia into the war as an ally. Besides, he was hopeful that the United States would soon take an equally decisive step, and was busy preparing the ground with President Roosevelt. De Gaulle was, in the midst of these great affairs, just a minor irritant, and Churchill could not be bothered even to reply to his telegrams.

This attitude changed abruptly with the publication of the 27 August issue of the *Chicago Daily News*. The paper contained an account of an interview General de Gaulle had given to its foreign correspondent, George Weller, a few days previously in Brazzaville. It was certainly heady stuff: ' "England is afraid of the French fleet," ' the General was reported as having said. ' "What England is carrying on is a wartime deal with Hitler in which Vichy serves as a go-between . . . What happens, in effect, is an exchange of advantages between hostile powers which keeps the Vichy government alive so long as both Britain and Germany are agreed that it should exist." '[7] As a piece of analysis, it had something to commend it. As a political gesture, if that was what it was, it was the sheerest idiocy.

Churchill first received news of the article in a summary sent to him from the United States, which reported the paper as saying that he had done a 'wartime deal with Hitler'.[8] His rage, as might be expected, was spectacular. 'He has clearly gone off his head,' he wrote to Eden. 'This would be a very good riddance and will simplify our further course.'[9] He ordered all cooperation with Free France to cease instantly. Intelligence help was suspended; there were to be no broadcasts on the BBC; all relations were cut. 'No one is to see General de Gaulle . . . if he asks to see Sir A. Cadogan, Sir A. Cadogan should not see him . . . no one should see any of General de Gaulle's subordinates either.' In short, de Gaulle was to be ostracised, to be left to 'stew in his own juice'.[10]

At first, de Gaulle tried to deny that the interview had ever taken place. But the damage had been done, and he had to fall back on the claim that his words had been misinterpreted. He disputed the remark about British fear of the French fleet, he threatened to have Weller expelled from Free French Africa. But even that would not stick, and it was left to colleagues in London to try to clear up the mess. Maurice Dejean,★ the head of de Gaulle's political secretariat, went to see Desmond Morton, to explain that de Gaulle 'had no political experience whatever and was quite a child in politics; [that] he would have to be educated and it would have to be impressed on him that he could not make statements of this kind'.[11] On the British side, Eden tried his best to mollify Churchill: 'It may well be that de Gaulle is crazy; if so, he will have to be dealt with accordingly . . . if, however, he shows indications of repentance, I hope that you will not underestimate your power to complete the cure.'[12] It was a clever try, but Churchill was far too angry to take any notice.

The object of all these comings and goings, meanwhile, was on his way back to London. In truth, he was probably rather pleased with

---

★Maurice Dejean (1899–1982): Career diplomat. Clever, emollient and generally anglophile. Free French Director of political affairs 1941; Minister to Allied Governments in London 1943–4; then Ambassador, Prague 1945–9, Tokyo 1952 and Moscow 1955–64.

himself at having caused such a stir; nothing is worse than being ignored, and perhaps de Gaulle felt that he had been too long ignored. But on the plane not long before arrival in London, he received a message from Cassin and Pleven conveying their dismay. At first he swore at his ADC, Coulet, for having let the text of the article go through uncensored, and then made up his mind that he would have to brazen it out.

The freeze was on. The British would not talk to him or even officially acknowledge his return to London. Wherever the Free French went, they were told, sometimes violently, that the General was not 'behaving', and the same message went out to foreign journalists in London. The question of a possible interview with Churchill was in suspense: 'Until I am in possession of any explanation you may do me the honour to offer, I am unable to judge whether any interview between us would serve a useful purpose.'[13]

But it could not possibly last, and de Gaulle knew it. Contacts were gradually resumed. Morton made a studiously informal call at Carlton Gardens; in turn, de Gaulle went out of his way, after listing his complaints against Maitland Wilson and Spears, to praise Lyttelton and Churchill himself; he then sent a personal letter to Churchill along the same lines. Finally Churchill gave way, and a meeting was fixed for 3 p.m. on 12 September, in the Cabinet Room at 10 Downing Street.

The meeting, when it came, went through many phases, from farce to fury and back to farce again. Before de Gaulle arrived, Churchill summoned Colville, his private secretary, to explain the procedure that he envisaged for the meeting. When de Gaulle came in, Churchill said, he would rise and bow slightly but would not shake hands. He would not speak to him in French – no doubt, Colville wrote, as a supreme mark of disapproval – but would converse through an interpreter. 'And you,' he said to Colville, 'will be the interpreter.'

De Gaulle arrived precisely on time. Churchill duly rose to his feet, inclined his head slightly towards him and gestured to the selected seat on the opposite side of the Cabinet table. De Gaulle walked to his chair, sat down, gazed at Churchill and said nothing. 'General de Gaulle, I have asked you to come here this afternoon – '. Churchill stopped and looked fiercely at Colville. '*Mon Général,*' he translated, '*je vous ai invité de venir cet après-midi*' – 'I didn't say "Mon Général",' interrupted the Prime Minister, 'and I did not say that I had invited him.' After a few more sentences it was de Gaulle's turn. He too found Colville's translation defective. '*Non, non,*' he interjected after only one sentence, '*ce n'est pas du tout le sens de ce que je disais.*'[14]

Churchill said it was clear to both of them that if Colville could not do better than that he had better find somebody who could. Colville retreated and telephoned a Foreign Office official whose French was immaculate. Not a word was spoken in the Cabinet Room while they waited. The official soon arrived, but it seemed to Colville that no time at all had passed before he emerged, red in the face, protesting that they must be mad; they had said that he could not speak French properly and they would have to manage without an interpreter.

These preliminaries over, the two men got down to their row. Churchill told de Gaulle that, after the trail of anglophobia that the General had left behind him in the Near East and Africa, in particular the offending newspaper article, he now felt that he was no longer dealing with a friend. This was a serious matter in all the circumstances and Churchill was 'greatly pained'. De Gaulle replied that it could not be seriously maintained that he was an enemy of Great Britain, but recent events, especially in Syria, had profoundly disturbed him and cast doubts in his mind about the attitude of many British authorities towards him and the Free French movement. These events, he went on, added to the great difficulties of his personal position, to his isolation, and no doubt to the factor of his own personal temperament, had led him to utterances which must clearly have been disagreeable to British ears. He said that he wished to express his 'frank regret for these utterances'.[15]

Taken all in all, it was a handsome enough apology, and was accepted as such. Furthermore, de Gaulle seemed to acknowledge that in his isolation, particularly when he was away from London, he tended to invent demons where none existed, and that there were strains in his own character that led him to ill-considered outbursts. It was a surprising, courageous – and untypical – piece of self-analysis.

After that, the atmosphere improved considerably, and the conversation turned to the organisation of the Free French. Churchill was anxious to see more of a committee structure, in the hope that some of de Gaulle's more wayward tendencies might be brought under collective control. De Gaulle, on his side, was equally anxious to ensure that all his colleagues followed the same policy as him, and with equal determination. He therefore agreed to consider Churchill's suggestion.

More than an hour passed, and Colville, sitting in the next-door office with Courcel, began to worry – even, he wrote, 'to fear violence. I tried to eavesdrop . . . I could hear nothing . . . I walked out into the hall and tried on General de Gaulle's cap, registering surprise at the smallness of his head . . . I had decided that it was my duty to burst in, perhaps with a bogus message, in case some dire act had been committed. Perhaps they had strangled each other?' At that point, Colville was summoned by the bell, and when he went into the Cabinet Room he found the two of them sitting side by side 'with amiable expressions on their faces' and de Gaulle, 'no doubt for tactical reasons', smoking one of the Prime Minister's cigars.[16] All, at least for the moment, was sweetness and light.

As it happened, de Gaulle's decision to consider a more collective organisation for the Free French came not a moment too soon. For some time, Admiral Muselier had been causing trouble. He had told the British Admiralty, with which he had built up an excellent – perhaps too excellent – relationship, that he thought that de Gaulle was 'suffering from megalomania' and that 'either they must change their leader or the leader must change his ways'.[17] Muselier was not alone. Morton, ever the assiduous watcher of Free French affairs, was told by two members of Muselier's staff that the members of the Free French headquarters, apart from a few 'yes men', chiefly in the military bureau, were determined to force the General to set up a council. But forcing the General was not an easy operation.

A conspiracy was under way. Muselier wrote to de Gaulle on 18 September requesting him to form immediately an executive council, which would approve in advance all announcements and all policy initiatives. He, Muselier, would be president of the council, with all effective power, while de Gaulle would remain as a figurehead. Muselier's friends were to take charge of the organisation, and André Labarthe, the unfortunate victim of the previous Muselier affair, would return to the fold in charge of propaganda.

This was tantamount to a revolution. Muselier revealed his plan the next day to a group of his allies and, oddly enough, Dejean – who was in charge of de Gaulle's political secretariat and not an obvious Muselier supporter. The occasion was a lunch at the Savoy (hence the name 'Savoy plot'), and the host was none other than the Earl of Bessborough, a close friend of Churchill; not only that, but Desmond Morton was also in attendance, The lunch, it must be admitted, took a long time, and Bessborough was heard later to remark that he 'never knew that a revolution required so much brandy'.[18]

Morton reported all this to Churchill, who was quite satisfied with the turn of events, provided that the dissidents did not intend to press de Gaulle too far, since in that case he might have to intervene, 'for example to send for General de Gaulle and Admiral Muselier and knock their heads together . . . to prevent a serious bust-up'.[19] In the event, none of this was necessary, since de Gaulle had already planned his next move, with which he intended to take Muselier out of the game altogether.

The following day, not having received an answer to his note of the 18th, Muselier again wrote to de Gaulle with a slightly modified version of his plan, under which he would only hold the vice-presidency but would supervise 'political' decisions. Even that was no good. When Muselier and Labarthe went to see de Gaulle on the evening of the 21st, they were told that there was no question of de Gaulle relinquishing control of the committee or council, whichever it might be. Muselier replied that under those circumstances he would refuse to join whatever body it was.

The next morning, Muselier telephoned Dejean to find out whether de Gaulle had changed his mind as a result of their meeting and Muselier's parting shot. Far from changing his mind, Dejean replied, the General was preparing to announce the formation of a French National Committee, and that neither Muselier nor Labarthe was on it. This was too much for the Admiral, who announced that, in that case, the fleet would declare its independence and continue the war. Later, he told the British Admiralty, much to their embarrassment, that the Free French fleet was at their disposal.

This was going too far. De Gaulle gave the Admiral twenty-four hours to recant, or face the consequences. By this time, the British were alerted to the major row simmering among the Free French. It was becoming the 'serious bust-up' that Churchill had feared. He immediately sought from de Gaulle a postponement of the announcement of the committee for twenty-four hours. There was a great deal of diplomatic activity. Anthony Eden led the British group of conciliators; there were meetings; the meetings were reported to other meetings, which led to more meetings. In the end, on 25 September, de Gaulle announced the formation of the Committee; he was to be president, and all commissioners, as they would be called, were to be responsible to him personally. Muselier was on the list. The British heaved a huge sigh of relief.

Not so Churchill. 'This is very unpleasant,' he wrote to Eden. 'Our intention was to compel de Gaulle to accept a suitable council. All we have done is to compel Muselier and Co. to submit themselves to de Gaulle. I understood you were going make sure that the resulting government represented what we want.'[20] Eden, of course, had no answer. The General, on the other hand, was quite content with the result. He had neutralised the dissidents, while securing for himself the control of Free France on a basis that the British had themselves suggested. All in all, a happy outcome. It is no wonder that relations between Free France and Britain at this point entered a period of comparative serenity.

General de Gaulle was now able to turn his attention fully to the foreign relations of Free France. Operation Barbarossa, the German assault on the Soviet Union, had, in de Gaulle's own words, 'opened up the greatest hopes for a shattered France'. Besides, the Soviet presence in the Allied camp brought Free France a 'counterpoise' with regard to the 'Anglo-Saxons', a factor which he 'certainly counted on making use of'.[21]

He had already made the first moves. Two days after the German attack on the Soviet Union on 22 June 1941, de Gaulle had signalled from Damascus, instructing Cassin and Dejean to make 'discreet but distinct' contact with Ivan Maisky, the Soviet ambassador in London. This was done on 28 June. But, although the reception was cordial, the Russians were in the process of forming a completely new series of relationships, and were therefore treading on diplomatic tip-toe. Maisky was able to take refuge behind the legality of the existing link with Vichy, which, of course, conveniently excluded any simultaneous and equivalent link with Free France.

The true reason for Soviet caution was more down to earth. The Russians were in the process of concluding their alliance with Britain, and, to say the least, found it difficult to assess the true Free French standing with the British. Furthermore, they suspected that Free France was not much more than a one-man effort – and the man, they knew, was awkward.

This caution was again apparent when in August de Gaulle sent one of his colleagues to see Ivan Vinogradov, the Soviet ambassador to Turkey. This time de Gaulle had a positive suggestion: Free France would send two or three representatives to Moscow so that there could be direct, if informal, relations rather than everything being conducted through the British. But Vinogradov's reply was no more encouraging than Maisky's.

Two events changed the Soviet attitude. First, Vichy broke off diplomatic relations with the Soviet Union; and, second, de Gaulle announced the formation of the National Committee to the accompaniment of

British smiles. Maisky's reaction to a further visit from Cassin and Dejean was much more constructive, and he let it be known that the Soviet Union might follow Britain in recognising de Gaulle as leader of all the Free French. The follow-up was immediate. An announcement was made on 26 September, the day after the publication of the establishment of the Committee, by which Moscow accredited Alexander Efromovich Bogomolov, formerly at Vichy, as ambassador to the refugee governments in London and to the Free French. The Soviet Union, in a letter from Maisky to de Gaulle, undertook to ensure 'the restoration of France's independence and greatness' after the war. For what it was worth, the promise was clear and unequivocal.

The reaction of the United States to the formation of the National Committee was quite different. The Americans could not have cared less. To be sure, the State Department expressed 'appreciation' that they had been informed, and this was one better than the previous attitude of disregarding the Free French altogether, but it can hardly be said to have been encouraging.

By the autumn of 1941, the Roosevelt administration had a settled policy towards France. The groundwork had been laid by William C. Bullitt, ambassador in Paris during the years 1935–40, who had, by the force of his personality and the outspokenness of his opinions, almost singlehandedly set the US diplomatic agenda in Europe. Roosevelt's Secretary of State, the ageing and irascible judge from Tennessee, Cordell Hull,* did nothing to control or restrain Bullitt. Indeed, when Bullitt stayed behind in Paris rather than follow the Reynaud Government to Tours in May 1940, Hull excused this breach of discipline to his Assistant Secretary of State, Adolf Berle, with the comment that, if he had gone, he would have been 'spinning around like a goose that had been hit on the head with a corn cob'.[22] At this point, it was clear that a refreshing new language was entering international diplomacy.

When Ambassador Bullitt, having supervised the declaration of Paris as an open city, finally caught up with the French Government in Vichy, Pétain was in charge and the chief resisters – Daladier, Reynaud and Mandel – were out of it. By the time he returned to the United States, on 10 July 1940, he was quite clear on two fundamental points:

---

* Cordell Hull (1871–1955): Lawyer and politician. Testy, with tendency to drink too much, but undoubtedly shrewd. Practised law in Tennessee; Judge 1903–7; House of Representatives 1907–21 and 1923–31; Senator for Tennessee 1931–3; US Secretary of State 1933–44. Nobel Peace Prize 1945.

first, that the armistice had allowed Vichy to exercise genuine sovereignty; and, second, that Pétain was not unsympathetic to the Allied cause, and indeed was the one factor that restrained Darlan and Laval from more active collaboration with the Nazis.

Roosevelt and Hull accepted Bullitt's view and set about cultivating the relation with Vichy, with the specific aim of keeping Pétain in control and Vichy out of the war. From their point of view, it was the only sensible policy. Besides, it had the advantage of commanding widespread public support, particularly in the isolationist Mid-West – an important, perhaps overriding, consideration for a Democratic President seeking re-election. There was some support for the Free French in the press, especially in New England, but the Americans were used to dealing in big numbers, and in terms of numbers de Gaulle was not yet in any league worthy of serious notice.

Pétain on the other hand was the object of respect rather than of contempt. Americans looked back to the First World War and Verdun: General Pershing was still alive, although by now very old, living in an autumnal glow of universal admiration. He, of course, had been Pétain's great friend. Even after Montoire, photographs of which were flashed by the Germans around the world's press, Pétain's reputation in Washington held firm. It was felt that he had done his best in difficult circumstances, and had prevented the collaborationist Laval from pulling France in the wrong direction.

The first outward manifestation of Roosevelt's Vichy policy was the exchange of ambassadors in November 1940. His choice was typical of the man. Instead of appointing a State Department worthy, he plumped for a retired admiral, William D. Leahy. Roosevelt had known Leahy in 1913 when he was a young assistant secretary of the navy. Leahy, who had seen action in the Spanish–American War, the Philippine rebellion and the Boxer Wars in China, was an experienced and calm adviser whom Roosevelt had learnt to trust. He was one of the few who had known Roosevelt before he was stricken by polio.

Leahy's subsequent career had been measured rather than meteoric; by 1937, just two years before his retirement, he had risen gently to become chief of naval operations. When he was made Governor of Puerto Rico in 1939, Roosevelt decorated him with the US naval equivalent of the gold watch, the Distinguished Service Cross; as he pinned it on, Roosevelt is reported to have said, 'Bill, if we ever have a war, you're going to be right back here, helping me to run it.'[23] Roosevelt used to speak like that. It did not necessarily mean anything.

The choice of Leahy was welcomed both in Vichy and in London, at least by the British there. It was felt that by appointing someone whom he obviously trusted Roosevelt was making it clear that he attached the highest importance to the post. Moreover, and equally realistically, those with some experience of Washington politics realised that, if the policy ran into trouble, it would be difficult for the President simply to dump his appointee and blame the State Department, as he was wont to do. It was perhaps a pity that the Admiral held such robust views on civil rights – in the times of unrest in Puerto Rico, his standing instruction to the police was said to be 'to shoot first and investigate later'.[24] But that did not do more than cast a slight shadow.

All in all, it was a popular appointment, except in the State Department and with the Free French. The State Department objected on the grounds that Leahy was just one of the President's old cronies, that he had no experience whatever of international politics and had never been near France. Besides, the Department had no clear idea of the Admiral's terms of reference, and had to ask him to set them out after he had seen the President, so that they could work up an official brief for him. In the event, Leahy was surprisingly successful in his post, reading the politics of Vichy better than most, and certainly better than Hull and the State Department. Given the limited nature of his role and the constraints imposed by Roosevelt's general policy decision to support Vichy, Leahy did a good job.

Neither the appointment nor the policy was to the liking of General de Gaulle, who had to make do with short informal discussions with the US ambassador in London, John Winant. In fact, de Gaulle at this time knew as little about the United States as he had known about the United Kingdom in 1940. He had never been there and had been in prison camp when the American forces were in Europe in 1917–18. Furthermore, his English was still not very good, and the idiom of Washington politics was strange. Yet he was convinced that Roosevelt's Vichy policy was based on a misunderstanding of the real state of affairs, and that by patient diplomacy the President could be won over.

The truth is that de Gaulle never fully grasped the extent of the pragmatism, even the cynicism, that lay behind Roosevelt's policy. The President took the view that the war must first be won, and any amount of devious dealing was justified if it contributed to that end. The politics of the post-war world would wait until peace had been secured. Any attempt to form views about that world while the war was on was not only a distraction from the war effort but counter-productive. The

General's view was, of course, quite the opposite. Unless there was a clear perception of the post-war world, particularly as regards France, the war was hardly worth fighting. It was the moral basis for Free France that he constantly stressed. To Roosevelt this seemed absurd and, coming from a two-star general in a defeated army, pretentious. The two positions were irreconcilable, and, with two such egocentric men, led to mutual incomprehension and, in the end, at least on the President's side, personal dislike.

De Gaulle had sent a number of emissaries to the United States over the previous few months, but the objective had been to try to bring some order into the Free French movement there rather than to try to approach the US administration directly. Order was very much needed. As in London, a number of disparate individuals had set up different ventures in support of de Gaulle, and there were the usual jealousies and squabbles. At one point there were three organisations competing with one another: France Forever, a group largely composed of American citizens and organised by a well-known businessman, Eugene Houdry; the official office of Free France, run by the former commercial attaché in the French embassy in Washington, Marie-Adrien Garreau-Dombasle, with offices in the Rockefeller Center; and de Gaulle's personal representative, Jacques de Sieyès, who had an office on Fifth Avenue.

Furthermore, there had been a financial scandal. In February 1941, de Gaulle had sent a Lieutenant de Saint-André to New York to help with Free French public relations in America. The lieutenant had been unwise enough to enter into an agreement with an eccentric New York businessman by the name of Alfred Bergman, under which Bergman would act for the Free French to obtain the release in their favour of assets blocked by the US Treasury. The plan might have been sensible enough if it had stopped there; but Bergman's commission arrangements were particularly favourable, and anyway the whole deal had been arranged without the knowledge of Free France in London. It was all very embarrassing.

To clear up the mess, and to establish permanent relations with the State Department, de Gaulle decided in May 1941 to send René Pleven on a mission to the United States. Pleven had several advantages: he spoke fluent English, was a friend of Jean Monnet — who was now in Washington and, although not a supporter of the General, anxious to promote the cause of France in whatever way possible — and he had had experience of American business before the war. Pleven's brief was twofold: to set up a mechanism for representation in Washington, and to sort out the Free French support groups.

In the second task, Pleven succeeded admirably. By the time of his departure in October, there was a reasonably professional organisation in place instead of the haphazard group of amateur enthusiasts who had been so ineffective before. A Catholic trade unionist, Adrien Tixier, was chairman of a properly constituted delegation, with Raoul Aglion as secretary, and Raoul de Roussy de Sales in charge of information – a particularly good appointment.

In the first task, he was much less successful. He was very popular in Washington, except where it mattered, in the White House and the State Department. Henry Morgenthau at the Treasury was particularly taken with him, and John J. McCloy, the Under-Secretary of War, introduced him to his superior, Colonel Stimson. Pleven met Harry Hopkins,* the President's personal adviser, and the Vice-President, Henry Wallace. But he never managed to see the President, who replied, curtly enough, to Morgenthau's request for a visit: 'I cannot see Pleven. The matter has been taken up before.' Nor did he manage to see Sumner Welles, the Under-Secretary of State, until it was almost time for him to leave; and then Welles told him only that the relationship with Vichy was of the greatest importance. Finally, on 7 October, days before his departure, he was granted an interview with Hull, but the Secretary of State confined himself to windy generalities.

The Pleven mission succeeded, it is true, in securing some useful concessions from Washington. The State Department offered Red Cross assistance for Free France and sent a Colonel Cunningham to Africa to look at the bases that de Gaulle was suggesting for American use. Furthermore, they did accept the presence of the new Free French delegation in Washington, although there was no question of diplomatic status. Finally, after Pleven's departure, the Lend-Lease Act was extended to include direct credits for Free France. The Cunningham mission and the extension of Lend-Lease direct to the Free French were promising enough – Cunningham was given the red-carpet treatment on de Gaulle's specific instruction when he and his mission arrived in Africa. But nobody could pretend that Pleven had conquered Washington, or

---

*Harry L. Hopkins (1890–1946): Diplomat. Son of a saddle-maker in Sioux City, Iowa; thin, untidy but with piercing eyes and winning smile. Board of Child Welfare 1915–17; Red Cross 1917–22; various bodies for relief of poverty 1923–38; Sec. of Commerce 1938–40; Special Adviser to President 1940–5.

that relations between Free France and the White House were other than extremely cool.

De Gaulle was able to ponder on this during the autumn and early winter of 1941. He was perhaps able to ponder more calmly now that his family had moved nearer him and London. The house where they now lived, known as Rodinghead, was rented from a landlord who lived, it appears, in Scotland. Smaller than Gadlas Hall, it was comfortable enough, had an attractive garden with a pool – like Gadlas Hall – and it stood at the top of a slope leading down to a wood full of wild flowers. A calm and gentle place, it was not only suitable for little Anne, but was within easy reach of London. De Gaulle was able to see his wife and daughters – especially Anne – much more than he had in the previous year. Berkhamsted was only three miles away and the roads to London were quick and good. The days of bachelor life in Grosvenor Square were now over.

Although the de Gaulle family did not stay more than a few months at Rodinghead – it is said that they had trouble with the landlord, not least because the General broke the bath when he got into it – they were some of the most momentous of the General's whole war. The Japanese attacked Pearl Harbor on 7 December; Germany and Italy declared war on the United States on the 11th. Here at last was the moment for action – the chance for the General to reassert his position as the only leader of France, who was a true friend, and to cultivate his relationship with the great new ally. Instead, quite astonishingly, he chose to occupy, by force and against Washington's express wish, two insignificant little islands off the coast of Canada. He could not have done more to provoke the United States to rage, and the United States duly obliged.

5

RESISTANCE ON ALL FRONTS

*It is intolerable that the great movement of events should be obstructed,
and I shall certainly not intervene to save de Gaulle or other Free French
from the consequences.* ★

On Christmas Eve 1941, Admiral Muselier, in command of a small Free
French naval flotilla, sailed into the harbour of the tiny island of St
Pierre. On Christmas Day, he held a plebiscite, announced an overwhelming vote for de Gaulle, and immediately declared that the island
and its neighbour Miquelon were now part of Free France. In itself it
was an action of no particular consequence, but, coming at the time it
did, it was nothing if not provocative.

The islands of Miquelon and St Pierre lie some twenty miles off the
tip of the Burin peninsula on the south-eastern coast of Newfoundland.
They guard, if that is the right word in such a climate, the eastern outlet of the Cabot Strait, which at its western end separates the province
from the mainland of its nearest neighbour Quebec. Miquelon is the
larger of the two islands. It consists of two almost circular rocky out-
crops, each with a diameter of 10 miles or so, linked by a narrow spit of
land. To the south-east, but clearly visible in good weather, is St Pierre,
small, pear-shaped, measuring not more than 5 miles from coast to
coast; but with a safe anchorage on its eastern flank, sheltered from the
prevailing westerlies. Around the little harbour is clustered, huddled
together, a collection of low houses and huts. This is the town of St
Pierre, the main centre for the 5000-odd fishermen and their families
who inhabit this bleak and isolated land. The weather is cold to the
marrow in winter and sticky in summer, the surrounding seas rough and
inhospitable. Life there can only be described as extremely harsh.

St Pierre et Miquelon, as the archipelago is called, was originally

★ From a signal of 13 January 1942 from Winston Churchill to Anthony Eden. Quoted
in F. Kersaudy, *Churchill and de Gaulle,* page 179; Fontana, London, 1990.

settled by thirty Basque and Norman fishing families in 1604. By 1713, when Britain claimed the two islands under the Treaty of Utrecht, the original settlers, or their descendants, had given up, and the islands were again uninhabited; the whole thing had obviously proved too much.

The British relinquished their claim, for what it was worth, in the negotiations with France which led in 1763 to the Peace of Paris at the end of the Seven Years' War between the two kingdoms. The treaty laid down that all territories in the northern part of the American continent to which the French crown had claim should be ceded to the British – except for St Pierre et Miquelon.

The islands were then resettled by French deportees from New Brunswick, were twice occupied by the British, in 1780 and 1793, and finally achieved a settled status with France under the Treaty of Ghent in 1814. These two tiny and rugged islands thus came to form, by a circuitous historical route, the totality of the French Empire in North America; and at the armistice in 1940 that Empire came under the control of Vichy.

Muselier's expedition to occupy the archipelago, planned as far back as June by the Free French, had been approved in outline by the British chiefs of staff in September, on the grounds that there was a shortwave radio transmitter on St Pierre that could be used to broadcast Allied shipping movements to German submarines. But the plan had run up against American and Canadian hostility. Indeed, Roosevelt himself had become involved and said he was 'strongly opposed to the suggested action'.[1] The British were surprised and, since they had already approved the plan, not a little embarrassed.

There were several good reasons for American opposition. First, they had just concluded an agreement with the Vichy Admiral Robert, the High Commissioner for all French possessions in the western hemisphere, including St Pierre et Miquelon, which reaffirmed the Havana Convention of June 1940 maintaining the status quo in the area, including the continued immobilisation of the French Caribbean fleet. The specific reaffirmation of the Havana Convention was given by the President himself, in the clearest possible terms, to Marshal Pétain on 13 December 1940. Second, discussions were already in progress with the Canadians on how to neutralise the transmitter. Third, Roosevelt was acutely sensitive to the traditional American objection to any incursion by European imperial powers into the western hemisphere, embodied in the Monroe Doctrine. The 'Doctrine' itself, formulated as it was in the nineteenth century, might be ridiculous in the wartime conditions of 1941, and in this case it might anyway have been irrelevant, but it was part of the emotional substructure of American politics, and not to be trifled with.

When the American opposition became known, British support was immediately withdrawn. On behalf of the Free French, and after consultation with de Gaulle, Dejean gave the British an assurance on 17 December 1941 that 'no orders would be issued for this operation'.[2] There remained, however, the matter of the transmitter. On the assumption that it was a danger, the Allies could not allow it to continue broadcasting freely. The Canadian solution was to send their own personnel to take charge of it, and, if they were not welcome, the Canadian navy would simply blockade the islands until they were. It was a sensible plan, and Washington approved of it.

But General de Gaulle certainly did not. When he heard about the Canadian proposal, he considered it, as he later wrote, 'a question of foreign intervention on French territory',[3] and quite intolerable. He therefore ordered Muselier – who was on his way to Halifax, Nova Scotia, to inspect the submarine *Surcouf* – to proceed at once to the 'rallying' of the islands, 'by your own means and without saying anything to the foreigners'.[4] After some hesitation, and after private consultation with the Canadians, who told him of their disapproval, Muselier obeyed his orders and headed for St Pierre, his little fleet bucking through a bad storm in which Muselier himself lost his cap. On arrival, he immediately signalled his friends in the British Admiralty – adding, of course, that he had done what he had done in compliance with the order 'quite recently received from General de Gaulle'.[5]

On the same day the news reached Washington, where Churchill and Roosevelt were in the middle of cordial discussions on the great issues of the war, which could be discussed openly now that the United States were officially belligerents. At first, the two leaders were prepared to brush the whole matter aside, but the anger of the State Department caught them off balance. Cordell Hull appeared almost unhinged. He immediately issued a statement claiming that 'the action taken by the "so-called" Free French ships at St Pierre et Miquelon was an arbitrary action contrary to the agreement of all parties concerned'.[6] He suggested to the President that the seizure had given the Germans a perfect pretext for occupying North Africa, and that the British had probably egged on de Gaulle; and he wrote to Eden to say that the coup had jeopardised the whole structure of inter-American relations. In view of the negligible size and limited strategic importance of the archipelago,

Hull's reaction can only, at best, be described as exaggerated.

Unfortunately for Hull, Muselier had, almost by chance, taken on board his ship a journalist, Ira Wolfert, who described the heroic action in full detail in a series of reports for the *New York Times*. The story quite clearly touched in Americans a nerve of sentimentality. Possibly it reminded them of the folklore of their own Wild West. But, for whatever reason, they were moved and impressed; and reacted with outrage to their Secretary of State's slurs on the gallant fighters for freedom. In the following days, Hull received a huge mail, mostly addressed to 'the so-called Secretary of State' at the 'so-called State Department'. He tried to recapture ground by pointing out his use of 'so-called' had applied to the ships, not to the Free French, but it was no good. The press was enjoying itself. 'Perhaps they were actually pink elephants,' sneered the *New York Herald Tribune*.[7] The 'mud batteries', as Hull called them, were going full blast.

Hull was not deterred. He imperiously asked the Canadians what they were going to do to restore the status quo. The answer was not encouraging. The Prime Minister, Mackenzie King, would not move: Canadian feeling, he hinted, was rather pleased at the Free French achievement. Hull then pestered Churchill to instruct de Gaulle to remove his forces from the islands. Churchill was far from enthusiastic, knowing perfectly well that any move in that direction would involve at least another bruising row with de Gaulle, and possibly a serious breach between Britain and Free France. It was something he was very anxious to avoid. The truth was that de Gaulle had won the support of public opinion, not only in the United States but in Britain as well.

The General himself poured salt on the wound by writing personally to Churchill, pointing out, perfectly reasonably, that the present attitude of the United States State Department was doing a great deal of harm to morale within France itself. 'It does not seem to me a good thing,' he said, 'that, in war, the prize should be handed to the apostles of dishonour.'[8] He had by now certainly mastered the art of provoking Churchill, who was ever sensitive to dishonour, wherever it was to be found.

It was that that prompted Churchill, in a speech to the Canadian Parliament in joint session, to go out of his way to support Free France and de Gaulle. He was at his most eloquent: 'They have been condemned to death by the men of Vichy, but their names will be held in increasing respect by nine Frenchmen out of every ten throughout the once happy, smiling land of France.'[9] De Gaulle was, of course, delighted with the speech, and said so in a BBC broadcast to France.

But Hull still would not give up. He threatened to resign unless the President took him more seriously. Whether he was worried by the threat or, perhaps more likely, bored with the whole affair, Roosevelt started to press Churchill, who was still in North America, to take action. There followed a long-range negotiation between Churchill and de Gaulle, with Eden acting as the unhappy intermediary in London. Churchill told Eden that the Free French must leave the islands: 'However you dish it up he has got to take it,' he wrote.[10] The General made a counter-proposal: there would be withdrawal officially, but there would be secret clauses to the agreement which allowed Muselier to remain as part of a Consultative Council. This was quite unacceptable to Churchill, who said that Eden had failed lamentably with de Gaulle. Hopkins considered the proposal 'ludicrous'.[11]

The upshot was that it was agreed that Churchill would do his best with de Gaulle when he got back to London. This he did. The General was summoned to Downing Street for another dressing-down. This time Frank Roberts of the Foreign Office was called in to interpret. The interview was as stormy as expected. Churchill accused de Gaulle of breaking his word, of having no consideration for the Alliance, and of various other sins. He demanded an explanation. But de Gaulle was not in a mood to explain. Indeed, there was no explanation. Apart from asking one or two questions about the meaning of the text of a compromise communiqué that Churchill placed in front of him, he remained silent. Churchill was taken aback; but, after de Gaulle had got up, asked politely for permission to leave, given a short bow and left without further comment, he turned to Roberts, beaming, and said about de Gaulle's performance, 'That was really very well done. I could not have done better myself.'[12]

In the end, as de Gaulle wrote, it was a question of saving the face of Cordell Hull and the State Department. The storm subsided as quickly as it had blown up. Events moved on, and the compromise communiqué, which allowed for a Consultative Council excluding both Muselier and the Vichy administrator, and for the withdrawal of Free French ships, was never published. Hull had called the dogs off for the moment, but he was a man with a long memory and did not like being made a fool of. Whatever his views on the event itself, Roosevelt did not like his Secretary of State being made a fool of either. The price to be paid in the future would be high.

Admiral Muselier, the hero of the hour, returned to London on 28 February 1942 and was met in person by General de Gaulle at Heston airport. In the middle of all the congratulations, de Gaulle suggested to Muselier that he should take charge of the next adventure, the liberation of Madagascar. The General added that he would also like him to get rid of Moullec, who had been in on the 'Savoy plot' and was known to be one of Muselier's closest colleagues.

The victor of St Pierre et Miquelon was certainly not going to stand for that. He turned up at the meeting of the National Committee in Carlton Gardens on 3 March and, to general astonishment, announced his resignation. Furthermore, he accused de Gaulle of withholding the truth from him about Dejean's undertaking to the British that the St Pierre et Miquelon operation would not go ahead without their approval, and he produced a minute to support his case. Finally, he said that he was not only resigning but taking 'his' fleet with him.

This was the third Muselier crisis, and the veterans of the previous crises, Eden, Cadogan and the British Admiralty, girded themselves again for action. The War Cabinet met on 6 March, the day after de Gaulle had appointed Philippe Auboyneau to replace Muselier. They resolved to insist upon Muselier's retaining his post as Commander-in-Chief of the Free French navy. If General de Gaulle would not agree to this course, they should have to take the necessary action themselves. Eden summoned de Gaulle to tell him of the War Cabinet's decision. The interview, as might be expected, was fruitless. De Gaulle was adamant.

This was perhaps the most serious internal crisis that de Gaulle faced in the whole war. After all, he was the Commander-in-Chief, and he was confronted by open disobedience. When he tried, on 10 March, to speak to Free French naval officers at Westminster House, Muselier refused to let him do so by himself and insisted on being present, even though he had been given twenty days leave on condition that he stayed away. De Gaulle managed to win over only three senior officers; the rest stayed loyal to Muselier. On 11 March he asked the British Government to put Muselier under close arrest, but there was no response.

The General again fell victim to acute depression. As after Mers el-Kébir and Dakar, he was on the point of abandoning the whole enterprise. He left London and stayed at home in Berkhamsted, waiting gloomily on developments. He even left with his most loyal colleagues, René Pleven, André Diethelm and François Coulet, a secret political testament. 'If I am led to give up the work that I have undertaken, the French nation must know why,' it starts, and goes on to denounce British intervention in the Muselier crisis. It ends with the words: 'France already understands by what path and in what manner I have done everything to serve her. She will understand that if I stop it is because my duty to her forbids me to go farther. She will choose her road accordingly. Men pass. France continues.'[13]

Fortunately for the General, Muselier went one step too far. On 19 March he called on the Free French navy to go on strike. The British were horrified. They regarded this as an incitement to mutiny. Muselier had destroyed his own case, and the Admiralty moved hastily to dissociate themselves from the mutineer. On 23 March de Gaulle was informed that the British Government no longer insisted on the Admiral's retaining his post as Commander-in-Chief of the Free French navy. The last, and decisive, Muselier crisis had passed. De Gaulle had won. Muselier himself ceased all cooperation with Free France – indeed, he became an enemy.

It had been a close-run thing, but de Gaulle was now back in charge and able to turn his attention elsewhere. In his political testament, written when he thought that things were going badly and that the British were conducting a campaign to unseat him, de Gaulle had emphasised the role of 'France'. Now that he had returned to Carlton Gardens, and the crisis was over, it was time to consider what was happening in the real France, as opposed to the abstract France of his imagination.

The truth was that de Gaulle knew very little about the real France of 1942, just as had known very little about the real Britain that he had found in 1940 and the real America that he was to find later. After all, in his education there had been no pretence that what was being studied were contemporary French problems; his father had still been fighting in his mind the old battles of 1870. De Gaulle had never, since he was a child, lived as a civilian in a French community outside Paris; nor, since childhood holidays in the Dordogne, had he even visited, other than on military manoeuvres or in hospital, the broad France that lies south of Paris.

It is therefore no wonder that when Christian Pineau, one of the leaders of the Resistance in France, arrived in London in March 1942 and visited de Gaulle in Carlton Gardens, he was seated in a chair and faced with the abrupt request: 'Now tell me about France.' After hearing the description of Resistance activities, de Gaulle, when he came to speak, simply rehearsed grievances against the Allies. He had nothing to say in reply to Pineau, because he had not followed what had been happening in France itself; for him the struggle had taken place in the Empire. But he was about to learn.

At first, life in the unoccupied zone had not been too difficult. Pétain was still popular – he was perceived as not having 'allowed' the Germans to occupy the whole of France – and economically things were not too bad. There were, of course, people who wished to protest against what had happened, and they found their own, relatively harmless, methods of expression. Newsletters were produced, usually on primitive roneotype; small demonstrations were organised. It was not very taxing, or very dangerous.

Gradually, the groups in the zone had coalesced. By the end of 1941, there were three major organisations, each with between 20,000 and 40,000 members, with a few smaller groups staying outside. The largest of the three, Combat, was predominately composed of left-wing Catholics, led by a committee dominated by Henri Frenay, called 'Charvet', Pierre-Henri Teitgen, known as 'Tristan', and Georges Bidault.* Then there was a secular left-wing group, known as Libération, led by Emmanuel d'Astier de la Vigerie, whose ambition was to foment a working-class revolt, and who was the first to form a purely guerrilla arm. A third group Francs-tireurs et Partisans Français was led by anti-clerical radicals from Paris such as Bayet, Farge and the historian Marc Bloch. All of these groups were centred on Lyons, which was the centre of Resistance in the south, and all of them were in touch with one another. It was diffuse, and to some extent chaotic, but that was in the nature of the Resistance movement itself.

In the north, the occupied zone, everything had been much more hazardous. There, resistance was not just a question of irritating fellow Frenchmen; it was a matter of life and death, and probably death after torture at that. At first, resistance was confined to making life mildly uncomfortable for the occupiers: they were given wrong directions on the Métro; bus drivers missed out stops at which they wanted to get off; shops would deliberately sell them faulty goods. It was not very damaging, or even very serious, but there was no particular will to do much more.

Slowly, a few small Resistance groups had been organised. They had to be small, in order to keep to the minimum any damage to a group that might follow the arrest of one member – it was hard not to break

---

* Georges Bidault (1899–1983): Academic, journalist, then Resistance, finally politician. Jesuit educated; never quite trusted by de Gaulle. President of the Provisional Government 1946; Foreign Minister several times 1944–54; Prime Minister 1946, 1958. Supported de Gaulle in 1958 but fell out with him over Algeria. Founder of OAS; charged with treason 1962; fled to Brazil; returned to France on amnesty 1968.

down under Gestapo torture. Arrests were frequent; the Germans operated an effective and ruthless policing system. An early group, for
example, called the Comité National de Salut Public, which was
formed in December 1940, was discovered by the Germans in February
1941 and seven of its members were executed; it was reformed, but discovered again two months later, when two more were shot; and finally
rounded up in November, when six more were shot, a further six brutally decapitated and the rest shipped off to Germany.

In London, de Gaulle had, as early as the summer of 1940, given
Passy the job of trying to make contact with the Resistance groups in
both zones. It had not been easy. Quite apart from the difficulty of who
and where they were there was absurd competition for agents between
the British Special Operations Executive (SOE) and Passy's Bureau
Central de Renseignement et d'Action Militaire (BCRAM). There
was obstruction and bad temper, bringing great danger to those on the
ground in France. The Confrérie Notre-Dame, for instance, founded
by Gilbert Renault, alias 'Rémy', was a network run by the BCRAM,
while Alliance, formed by Marie-Madeleine Méric, alias 'Fourcade',
was controlled by the SOE. Both networks ran agents into and within
France, primarily for the gathering of information, but also acting as
liaison with the Resistance groups on the ground. It was not a sensible
way for them to conduct their business.

But with the entry of the Soviet Union into the war against Germany
at the end of 1941, the whole situation inside France had been transformed, and both the SOE and the BCRAM had had to adjust. The
Resistance, having started as a diffuse group of protesters, was about to
change its nature. The Communist Party, by far the most cohesive group
of militants, was now able to organise officially against the Germans. The
underground system that they had developed over the years for the overthrow of capitalism was now available for the overthrow of the Reich.
Furthermore, they were going to use it, and use it politically.

The Communist Party set up the Front National, intended as a political movement to include Resisters of all views from centre to extreme
left, and, under Charles Tillon, a party official in the south-west, the
Francs-tireurs remaining as a guerrilla arm. Both groups operated in the
north and the south – indeed the Front National, under Pierre Villon
in the north and Georges Marrane in the south, was probably the most
influential body in the whole Resistance by the end of the war.

But even with the full participation of the Communists, the
Resistance was poorly organised and coordinated; and not everybody

liked the Communists, who made it their business to infiltrate groups that had been started by others. The Organisation Civile et Militaire, for instance, consisting mainly of soldiers and civil servants, and operating in the north, would have nothing to do with them; and another northern group, Libération-Nord, a mainly trade-union-based organisation run by the socialist Christian Pineau, kept its distance as well.

Clearly, sooner or later some order would have to be brought into this confusion, and the General was the obvious person to do it. The Free French were, after all, in a good position. They refused to accept the armistice and all that went with it; they were against the Germans and against Vichy. Also, the Free French broadcasts of the BBC, led by Maurice Schumann, were listened to widely in France, and the strange messages read out in sombre voices – 'the dandelions do not like the sardine' or 'Father Christmas is dressed in pink' – served to convey information not just to the SOE and BCRAM agents, but to the Resisters as well.

But there had been two snags. First, de Gaulle had not endeared himself to many in the Resistance by appealing on 23 October 1941 for patience and for preparation for the great day of liberation. He had issued an instruction in the name of the French National Committee 'which directs the nation in its resistance'. The instruction was not 'openly to kill' Germans, since, he went on, it was at that time too easy for the enemy to respond by massacring French hostages who were 'for the moment disarmed'.[14]

In truth, it had been a reasonable request, coming as it did the day after the shooting of forty-seven hostages – mostly Communists – at Chateaubriant near Nantes in reprisal for the assassination of a German officer in Nantes two days earlier, and of fifty hostages at Souges near Bordeaux following the killing of another high-ranking German in Bordeaux on the previous day. But the 'instruction' had not been popular with many in the Resistance in France. It was not just the peremptory tone in which it was issued, or the assumption of leadership which de Gaulle did not at that time have. The message itself was unattractive; if they were not to kill Germans, what were they meant to do? Were they to wait for ever until the General appeared over the horizon? It certainly was not what they had joined the Resistance, with all its daily dangers, to do – just to sit and wait.

The other problem was that there had been nobody in the Free French movement who knew anything about these people or who could talk to them in their own particular, and necessarily private, language. Fortunately, there arrived in London, on 20 October 1941, after a risky sea journey which ended at Bournemouth, the man who was to be the answer to that problem: Jean Moulin.

Of all the heroes of the Second World War, Moulin must be numbered among the bravest. Slim, dark and small, with fierce brown eyes, he had already, by the time of his arrival in England, suffered torture at Nazi hands. Before the war, as a Socialist, he had been private secretary to Pierre Cot, the Aviation Minister in the Popular Front. He had subsequently been appointed Préfet, and had so far protested against the armistice as to cut his own throat to avoid signing the documents that, as an official, were placed in front of him. Dismissed by Vichy, he had been arrested by the Germans and tortured. When released, he took on the role of a picture dealer in Provence, in order to make contacts with those who felt like him. In the end, after playing the leading role in unifying the whole Resistance, he was arrested on 4 June 1943, handed over to the Gestapo and tortured so savagely that he died, while still under torture, in merciful relief. He had not spoken a word.

In November 1941, de Gaulle chose Moulin for the task of unifying the Resistance in the south under his leadership. He was parachuted into southern France, near Arles, on New Year's Day 1942. Under the code name 'Rex', he carried with him his commission from the General in a matchbox: 'I appoint M. Jean Moulin, Préfet, as my representative . . .'

The job was fraught with difficulty and danger. De Gaulle was not trusted, nor were the British, nor were members of rival groups. Nevertheless, by the end of April 1942, Moulin had succeeded in establishing a Délégation Générale du Général de Gaulle en France – which de Gaulle was able to present as an umbrella organisation for the whole Resistance – and also, perhaps with more practical effect, in forming three committees to coordinate Resistance activity. They were the Armée Secrète, which was be the nucleus of a French uprising at the Liberation, but would not engage in guerrilla activity, which would be left to the Francs-tireurs; the Bureau d'Information et de Presse, whose job was to disseminate propaganda, and the Comité Général d'Etudes, to prepare for post-war France.

Moulin's activities prompted approaches by leaders of the Resistance in the north. Christian Pineau came to see de Gaulle in March 1942, Pierre Brossolette came in April, and André Philip* in July. It looked,

---

* André Philip (1902–1970): Academic and politician. Editor of Resistance newspaper *Libération* before escaping to London in 1942; co-ordinated Resistance groups until end of war; Commissioner for the Interior in Algiers; Minister of Finance in three

at last, as though Free France would be accepted as the anchor of the Resistance in France itself. When Pineau returned to France with a message from de Gaulle to his colleagues in the Resistance paying tribute to 'the age-old French ideal of liberty, equality and fraternity', he found that it was enough to bring them into Moulin's scheme for unity, which by then was starting to extend to the north. The arrival in London of Philip, and his appointment to the National Committee as Commissioner for the Interior, put the seal on the new relationship between the Resistance and Free France. It was never easy. Indeed, it could never be easy with the Communists. It was always to be stormy, but it was always to hold, if at times only just.

But there was trouble elsewhere in the world. Along with the task of unifying the Resistance within France, there remained the objective of securing the French Empire. As the St Pierre et Miquelon episode had shown, de Gaulle was prepared to go to extraordinary lengths to do so, even at the risk of infuriating his supposed Allies. Pierre Brossolette told a colleague that the General must be constantly reminded that their number-one enemy was Germany. If he followed his natural inclination, in Brossolette's view, 'it would rather be Britain'.

There were occasions, however, when the General obviously had right on his side, and one of those was the British invasion of Madagascar. De Gaulle had on several occasions submitted plans to the British for a joint expedition as early as December 1941, and again in February and April 1942. His idea was that Free French ground troops should land on the island, covered by British air and sea support. It was to be another Dakar, only this time a successful one, since after the Levant there was no denying the will of Vichy forces to fight even against their own countrymen.

Almost twice the size of Britain, Madagascar is one of the largest true islands in the world. It is mostly covered by rainforest, but there are good anchorages at either end. Lying as it does off the eastern coast of southern Africa, the island was in a position to dominate the sea route round the South African Cape. At the end of 1941, after the fall of Singapore to the Japanese, and with Rommel's threat to the Suez Canal, it was clear that the lifeline to the Far East and Australia would be cut if, as they threatened, the Japanese went on to occupy the island. Indeed, it was to prevent the Allies being forestalled by the Japanese in the occupation of Madagascar, as Churchill told the War Cabinet on 24

post-war cabinets, finally opposing de Gaulle.

April 1942, that Operation Ironclad, as it was called, was approved.

The decision had been far from easy. General Sir Alan Brooke, the Chief of the Imperial General Staff, thought that Vichy might invite the Japanese in; Eden demurred on the grounds that Vichy would not wish to offend the Americans; Churchill thought it would be a much easier course to do nothing, but he had already told Roosevelt and the South African Prime Minister, Jan Smuts, that the British were resolved to carry out the operation and if the decision were reversed 'and the Japanese walked into the island, our inaction would take a deal of explaining away'.[15] Besides, the Ironclad force had now turned the Cape of Good Hope and was entering the Indian Ocean.

On 29 April, Roosevelt gave virtual public support to Ironclad in a speech in which he said, with ominous signals for the future, 'The united nations will take measures if necessary to prevent the use of French territory in any part of the world for military purposes by the Axis powers. The good people of France will readily understand that such action is essential for the united nations to prevent assistance to the armies and navies or air forces of Germany, Italy and Japan.'[16] The good people of Free France, needless to say, had not been consulted.

The Ironclad ships were by then assembled at Durban. It was a substantial force, including the battleship *Ramillies* and the aircraft-carrier *Illustrious*, and it was ready to move. On 30 April, Churchill instructed the chiefs of staff not to lay too much stress on 'gaining control of the whole island'. It was 900 miles long, and all that really mattered were the two or three principal centres, above all Diego Suarez. They were not setting out to subjugate the whole of Madagascar.

At dawn on 5 May, the attack went in, against what Churchill, in reporting to the Pacific War Council that evening, called 'slight' opposition from Vichy troops. By early on 7 May, the Vichy naval and military commanders had surrendered and the British troops entered Diego Suarez. In line with Churchill's instructions, no attempt was made to occupy the rest of the island. Indeed, Rear-Admiral Syfret, Ironclad's commander, when seeking further instructions from London, was surprised to be told to seek a *casus belli* with the Vichy authorities. Prudently he asked for a repeat of the message, which now came back as 'seek a *modus vivendi*'. When an inquiry was made into the mistake, the staff officer responsible shouted, 'Why the hell should I be expected to know French?'[17] It was a near thing, since Syfret wanted to move south from Diego Suarez to occupy the whole island. Churchill would have none of it. He wanted the troops in Madagascar to be moved as soon as possible to India, as he signalled to Syfret on 15 May. By that time, the '*modus vivendi*' had been reached with the Vichy Governor-General, Annet, and a period of uneasy stalemate followed.

General de Gaulle heard about Ironclad from a journalist, at three o'clock in the morning of 5 May, by telephone. There had not even been the courtesy of an official communication from the British Government. He was extremely angry and very depressed – angry because of the event itself and at the violation of French sovereignty; depressed because of the obvious disregard in which the British, and Churchill in particular, now held Free France. His immediate reaction was to send a note of protest to the Foreign Office – the language suitably doctored by his chief of staff, Pierre Billotte,★ who was made to sign it – and then to engage in an ostentatious sulk.

When he finally agreed to see Eden, on 11 May, de Gaulle's manner was glacial. He noted Eden's excuses for not telling him about Ironclad – 'we were afraid that you would insist on joining the operation, and we did not want to take responsibility for sending Frenchmen to fight against Frenchmen' – and took them 'for what they were worth'.[18] As both men knew, they were worth nothing, since the real reason had been that neither the British nor the Americans could face a repeat of Dakar, and the Americans, particularly, wanted to keep de Gaulle away from any military operation that might threaten their friendship with Vichy. De Gaulle went on to protest about the British negotiations with Governor-General Annet, since they were in effect offering him, and hence Vichy, security until the end of the war. It was nothing less than a betrayal of Free France.

He was, of course, right. He was also determined to make the most of it. He demanded from Eden a communiqué to the effect that the British Government intended Free France to play 'its due part in the administration of the liberated territory'. Eden agreed, but nothing came of it. The General thought of moving out of London, to Brazzaville or even Moscow; of using one of his BBC broadcasts to denounce Churchill and Roosevelt; or of ceasing all cooperation with the Allies. He was obviously in the middle of a period of acute stress and strain, which is little wonder, since he was still convalescing from an illness which had brought him perilously close to death.

★ Pierre Billotte (1906–1992): Soldier through and through. Free French military representative in Moscow 1941; chief of staff in London 1942; commanded brigade at Liberation 1944; Military Representative at UN 1946–50; Minister of Defence 1955–6, of Overseas Territories 1966–8; Mayor of Creteuil 1965–77.

6

MEDITERRANEAN STORMS

*Pray be easy. The quarrel is a very pretty quarrel as it stands; we
should only spoil it by trying to explain it.** *

Malaria is, in all its variants, a serious illness. It results from the injection
into the human blood stream of large quantities of micro-organisms,
previously encamped, in readiness, in the salival glands of pregnant
females of certain species of the anopheles mosquito. These armies are
released at the point at which the mosquito's proboscis has passed
through the protective layers of the skin and penetrates the wall of the
vein that is to be the source of the insect's nourishment. The sporo-
zoites, as they are called, quickly leave the blood stream and invade the
liver. From there they deploy to attack and damage the victim's red
blood cells.

Malaria is also a most unpleasant illness. There are periodic paroxysms
of shivering, fever and profuse sweating; and clinically, there is an
accompanying enlargement of the spleen and severe anaemia. All forms
of malaria are unpleasant, but in its extreme form, known as malignant
tertian malaria, it may induce a blockage of the capillaries of the brain,
leading to coma and, in some cases, death.

In mid-April 1942 – the date is not yet precise – de Gaulle suddenly fell seriously ill. There was consternation among his colleagues.
Nobody knew what to do. None of the doctors among them knew
what was wrong. The only thing that was clear to them, in their state of
disarray, was that in the interests of Free France the General's illness had
to be kept secret. There must be no leakage of information about his
condition, or indeed of the fact that he was ill at all. Relations with the
British were tense in the aftermath of the third 'Muselier affair', and
promising negotiations with the Resistance groups were under way.

* Sir Lucius O'Trigger, in Sheridan, *The Rivals*, Act IV, Scene 3.

There could be no question of revealing that the standard-bearer of Free France was severely ill.

Billotte and Diethelm, at that time the Commissioner for the Interior, decided to carry on as if nothing had happened. They issued orders as though they had come from de Gaulle himself – indeed, they issued them in his name. Even the British Government had no idea what was going on, or, indeed, that anything was going on at all. The patient lay at home in Berkhamsted, nursed by his wife and one or two Free French helpers. Nobody knew whether or not he would pull through.

As luck would have it, Billotte had heard of the arrival in London, after a tortuous journey by way of Lisbon, of the former personal physician to Reynaud himself, Dr André Lischwitz – reputed to be one of the best doctors in France. Lischwitz was immediately located, and summoned to examine de Gaulle. The verdict was clear. After examining the patient for half an hour, when he was 'pale, motionless, almost in a coma',[1] Lischwitz pronounced a case of malignant malaria, exacerbated by lack of exercise, excessive smoking and nervous exhaustion. But, the doctor went on, because of his robust constitution the patient would survive.

The doctor was right. That was precisely what happened, and Free France breathed again. De Gaulle did recover quickly; and, being who he was, carried on as though nothing had happened. But malaria is a debilitating and draining illness, and, even with his powerful constitution, there were after-effects, or, at least, there were odd consequences that could be considered as such. In mid-May, he put off a proposed trip to Africa, fortunately perhaps, because Churchill would not have let him go. Similarly, some wild ideas emerged in early June 1942: that the British were planning an expedition to Senegal and Niger; that he would break with the British and move, along with his whole headquarters, to Moscow. They seem too eccentric for a de Gaulle in normal health. Even the style of his telegram of 6 June to Catroux and others describing his reaction to the Madagascan affair is uncharacteristically vague and there are mistakes in the drafting.

But both his health and his spirits were transformed by news of a successful military engagement by Free French forces in the Western Desert. On 26 May Rommel's long-awaited offensive in Libya had been launched, and Auchinleck's armoured line had begun to crack. To prevent his forces from encirclement, General Ritchie, commanding the British 8th Army, ordered a Free French light division under General

Koenig* to hold the southern flank at Bir Hakeim. He needed Rommel contained for least a week.

The Free French did better than that. Koenig and his men stayed put, surrounded for sixteen days, against enemy forces more than three times their number, and in spite of repeated German requests that they should surrender – finally breaking out at night on 11 June. With three-quarters of his troops safe, Koenig made the rendezvous with the British transport column that had been sent to collect them. The operation had been a spectacular success.

When the news of Bir Hakeim broke, the British press was ecstatic. The Free French had shown, for the first time, the spirit and courage to face the toughest enemy and hold him at bay. Dakar had been forgotten and they were heroes again. Perhaps for the first time since his arrival in England in June 1940, de Gaulle was able to let himself go. 'You are France's pride,' he wired Koenig the day before the breakout; when a messenger came from General Brooke to tell him that Koenig and his men were safe, he thanked the messenger, and then told him he could go. He went back into his office, shut the door – and wept.

'It is', Churchill said when the two men met again on 10 June, 'one of the finest feats of arms in this war.' As might be imagined, that got the meeting off to a good start. The conversation then turned to Madagascar, which Churchill agreed was an unsatisfactory situation. They reviewed de Gaulle's complaints about the Americans – 'their policy towards us is atrocious'; touched on the Muselier affair – 'Mr Churchill smiled and did not insist'; and ended with a Churchillian vision of the two 'being in France perhaps next year; in any case, we shall be there together'.[2] It had been without doubt one of their most friendly encounters since their first meeting in June 1940.

Eden followed up, not only in continuing close contacts with de Gaulle, but also asking the chiefs of staff to be more cooperative with the Free French. Charles Peake, the British representative to the French National Committee, reported on 17 June, '[He] has often expressed the wish to help and advise in any way possible, and he has sat up, night after night, assembling data and making notes in case his advice should he needed.'[3] Lyttelton in Cairo also reported Catroux as telling him that he was convinced that de Gaulle would be far more reasonable and easy to

* Marie-Pierre Koenig (1898–1970): Soldier. Norman origin. Unspectacular military career until joined Free French; commanded at Bir Hakeim; C.-in-C. all French forces in UK, then all French forces in France after D-Day, then French occupation zone of Germany 1945–9; RPF Deputy 1951–2.

handle if he could be seen by Cabinet ministers in London at frequent intervals. 'He also suggested,' the report went on, 'that whenever it could be done, his advice should be sought. General de Gaulle's character should always be borne in mind. He [is] a very vain man and as such [can] be relied upon to respond to the above treatment.'[4] The British took note, and for a while the atmosphere improved markedly; indeed, de Gaulle went out of his way to praise the British in his speeches.

The action at Bir Hakeim also served to improve Free France's relations with the United States. It had been widely and favourably commented on in the American press. Furthermore, American military planners were also taking an interest in the activities of the Resistance inside France, not least in Moulin's role in bringing the diverse groups together under de Gaulle's leadership.

This new mood coincided with a period of American disillusion with Vichy. Laval had come back into power and his Government had made the mistake of prosecuting those whom they considered responsible for France's collapse in 1940. The trials, held before a special tribunal at Riom, a small town in the Auvergne just north of Clermont-Ferrand, were intended as justification for Pétain's assumption of power in June 1940 and the subsequent armistice, but the plan backfired. Léon Blum, charged with 'disrupting production by nationalising war industries' and 'subordinating work to leisure as a national creed', claimed that democracy itself was on trial, and produced such a resounding and eloquent defence that he stole the show. Daladier, another accused, regarded the trials as no more than a German manoeuvre. The proceedings were widely reported in America, and Roosevelt even asked for a private transcript. Vichy looked both absurd and unpleasant.

The upshot was a noticeable change in Washington's attitude towards Free France. John Winant, the US ambassador to Britain, saw de Gaulle twice and indicated that he would be consulted on the general direction of military strategy; a consulate was opened in Brazzaville; the American press gave extensive coverage to a rally held in the Albert Hall on 18 June 1942 to mark the second anniversary of de Gaulle's original call to arms. Some 10,000 French men and women had listened to a bravura speech from the General and roared out the 'Marseillaise' and the 'Marche Lorraine'. General Dwight D. Eisenhower, the commander of US forces in Europe, reviewed the 1942 Bastille Day parade in London; Emmanuel d'Astier de la Vigerie visited America to discuss with the War Department the possibilities of clandestine operations in France; and, most significant, the United States accredited representatives to the

French National Committee. Admittedly, those chosen for the task, Admiral Stark and General Bolte, were presented as on a military mission, so as not to offend Vichy, but it was a clear advance nonetheless.

Washington, however, was not speaking with one voice. The Secretary of State, Cordell Hull, had not forgotten St Pierre et Miquelon. The State Department was consequently dragging its feet, saying that the new policy was the responsibility of the War Department. Sumner Welles, in particular, was very unhappy. 'I was unable to see . . .', he wrote subsequently about a conversation he had had at the time with Lord Halifax, 'that the Free French movement . . . had anything very much to recommend it from the practical standpoint'.[5] But Washington's continuing ambiguity did not daunt de Gaulle. He was full of optimism. On Bastille Day, 14 July 1942, he announced that in future his movement would be known as 'Fighting France'. On 18 July, he told Tixier that negotiations with the United States should henceforth be on a 'government-to-government' basis.

Support from the American public was vocal. Bir Hakeim had worked wonders. There were social functions and more committees were formed. Free French Week, in New York in July, was generally considered to be a great success, supported as it was by Mayor La Guardia and Eleanor Roosevelt, the President's wife. Old-fashioned American sentimentality was at work. It was a time of intense and, as it turned out, exaggerated euphoria.

But the White House had a serious purpose. The President was very anxious to see United States troops in action in the war against Germany, and instructed his chiefs of staff accordingly. Both General George C. Marshall, the chief of staff of the US army, and Admiral Ernest J. King, chief of naval operations, thought that the right strategic course was a cross-Channel invasion of northern Europe. They were under no illusions about the strength of the enemy defences. To overcome them, they badly needed the Resistance; and the key to the Resistance was General de Gaulle.

Marshall and King, together with Harry Hopkins, arrived in London on 18 July to confer with the British. They proposed creating and holding a bridgehead on the Cherbourg peninsula. The British chiefs of staff were against the whole idea, preferring instead a plan to invade North Africa; the War Cabinet agreed with them. The crucial meeting took place between the three Americans and the British on 22 July. Churchill, knowing that he had support, was categoric: British territory would not be used for such a risky adventure, and he would like that message conveyed to the President. Late that evening Marshall reported the British position back to Roosevelt. Theoretically, Roosevelt still had a choice, but Marshall already knew what the verdict would be.

De Gaulle had discovered that Marshall and King were in London, and that their visit marked an early decision on a major strategic move in the war. Not unnaturally, he was full of curiosity to know what it was to be, and indeed wanted to be involved in the planning, as he had been led by Winant to expect. He met Marshall at Claridge's hotel on 13 July. As it turned out, Marshall was not by himself, as de Gaulle had believed he would be, but had with him not just King, but Eisenhower, Eisenhower's deputy, General Mark Clark, Admiral Stark and General Bolte. De Gaulle had with him only his ADC François Coulet, to act as interpreter.

In the end, there was really nothing to say. De Gaulle had assumed that he was to be told details of a great operation, but for the Americans the meeting had lost its point. They knew that they were going not into Europe but North Africa, and for that they did not need de Gaulle. Quite the contrary.

Marshall tried to be polite, offering champagne and complimenting de Gaulle on Bir Hakeim, but that did not take long, and an embarrassed silence followed. De Gaulle then gave an account of the strength of Fighting France and of the Resistance. There was another silence. Finally, de Gaulle proposed a discussion of the plan that he had devised for a second front in northern Europe. Eisenhower said that he had seen it. More silence. There was nothing for it but to call a halt, and de Gaulle and Coulet politely took their leave.

The General was, not surprisingly, irritated. After all, it had been the Americans, not he, who had been trying to mend fences in the previous weeks. He now found himself again frozen out of all discussions. It was time, he thought, to be out of London again, and he requested, and was granted, British facilities to travel to Africa. After a cordial meeting with Churchill, he left on 5 August for Cairo.

Yet again, and for the third time, it was the Levant that was to be the battleground between Britain and Fighting France, and to sour relations between de Gaulle and Churchill. In reality, nothing much had changed since the previous year: Catroux was installed as military commander of the French forces, and General Spears had been in place for several months as British minister in the Levant, heading what he liked to call the 'Spears Mission'. Catroux and Spears had even achieved a measure of cooperation over what was called 'Spears' Plan' to provide supplies of wheat to prevent what threatened to be a famine in Syria and the Lebanon.

Admittedly, it had taken time and effort to achieve that cooperation. Auchinleck, 'a big, powerful and very handsome man with a flat forehead which gave the impression that it might have been used effectively as a battering ram against a castle wall', had had to take a hand; and 'Jumbo" Wilson – looking 'as would any cave owl driven out of his shelter into daylight' and 'eyeing Catroux as if he were a mouse, which, although emaciated, was nevertheless a tempting morsel'[6] – had been forced to intervene. All this had happened at Spears's request, and Catroux's resentment was understandable.

Nobody was very happy about it; and the personal relations between Catroux and Spears were at this point anything but good. Catroux seemed too frightened of de Gaulle to be anything other than prickly and defensive. But, as always, it was de Gaulle's own arrival on the scene that raised the temperature.

It all started calmly enough. The General arrived in Cairo on 7 August. Somewhat unexpectedly, he found Churchill there, on his way to Moscow, and the two lunched together, Churchill promising to 'look into' their quarrels over Syria. The trouble now was that Catroux – having announced Syria's 'independence' in September 1941 and Lebanese 'independence' in November – had, on de Gaulle's instructions, then proclaimed that the mandate had not yet ended and that he would therefore rule by decree. There was to be no question of elections. The local politicians had been furious, appealing to Spears and to the new Minister of State in Cairo, the Australian Richard Casey. Both of them tried to put pressure on Catroux before de Gaulle's arrival, and then on de Gaulle himself, to organise elections so that the two countries' independence could be genuine. Nothing was more likely to provoke a row, and a row there duly was.

It occurred between de Gaulle and Casey the following day. The General accused the Minister of 'trying to oust the French from their position in Syria and the Lebanon' and of a great number of subsidiary sins. Casey replied that the British had no ambitions in the Levant. De Gaulle said that whatever might be true in London it certainly was not true of British authorities on the spot. It all ended, predictably, in 'a shouting match',[7] de Gaulle in French and Casey in English.

Churchill flew into a temper when he was told; his mood was not improved when Catroux suggested at dinner that night that Churchill take Spears out of the Levant and put him in the House of Lords. 'He's my friend,' growled the Prime Minister,[8] and that was that.

But that was certainly not that as far as General de Gaulle was concerned. He was 'appallingly rude' to the British representative in Aleppo, telling him 'not to meddle in French affairs';[9] he inveighed furiously against the British in an interview with William Gwynne, the American representative in Damascus, saying that he would go to war with them; and he informed Casey that, as French troops now out-numbered British troops in the Levant, it was natural that the French should take over command.

Just as in the previous year, Spears reflected, de Gaulle's mood and manner over the Levant was one of an almost insane anglophobe. He had changed much, Spears thought, since June 1940. General Brooke said that the greatest public service Spears could render would be to knock him on the head. Once again, as in 1941, de Gaulle's London colleagues were nervous, and once again, full of the heady air of the Levant, he slapped them down. 'The attitude I have adopted with regard to the British Government in the Levant,' he wrote, 'is the only one that corresponds to our dignity and our responsibilities . . . I mean to be upheld by the Commissioner for African Affairs [Dejean] in what is once again a difficult task . . . If you do not feel able to do this, it is your duty to tell me so.'[10]

In fact, de Gaulle had never changed, as Spears claimed. He had never wavered in his belief that French foreign territories, whether administered directly or by mandate, were an integral part of the wider France, and any attempt to dislodge French authority was an attack on French sovereignty itself. Spears, in supporting the local nationalist politicians in their demand for elections, had mounted just such an attack. In truth, it could be argued that it was Spears himself who had changed, becoming ever more sympathetic to the move to independence for Syria and the Lebanon and consequently ever more anti-French. The root of the dispute lay in Catroux's independence pledge, which at the time had been little more than an expedient to win the Levant for Free France rather than Vichy, but which backfired when the local politicians – with Spears's support – sought to have the pledge honoured. The British had underwritten the pledge, and as a result found themselves caught in an unpleasant trap.

The British Government thought that it was high time for the awk-ward General to be recalled to England before he did any more damage, but de Gaulle was in no hurry, and replied politely to Churchill that he was 'too busy'. He then proceeded on a leisurely tour of French Equatorial Africa. But on 6 September Eden called Dejean to his office to tell him that negotiations with the Vichy Governor of Madagascar had failed, and that the British were about to take the rest of the island. Under those circumstances, Fighting France would be invited to take over the administration of the island, and the British Government wished to reopen negotiations to that end. That suggestion itself was enough to tempt de Gaulle back to London, and he duly made preparations for his return.

Whatever else de Gaulle was in this period, convalescing, hyperactive, or simply bad-tempered because of the heat, he was certainly no fool. He knew perfectly well that there was something afoot, and that that something was probably to do with North Africa. He realised, too, that if that was what it was, the British and the Americans would not want him wandering around Africa, free to comment in whatever way he thought fit. But there was a price for his cooperation, and that price was higher than the mere administration of Madagascar.

What the price was de Gaulle did not yet know. What he did know was that his bargaining strength was greater than it had ever been – and that he was going to use it. He therefore resorted, as before in the build-up to the meeting with Lyttelton a year earlier, to the tactic of maximum irritation of the British, and indeed the American, authorities. When Pleven and Dejean told him that the British were thinking of retracting their offer over Madagascar following Gwynne's report of the Damascus interview, he replied that it was monstrous that they should appear to be going back on their word on the pretext that he had not come when they whistled. Furthermore, on the same day, 19 September, he wired instructions to Tixier not to proceed further with the American administration for the time being. France, he told Tixier, was not a candidate sitting an examination.

But de Gaulle very nearly overplayed his hand. The difference between this row and the previous rows was that the United States was now in the war rather than sitting on the sidelines, and the British Government was far more concerned to ensure a tranquil relationship with its new senior ally than it was to protect its awkward French protégé. In the eyes of the United States, de Gaulle was not 'France' in any sense whatever, and this meant that he was not 'France' in Churchill's eyes either. Of this important fact Churchill was about to remind him in case he had misunderstood.

De Gaulle arrived back in London on 25 September 1942, determined, as he had told Catroux, to settle the matter once and for all. Instead of the loyal troops and enthusiastic crowds of Africa, he found, as he was to write, 'once again . . . what is known as power, stripped of the contact and the recognition that occasionally manage to soften it'. The resumption of contact with the British Government he went on, 'was bound to be rather rough'.[11]

It certainly was. The stage was now set, yet again, for psychological warfare. De Gaulle was summoned to Downing Street on 30 September. The Prime Minister had with him Eden and Morton; the General had Pleven. It was, as de Gaulle told Catroux in a telegram after the event, a very bad meeting. Even Eden lost his temper. The difference between the two sides was never more evident. 'You are not France,' Churchill shouted, 'I do not recognise you as France.'[12] Why were they discussing matters with him, de Gaulle retorted, if he were not France? Churchill explained that all this was written down: General de Gaulle was not France, but Fighting France. Again, de Gaulle came back, maintaining that he was acting in the name of France. He was fighting with, but not for, 'England'. He spoke for France, to whom he was responsible. His attitude, he went on, was borne out by that of the French people, who believed that he spoke for France and would support him only as long as they believed this.

So it went on. In the end, the meeting broke up without any conclusion other than continued British anger. Churchill told Eden he 'was sorry for the man, he was such a fool', and Eden said later that he 'had never seen anything like it in the way of rudeness since Ribbentrop'.[13] There was the usual follow-up: communications were cut between Fighting France in London and Fighting France in Africa, the Levant and the Pacific, and intelligence assistance was suspended.

This time, however, it nearly did come to complete rupture. Churchill knew that that would please Roosevelt, and was tempted. De Gaulle even had to resort to offering his resignation to the French National Committee, but it was unanimously rejected. Dejean succumbed to the pressure and resigned, leaving Pleven to take over Foreign Affairs temporarily, pending the arrival from France of René Massigli. Palewski, now de Gaulle's personal assistant, went to see Morton to tell him that the General felt outraged by the meeting of 30 September. Churchill, meanwhile, could hardly hear de Gaulle's name mentioned without exploding.

The freeze was on again. But there were some subtle differences from the year before. After all, the British knew through their intelligence sources that de Gaulle's BBC broadcasts had audiences in September 1942 some ten times larger than the audiences of September 1941. Figures, from Vichy no less, suggested that somewhere between 3.5 and

4 million listeners tuned in, illegally, to the opening drumbeats which announced that London was on the air. It was a formidable weapon.

Then there was the Resistance. Gradually it became clear to the British that de Gaulle was becoming the rallying point for the Resistance as well. Moulin's efforts were bearing fruit; and it was in London, in October, under de Gaulle's auspices, that a conference of Resistance leaders took place – under the noses, as it were, of the British, who knew nothing about it.

The talks lasted from 3 October to 15 October. Frenay (Charvet) of Combat was there, as was Emmanuel d'Astier de la Vigerie of Libération. The London team was André Philip, Passy, Pierre Brossolette and, in its later stages, among others, de Gaulle. The discussions centred on the role of Moulin and the future leadership of the secret army. They were not easy, not least because Jean-Pierre Lévy, the leader of the Francs-tireurs, could not be there, and he if anybody was the one to challenge the General's view that the role of the Resistance was not to kill Germans now but to wait for the coming invasion.

By the end of the long series of meetings, however, there was no doubt that Fighting France had asserted its ascendancy over the Resistance in France itself. Moulin's authority had been confirmed. General Delestraint, an old associate of de Gaulle's from pre-war days, had been appointed head of the secret army, and the French National Committee in London was recognised as the authority around which all Resistance groups could coalesce. Moulin was authorised to proceed to the formation of a national council of the Resistance. 'Of course,' de Gaulle later wrote, 'we let Washington and London know what we had heard from France.' Indeed he did, and this led to an instant thaw in his relations with the two Allies. 'Nevertheless, and according to the usual custom', de Gaulle went on, 'the tempest soon subsided.'[14] Again the dove of peace was Desmond Morton, dispatched by Churchill to Carlton Gardens on 30 October on the pretext of congratulating de Gaulle on the achievements of the Fighting French submarine *Juno*, which had just sunk two enemy ships off the coast of Norway. One thing led to another. De Gaulle congratulated Morton on the achievements of the British at El Alamein; Morton deplored the fact that relations were not closer and expressed the hope that efforts would be made, on both sides, to bring about 'a more favourable evolution'. De Gaulle was pleased that the crisis had passed, and on 6 November, the day after the Madagascan armistice, agreed to a joint communiqué with the British announcing that General Legentilhomme had been appointed High Commissioner and was leaving immediately to take over the administration of the island. Eden, as de Gaulle wrote, was 'all sugar and honey'.[15] By this time, preparations for Torch, the codename for the North African landings, were in full swing, and the Allies could not afford to have an unfriendly Fighting France at their backs when the day came.

De Gaulle was kept away from Torch because Roosevelt wished it. The President regarded Torch as the ultimate justification of his Vichy policy. The French, he believed, or was persuaded to believe, would not put up any resistance, but would welcome Allied intervention, provided that it was an essentially American operation. The British were suspect because of their association with General de Gaulle.

In this, at least, the White House and the State Department were working as one. Roosevelt and Hull both believed that it was America's Vichy policy that had allowed them to keep Robert Murphy★ as consul-general in Algiers, and they were almost certainly right. Murphy, a State Department career diplomat of Irish origin, had been very active in his appointment. He was, perhaps, a bit of a snob and led an over-active social life – de Gaulle remarked cuttingly that he 'apparently rather inclined to believe that France consisted of the people with whom he went out to dinner'.[16] But he had set up, and continued to direct, a substantial intelligence operation throughout North Africa, mainly through a series of 'vice-consuls', in reality agents, whom he had placed in all the major cities, who in turn cultivated Frenchmen sympathetic to the Allied cause.

Murphy had also been in charge of efforts to find a French leader of suitable standing who would support Torch, and thereby make the operation look like an act of liberation rather than an invasion. It had not been an easy task. De Gaulle was obviously not a candidate. Roosevelt simply would not have had him, even if Murphy had wanted to put his name forward, which he did not. Weygand was tried, and not only refused but reported the whole thing to Pétain, who summoned William Leahy, the US ambassador to Vichy, and told him that French territory would be defended against any foreign intervention, including American. General Odic, a former air force commander in

---

★Robert Murphy (1894–1978): Diplomat, mostly in US Consular service. Strange, stubborn and given to doubtful enthusiasms from time to time. Chargé d'Affaires for US at Vichy 1940; Special Mission in Algiers 1941; President's personal representative Algiers 1942–3; US political adviser to Allied forces in Europe 1943–4, to military govt. in Germany 1945; Ambassador, Brussels 1949–52, Tokyo 1952–3; Dep. Under-Sec. of State 1954–9.

North Africa and now in Washington, was looked over, found wanting and discarded. The list of serious candidates was becoming depressingly short.

Fortunately for Murphy and the Americans, the pantomime trapdoor flew open and out came an almost perfect candidate: General Henri Giraud. Giraud had been taken prisoner in May 1940, had escaped in April 1942 from a German prison at Königstein and had turned up in Vichy a week or so later. Laval tried to persuade him to give himself up to the Germans, and to go back to prison, but Giraud understandably found the suggestion insulting. 'This man,' Churchill informed Roosevelt, 'might play a decisive part in bringing about things of which you had hopes.'[17] American agents were immediately dispatched to talk to him.

Giraud was flattered by the American approach and ready to cooperate, even though he had taken an oath of loyalty to Pétain a few days previously. Nevertheless his terms were onerous: namely, that he, General Giraud, should be given command of all forces invading French territory, including, of course, the American expeditionary force for Torch. It was an impossible demand, but such was the momentum behind the campaign to recruit Giraud that the matter was apparently, and feebly, put on one side.

One of Murphy's co-conspirators in North Africa, Jacques Lemaigre-Dubreuil, was delegated to see Giraud and sort out the details. The choice of ambassador was bizarre. Before the war Lemaigre-Dubreuil had been in charge of France's largest producer of vegetable oil, Lesieur. After the fall of France, he had reopened his refineries to supply the occupying forces, and was therefore able to travel freely in France. On the other hand, he was, in Murphy's own words, 'sure of himself, speaking loudly, his angora hat at a tilt and displaying an innate taste for being observed', and 'he moved about freely disguising his conspiracy, like Ali Baba, in so many barrels of oil'.[18] To say the least, he was not exactly Giraud's type.

What happened at his meeting with Giraud remains obscure. Giraud appeared convinced that his role was to be commander in chief, while Lemaigre-Dubreuil reported that no such commitment had been made. By mid-September the situation was still confused, although Murphy had given assurances to Giraud, on behalf of the President, that France would be treated as an ally, that the country's pre-war frontiers would be restored, and that there would be further aid for the French North African army. But neither Giraud nor his chief ally in Algiers, General

Mast, were told by Murphy or anybody else what Giraud's true role was to be, if indeed, at that point, anybody really knew.

Although the details of Torch remained secure, rumours abounded of a major Allied operation, and, needless to say, the rumours reached Vichy. The result undermined all Murphy's previous efforts, since in early October he received a new offer, from a wholly unexpected source. He was asked what price the Allies would pay for the defection of the French fleet, at present holed up in Toulon. The hint was heavy: the real price for what was on offer was that none other than Admiral François Darlan should be accepted as the Allied commander in North Africa.

The Americans faced a serious problem: whether to deal only with Darlan, or only with Giraud, or with both. Far from a lack of candidates they now had a superfluity. Murphy was in favour of Darlan, with Giraud in reserve, as it were, but Eisenhower was wary of trying to run Darlan and Giraud at the same time. They decided to consult General Mast, who rejected outright any idea of cooperation between the two. Worse still, he started to doubt the Americans' good faith. On no account must Giraud be lost, since the approach to Darlan was tentative, and might easily fail. Murphy had therefore to recreate the trust that had been damaged. The whole business was already bordering on the absurd, but the way Murphy chose to recreate that trust led to one of the most ludicrous episodes of the whole war.

The plan – which, astonishingly, was agreed by Eisenhower – was for Eisenhower's deputy, General Mark Clark, the Deputy Supreme Commander of Torch, together with other high-ranking specialist officers from London, to land from a submarine at dead of night and in secret on the Algerian coast. There they would meet Murphy, Mast and others from among Murphy's French co-conspirators – one of whom, Jacques Tessier, had put his beach villa, about sixty miles west of Algiers, at their disposal. In order to allay suspicions, Tessier invented an elaborate cover story. He gave his Algerian servants three days' leave, then explained to the local commissioner of police that he was giving a party for some senior officials and the American consul-general. Ladies would be present, he said, and it would be better if the party were left undisturbed.

The American officers, after flying out from London, duly embarked at Gibraltar on a British submarine, HMS *Seraph*, and sailed for the Algerian coast. The rendezvous was set for the night of 20–21 October, the submarine going in as close to the shore as was prudent, whereupon the distinguished party would paddle themselves ashore in inflatable boats. They missed the appointed night because of bad weather, but made it the following night, all arriving ashore safe and dry except for the Deputy Supreme Commander, whose boat overturned in the rough surf, forcing him to scramble to the beach wet to the skin.

The meeting started as planned, Clark telling the French that a landing had been decided on and that it would be in strength. He omitted to tell them the date, or that the Torch armada was already at sea. While it was in progress, however, one of the Algerian servants unexpectedly returned, saw what was happening and went off to tell the commissioner of police. Fortunately, he saw only the commissioner's secretary, who happened to be a member of a Resistance group, and who was quick-witted enough to calm the man down.

But this did not entirely satisfy the Algerian, who waited for the commissioner and told him about the whole thing in person. The commissioner was about to rush off to investigate when he ran into his deputy, Leven, who was also in the Resistance and whom Tessier had told about the meeting. Leven jumped onto his motorcycle and headed for the villa to warn the group of a raid. He was only just in time. There was nothing for it but to hide the Americans in the cellar, the French making off as best they could. While the search went on above, the Deputy Supreme Commander and his colleagues hid below. At one point, one of the American officers found his teeth chattering uncontrollably. Clark jammed a lump of chewing gum in his mouth. 'But it has no taste,' the poor man whispered. 'I know,' Clark replied, 'I've been chewing it since this morning.'[19]

Finally the search party left. The *Seraph* arrived back to collect its distinguished cargo, but the sea was too rough for them to reach the ship without difficulty, and all eight of the Americans took to the oars in one boat. Needless to say, it capsized and, as Clark wrote, 'clothes, money, colonels, generals, plans and papers found themselves floundering about in the cold water'.[20] In the end, the crew of the *Seraph* fished them out with boathooks.

HMS *Seraph* dropped its passengers, somewhat sobered after their undignified adventure, safely back at Gibraltar, and set off almost immediately on another assignment. This was less ridiculous, but it was to lead to almost equal confusion. The mission was the collection from the southern coast of mainland France of the man who was to be the Allies' trump card, 'Kingpin', as he was codenamed, alias General Henri Giraud. For the moment Admiral Darlan had to wait. His day – and indeed his death – was to come.

7

THE DARLAN DEAL

Et voilà que je suis tué dans une embûche,
Par derrière, par un laquais, d'un coup de bûche!★

The Torch armada started its land assault in the early hours of Sunday 8
November 1942. There had been rumours at the Soviet embassy reception in London the previous evening, but nothing certain, and de
Gaulle had left early. Just after midnight, Ismay called Billotte, to tell
him officially that in three hours time American troops were to land in
strength at several points in Morocco, at Oran and at Algiers. Prudently,
Billotte decided to do nothing until morning. After all, he reasoned,
there was nothing he or the General could do, and the tempest of rage
which was sure to come could wait.

At six o'clock the next morning Billotte went to wake the General
up and tell him the news. It was not a task that Billotte enjoyed. De
Gaulle gave his temper free rein. 'Well,' he shouted, as he put on his
dressing gown, 'I hope the Vichy people are going to throw them into
the sea. You can't get into France by breaking and entering.'[1] He then
proceeded to give Billotte a foretaste of what he would say to Churchill
when he saw him. It lasted two hours.

But by the time Charles Peake arrived in mid-morning at Carlton
Gardens to confirm a previous appointment to lunch with Churchill, de
Gaulle's temper had improved. 'If a genial note can be struck at the
beginning of the meeting,' Peake reported to the Prime Minister, 'the
General may be put into the right mood at once and the luncheon may
pass off fairly successfully.'[2] Churchill took the advice, and was at his
most genial. He was, to be sure, a trifle embarrassed as he told de
Gaulle of the American insistence on the exclusion of Fighting France,

★ 'And there I am – killed in an ambush, from behind, by a lackey, with a blow from
a piece of wood!' Edmond Rostand, *Cyrano de Bergerac*, Act V, Scene 6.

but he reaffirmed his commitment to it. 'I shall never forget those who did not desert me in June 1940, when I was all alone,' he said, yet again. 'You'll see. One day, we'll go down the Champs Elysées together.'[3]

The General was delighted with Churchill's reassurance and, it was said, left lunch wreathed in smiles. Churchill's expression of loyalty had calmed him. Of course, Churchill had also told him of the progress of the operation, which was far from smooth, and of the arrival of Giraud in Gibraltar and his – purely military – future role. That was no problem for de Gaulle; he had always had a great respect for Giraud as a soldier.

On the evening of 8 November, de Gaulle broadcast on the BBC. As after Mers el-Kébir, two years earlier, he was inspired. There was no question of complaint that the Americans had barged into French territory; there was no attempt to outflank possible rivals, although he knew the Allied plans for Giraud. There was a fulsome tribute to the triumphs of British and Russian forces in other theatres; and there was finally a ringing call to Frenchmen in North Africa to rise in arms. 'Let us return through you to the line of battle, and there it will be: the war won – thanks to France!'[4]

So far, so good. But at their meeting Churchill had slipped in a question: was de Gaulle aware that Darlan was now in Algiers? It was the truth. Whether by accident or design, the Admiral had arrived just before Torch was launched to visit his son, who was ill in an Algiers hospital with poliomyelitis. The Americans had discovered his unexpected presence after he had been arrested by a group of young Gaullists on the first night of the landings; but they had arrived too late and Darlan had been freed by the police. Yet there was no doubt that he was there, or that he was the highest ranking Vichy official in North Africa. Indeed, he was second only to the Marshal himself in popular eyes, although Laval was Prime Minister.

As such, Darlan was the obvious person for the Allies to deal with, particularly since Giraud was still in Gibraltar arguing about his future role. Indeed, the idea had already been discussed at a meeting in London between Churchill and General Eisenhower, with Eden and Sir Alan Brooke in attendance, three weeks before the Torch landings, when Darlan had sent a hint that he might come over. The conclusion of the meeting, as relayed to Roosevelt, was that Darlan might be considered seriously as a Deputy Commander to Eisenhower in North Africa if Giraud, the preferred candidate, were not available.

But dealing with Darlan was never easy, since he always took refuge behind what he considered to be the view of the Marshal. It was a clever ploy, as nobody was sure at that time what the Marshal's view was on any matter that was put before him. Perhaps even Pétain himself did not know, as his concentration, and his ability to recollect events, was beginning to fade, particularly in the afternoons. Dealing with his lieutenant was therefore doubly difficult.

On the matter of Darlan, de Gaulle had been quite clear to Churchill at their lunch on the day of the Torch invasion. If Darlan were put in charge of North Africa, he had said, no agreement would be possible between him and Fighting France. Similarly, Giraud, when he finally arrived on 9 November, was equally adamant. But Roosevelt was getting tired of the antics of the 'three prima donnas', as he called them. 'Put all three of them in one room alone,' was his recommendation, 'and then give the government of the occupied territory to the man who comes out.'[5] It was not an unreasonable reaction in Washington, but was far from helpful to his commanders in the field.

The fact was that they had to do something and do it quickly. Torch was not going well. Vichy resistance was much tougher than expected, and the arrival of Giraud, as commander in chief of French troops, complicated matters further. Clark and Murphy had by now got hold of Darlan, and were offering him precisely the same powers as Eisenhower was offering Giraud. The confusion was compounded when Giraud broadcast his assumption of leadership of French North Africa and ordered a ceasefire. Nothing happened. He was simply ignored. It was, as Eisenhower mildly noted at the time, a bad blow to American expectations.

So it was, and the Americans were now faced with a situation which was not far from desperate. There were 120,000 Vichy troops in North Africa, an army more than twice the size of the landing force. The French aircraft were superior to anything the Americans could put in the air. German air assistance had been offered and accepted. Battle-hardened German troops were pouring into Tunisia. The United States army was in battle for the first time since 1917, and on territory that was wholly strange. Murphy's elaborate network of 'vice-consuls', which had led the Americans to believe that the French would come over to their side without a fight, had been revealed as a paper army. In short, it had been another Dakar.

In practice, therefore, there was only one thing to do to avoid massive American casualties, and possible military defeat; and Eisenhower did it. Darlan signed an armistice 'in the Marshal's name' at midday on 10 November. He claimed to have received a secret telegram from

Pétain authorising him to sign. It has never been found. In return, Darlan became 'High Commissioner for North Africa'.

There was uproar in Britain, in the United States and, above all, in Fighting France. Politically, the 'Darlan deal', as it was immediately dubbed, was a disaster. Churchill, Eden and Brooke were all deeply embarrassed, since they had been well aware of the proposed deal, and had indeed endorsed it. For public consumption Churchill affected fury: 'Darlan ought to be shot.'[6] Eden let it be known that he believed that any permanent Darlan settlement would be catastrophic. Winant cabled Roosevelt that there was 'considerable agitation' in Britain; trade unions, Jewish organisations, the press and members of both Houses of Parliament protested angrily and vociferously.

The reaction in the United States was similar. Darlan was described in the press as 'one of the greatest living traitors' and 'America's first Quisling'. The flood of mail to the White House was almost universally hostile. Politically, and Roosevelt was for ever a politician before all else, it began to look nasty; he started to retreat. In a press conference on 18 November, he announced, prompted by Churchill, that the deal was 'only a temporary expedient, justified solely by the stress of battle'.[7] It was not at all clear what that meant, but, not for the first time, he managed to imply that Hull and the State Department were in some way responsible for the fiasco, and that all questions should be addressed to them.

Fighting France's reaction was one of intense anger, mixed with depression. The reason for the anger was obvious: they felt betrayed. The depression was due to the nagging thought that the Americans might be preparing, not just an agreement, both political and military, with Darlan, or indeed with any Vichy official of authority who happened to be there. It was conceivable that they could go on from there to negotiate with Hitler himself. De Gaulle's own reaction, however, apart from a private outburst to Admiral Stark, the American representative with Fighting France, was more measured. He made no reference to the deal in his speech to the Fighting French in the Albert Hall on Armistice Day, 11 November – the day, as it happened, on which the German army was busy occupying France's unoccupied zone.

Quite clearly, he had understood Churchill's dilemma, without, be it said, sympathising much with it. Churchill, after all, had undertaken to be Roosevelt's lieutenant in Torch, and once that position had been accepted it was difficult to change it. What de Gaulle did not know was that Churchill had agreed in advance to the Darlan deal – and was not telling the General the whole truth. Had he known that, his behaviour would have certainly been different.

But it was worse, much worse, when Darlan invited the French forces in North Africa to obey him 'in the name of the Marshal', and de Gaulle told Churchill in their meeting of 16 November that he could no longer have anything to do with it. He showed him the messages that he had received from France – of disillusion and incredulity – and went on to say, as he later recorded, 'If France one day discovers that because of the British and the Americans her liberation consists of Darlan, you can perhaps win the war from a military point of view but you will lose it morally, and ultimately there will only be one victor: Stalin.'[8]

Churchill advised him to hold firm. 'You stand for honour. Yours is the true path; you alone will remain.'[9] The General, in spite of his doubts, did hold firm. In his broadcast that evening he again put France above his disappointment and his own personal ambition. He simply let it be known that he and the National Committee had no part in the negotiations with Darlan and disclaimed any responsibility for them. If those talks were to bring about the 'consecration' of the Vichy regime in North Africa, they were obviously unacceptable to Fighting France.

In the middle of November 1942, another recruit to Fighting France slipped into London: General François d'Astier de la Vigerie. Whether he was sent for is unclear, but his arrival at this particular time, and in the light of later events, takes on special significance. François was one of three brothers, the others being Emmanuel, the Resistance leader, and Henri, who – most important – was the Secretary-General of Police in Algiers. Emmanuel had played his role as emissary to the United States, and was still at work in France; the other two brothers were to play their role in a much more sinister drama, the first act of which had already begun.

Although they dealt with him, Darlan was never really trusted by the Americans – Roosevelt had written as much to Eisenhower on 16 November. Not only was Darlan not trusted, but he knew it, and resented it deeply. 'I am,' he wrote to Clark the following week, 'only a lemon which the Americans will drop after they have squeezed it dry.'[10] He wrote a similar letter to Churchill, but such was Churchill's dislike and contempt of him – he referred to him as 'that rogue Darlan' – that he did not bother to answer. There was, however, one success: Boisson, the old Vichy general who had put up such fierce resistance to the British guns at Dakar in September 1940, came over to Darlan with 50,000 troops. It was something, but the Allies wanted more. What they wanted was lying serenely at anchor in Toulon harbour – the rest of the French fleet.

The fleet had, of course, been Darlan's special child. At Mers el-Kébir it had been severely depleted, but the Toulon squadron, under Admiral Laborde, had survived. Two battleships were there, as well as the survivor of Mers el-Kébir, the battlecruiser *Strasbourg*, along with seven cruisers and as many as thirty destroyers and sixteen submarines. In addition, the old battleship *Lorraine,* four cruisers and three destroyers were lying in Alexandria under the command of Admiral Godfroy, while a further squadron of one aircraft-carrier, two cruisers, five destroyers and five submarines formed the Atlantic fleet, stationed in Martinique under Admiral Robert. All in all, it was a formidable force, at least on paper, although enforced idleness had inevitably damaged both its operational efficiency and the morale of its sailors.

But, formidable or not, Darlan was unable to deliver it to the Allies. Godfroy and Robert paid no attention to his instruction to sail to Algiers. Laborde at Toulon replied simply – like Cambronne at Waterloo – '*Merde*', and when, on 25 November, German armoured troops broke through the perimeter and raced onto the jetties, he gave the order to scuttle. One hundred and seventy-seven ships blew themselves up. 'In that one instant of time', de Gaulle broadcast on the BBC that night, 'the commanders, the officers, the sailors saw torn in pieces the terrible veil which, since June 1940, falsehood had stretched before their eyes . . . A shudder of pain, of pity and of fury ran across the whole of France.'[11]

Not only did Darlan fail to deliver the fleet; his administration in North Africa turned out to be no better than its Vichy predecessor. There was near anarchy in civilian life. Nobody knew whom to trust. Informers were everywhere; nothing could be done without intrigue. In short, it was only the strong Allied military presence that prevented riot and possibly civil war.

Anti-semitic laws remained in force; de Gaulle's supporters languished in gaol; and even those who had helped the Allied landings were arrested for 'desertion'. The camps in the desert where they were kept were filthy and disease-ridden. Known German sympathisers were reinstated in their jobs. At the end of November Marcel Peyrouton, a former member of the Vichy Cabinet who had been one of the leaders in the effort to stamp out the Resistance in France, had been hauled out of retirement in Argentina by Darlan, with Murphy's approval, to become Governor of Algiers. Even Hull thought the appointment went a bit far; there was a large Jewish population in Algeria, and that, as always, touched a sensitive nerve in domestic American politics.

The fact was that North Africa was going in a direction precisely opposite to the one the Americans had intended. Darlan even embarked on a scheme which he called the 'Imperial Federation', whereby a Vichyite empire would be set up in Dakar, Martinique and Djibouti. Eisenhower was fed up with it all, since he was having to spend far too much time on civil affairs rather than fighting the Germans, and so, now, was Roosevelt.

Again the Americans changed tack and, encouraged by the British, started to make overtures to Fighting France. In the event, they did not amount to much. There was one false start, which virtually stopped the whole initiative. Adrien Tixier, de Gaulle's Washington representative, was invited, together with André Philip, who was in Washington at the time, to an interview with the President. It did not go well. Roosevelt told them that he would like Fighting France to cooperate with the Americans, but 'so long as the United States was the occupying power in North Africa, the final decision would be reached solely by the occupying power'.[12] Nothing could have been less palatable to de Gaulle. Tixier became angry, and started shouting. Roosevelt was furious that an upstart trade unionist from a defeated country could adopt such a tone with the President of the United States. It was stalemate again.

But the American initiative brought one crucial benefit to de Gaulle. Eisenhower, in the new spirit of cooperation, but against the advice of Roosevelt and Leahy, who thought it would stir up trouble, invited Fighting France to send a mission to Algiers, and de Gaulle accepted. His choice of emissary was curious, to say the least – perhaps significantly so. It was none other than General François d'Astier de la Vigerie. It is far from easy to see how this new recruit – he had only been in London a month – could have gained sufficient knowledge of Fighting France to devise a method of cooperation with the Darlan administration (on the assumption that de Gaulle had had that purpose in mind); but he was, and here lay his importance, the brother of the Secretary-General of Police in Algiers.

François d'Astier's visit to Algiers was part of a strategy, support for which had been gaining strength in London and with the British clandestine services in Algiers, that Darlan had to go. By the end of November 1942 signals from the Special Operations Executive in

Algiers were already urging action. These signals found their way to the offices of Fighting France, and were duly noted. By the time Churchill and Eden recognised that no diplomatic effort would persuade Roosevelt to abandon Darlan, and Catroux had added his voice – a voice which was respected by the British chiefs of staff as much as de Gaulle's was disliked – both Britain and Fighting France were ready for conspiracy, and de Gaulle had his conspirator ready.

On the surface, d'Astier's trip went badly. Darlan would have had him arrested immediately if Eisenhower had not intervened. D'Astier had a full visiting list, but only once saw Darlan. The meeting can only be described as one of extreme hostility. There was no prospect of a compromise, and Eisenhower concluded that from his point of view the mission had achieved nothing; Roosevelt and Leahy had been right. Darlan ordered d'Astier to leave. He took off for London on 24 December.

But d'Astier's visit was wholly successful in its real purpose. He was shepherded about by his brother and saw, not just Gaullist sympathisers, but the pretender to the French throne, the Comte de Paris, who was in Algiers to see if there was advantage to be gained for his own ambitions, Lemaigre-Dubreuil, as well, of course, as Murphy himself. But above all he had long conversations with his brother.

Henri d'Astier had been in touch with a number of groups of hot-headed young Gaullists, known as *corps francs*. They regarded themselves as paramilitaries, and had indeed been useful in disrupting communications at the time of the Torch landings. One such group comprised twelve young men in their early twenties, led by an officer-cadet by the name of Ragueneau. The group's original plan had been to escape to join the British army in Tunisia, but when four of them, all of whom had taken part in Darlan's capture on the night of the 8th, met on 20 November in a barn just outside Algiers, they were told by Ragueneau that there was a new plan: no less than the assassination of Admiral François Darlan.

The short straw was drawn by a twenty-year-old boy, Fernand Bonnier, who liked to add 'de la Chapelle' to his name – his mother's maiden name was della Capella. While his companions stuck to their original plan and went eastwards towards Tunisia, Bonnier returned to Algiers. In the following weeks, he made contact with, among others, Jean-Bernard d'Astier, Henri's son. Through him Bonnier met an army padre, Father Cordier, and the Secretary-General of Police himself, and he was introduced to the British SOE.

Bonnier was put through a two-week training course, which included shooting with a Webley .38 pistol, by the SOE at the Club des Pins. The Webley was later switched to a Colt .45, although neither of these were to be used in the event, for fear that they could be traced back if Bonnier were caught. By the time General François d'Astier arrived in Algiers on 19 December, the plot was well under way. Even in London there were rumours. Virginia Cowles, acting as personal assistant to Ambassador Winant, remarked casually at a dinner party that 'the French ought to be able to deal with [Darlan] themselves'.[13] She was called a few days later by an anonymous member of Fighting France and told that if she kept an eye on the newspapers she would soon see that her advice had been taken.

Algiers was, as always, full of conspiracy and intrigue, and it seemed only a matter of time before the volcano erupted. On 23 December 1942, Darlan gave an official lunch for General Clark and the Allied staff. The main topic of conversation was the arrangement to fly Darlan's son, Alain, from Rabat, where he was then in hospital, to the United States for further treatment for his polio; Roosevelt, as a sufferer himself, had taken a special interest. The subsidiary, and more delicate, matter was the future of the father himself. Clark hinted that it might be possible for a passage to be arranged for the Admiral as well, to which Darlan replied, much to Clark's astonishment, 'Yes, I'd much like to hand over to General Giraud. He likes it here. I don't.'[14]

After lunch, Darlan asked Murphy to come to his office. There were one or two things, he said, that he would like to discuss. When there, Darlan said that he knew of four separate plots to kill him and asked Murphy whom the Americans would choose as his successor. Darlan himself produced a list of possible candidates. Giraud headed it, but Murphy was surprised to see another name on it – that of General de Gaulle. 'But not yet,' Darlan said, 'it would be too soon. In the spring of 1943 perhaps. If de Gaulle took over now, he'd cause you a great heap of trouble.'[15] All in all, it was one of the most surprising comments of the whole affair.

In the event, Darlan was not to make many more comments at all, surprising or otherwise. On the following morning, General d'Astier de la Vigerie having left for London to report back to de Gaulle – and Churchill – Bonnier arrived at Darlan's office in the Summer Palace, a building in the high Moorish style in which the High Commissioner had set up his office, armed with an identity card in the name of Morand and a revolver given him by Father Cordier. He said that he had an interview with the Admiral 'for personal reasons', but was told that Darlan was out and would not be back until the afternoon.

Just before three o'clock Bonnier/Morand got out of a black Peugeot which had parked near the Summer Palace, said goodbye to his friends in the car, was recognised by the palace official he had met that morning, and sat down to wait in the anteroom. He did not have to wait long. Soon afterwards, Darlan returned from lunch, accompanied by his ADC, Commander Hourcade. Hourcade opened the door of his own office and Darlan went past. As he did so, he heard a noise behind him and turned – to see Bonnier coming directly at him. Bonnier raised his revolver and fired two shots, hitting the Admiral in the stomach. Darlan staggered towards his office, but failed to reach it and fell unconscious to the floor.

Bonnier's plan had been to escape through a corridor window but it was barred from the outside. He turned, fired two shots at Hourcade, who was bravely in pursuit, hitting him in the thigh and the ear, and then gave himself up to the guards who had by now surrounded him. The arrest was short, sharp and merciless.

Darlan never regained consciousness. He was taken to the Maillot hospital, where he died three hours later. Allied headquarters in Algiers immediately declared a state of emergency, and there was a news black-out. Bonnier was beaten up and then handed over to the police. He was interrogated by Police Commissaire Garinacci, and seemed quite willing to confess, even to the point of naming names. He was quite clearly expecting the intervention of a high authority, and seemed unperturbed by the whole process. But when Garinacci read the confession that Bonnier had signed, he was so appalled that he grabbed the document and burned it.

Bonnier was placed in solitary confinement and a court-martial was arranged for the night of 25–26 December. It was held in camera and only Bonnier's lawyer was admitted. After a short hearing, the young man was condemned to death. He still believed that he would be saved, but as the hours wore on he came to realise that he was to be sacrificed. He asked for paper, but the prison chaplain had none; so he wrote a final confession on the back of a visiting card that he happened to have on him. The name on the visiting card was Henri d'Astier de la Vigerie.

Bonnier was shot at 7.30 a.m. on 26 December 1942 in the courtyard of a police barracks on the edge of Algiers. His coffin had already been ordered before the court-martial started. He was buried without delay in an anonymous grave. The press were forbidden to reveal his name. It was as though he had never existed.

There was, of course, an enquiry, but it was not pursued with great diligence. Eisenhower was anxious to avoid any suggestion of British involvement and his staff circulated stories to the effect that Darlan had been killed by Axis agents. French agents in Algiers were told quietly to disappear, and the fact that Bonnier wrote his last message from a prison cell on Henri d'Astier's visiting card, and that he had $2000 in his pocket when he was captured which could be traced back to the financial services department of Fighting France, was covered up. De Gaulle took his own measures to distance himself from the affair. He cabled all Fighting French authorities that 'neither he nor his fellow-workers' were involved in the murder.[16] But by 29 December he was referring in a further telegram to his proconsuls to Darlan's 'execution'.

'No private person,' de Gaulle wrote, 'has the right to kill other than on the field of battle.' But, he goes on later, the secrecy and haste in the execution of the murderer 'and the orders given to the censors that not even his name should be known – all pointed to the suspicion that someone wanted to conceal at any price the origin of his decision, and constituted a kind of defiance of the circumstances which, without justifying the drama, explain and to a certain degree excuse it'.[17] It is a strange comment; but, on the face of it, there is no doubt that it lends weight to the view that de Gaulle knew all along about the plot to kill Darlan.

Whatever the rights and wrongs, or who was or was not in the know, the Darlan assassination marked a crucial stage in de Gaulle's rise to ultimate power in French North Africa, and subsequently in France itself. As the General cabled Catroux in Accra on 26 December, Darlan's 'disappearance' placed the North African situation 'in a new perspective'. With his usual speed at grasping the significance of events, he had seen three things: first, that the American Vichy policy had suffered a mortal blow; second, that it was only a matter of time before Darlan's successor, Giraud, could be outmanoeuvred; and, third, that Fighting France continued to enjoy British support even to the point where the British were prepared to defy the United States.

De Gaulle's message of Christmas 1942 and his message after Darlan's assassination were both brimming with confidence. Things were going well. 'On this day of Christmas 1942, France sees, on the horizon, her star rising again.' Home life, too, was much more settled. In February his family had moved from Ashridge to a house in Hampstead – 65 Frognal (or Frognal House, as it is known by the Sisters of Dorothy, who now run it as a hostel for young women). The General was able to go home in the evening when he was in London and spend his hour with little Anne and the evening with his wife.

Elisabeth, too, was there from time to time during the Oxford vacations. She was now well advanced in her studies and had made her own friends. Like many young women of the day, she had developed an innocent passion for Winnie the Pooh, and gave each of her friends names that she thought corresponded to their characters. In early December 1942 Elisabeth wrote a letter – to 'Roo' – that illustrates the busy complexities of Frognal life. In explaining why she had had to cancel an invitation to 'Roo' to luncheon, she said that 'Daddy' had some 'official people' to lunch at 1.30 p.m. The two could have had an early meal, she went on, but that would have meant that 'cook' would have had to prepare five different lunches: Anne's, her governess's, Elisabeth and her friend's, the 'official' lunch and, at the end of it, a meal for the maids. It was all too much, and she was very sorry that it had not worked out as planned.

Whatever the complications of life, all the de Gaulles seem to have liked Frognal. At that time Hampstead was pleasantly remote and peaceful. It was a short walk from home to the little church of St Mary's, Holly Place, where the de Gaulles worshipped every Sunday, not least because of the church's close historical connection with France. Hampstead also seems to have liked them. The General was perhaps 'aloof', as one of the neighbours put it. 'He was always smartly dressed in uniform,' another said. 'I don't think I ever saw him in civvies.' 'Our General,' said a third, 'that's what we called him then.'[18]

But most noticeable of all, in late 1942 and early 1943 de Gaulle's self-doubt, the dreadful thought that the whole enterprise might fail, was, at least for the moment, starting to fade. 'He was really and truly a humble man at heart,' said the priest in charge at St Mary's, Canon Geraerts, '[but] I observed his unshakeable confidence in final victory for France'.[19] De Gaulle's acquaintance, particularly the British, might have been surprised at the first part of the Canon's judgement, but there was no doubt that he was right in saying that the General's confidence in final victory was absolute. The real question in his mind now was what role he himself would be playing when victory came.

8

FROM ANFA TO ALGIERS

I warned W. not to be too hasty with de G. and the F. Fr.
Nat. Comee. ★

General Henri Honoré Giraud has frequently been portrayed by Gaullist historians as something of a figure of fun. The portrait could hardly be further from the truth. As an officer in the French army, he had conducted himself in both wars with brilliance and courage. In the First World War, he had been left for dead on the battlefield, had been captured, had escaped and then operated clandestinely behind enemy lines – his description of those adventures had enthralled Churchill when he visited Giraud's positions on the Maginot Line in 1937.

In the Second World War, he had been in the northern sector, commanding first the 7th and then the 9th French armies in May 1940 with as much distinction as was possible under the circumstances, until he was captured on 19 May. A carefully guarded prisoner-of-war, he slid down a 150-foot rope to escape from his fortress prison, in spite of lameness from an earlier wound that had healed badly. When he heard of Giraud's arrival in Algiers some months later, Hitler cabled Otto Abetz, his ambassador in France: 'Why have you let Giraud get away? This man is worth thirty divisions!'[1]

Tall and dapper, Giraud resembled every officer cadet's image of a successful general. He wore his moustache in the shape of a sabre, strode purposefully wherever he went, was friendly to his subordinates and kind to his colleagues. Although his face tended to roundness, with 'Siamese cat's eyes', and although his voice was that of a high tenor, there was no suggestion that he lacked authority. In short, he was a military man through and through. To a British observer, he was an

★ Diary of King George VI, 9 February 1943. J. W. Wheeler-Bennett, *King George VI, his life and reign*, page 560; Macmillan, London, 1958.

'old-fashioned but charming colonel, who would grace the Turf Club . . . he is really so nice and also so stately and stupid.'[2]

With Darlan out of the way, the Americans were able to retrieve political respectability at a stroke by cultivating the untainted General Giraud. A group of senior figures was assembled, including General Boisson from Dakar and General Noguès from Rabat, and Giraud was declared High Commissioner and Commander-in-Chief in North Africa. Peyrouton was asked to stay on as Governor General of Algeria. It was all done quickly and with the minimum of fuss.

None of this was wholly welcome to de Gaulle, but it was not unexpected; at least Darlan had gone, and there were some possibilities he could see for the future. As an opening gambit, he sent a message to Giraud, in the politest terms, suggesting a meeting on French soil to study how to group together all French forces, inside and outside France, under a 'provisional central authority'. It was a simple enough move, but he knew perfectly well that Giraud was controlled by the Americans, and that nothing of moment could happen without their approval. However, he was due to leave on 26 December for the United States and his first meeting with Roosevelt; and he was confident that 'a simple and sincere conversation' would be enough to change the President's view of the situation and pave the way for a de Gaulle–Giraud partnership.[3]

In the event, de Gaulle's visit to Washington was postponed yet again, and Giraud refused his invitation to meet, suggesting that he send an emissary in his place. De Gaulle suspected, rightly, that the two matters were linked, and that the British and Americans were preparing to do a deal with Giraud over his head. He decided to air his grievance in public. On 2 January 1943, he broadcast on the BBC his plan for a provisional authority to unite all Frenchmen; he cited historical precedent in support of the proposal, and went on to reveal that he had requested a meeting with Giraud, on French territory, to sort the matter out between Frenchmen.

The broadcast, of course, irritated almost everybody, as it was probably meant to do. The Americans were upset because they considered that he was undermining Eisenhower's authority as Supreme Commander; the British were annoyed because they were having enough difficulty defending de Gaulle's position to the Americans as it was; and Giraud simply thought it impertinent. It did not help that the dispute was widely discussed, in each phase and with loving detail, in the British and American press, as de Gaulle had certainly intended.

The broadcast, and the subsequent fall-out, had its desired effect. The question of the future management of the liberated French Empire, part of which owed allegiance to de Gaulle and part to the former Vichy administration in Algiers, floated again to the top of the Allied agenda. It was therefore added to the list of topics that Roosevelt and Churchill would discuss at their forthcoming meeting at Casablanca.

The main object of the Casablanca summit was to map out the future of the war. It was perhaps unfortunate that Stalin had turned down an invitation to attend, on the grounds that the Russian situation was still too tense for him to leave, but Roosevelt and Churchill carried on regardless. Roosevelt, indeed, was in a particularly carefree mood; he seemed to treat the whole thing like a junior school treat. He arrived with a troop of secret service bodyguards, armed conspicuously with 'tommy guns and sawn-off shotguns and all sorts of weapons of that kind',[4] for all the world like extras in a Chicago gangland movie. Several villas in the elegant suburb of Anfa, as well as the Anfa Hotel, had been taken over for the duration, and Roosevelt, together with Hopkins and Averell Harriman, and Generals Marshall and Eisenhower in attendance, made themselves at home in a heavily guarded but spacious villa in the middle of the compound.

Churchill's accommodation was equally luxurious. He was not quite so well attended at the highest level, but he did have with him the newly appointed British Minister Resident in Algiers, Harold Macmillan. It was Macmillan's first real contact with Roosevelt. At their first encounter, he recalls the President lying 'in a great bed on the ground floor'. 'He was indeed,' wrote Macmillan, 'a remarkable figure: the splendid head and torso full of vigour and vitality; below, concealed by the coverings, the terrible shrunken legs and feet . . .'. Roosevelt 'threw up his hands when I walked in, and he said, "Harold, I am glad to see you." Well, that was absolutely insincere . . . he tried to charm everybody . . . he lived on charm . . . Even thought he could charm Stalin.'[5] From then on, Macmillan never trusted Roosevelt. That mistrust was itself to have its impact on the course of events in Algiers in 1943.

The discussions at the summit started with the main business of the war, and naturally took some time to get around to the problem of French unity. When the subject arose, Roosevelt chose to turn it into an elaborate schoolboy joke. 'We'll call Giraud the bridegroom,' he proposed to Churchill, 'and I'll produce him from Algiers; and you get the bride, de Gaulle, down from London, and we'll have a shotgun wedding.'[6] It would all be great fun and the Roosevelt charm would ensure a happy outcome. Churchill, it need hardly be said, was less convinced.

Everything went about as badly as could have been expected. Giraud duly arrived in Casablanca on 17 January, with his two advisers, André Poniatowski and Jacques Lemaigre-Dubreuil, and went to see Roosevelt. The interview was cordial, and Roosevelt said that he hoped to see Giraud as military chief with de Gaulle as second in command and someone else, unspecified, as political head. But even as he spoke Roosevelt was forming a bad impression of Giraud – 'I am afraid we're leaning on a very slender reed,' he later told his son, who had been with him. 'He's a dud as an administrator; he'll be a dud as a leader.'[7] The wedding had got off to a bad start.

It went from bad to worse. De Gaulle was asked in London the same day by Eden and Cadogan whether he would be prepared, on the Prime Minister's invitation, to go to Algiers. After a period of reflection, he replied later in the day that he was quite ready to meet Giraud on French territory, but that he did not think that 'the atmosphere of an exalted Allied forum . . . [was] . . . the best for an effective agreement'.[8] In other words, he would not go.

Churchill was understandably put out. Roosevelt was still enjoying the joke, and told Murphy that he rather enjoyed Churchill's discomfiture. He cabled Hull: 'We delivered our bridegroom . . . However, our friends could not produce the bride, the temperamental lady de Gaulle. She has got quite snooty about the whole idea and does not want to see either of us, and is showing no intention of getting into bed with Giraud.'[9] The joke continued laboriously until Churchill was so goaded that he sent Eden a further message, for onward transmission to de Gaulle, instructing him that if he did not turn up in Casablanca it would be the worse for him; that arrangements for the future administration of North Africa would be made without him; and finally that he, de Gaulle, would have to be removed as head of Fighting France. 'I hope you will put as much of this as you think fit to him. For his own sake you ought to knock him about pretty hard.'[10]

The message was considered in London by the War Cabinet. It put them in a difficult position. The truth was that they had followed the policy of support for Free – and then Fighting – France consistently since Churchill had announced it in August 1940. Admittedly, the clash of personalities between the two leaders, and the consequent volcanic rows, had made life difficult; but there was no question either of abandoning de Gaulle at this point or of ceasing to protect him and his movement against the Americans. Eden was the General's foremost supporter in Cabinet, and he was certainly not going to abandon what he saw as the prospect of a stable France of the future just because Churchill was temporarily out of sorts. As for his colleagues, they were well aware that the General's position was now so strong with British public opinion and with the French Resistance that it was politically no longer sensible to think in terms of deposing him.

Not for the last time, the War Cabinet decided to ignore Churchill's intemperate instruction. His message was therefore delivered to de Gaulle in very much less aggressive language than the original. It was duly considered by the French National Committee. This time it was the General who felt himself insulted – to be invited to French territory, indeed! – and his instinct was to stick to his position and refuse again. Exactly the same debate took place in the committee as had taken place in the War Cabinet, only in reverse. The majority on the committee argued that, whatever the suspicions of Churchill, it was in the interests of Fighting France to stick as closely as possible to the British, who were their closest allies and still giving them substantial material help. The only alternative would be to rely on the Americans – a policy which the Torch affair and the Darlan aftermath had shown to be out of the question.

The General was finally persuaded, but he was not going to go without reservations. He went to see Eden to tell him that he accepted, but also to give him a message for Churchill: that although he was being invited, without warning, to discussions of which he knew neither the programme nor the conditions, he was only going because he could not decently refuse an invitation to meet the President and the Prime Minister. When Roosevelt heard the news he congratulated Churchill with heavy sarcasm, saying that he had always known that 'Winston' would swing it in the end. The gulf between the President and the General was already a chasm. They lived in two different worlds.

De Gaulle arrived at the military airfield of Fedala, near Casablanca, at about eleven o'clock on 22 January 1943, just as the summit was concluding talks on the future conduct of the war. He had with him Catroux and d'Argenlieu, as well as Palewski, his personal assistant, and Hettier de Boislambert for his knowledge of English. The General was never at his best after flying: he was nervous and smoked heavily during the whole trip. When he was met at the airfield by a French colonel and an American general, with no troops to present arms and American armed sentries everywhere, he began to regret his decision to come. He was driven – in an American car with the windows smeared with mud to prevent him being seen – and lodged in a specially requisitioned villa at Anfa which American soldiers looked after and guarded, and which was surrounded by a high barbed-wire fence. As he said himself, it was captivity, and a sort of insult. Indeed, it could hardly have been more insulting.

De Gaulle had a busy afternoon ahead of him. He was due to lunch with General Giraud and, in the evening, have his first meeting with Roosevelt. The lunch started coolly. Giraud, whom he had not seen since before the war in Metz, brusquely greeting him 'Bonjour, Gaulle,' and de Gaulle remarking sardonically that he hoped the 'Americans' had been treating Giraud well, going on to protest that he had offered to meet him four times and that they now had to meet among foreigners in a barbed-wire camp. De Gaulle then refused to sit down to lunch until the American sentries had been replaced by French ones, and capped it all by responding to Giraud's account of his escape from Königstein with an acid observation that perhaps General Giraud would now tell them how he had been taken prisoner.

In his memoirs, de Gaulle describes the meal as 'cordial'. Perhaps it was, but he did not always appreciate the bruising effect of his sardonic sallies, and Giraud was obviously taken aback by them. He said that he was not interested in political matters, and that while he was intent on pursuing the war against Germany he had no complaint to make about Vichy, and would support the authorities already in place, in particular Noguès, Boisson and Peyrouton. The meeting broke up inconclusively without any date being set for a further encounter.

De Gaulle returned to his villa and waited. His first visitor was Macmillan, who had come to persuade the General to see Churchill. Still not in the best of moods, de Gaulle agreed. It was, Churchill wrote, 'a very stony interview'.[11] The General complained bitterly about the American bayonets that surrounded him on French soil; if he had known, he certainly would not have come. 'This is an occupied country,' Churchill shouted back;[12] and went on in his own brand of French, '*Si vous m'obstaclerez, je vous liquiderai.*' At that point, it looked like turning into another furious row, but both men managed to calm down in time.

Churchill then outlined the solution to the problem of the French Empire that he and Roosevelt proposed. Giraud would be supreme military commander, but he and de Gaulle would be joint chairmen of a governing committee, all of whose members would enjoy equal respect. General Georges would join the committee, as would the 'proconsuls', Generals Noguès, Boisson, Peyrouton and Bergeret.

It is a measure of the Allies' failure to understand either de Gaulle or Fighting France that this plan was ever put forward in the first place. As de Gaulle pointed out, it was a plan at the intelligence level – quite respectable, he said – of American sergeant-majors, but nothing to do with reality. To expect the Fighting French, after all they had been through, to submerge themselves in a Vichyite-dominated committee under permanent American control was nothing less than absurd. That was the end of the interview. De Gaulle simply got up and, very politely, took his leave. All Churchill could do was to stand in the hall of the villa 'watching the Frenchman stalk down the garden path with his head in the air'.[13]

The meeting with Roosevelt was rather better in tone, but similar in substance. The President was wearing his white tropical suit and had arranged himself on a large sofa. When de Gaulle came in, 'giving the impression that thunder clouds were billowing around his narrow skull',[14] Roosevelt invited the General to sit next to him. With the famous charm turned full on, he said that he was sure that the United States would be able to assist France in re-establishing her destiny, and he assured the General that it would be an honour for the United States to participate in the undertaking. De Gaulle could not resist the sardonic reply that it was nice of him to say so.

The President went on to suppose that the collaboration on the part of General Eisenhower with Admiral Darlan had been the source of some wonderment to General de Gaulle. De Gaulle's reply to this masterly understatement was inaudible, perhaps fortunately. But, the President went on, progress had been made before the Admiral's untimely death – although he failed to specify exactly what progress – and the only course of action now was for all France's loyal sons to unite to defeat the enemy. It was, in short, exactly the same formula that Churchill had outlined in the afternoon, but as de Gaulle put it, wrapped in charm rather than reason. What the General did not know was that behind the curtain in the room, and at all the doors leading into the room, lurked secret service men with loaded tommy-guns 'not taking', they told Hopkins outside, 'any chances on anything happening to the President'. Hopkins found the armed men 'unbelievably funny' but did remark that it was simply an indication of the atmosphere in which de Gaulle found himself in Casablanca. None of this 'hocus-pocus'[15] had gone on when Giraud saw the President.

De Gaulle thought the meeting had gone well. 'You see,' he said to

Boislambert, who had acted as his interpreter, 'I have met a great statesman today. I think we got along and understood each other well.'[16] He
was over-optimistic. Roosevelt regarded de Gaulle as just another difficult French general, and a particularly stiff-necked one at that. All the
President wanted was to be able to announce to the world that he had
brought the two warring French factions together; and his main purpose in that was to demolish his critics in the American press.

The following day, Giraud and de Gaulle, together with their
advisers, met again. There was again no progress. Giraud demanded the
implementation of the Roosevelt–Churchill plan, and de Gaulle invited Giraud to join Fighting France as commander-in-chief. The circle
could not be squared. There was no possible compromise, and the
meeting broke up with only the vague agreement that liaison officers
would be exchanged. The final handshake was icy.

But Roosevelt needed his communiqué, and during the night of the
23rd Murphy and Macmillan strove to persuade de Gaulle to agree to an
announcement to set up a war committee under the joint chairmanship
of the two generals. They went through draft after draft, all of which
Giraud accepted, and all of which de Gaulle turned down. By this time
de Gaulle had learnt that Roosevelt had been dining with the Sultan of
Morocco and General Noguès the previous night, just before their own
meeting, and had discussed the post-war future of an independent
Morocco free from French influence. Furthermore, it appeared that
Roosevelt had signed – some said he had not bothered to read it, but
that hardly seems credible – a document recognising, on behalf of the
United States and the United Kingdom, that General Giraud had the
'right and the duty of acting as trustee for French interests'. At the same
time, the United States committed herself to re-equipping the French
army in North Africa.

None of this had been shown to Churchill in draft, and it was
Macmillan who got hold of a copy and gave it to him. Churchill immediately set himself to amend the document. He knew perfectly well that
de Gaulle could not possibly accept it as it stood. But he failed to
remove from the document the recognition of Giraud as 'director of
French interests'.

By now de Gaulle had had enough. After consulting his colleagues,
all of whom agreed with him, he told Murphy and Macmillan in the
morning that 'an enlargement of French national authority could not be
brought about by foreign intervention, no matter how high and how
friendly'.[17] He would therefore not put his name to Roosevelt's

document. Nor would he sign the communiqué that Murphy and Macmillan had drafted to reflect it.

Churchill was also at the end of his patience. The Allies were trying to fight a war. He was doing his best to deal with Roosevelt, not always the easiest of men. At the same time he was attempting to defend his protégé, de Gaulle, against Roosevelt's snide jokes and growing personal dislike. Far from helping, de Gaulle was actually impeding his efforts, first refusing to come to Casablanca, then refusing to get on with Giraud, and now rejecting arrogantly all attempts to work out text of a face-saving communiqué. Churchill was mortified by de Gaulle's behaviour and when Churchill was mortified he was also very angry.

'Owing to Mr Churchill's dispositions, we had an extremely bitter interview. It was to be the roughest of our encounters in the whole war.'[18] Thus starts de Gaulle's own account of the meeting at which he was to say his farewells before leaving Casablanca. Churchill heaped reproaches on the General, and said that on his return to London he would denounce him in the Commons as the main obstacle to an agreement between the French factions. De Gaulle was by now used to this sort of treatment and affected, while replying with some sallies of his own, not to pay too much attention.

The Anfa meetings had ended, but there was to be one more note of sour comedy. De Gaulle's final visit to Roosevelt was friendly enough; the fact was that Roosevelt had already written him off, and there was no point in being rude. He was sorry, he said, that agreement between Frenchmen should remain uncertain, and that he had not been able to persuade de Gaulle to accept even the text of a communiqué, but there it was and there was nothing to be done. De Gaulle promised that he would arrange some sort of communiqué with Giraud, and the meeting quietly fizzled out. But it was just at this point, outside, that things started to move fast.

'At this moment,' wrote Harry Hopkins, 'the Secret Service called me up to say that Churchill was outside.'[19] He was saying his farewells to Giraud. While Hopkins went after Giraud, thinking that if all four men got together for one last time something might emerge, Churchill came in. He was still, in Murphy's words, 'in a white fury over de Gaulle's stubbornness . . . he shook his finger in the General's face . . . In his inimitable French . . . Churchill exclaimed: *"Mon Général, il ne faut pas obstacler la guerre!"* '[20]

Roosevelt, still exuding charm, asked de Gaulle if he would mind being photographed shaking hands with Giraud. De Gaulle replied, in

English, 'I shall do that for you.' Whereupon Roosevelt had himself carried out into the garden, where a crowd of photographers was waiting. He was followed by Giraud, de Gaulle and, still in a black humour, Churchill. The astonished photographers fired away at an unsmiling General Giraud and an unsmiling General de Gaulle shaking hands. Roosevelt thought it so funny that he shouted *'Encore!'* and the two French generals went through the bizarre routine again. It was humiliating, but Roosevelt got the picture he wanted.

He also got a communiqué, of sorts. De Gaulle drafted, and Giraud accepted, a limp statement to the effect that the two generals agreed on their goal – the liberation of France. It was not a very grand ending, but it contained one moment of significance. De Gaulle's original draft referred to the triumph of democratic principles. 'Do you believe in them yourself, these "democratic principles"?' Giraud asked Catroux when he saw the draft. 'Yes,' replied Catroux. 'But if you wish we can substitute "human liberties".'[21] The revision was agreed, but the difference between the two versions did not go unnoticed.

General de Gaulle arrived back in London to assess with his colleagues the results of the Anfa meetings. They were in his view 'modest'. There had been no agreement with General Giraud. The attempt by the United States and Britain to submerge Fighting France into a North African-based American satellite regime had been crass and obviously unacceptable, but the mere suggestion, and the fierceness with which it was urged, had soured relations not just with Giraud, which did not matter very much, but with the British, which did – and with Churchill in particular, which mattered very much indeed.

On the credit side, de Gaulle had come out of Anfa with his pride more or less intact, in spite of obvious attempts by both Allies to pull him down; and he had won two important friends, Hopkins and Macmillan, both of whom saw in him the qualities of persistence and courage that were missing in so many of the defeated French. The two codenames given him by the Allies, 'Ramrod' and 'Wormwood', told their own story about other participants' attitudes towards him, and certainly reflected the view of both the American and British general staffs. Hopkins and Macmillan knew better.

Thus, although he was in bad odour again with Churchill, de Gaulle's showing at Casablanca had won him more support than he thought. Macmillan now perceived him as a 'statesman', and even Murphy recognised the force of de Gaulle's ambition – to return France to the rank of a great power – and the speed of his tactical perception that the war was now effectively won. It was true, but nobody at Casablanca fully appreciated de Gaulle's conclusion, which seemed to him obvious, that he had limited time in which to extract concessions in France's favour from the Allies, and that on no account could he surrender any of the ground that he had won. The Allies were fighting the Germans; he was fighting for France.

De Gaulle's one serious error was to misread completely the effect of Anfa on his relations with President Roosevelt. Having originally regarded him as yet another failed French general, Roosevelt now found him personally detestable – arrogant, argumentative, egocentric and opinionated. The same epithets could be, and indeed have been, applied to Roosevelt himself, and that may be why the President came to dislike de Gaulle so much – they were two of a kind.

De Gaulle himself thought that he had got on rather well with Roosevelt. But even while they were still at Anfa Roosevelt had been telling jokes about him. De Gaulle had explained at their meeting that Joan of Arc had established her legitimacy by taking up arms against the English invader. But on the following day the General had suggested that he was to be a Clemenceau and Giraud a Foch. Roosevelt immediately invented a story that de Gaulle claimed to be both Joan of Arc and Clemenceau at once. By the time he had returned to Washington the already apocryphal story had been embroidered by the President to ludicrous lengths. For instance, he told Hull that de Gaulle, 'walking up to [me] rather stiffly, had remarked: "I am Joan of Arc, I am Clemenceau." '[22] Roosevelt thought it all tremendously amusing, and so, with less conviction, did Washington society.

Nevertheless, in a press conference in London on 9 February, de Gaulle went out of his way to praise Roosevelt as the man who had the highest aims in the war, while patronising Churchill. Furthermore, he wrote on 14 February to Hull, of all people, an unctuous letter asking him to convey to the President the expression of his great pleasure in having established a first contact. A Frenchman, the letter went on, could not but be deeply touched by the President's feelings of 'ardent sympathy towards France'.

This 'ardent sympathy towards France' certainly did not extend to Fighting France. Both Roosevelt and Hull had been irritated by de Gaulle's press conference of 9 February, in which de Gaulle had said that what he wanted, and what France wanted, was not just an agreement between two generals, but a union of France's Empire for the liberation of France. That was not what Roosevelt wanted at all; he wanted an agreement between the prima donnas so that everybody else could get on with the war and the American press would stop harassing him.

The fact was that Roosevelt and Hull were becoming increasingly nettled by press criticism of their French policy, criticism which they believed was provoked by de Gaulle's information service in London, and which found fertile material in the defection to Fighting France of French sailors from former Vichy ships immobilised in American ports. Hull sent Eden a stiff request to take steps to tell them to stop. But there was nothing that he or Churchill could do, since the British and de Gaulle were hardly on speaking terms.

Worse still, when Eden visited Washington the following month, President Roosevelt unburdened himself at a private dinner on 22 March of his views on the future of post-war Europe. 'Armaments should be concentrated in the hands of Britain, the United States and Russia,' he argued. 'The smaller powers should have nothing more dangerous than rifles . . . the three powers should police Europe in general . . . a new state called "Wallonia" would include the Walloon parts of Belgium with Luxembourg, Alsace-Lorraine and part of Northern France.'[23]

So much for Roosevelt's 'ardent sympathy' for France. But at least Casablanca had one favourable result. At the end of February 1943 Roosevelt sent Jean Monnet to Algiers, ostensibly to supervise the shipments of arms to French forces but in practice to act as Giraud's political guide and mentor. Monnet had earned great respect in Washington for his inventive intelligence and his diplomatic skills, and it was felt that he, of all people, could give Giraud the dimension of political awareness which he so obviously lacked. On his arrival, Monnet struck up a friendship with Macmillan, and it was Macmillan who convinced the initially hostile Monnet that de Gaulle was the only figure around whom a credible future administration could be built. As Roosevelt had said, Giraud was a dud.

But the future was one thing. The present was another, and was decidedly bleak. General de Gaulle had requested facilities to go to Cairo on 22 January, and was met with a violent refusal from Churchill. The same response came back, to the same request, at the end of February. 'The old boy is in a rage again with de Gaulle,' wrote Oliver Harvey. 'He wishes force to be used if necessary to prevent his leaving the country to visit Syria and Africa . . . declares that he is our foe.'[24] René Massigli, now the commissioner for international affairs in the French National Committee, did all he could, but Churchill and the

War Cabinet were adamant. De Gaulle moved out of his office in a fury and went home to Hampstead. 'I hold you responsible,' Churchill bellowed down the telephone to Charles Peake, 'that the Monster of Hampstead does not escape.'[25]

De Gaulle had been, and still was, very anxious to get to North Africa. Monnet had been working on Giraud – with some success. Much of the Vichyite legislation had been repealed, officials resigned and, to crown it all, Giraud had delivered a speech, somewhat against his own inclinations, asserting the democratic and republican basis of any future French government. Monnet had written the bulk of it; but under Monnet's influence Giraud was, at least in public, moving more and more towards de Gaulle's view.

Yet neither Giraud nor his staff were prepared to concede in advance much political territory to de Gaulle. Indeed, they were planning a manoeuvre of their own to block the General's progress decisively. The manoeuvre could not have been more surprising; it was no less than a plan to bring over to Algiers the one man who still commanded the loyalty of the bulk of the French army: Marshal Pétain himself.

The British got wind of this plan from André Poniatowski, Giraud's ADC, some time in April 1943. The Americans were presumably aware of it as well, but there is no written record of the plan, for the simple reason that, at least on the British side, the memorandum recording the information that they had had from Poniatowski was burnt immediately, with strict instructions from Macmillan's political office that on no account should London be informed. Churchill, they thought, would have had a seizure at the mere idea. On the American side there was presumably similar discretion, on the grounds that even Roosevelt would have felt that putting Pétain in charge of the French Empire would be going too far.

In the event the plan came to nothing, not because Pétain was not prepared to come over – Giraud and Poniatowski must have assumed that he was – but because of the logistics of the operation. The fact was that the old Marshal was incontinent, and while an aeroplane could be found to lift him from Vichy to Corsica, which was a relatively short hop, there was no aeroplane with the facilities that Pétain required to continue the journey on the longer leg from Corsica to North Africa. Clearly, the Marshal could not be expected to suffer the indignities that would have resulted, so the whole operation had to be called off.

It was therefore no wonder that de Gaulle wanted to get to Algiers as quickly as possible. Of course, he had no knowledge – as far as is known – of the Pétain plan, but he was in no doubt that London was not the place to be while Giraud was in sole charge in Algiers. In the end, it was Massigli who finally managed to break the diplomatic log-jam, by reminding the British, in the politest possible way, of General de Gaulle's position with the Resistance in metropolitan France. It was becoming de Gaulle's strongest card, and became even stronger as Moulin's mission came nearer to success.

On 2 April Churchill agreed to see the General as a prelude to his going to Algiers. The interview was free from explosions, at least. But the explosion came two days later, when a message came, purporting to be from Eisenhower, asking de Gaulle to postpone his trip in view of the impending battle for Tunisia. Of course, it did not originate from Eisenhower at all, but from the British Foreign Office, as later became apparent. De Gaulle was convinced that Churchill was behind it all, and, when he found out about the British involvement, responded on 4 May with a ferocious attack on Giraud's administration, which reminded Monnet, as he wrote to Hopkins, of the speeches that Hitler made before the Czechoslovakian affair.

It was in this atmosphere of bad temper and mutual suspicion that Churchill visited Washington for his next round of discussions with Roosevelt. On arrival, it was clear that he was to be treated to the same tirade against de Gaulle as Eden had endured two months earlier. 'De Gaulle,' Roosevelt wrote in a memorandum to Churchill, 'is without question taking his vicious propaganda staff down to Algiers to stir up strife . . . he has the Messianic complex . . . I do not know what to do with de Gaulle. Possibly you would like to make him Governor of Madagascar!'[26] Hull was sent to soften up Churchill with stories of the iniquities of the Fighting French.

Roosevelt went on and on, and in the end Churchill bowed to the pressure. On 22 May Churchill wrote three long telegrams to Eden detailing the American complaints against de Gaulle. The allegations were numerous and specific. For example, the FBI had discovered that sailors from the *Richelieu*, then in New York harbour, had been bribed to desert to Fighting France, and that the source of the funds was British. It was an impressive indictment, and ended: 'it seems to me most questionable that we should allow this marplot and mischief-maker to continue the harm he is doing.' But in one sentence the Prime Minister betrayed himself: 'He has never fought since he left France and took pains to have his wife brought out safely beforehand.'[27]

It was not true – and Churchill's memory, normally so reliable, had curiously failed him.

As luck would have it, these infuriated telegrams arrived just at the time that the tide was running in de Gaulle's favour. To start with, whole units of troops in North Africa were abandoning Giraud's army and joining Fighting France. Then, in mid-May, he received news from Moulin that the National Council of the Resistance had been formally created. In its first declaration, it affirmed that 'the people of France will never agree to General de Gaulle being subordinate to General Giraud, and demand the immediate installation of a provisional government in Algiers under the presidency of General de Gaulle, with General Giraud as military chief'. It was game and set, if not yet match, to de Gaulle. Giraud and Monnet recognised as much, and on 17 May Giraud invited de Gaulle to come to Algiers, on two conditions: first that a future government would be headed by a Cabinet rather than a single individual; and, second, that the terms of the French constitution would be observed – in other words, there would be no personal dictatorship.

If these conditions were agreed, Giraud suggested, a central committee could be formed, over which de Gaulle and Giraud would preside alternately. It would be composed of six members, with each of the two generals choosing two of the other members. It was a perfectly satisfactory basis for negotiation. De Gaulle intended to accept Giraud's conditions and his invitation, and accordingly applied to the British for transport facilities.

It was now very much in the balance. The War Cabinet met on the evening of 23 May 1943 to consider a recommendation from the Prime Minister that relations with de Gaulle should be broken. At the same time, they had before them absolute evidence that de Gaulle's position within France was unassailable, and that Giraud was now prepared to do the deal for which they, particularly Eden, had worked so long and hard. The War Cabinet deliberated conscientiously, but were quite firm. Eden wrote in his diary that evening; 'Cabinet at 9 p.m. re de Gaulle and Winston's proposal to break with him now. – Everybody against and very brave about it in his absence.'[28] They had decided in favour of de Gaulle and against Churchill. As Churchill later wrote, 'It hung in the balance whether we should not break finally at this juncture with this most difficult man. However, time and patience afforded tolerable solutions.'[29] Indeed they did, but only thanks to Churchill's colleagues in the War Cabinet.

General de Gaulle left London for Algiers on 30 May. 'Before leaving England,' he recorded later, 'I wrote to King George VI to tell him how grateful I was to him, to his government and to his people for the reception they had given me during the tragic days of 1940 and for the hospitality they had subsequently accorded to Free France and its leader. Intending to pay a visit to Mr Churchill, I learned that he had just left for an "unknown destination". It was therefore Mr Eden to whom I made my adieux. The meeting was a friendly one. "What do you think of us?" the British Minister asked me. "No one could be more agreeable than the British people," I observed. "As for your politics, I cannot always say the same." When we were discussing the many occasions on which I had had dealings with the British Government, Mr Eden good-humouredly asked: "Do you know that you have caused us more difficulties than all our other European allies put together?" "I don't doubt it," I replied, smiling in my turn. "France is a great power." '[30]

9

CHECKMATE FOR 'KINGPIN'

Je suis ici chez moi.★

For the casual traveller, the most rewarding approach to Algiers is from the sea. The view from the deck of a ship entering the large harbour stands comparison with any of those of the more famous ports of the northern Mediterranean. The city lies in the foreground, rising sharply from the docks and the business district to the spacious residential boulevards which run along the contours of the surrounding steep slopes, which in their turn lead the eye upwards to the mountains behind. The strength of the sun lends sharpness to the contrast between the blue of the sea, the white of the colonial villas and the green of the palms and pine trees in the parks and on the hills. Set in its great natural amphitheatre, 'Alger la Blanche' was, and still is, one of the loveliest cities on the Mediterranean littoral.

General de Gaulle, of course, was no casual traveller, and his arrival, at about midday on 30 May 1943, was not by sea but at the dingy military airport of Bufarik, some way outside the city to the south. It was hot and dusty, and the sun was fierce. But the photographs of his arrival show quite distinctly that, after emerging from the aircraft's low door and pausing for a moment to stretch himself to his full height after what had been several hours in a cramped seat in the small aircraft, there was a smile on his face as he moved forward to salute and shake hands with General Giraud who had come to meet him. It was a moment to savour.

Indeed, the reception was in marked contrast to his experience at Casablanca in January. There was a guard of honour to present arms and

---

★ 'I am here at home.' Charles de Gaulle to Henri Giraud on his arrival in Algiers, 30 May 1943. Quoted in C. Paillat, *L'Echiquier d'Alger*, page 251; Laffont, Paris, 1967.

be inspected, and a band to play the 'Marseillaise'; Giraud was there to greet him as well as Catroux; Murphy and one of Macmillan's aides stood discreetly behind the French officers; and they were all driven away not in American but in French cars. To be sure, there was one irritant; much to his annoyance, Giraud had ordered a news blackout, and the public were unaware of the fact that General Charles de Gaulle was once again on French soil, this time for good. It was a nuisance, but one that could be corrected later.

'General de Gaulle's mood seemed to vary from comparative calm to extreme excitability,' Macmillan wrote to his wife the day after de Gaulle's arrival. 'He was clearly very hostile to the Americans and, to a somewhat less extent, to the British . . . Monnet still finds it difficult to make up his mind as to whether the General is a dangerous demagogue or mad or both.'[1] But the General's mood was softened by a great luncheon banquet – 'this good French custom', as he called it[2] – served in honour of the occasion at the Summer Palace, the most opulent construction in Algiers. In the Great Hall, Giraud sat opposite de Gaulle, who was flanked by General Georges, a recent arrival from France, on one side and by Monnet on the other; forty other guests sat down with them. By the time the feast was approaching its stately conclusion, word had spread through the city of de Gaulle's arrival, and there were popular demonstrations of welcome that continued well into the scented Mediterranean evening. As might be imagined, de Gaulle enjoyed this carnival much more than his host.

General Giraud had set up his headquarters in the Summer Palace and was guarded by a detachment of former Vichy troops. De Gaulle, on the other hand, set up his headquarters in a much more modest villa nearby, known as Les Glycines, and was guarded, as might be imagined, by a detachment of Fighting French troops. The question that now had to be resolved, indeed the question that had dominated discussion in Algiers in the weeks leading up to de Gaulle's arrival, was simple: could the two sides possibly come together in any sort of harmony?

The question was also intriguing the rest of the world, and by far the most surprising visitor to Algiers, landing on 28 May having left London for an 'unknown destination', was the British Prime Minister himself. Ostensibly, he was in Algiers to keep an eye on the development of Operation Husky, the assault on Sicily, but his real motive was to witness, in a state of excitement that was almost boyish, the 'nuptials', as Roosevelt called it, of the two opposing French generals. He could not wait to be best man at this uniquely interesting wedding.

But no sooner had Churchill arrived than he started to doubt his own ability to play the role. To start with, he was very tired. He needed a rest. He was 'quite dead when he first arrived from America,' Eden told Harvey a week later, 'and could hardly move, but the sun and the bathing had gradually revived him'.[3] The memory of the rows at Anfa was revived by his return to North Africa, and he was not in the mood for more of those. Eden was therefore sent for. In his telegram to the Labour leader and deputy Prime Minister, Clement Attlee, asking for Eden to join him, Churchill wrote that the Foreign Secretary would be much better fitted to be best man at the Giraud–de Gaulle wedding than he was. Later, at dinner with Admiral Cunningham, Macmillan and Murphy, Churchill was more direct, claiming again that de Gaulle was anti-British and anti-American and, furthermore, that they could count on him 'to play the fool'. De Gaulle was fully capable of a *putsch*, and there should be no illusions about his thirst for personal power. With the Prime Minister in such a mood, Eden would be a better best man, but Churchill wanted to be there in the background; there was too much at stake for him to leave everything to the Foreign Secretary.

Negotiations between the two French protagonists began in earnest on the morning of 31 May at the Lycée Fromentin. On Giraud's side of the table were Georges and Monnet; on de Gaulle's were Catroux, Massigli and Philip. After an initial agreement that those present would be constituted into a committee, to be enlarged later, de Gaulle played his first high card. He had, he stated firmly to the new committee, two requirements: first, that the military command structure be subordinated to the political will as expressed by the committee; and, second, that under no circumstances could the prominent former Vichy officials, Noguès, Boisson and Peyrouton, be allowed to continue in their jobs.

There were, of course, perfectly good grounds in principle for de Gaulle's demands. The subordination of the military to the civil power, provided that the civil power was able to give coherent instructions, had long been the basis of the relationship between army and state, and that relationship had served France well over the years. All officer cadets at St Cyr had been carefully schooled in the doctrine. As for the three offending Vichyites, each of them had war records that in the eyes of the Fighting French amounted to nothing less than treason. Peyrouton had tried to crush the Resistance – and incidentally had signed de Gaulle's death warrant. Noguès, as commander in Morocco, had refused the *Massilia* passengers a safe haven in 1940; he had sent Daladier and Georges Mandel back to prison; and he had turned French guns on the

Americans in the Torch landings. Boisson had fought, with determination and ruthlessness, against the Free French in the Dakar fiasco. All three had French blood on their hands.

But however good the grounds, such demands at this point constituted a clear challenge to Giraud. These were issues that were thought to have been conveniently buried. In fact, they had been swept aside by the Americans and British at Casablanca. It had simply been assumed that Giraud would be commander-in-chief, and that America's Vichy friends would be suitably accommodated. Indeed, it was on that basis that de Gaulle had been invited to Algiers in the first place, and it was precisely that basis that was being challenged.

The crisis erupted quickly. Giraud was outraged, but this only had the effect of allowing his fellow general to provoke a heated discussion, and finally to get up and march out of the room, slamming the door as he went. Giraud retaliated the next day. He claimed that de Gaulle was indeed planning a *putsch* and put armoured units near the capital on high alert. A state of emergency was declared in Algiers itself; all public meetings and parades were forbidden, and all troops were confined to barracks. As a final gesture, Giraud appointed as emergency commissioner for security none other than de Gaulle's old enemy, Admiral Muselier, who at once commandeered a warship with a view to spiriting de Gaulle off to Tangiers.

De Gaulle in turn sent messages to the Fighting French troops under de Larminat and Leclerc to make for Algiers at top speed. Much to the dismay of Macmillan and Murphy, and to all the other onlookers, it seemed not just as though the talks had already broken down, but that there was a serious possibility of armed clashes between the rival camps.

But the eccentric appointment of Muselier had an unexpected outcome. Peyrouton, still officially the Governor General of Algiers, was so put out that he abruptly resigned. He sent two letters, one to Giraud and – quite unnecessarily since he had as yet no legal standing – to de Gaulle. Even while Giraud was trying to persuade Peyrouton to reconsider, de Gaulle announced the resignation to the press. This was too much even for the faithful Catroux, who demanded an interview with de Gaulle, told him that he had usurped the legal authority, and then himself straightaway resigned.

Catroux's anger did not last and he soon pulled himself together. But Giraud had missed the critical moment in which to assert his authority, which he could have done, quite legally, by arresting de Gaulle. Having missed that chance, he would thereafter have to accept the consequences. In announcing Peyrouton's resignation, de Gaulle had publicly assumed a political role for which there was not a shred of legal support, and Giraud had done nothing about it. He was, as a result, no longer in a position to claim to be the supreme authority in Algiers. The cuckoo had forced its way into the nest and, once there, was not to be moved.

The Peyrouton affair presented de Gaulle with an important tactical advantage, but in reality no issue of principle was involved. The fundamental difference between de Gaulle and Giraud concerned not just the shape of a future administration but also its ultimate aim. Giraud wanted peace and order in North Africa, so that he could get on with what really interested him – the serious military business. De Gaulle's ambitions were of a different order, as he carefully explained to Murphy and Macmillan when they called on him on 1 June, in an effort to patch up the crisis that de Gaulle himself had manufactured.

'He was at his best, and [Murphy] was much impressed,' Macmillan recorded. 'He set out his feelings in a powerful and even noble way. Naturally there were some harsh phrases. But it was clear to us both that here was a more powerful character than any other Frenchman in or outside France.' De Gaulle described to them the humiliation of 1940 and the regeneration for which he and Fighting France were working. As the meeting finished, he took Murphy's arm and said, 'Why do you not understand me? Why do you always interfere with me? It is a mistake France will not understand, why your politicians are against me. I represent future France, and it will be better for us all if you support me.'[4] Murphy had no answer, since in truth there was none.

The crisis receded and discussions between the two sides were resumed on the morning of 3 June. It was then that the new French Committee for National Liberation (FCNL) was born. The document setting up the committee had been drafted by de Gaulle and was hardly debated at all. Giraud, not for the first or the last time, hardly read what he was signing. The committee would be 'the central French power' directing the national war effort and exercising French sovereignty over all liberated territories. It would cede its powers only to a provisional government in a liberated France, in conformity with the laws of the republic.

As for the composition of the committee, Giraud and de Gaulle were to be co-presidents, Massigli would be commissioner for foreign affairs, Philip for the interior, Monnet for armaments, Catroux for Muslim affairs, and General Georges would be commissioner without portfolio. The Vichy 'proconsuls', Noguès and Boisson, were unceremoniously sacked as the first act of the committee, and there was no question of Peyrouton's reinstatement: in addition to his job as commissioner, Catroux was made Governor General of Algiers in Peyrouton's place.

It was a reasonable compromise. De Gaulle had felt obliged to make a concession in accepting a system of co-presidents, but he had secured most of his other objectives, with the important exception of the subordination of the military to the civil power. Giraud was to be commander-in-chief responsible to the full committee, of which he himself was co-president, which pleased him, but he in turn had had to drop the 'proconsuls'. There had been some compromise in each position, for which Macmillan was quick to claim the credit.

De Gaulle seems to have believed that the thing could be made to work, provided Giraud was prepared to stay within the rules – which was, as it happened, a rather ambitious proviso. Thus he felt able to write to Macmillan telling him 'how much I appreciated the action which you have exercised here in the name of the Government of which you are a part, and to what point your sympathy is precious to me, which permits me also to call it our friendship . . .'[5]

Such friendly sentiments, however, did not deter de Gaulle from continuing to pursue his course without consulting either Macmillan or Murphy. Indeed, it was at his instigation, and in total secrecy, that the committee on 7 June decided to double its size, to include Pleven, Diethelm and Henri Bonnet from London, for colonies, economic affairs and information respectively, Tixier from Washington for labour, and, on Giraud's side, René Mayer, Jules Abadie and Maurice Couve de Murville★ for transport, justice and finance.

It would take time for de Gaulle's supporters to get to Algiers to participate in the committee's deliberations. His solution to this problem was to try to make sure the committee did not meet in the interim. He therefore provoked a second crisis. On 8 June he reiterated his demand that the political and military powers should be separated, and that the second should be subordinated to the first. General Giraud, he said, must resign either as co-president or commander-in-chief. He could

---

★ Maurice Couve de Murville (1907–): Civil servant and politician. Civil service career until Second World War: then Vichy; then Gen. Sec. to Giraud in Algiers March 1943, member French Ctte for Nat. Liberation June–Nov. 1943; Ambassador, Rome 1945, Cairo 1950–4, Washington 1955–6, Bonn 1956–8; Minister Foreign Affairs 1958–68; Prime Minister 1968–9.

not hold the two posts at the same time. When Giraud refused point-blank even to discuss the matter, de Gaulle announced that he would attend no more meetings of the committee unless its structure were changed to that effect. He then retired to his villa in a highly contrived sulk.

News of all this manoeuvring came as an unpleasant shock to Churchill, who had considered that the original smaller committee was exactly what was required. The seven members had been invited to a celebratory lunch at Churchill's villa, at which he took the opportunity to explain to de Gaulle that the Allies were determined to protect their military interests, and that they might have had to 'take steps if too brutal a shock had occurred; if, for instance, you had devoured Giraud in one mouthful.'[6] Since this had obviously not happened, on his departure from Algiers, Churchill wrote to Roosevelt an encouraging report on the general North African situation, saying that should de Gaulle prove 'violent or unreasonable' he would be in a minority of five to two on the committee, and therefore could be considered to be satisfactorily under control.

He had spoken far too soon. Once the committee had been doubled in size, there was a distinct Gaullist bias, since both Monnet and Couve de Murville were now edging towards the de Gaulle camp, Monnet on the grounds that Giraud was incapable of any political decision, Couve in the belief that de Gaulle would win in the end and, reasonably enough, he wanted to end up on the winning side.

On 12 June the new members of the committee arrived in Algiers, and de Gaulle decided that he was now able to leave his self-imposed exile. He called a meeting of the committee for the 14th. By now both the American and the British Governments were aware of the enlargement of the committee, and its significance, and were becoming increasingly annoyed. Murphy and Macmillan were instructed to stop the meeting of the 14th from taking place. Roosevelt cabled Eisenhower, telling him to plan an occupation of North and possibly West Africa if de Gaulle succeeded in arrogating to himself the position of commander-in-chief of the army, and to take any action he deemed appropriate if de Gaulle assumed total political power. Churchill cabled Macmillan supporting these American moves, and sent a secret circular to the British press to the effect that he was concerned about the enthusiasm being shown by them to de Gaulle and Fighting France, and they should be much cooler.

None of this agitation had any great effect, largely because de Gaulle was out of range. What might have worked with him in London did not work with him in Algiers. In fact, even de Gaulle's opponents were irritated by this blatant interference in French affairs; nor did the British and American press pay a whit of attention to the official 'guidance' they were receiving. Monnet seemed now to be distancing himself from his former American protectors; he himself recalled Murphy coming to see him at that time with Macmillan to reproach him for allowing de Gaulle to establish his ascendancy, but that he told them, in effect, to mind their own business. 'Murphy', he wrote later, 'drew the correct conclusion that a new epoch had begun . . . and subsequently observed: "Monnet thus politely declared French independence." '[7]

Roosevelt himself was in a fury. 'I am fed up with de Gaulle . . .' he wrote to Churchill on 17 June 1943. 'We must divorce ourselves from [him] . . . unreliable, uncooperative, and disloyal to both our governments . . . interested far more in political machinations than . . . in the prosecution of the war'.[8] He cabled Eisenhower again: 'It is important that you should know for your very secret information that we may possibly break with de Gaulle in the next few days.'[9]

But Roosevelt was no more successful now in 'breaking' with de Gaulle than Churchill had been a month earlier. To give him his due, he tried hard. On 19 June, on explicit instruction from Washington, Eisenhower summoned de Gaulle and Giraud to tell them that he was prepared to deal further with the French, and in particular to supply the arms that were required, only if Giraud was quite clearly commander-in-chief. He was not prepared to deal with anybody else. De Gaulle replied immediately that he, for one, refused to accept American dictation of the French military command structure. That was the end of the meeting.

Two days later the full Committee for National Liberation met to consider Eisenhower's message and after long deliberation produced their response. They set up another military committee, of which both de Gaulle and Giraud were members but with de Gaulle as chairman. The military command was split, with Giraud as commander of the North African army and de Gaulle as commander of all other forces in the Empire. It was absurd, and would never work, as de Gaulle knew full well. But at least it was enough to keep the flow of American arms coming. In the next few months, 450,000 tons of military equipment were delivered, enough to equip four infantry divisions, two armoured divisions and four tank battalions.

The attempted American 'break' with de Gaulle had failed. The

British could not break with him, as had been shown in May, and Roosevelt was much too shrewd to pursue the matter too far alone, and with sole responsibility. De Gaulle's standing with public opinion, in Britain, in America, and in France itself, was the card with which he could trump both the Prime Minister and the President.

The frustration, both in Washington and London, was evident in bad-tempered discussions about whether or not the French Committee for National Liberation should be 'recognised'. It was only Eden's persistence, with help from Cadogan and Oliver Harvey, and finally from Eisenhower, who, after all, had to work with them, that won Churchill round; but nothing would move Roosevelt, and the argument whether or not there should be a common Allied position dragged on into the summer.

Suddenly, on 2 July, General Giraud left for Washington. It was, to say the least, a tactical error. He had hoped during his visit to firm up arrangements for the arming of eleven French divisions that he believed Roosevelt had promised him at Casablanca. Roosevelt in his turn was determined to grant Giraud the sort of reception that would give him the aura of a favoured prince. There was tea with the Roosevelt family in the garden of the White House on his first day and an official dinner at the White House the following day; there were talks with high officials at the State Department and the Department of Defense, visits to munitions factories, press conferences, and so on. Giraud himself was mightily impressed.

Meanwhile, de Gaulle had been left with sole authority in Algiers, and he had made good use of it. There was a purge of former Vichy supporters in the administration. Indeed, the most active collaborators, particularly those in charge of the notorious Camp Hadjerat in the Sahara, where pro-Allied and Gaullist sympathisers had been kept in appalling conditions, were arrested. The administration was now firmly Gaullist, and efficient as well – Allied representatives at all levels recognised that the committee was more effective than any government France had had for many years.

As a further gesture, de Gaulle toured North Africa to show himself to the people whom he was now obviously governing. The response was overwhelmingly enthusiastic, and this in turn increased de Gaulle's own confidence in his position. The rhetoric became less restrained. The gestures were more flamboyant – his arms stretched wide and high above his head in salutation of the crowd – and his voice grew more trumpet-like in tone. The high point of the tour was his speech in the

Place du Forum in Algiers on Bastille Day, in which he proclaimed national renewal and the unity of a whole people at war. 'Let us lift up our heads, let us close our ranks in the spirit of brotherhood, let us all march together, through the struggle and the victory, towards our new destiny!'[10]

By the time Giraud arrived back on 25 July, after a leisurely tour through New York, Ottawa and London, his position in Algiers had been fatally undermined. The Gaullist pack closed in. He had made the mistake, he was told by the committee at its meeting of 31 July, of representing himself in Washington as the army's commander independent of the authority of the committee. It was therefore decided that although he would remain co-president he would give up the right to preside over the committee's sessions. General de Gaulle was henceforward to be not only the one effective co-president but would also remain chairman of the military committee, which was now transformed into the Committee for National Defence. General Giraud was to be commander-in-chief of all French forces – subordinate, of course to the Committee for National Defence. Again, Giraud signed the decree almost without reading it.

De Gaulle was quite content with the outcome. If Giraud really accepted the supremacy of the committee, it had many advantages: Eisenhower could deal with his preferred commander, and one who commanded all the army instead of part of it; de Gaulle himself retained political power; and, organisationally, there was more than enough work for a commander-in-chief, now that Admirals Robert in Martinique and Godfroy in Alexandria had joined Fighting France, and the Italian campaign was being planned. Indeed, once Eisenhower had accepted de Gaulle's argument that Fighting France should be part of the Italian force and not, as originally intended, left behind in North Africa, Giraud was able to look forward to the greatest command of his distinguished military career.

There remained the knotty issue of 'recognition' by the Allies, which became even knottier as de Gaulle strengthened his grip on the committee. It surfaced again at the Anglo-American summit at Quebec in late August 1943. Churchill and Eden were becoming seriously concerned about arrangements for post-war France. In their opinion, a strong France was vital to the success of a post-war Europe, and the French Committee for National Liberation in Algiers, whether they liked it or not – and Churchill at the time certainly did not – was the only possible basis for such a France. Other governments in exile, those

of Poland, Belgium, Norway and Greece, had come to the same conclusion and had extended recognition to the FCNL.

The United States, on the other hand, was determined to remain out
of step. The State Department had hardly given any thought at all to the
problem of post-war Europe, and there was no sign that Roosevelt disliked de Gaulle any less than he had at Anfa. Hull and Eden started a
desultory discussion of the issue at the beginning of the Quebec conference, but Hull brought up all the old complaints, adding that 'the
Committee in Algiers would be ephemeral, and would destroy itself'.[11]
It was obvious that they were not going to agree, and it was left to
Churchill to raise the issue direct with the President. He fared no better with Roosevelt than Eden had with Hull. By the last day there was
still no agreement, and the summiteers decided to go their own ways.

On 27 August the British announced recognition of the FCNL as
'administering those French overseas territories which acknowledge its
authority . . . [and] . . . as the body qualified to ensure the conduct of
the French effort in the war'.[12] The United States announced that it
'takes note, with sympathy, of the desire of the Committee to be regarded as the body qualified to ensure the administration and defense of
French interests. The extent to which it may be possible to give effect
to this desire must however be reserved for consideration in each case as
it arises.'[13] The Soviet Union, on the other hand, recognised the FCNL
as 'representing the state interests of the French Republic' and as 'the
sole representative of all French patriots in the struggle against
Hitlerism'.[14] There was no doubt which version de Gaulle preferred.

By early September, twenty-six states had recognised the FCNL, and
de Gaulle was able to claim, reasonably enough, that this was convincing proof of their solidarity for 'victory and peace'. But there was still
the nagging problem of the co-presidency. De Gaulle's co-president was
showing himself dangerously independent of the committee. The liberation of Corsica, for instance – a brilliant military operation
completed in September by Giraud with help from local communist
insurgents – was planned and carried out without the knowledge of the
FCNL in Algiers. That was bad enough, but worse was to come. The
Italians signed an armistice on 4 September, without any French representative present and without de Gaulle's knowledge, although he had
earlier been promised a presence at the event. It turned out that the
Allies had kept General Giraud informed all along, and that Giraud had
omitted to inform the committee. To a man, they were furious.

On 25 September, the committee struck again. The co-presidency was abolished and de Gaulle was voted sole president. After consultations with a wider group of Fighting French, particularly Resistance leaders who were in Algiers at the time, on the pretext of making the procedure appear more democratic, they voted Giraud off, along with Georges, Abadie and Couve de Murville, all Giraud nominees. The upshot was now plain: either Giraud accepted the orders of the committee or he would be sacked. He had no power left to prevent it.

Even by the autumn of 1943, therefore, it was clear that de Gaulle had decisively won the battle for supremacy, and had won it not just against the Giraudists but against fierce and sustained American opposition. The British had been less hostile, but as always their main preoccupation was the alliance with the United States. Nevertheless, it was with the British that the next conflagration broke out, and, as before, it all started in the Levant.

General Catroux had left Beirut for Algiers when de Gaulle moved there from London, leaving as his successor as French delegate-general in the Levant Jean Helleu, the former Vichy ambassador to Turkey. It was ambassador Helleu, therefore, who supervised the promised elections that finally took place in Syria and the Lebanon in July 1943. Needless to say, the French made every effort to swing them their way – as indeed did the British. Neither intervention had much effect, and the result was a massive victory for nationalist and anti-French parties in both countries.

The new Lebanese parliament did not take long to assert the Lebanon's independence from France and the dissolution of the mandate, which they did on 8 November. Ambassador Helleu riposted by moving in troops and putting the President and his senior ministers in jail. For good measure he suspended the Lebanese constitution and dissolved the parliament. There were riots in Beirut and in other major cities, which were put down with ferocity, mostly by Senegalese troops. The United States, the Soviet Union and Arab neighbours protested vigorously. Spears wrote to Helleu in strong terms, referring to 'inadmissibly dictatorial measures, taken against a small and defenceless people'.[15]

De Gaulle had convinced himself that the whole affair was part of a plot by the British to remove France from the eastern Mediterranean. On 11 November he cabled Helleu: 'The forceful measures you have seen fit to take were no doubt necessary. At any rate, I consider that they were necessary, since you have taken them.'[16] It was no doubt the best he could do under the circumstances, however bizarre his argument, but the committee were not so convinced, and Catroux was sent to resolve the matter as quickly as possible. He was sure he could sort it out; Helleu, he told Macmillan, had made a complete fool of himself and had not even telegraphed Algiers for instructions. Besides, he may well have been drunk when he gave the arrest order – he was known to 'cease to be lucid at certain hours of the day'.[17] Macmillan was quite satisfied that Catroux would settle matters, particularly if it meant putting down Spears, whom he found boring and pompous.

At this point, the British in Cairo intervened. Their entry on the scene could hardly have been more clumsily managed. Richard Casey, Lyttelton's successor in Cairo, arrived hotfoot and delivered a note to Catroux: he had three days to release the prisoners before the British declared martial law and sent in their own troops. It was, Catroux exclaimed furiously, 'another Fashoda'. 'What does he mean by "Fashoda"?' Casey asked Spears.[18] In Algiers de Gaulle, while in public defending Helleu's action – on the grounds that the mandate could not be unilaterally terminated, and that therefore the decision of the new Lebanese parliament had been unconstitutional – in private thundered against the British in general and Spears in particular.

In the end, the dispute blew over after the usual period of bickering between the two sides. Helleu was brought back to a minor job in Algiers, the prisoners were released, and things gradually returned to normal in the Lebanon. But no sooner had that fire been extinguished than another broke out, this time in Algiers itself.

In its pursuit of Vichyites, the French Committee for National Liberation had ordered the arrest of Peyrouton, Boisson and a former Vichy Foreign Minister, Pierre-Etienne Flandin. Again, from the Gaullist point of view, the arrests of these traitors, as they were considered, was perfectly reasonable. The difficulty was that all of them had been afforded some form of Allied protection, Peyrouton to bring him back from Argentina, Boisson to persuade him to bring Dakar and West Africa over to Darlan, and Flandin as a potential member of the Darlan government in North Africa. Roosevelt, prompted in this case by Churchill, instructed Eisenhower to 'direct' the FCNL to take no action against the three unfortunates. The 'instruction' was headed off by Macmillan, who realised the effect it would have on de Gaulle and the committee, and in the end, after a flurry of diplomatic activity, it was cancelled. The excuse for the Allied retreat was that the committee had acted under pressure from the Resistance within France. But Roosevelt and Churchill knew that they were powerless to do anything to help their protégés, and both felt guilty and angry that their protection had proved so meaningless, and they blamed de Gaulle all the more.

The year 1943 ended in some respects on a surly note. Churchill was irritated by the arrests and by what he called the 'persecution mania of the committee', and 'their violent assertion of French dignity'. It needed all the persuasive powers of Macmillan and Eden to keep him calm. Roosevelt, egged on by Cordell Hull, was still determined to 'eliminate de Gaulle and [to] give the Committee a sense of the realities of the situation'. De Gaulle, for his part, was convinced that 'Roosevelt and Churchill have corrupted this war . . . they have chosen the easiest way and that should never be done in war . . . the result: Pétain, Badoglio, von Papen . . . and it isn't yet over.'[19]

But in other ways 1943 ended with a much improved position for General de Gaulle and Fighting France. The former Vichy army and the army of Fighting France had been amalgamated – de Gaulle had been particularly generous to General Juin,★ his former colleague at St Cyr who had become the right-hand man first to Weygand and then to Darlan. There were now nearly 400,000 men either already under arms or waiting for the shipments of American weaponry that were on the way, and their fighting qualities had been demonstrated, not just at Bir Hakeim but in Italy, Corsica and Tunisia. Equally, there was now a unified command system operating out of Algiers. In the army itself, the troops were hard and fit; they took their example from the British 8th Army – Leclerc astonished his quartermasters in Tunisia by refusing to allow his tank crews to carry wine with them. A new toughness, almost an arrogance, was in the air.

This sense of purpose had spilt over into the administration, which started to resemble a real government machine. Activity was hectic. Everything was done at the run; staff worked in their offices well into the nights and slept on camp beds that were folded up during the day. Even the Consultative Assembly, the motley group of Resistance leaders and former parliamentarians assembled in September by de Gaulle, whose first session was opened by him on 3 November, started to look like a fledgeling parliament; and the members of the FCNL started to

---

★ Alphonse Juin (1888–1967): Soldier. Very much old style; contemporary of de Gaulle at St Cyr; fought through Morocco 1912–14, First World War and then Morocco 1925; commanded Vichy forces in North Africa 1941, then all French forces in Tunisia 1942–3 and Italy 1943; C-in-C Allied Land Forces 1951–3, then all Allied forces 1953–6, Central Europe. Académie Française and Marshal of France.

look like ministers, as indeed many of them were later to become.

By contrast, the Resistance in France, so carefully brought together by Jean Moulin, had suffered a series of hammer blows. All but one of the members of the Conseil National de la Résistance had been ambushed, arrested and killed. Charles Delestraint had been taken as well; Brossolette was on his last 'run', which ended in his suicide. Throughout the summer and autumn arrests continued. In short, there had been too many disasters. The central organisation of the Resistance was in danger of breaking apart, in spite of its spectacular growth in numbers as a result of the introduction by the Germans in February of deportation for forced labour. It was, of course, stitched together again under the leadership of Georges Bidault, but the unity was still fragile at the end of the year.

For General de Gaulle, life had brought contentment. He was back on French soil, amid familiar sounds, smells and, better still, food. Politically, he was firmly established at the centre and his authority was unchallenged. Admittedly, his office was cramped and uncomfortable – he worked in a small drawing-room in Les Glycines, often in summer temperatures of over 100°F – but he had never paid much attention to his surroundings, and he was well served, and protected from unnecessary interference, by an efficient staff, led by Palewski, Louis Joxe★ and Courcel.

Domestic life in Algiers was also more settled. His wife and little Anne had arrived from London during the summer, and Elisabeth would soon leave Oxford to take a job in one of the offices of the committee monitoring the foreign press. The family had taken a three-storey villa overlooking the city, known as Les Oliviers, about two miles from the centre. It was, as Elisabeth wrote to her friend 'Roo', large and pleasant. There was a music-room as well as a drawing-room, dining-room, hall and patio on the ground floor. On the first floor were two offices – one, rather large, for de Gaulle himself, although he hardly ever worked at home (fortunately, Elisabeth thought) – in addition to Anne's room, a sitting-room and bathroom, Yvonne's room with two more bathrooms, a spare room and a terrace; and on the second floor there was cook's room and bathroom, two maids' rooms and another

★ Louis Joxe (1901–1991): Academic and diplomat. University lecturer in history, Paris 1925–32; minor left-wing political posts; then Algiers University; Sec.-Gen. of Committee of National Liberation in Algiers 1943, Provisional Govt. 1944–6; Ambassador, Moscow 1952–5, Bonn 1955–6; Minister Education 1960, Algerian Affairs 1960–2, Justice 1967; Deputy Prime Minister 1968.

spare room and bathroom. All in all, the villa, when compared with other houses in which the de Gaulles had lived, provided a welcome haven of space and comfort.

Their private life was simple, as always. There was little entertainment, and not much room for luxuries; sometimes even the basics of life were hard to come by. There were frequent power cuts and telephones seldom worked properly. But Mme de Gaulle made do, and the General was too busy at work to notice the sparseness of his home. The family's one diversion was the weekend drive to a cottage in the Kabylia mountains behind Algiers, where they indulged in carefully planned picnics.

On the other hand, the family news from France was depressing. De Gaulle's sister, Marie-Agnès, had been arrested and imprisoned and her husband sent to Buchenwald. Xavier, his eldest brother, was on the run, but Xavier's daughter Geneviève was in Ravensbruck. His brother Pierre had been taken to Eisenberg, and the youngest, Jacques, paralysed as the result of a polio attack, had been smuggled across the border into Switzerland. The rest of the family – their eldest son Philippe and Yvonne's brother and cousins – were serving with Fighting France.

But, at least, as they celebrated the New Year, General de Gaulle, his family and colleagues could at last reflect with some satisfaction not only that they were at last on French territory and showing every sign of staying there, but also that they were now able to look forward with confidence to 1944 as the year when the real business of the war was going to start; and the real business of the war, of course, was the liberation of France herself.

10

WAITING FOR OVERLORD

*FDR's continued hostility toward the General was primarily
due to antipathetic personal chemistry.* *

By the beginning of 1944 the focus of the war in Europe had moved
decisively northwards. Italy was the main battleground on land, but
soon it would be northern France, followed by the assault on Germany
itself. North Africa, and consequently Fighting France, had moved to
the periphery of the Allies' attention. The whole African continent was
clear of enemy forces, and the problem of political authority in French
North Africa had been solved, whether the Allies, in particular the
Americans, liked it or not. Purely French problems could, at least for
the moment, be put to one side; for the Allies at least, if not for de
Gaulle, that was something of a relief.

There were, however, some advantages for the General in the new
situation. It allowed him and the French National Committee a period
of months, albeit not very tranquil months, in which to become accustomed to the process of governing, an experience which its turn would
add force to their claim to be the legitimate government of France once
the moment came. They were able, too, to deliberate, in their own time
and rhythm, about the future administration of France and of her extensive and in some ways problematic Empire, in other words to think
about what was to happen after the war.

One consequence of the downgrading of Algiers in Allied political
and military priorities was a changing of the guard among senior Allied
personnel. Most importantly, General Eisenhower returned to England
to take command of the planned cross-Channel invasion. It was, from
the Fighting French point of view, a sad leavetaking. To be sure, there

---

* Unpublished letter from George W. Ball to the author, 8 February 1991.

had been difficulties in 1943, largely because of Roosevelt's insistence that while America was providing arms to the French they were to be considered a subordinate military agency obliged to accept American orders without question. But by the time Eisenhower left Algiers, on 30 December 1943, relations, particularly personal relations between the two generals, had improved to the point where he could assure de Gaulle confidentially that the Fighting French would be fully involved in the invasion of southern France that was to follow the cross-Channel attack. He also said, although this was more tentative, that Leclerc's 2nd Armoured Division would be included in the force that would fight in northern France. Those assurances, even if there had not been a warm friendship and respect between the two men, were enough to ensure the 'love feast' that, in Eisenhower's diarist's words, his farewells became.[1]

Eisenhower was replaced in North Africa by, of all people, the hammer of the French in the Levant, General 'Jumbo' Wilson. De Gaulle could afford to ignore him, and did. The difficult, pro-Vichy Robert Murphy left too, and in his place came the more sympathetic Edwin C. Wilson. Lastly, Macmillan was due, first to take home leave, and then move on; and his replacement, with ambassadorial rank, was an old friend of the Free French of 1940, Alfred Duff Cooper, who came with his brilliant wife to liven up the rather bleak Algiers social scene. There was now a great deal of official entertaining – and informal parties as well. The two queens of society were Lady Diana Cooper and Mme Catroux, the latter known universally as 'La Reine Margot'; their joint endeavours made a posting to Algiers much coveted among young unattached Allied officers.

The de Gaulle receptions were less elaborate and more awkward than those of Mme Catroux. The General himself was a considerate host, although apt to be rather clumsy, even gauche, in large gatherings, while Yvonne was shy and difficult to talk to. Her heart was not in it. She was much preoccupied with caring for Anne: 'She had a sad look, and sometimes the shutters came down on her mind and she lapsed into silence.'[2] The Catroux parties were quite different. '*Très snob*,' reported the British diplomat Roger Makins to his wife. 'Senegalese guards presented arms, Annamite stewards moved noiselessly about the halls and ADCs responded to the Châtelaine's slightest whim . . . I rather like the old woman and Catters himself was most amiable.'[3] Mme Catroux also enjoyed dancing, which she did 'surprisingly well'. Mme de Gaulle did not, of course, even try to compete.

All in all, social life in the Algiers of early 1944 was looking up, and was certainly a great improvement on 1943. But politically, the changes in the cast, and particularly Eisenhower's departure, made the task of fence-mending with the Allies – necessary after the bruising experiences of the Anfa summit and the de Gaulle-Giraud confrontation – more rather than less difficult. As for Washington, hopes were now pinned on Jean Monnet, who was entrusted with the task of achieving a reconciliation. In this, at lower levels, he made considerable progress, by using to good effect all the friendships that he had established earlier in the war. But, whatever his friendships, he had not Eisenhower's position or authority, and changing the view in the White House was quite another matter.

Here Monnet failed completely. Indeed, the situation was far worse than imagined. Roosevelt's opposition to de Gaulle was still uncompromising, and expressed in very personal terms. When the question of how liberated France was to be run came to be considered in Washington towards the end of 1943, the President wrote to Hull: 'De Gaulle now claims the right to speak for all of France . . . the thought that the occupation when it occurs should be wholly military is one to which I am increasingly inclined.'[4] Furthermore, Admiral Leahy was still advising him in February that 'the most reliable person' to whom the Americans could look for help in rallying the French was Pétain. A great deal of time and effort was being expended in the United States to train administrators to go to France – 'sixty-day marvels' they were called, after the length of time they took in training – and currency was being printed to be issued in France by the Allied commander-in-chief.

In the face of such unrelenting hostility from the President, de Gaulle at least needed to patch up matters with the British Prime Minister. As it happened, Churchill had unexpectedly appeared again in North Africa. On his way back from the Teheran conference with Roosevelt and Stalin he had fallen seriously ill with pneumonia and cardiac complications, and had stayed to recover at Eisenhower's villa at Carthage near Tunis. It was only in mid-December that he had been able to move for his convalescence to another luxurious villa, also owned by the United States army, in Marrakesh.

General de Gaulle was not altogether pleased by the behaviour of his distinguished visitor, who seemed to him to be treating the norms of international courtesy with scant respect. On his way out to Teheran, Churchill had called at Algiers in a British warship, and had not only failed to see de Gaulle but had invited on board General Georges, an old acquaintance of his from pre-war days. Georges had been keeping Churchill closely informed of events throughout the whole struggle between de Gaulle and Giraud, and was now able to report on the outcome – as well as to explain why he was no longer on the FCNL. Then, on his way back, Churchill had ignored the Governor-General of Tunisia, and was now in Marrakesh ignoring the Governor-General of Morocco. In short, he gave every appearance of treating North Africa as part of the British Empire.

On New Year's Day 1944, Churchill sent de Gaulle a message inviting him and Mme de Gaulle to lunch with himself and Mrs Churchill. The day suggested was 3 January, only two days later. The General declined on the grounds of pressure of business; the reason was probably that Yvonne did not want to go and, if there was going to be an argument, he did not want her there anyway. Undeterred, Churchill sent Macmillan to see de Gaulle to renew the invitation, this time, perhaps, to an afternoon's discussion followed by dinner. Mme de Gaulle was not included; Macmillan was experienced enough in his dealings with the General to know that he did not like mixing business and social occasions. Macmillan had also had the sense to make sure that Massigli was aware of the invitation, and that he approved of it.

De Gaulle's acceptance came as a relief to the British party at the Villa Taylor, as Churchill's convalescent home was called, and all concerned could now concentrate on making the event as productive and agreeable as possible. The date was fixed for 12 January; the General would fly to Marrakesh that morning. He pointed out to the FCNL that he was making this gesture because he did not think that Churchill would ever fully recover from his illness. 'He is on the wane,' he told them.[5]

There was the inevitable hitch. Churchill had earlier invited General de Lattre de Tassigny,* the only French general who had put up resistance to the German seizure of unoccupied France at the time of Torch, to come and see him in Marrakesh the following week. It was no more than a goodwill gesture, but the visit required de Gaulle's permission, which was refused. Churchill, irritated by such interference, immediately wanted to send a message to de Gaulle himself telling him not to

---

*Jean-Marie Gabriel de Lattre de Tassigny (1899–1952): Soldier. Vichy C.-in-C. Tunisia 1941; arrested for opposing German occupation of Free Zone 1942; escaped to London; commanded division in Algeria 1943, army in invasion of Southern France 1944; C.-in-C. Western European Union land forces 1948, then Indo-China 1950–1. Marshal of France.

come either; but he was calmed down by Duff Cooper, and in the end, somewhat grumpily, accepted that the visit should go ahead as planned.

These explosions had been observed by Mrs Churchill and her daughter Sarah, both of whom had accompanied Churchill to Marrakesh. When the General arrived, Mrs Churchill, who spoke almost faultless French, invited him to take a walk with her and Sarah in the garden. The General accepted, not just out of courtesy, but because he had a genuine affection for Mrs Churchill, as she had for him. Behind the awkward and frequently arrogant exterior she could see the passionate and single-minded commitment of the man, and it was attractive. Besides, she was upset at her husband's bouts of anger and was forever trying to calm him down. As they walked around the semi-tropical garden, the conversation became sticky. Mrs Churchill stopped and turned to the General. '*Mon Général,*' she said, 'you should be very careful not to hate your friends more than your enemies.'[6] It was wise advice.

The lunch turned out to be a great success, with good humour on all sides. It went on until five o'clock, covered the usual complaints with less than the usual rancour, and ended with an invitation by de Gaulle to Churchill to review the next day the French troops in Marrakesh. Nothing could have pleased Churchill more, and the following morning the Prime Minister, in his air commodore's uniform, and the General stood together on a hastily erected saluting base. There were only three small contingents, a mixed bunch of French, Moroccans, Algerians, Senegalese, Spahis and Zouaves; and the formation 'shoot-ups' performed by the local French flying training school terrified everybody. But none of that mattered. What mattered was that the scene recorded by the newsreel cameras showed a picture of smiling harmony between the two leaders, and of crowds shouting, '*Vive de Gaulle!*' and '*Vive Churchill!*'

It was no wonder that the General was pleased with his visit to Marrakesh. As he told one of the French officials there: 'My reason for coming to see [Churchill] was to try to effect a reconciliation – and I think I have succeeded.'[7] The General impressed the official by 'his look of satisfaction and pleasure'; he had met de Gaulle on previous occasions, but 'never had he seen him so happy'.

He had every reason. Not only had de Gaulle mended fences with the British Prime Minister, but he had secured further armaments for the Resistance and agreement that French forces should participate in the coming liberation of France – all without making any concessions over the fate of the three Vichyites, which Churchill was still fussing about. At least he now had the British on his side, which went some way to make up for the failure to move Roosevelt from his attitude of apparently irreconcilable hostility.

Indeed, that attitude had hardened further as the results came through of a conference of Governors of French African territories, held in Brazzaville in January and February 1944 and presided over by Pleven, the object of which had been to discuss the future of the French Empire. The conference had been opened by de Gaulle himself, whose speech looked towards the day when the people 'would raise themselves little by little to the level where they [would] be capable of participating in the conduct of their own affairs'.[8] The General went on to point out that it was France's duty to encourage this process. It was a speech that would be much quoted twenty-five years later when de Gaulle was struggling with the Algerian problem. But he left Brazzaville immediately after delivering it, and after that Pleven was unable to keep the conference to the line that de Gaulle had initially set. The result was a reaffirmation of France's overseas mission in terms that might have come from the previous century, and a vigorous reassertion of French sovereignty. Roosevelt, whose general policy was to break up all remaining European empires after the war, was far from impressed with the outcome of the Brazzaville conference. It was another black mark for Fighting France.

In late January in Algiers, however, there were more pressing problems. De Gaulle was suffering from another attack of malaria, this time complicated by kidney trouble, and there was worrying news from France. The German campaign against the Resistance was proving more effective. Moreover, within the Resistance itself the best organised groups were communist, and they were increasing their influence. Those who had avoided forced labour were flooding into the underground movement known as the Maquis which, at least in many areas, was communist-dominated. De Gaulle was well aware of the implications of this for the Liberation. It was an extra reason, much more down to earth than mere sentimentality, for Fighting French troops to spearhead the Allies forces in France.

These were the issues that preoccupied the French Committee for National Liberation in the months to come. It was becoming obvious, as the winter of 1944 turned into spring, that the real question was not whether France would be liberated, or even when, but how the country would be administered after the event. In de Gaulle's view, the danger of communism was all too apparent. Even if he were prepared to make use of the communist organisation for the Liberation, he would not tolerate another totalitarian regime in France afterwards, particularly a communist one.

Roosevelt, on the other hand, mainly because of his dislike and distrust of de Gaulle himself, considered that the FCNL itself represented the major totalitarian threat which had to be avoided at all costs. He believed that there should be a military occupation of France until such time that the French people were in a position freely to choose both the kind of government that they wanted and whom they wanted to run it.

The clash between these two views dominated relations between Fighting France and the two western Allies right up to D-Day and beyond. Roosevelt's draft directive to Eisenhower, issued on 15 March 1944, set out the American position clearly. Once in France, the Allied commander-in-chief would be responsible for the administration of the country. 'He may consult the French Committee for National Liberation,' it went on, but he could also make whatever arrangements he thought fit with other groups – and, although this was not specified as precisely as it might have been, with individuals, including members of the Vichy Government. The only thing that he could not do was to deal with 'the Vichy government as such'.[9]

It did not take long for this draft directive to leak out and to become known in Algiers. Naturally, it caused the greatest offence. The committee's representative in London, Pierre Viénot,★ was sent to protest to Eden. It was, he pointed out, not only wrong, but absurd. If the commander-in-chief was to shoulder the whole responsibility it would be an enormous burden for him. In practice he would be appointing a Vichyite in one district and a communist in another. It was a recipe for disaster, and would end either in France being handed over to Stalin or in civil war.

Eden was inclined to agree with Viénot, but their difficulty was how to persuade Churchill to use his influence with Roosevelt to have the directive modified. In their view, it was vital to alter the words 'may consult [the FCNL]' to 'must consult'. Eden was pessimistic, but he offered to make an attempt. It was unsuccessful, and Viénot decided to see Churchill himself, which he did on 4 April.

★ Pierre Viénot (1898–1944): Politician. Able, smooth and anglophile. Socialist; Under-Secretary of State in Popular Front government; joined Free French in 1942; represented Algiers National Committee in London 1943–4; died of heart attack before Liberation.

By an accident of timing, Viénot's visit to Churchill came only a few days after news had reached London of the execution in Algiers on 20 March 1944 of a former Vichy Minister for the Interior, Pierre Pucheu. Pucheu had arrived in North Africa in mid-1943 under the impression that he had been promised immunity by Giraud. But the communists were after him, and he was arrested that August. By normal standards, what followed was quite scandalous. The charges, relating to a reprisal shooting at Chateaubriant in October 1941 of a number of communist hostages – the list of names Pucheu was said to have drawn up – rested on the flimsiest of evidence. The trial itself had been largely conducted in the press in advance, and was almost certainly rigged. Indeed, proof of Pucheu's guilt only came out after the Liberation. Nevertheless, Pucheu was duly sentenced to death and shot. Neither de Gaulle nor Giraud intervened. 'Reasons of state required that an example should be made rapidly,' wrote de Gaulle later. In other words, he had been told from France that, if the court were lenient, the communists would not only take the law into their own hands but would no longer be prepared to cooperate with Fighting France.

Pucheu may indeed have been guilty, but the procedure was wrong, and de Gaulle knew it was wrong. Only a few hours after Pucheu's dawn execution, de Gaulle, 'his eyes hollow with lack of sleep', as Louis Joxe reported, stated that if he had exercised his power to pardon Pucheu 'all the criminals of that category would have arrived in Algiers' to wait for the end of the war.[10] It was a political trial and a political execution, to which both de Gaulle and Giraud were accomplices.

Its effect was to reinforce the view of those, particularly in Washington, who believed that de Gaulle was no respecter of justice, and that he would, if given even a share of power in post-war France, embark on a series of purges there. All Roosevelt's worst fears were in his own mind thus confirmed, and the result of all interventions over the March directive was exactly as Eden had predicted. In spite of Churchill's pressure, since he too had recognised that the directive was untenable, in spite of an increasingly boisterous campaign in both the British and American press for greater cooperation between the Allies and the FCNL, and in spite of the fact that D-Day was fast approaching, Roosevelt refused to be moved. 'General Eisenhower should have complete discretion in the matter of civil government,'[11] he wrote to Churchill on 17 April. The 'pig-headed Dutchman', as Roosevelt was fond of calling himself, had spoken.

Churchill made one last effort. He suggested to Roosevelt that it might be appropriate for General de Gaulle to visit Washington. The President replied that he had 'no objection', which sounded promising. But as the diplomatic exchanges between London, Washington and Algiers continued it became evident that the cause was hopeless. Roosevelt, supported by Hull, suspected that Churchill was trying to tie them to de Gaulle before D-Day, and became more and more negative. Churchill finally abandoned all hope on 24 April. 'I press it no more,' he wrote forlornly to the President.[12]

But in reality the problem of the March draft directive had become academic. Events had moved on. The important breakthrough for the FCNL had come almost four months earlier, on 1 January 1944, when the Communist Party in Algiers had written to de Gaulle expressing their wish to 'help the government'. The approach had clearly been sanctioned by the Communists of mainland France; and when de Gaulle replied to the Algiers branch, in the coded language of the time, praising unreservedly those 'French Communists' who 'served their country well, placing national duty before every other consideration',[13] the deal with the Communist Party was as good as done. On 18 March de Gaulle announced that he would include in 'the Government' all those forces who were fighting for the Liberation. On 20 March, Pierre Pucheu was executed; and on 4 April three Communists joined the French Committee.

It was a decisive step for France, since the FCNL could now claim to represent all major French interests. But the gulf between the committee and the western Allies widened further. On 6 April Churchill pointed out to Duff Cooper that, if the French Committee or any representatives sent to London were 'infected' with communism, they would certainly not be made party to any British or, he confidently expected, American secrets. The divergence was clear. It was almost a side issue that General Giraud was removed by the newly enlarged committee from the post of commander-in-chief, replaced by de Gaulle and put on the retired list ten days later. That only served further to irritate Giraud's former sponsors, Roosevelt and Churchill.

However it may have seemed at the time, the elaborate dance between the American and British Governments over the future administration of liberated France was no more than an irrelevance. The FCNL had already put in place a shadow administration. On 10 January the committee appointed eighteen commissioners of the republic, who would replace the eighty-nine prefects of the Third Republic. On 14 March the committee decided that each section of liberated territory would be administered by a committee appointee but that the municipal and departmental councils that had been in office in 1939 would be recreated. Finally, it was decided that the Consultative Assembly would move to France at the earliest opportunity and remain in being until a Constituent Assembly could be elected.

Once the communists had joined the FCNL – after Pucheu's execution – it was in all but name a provisional government. It remained to convince the Allies of the reality, that the FCNL's formula for the future administration of liberated France was the only one possible. De Gaulle tried to do so in a speech in Tunis on 7 May. After a long prologue, which dwelt at some length on the future of a reborn France, and went on to describe the state of the French forces fighting gallantly against the common enemy, he ended with the pointed expression: 'We most fervently wish that French realities may be clearly recognised.'[14] He might just as well have saved his breath. There was no response at all to his message, even if it had been heard, which is doubtful. There was only one other course, which was simply to go ahead regardless. This was now what happened.

The Consultative Assembly convened on 13 May 1944, and a former Popular Front minister, the socialist Vincent Auriol, was put up to speak. It was an emotional occasion; there was not a seat free. Auriol rose and pronounced that there was only one authority which could speak for France: the French Committee for National Liberation. This was the only government that the people would accept, because it was faithful to France, to its Allies and to the republic. Auriol waved in front of the crowded Assembly a document – which he had read, he said, 'with tears in his eyes' – from the National Council of the Resistance. It said, 'The French Committee for National Liberation is the legitimate government of France.'[15] He was cheered and cheered again.

On 3 June 1944 a decree was issued stating that 'The French Committee of National Liberation takes the name of Provisional Government of the French Republic.'[16] The deed had been done. In the event, it passed entirely without comment. This was perhaps not surprising; it came only three days before the Allied invasion of Normandy: Operation Overlord.

Preparations for Overlord had been going on for months. By the end of May 1944, over a million American and Allied troops were assembled in southern England. Fighting France made a modest contribution to this total; the 2nd Armoured Division under Leclerc had arrived in Britain at the beginning of April, or, to be more exact, the officers and men had arrived, to be re-equipped with American weapons. In support of the operation – although officially they were supposed to know nothing about it – the FCNL on 28 March chose General Koenig, the hero of Bir Hakeim, as its delegate to what was described as the 'operation of the North'. He was also the FCNL's liaison with the Resistance in France, a role which was much more easily conducted from London than from Algiers.

It was an ingenious appointment. Koenig's double responsibility made life extremely difficult for the Overlord planners and Eisenhower, the Supreme Commander. They needed to discuss with Koenig, in his liaison capacity, detailed arrangements to coordinate Resistance activity with the assault on the beaches. On the other hand, they were forbidden to discuss anything at all with Koenig in his capacity as the FCNL's delegate. Roosevelt had insisted, and Churchill had reluctantly agreed, that de Gaulle should be kept in complete ignorance of the whole Overlord operation.

This ludicrous state of affairs persisted throughout May. By now, it had become apparent to the British press and to parliament that something was wrong. Eden had great difficulty in defending the position in the House of Commons; and the press took up the campaign, which intensified after another Fighting French military success on 14 May when General Juin broke the German line at the river Garigliano. Why, everybody asked, were there not direct and close consultations with the FCNL, which was now quite clearly the authority with which the Allied command was going to have to deal once France was liberated?

The pressure continued to build, and threatened serious embarrassment for Churchill, but it was not at all clear what he could do which would not in its turn offend Roosevelt. On 24 May he reluctantly invited General de Gaulle to London to discuss matters. When he informed the House of Commons that he had done so, the Prime Minister was given a difficult ride by his own backbenchers. Harold Nicolson, for instance, described the Government's behaviour towards the FCNL as 'grotesque' and 'discourteous'.[17]

De Gaulle's reply to the invitation was a reply from strength. Yes, he would go to London provided communications between London and Algiers were not obstructed and could be sent in code. He sent Viénot a telegram saying, 'We are asking nothing. There is ourselves or else chaos. If the western Allies provoke chaos in France, they will be responsible and they . . . will be the losers.'[18]

At the same time, there was an approach from Washington so discreet as to be almost unnoticeable. On 27 May Admiral Fenard, the French Committee's naval expert at their delegation in Washington, was requested by the White House to inform de Gaulle that a visit by him would be quite acceptable, without its being necessary to say which side had taken the initiative in arranging it. There was now no doubt about it. Eisenhower's complaints that the success of Overlord could be jeopardised by a continued boycott of the FCNL had finally reached the ears of the President. He was not prepared to abandon his previous attitude, but he was prepared to give an inch. As de Gaulle later wrote, 'The President's approach made things quite clear to me. I saw that the long, hard-fought match with the Allies for French independence was reaching the desired conclusion.'[19]

He did not go to Washington because he was on the point of leaving for London. But even now it was with reluctance, for he feared a trap. He was worried that, without achieving any concessions from the Allies on the status of the FCNL, he would be manoeuvred into making a speech in support of Overlord simply because, being in England at the time, he could not decently refuse. On 2 June the formal invitation from Churchill was conveyed to de Gaulle by Duff Cooper. After two argumentative sessions of the FCNL, de Gaulle sent his acceptance back through the same route. But it was at that same time, and certainly not coincidentally, that the French Committee for National Liberation declared itself to be the Provisional Government of the French Republic. The General's point was well made.

11

WHO WON THE BATTLE
FOR FRANCE?

Quelli i quali per vie virtuose . . . diventano Principi,
acquistano il principato con difficoltà. ★

The new head of the Provisional Government of France, General de Gaulle, arrived at Heston airport on the morning of 4 June in the York aircraft that Churchill had put at his disposal. The weather was rough and there was a makeshift band to play the 'Marseillaise' as the plane taxied up to the airport building. In London, however, the reception was much warmer. He was handed a letter from Churchill, beginning 'My dear General de Gaulle, Welcome to these shores!' and inviting him to travel down to see the Prime Minister in his train for '*déjeuner*', after which they would go together to Eisenhower's headquarters to hear about the 'military position which is momentous and imminent'.[1]

The train – 'an original idea', as de Gaulle remarked[2] – was Churchill's office and living quarters. It was stationary in a siding near Portsmouth – Churchill thought that the closer he was to the action the more effective he would be – and was extremely uncomfortable for everybody except the Prime Minister. 'There was only one bath,' Eden recalled, 'and one telephone. Mr Churchill seemed to be always in the bath and General Ismay always on the telephone.'[3] Nevertheless, when de Gaulle arrived with Viénot and General Béthouart, and walked down the track with Eden towards the train, Churchill was sufficiently moved to leave his bath and go out onto the track to welcome the General 'with arms outstretched'.[4]

Although de Gaulle recoiled from this almost Latin expression of emotion, the subsequent discussion went smoothly. The General later recorded his admiration of the Prime Minister and his efforts throughout the war which had led to this outcome: 'It was a striking justification of

★ 'Those who become princes . . . by virtuous means . . . achieve their princedom with difficulty.' Niccolò Machiavelli, *Il Principe*, ch.6.

the policy of courage which [Churchill] himself had personified since the darkest days.'[5] So far, so good; and at about 2.15 p.m. they sat down to lunch in the best of humours.

At about the time dessert was being served, things started to go wrong. Churchill suggested that they talk about 'political matters'. The idea fell on stony ground. It was precisely those 'political matters' that the General refused to discuss. He was only prepared, as indeed he had told Duff Cooper before he left Algiers, to discuss military matters. 'It is war,' he replied to Churchill, 'the rest we will see about afterwards'.[6] In vain first Churchill and then Eden tried to persuade him to visit Roosevelt – or, as a fall-back position, to accept political discussions with the British in the presence of the American ambassador. But the General was not to be moved. He had made proposals to Washington six months earlier, but had not even received a reply. 'Why do you seem to think that I need to put before Roosevelt my candidacy for authority in France?' he demanded. 'The French Government exists. I have nothing to ask, in this respect, of the United States of America or of Great Britain.'[7] He could not resist a sarcastic reference to the banknotes that the Americans had been busy printing. His voice rose in pitch and volume at the enormity of it all.

Of course, Churchill started shouting back. 'We are going to liberate Europe, but it is because the Americans are with us to do it . . . no quarrel would ever arise between Britain and the United States on account of France . . . every time I have to choose between you and Roosevelt, I shall choose Roosevelt.'[8] This was going too far for Eden, who was shaking his head in despair. Even Ernest Bevin, who was also present, suddenly spoke up to say bluntly that the Prime Minister had been speaking for himself and not for the whole Cabinet.

The conference was over. It had ended in a row, just at the point when, forty-eight hours before D-Day, all the Allies should have been pulling in the same direction. As the meeting broke up, Churchill gloomily proposed a toast: 'To de Gaulle, who never accepted defeat.' De Gaulle replied. 'To England, to Victory, to Europe.'[9] They then drove off together – in silence – to Eisenhower's headquarters.

Again, the reception at first was cordial and courteous. Eisenhower and his chief of staff, General Bedell-Smith, took de Gaulle into their map tent and explained in great detail the plan for Overlord. De Gaulle was most impressed by the planning of the operation. The precise date had not, however, been fixed, and Eisenhower was diplomatic enough to ask de Gaulle his opinion. De Gaulle, obviously flattered by this attention, urged minimum delay. It was all most friendly until, just as de Gaulle was getting ready to leave, Eisenhower dropped his bombshell. On the day of the landings, he said, he would be broadcasting a proclamation to the French people, and he would like de Gaulle to do the same.

So that was the plot. It was exactly as de Gaulle had suspected. The Americans had decided to take over France. When he was shown the text of the proposed proclamation, in which Eisenhower urged the French nation to 'carry out [his] orders', de Gaulle's suspicions were confirmed: 'He appeared to be taking charge of our country even though he was merely an Allied general entitled to command troops.'[10] All that had been fought for since June 1940 was to go for nothing. There was not a single word in the document about Fighting France, the FCNL, or even about the French troops who were preparing to fight alongside the Allies. It could hardly have been more wounding or more offensive.

Eisenhower tried to rescue the situation. It was, he said, only a draft, and it could be changed. De Gaulle replied that he would suggest changes, and then left with Churchill to return to the train – leaving Churchill, during the short journey, in no doubt about what he felt about the American 'pamphlet', as he called it. Churchill had expected that de Gaulle and his colleagues would stay to dinner before returning to London, but 'he drew himself up and stated that he preferred to motor with his French officers separately'. 'I feel chilled,' Churchill said to Eden.[11]

The next morning, 5 June, de Gaulle sent Eisenhower an amended version of the proclamation. It was carefully constructed. It did not even mention Fighting France, only asking the liberated French to 'comply with the orders of the qualified French authority', with a view, when all was over, to winning the means 'for you yourselves to choose your representatives and your government'.[12] It was not only carefully constructed but studiously moderate in tone, and no more than the Americans had been insisting on. But de Gaulle's version was rejected. Eisenhower had been either lying or unforgivably naive. The original draft had already been approved in Washington and could not under any circumstances have been changed.

Later that morning Charles Peake called on General de Gaulle in Carlton Gardens to inform him of the role he would be playing once the landings had taken place. First, he announced to the General, the exiled heads of state would broadcast, then Eisenhower would read out his proclamation; then de Gaulle himself would speak. Peake must have been unaware of the Eisenhower text and the fate of de Gaulle's amendments, or he had badly misjudged the depth of de Gaulle's anger. The General's reply was brusque. He would agree to make a broadcast, but not one which in any way, or at any time, might imply approval, or even endorsement, of what Eisenhower had said. His broadcast would be at a time and in a manner of his own choosing. If the Allies did not like it his way, it was all one to him, and there would be no broadcast.

The news reached Churchill in mid-afternoon. It was presented as though de Gaulle had refused to broadcast at all. The Prime Minister was enraged and spent most of the opening hour of the War Cabinet meeting that evening berating de Gaulle and all his works. Cadogan noted, 'Cabinet 6.30 p.m. We endured the usual passionate anti-de Gaulle harangue from the PM. On this subject, we get away from politics and diplomacy and even common sense. It's a girls' school. Roosevelt, PM and – it must be admitted – de Gaulle, all behave like girls approaching the age of puberty. Nothing to be done.'[13] In the middle of all this, word came through that de Gaulle was also ordering the 200 French liaison officers not to go on board ship for France, since there had been no agreement about what they were meant to be doing. For Churchill, this was the last straw.

During that night, the massive invasion armada sailed across the Channel towards France. But that night also saw intense shuttle diplomacy between various members of the British Government and de Gaulle, who had retired to his room at the Connaught Hotel. Viénot was the unfortunate who had to run errands between the two sides. At 10.30 p.m. he was summoned by Eden to the Foreign Office, where he confirmed that the General would broadcast but that the liaison officers would not be going. He was sent to try to persuade de Gaulle to change his mind. At 11.30 he saw de Gaulle again at the Connaught, listened to a long diatribe against the British, and Churchill – 'that gangster' – in particular, and was then given the dressing-down of his life for his pains: 'They wanted to trick me. I will not be tricked.'[14]

At one o'clock in the morning Viénot was back at the Foreign Office, where he found not only Eden but Churchill himself, by that time in his most belligerent mood. Viénot explained that de Gaulle had considered the situation further but was not to be moved. This provoked a furious explosion from the Prime Minister, who cursed de Gaulle bell, book and candle, and for good measure bellowed at Viénot. Viénot retired in high dudgeon and Churchill immediately sent for

Desmond Morton, instructing him to tell Walter Bedell-Smith, Eisenhower's chief of staff, to put de Gaulle in a plane and send him back to Algiers – 'in chains if necessary'.[15]

By 3 a.m. Viénot had returned to the Connaught, where he found de Gaulle somewhat calmer. He had spent the hours since their last meeting with his son Philippe, who was on shore leave for a few hours. It was an emotional moment for both of them. The General told his son that the invasion was about to start; both of them were entering a period of great danger and this might be the last time they would meet. The relationship had never been easy, but the moments of farewell brought them closer.

The order to deport de Gaulle was still in effect, and it required all Eden's tact and persuasiveness to get the Prime Minister to cancel it, which he managed to do just after dawn on 6 June. Churchill's intemperate letter to de Gaulle instructing him to leave the country was burnt. As a further reward for Eden's nocturnal diplomacy, de Gaulle sent him a message that he would agree to make a broadcast. 'Well,' Eden said later that day, 'we've had a crazy night.'[16]

The Normandy landings went well – according to plan and with fewer casualties than expected – much to everyone's relief. Eisenhower delivered his proclamation, and it was now imperative to get General de Gaulle to the BBC microphone at Bush House. There was no chance of seeing his text in advance; indeed, Viénot did not dare ask him for one. The British decided that they would have to listen to the recording and stop it 'if', in Cadogan's words, 'it was too bad'.[17]

As so often, de Gaulle rose to the occasion and made one of his most inspiring broadcasts. 'The supreme battle is joined. Of course, it is the battle of France, and it is France's battle!' But he was also determined to make his point. In the middle of his speech he said quite clearly: 'The instructions given by the French Government and by the French leaders whom it has designated for the task must be followed exactly.' He ended with an emotional climax: 'In the nation, the Empire and the armies there is now only one hope, the same for all. Behind the cloud, that has been so heavy, of our blood and our tears, look! – the sun of our greatness is shining once again!'[18]

It was a masterpiece. But it did refer to a French Government, not even a Provisional French Government, and this certainly did not pass unnoticed. Eden realised that it would create another storm, but decided to let it go. The storm lasted throughout the afternoon and evening of 6 June. Eden was determinedly trying to persuade Churchill to discuss the civil administration question with de Gaulle, while Churchill was accusing him, and Attlee and Bevin as well, since they took Eden's side, of trying to break up the Government. He said that nothing would induce him to give way and that de Gaulle must go. Eden stood his ground, and was saved just after midnight when a message came through from Roosevelt suggesting that a definite date should be set for de Gaulle's visit to the United States. Roosevelt had conceded a point – just in time.

In the meantime, Eden had sent Duff Cooper to see the General on the afternoon of the 6th, to try to soften him up. It was not easy. De Gaulle was depressed. He felt that he had been brought over to London solely with the object of telling the French people that the Allies and the Provisional Government were in agreement, which they were not; but he obviously could not say so. It had all been a trick. Duff Cooper raised the matter of the liaison officers, pointing out that any refusal to allow them to go to France would be considered a sign of reluctance to help the Allies in the Liberation. In the end, de Gaulle recognised the force of the argument and agreed to consult Koenig about the number that could be sent immediately. He felt, Duff Cooper reported, that he was making a concession and a 'gesture' and complained that he was always making concessions but that nobody ever made them to him.

De Gaulle was still angry and depressed at a dinner he gave on the evening of 8 June at Carlton Gardens in honour of Anthony Eden. What should have been a celebration – Duff Cooper and Charles Peake were there for the occasion, as well as Viénot, Palewski and de Gaulle's new ADC, Léo Teyssot – degenerated into another sullen lament about British and American behaviour towards the French. Eisenhower, he said, planned to issue a series of edicts about France without knowing what he was doing; and the 'false money' that the Americans had invented would not just be insulting but would cause chaos and confusion. In the end, Viénot asked permission to start discussions with the British, to which de Gaulle replied that he could do so if he really wished.

It took another three days for Eden to persuade Churchill to allow him to embark on the discussions with Viénot. But by then there was a new matter of contention. Not unreasonably, the next request from Viénot had been for a visit by General de Gaulle to the Normandy bridgehead. 'Wait and see how he behaves,' shouted Churchill. 'Remember,' he wrote to Eden, 'that there is not a scrap of generosity about this man, who only wishes to pose as a saviour of France in this operation without a single French soldier at his back.'[19] Conveniently, Churchill had forgotten that de Gaulle had been pressing for the inclusion of French forces in Overlord but that, at Roosevelt's insistence and with Churchill's connivance, he had been kept in the dark about the whole operation.

In the end, the head of the Provisional French Government, by now recognised by all the governments-in-exile in London except the Netherlands, was permitted to visit France by the British Prime Minister. But there would be restrictions: he could not hold a public meeting or gather crowds in the streets. 'I suggest that he should drive slowly through [Bayeux], shake hands with a few people, and then return, leaving any subsequent statement to be made here,'[20] Churchill minuted Eden on 13 June.

On the same day, de Gaulle appointed his former ADC François Coulet Commissioner of the Republic for the liberated sector of Normandy, and Colonel de Chevigné, the former military attaché in Washington, as the senior French military authority. Needless to say, the appointments were kept confidential, and not communicated to the British. He then went to a celebratory dinner with Eden, Attlee and Bevin. A letter arrived from Churchill with last-minute objections, but they were brushed aside by the Cabinet ministers present and the plan went ahead. De Gaulle left for Portsmouth.

At dawn on 14 June the French destroyer *Combattante* sailed for France. General de Gaulle was on board, with his closest colleagues, not least Geoffroy de Courcel, who had been his companion on the flight from Bordeaux almost exactly four years back. But they hardly spoke. The party landed just after 2 p.m., de Gaulle still silent and nervous, smoking heavily. Their first call was on General Montgomery, Eisenhower's British deputy, at his headquarters; the reception was cordial but Montgomery was busy – he had other things to think about. They then drove on to Bayeux.

This was to be the ultimate test of the crusade of June 1940. It was the first time de Gaulle had been seen by Frenchmen in France. Up until then, he had only been a voice on the radio. Nobody had seen the immense, awkward figure in the flesh. As they approached the town, the party had to stop two gendarmes, tell them who they were, and ask them to go into Bayeux to warn people of the General's visit. While he was waiting, de Gaulle sent Coulet on ahead to take up his appointment as commissioner.

By the time the General and his party arrived in Bayeux, the town had been alerted. 'We proceeded on foot,' de Gaulle later wrote, 'from street to street. At the sight of General de Gaulle, a sort of amazement seized the inhabitants, who then burst into cheers, or into tears. Coming out of their houses, they escorted me amid an extraordinary display of emotion. The children surrounded me. The women smiled and wept. The men stretched out their hands. We thus walked on together, fraternally, overwhelmed, and feeling the joy, pride and faith in the nation surging again from the abyss.'[21] After a short speech it was all over. Charles de Gaulle knew that his crusade had not been in vain. The scenes at Bayeux, he knew, would be repeated throughout France as liberation moved forward. The great gamble of June 1940 had paid off. The exile had returned as a hero.

PART FOUR

HERO

1

A PARISIAN SUMMER

Magnificat anima mea Dominum; et exultavit
spiritus meus in Deo salutari meo. ★

General Charles de Gaulle was in many ways an unlikely hero. To begin
with, his physical presence, although undoubtedly impressive, was distinctly awkward. Even by mid-1944, at the age of fifty-three, his body
had not yet softened, as it was to do in later life. His hair and moustache
were now flecked with grey, and the tensions and illnesses of the past
four years had left lines on his face and tiredness in his eyes, but his figure was not yet one of a statesman; it was still ungainly, spare and
uncompromising. From his great height he appeared to look down his
large nose, as though from a high mountain, at those whom he was
addressing. He seemed lofty, suspicious, cool and remote.

Added to this uncomfortable physique, and perhaps accentuated by it,
was the shyness that he had noted in himself during his period as a prisoner in the First World War. Quite unlike Churchill, Roosevelt or
even Stalin, he was not able to produce at will the charm that reaches
out and captivates. He was still too much of a soldier, used to giving
peremptory orders rather than winning hearts and minds. Although his
rhetorical technique had come a long way from the stilted, almost prim,
performances of June 1940, it was only when addressing a distant and
almost invisible presence, and speaking of abstractions such as the 'eternal France', that he was able to generate the particular kind of
psychological electricity that those who want to be loved, as opposed to
be respected, have to be able to command.

This shyness, and his own knowledge of it, spilled over into personal relations. With his family and intimates, the de Gaulle of mid-1944

★ 'My soul doth magnify the Lord; and my spirit hath rejoiced in God my Saviour.'
Opening words of the Magnificat; St Luke's Gospel, ch. 2.

could relax, be humorous and even, occasionally, self-mocking. His relationship with his daughter Anne was more than just movingly affectionate; it was as though she, because of her defencelessness, helped him to unbend. The hour that he reserved for her each day when he was at home showed a quite different side to de Gaulle. When the family lived in Frognal, for instance, in 1942 and the first months of 1943, he used to invite his neighbours to a game of rummy in the evenings. But it was no ordinary game. He used to sit Anne in her place at the card table, deal her a hand and gently play the cards for her. Such tenderness was in marked contrast to those characteristics which had led the British, maliciously but accurately, to award him the codenames of 'Ramrod' and 'Wormwood'.

To those outside his close circle de Gaulle showed a thick protective skin; he was stiff and difficult, and to his subordinates was frequently no more than morose, hectoring and abrasive. Indeed, as the war progressed, and his position became more secure, his worrying seemed to increase rather than to diminish. To the outside world, even in his triumphs, he appeared to be at worst suspicious and pessimistic, and at best only fleetingly able to enjoy his own successes. For him, the hill that had just been climbed always had another higher one behind it.

It was not that the outside world, in terms of his appeal to popular opinion, was against him. On the contrary, the press of all Allied countries found the hostility of their governments to the French Committee for National Liberation almost incomprehensible. Nor was there inability or reluctance on his part to learning the techniques of communication. Far from it; he studied hard, and successfully. It only seems, from watching his movements and listening to his voice, that he did not enjoy using them. The response of a cheering crowd did not yet move him to inspiration. That, when it came, came from elsewhere.

For example, a hero's welcome awaited him on his first visit to the United States in early July 1944. As far as the press was concerned, glory was his for the taking; and at the start the General behaved as one who would take it. He set precisely the right tone on arrival. His televised statement was delivered in impeccable English with a clear, but not too thick, French accent, straight to camera, with only an occasional glance at his notes. The General sat, apparently relaxed, in a wicker chair on the White House lawn. He referred with carefully studied emotion to 'those brave American boys . . . who abroad are fighting our common enemies . . . The whole French people is thinking of you and salutes you, Americans, our friends.'[1] It was just the right way to speak to

America. It was broadcast from coast to coast, and went straight to the heart. America responded with its own unique brand of heartfelt enthusiasm. But de Gaulle himself was somewhat bemused.

Of course, the start of his visit had been rather overwhelming. He had been met at Washington airport, and had been driven immediately to see the President, who greeted him with what looked to all the world like an enormous beam of pleasure. Certainly, the photograph that was published in the world's press the following morning showed it as such. Cordell Hull stood behind the President, old, impassive and worldly-wise. He knew perfectly well that Roosevelt was facing re-election in a few months; any card was worth playing.

But if Roosevelt was using de Gaulle, de Gaulle seemed to be prepared to be used, and was quite amenable to being carried along on the whirlwind. He appears to have found it easier to respond to Americans, to abandon some of the restraint he showed his own countrymen. By the time he reached New York, the crowds who wanted to see him and touch him could hardly be contained. He was received at City Hall by the Mayor of New York, Fiorello La Guardia, who had been a constant supporter of the Free French in the dark days, and the reception was a triumph. There was another speech in English – 'how often we have seen encouragement, sympathy and help coming from New York' – and in the evening there was dinner with Cardinal Spellman, followed by a rally at Madison Square Garden at which the contralto Marian Anderson sang the 'Marseillaise' in his honour. It was nearly too much for de Gaulle, who was very close to tears. America, for the first-time visitor, can be a powerful drug.

A great deal had happened since his last hero's welcome, at Bayeux on that grey day of 14 June. On his return to England he had found the British press full of his visit and delighted with the reception he had received. From then on it had been clear that the American plans for the administration of liberated France were slipping off the agenda. The General himself had been readier to lower his guard, taking Eden by surprise when he had paid a farewell visit to Carlton Gardens, on 16 June, before de Gaulle's departure for Algiers. 'I was received with some ceremony,' Eden recalled, 'a guard of honour being drawn up outside, with officers posted at intervals up the stairs. De Gaulle talked easily for twenty minutes. As I commented at the time, "He is at his best as host." '[2]

Before he left England, de Gaulle had endorsed the discussions between Eden and Viénot on the future administration of France; and he had written generously to Churchill, assuring him, among other things, of 'the deep confidence and unbreakable attachment which France feels towards Great Britain'. Churchill had still not got over the exhausting rows before and during D-Day, and had written a cool response. 'I am sorry,' he had said to Duff Cooper after he had dictated it, 'but that's the best I can do.'[3]

By the end of June, Roosevelt's invitation had been accepted and the dates of de Gaulle's visit to the United States fixed for 6 to 10 July. Viénot had reported '90 per cent success' in his negotiations with Eden, in other words formal recognition by the United Kingdom of the French Provisional Government, with the implication that it would be responsible for the administration of the country; and de Gaulle had found time to visit Pope Pius XII. It had been a strange visit: the Vatican's record in the war had been dubious, to say the least, particularly with regard to the blind eye that had been turned to the massacre of Jews, but de Gaulle had been much more impressed with the spirituality of the Pope and had ignored entirely his record on human rights. In this case, certainly, the Jesuit Fathers had left their mark on their pupil. The Holy Father could only be beyond all reproach.

On 5 July, the General had set off for the United States, accompanied by Palewski, Béthouart and Teyssot, in an aeroplane put at his disposal by the United States Government. Just before leaving, he had sent a cordial message to the President to mark the Fourth of July. But none of this new friendliness was more than skin-deep, at least on Roosevelt's side. The President disliked de Gaulle as much as ever – he described him as 'a narrow-minded French zealot with too much ambition for his own good and some rather dubious views on democracy',[4] and on another occasion, just before de Gaulle's visit, 'he's a nut'.[5]

As a result, the official conversations in Washington did not go particularly well. Roosevelt turned on the famous charm, but disconcerted his visitor with his – admittedly rather unrealistic – views on how the United States would rule the world after the war, by means of a four-power directorate of themselves, the Soviets, China and Britain, with a series of bases encircling the globe, many of them on French territory. De Gaulle heard all these fantasies almost without a murmur. The fact is that he was rather overawed by the President, as he had been by the Pope. Tea at the White House, dinner with Cordell Hull, lunch the next day again at the White House, dinner with Henry Stimson, visits to Arlington Cemetery and the Lincoln Memorial, receptions, parties – it was all very dazzling, and de Gaulle, without a doubt, was duly dazzled. In his memoirs, all the villains of the previous years somehow become stars: Roosevelt has a brilliant personality; Hull is magnanimous; and so the catalogue continues.

The explanation for Roosevelt's double dealing – charm to de Gaulle's face and snide remarks behind his back – was not far to seek. The election in November, with Thomas Dewey, the Governor of New York State, putting up strong Republican opposition, was troubling him; and he had scented a shift in public sentiment. America loved de Gaulle; so America would get de Gaulle. That was how American politics worked. Meanwhile, as Hopkins, Morgenthau and McCloy made clear in private to the General, it was agreed to bury the idea of an American-occupied France.

But de Gaulle was not only dazzled by America. He was also fascinated by the confidence that the America of that period displayed. It really was a New World. There was optimism, promise, confidence in the future. When he arrived in New York, on 10 July, he was astonished, and taken aback, by the frenetic energy of the place. It was almost a relief to move on the next day to the more sedate atmosphere of Canada. Ottawa was friendly, but Quebec had been firmly Vichyite and the reception there was more cautious.

On 13 July, de Gaulle returned home to Algiers. His visit to the United States had paid the dividend that he had been seeking. At a press conference on 11 July, Roosevelt had turned about. It was not, he said, a question of 'recognising' the French Committee for National Liberation; it was rather that the United States would accept the committee as 'the de facto authority for the civil administration of France'.[6] There had been what was described as 'a fresh approach to the French situation' – in practice no more than a reshuffling of the old arguments by de Gaulle's supporters Morgenthau, Stimson and McCloy, but now with tacit support from Hull.

It had also been a question of selling the proposition to the President. Morgenthau had insisted that it had to be presented as something completely new. McCloy agreed, but also said that there had to be some points in the declaration that would attract the President's favourable attention. 'I mean,' he said, 'those things that he clutches at, and if you put them in there, he's awfully apt to say "Yes, that's right" and take an awful lot of other stuff along with it.'[7] The technique had worked: the 'de facto' authority was born.

But Roosevelt's about-turn had taken the British aback. Eden and Viénot had, after all, been patiently putting together a detailed agreement

on civil administration, and the President had, by his public announcement, made it appear that it was the Americans who were taking the lead
in supporting the French Committee for National Liberation. As Oliver
Harvey wrote at the time, Roosevelt made it appear 'that it has been
himself and nobody else who has got us all out of the jam, in order to
acquire for himself credit by removing it. What a slippery politician he
is!'[8] Eden was understandably furious. 'Can't we really have a foreign
policy of our own?' he asked.[9]

The effect of the American acceptance of the 'de facto' authority of
the French Committee was to encourage Churchill and Eden to
improve relations between the British Government and de Gaulle.
Churchill praised the success of the General's visit to the United States
in a speech to the House of Commons on 2 August, and suggested that
on his way to Rome on the 11th he would stop in Algiers, where he
would welcome a meeting with de Gaulle. Duff Cooper transmitted this
message to de Gaulle, but was told curtly, 'I have nothing to say to
him.'[10] Spears had been causing more trouble in the Levant, offering to
supply arms to the Syrian police, who wished to be independent of
French interference. De Gaulle was angry about that, but he was also
still harbouring resentment over his treatment by the British during and
after the Normandy invasion. The result was that all Churchill received
at Algiers airport was a letter from the General, delivered by Palewski,
which conveyed the message that it was, in the General's view, preferable that they should not meet at that point, so that Churchill might get
some rest between flights.

It was a snub, and a particularly unpleasant one, considering that
Churchill was, as he wrote to Eden the next day, 'the head of a government which has three-quarters of a million soldiers fighting, with
heavy losses, to liberate France'.[11] The mere thought of de Gaulle was
enough to irritate him. 'I didn't do at all well with Duckling,' Diana
Cooper recalled of a dinner in Rome a few days later – 'Duckling'
being Churchill's rather fanciful codename at the time – 'because my
face reminds him instantly of de Gaulle. This gives him apoplexy, so I
turn from him to Ambassador Kirk . . . I turn with a new subject to
Duckling, but again my face transports him back immediately to de
Gaulle, and apoplexy envelops him. It's made our meeting impossible.'[12]

There is no doubt that de Gaulle was at this time worried and
depressed. His attention was wholly taken up by the situation inside
France itself. Ever since the formation of an umbrella organisation for
the Resistance, there had been tension between those who wanted

immediate and decisive action and those who urged restraint until Allied forces had completed the initial phase of the Normandy landings. This tension, which erupted like a volcano from time to time in violent uprisings – mercilessly suppressed by the German occupying armies, most notably in the Vercors in late June 1944 – was aggravated by the increasing influence of the Communist Party within the movement. The communists wanted action, and de Gaulle became increasingly suspicious that they were preparing a post-war takeover. Even at the eleventh hour, he thought, France could slip out of his, and into Stalin's, hands.

On 11 August 1944, the FCNL sent an instruction to the Resistance, in a very muted tone, to confine its activities for the moment to strikes and possible taking of hostages if the enemy showed signs of weakness. It was not a very inspiring call to arms, to say the least; and it was followed by the appointment of Alexandre Parodi* as delegate-general in France and full member of the FCNL, a position previously enjoyed, if that is the right word, by Jean Moulin the year before. Parodi's job was to keep the situation under control.

At the same time as the real or imagined threat from the left loomed large, another threat made itself felt, this time from the right. It was in truth a strange affair. It originated with Laval, who had begun to sense a German defeat. For some reason, Laval thought that he could frustrate a Gaullist government in France, and at the same time save his own skin, by resuscitating the 1936 Assembly of the Third Republic – which he himself had been instrumental in killing – and then claiming that it was the legitimate authority in the new France.

Bizarre as it now seems, the plan came within sight of success. Laval was clever enough to choose Edouard Herriot, the President of the 1936 Assembly, to lead the movement; at his side would be Jules Jeanneney, the former leader of the Senate. There were, to be sure, some difficulties: Herriot was in prison, and had anyway come out in favour of de Gaulle; and Jeanneney, although he had not been put inside, was also known to be a Gaullist and a rather awkward character.

Laval arrived in Paris on 10 August, apparently after having in vain tried to persuade Pétain to put himself under Allied military protection. He sought and obtained the approval of the German ambassador in

---

* Alexandre Parodi (1901–1979): Politician. Came to prominence in Resistance; Delegate General of Provisional Government for Occupied France 1944; Minister of Labour 1944–5; Ambassador to Italy and French representative to UN Security Council 1946–9; French representative to NATO 1955–7.

Paris, the ever-faithful Otto Abetz, and made contact with the Americans through Allen Dulles, the head of American intelligence services in Europe. The American response was equivocal – much less positive than de Gaulle was later to claim.

Laval went to Nancy on 12 August, removed Herriot from his prison hospital and took him off to Paris. But the old warrior was not so easily fooled. He said he would do nothing without first consulting Jeanneney. By this time, events had moved forward. The Allies had broken out of the Normandy bridgehead and were moving apace into the heart of France; Hitler had got to hear of the Laval plan; and the French Nazis, Marcel Déat, Joseph Darnand and Fernand de Brinon, had mobilised opposition to the scheme. It was immediately knocked on the head. Laval was told to keep quiet, and Herriot was arrested again and taken off to Germany. He was finally freed by the Red Army, near Potsdam, in April 1945.

That was the end of the threat from the right. De Gaulle could now be relieved that a combination of old Third Republican politicians, Pétain, and – quite possibly – American support could not succeed. But the threat from the left remained. At all events, the Allied armoured offensive in France – both in the north and also in the south, following the landings in Provence – was moving so quickly that, whether or not there was a communist plot, it was clearly time for the head of the Provisional Government to be in France. De Gaulle therefore requested permission from the Allied high command to visit France, as protocol still required him to do; he was granted it after giving an assurance, requested by Washington, that he was only making a visit and did not intend to stay – which was less than the truth. He then left Algiers on 18 August 1944, bound for Normandy.

As it turned out, the flight was hazardous, to the point where the aircraft and its passenger were nearly lost. It took two full days to reach France. There were stops at Casablanca and Gibraltar. There were mechanical failures in the American aircraft that had been sent to fetch de Gaulle and Juin, who was with him, leaving Juin stranded at Gibraltar airport; and de Gaulle's own smaller Lockheed nearly ran out of fuel over the Channel, where they had lost their way. It was de Gaulle himself who, having forbidden his pilot to land in England, had to identify visually various points on the Cherbourg peninsula and order his pilot to land, in mist, at an improvised strip near Maupertuis in Normandy. It could have been anywhere, even in German-occupied territory. Koenig and Coulet, who were to greet him, had to scurry about to find out where the aeroplane had come down. In the end, the General was driven into Cherbourg, and Koenig and Coulet were summoned to meet him there. The General had had luck on his side, but he was nervous and bad-tempered at the near-miss.

The reports from Koenig and Coulet brought mixed news. Coulet told the General that the administration was working well, that the Allies had accepted the de facto position and that there was no longer any question of 'bogus currency'. The 'sixty-day marvels' had not appeared. Koenig's report, on the other hand, was less satisfactory. The tensions in the Resistance movement had finally boiled to the surface in Paris. The Forces Françaises de l'Intérieur (FFI), as the Resistance was now collectively known, were deeply divided between the communists, who considered themselves the heirs of the Commune of 1871, and the 'attentistes', the moderates, supported by the FCNL, represented by Parodi and de Gaulle's military delegate-general, Jacques Chaban-Delmas. There had been one crisis immediately after the Normandy landings, when, in response to what was perceived as a call to general uprising, a number of groups had taken violent action, only to be dismayed by later messages, both from Koenig in London and de Gaulle in Algiers, telling them to hold back. Another crisis was now threatening. At any moment there would be an uprising in Paris itself, which Parodi was powerless to prevent.

The fact was that Parodi and Chaban-Delmas had only been able to hold the line at all by agreeing to a general insurrection in Paris, in the knowledge that American armoured columns were within striking distance of the capital and would arrive within forty-eight hours. The German general in command of Paris, General von Choltitz, had disobeyed Hitler's order to destroy the city and agreed a truce on 19 August, but it had been broken the next day. The police had gone on strike; barricades had been thrown up in the working-class areas of Paris; the traditional revolutionary arrondissements, those around the Bastille, were fighting the Germans with any weapon that came to hand, even kitchen knives. There had been hundreds of skirmishes; bodies were piling up in Notre-Dame des Victoires and starting to stink in the heat. Even the bourgeoisie were beginning to fear another 1871 and sent a delegation to de Gaulle asking him to come quickly.

It was now clear that the situation in the capital was one of great danger. There was, of course, the usual confusion, and nobody fully knew the extent of the uprising. But the truth was probably best summed up a year later in an editorial in Combat, generally supposed to have been written by Albert Camus; that initially some 4000 to 5000 men, with a few hundred firearms between them, came out, in accordance with a well worked out plan, to hold up the retreating remnants of the German 7th Army. After less than a week 50,000 Parisians were at the barricades, in the districts of the Revolution, and were fighting with arms captured from the enemy. Nearly 3000 Parisians died and there were some 7000 wounded. But Paris had slowed down the German retreat.

'Such is the truth,' the editorial went on. 'But one should add to it the colours of a Paris summer, the thunderstorm of that Wednesday night, and the young people manning those barricades and laughing at last, for the first time in four years.'[13]

Quite unlike Churchill, General de Gaulle was unmoved by these romantic notions. He could weep at the news of an act of French military heroism, as at Bir Hakeim, but young Parisians at the barricades had nothing to do with heroism, and far more to do with the ultimate sin – anarchy. Indeed, they represented something more sinister – a carefully controlled challenge to properly constituted authority. It was now vital to take speedy action to bring matters under control.

The immediate task was to see the Supreme Commander, General Eisenhower, and late in the evening of 20 August they had their first interview. Eisenhower explained his strategic plan: Montgomery's army group would strike north-east towards Rouen, and General Bradley's army group would move south of Paris, heading as fast as possible towards the Rhine. Paris would be encircled, and would fall without unnecessary loss of life. The plan was eminently sensible in military terms, but ignored the political significance of the capital, let alone the possibility of a second Commune.

For two days, the issue hung in the balance, while the fighting in Paris continued from street to street. De Gaulle was sure that Eisenhower's strategy was wrong, but he was in no position to force a change. His only weapon was, as always, a demonstration that he was supported by public opinion. In this case, it was the public opinion of liberated France. The next day, although he was only on temporary permission, he decided to make personal visits to as many cities and towns of liberated France as he could. His reception everywhere was no less enthusiastic than it had been in Bayeux two months earlier, and now it was less restrained.

Buoyed up by his day's tour of liberated Normandy and Brittany, de Gaulle sent messages from Rennes to the FCNL in Algiers, reporting on the state of popular morale in liberated France, and, more important, to General Eisenhower, again emphasising the danger of delaying the liberation of Paris.

The following day, 22 August, he heard at Le Mans from Parodi that the situation in Paris was worsening, and that German forces were regrouping for a counter-attack. As it happened, Eisenhower was getting the same message from his own intelligence sources and from Bradley's staff. At that point, he reversed his previous decision, ordered the attack on Paris, and agreed that General Leclerc's 2nd French Armoured Division would be given the task. It was a wise decision, both politically and militarily. Leclerc's division had already pushed units towards Paris beyond orders, much to the irritation of the Allied high command, but de Gaulle had informed him by cable, 'I approve of your intentions.'[14] In Paris itself, the situation was full of danger. Any other decision would have involved an inter-Allied row and Eisenhower was understandably anxious to avoid that.

Leclerc's division approached Paris from the south-west. De Gaulle caught up with the headquarters unit at Rambouillet, and in the evening of 23 August had his final meeting with Leclerc to hear his plan of assault. There would be three main thrusts: one through the Porte de Gentilly in the south west and heading northwards into the heart of the city, with the objective of taking von Choltitz's headquarters at the Hôtel Meurice in the rue de Rivoli; a second coming in from the west and storming the Pont de Sèvres; and a third moving further east and entering the capital through the Porte d'Italie and the Porte d'Orléans. De Gaulle approved. The real battle for Paris had started.

Throughout the day of 24 August, as Leclerc's tanks were rumbling to their positions, street fighting in the city continued. The insurgents were in control of the east of the city and most of the Left Bank, but von Choltitz's armour still held the Right Bank and the suburbs. Free newspapers were now being published, and the morale of the insurgents was raised by the sight of one of Leclerc's reconnaissance planes, which flew over the Ile de la Cité and dropped a message – immediately broadcast over the rebel radio. 'Keep holding out,' it read, 'we are coming.'

But it was not as easy as that. Leclerc's main force, under de Gaulle's old chief of staff Colonel Billotte, came under heavy fire ten miles south of its first objective, suffered heavy losses, and by nightfall had only reached Fresnes, six miles from the city. It would have been foolish to try a night attack and Billotte called a halt. Leclerc was bitterly disappointed and ordered a Captain Dronne to take three light armoured cars into the centre of Paris on reconnaissance. Dronne reached the Place de l'Hôtel de Ville late that night without incident, and told the Parisians who were there at the barricades that the next day would see the whole division in Paris.

Billotte's decision to wait for daylight caused confusion in more ways than one. De Gaulle, unaware of the situation, had cabled Algiers that the 2nd Armoured was entering Paris on the 24th, and that Parodi had the capital well under control. The BBC had already announced late on the 23rd that Paris had been liberated, which in turn prompted a congratulatory telegram from King George VI and public demonstrations of delight in London.

Fortunately, 25 August dawned brilliantly clear and Leclerc's tanks were on the move again. They quickly broke the remaining German resistance in the suburbs, and by nine o'clock Billotte was in the centre of the city. The commanders of the other columns were not far behind: Massu* arrived at the Place de l'Etoile at half-past nine, and Georges Buis at the Place de la Concorde at ten. Leclerc himself followed soon afterwards and set up his headquarters in the Gare de Montparnasse. The Meurice was stormed early in the afternoon, and General von Choltitz was hauled off to a meeting with Leclerc. The document of surrender of the German garrison had already been prepared. It was signed without further delay. Paris was liberated.

De Gaulle's own entry into Paris was timed and executed with exquisite theatricality. He left the château of Rambouillet at almost exactly 3 p.m. and was driven eastwards through the southern suburbs, turning north at Longjumeau to follow the line of the modern Autoroute du Sud into Paris at the Porte d'Italie. None of this was accidental. The crowds, the 'exulting tide' as he would call them,[15] were waiting, becoming more excited the nearer he got to the boundaries of the city, and already threatening to hold him up. By the time he reached the Porte d'Italie it was obvious that he was in danger of being brought to a standstill. But it was a simple matter to take a left fork up the Avenue du Maine rather than continue along what is now the Avenue du Général Leclerc and on to the Boulevard St Michel.

---

*Jacques Massu (1908–1992): Soldier. Sometimes crude but always effective paratrooper; took part in all Free French African campaigns in Second World War; commanded French forces first in Indo-China and then at Suez 1956; Prefect Algiers 1958; C.-in-C. French forces in Germany 1966–9.

e de Gaulle children in 1900: from left to right - Xavier, Marie-Agnès,
arles, Jacques and Pierre.

harles de Gaulle at sixteen.

The de Gaulle, Maillot and de Corbie children on
holiday at Wimille, about 1900.

The Rhetoric class at Vaugirard: Henri, Charles' father, sits in the centre; Charles is in the second row, third from left.

Second lieutenant de Gaulle with fellow officers of the 33rd Regiment of Infantry, 1913.

De Gaulle at St Cyr, 1910.

Captain de Gaulle, in the First World War, before being taken prisoner, 1916.

The wedding of Charles de Gaulle and Yvonne
Vendroux, 6 April 1921, in Calais.

De Gaulle with his daughter Anne on the beach at Bénodet in Brittany, summer 1933.

Colonel de Gaulle showing off his tanks to President
Lebrun, October 1939.

Defeat: May 1940.

The 'Appel' of 18 June 1940.

Rallying French Africa: Brazzaville, 1940.

De Gaulle with the Free French
Navy, 1941.

De Gaulle as leader of Free French, 1940.

Arrival in Algiers: May 1943

Exhaustion and stress: de Gaulle's first visit to
France after the Normandy landings, June 1944.

Liberation: Paris, August 1944.

Armistice Day 1944: Churchill and de Gaulle
in Paris.

De Gaulle leaves the National Assembly,
November 1945.

De Gaulle's speech at Bruneval: March 1947.

RPF rally at Bagatelle: May 1952.

The family (clockwise from top left): Charles de Gaulle, Yvonne de Gaulle, Philippe de Gaulle, Elisabeth de Boissieu and Anne de Gaulle.

Return to power: May 1958.

De Gaulle and Kennedy: May 1961

Press conference: November 1962.

"VOILA, THIS IS WHAT YOU CALL 'HIT FOR SIX', NON ..?"

In power: May 1966.

Ireland, 1969.

The head of state in formal dress.

The coffin passes by Anne's grave: 12 November 1970.

Leclerc himself was waiting for him at the Gare de Montparnasse. It was familiar territory for de Gaulle; just around the corner was the Jesuit school in the rue de Vaugirard, and the Collège Stanislas was no more than a stone's throw from the Gare de Montparnasse. Forty years earlier, the young Charles had known this quarter of Paris better than any other place on earth. Not only that, but the Ecole Supérieure de Guerre was only a few minutes' walk away.

Once there, he shook hands with Chaban-Delmas, the French National Committee's military delegate, and Colonel Tanguy, a fiery communist, known simply as 'Rol', who had been the leading organiser of the Paris uprising – and who had been, much to de Gaulle's displeasure, a co-signatory of the surrender document. There were greetings and mutual congratulations – and a chance to see his son Philippe, who had been seconded to the 2nd Armoured; then, at about 5 p.m., he left the Gare de Montparnasse.

His next destination was the office of the Ministry of War in the rue St Dominique, just by the Invalides. Normally, he would have gone straight up the Boulevard de Montparnasse and crossed the rue de Sèvres into the Boulevard des Invalides, but there was a pocket of resistance around the church of St Francis Xavier – his own parish church during his schooldays – and he took the smaller rue Vanneau. He sat in his old office, which he had left more than four years previously. Not a piece of furniture had been altered. Even the telephone had the names of 1940 on its register. The ghosts had now returned.

Not unnaturally, the National Council of the Resistance and their Parisian branch, the Paris Liberation Committee, who had led the uprising, were becoming rather irritated at what they regarded as the General's sentimental journey. Parodi and Léon Morandat, both of whom had worked closely with the Resistance, and in Morandat's case with the British as well, explained the situation in the clearest possible terms. De Gaulle should go immediately to the Hôtel de Ville.

He refused, moving on instead to the headquarters of the police with Charles Luizet, who had led the police strike against the occupation in the final days, and who was a committed supporter. It was a sensible enough move. Before meeting the Resistance leaders, de Gaulle wanted to make sure that the Paris police were on his side. He knew perfectly well that the president of the Paris Committee of Liberation, Georges Marrane, was a communist.

He need not have worried so much, although it is typical of the man that he did. When he finally arrived at the Hôtel de Ville, after walking there from the police prefecture through a large crowd, he was welcomed by both Bidault and Marrane in the warmest possible way. But he was ill at ease in the atmosphere. He made a speech, one of his few wholly impromptu speeches – which, as it turned out, was among the greatest of his life. At the start his head moved from side to side as he eyed, almost suspiciously, the crowd surrounding him. Then, when he spoke of the 'eternal' France, his head went back and his eyes closed, in the manner of a mystic. Suddenly, towards the end of the speech, he started using quick and dramatic gestures with his arms, to illustrate the fact that the liberation had been achieved with the help of the whole of France. On film, it is as striking today as it must have been then. It was Gaullist oratory at its most inspiring.

Carried away, Bidault pressed de Gaulle there and then to 'proclaim the Republic', a phrase resonant with the echo of revolutionary France. De Gaulle cut him down. 'The Republic,' he said, 'has never ceased to exist . . . Why should I proclaim it?' One hour later, de Gaulle was back in his office at the Ministry of War. There he told Maurice Schumann, who had managed the French radio service on the BBC almost throughout the war, 'You will never get me to do that again.'[16]

The following day, 26 August 1944, there was a parade such as Paris had never seen before. Militarily it was the sheerest folly. There were still German snipers all over the city; the German rearguard was still just east of Paris; the German 47th Division was moving in from the north; and there were ninety German bombers sitting on the airfield at Le Bourget waiting for the order to attack. Yet de Gaulle had announced a Parade of Liberation, and as the announcement was repeated on the radio during the morning nearly a million Parisians responded by coming out onto the streets.

It started at the Etoile in early afternoon. General de Gaulle, surrounded by his closest colleagues, stood in silence at the Tomb of the Unknown Soldier before laying a Cross of Lorraine made of flowers on the plaque and relighting the flame. The procession then moved down the Champs-Elysées towards Notre-Dame. The General, after curtly telling Bidault to keep a few paces behind him, set out at a brisk pace. As he went, he acknowledged the cheers of the crowd with short, jerky movements of his arms from the elbow, as though he were throwing something away. But for one of the few times in his life, he was smiling in public – not a broad smile, to be sure – but smiling nonetheless.

The procession passed through the delirious crowd to the Grand Palais and the statue of Clemenceau, continued down to the Hôtel de

Ville and from there to Notre-Dame. The crowd held back, chanting de Gaulle's name in unison as the tall figure passed, then fell in behind him. In the rue de Rivoli the General got into a car to drive the rest of the way to the cathedral. Even then there was danger. Shots were fired by snipers on the way, and it was even said that a German sniper had had de Gaulle in his sights but had known that he would never escape if he were mad enough to pull the trigger. The crowd was on the verge of panic, but de Gaulle left his car and walked slowly to the west door. Once inside, there were more shots from the roof of the nave as the assembled company took cover under their seats. De Gaulle was unmoved. Although it was thought wise to keep the proceedings as short as possible – the grand 'Te Deum' was put off for another day – he calmly stood through the service, joining fervently in the 'Magnificat': 'For he that is mighty hath magnified me; and holy is his name.' The words were more than usually appropriate.

2

GOVERNMENT MUST GOVERN

Que Charles ne se croie pas attendu comme le Messie. Certes il sera, à juste titre, très bien reçu ici, et les espoirs de millions de Français et de Françaises sont attachés à ce qu'il fera. Mais son credit n'est pas illimité, loin de là.★

'I am at the Ministry of War,' de Gaulle wrote to his wife on 27 August 1944, 'in rue Saint-Dominique. But it is a temporary arrangement. When you come, we will take a house with a garden next to the Bois de Boulogne, and I will have offices somewhere else.'[1] The General was signalling his firm belief that he had become indispensable to the future of his country. Since June 1940, his prime task – self-imposed, it must be admitted – had been to preserve the honour of undefeated France and to challenge the shame of the armistice. There had always been a risk that he would fail or be elbowed aside. That risk had finally been removed. He was now, without doubt, destined to head the Government of France.

This being so, there were three clear priorities. The first was to establish the authority of the Government after four years of enemy occupation and the inevitable confusion of liberation; the second was to finish the war, and to achieve for France the post-war position that her historical greatness, at least in the General's view, merited; and the third was to recreate the economic infrastructure that would serve as the basis for post-war prosperity.

The first and third were priorities for peace, and, for all his wartime achievements, the truth is that General de Gaulle had had no experience at all of peacetime government. He had spent only a few days as a min-

---

★ 'Charles should not think that he is waited for like the Messiah. Certainly, and rightly, he will be well received here, and the hopes of millions of French men and women are founded on what he will do. But his credit is not unlimited; far from it.' Message to Charles de Gaulle from Jacques Bingen, 14 April 1944, a few weeks before his arrest and murder by the Gestapo. Bingen's letters, quoted in Jean Lacouture, *De Gaulle*, vol. 1, page 731 (tr. author).

ister, and those were in the chaos of June 1940. He had no knowledge of, or much interest in, the issues of economics and public welfare which preoccupy modern peacetime administrations. True, he had been the head of the FCNL in Algiers, but that had been at best a colonial administration deprived of its metropolitan centre; at worst an ill-assorted group of men chosen more on grounds of personal loyalty than ability or political distinction. Now he was confronted with the task of running a real government of a real country.

The problems facing de Gaulle in August 1944 were daunting. War was still raging, and the part of France that was now free was only just beginning to come to terms with the end of four years of oppressive occupation. De Gaulle himself was only on a 'temporary visit', by leave of the Allied high command. The Government of which he was head was only provisional, and was not recognised even as such by his most powerful Allies, Britain, the United States and the Soviet Union. There was no constitution by which to be guided, other than that of the discredited Third Republic. The Provisional Government had no clear political programme, since all its efforts to date had been directed along the single track of liberating the country from the occupying enemy.

But perhaps of even greater significance than any of these difficulties was that the new head of Government had – by force of circumstance – been out of touch with the large majority of his fellow Frenchmen for four full years. He had not shared either the dangers of Resistance, and the camaraderie which they generated, or the resignation of the defeated, and the consequent desire to be left in peace. All his information about living conditions under the occupation had come to him at second hand. It was not his fault, and even for the most perceptive and experienced politician the undercurrents of the time were hard to detect, let alone analyse. Furthermore, if the truth be told, he did not particularly like his compatriots. They failed too often, in his view, to match up to his perception of the grandeur of France. It is little wonder that inexperience, and perhaps an instinctive inability to adapt to the diversities of peacetime politics, led him to mistakes, and in due course to failure.

The first priority, that of establishing the authority of the Government, was addressed immediately, although de Gaulle's method of going about it led him into strange political territory. There was, in his view – and, to be fair, that of many others – a direct conspiratorial threat from communism, which he instinctively detested by temperament and upbringing, and which he had learnt from his Jesuit education to consider as atheist and therefore inherently evil. But to counter that threat, if indeed a threat existed outside the General's imagination, he was compelled to adopt a strategy that carried a high degree of risk.

The strategy was in essence simple. It was to keep the official Communist Party quiet by offering it a share in the Government and stealing many of its policies, but at the same time to suppress the Resistance and incorporate its fighting men into the regular army. As both head of government and a soldier, de Gaulle could not countenance the continued military presence of a Resistance side by side with the official French army. Besides, he regarded the Resistance as being heavily dominated by communists – the National Council had after all produced the 'CNR Charter', which read in places as though it had been dictated from Moscow. But to defeat the Resistance he had first to secure the full support of the Allies, so that he had visible strength on his side. Then, with that support, he had to appeal directly to the passive majority that had previously sought, and gained, its reassurance from Marshal Pétain.

'If the Government wishes to kill the Resistance,' one of his critics wrote, under the pseudonym 'Indomitus', 'it can do it by following the logic of the policy that it has set in train, that is to play the card of the "Nation" against that of the "Resistance". In other words, in domestic policy, it is enough for it to assume the role of the Pétain Government . . . The secret wish of many . . . is to follow what he represented . . . Such a policy would receive massive support from right-thinking people.'[2] Indomitus was right; and, by an ironic twist of circumstance, the rebel General was forced to abandon those who had brought him to power and assume the mantle of the defeatist Marshal.

It was not easy for General de Gaulle to appeal to the Allies for support in what were, after all, French domestic matters. He had never done it before. On the contrary, he had always fought to keep them out. Not surprisingly, the General failed to mention the episode in his memoirs. Yet, so fragile was his hold on power, and so great his fear of an armed communist takeover led by the Resistance, that for once he had to overcome his own pride.

In this he had a piece of luck. On Sunday 27 August 1944, the day after the Magnificat in Notre-Dame, General Eisenhower arrived in Paris. 'I went to call on General de Gaulle promptly,' Eisenhower said after the war, 'and I did this very deliberately as a kind of de facto recognition of him as the provisional President of France.'[3] De Gaulle asked for two American divisions to help him enforce authority in Paris, and for uniforms for the lower echelons of the Resistance, who were to be incorporated into the French army. It was the first time, Eisenhower noted sardonically, that de Gaulle had ever asked for help from Allied forces to bolster his own authority, and it had happened in France itself. 'But,' he went on, 'I understood de Gaulle's problem.' The request was granted.

With this support secure, General de Gaulle moved into action. The very next morning he summoned to his office the military leaders of the Resistance, together with the officers of their general staff. He had the officers lined up in an ante-room, into which he marched loftily – remarking as he came in, 'There are a lot of colonels here' – and then shook each by the hand. As he did so, he asked, 'What is your job?' To a reply 'mechanic', de Gaulle simply said, 'Well then, you must go back to the factory'; to a reply 'teacher', it was 'back to school'. Pierre Villon, the Communist leader of the military committee of the National Council of the Resistance, was outraged. One of his aides said to him as they left, 'I knew about human ingratitude, but I never imagined that it could reach such a level.'[4] It was obviously the first time he had seen the General deploy the full range of his formidable psychological weaponry.

In the afternoon, it was the turn of political leaders of the National Council. They were told firmly that the senior command of the Forces Françaises de l'Intérieur was to be disbanded and the FFI itself absorbed into the army. In vain they argued that, if that were to happen, morale would collapse. De Gaulle simply would not listen to any opposition.

The dispute continued at a further meeting the following morning. By that time the two American divisions that Eisenhower had promised were lining up to parade through Paris, with de Gaulle alongside General Bradley on the saluting base. The Resistance leaders realised that the game was up. They could not fight de Gaulle and the Americans as well. Besides, both Bidault and Villon, the two most influential, had been offered places in de Gaulle's new Government. From then on, the Resistance as such disintegrated as a centralised and coherent political force. But even with very visible American support, de Gaulle had had to concede a place for the remnants of the National Council in his new Government. He could not exclude them entirely without risking a confrontation with the official Communist Party – and that was one which he could not possibly win, even with Eisenhower on his side, without pushing the country into civil war.

The next step was to form his new Provisional Government. It was not at all easy, as his notes of the time show. By temperament, he wanted a Council of Ministers that would reflect without question his own views. But he had enough sense to see that there were interest groups that had to be placated, by far the most important of which was the Communist Party. After much pondering, de Gaulle finally asked Jacques Duclos, the representative in France of Maurice Thorez, who was still in Moscow, to suggest a replacement for Villon, who had turned down de Gaulle's offer of a job. It was a sensible move, but not one of which the General, normally so decisive, was particularly proud.

A Government of 'National Unanimity' was announced on 5 September 1944, although the list of ministers was not finalised until 9 September. The version that emerged was, as a result, and in spite of many hesitations and last-minute doubts, probably the least unsatisfactory that could be achieved under the circumstances. Bidault was entrusted with foreign affairs, and other active members of the Resistance, François de Menthon, Teitgen and Charles Tillon, were included, but Tillon was there on the grounds that he was a communist – there was only one other. Pierre Mendès-France came in to take control of finance. The rest were old faithfuls from Algiers days such as Diethelm, Pleven and Catroux, or representatives of the 'old' parties. All in all, it can be said to have been enough to hold France together, but was certainly not to de Gaulle's own private taste. In fact it was, as was noted at the time, a transparent and old-fashioned political fudge. Almost without being aware of it, the General had not just readmitted party politics by the back door but had made them central to the whole political process of post-war France.

With the new Government now in place, it was time for its new head to define its general policy stance, and in particular to explain his thoughts on his three priorities, the authority of the Government, France's place in the world and the state of the French economy. This he did in a speech to a mass meeting at the Palais de Chaillot on 12 September, organised for him by the National Council of the Resistance – rather oddly, given his brutal treatment of its leaders. Although the speech reflected the ideas that he had put to the Resistance leaders in 1942, when he was canvassing their support, he found it difficult to make and it took him the best part of four days to draft.

The start was straightforward enough. There was the assertion of the authority of the state over the judicial system, the administration of the country and the armed forces. He insisted that France, by her own exertions, merited a place high among the great powers. All that was classic Gaullism. But what came next was surprising. He proclaimed that private interest must always be subordinate to public interest, that the major sources of wealth must be exploited, not for the profit of a few, but for the advantage of all, that the private monopolies which had 'weighed so heavily on our human condition and even on the policy of the State' must be abolished once for all, and that all French men and women had the right to live, work, and bring up their children, in 'security and dignity'.[5] It was as near to socialism as it could be without the name itself.

The Chaillot speech was intended not just as a string of generalities. It marked the beginning of a formidable programme of action. Work was put in hand for the nationalisation of coal, gas and electricity, the banks and insurance companies, and the great companies of Renault and Berliet. There was to be a system of family allowances, of unemployment and sickness pay, as well as employee involvement in the management of industry. The civil service was to be reorganised and an Ecole Nationale d'Administration founded. Although a great deal of the programme remained to be completed when de Gaulle left office, there is no doubt that his Provisional Government did the groundwork. A Jesuit-educated general set France on the road to socialism.

Much of that, however, lay in the future. In the autumn of 1944, the problems were more pressing and immediate. In Paris, although the situation seemed at least stable, it was far from normal. There was no public transport; the first trains on the Métro did not start running until 11 September. Food was in short supply and the black market was thriving. The euphoria of liberation was quickly giving way to discontent.

Nevertheless, de Gaulle felt able to move to his new home in Neuilly, a leisurely suburb just to the west of the boundaries of Paris proper. The house which had been found for him was, in his view, appropriate to his new estate, sitting as it did in the rue du Champ d'Entrainement overlooking the Bois de Boulogne – as he had promised his wife; it was elegantly furnished, mostly by Palewski, with pieces that were largely the property of the state. De Gaulle was doubtful about the propriety of this – he was always punctilious about taking advantage of his official position – but let it pass. He was joined there – at last, since it was their first taste of France since the hectic escape of June 1940 – by his wife and daughters, although the house was not entirely to Yvonne's liking. It was, she confided to a friend, 'a bit above what I would have wished'.[6]

But even if Paris seemed stable, and the Resistance leadership neutered, a Government formed and a home established, there remained the rest of France. By now, apart from some remaining German garrisons in the harbours on the Atlantic coast, the whole of the country to the west of a line from Normandy to Provence was free of enemy troops and in the hands of local Resistance groups. Many of these were communist or communist-led, and were by no means enthusiastic about the 'commissioners of the republic' whom the Provisional Government sent to take control of their areas in the name of de Gaulle. Indeed, had it not been for divisions and jealousies within local groups, and a general directive from Moscow to the French Communist Party to make no trouble until the peace, there might have occurred just the kind of sporadic civil war that the Allies, as well as de Gaulle, had been so anxious to avoid.

So if the Pétain role, of national unity against factional disturbance, of proved military discipline against anarchic uprisings, had to be played again, General de Gaulle had to be ready to play it in the wider France, outside Paris. Like Pétain in 1940, his strength lay in direct and popular appeal to the provincial French on the grounds that he, and he alone, could bring peace and tranquillity to their lives. He therefore proceeded to spread that appeal through personal appearances throughout the country, and, in a direct imitation of the Pétainist technique, by distributing idealised photographs of himself up and down the length of liberated France. Portraits of the Marshal were quickly removed from hundreds of thousands of mantelpieces, and replaced by portraits of the General.

Of course, it was not just a question of propaganda, important as that was. There were real and pressing problems, and de Gaulle showed himself able to deal with problems in a decisive, and frequently ruthless, manner. At Toulouse, for instance, Commissioner Bertaux was faced with what looked suspiciously like a soviet on the model of Petrograd in 1917; it was under the control of a twenty-six-year-old Colonel 'Ravenel', whose command, and rank, had been confirmed by General Koenig himself just before Overlord. To complicate matters, a British agent called 'Colonel Hilary' had been operating with the Toulousain underground, and now commanded a force of some 6000 Spanish republicans who wanted either to support a Communist government in France or, in a fit of enthusiasm which now seems hilarious, to march boldly across the Spanish frontier and on to Barcelona. On de Gaulle's arrival, Colonel Hilary was packed off to England in an aeroplane within twenty-four hours and Ravenel was told curtly, 'The role of the Resistance is finished . . . as for the FFI, those who wish to remain in the army should join the fighting forces once they have received the necessary orders.'[7] Ravenel, who had fought for two years with outstanding courage against the German occupiers, could hardly believe his ears. But the Toulousains showed themselves, very vocally, to be on de Gaulle's side.

There was a similar story at Bordeaux. After making a speech to a huge crowd from the very balcony from which Léon Gambetta, one of the leaders of the 'hawks' in the Franco-Prussian War, had spoken in 1870, de Gaulle found that the local Resistance leaders were in no mood to compromise. Their case was the stronger in that there were still some strong German units occupying pockets on the Gironde estuary, but weaker in that there had been a strong collaborationist faction in Bordeaux, personified in the Mayor, Adrien Marquet, a personal friend of Laval. De Gaulle's tactics were the same. The offer – take it or leave it – was either incorporation into the army or prison. They took it.

Marseilles was much more difficult, since the communists were virtually in control, and de Gaulle's commissioner, Raymond Aubrac, was himself something of a communist sympathiser. This time, the answer was to bring across a regiment of infantry from Algiers before making his usual offer. But the offer was made not in a spirit of conciliation but of hostility and disdain. When the Marseillais put on a parade, with the Maquisards in open collars and flowers in their rifles dragging a German armoured car on which were perched some young Marseillaises in admittedly somewhat immodest summer dresses, all screaming happily and waving flags, General de Gaulle sat glumly throughout, muttering: 'Quelle mascarade, quelle mascarade!'[8]

Lyons was easier, but still the message was uncompromising – incorporation or prison – and the message itself was delivered with the same mixture of arrogance and sarcasm that only the General was capable of when dealing with his fellow countrymen. At the banquet given for him, de Gaulle wanted to sit between the Préfet and his own commissioner. Instead, they put him between two Resistance leaders. He took it badly, turned up his nose, and did not speak at all during the meal.

General de Gaulle arrived back in Paris in early November 1944. His authority had been imposed in the major cities and towns of liberated France, but at a cost. He had achieved success with the Pétainist majority, but the Resistance leaders had been deeply offended, and the offence was felt by many people whom the General had needed to woo.

The cost would be counted in later months when he needed support more than he had in the autumn of 1944. He had made mistakes that the old Marshal would never have made.

The picture presented to the General by his ministers on his return was bleak indeed. It was perhaps best summed up by François Mauriac, the editor of Le Figaro, at the time of the first meeting of an enlarged Consultative Assembly that met at the Palais Luxembourg. Mauriac quoted one of the Revolutionaries of 1792: 'Everybody wants the Republic, but nobody wants either poverty or morality.'[9] People wanted to know where the food was coming from and how they were to get decent housing.

Not only were the economic portents menacing, but there were serious political problems as well. Indeed, the whole political climate in France in the late autumn of 1944 was depressing. The country needed healing after the trauma of occupation; even if de Gaulle had been by nature a healer, the process would have been long and difficult. It was not just the shortage of food and the prospect of a hard winter. The bitterness of those who had resisted, even passively, toward those who had collaborated was given full rein. The reprisals had started immediately, and continued unabated. Traitors, particularly the pro-Nazi para-military police, were summarily executed. Women who had shown even friendliness to the German occupiers had their heads shaved in public, were tarred and marched through the streets. Old scores were paid off, old insults avenged.

In the latter days of the occupation the Germans had behaved with dreadful brutality, and their French accomplices had urged them on. According to de Gaulle's own numbers, 60,000 French men and women had been executed, with a further 150,000 dying in German camps or as the result of forced labour; 15,000 fighting men and women were condemned by the Vichy courts as traitors. 'Wiping away so many crimes and abuses of justice with a sponge,' he wrote, 'would have been to leave a monstrous abscess infecting the country for ever. Justice had to be done. It was done.'[10] Perhaps so; but the cost, both in terms of the lives of Frenchmen summarily murdered by French – perhaps as many as 40,000, and some say more – and in terms of the resentments engendered in almost every community in France, was fearful.

Gradually, but only gradually, the tide of revenge that swept France after the Liberation was brought under control. Emergency courts, set up under the authority of an Algiers decree of 1943, started to function. But it was a slow and uncertain process. Witnesses for the defence were hard to find. The trial and execution of Pierre Pucheu in Algiers seemed to have given official sanction to a general pursuit of Vichyites and collaborators in France itself; and the head of the Provisional Government kept his silence.

Nevertheless, on his return to Paris, de Gaulle realised, not necessarily that enough was enough, but that unless the Allies could see law and order properly upheld, there was a danger that they would intervene to prevent what could quickly develop into civil war. Whatever he himself felt, politically it was time to call, and enforce, a halt. It was not easy – indeed it was often difficult, and always time-consuming – but from then on the processes of law started to take hold. The courts, whatever their shortcomings in the aftermath of war, asserted their control of judicial procedure. Law and order were beginning to prevail again in France.

There was not yet, to say the least, a fully-fledged judicial procedure, working on proper rules of evidence, but the wholesale arrests of suspected collaborators on any grounds that seemed reasonable to random Resistance marauders was stopped. On 28 November courts of justice were set up to try cases of treason and 'collaboration', and special departmental committees were formed to deal with 'illicit profits' made during the occupation. On 27 December a High Court was established specifically to try Vichy ministers.

As might be imagined, none of these institutions moved smoothly and swiftly into action. To start with, there was a shortage of lawyers. The large number of cases coming up immediately clogged up the whole system. Besides, many of the magistrates were disqualified for having taken the oath of allegiance to Pétain during the occupation. Critics soon made themselves heard. *Le Franc-Tireur* was robust: 'It is not merely a matter of justice, but of national dignity.' The newspaper was particularly fierce about 'economic collaborators': 'They have made milliards; they bought themselves châteaux, and shares, and diamonds, and furs and gold . . . in the hungry and blacked-out Paris of the occupation they feasted behind the curtains of night clubs . . . rubbed shoulders with the masters of the New Order, with crooks and "collabo" journalists and Gestapo tarts.'[11] The whole process was, it claimed, sluggish and inadequate.

Nevertheless, the system did start to work, albeit laboriously, and there were some spectacular trials of Nazi sympathisers during the winter of 1944–5, which revealed the dreadful treacheries of the occupation. In one of the most prominent cases, the two heads of the

French Gestapo, Bony and Laffont, were sentenced to death and shot. So were the Nazi writers Georges Suarez, Paul Chack and – perhaps not a Nazi but certainly a collaborator – Robert Brasillach. Henri Béraud received the same sentence, but was reprieved by de Gaulle.

The reprieve had been a difficult decision for the General, and one for which he was much criticised. As head of the Government, he had to take responsibility for final judgement. In this, as always, he showed courage. He refused to delegate this most fearsome of tasks, even when it was suggested that the number of cases coming before him was imposing too heavy a burden. He himself admitted that he found it difficult to sleep. Of those condemned to death by the courts whose cases were put before him, he reprieved more than two-thirds.

The ritual was the same each day. In the evening the director of criminal affairs, Maurice Patin, used to bring a pile of documents into de Gaulle's office. They would discuss them together, and then de Gaulle would take the most difficult cases back with him to his home in Neuilly. It was a dreary and painful process, and one in which, as de Gaulle himself pointed out, there was no political accountability; he was accountable only to God.

On top of all these difficulties, the winter of 1944–5 also saw the first cracks appear in the Provisional Government. In large measure, the problem was the General's own personality and style of government. However suitable they had been to the war years, in the process of liberation they were resented, not just by the Resistance, which felt ignored, but by his own ministers. To be sure, he worked as hard as any of them. When he was not away travelling, he left his wife and daughters early for his office in the rue St Dominique, returned late, and often with work to do, seeing little of either his family or his home. The discipline in his office was harsh. The Council of Ministers met twice a week in the Matignon, in a room whose walls were left without ornament so as not to distract ministers from their tasks. Agendas were prepared with great care and detail by Joxe, the Secretary to the Council. Ministers were required to give reports, to which de Gaulle would listen, occasionally raise questions and then announce a decision. Nobody was allowed to argue. There was no humour, no intimacy.

By November, the Communists were starting to fret. Supported by the Resistance press, they claimed that too many Vichyites had been taken into the reformed civil service. There was threat of a breakaway. Even Léon Blum and Edouard Herriot, the two old soldiers of the Popular Front, who had supported the General during their years in prison in the war, made acid comments about de Gaulle's Bonapartism. The winter was hard, too, and the economy was slipping.

Temporary help came from an unexpected quarter. Maurice Thorez, the Communist Party's king across the water – the water in this case with its shoreline in Moscow, where Thorez had taken refuge in 1939 – returned to Paris in November. Thorez was, in the crudest way, an uncompromising Stalinist, ever faithful to the Moscow line. In French eyes, his crime was that he had deserted from the army, which indeed he had, and he had been condemned to death for the offence. It was Stalin himself who had advised de Gaulle to secure an amnesty for him. The advice was taken, and a special decree passed to that effect. It was a sensible move, for, when Thorez returned, he astonished the Communist Party leaders by telling them that they were quite wrong to complain about the Government and that they should give it their enthusiastic support. Moscow was apparently not prepared to see France disintegrating politically while the war was still on.

The line was held for the time being. But the underlying problems would not go away, and rows over the major domestic issue of the day, the conduct of the economy, finally culminated in the first ministerial resignation. Pierre Mendès-France, the Minister of National Economy, had been a Free French fighter pilot in the war, flying out of English airfields. He had never been involved in the intrigues of Carlton Gardens, and was never close to de Gaulle. But as the youngest, radical deputy in the Assembly of 1932, he had had political experience. 'Brilliant, but rather wild', they called him.[12] Small in stature, with clearly Jewish features, he was the antithesis of the towering Catholic General.

Mendès-France believed that the French economy needed a stringent monetary policy. Above all, he was determined to break the black market by monetary reform. He proposed calling in all notes and coin, and blocking bank deposits and all foreign exchange, with a view to resupplying money as production rose. It was all too much for his fellow ministers. By April 1945 they had had enough. There was a long, acrimonious discussion in the Council of Ministers, with de Gaulle obviously out of his depth. In the end they voted against Mendès-France and he resigned. The weaker, more sentimental Pleven took over, and the black market continued to flourish. There were protests and then riots. Liberation did not seem any better than occupation; and there was only one person to blame: the head of the Provisional Government.

Politically, there were now clear danger signals. Within eight months of the joyous scenes of the liberation of Paris, France was rebellious and morose. The truth was that people simply wanted to eat, and had expected food to follow quickly on liberation. They were not interested in projects of grandeur. But the General was. He seemed unable to understand why the gratitude of August 1944 had not been translated into enthusiasm for what he called, in his Chaillot speech, 'renovation'.

In this atmosphere of mutual incomprehension between France and her leader, it was therefore almost a pleasant diversion for de Gaulle to turn to his greatest priority and abiding passion, France's place in the world; and his technique was the same as it had been throughout the war – pushing awkwardness and discourtesy towards his Allies to the brink, but never over the brink, of complete and angry rupture.

3

THE END OF THE GENERAL'S WAR

*France . . . was like a man emerging from a
darkened room into a blaze of light, dazed
for a moment and grateful still to his friends
for understanding and encouragement.* [*]

The liberation of Paris at the end of August 1944 had, in terms of the
grand military strategy of the Allies, been little more than a sideshow.
Indeed, the two American divisions that had come to the aid of the
General in his assertion of authority over the Resistance had been on
their way to the front line, and marched through Paris in full battle
order. Not only that, but they had carried on marching, figuratively
speaking, straight through Paris and on to join General Patton's thrust to
the Rhine. That was their proper task, and the Paris parade was for
them merely an interesting diversion. As for the relatively small French
army, the view of Eisenhower and the Allied chiefs of staff was that it
needed a rest. The French had been fighting hard in Italy, and the
North African troops, in particular, needed a period of respite. Besides,
the French troops, courageous as they were, fitted uneasily into the
American and British chain of command. In other words, they were
something of a nuisance, and would do better to make themselves ready
for internal duties in France. Furthermore, all available American and
British shipping was occupied in supplying their own forces.

As might be imagined, none of this was to General de Gaulle's liking.
To retrieve the honour of France, French troops had to be in at the kill.
The army had to be built up, and the incorporation of Resistance
groups into the regular forces was the chosen, indeed the only, method
of achieving this. Some 400,000 men were recruited in September
1944, and the best trained of those, which was not saying much, about
100,000 in all, were sent to de Lattre de Tassigny's 1st Army. They were

[*] Anthony Eden, *The Eden Memoirs, The Reckoning*, page 492; Cassell, London, 1965.

equipped with arms captured from the Germans and with what they had managed to 'adopt', to use de Gaulle's own phrase, from Allied arms depots.

This effort was designed to ensure that the prestige of France was maintained to the end of the final battle. The Allies were irritated, but they were gradually coming to recognise that France, under the leadership of the General, could not simply be brushed aside. This in turn raised the question of the status of the 'Provisional Government' of France.

The matter had been discussed at the meeting between Roosevelt and Churchill at Quebec in September 1944. It was, as Eden reported on 15 September, 'a pretty hopeless discussion, each going off in turn on a tirade against de Gaulle', although Churchill did admit – 'a distinct advance' – that he would rather have a de Gaulle France than a communist France.[1] But it was a small concession, and Roosevelt wrote to Cordell Hull, on 19 September, that he had had 'lengthy talks with the PM in regard to recognition of provisional government in France. He and I are both very much opposed to it at this time. The provisional government has no direct authority from the people.'[2]

That was all very well. But on 28 September, Churchill announced to the House of Commons that the British Government was extending recognition to the new Italian Government. That in itself raised two problems – apart from a hostile reception in the House. The first was that Duff Cooper had been sent to Paris a month before with the rank of ambassador, and there was an obvious difficulty if the Government to which he was supposed to be accredited was not recognised by the Government that had appointed him. The second problem was best expressed in an editorial of 5 October in Le Franc-Tireur, one of the newspapers of the old Resistance. 'The US and Britain,' it commented acidly, "have recognised the Italian government. That is good news for the latest country to join the United Nations. It is probable that the Romanian government . . . will also be recognised . . . then it will be the turn of Bulgaria, and one day, let us hope, of Hungary . . . after the final victory, governments set up in Berlin and Tokyo will also be recognised . . . Then . . . normal relations with the Papuans, the Hottentots and the Lapps. After which – who knows – we French may at last get a look in.'[3]

To Anthony Eden's embarrassment, this line was taken up by the House of Commons. 'More argument about France,' he wrote on 12 October, referring to the continuing disagreement with Churchill, 'which didn't advance matters much; the drip-drip of water on a stone.'[4] But the stone was starting to soften, and on 14 October Churchill wrote to Roosevelt suggesting recognition. Roosevelt was still reluctant, but, as Cadogan minuted Eden on 20 October in the unmistakably urbane tones of a senior British civil servant, 'It may possibly be that the imminence of [the presidential election] might make the President hesitate to be isolated on this question.'[5]

However phrased, there was truth in Cadogan's remark. The President had taken the point and was not prepared to be upstaged by the British when it came to claiming political credit. The State Department was instructed to move, and on 22 October Jefferson Caffery, the United States ambassador in Paris, was told to take the formal steps for 'recognition' the following day. The British, and the Russians, were taken unawares by the suddenness of the American volte-face. 'But I don't care,' wrote Cadogan, 'we're not going to be left out on a limb in this show.' The next day, he wrote on the same theme: 'We plainly can't stop Duff and let the Americans get in ahead of us.' There followed an undignified scramble among the diplomats to see who could get there first. Finally, as Cadogan related, 'things took their course and we have all, thank God, Americans, British and Russians, recognised de Gaulle.'[6]

In fact, the General had no reason to be particularly impressed. His domestic problems at that moment were far more pressing, and the matter of the diplomatic status of his administration was of peripheral importance. To Allied pressmen accompanying him on his tour of the French provinces, he simply commented that the French Government was 'satisfied' to be called by its rightful name.

The truth was that de Gaulle, although secretly pleased at the news, was much more interested in building up the French army so that it could take what he regarded as its proper share in the final phase of the war. The whole drama of 'recognition' seemed to him to be a diversion. Worse still, he suspected that it was a clever manoeuvre by the Americans, made in the hope that he would be satisfied by the new status and stop his irritating insistence on further supplies of arms to the French army. He was planning to bring into action ten properly equipped divisions within the next six months, and in further comments to the press on the Allies' recognition of his Government he could not refrain from pointing out that the armaments to do so had not yet arrived, implying that this was not entirely due to difficulties of transport.

His immediate target was Strasbourg. Militarily the city was of little consequence, other than as the site of a major Rhine bridge. But for the French it was the capital of Alsace, which, together with Lorraine, had been absorbed, under the names of Elsas and Lothringen, into Hitler's thousand-year Reich. As early as 12 September 1944, de Lattre de Tassigny's 1st Army, after sweeping with the Americans 500 miles up the Rhone valley in three weeks, had made the link with Leclerc's 2nd Armoured Division thrusting due east from Paris. All seven divisions of the regular French army were now together, facing eastwards towards Strasbourg itself.

But by that time the general Allied advance had run into problems. The troops were tired; there was no petrol for the tanks and spare parts were hard to come by. Besides, the French press thought that the war was over. Even when Leclerc took Strasbourg on 23 November, there was little enthusiasm; the editors of the main newspapers, when called to account by the General, pointed out that they were concerned about their circulation figures, and that their readers considered that, with so many British and American troops around, the war was already won. The part played by French forces was simply not big enough to be good copy.

What was good copy, however, was proposed visit by the British Prime Minister to Paris on Armistice Day, 11 November 1944. The original suggestion had come from London, but the omens were not particularly favourable. Armistice Day was, after all, a national day, redolent of Verdun and the heroism of the *poilu*; de Gaulle was worried that Churchill would steal the show. Then again, relations between the two leading actors were far from cordial; France had been excluded from the Quebec Conference, the meeting at Dumbarton Oaks on a post-war settlement, and the European Advisory Commission to determine the future of Germany after the war. Furthermore, de Gaulle did not want Churchill prying into the internal problems of France.

But it was difficult to stop Churchill coming to Paris, if that was what he wanted to do. Even though he had not been invited, he was 'thinking' of going anyway, the Prime Minister told Duff Cooper, 'to see General Eisenhower'. Duff Cooper replied that that 'would be the last nail in the coffin of his relations with de Gaulle', and set about procuring the necessary French invitation.[7] It was a tricky business, but in the end the diplomats' efforts bore fruit. 'We gave them the best possible reception,' the General later wrote. 'With Bidault and several other ministers, I went to meet them at Orly and drove the Prime Minister to the Quai d'Orsay where he was to stay.'[8] The arrangements could not have been better. 'The Prime Minister was delighted to find that he had a golden bath, which had been prepared by Goering for his own use,' Duff Cooper went on to record, 'and still more delighted that the Foreign Secretary's bath was only silver.'

It was a good start, and the parade the following day was even better. 'The reception had to be seen to be believed,' Duff Cooper reported. Churchill and de Gaulle laid wreaths at the Tomb of the Unknown Soldier under the Arc de Triomphe, and then walked together down the Champs-Elysées. Half a million Parisians were there to cheer; the march-past of French and British troops lasted a full hour. Then Churchill laid a wreath beneath the statue of Clemenceau, 'who was much in my thoughts on this moving occasion'.[9] 'On my orders,' de Gaulle wrote, 'the band played "Le Père de la Victoire". "For you," I said to him in English.'[10]

There was a visit to Foch's grave and Napoleon's tomb at the Invalides, and then lunch at the Ministry of War in the rue St Dominique. De Gaulle made a generous speech, and Churchill an emotional one, full of tears. After lunch a few on each side – de Gaulle, Bidault, Massigli and Palewski for the French, Churchill, Eden, Cadogan and Duff Cooper for the British – spent two hours reviewing the state of the world in the best of humours. The discussion was relaxed and friendly. Churchill told de Gaulle of his impressions of the day. 'I felt as if I were watching a resurrection,' he declared.

It was perhaps not the right climate in which to raise great issues. It might have been better to have waited until the sentiment of popular acclaim had had time to wear off. But it was Churchill who started it later in the day by suggesting, in private talks, that Britain and France should conclude a treaty of alliance. 'On this occasion,' de Gaulle wrote, 'we were concerned with business, and no longer with sentiment.'[11]

A meeting took place in the early evening in de Gaulle's office. Churchill had with him Eden and Duff Cooper, de Gaulle had Bidault and Massigli. In response to Churchill's proposal, the French made it clear that the only acceptable position to them was that of a full partner. With the irony of history, they were almost back to the Monnet scheme of June 1940 for Franco-British union.

Over the next two days, in a series of conversations, de Gaulle elaborated his offer. What Churchill had suggested was not enough. A much closer relationship was the only one which made sense. 'If,' he said – in his own account of the meeting – 'England and France agree and act together on tomorrow's settlements, they will wield enough power to prevent anything being done which they themselves have not accepted or decided. It is this mutual resolve which should be the basis of the alliance you offer us . . . If you are willing . . . I am ready. Our two countries will follow us. America and Russia, hampered by their rivalry, will be unable to counter it. Moreover, we shall have the support of many states and of world opinion, which have an instinctive fear of giants. Eventually England and France will create peace together, as twice in thirty years they have confronted war.'[12]

As the General later pointed out, it was perhaps the last occasion to seize the possibility of a genuine and substantial agreement between the two countries. 'I made every effort,' he wrote, 'to do so during the conversations we had alone together',[13] and there is no reason to doubt his word. But it was going too far for the British. All Churchill would offer in return was an 'alliance in principle', but even this was conditional on American approval. Churchill's loyalty to Roosevelt was too strong for him to make the leap into uncertainty that de Gaulle was offering.

So that was that. The British had drawn back, and de Gaulle's natural reaction was to pursue an alternative. Immediately after Churchill's departure, the General arranged a visit to Moscow. He explained his reasons in a speech to the Consultative Assembly just before leaving: 'We have just had a series of frank, extensive and friendly meetings with the British Prime Minister and Secretary of State for Foreign Affairs. We propose to have the same kind of meetings with the Soviet Government during our imminent visit to Moscow.' He went on to claim a role for France in the 'imposition of a peaceful fate' on Germany in the future, and said that by these means France intended to lay the foundations for that valuable edifice: the unity of Europe. 'We believe in this unity,' he proclaimed, 'and we hope that it will be translated, to begin with, into specific acts binding its three poles: Moscow, London and Paris.'[14]

It is not at all clear what de Gaulle meant at this time by 'the unity of Europe'. He could not seriously have thought that the Soviet Union would form part of any such unity. But his objective was to re-establish France as a major power in Europe and, having failed with the British, at least for the moment, a Franco-Russian treaty was as good a start as any. The Consultative Assembly dutifully agreed.

De Gaulle and his now customary retinue of ministers took off for Moscow on 24 November 1944, stopping on the way at Cairo and Teheran. While they were in the air, Stalin asked Roosevelt and

Churchill for their views on a Franco-Russian treaty. Roosevelt, naturally, showed no interest, but Churchill replied by suggesting a
three-cornered pact of friendship and alliance – precisely what de
Gaulle himself had suggested to the Consultative Assembly a few days
before.

The French contingent was kept waiting in Baku for two days. The
Soviet authorities refused to allow them to fly on to Moscow, on the
grounds that the weather was too bad. Instead, they sent a train to collect them – the same train that the Grand Duke Nicholas had used to
transport himself and his court around in the First World War – which
then took four uncomfortable days on the journey north to Moscow,
arriving on 2 December in bitter cold.

They stayed for a full week, and de Gaulle had some fifteen hours of
discussion with Stalin. 'A communist dressed as a Marshal,' de Gaulle
recalled, 'a dictator skilled in guile, a conqueror with an air of cheer-
fulness, he was a past master of deception.'[15] The truth was that Stalin
was rather bored. For most of the time, he sat doodling with his pencil.

De Gaulle raised the future of Germany; Stalin said that that was a
matter to be studied with Britain and the United States. In turn, Stalin
proposed that France 'recognise' the Soviet-backed puppet government
in Poland, known as the Lublin Committee; de Gaulle could not do this
without abandoning the Polish government-in-exile. Stalin then produced Churchill's proposal of a tripartite treaty; de Gaulle turned it
down, without explaining why he had, as Stalin knew perfectly well,
made precisely the same proposal to the Consultative Assembly only
two weeks before.

Stalin then brought in a delegation from the Lublin Committee to
call on de Gaulle at the French embassy. On the defensive, de Gaulle
consulted Averell Harriman, the American ambassador, and John
Balfour, the minister in the British embassy. Neither was particularly
helpful, since both regarded the problem as being of de Gaulle's own
making. There was no reason, they felt, for de Gaulle to be in Moscow
in the first place.

On 8 December, there was an elaborate banquet at the Kremlin.
Stalin got drunk, proposing no fewer than thirty toasts to various senior
generals, the toasts being mixed with threats, such as that to Alexander
Novikov, the chief of the air staff: 'To you! You are the one who uses
our planes. If you use them badly, you should know what's in store for
you!' De Gaulle tried to get his own back by asking in a loud stage
whisper whether Nikolai Bulganin, then a member of the Soviet war

council, was not the man who had killed so many Russian generals. Perhaps he had in mind Tuchachevsky, his fellow-prisoner in Fort IX at Ingolstadt in 1916, perhaps not; but Stalin's interpreter picked up the remark, and translated it. Stalin's riposte was uproariously crude: 'Yes! There's only one way to deal with [them] . . . with a machine gun! Bring one in!'[16] De Gaulle was repelled, but before he could leave, as he was inclined to do, his host shepherded everybody into his private cinema to watch movies. For the moment. de Gaulle was unable to escape.

After the first film, de Gaulle had had enough, and got up to leave. Stalin was in the mood for another film, but was just able to shake his visitor's hand, and Molotov was left to see de Gaulle out. The text of a Franco-Russian treaty had by that time become a wrangle about words, in particular about Poland, and Molotov and Bidault argued on through the night. By 4 a.m. they had agreed a new draft, and de Gaulle returned to the Kremlin to sign the document. That done, Stalin ordered more refreshments. The tables were set up. Courtesy required that de Gaulle stay for an hour or so, but at about six o'clock he could not take any more. 'I left the room,' he wrote, 'with my ministers. Turning back at the door, I saw Stalin sitting, alone, at the table. He had started eating again.'[17]

De Gaulle's train rumbled out of Moscow's Kursk station later in the day. The General thought that he had scored a triumph by out-negotiating Stalin. But in reality the treaty did not amount to much. In view of Stalin's known habit of assessing a country's importance by its military strength, the French view was of minor significance to him. Later, Stalin said that he 'had not found de Gaulle a very complicated person', which may be due to the fact that he had not been paying much attention. He gave the impression of being bored, and certainly his hostility towards France was one of the features of the Yalta conference of February 1945.

It was a laborious journey home, back through Teheran, Cairo and, this time, Tunis. They finally landed in Paris on 16 December 1944, to be confronted with a serious, and immediate, military problem. For it was on that very day that Field Marshal von Rundstedt, achieving complete surprise, launched a German counter-offensive with twenty-three divisions against the American lines in the Ardennes. The 'Battle of the Bulge' had started.

South of the 'Bulge' was the city of Strasbourg, which had been liberated by Leclerc's 2nd Armoured Division three weeks earlier; and along a line south of Strasbourg the French 1st Army under de Lattre de

Tassigny was pushing forward with difficulty towards the Rhine. Strasbourg looked dangerously vulnerable, well to the east of the French troops in southern Alsace and in danger of encirclement should the Germans achieve their planned breakout from the Bulge. Eisenhower decided to shorten his line by evacuating Strasbourg and withdrawing de Lattre's army.

Militarily, it was a perfectly sensible decision. The problem was that Eisenhower had reached his decision on 26 December, the day after General de Gaulle had made a much-publicised congratulatory visit to Leclerc in Strasbourg and de Lattre near Colmar. The political effects of withdrawal from Alsace at this moment would have been volcanic, and de Gaulle proceeded to say so. He cabled de Lattre, ordering him to 'guarantee the defence of Strasbourg'. He wrote to Eisenhower, 'Whatever happens the French will defend Strasbourg.' Finally, he cabled both Roosevelt and Churchill, explaining 'the extremely serious consequences which would result for France'.[18]

Roosevelt would not intervene, quite properly – and conveniently – replying that it was a military matter, but Churchill immediately flew with his chief of staff Sir Alan Brooke to Eisenhower's headquarters at Versailles, arriving on 2 January. De Gaulle was there, with Juin, and a long meeting followed. De Gaulle argued his point fiercely and in detail. Churchill supported him, and in the end Eisenhower gave way. To general relief, the decision was reversed. But de Gaulle was hardly gracious, even when he had won his point. On the return journey, Juin ventured to say that that de Gaulle should at least have expressed his thanks to Churchill. ' "Bah," he answered, and with a gloomy expression he went back to his thoughts.'[19]

'The General,' Duff Cooper recalled later, 'was not in the sunniest of moods during these early months of 1945.'[20] It was certainly no more, and perhaps considerably less, than the truth. Apart from the domestic difficulties of France, diplomatic and military problems were piling up. Soon after the meeting with Eisenhower, it was announced in the British and American press that Roosevelt, Churchill and Stalin would meet at Yalta on the Black Sea to discuss a post-war settlement in Europe and the creation of a United Nations organisation. De Gaulle was not invited. Furthermore, negotiations for a less ambitious Franco-British treaty, already desultory, had now completely stalled. Churchill was in a bad mood. 'I cannot think of anything more unpleasant and impossible,' he minuted Eden on 19 January 1945, 'than having this menacing and hostile man in our midst, always trying to make himself a reputation in France by claiming a position far above what France occupies, and making faces at the Allies who are doing the work.'[21]

In the event, France did well out of the Yalta conference, thanks entirely to Churchill's advocacy, and the support, behind the scenes, of the President's adviser, Harry Hopkins. Eden had continually reminded Churchill, in the weeks leading up to the conference, that France was a necessary part of a stable settlement in Europe, and Churchill was, after long debate, in turn able to convince his two Allies of the point. France, it was in the end decided, would have a place on the commission that was to control Germany, would have her own zone of occupation, and would be one of the powers issuing invitations to the San Francisco conference that was to establish the United Nations. It is perhaps not too much to say that France would never have achieved as much if the General himself had been present at Yalta in person.

General de Gaulle's response was ungracious – as well as politically inept. He rejected the idea that France should be an 'inviting power' in convening the San Francisco conference. Then, on 13 February, the day after Ambassador Caffery had reported to him on Yalta, he refused to meet Roosevelt on board the cruiser *Quincy*, which was to call in at Algiers on its way back to the United States. The invitation had been – for Roosevelt – surprisingly cordial, and it was common knowledge that the President was seriously ill. Not only that, but another passenger in the cruiser, Harry Hopkins, one of de Gaulle's defenders at Yalta, was also confined to his cabin with the cancer that was shortly to kill him.

De Gaulle's refusal reached Roosevelt while the USS *Quincy* was lying at anchor at Alexandria. The President lost his temper and dictated what his adviser, Charles Bohlen, described as a 'terse and insulting statement'. He refused to listen to any argument that it should be toned down. Hopkins urged Bohlen, 'Chip, go and see what you can do with the President.'[22]

Bohlen relayed Hopkins's view that Roosevelt could not hit at de Gaulle without hitting at France herself. As he worked on his stamp collection, the President again refused to entertain the argument, until Bohlen expostulated, in language after Roosevelt's own heart, 'Mr President, we can all admit that de Gaulle is being one of the biggest sons-of-bitches that ever straddled a pot.' Roosevelt was so amused that he gave in. 'Oh, go ahead, you and Harry try your hand at a draft.' The President's version was quickly modified and agreed.

Even the modified American response had a powerful effect. For the first time since the Liberation the General was faced by a French press that was universally hostile. Ingratitude to the Americans had been carried to extremes. As the press predicted, the affair did nothing but harm to France. Hopkins had to be flown home to hospital – and death; and Roosevelt himself died two months later, on 12 April 1945. The incident not only dented de Gaulle's own reputation in France, but affected Franco-American relations for years to come. The American press turned unanimously anti-Gaullist for the first time. It was a bad omen for the future.

Furthermore, still 'not in the sunniest of moods', de Gaulle was not satisfied with the honorary award of an occupation zone. He was still determined to see that the French army played a full part in the final stage of the European war. General Patton crossed the Rhine at Mainz on 22 March, and Montgomery crossed to the north on 23 March. Not to be outdone, de Gaulle ordered de Lattre de Tassigny, on 29 March, to make his own crossing, 'even if the Americans do not help you', and head for Karlsruhe and Stuttgart.[23] On 30 March, de Lattre, using boats and bridging of French construction, obeyed. By 4 April he had some 125,000 men on the eastern side of the river, and on 7 April he occupied Karlsruhe. De Gaulle's reaction was to visit the army on the same day, congratulate them and order them to defy the explicit orders of Allied headquarters and to make for Stuttgart.

De Lattre reached Stuttgart on 23 April. The following day, the US 7th Army under General Patch, which had been assigned to take the city, arrived. There they found de Lattre, who refused to budge. The situation would have been ridiculous had it not been so dangerous. De Gaulle had deliberately ruptured the command structure of the Allies. It was the first test for the new President, Harry Truman. He proved up to it. He intervened to tell de Gaulle that all supplies to French forces would be cut off. The General was satisfied that he had made his point. French forces in Stuttgart were reduced to a nominal presence and the Americans took control.

The story was repeated in northern Italy, where Field Marshal Alexander was in command of the Allied forces advancing from the south. Without consultation, de Gaulle ordered French troops under General Doyen to cross from France into Italy and take Turin. This they did, arriving at the outskirts of Turin on 27 April. Alexander told Doyen to withdraw. Doyen refused, threatening what appeared to Alexander to be armed resistance against the Allies. Again, Truman was alerted, made the same threat to cut off supplies, and the French pulled back.

Finally, there were crises in Algeria and in the Levant. Algeria was particularly menacing. New leaders of the Muslim population had emerged, with a new determination to achieve independence and Arab unity. Ferhat Abbas, Sheikh Brahimi and Hadj Messali were preaching revolution, and on 1 May there were riots in Algiers and Oran. On 8 May twenty-seven Europeans were murdered, and on the following day a further seventy-five, many of them hacked to death. General Duval, commander of the Constantine region, was ruthless. Whole villages were razed to the ground, and it was said that German and Italian prisoners-of-war were armed by the French to put down the insurrection. Even in 1945, the long and bloody Algerian war had begun.

In the Levant the problem was the familiar one. French troops were still in occupation, and there was no sign of the promised treaty of Syrian independence. The Syrian President, Choukri Kouatly, had been persuaded by Churchill, on his way back from Yalta, to attempt negotiation with the French, but de Gaulle would have none of it, sending French reinforcements. They landed on 17 May, provoking immediate rebellion in Syria. Over the next two weeks there were pitched battles in the streets. Order was restored only after Churchill, on appeal from the Syrians, had instructed General Paget, the Commander-in-Chief Middle East, to intervene and ensure that French troops were confined to barracks. Needless to say, de Gaulle considered this an unwarranted intrusion, and announced it to be yet more evidence of British imperial ambitions.

None of these adventures reflects great credit on de Gaulle. Indeed, it seems that he was, as in June 1942, going through a strange period of isolation, which led him to take decisions that to the rest of the world, including his compatriots, seemed to be the product of inexplicable obstinacy and spite.

The darkness of the General's mood is best illustrated by an incident during the VE Day parade in Paris on 18 June 1945. It was to be a splendid occasion. The French army was to march down the Champs-Elysées, as it had at the end of the First World War; and the General would take the salute. Opposite his saluting base a stand had been put up for the wounded. As the parade proceeded, the wounded soldiers saw driving past, in perfect formation, twelve ambulances of the hospital unit of the 1st Free French Division, the unit that had been responsible for looking after hundreds of their number in the Western Desert and the Levant. The injured soldiers raised a great cheer. All would have been well had not the ambulances been sporting British and French flags side by side, and had not the unit been organised and run by Lady Spears, who was sitting in one of her ambulances. Once the General heard the name 'Spears' acclaimed by the French wounded – '*Voilà Spears; vive Spears!*' – he turned furiously to Koenig, who was standing just behind him, and ordered him to see to it that the unit was disbanded and its British members repatriated without delay.

So it was that the General's war, which had started with his journey to England with Spears in June 1940, ended with his abrupt and hostile dismissal of Spears's wife at the moment of victory. All the French officers in the hospital unit returned their medals immediately. 'A pitiable business,' Lady Spears wrote, 'when a great man suddenly becomes small.'[24]

PART FIVE

POLITICIAN

1

WITH PEACE COMES POLITICS

*Je devrais devenir président de cette République
pour recommencer la IIIe en pire. Pour cela, on n'a
pas besoin de moi.* ★

June 1945 saw the high-water mark of Charles de Gaulle's first political career. He was by then universally recognised as the liberator of France and head of the French Government. His political base, nationally and internationally, was secure. He had neutered the Resistance, then lifted from its programme his agenda for government. He had hectored the Allies into recognising France as a major post-war power. Finally, he had manoeuvred his main potential opponent, Thorez, into swinging the Communist Party into line behind his Government. Altogether, it had been an impressive performance. There was now no doubt, if there had indeed been any doubt before, that the General was a master of the art of political in-fighting.

Furthermore, in spite of the continuing poverty and corruption of much of post-war France, and in spite of the physical difficulties of reconstruction, his Government was generally felt do be doing rather well. The underlying economic problems which had provoked a row between Mendès-France and Pleven in April had not yet penetrated the public consciousness. Pleven's more relaxed policies were popular. Above all, and towering over them all, de Gaulle retained, like a halo around his admittedly odd-shaped head, the aura of the symbol of French Resistance. It was formidably attractive and continued to mesmerise a France that was still happy to find itself free from the occupation.

Six months later the General walked out. To universal stupefaction,

---

★ 'I was supposed to become President of this Republic to start again the Third Republic, only worse. For that, there is no need of me.' Charles de Gaulle to his son Philippe, as reported by him. *Le Figaro, L'Actualité,* 13 April 1990.

he simply downed tools, leaving the Government stranded and France leaderless. It was not just a resignation for temporary tactical convenience; nor was it a sudden decision or a rush of blood, or a gesture of attempted political blackmail. He was far too experienced by now to bank on an immediate return, in spite of subsequent tittle-tattle. It was no more and no less than he said: a clear and deliberate admission of his inability to work within the political structure that was emerging from the wreckage of wartime France. The only thing to do, he felt, was to wait on the sidelines, in the firm belief that it would all end in tears. What he did not foresee was the length of time he was to have to wait.

Leading up to his decision, surprising as it was at the time, was a series of events which, in retrospect, made his decision almost inevitable – not wholly inevitable, since the events themselves were provoked, and their impact coloured in his mind, by his own personality, but almost inevitable. To be sure, his perception of the grandeur of France was noble, but he did not see that the French only wanted peace. He was aware, too, of the extent of his wartime triumph, but he was unable to reconcile himself to the limited ambitions of peacetime politics. Perhaps most important, although he had certainly mastered the politics of manoeuvre, the General was a long way from grasping the politics of flattery, and one without the other can in peacetime quickly lead to downfall. Nor was Mme de Gaulle much help. She was far from being a 'political' wife, warning her husband of the traps that were being laid, of the mutterings behind his back – reminding him, in short, of his own mortality.

Mutterings there certainly were. In the latter half of 1945 the French started to rediscover democracy and, on the whole, they liked what they found. As the old political soldiers of the Third Republic came home, along with the deportees and prisoners, the old rows came home with them. The debate moved away from the attempt to overcome the differences between those who had resisted the Germans in France itself and those who had joined Fighting France. It moved on to the whole question of the political geography of post-war France.

During the summer of 1945, the four major political groupings, Communists, Socialists, a new party – perhaps best described as Christian Democrat – known as the Mouvement Républicain Populaire (MRP) and the Radicals, held their party conferences. Herriot was back among the Radicals, Blum with the Socialists. Thorez and Duclos were articulating the Communist view. On one point they were all agreed. They wished to see a break with the Third Republic and a new constitution based on the supremacy of a single elected chamber; none of them wanted anything to do with government by plebiscite. For de Gaulle, this clear statement of view was, to say the least, inconvenient, since he wanted precisely the opposite: a strong presidency confirmed by plebiscite.

It was not a debate that the General either enjoyed or, indeed, at this stage was much interested in. Up until VE Day, as his future Prime Minister, Michel Debré,★ perceived, he only thought about France being present at the top table of the victors. Those around him at the rue St Dominique took a different view. Debré, Cassin, Teitgen and Parodi were all deeply involved in the debate. De Gaulle's immediate reaction, to try to finesse the problem by absorbing Herriot, Blum and Jeanneney into his Government, failed when only Jeanneney accepted office. It was becoming rapidly clear that no easy compromise would be possible with the 'old parties'.

When he finally addressed the matter seriously, the General's response was typical. Against the advice of his closest colleagues in the rue St Dominique, he simply ignored the views of the political parties and, on 9 July, presented to the Council of Ministers his own version of a future electoral statute. Elections were set for October, together with a referendum to decide whether there should be a new constitution. The gauntlet had been well and truly thrown down, and was equally well and truly picked up. It was the start of the real political war between the General and the parties, which was to lead, first to acrimonious confrontation and ultimately to their victory and his defeat.

Debré's perception was all the more pointed in that the General had set his heart on being present at Potsdam, where the Big Three, the United States, the Soviet Union and Great Britain, were having their last meeting of the war – and he had been excluded. In practice, it did not much matter: the major decisions about the future of Europe had already been taken at Yalta in February. But it was the top table, and de Gaulle took the rejection badly, immediately dissociating France from any and all of the Potsdam conclusions.

Exclusion from Potsdam, a show of defiance from the old guard of

★ Michel Debré (1912–): Civil servant, soldier and politician. One of the genuine intellectuals of Gaullism (and one with real charm). Served in Finance Ministry before 1939; called up 1939; taken prisoner 1940; escaped 1943; member Provisional Government in Algiers 1944; Senator (Indre et Loire) 1948, 1955; Deputy (Réunion) 1967 onwards; Prime Minister 1959–62; Minister for Finance 1966–8, Foreign Affairs 1968–9, National Defence 1969–73. Académie Française.

the Third Republic, inflation now rising alarmingly, the prospect of a bruising political battle over the new constitution: any one of these would have been enough to dent even the formidable willpower of Charles de Gaulle. But there was an added complication. On 26 April the usually sleepy Swiss frontier town of Vallorbe had witnessed a strange event. Marshal Pétain had decided to return to France from Germany, where he had been secluded since August 1944, to face trial. 'I can answer for my actions,' he wrote in his petition to Hitler, 'only in France. At my age the only thing one fears is not to have done one's full duty; I wish to do mine.'[1]

It was, by any standard, a dignified performance. The old Marshal, now eighty-nine years old, almost entirely deaf and partially blind, was put on trial at the Palais de Justice on 23 July 1945. The trial, which lasted three weeks, was beset by judicial confusion. To start with, the presiding judge, as well as the prosecutor, had previously sworn alle-giance to the Marshal himself as head of the Vichy state. It then turned out that the prosecutor, Mornet, had also prosecuted the glamorous Mata Hari, the spy of 1917. Much was made of that. Finally, Pétain decided that he would make only one statement, at the beginning of the trial, and then say nothing. At the end, the judge recommended ban-ishment for five years and loss of civil rights. Undeterred, the jury decided on the death penalty but with an immediate recommendation for reprieve. De Gaulle granted the reprieve.

The whole episode of Pétain's trial was extremely painful for the General. Daily reports by Teitgen, the Minister for Justice, met with an abrupt response. 'Do your duty,' de Gaulle told him. 'Do your duty.'[2] De Gaulle never wanted the trial. After all, Pétain had been his protector during thirty-odd years of his army career, and memories of dinners with the Marshal – when Nini, the Marshal's wife, was kept discreetly apart – must have been very much alive for the de Gaulles. 'His decision [to return],' de Gaulle wrote, 'was a courageous one.' Moreover, Pétain was still, for de Gaulle, 'a leader once distinguished by the most excep-tional powers, an old soldier in whom at the time of catastrophe many Frenchmen had put their trust and for whom, in spite of everything, many still felt respect or pity.'[3] It was true. But truer still was the knowl-edge that Pétain, the 'victor of Verdun', had been the hero of de Gaulle's earlier years. Certainly, Pétain had betrayed France by his accep-tance of defeat at the armistice, but that was not what the trial had been about. It had been about what had happened under Vichy, and de Gaulle regarded that as irrelevant.

Soon after the Pétain trial, de Gaulle secured an invitation to visit the United States. It came as a relief from domestic French problems. At least in America he could walk again as a world statesman and forget for the moment the inconveniences of French internal politics. President Harry Truman was ready and willing to see him, and his reception was much more cordial than during the Roosevelt era. The General arrived on 22 August with his usual train of colleagues and advisers – Bidault, Juin, Palewski, as well as several diplomats – to be met at the airport by James Byrnes, the new Secretary of State, General Marshall and Jefferson Caffery, the United States ambassador to Paris. It was all smiles.

On the surface, official relations between the two countries had improved. At least the personal antagonisms had disappeared with Roosevelt's death. 'Throughout his stay,' the dispatch from the British embassy records, '[de Gaulle] was never deflected from an obvious and almost painful desire to please. He not only kissed babies, as every zealous politician must, but Mayor La Guardia . . . and the American Chiefs of Staff as well.'[4] Truman gave de Gaulle seven hours of his time, as the General carefully records, and at the end of his stay in Washington presented him with a decoration and a four-engine DC4 Skymaster transport for his personal use. Truman knew his man. 'On subsequent occasions,' de Gaulle wrote later, 'no hard words ever passed between us.'[5] Understandably so; but on the American side, at least, the official view was that none of the serious issues had been addressed, and that there was total disagreement about the future of the defeated Germany. Truman, certainly, did not think the visit important enough to be mentioned in his own memoirs.

In the long run, perhaps the most important meeting de Gaulle had in Washington was with Jean Monnet, which was wholly concerned with French domestic affairs. The conversation was intense and detailed. Monnet had just negotiated a $650 million credit line with the Export-Import Bank, which de Gaulle signed during his visit, and had very firm views on the way forward for the French economy. Put simply – and Monnet was an expert at putting things simply – his view was that unless there was a coordinated and planned approach to the problems of the French economy and its modernisation, things would not get better by themselves; they would only get worse. The General was impressed, and asked Monnet to put his thoughts in writing. It was to prove a crucial step in the economic development of post-war France.

A moment of political seriousness was followed by the cavalcade going back on the road. On 26 August the French party drove to New

York, stopping on the way at West Point Military Academy and Roosevelt's grave at Hyde Park. As always, the reception given to the General by the American public was rapturous, and, as always, he could not resist it. It so happened that that day was the first on which petrol was off ration; thousands of day-trippers turned out on the roads, and the French were greeted by a cacophony of car horns – 'for about one hundred kilometres', the General recorded.[6] When they reached New York, Mayor Fiorello La Guardia was there to embrace the General – provoking a cartoon on the following day with the caption 'The Great Asparagus kisses the Little Flower' – and as they drove together through the city the New Yorkers yelled 'Hello, Charlie' and showered them with tickertape.

It was the same story in Chicago, although the plane was delayed. By the time it arrived, the welcoming party had had far too much to drink, and the speeches suffered from being both overlong and indistinct. Montreal was more dignified; Ottawa even more so – de Gaulle recorded with satisfaction a meeting there with the Governor-General and Princess Alice.

But it was time to go home. By now, the French press had begun to show irritation with the General's strutting around the New World and were criticising him by name. But no sooner had he arrived home than there was another conference about the future of Germany, this time in London, which lasted from 11 September to 3 October. Although de Gaulle himself did not attend, he took a minute-by-minute interest in what Bidault was saying on his behalf. Then, to cap it all, the General himself set off on yet another trip, this time a three-day excursion to the German Rhineland before returning to France at Strasbourg, whence he travelled in the Belgian Prince Regent's private train to Brussels, to receive an honorary doctorate. In Brussels he caused some puzzlement by expounding his views on a 'western grouping having as its arteries the Rhine, the Channel and the Mediterranean'.[7]

The French press and the politicians were dismayed by the General's apparent lack of concern about France's domestic problems. Pleven's economic policies were failing and price rises were being fuelled by increases in indirect taxation. There were strikes in major industries. Protests became more violent, and on occasions had to be dealt with by the police. Everything seemed to be in short supply on the official market and the black market consequently flourished. Furthermore, on his return to Paris, de Gaulle was confronted with another problem.

On 5 October the trial opened of the Vichy leader and Nazi collaborator, Pierre Laval. It was quite different from the earlier trial of Pétain, partly because there was only one conceivable result. But Laval was nothing if not skilful, and he conducted his own defence with verve and dramatic flair. The cause was, of course, hopeless. When, after three days of argument, Laval wanted to return to the stand, the presiding judge simply said to the clerk – in a loud aside, 'No, he's getting up my backside; we must finish it off.'[8]

Laval was condemned to death on 9 October. A retrial was demanded, in view of the hysteria surrounding the trial, but de Gaulle refused. Just before the hour of his execution on 15 October, Laval managed to swallow a cyanide pill, but the poison somehow failed to work. He was rushed to hospital, where his stomach was pumped out. He was then rushed back to be shot, but was still retching and in great pain. Luizet, the chief of police, thought that he ought to take the advice of the head of Government on whether to proceed with the execution of someone so obviously in agony. De Gaulle replied, his eyes half shut, 'Pierre Laval no longer belongs to us. The officer commanding the firing squad must do his duty.'[9] Laval died shouting '*Vive la France*'. It was noted that, because of shortage of equipment, the firing squad wore British tin hats.

Both the Pétain and the Laval trials weakened de Gaulle's position, Pétain's because of the dignity of his behaviour and the residual affection in which he was held, albeit secretly now, by a large section of public opinion, Laval's because of the obvious vindictiveness of the whole event, and because of the generally accepted view that de Gaulle wished to have the thing over and done with before the elections on 21 October. After all, it was on 17 October that the General was due to make his final appeal to the electors, and it would have been inconvenient, to say the least, if Laval's fate had still been undecided by then.

The vote, on 21 October, was both a referendum – on whether there should be a new constitution, to be devised by an Assembly with a limited life – and a parliamentary election. It was, to say the least, confusing, and the result had been made more difficult to predict by the enlargement of the electorate, following the enfranchisement of women.

In the event, de Gaulle won the referendum easily: 96 per cent in favour of a new constitution and 66 per cent in favour of a Constituent Assembly of limited life. But the result of the election to the Constituent Assembly was little short of a disaster for him: the Communists won 26 per cent of the vote, the Socialists 25 per cent and the new Mouvement Républicain Populaire, on which he had pinned high hopes, also 26 per cent. It was an Assembly dominated by the traditional left. Old party loyalties had proved stronger than the new wave. The mould of the Third Republic had by no means been broken.

The new Constituent Assembly met on 6 November and re-elected Félix Gouin as its President. It then turned to the election of the head of the Provisional Government. As a demonstration of their newly won electoral legitimacy, the parties within the Assembly took a week to make up their minds, a week spent in long meetings and secret caucuses. Armistice Day came – and with it another visit from the now deposed Churchill. The General had time to entertain his old ally and antagonist, and to regret his loss of office in the British general election of the previous July. 'I saw it with melancholy,' de Gaulle wrote in his memoirs. ' . . . Having seen a great deal of him, I had greatly admired, though quite as often envied him . . . Different though the conditions were under which Churchill and I had to operate, fierce though our disputes had been, for more than five years we had nonetheless sailed side by side, guiding ourselves by the same stars on the raging sea of history.'[10] It was an eloquent summary of their stormy yet affectionate relationship. But even the old warrior's visit failed to calm the domestic political atmosphere. It was not until 14 November that everybody became bored with the game, and the Assembly elected de Gaulle – unanimously, as it happened – President of the French Republic and head of the Provisional Government.

The game resumed when de Gaulle tried to form a government. Herriot and the Radicals refused to get involved. The Communists demanded one of the three most important ministries, defence, foreign affairs or the interior. It was a ridiculous demand, and de Gaulle told them so. Thereupon they stormed out of negotiations, relying on the support of the Socialists, who said that they would not serve in any government that did not include the Communists. De Gaulle took the only course open to him. He sent a message to Gouin, the President of the Assembly, that he was unable to form a government.

There was, of course, consternation, and the game again ceased abruptly. On 19 November, the Assembly renewed their election of de Gaulle as President, in spite of Communist opposition. Once that was done, however, the Communists capitulated, and Thorez came to see de Gaulle to tell him that his party would enter the government without any preconditions.

De Gaulle's second Provisional Government was announced on 21 November. As before, it was a mixture of left and right, the balance dictated by the politics of the moment. It got off to a reasonably harmonious start, particularly since the first measures introduced were to nationalise the banks, insurance companies and the major utilities; but it could not last, and de Gaulle knew it. Even with the benefit of hindsight, it is difficult to disbelieve what he wrote in his memoirs: that it was during November that he took the decision to throw in his hand. It was clear at that point that the Fourth Republic would be, to all intents and purposes, a replica of the Third, and the General, after all he had done to save France's honour from collapse, could not agree to what he saw as a disastrous repetition of history.

In the two months from 21 November 1945 to 20 January 1946, the date of his resignation, the situation veered ever more swiftly out of de Gaulle's control. Having scented blood, his political enemies in the Assembly time and again attacked him, for the most part indirectly and by innuendo. In the Council of Ministers there were endless arguments about the level of public sector salaries, the threat of a general strike by civil servants, the organisation of social services in the provinces, the intricacies of agricultural price support and the annual rate of inflation, which was now touching 60 per cent. De Gaulle was bored beyond measure by these sessions. Worse, he had rows with his ministers, particularly with Bidault over the conduct of foreign policy, which he regarded as his own fief. Bidault for his part was not slow to let the press know about their disagreements.

Nevertheless, in December 1945 de Gaulle approved what was to be, apart from the foundation of the Ecole Nationale d'Administration, the lasting achievement of his first political career. The conversation in Washington with Monnet had borne fruit. Monnet himself drafted for the General – in very simple terms, since he knew that Mendès-France had made the mistake in April of speaking to the General for no less than two hours on economic problems – a programme for the reconstruction of the French economy on the basis of what came to be known as 'indicative' planning. Monnet's ideas appealed to the General's military mind, and one of his last acts in office was to set up the commission that Monnet had proposed, with Monnet himself at its head. There is no doubt that the Planning Commission laid the basis for the French economic recovery that took place within the political chaos of the following decade. It proved itself indeed to be a method of bypassing the 'parties'.

But sooner or later there was bound to be an overt and major crisis, and sure enough it came. As it turned out, the issue was the defence budget, which General de Gaulle, for obvious reasons, felt to be a matter on which there could be no challenge. It was, of course, part of the general budget debate in the Assembly, which was in any case going to be difficult, but which the business managers fixed, for some obscure reason, for New Year's Eve. As it was obviously going to take a great deal of time, Gouin hit upon the idea of stopping all the clocks at midnight. For what it was worth, it was a reasonable device, but it unravelled when a Socialist member, one Capdeville, moved, in the early hours of the morning – the clocks still standing at midnight – an amendment to reduce defence funds by 20 per cent. The Communists, not wishing to be outflanked by their working-class Socialist brothers, supported the amendment, believing it to be a simple manoeuvre which the Government could easily see off. A vote was postponed to allow the General to have his say.

Early on the morning of 1 January 1946 the telephone rang in the General's house in Neuilly. It was Teitgen, who had been following events in the Assembly for the Government. He told de Gaulle to come immediately. The General refused. He was still half asleep, and anyway he was unaccustomed to being disturbed in such an abrupt manner. But Teitgen insisted, adding that the Socialist charge was being led by de Gaulle's old wartime companion, André Philip. De Gaulle rang him immediately, threatening a vote of confidence, but Philip simply replied that he did not want to bring down the Government but to make it bow before the will of the Assembly.

All this was almost too much for the General, who had obvious difficulty in restraining himself when he finally arrived at the Assembly. There was uproar – but it was uproar of a particularly malevolent kind, which only parliamentary assemblies are capable of when they wish to bring down one of their own. It was, in the words of one witness, as though 'a circle of hatred was closing round General de Gaulle'.[11] In the end, de Gaulle won the vote, but he was forced to make a commitment to introduce proposals for reform of the army within six weeks. It was a dirty compromise, and they all knew it.

It was time for retreat, and for taking stock. On 3 January de Gaulle's daughter Elisabeth married one of Leclerc's officers, Alain de Boissieu. That evening, after the ceremony, Charles and Yvonne de Gaulle left Paris for the south of France. De Gaulle had decided to reflect, and he felt that he could best do so in peace. Besides, his sudden departure would keep his opponents guessing.

The de Gaulles had been lent a villa at Cap d'Antibes, and they stayed there for a week, from 5 to 13 January. They were joined, for one of the few family discussions on record, by Pierre, de Gaulle's younger brother, and Jacques Vendroux, Yvonne's elder brother. They analysed the situation, but, from reading the accounts, it is difficult not to believe that de Gaulle had already taken his decision, and the period of 'reflection' was merely to ensure that his resignation was not seen as just a hasty act on the spur of momentary provocation.

The first person to be aware of the General's state of mind on his return was Jules Moch, the Minister of Transport, whose job was to see that the General, as President of the Republic, was properly received at whatever railway station he chose to use. That morning, 14 January, the presidential train was due to arrive at the Gare de Lyon but, for reasons known only to himself, de Gaulle wished to make a discreet entry into Paris, and decided to get out at Maisons-Alfort, a few miles outside the city. Moch rushed to meet him there, complained at the General's breach of security arrangements in his change of plan, and was rewarded with the news, in the car taking them into Paris, that the General had decided that it was time for him to go. He had found it impossible, and would continue to find it impossible, to govern alongside the political parties. There was no more to be said.

During the following week, de Gaulle continued to carry out his official functions normally, throwing in for good measure a stand-up row with Herriot in the Assembly, while gradually widening the circle of those in the know about his decision – the Information Minister, André Malraux, the Commissaires de la République, Alain Savary and Pierre Bertaux, Georges Pompidou, Gaston Palewski; then, on the evening of 18 January, Francisque Gay, Bidault's deputy.

The plans were made with military precision, although there was no hint about the succession. 'After me?' he said to Francisque Gay. 'That is not my business. You will do whatever you consider you have to do.'[12] On the afternoon of Saturday 19 January, he telephoned Louis Joxe, who was in bed with 'flu, and told him to get better, since he was required for a meeting of the Council of Ministers the following day at noon. The summons was enough to cure Joxe's illness and he leapt out of bed. Messages were sent to all ministers to be in attendance at rue St Dominique.

The General himself arrived for the meeting a little after 12 a.m., dressed in uniform, a little pale but as stiff-necked as ever. He shook hands with all those present and, before they had a chance to sit down, made a short speech announcing his resignation. He then walked out of the room, went upstairs, wrote his letter of resignation to the President of the Assembly, and went home to Neuilly. Nobody else had said a word.

2

THE GAMBLE THAT FAILED

Die Politik ist keine exacte Wissenschaft. *

Marly-le-Roi is nowadays not much more than a dormitory suburb on the western side of Paris. The old village was built up in the 1950s to form one of several new towns that cluster around the capital. It has tower blocks, hypermarkets, discos and bright, featureless parks; above all, it is served by the Métro Express, which conveys its inhabitants quickly and painlessly into and out of the city centre.

It was not like that in January 1946. The Marly of those days was an attractive village, perched on the edge of an extensive former royal domain. The park, where Louis XIV had hunted, was commodious and elegant. Just inside the park was a hunting lodge, built by the Sun King's architects, and it was here that General de Gaulle decided to withdraw after his resignation, renting it for a nominal sum from the Service des Beaux Arts. It was small – Mme de Gaulle much preferred it to the overblown house in Neuilly – and close to Paris, so that the General could keep his political telescope trained on the gyrations that followed his departure.

On the other hand, the place was shabby after years of neglect. It needed repainting, and there was no question of the Beaux Arts providing elegant furniture, as they had for the house in Neuilly. Furthermore, the heating did not work, and it was a cold winter. But the de Gaulles were never very particular about their domestic comforts, as long as Anne, now aged eighteen but still lost to the world, could be properly looked after. Besides, their home at Colombey had been

---

* 'Politics is not an exact science.' Otto von Bismarck in a speech to the Prussian parliament, 18 December 1863.

damage and vandalised by the retreating Germans in 1944, and was only now being repaired. So Marly it was.

Whatever was said afterwards, not least by the General himself, his resignation was greeted, once the initial shock had worn off, with a collective sigh of relief. Within a week his name had disappeared from the front pages of the Parisian press, and negotiations were already under way, not to invite him back but to settle the conditions of his retirement. He had to surrender his DC4 Skymaster to the French air force and give up the Cadillac which had been a present from Eisenhower; he even had to buy a small French car, and Mme de Gaulle had to learn to drive. Money was short, since they had nothing but his military pension. It was suggested that his rank be raised to full General, or even perhaps to Marshal of France, not least to increase his pension, but the idea was rejected with scorn. His situation and his rank, he wrote to the unfortunate minister detailed to conduct negotiations, had not needed to be changed for 'five years, seven months and three days' after 18 June 1940. 'Every "administrative solution" that might be attempted today would be strange, and even ridiculous.'[1]

But the General did not spend his time at Marly simply writing rude letters to his successors. He engaged Claude Mauriac, François' devoted son, to help him sort out his papers and, with much more serious intent, he made contact again with 'Rémy' of the Resistance, 'Passy' of the Free French counter-intelligence bureau and Maurice Schumann, who had run the Free French broadcasts from London. Even by the time that the de Gaulles celebrated their silver wedding at Marly on 7 April 1946, surrounded by twenty of their family, at an apparently happy and uncomplicated party, the General was already starting to intrigue. Taking aside his brother-in-law Jacques Vendroux after lunch, he encouraged him, as a new MRP deputy, to campaign against the constitution that the 'old parties' were proposing.

The truth was that de Gaulle, after the excitement of resignation, was already starting to get rather bored. Long walks in the park at Marly were no substitute for Cabinet meetings or tickertape rides down Fifth Avenue. Furthermore, the politicians seemed to be doing quite well without him, as were the French people themselves. An opinion poll in February had shown that a majority was pleased that the General had resigned. Worse still, many of his former ministers had stayed in office under his successor, Félix Gouin. In particular, Bidault was still in charge of foreign affairs, and still pursuing a policy that was, in de Gaulle's view, far too soft and anglophile. It was not just very irritating; it was a betrayal, which de Gaulle was not to forget.

The contacts that he made in the early spring of 1946 with his old Resistance comrades were not accidental, and it was not long before he started seriously to plan a political comeback At first, hints were dropped within the close circle that had remained faithful – Gaston Palewski, Claude Mauriac, Guy de Bonneval, Claude Guy and the first secretary to have joined the Free French in London, Elisabeth de Méribel. Together they went to visit the tomb of Clemenceau in the Vendée, on 12 May – the date of the anniversary of victory in Europe and the feast of Joan of Arc. As they stood in front of the great man's tomb, de Gaulle, very pale and obviously moved, spoke of Clemenceau's achievements in the First World War, noting – significantly, for those who had ears to hear – that 'we see better than ever that for us tomorrow, no less than in the past, there can be no security, no freedom, no efficiency, without the acceptance of great discipline, under the guidance of a strong State and with the enthusiastic support of a people rallied in unity'.[2]

By the end of May, Marly-le-Roi had served its purpose. The house at Colombey was ready, or to be more exact, just habitable. A tower had been added, but it was not yet complete; the house had not been decorated and the garden was a wilderness. But the de Gaulles decided to return there. They left Marly on 25 May 1946, travelling by way of the Ardennes and making a short stay with Yvonne's brother Jacques. They arrived at their home – their true home – on 1 June.

By then de Gaulle had been just over four months out of office, and had already started to reflect on the lessons of his first political career. 'There never was a time in my life,' he told Claude Mauriac, 'when I had any doubt that I would one day be at the head of France . . . but things happened in a way that I could not foresee. I had always thought that I would be Minister of War and that everything would flow from that.'[3] The conclusion is clear. His flight to London in June 1940, and his subsequent wartime battle for the leadership of France, had been something of an aberration – an improvisation that would never be repeated. From now on he would have to seize his opportunities in France itself, in the hurly-burly of peacetime politics. It was in the light of this conclusion that the General considered his next move.

For all the relief which had followed the de Gaulle's resignation, the birth of the Fourth Republic was proving remarkably difficult. The Constituent Assembly had produced a new constitution, but it had been rejected in a referendum on 5 May. There were new elections to a new Constituent Assembly on 2 June. The result was not very different from the last time: MRP 28 per cent, Communists 26 per cent, Socialists 21 per cent and the rest as before.

It was at this point that the General decided to make a move and set out his own ideas on the right constitution for France. He chose the most theatrical time and place to do so: 16 June, the second anniversary of his return from exile, at Bayeux, where he had made his first speech. As it turned out, the event was far from the great spectacle that he had hoped for. To be sure, the planning had certainly been careful – Rémy and his old Resistance friends had seen to that. In the same square in which the hitherto unrecognised brigadier-general had made his first public address on French soil two years earlier, a platform had been erected. On the platform now sat the great figures of Fighting France: d'Argenlieu, Koenig, Juin, Schumann and Soustelle,* and, of course, the faithful Palewski. De Gaulle entered the square escorted by a fleet of police motorcycles, to which, as a former head of government, he was entitled.

Unfortunately, it was pouring with rain, and many of the onlookers wanted to go home quickly. De Gaulle's speech was far too long – it had taken two months to draft, losing spontaneity in the process, and it took nearly half an hour to deliver. By that time his audience was soaked. The speech itself, on analysis, does not turn out to be among de Gaulle's best. He did, of course, refer to his recent resignation, claiming that once the French people had elected Constituent Assembly he himself 'withdrew from the scene, not only in order to remove entirely from the party struggle what we, in the light of events, can symbolise, and which belongs to the entire nation, but furthermore in order that no personal considerations, while we were governing the country, could prejudice in any way the work of the legislators.'[4] It was, to say the least, a highly coloured account, but for the moment it served his political purpose. It meant that he felt that he could now, without being accused of partisanship, set out his views on the constitution that France should adopt,

* Jacques Soustelle (1912–1990): Academic and politician. Southern French, brilliant, precocious (by age twenty-five was acknowledged expert on Mexican Aztecs) but erratic. Originally on extreme political left, but joined Free French 1940; various posts, including Dir.-Gen. Special Services Algiers 1943–4; Minister for Information 1945, for Colonies 1945; Sec.-Gen. RPF 1947–51; Gov.-Gen. Algeria 1955–6; supported de Gaulle's return in 1958, but opposed Algerian settlement 1962; connived at formation of OAS, then fled to Switzerland; returned after 1968 amnesty; Deputy for Rhône 1951–8, 1973–8.

without the inhibition of being a possible candidate for office. This he then proceeded to do.

What he suggested was in line with what he had said previously: there should be an Assembly directly elected by universal suffrage, and a revising second chamber, whose members would be elected for the most part by regional and municipal councils, but who might also be drawn from different organisations playing an important part in national life. The executive authority would lie with a President, elected by a college consisting of members of both chambers complemented by representatives from outside, for instance from the overseas territories. On the American model, the President would appoint a Cabinet of ministers who would manage the day-to-day affairs of the country. De Gaulle made no mention of the judiciary, other than to say in his preamble that it should be separate from the legislative and the executive branches of government.

There is nothing very revolutionary, or even Bonapartist, to be read into the Bayeux speech; and, if the truth be told, it was rather dull. But in the press the speech was immediately attacked as an affront to democracy. All de Gaulle wanted, it was said, was a Bonapartist dictatorship, with himself as the new Bonaparte. The General's reaction was one of ill-concealed irritation. Two days later he deliberately celebrated the 18 June anniversary of his call to arms from London in 1940, not at the Arc de Triomphe, where he had been invited, but at Mont Valérien, the place of execution where many Resistance leaders had died.

It was an emotional choice, and it produced the intended emotional effect. De Gaulle shook hands with those of his colleagues associated with the Liberation who were there, and embraced a child who had lost both his parents but was wearing his father's Liberation medal. It was an occasion for tears and remembered sorrow. Hesitantly, the crowd started to chant '*Vive de Gaulle!*' and, as the voices became louder and louder, pressed him to speak. As he made to respond to their call, a hush fell, and the crowd waited in silence. Suddenly de Gaulle raised himself to his full height, thrust his clenched fists into the air in a gigantic V, and shouted in a voice like that of the last trumpet, '*Vive la France!*'

It was a brilliant piece of showmanship, which should have provoked a clear riposte from the Government. But they were too busy nursing the new Constitutional Commission – and incidentally ignoring all de Gaulle's Bayeux suggestions – and nothing happened. This, in turn, encouraged de Gaulle's supporters. After a second speech, at Bar-le-Duc on 28 July, Debré came to see de Gaulle at Colombey to persuade him to throw in his lot with the MRP and lead the party to what, on all the evidence, would be electoral victory.

It was at this point that the General missed his first opportunity for a successful return to power. The Government were scared. The MRP was strong. The leadership of the party was his for the taking. Yet de Gaulle would have none of it. His decision was influenced partly by pride and partly by principle: pride, because the MRP was led by people whom he felt had betrayed him, Bidault, Schumann, Teitgen and the rest – he was, recalled Debré, 'more Louis XIV than Richelieu';[5] principle, because his instinct told him that the party system, which he was being encouraged to join, would never work in France, and he had said so too many times to make it possible to go back on his own views.

When the new constitution was finally produced for debate by the Constituent Assembly, it had all the weaknesses that de Gaulle had feared. The office of President was feeble; the only serious responsibility was to appoint the Prime Minister, and he himself was elected by the two chambers of the Assembly. Real power lay with the Assembly, which could be dissolved only if two governments had fallen in successive years. On 27 August, just before the debate, de Gaulle put out a statement condemning the whole thing root and branch. Nobody paid any attention; even the MRP was broadly in favour of it. The truth was that the whole constitutional debate was becoming boring, and they all wanted to be done with it.

De Gaulle made one more effort, at Epinal in the Vosges, where he had been invited to attend the second anniversary of the liberation of the town on 29 September 1944. It was too late. The Constituent Assembly had voted through the constitution the previous night, and it was to be put to a referendum on 13 October. The General's speech was full of majestic scorn. He dismissed the 'derisory suggestions' that were current about his alleged dictatorial ambitions.[6] Then, after asking whether the various provisions of the proposed constitution were sound, he replied to his own question: 'Frankly no! . . . It is not worthy of the Republic.'[7] But again it was no good. The ensuing referendum approved the new constitution – just. De Gaulle commented mournfully that a third of the French people were resigned to it, a third had rejected it and a third had ignored it. It was under these doubtful auspices that the Fourth Republic was born.

There was an immediate council of war at Colombey. The battle against the constitution had been lost. Elections for the new Assembly had been fixed for 10 November. The only course left was to try to influence their outcome. De Gaulle's old friends, known to the hostile press as the 'Imperial Guard', advised him to back a new group known as the Union Gaulliste, but the General refused. He was right. In the event, the Union Gaulliste failed to make any impact electorally, polling only 3 per cent of the votes.

The elections returned an Assembly that was almost wholly anti-Gaullist. In the eyes of the victors, France had shown that the General's day was over. They hoped that he would accept the verdict with good grace. As the final insult, there were serious suggestions in Paris that he might accept the Presidency. He put out a statement on the day after Christmas 1946: 'It would not be the right way for me to serve my country . . . to preside in impotence over an impotent State.'[8]

Nothing, however, was further from the General's mind than accepting the verdict of the country with good grace. Now aged fifty-six, he was certainly not going to lapse into the dignified retirement towards which he was being ushered. Sitting in his house at Colombey, listening to the news on his almost antique wireless, he heard nothing but unpleasantness. Yvonne de Gaulle would never interrupt during the news; she sat there knitting while her husband spat at the wireless in fury, in reaction to reports of his former colleagues taking office. Worse, the old politicians of the Third Republic – Herriot, Auriol, Blum, Ramadier★ – were once again playing the game of ministerial merry-go-round. As he listened, the barrack-room language he used to describe them became ever more colourful: 'eunuchs', 'gigolos', 'sodomites', 'drinkers of their own urine', 'eaters of their own vomit'; so it went on, and so did Yvonne go on knitting.

Obviously it could not last. De Gaulle was reaching boiling point. It was not just his exclusion from the politics of the day, or what he felt to be the ingratitude for what he had achieved. Nor was it, in all honesty, a rounded protest at the new constitution and all that it represented. All these were factors, and were genuinely felt. But what finally sparked him into action was the realisation that his life was slipping away, and that the future, unless he seized the initiative, would be nothing more than a steady decline, playing patience in his home of an evening, opposite his wife placidly knitting. He certainly was not ready

★ Paul Ramadier (1888–1961): Politician. Socialist; junior minister in Popular Front; voted against full powers for Pétain 1940; Minister for Food in Provisional Govt. 1944, for Justice 1946; Prime Minister 1946; opposed de Gaulle's return in 1958.

for that. But to get back into active public life there had to be a pretext. The fact that he was bored, or even depressed, as his visitors of the time noticed, was not enough. Moreover, after all that had happened, the pretext had to be good. He did not want to risk another defeat – and this time a defeat that could be final. There was no point in taking risks simply out of boredom. There had to be the prospect of success, and for the General success meant his return as legitimate ruler of France.

The pretext that he found was the best possible: the threat of war. Nor was the pretext an idle one. Churchill had already warned the world of the 'iron curtain' that was cutting Europe in two, and the countries of eastern Europe were slowly but surely being forced into the Soviet Empire. The Polish elections of January 1947 exemplified the ruthlessness with which Stalin was tightening his grip; many of the results – and the formation of a Communist-dominated government – were announced before the votes had even been counted. The eastern zone of Germany had by now become a vast training ground for the Red Army. Worst of all, the threat of a nuclear holocaust – the Soviet Union by that time was near to the development of an operational atomic bomb – hung menacingly in the air.

On 2 February 1947 de Gaulle told Claude Mauriac that he was deeply worried and depressed by the growing international tension and France's response to it. 'I am going to try a *rassemblement*,' he said. 'It's the only hope.'[9] The General's mind was made up. He was going to attempt not to found a new political party but to rally the whole French nation above and beyond party politics. He was going to lead mass resistance against the apathy into which he believed his country had sunk.

Work started immediately. Messages went out from Colombey to the old faithful of the Resistance. Some of them refused to join him, but many agreed: Soustelle, Palewski, Chaban-Delmas, Debré, Louis Vallon, Morandat and, above all, André Malraux.* The General was excited again. 'I am re-making Free France,' he told one of them.[10] Meetings were held in secret, at Colombey or in rooms which Rémy had arranged for the General's use in the Hôtel La Pérouse. A name was found for the new movement: Rassemblement du Peuple Français

---

* André Malraux (1901–1976): Writer and politician. Creative genius of Gaullism (de Gaulle: 'Ah, Malraux: clouds, clouds but sometimes clear skies'), theatrical, impressed by authority. Studied archaeology and orientalism; fought for Govt. in Spanish Civil War; Resistance 1941–4; Minister for Information 1945–6; RPF; Minister of State 1959–60; numerous degrees at various universities.

(RPF). An organisation was sketched out. The Compagnons, as the senior members were called, would be organised on a regional basis, but all would meet every year at a vast rally to be called the Assises Nationales.

It was to be a mass movement, but there was, as might be imagined, one difficulty. All authority, to make decisions on policy, administration, tactics or anything else, was vested in a small group around the President. The President's decisions were final, and could not be challenged. The President was, of course, to be Charles de Gaulle. For a mass movement, it was the most authoritarian apparatus that could possibly have been devised. Either of the two Napoleons would have been proud of it.

The build-up to the launch went smoothly and rapidly. De Gaulle had been invited to a ceremony at Bruneval, for 30 March 1947, to commemorate the landing of British and Canadian commandos and their successful destruction of a German radar station in February 1942. It was decided to make this the great occasion.

A crowd of some 50,000, mostly old comrades of the Resistance who had found their way along the muddy, and on that day hopelessly clogged, Norman roads, were there to greet him. He mounted a platform, placed at the foot of the cliffs and decorated with both the Tricolor and the Cross of Lorraine, and delivered his message. 'The day is going to come,' he announced in tones of great solemnity, relayed to the crowd by loudspeaker, 'when the vast mass of the French people, rejecting sterile games and refashioning the ill-constructed framework of the State within which the nation is now going astray, will rally round France herself.'[11] The message was obvious; it was the same as Bayeux, but more direct.

It was enough to provoke action. On the afternoon of the following day Ramadier, now Prime Minister, set out for Colombey to find out exactly what de Gaulle was up to. Ramadier did not arrive until about 9.30 p.m., just as de Gaulle was preparing to go to bed. When the visitor's car halted in front of the main door of La Boisserie, a servant called up to de Gaulle, 'General, there is a gentleman who wishes to see you.' 'Who is it?' A short pause. 'He says he is the head of the Government.'[12]

The outcome of the interview was explained by Ramadier at a press conference the next day. 'General de Gaulle intends to make in the future a certain number of speeches of a political character. These speeches express his personal opinions, and the Government has no intention of raising any objection.' But if Ramadier thought that that was all the General had in mind, he was to be quickly undeceived. On 7 April, at Strasbourg, the capital of Alsace and the national symbol of defiance to Germany, de Gaulle went much further.

He had arrived on the 6th, a Sunday, to attend a service to commemorate the some 6000 American soldiers who had died in the battle for Alsace in 1944; and the Mass had been celebrated with all the decorum of official state occasions. On the Monday, the tone was quite different. As *Le Monde* put it, 'After the national day of Sunday [came] the political day of Monday.'[13] Speaking from the balcony of the Hôtel de Ville to an excited crowd of nearly 50,000, the General was in his most aggressive mood. After castigating the Government for all its errors, his voice rose to storm force during the climax: 'It is time for French men and women who think and feel like this, that is, I am sure, the vast mass of our people, to rally to prove it. It is time to form and organise the Rally of the French People which, within the framework of the law, will promote and bring to fruition, over and above differences of opinion, the great effort of common salvation and the reform of the State.'[14]

Nothing could have been clearer than that, except the question, which was put by *Le Monde* the next day, of how in practice it could all be done 'within the framework of the law'. But that was too subtle a point for the moment. The General's oratorical power had worked its magic. As he stood there, with his arms raised in the now familiar V salute, they stamped and shouted, sang the 'Marseillaise' – de Gaulle himself joining in – and screamed, '*De Gaulle au pouvoir*', again and again.

The Parisian press was hostile; ministers were angry and frightened. Blum was especially critical; he told the President, Vincent Auriol, that de Gaulle was a prisoner of his own illusion and wanted to be an absolute monarch. Sadly, Blum went on, de Gaulle would cast 'a shadow over his glory which ought to have remained pure and above the mêlée of politics'. Auriol was more bitter in his reply: 'He told me in 1946 that he wanted to remain outside political battles. I am sorry he lied to me.'[15] But the General was now enjoying himself and in the best of humours. Jacques Vendroux found him 'twenty years younger', and the whole company at Colombey thought it a great joke when he gave instructions that his letters should no longer have the Colombey address printed on them. 'One day I am here,' he explained, 'another day I am there . . . I have the gift of ubiquity.'[16]

The third step in the formation of the RPF was taken on 14 April by means of a press release in Paris. It announced the formal creation of the organisation. The release was followed ten days later by a press conference – a forerunner of the majestic press conferences that the General would give more than ten years later. Dressed in a suit of navy blue, he sat in front of a light green curtain and behind a simple table, which he banged with his fist from time to time to emphasise a point. To be sure, he had not yet developed the technique to its final form. The questioning was hostile, and he was sometimes forced into giving answers that he did not want to give. But the General was still learning; and he had already acquired the gift of repartee. Afterwards, de Gaulle thought he had done quite well, but complained about attitude of the journalists present, which he was never to do later on.

By the end of April 1947, it was clear that the General had struck a chord. The RPF gathered momentum. Within a fortnight of his press conference, well over 100,000 had enrolled. Headquarters were set up in the rue de Solférino in Paris, and branch offices in major cities. There were rallies up and down France. Enthusiasm grew with the rejection by the Soviet Union of the Marshall Plan for European reconstruction. De Gaulle now turned his fire on the Communists, denouncing them in a speech at a rally in Rennes on 15 July as fifth columnists who were planning to hand France over to the Soviet Union as a satellite. For once the General sounded pro-American, claiming that the Marshall Plan was essential for the defence of Europe. But it was the 'old parties' that came in for his particular scorn, all of them, as he said at a rally in Vincennes, 'cooking their small soup over a small fire, in their little corner'.[17]

By early summer 1947, France was heading for a trial of strength between the RPF and the main parties. The Communists demanded 'committees of vigilance' for the defence of the republic; the Socialists and the MRP forbad their members to join the RPF; but the RPF continued to grow, and by September probably had as many as 400,000 members. The trial of strength came in the municipal elections of October 1947, in a way which was surprising to many RPF members. Until then it had been possible to think of the RPF as something other than a political party. Indeed, that idea had informed its whole origin and foundation. But suddenly de Gaulle, scenting his opportunity, decided – indeed the decision had been taken as early as the end of June, and against the advice of his old Resistance friends – to put forward candidates at the October elections. At a stroke, the RPF became just another political party, and the General just another Fourth Republic party leader. There could no longer be any pretence of being 'above party politics'. It was a tremendous gamble.

De Gaulle's gamble almost came off. At the elections the RPF swept all before it. It won 40 per cent of the vote, easily passing the next biggest party, the Communists, with 29 per cent. The RPF captured thirteen of the twenty-five largest cities in France, the greatest prize being Paris itself.

It was certainly a major political event, but it was not decisive, and it was at this point that the General overplayed his hand. He called triumphantly for the immediate dissolution of the Assembly, new elections – and, for good measure, a new electoral system. To say the least, it was not a programme designed to encourage ministers of the existing Government, shaken as they had been by the result. But President Auriol kept his nerve, noting that nobody had thought to put down a motion of dissolution in the Assembly, which was the proper place for it.

Nor was the General disposed to negotiate. As Vallon later pointed out, 'If we had had any idea how to negotiate we could have been in power in a fortnight.' All they needed to do, he said, was 'to put through a call to the porter at the Elysée'.[18] But that was not on the General's agenda. There was some discussion of seizing power by military intervention, but it was quickly ruled out.

The defenders of the status quo were not slow to shore up their position. Ramadier was eased out as Prime Minister. When Blum proved unable to form a government, Auriol turned to Robert Schuman.* A Lorrainer with a temperament more German than French, Schuman was certainly no demagogue, nor – and this was his merit in the eyes of Auriol – was he frightened of General de Gaulle. The stalemate between the RPF and the Government was clear. Both sides were watchful of the other, but neither was prepared to compromise. As 1947 moved into 1948, the impasse continued. Domestically, the Schuman Government was, in spite of a rowdy Assembly and sporadic industrial violence, showing success in breaking the strikes that were crippling the country. On the other hand, the international dangers had not diminished; the Soviet Union had taken control of Czechoslovakia, and the Cold War was becoming more bitter. As measured by opinion

---

* Robert Schuman (1886–1963): Lawyer and politician. Centrist in political views. Educated at universities of Bonn, Munich, Berlin and Strasbourg; practised at Bar in Metz; Minister for Finance 1946; Prime Minister 1947–8; then various ministries in successive governments; President European Parliament 1958–60.

polls, de Gaulle's popularity was always at its greatest when international danger threatened, Schuman's at its greatest when there was peace.

At this point a tragedy occurred in de Gaulle's private life. His daughter Anne – little Anne – about whom he cared perhaps more than any other human being, caught pneumonia and died in her sleep. She was in her twentieth year. 'Anne became more feeble and was finding it more and more difficult to breathe,' de Gaulle wrote to his daughter Elisabeth on 8 February 1948, two days later. 'She died in my arms.' Her mother and governess had been there, and the *curé* from Colombey church had blessed her. 'Her soul is now free. But the disappearance of our poor suffering child, of our little daughter who was without hope, has caused us immense pain.'[19]

Those words come straight from the heart. Little Anne was perhaps the only person in his life that Charles de Gaulle truly and unreservedly loved. His relations with others were never easy; almost by way of compensation, towards her he felt the intensity of love that only a parent of a mentally damaged child can give, and, even with only the smallest signs of recognition, he derived from her presence a corresponding sense of comfort and fulfilment. Her loss deprived him of a solace that no one, not even his wife, could replace. They buried her in the churchyard at Colombey, simply and movingly. 'Come,' he said to Yvonne by the graveside, taking her hand, 'now she is like the others.'[20]

De Gaulle went through a period of depression after Anne's death. Even his speeches seemed to suffer. At a huge rally in Marseilles on 16 and 17 April 1948, he seemed tired, and it was generally admitted that Malraux, who had spoken before him, had put on a better performance. To be sure, the excitement was still intense wherever the General appeared – at Marseilles he spoke from a boat moored just off the quayside, and those who had come early were simply pushed into the water by the crowd that came later. But as the rallies continued, through the spring and the summer, they grew more and more oppressive in their tone – and less popular with the public.

The worst incident was on 18 September at Grenoble, where a rally was held to gather support for the following month's cantonal elections. It ended in a fearsome riot. Cars were burnt, a communist supporter was shot dead and fourteen other people were badly injured. The subsequent inquiry revealed that the 'Service d'Ordre', the private RPF paramilitary force commanded by the former Resistance Colonel Rémy, numbered no fewer than 6000 in Paris and 10,000 in the provinces, and that they were supplemented by less disciplined 'shock formations' who carried firearms and had on occasions, particularly at Grenoble, driven their jeeps ferociously into the crowd.

It was too much for the French public, and when the General failed to disavow his followers' violence or, indeed, at a press conference on 10 October, refused to dismiss the possibility of a coup d'état, the RPF reaped its reward. In the council elections its vote dropped badly. Not only that, but membership fell away and as that happened the movement was infiltrated by hard-line militants. In June 1949 sixteen of its members were arrested on the grounds that they were preparing a coup.

The general election of 17 June 1951 saw the end of the RPF as an effective political force. There were squabbles already within the leadership, but when the results came in – 22 per cent of the vote and only 120 Deputies out of 627 – it became clear that the RPF was no longer in a position to influence events. By June 1952, Soustelle had been approached to form a coalition government. This, for the General, was the ultimate betrayal; and, although Soustelle had refused the invitation, only a few months later a government led by Antoine Pinay was voted in with the support of twenty-seven dissident RPF Deputies. By the end of 1952 forty-five had broken with the movement, and de Gaulle drew the unavoidable conclusion that, as a force for reform in the direction he wanted, the RPF was finished. In May 1953, after a drubbing in the municipal elections of April, he finally admitted defeat. He formally released the remaining deputies from their allegiance and the movement was wound up a year later. Finally, at a press conference in June 1955, he announced his retirement from public life. His second political career had come to an end.

The whole episode of the RPF was something of an embarrassment for the General's supporters. It was never clear whether at the outset he genuinely meant it to be a movement above the existing political parties – a 'rassemblement' – or whether it was always destined in his mind to become one of them; or, indeed, whether he himself had any fixed opinion.

But this was the crucial question. De Gaulle had the temperament to lead a national movement, in the way he had led Free France, and it is tempting to see in the creation of the RPF a bout of nostalgia for the glorious days of the war. In some moods the General himself saw it in that way. On the other hand, once he had decided to present candidates for the 1947 municipal elections, the RPF became de facto a political party, and temperamentally he was unable to accept the compromises inevitable in any party. The organisation came to look more and more like an unsavoury replica of the movements of the 1930s, with all its accompanying inflammatory rhetoric, its childish dressing-up for theatrical parades and the attraction it exerted on young roughs who simply enjoyed a good punch-up.

De Gaulle himself was obviously not proud of the RPF. In his memoirs the entire period only rates a few elliptical lines. Nevertheless, it brought three things to his political experience that had up until then been missing: first, he had had to go out and meet real Frenchmen in France, and find out what they were really like, as opposed to what he thought they were like; second, he came to know, and appreciate the abilities of, many of those who would become his ministers during his third political career, as well as the network of ex-Resistance partisans who formed the basis of the RPF organisation and who would do the same for him in 1958; third, he was brought face to face with the emerging European movement, and over the next few years this obliged him to think deeply about France's role in the modern world. Jean Monnet was, for the moment, in the ascendant; the foundation of the Coal and Steel Community in 1951 was only the start of supranationality. It was a challenge that de Gaulle had to face.

But the abiding impression of the Charles de Gaulle of the ten postwar years is that of transition. He had learned some, but not all, of the political arts. He needed a period of reflection to allow that learning to sink in. But another dimension was being added, and it is perhaps not too fanciful to imagine that it was the death of his daughter Anne that brought out in him a quality of human sympathy that had lain unnoticed by the outside world, and perhaps even by himself. It was when that quality tempered his strength of will and single-mindedness that he was able to show himself not only as a courageous and obdurate general or a vain and intemperate politician, but as a man of true stature in France and in the world.

PART SIX

PHILOSOPHER

1

A Certain Idea
of France

I have considered the days of old:
*and the years that are past.**

De Gaulle's 'years in the desert', as they are known by his followers –
with the gentlest of New Testament overtones – lasted until his return
to power in 1958. During those years he had plenty of time to himself,
and he used it to reflect. Indeed, reflection, in his almost endless walks
around his garden and the neighbouring countryside, was the way he
filled his days. He reflected on his career, his character, his successes and
failures, and on the past and future courses of history.

The major project of those years was to put those reflections onto
paper, to create what became his *Mémoires de Guerre*. It was not an easy
project. He had written four books (and many articles) between the
wars, from the early *La Discorde chez l'Ennemi*, published in 1924, to *La
France et son Armée* of 1938, but they had none of them been books of
recollection. They had all of them, in their own way, been works of
advocacy, of a particular point of view, whether military or political.
The purpose of the books had dictated the style; practical rather than
noble.

Writing had never been easy for him. Although his output was enormous for an active soldier and politician – thirteen published books, five
volumes of speeches, some 35,000 letters – it was only achieved with
great labour. He wrote entirely in manuscript, slowly, with a pen and
black ink, in a sloping script, frequently crossing out and amending,
with meticulous attention to punctuation – 'It allows the sentence to
breathe,' he used to say[1] – until he was finally satisfied with what was on
the paper in front of him.

By 1952, when de Gaulle started on his memoirs – even before the

* Psalm 77, verse 5.

RPF had finally collapsed – he had achieved a measure of peace at Colombey that allowed him to attain the heights of style and composition that had eluded him while he was actively engaged in the army or in politics. The *Mémoires de Guerre* are without doubt a major work of French literature in their own right. The language is noble, the analysis profound and the sweep heroic. Of course, it would be missing the point to take the General's account of his life up to that date as an attempt at unbiased and objective history. They are more to be regarded as a personal apologia for his own role in the great dramas through which he had lived. As such, it need hardly be said, they frequently seem to view events through a badly distorted lens.

De Gaulle starts his memoirs, as might be expected, by referring to himself. But this is not mere egocentricity, although there is plenty of that, of course, throughout the work. It is a genuine attempt at self-analysis, to discover and reveal the motive force in his life. He launches immediately into a moving passage about his perception of France itself. 'The emotional side of me naturally imagines France, like the princess in the fairy stories or the Madonna in the frescos, as dedicated to an exalted and exceptional destiny.'[2] It is a curiously childlike image for a man of over sixty, and strangely reminiscent, too, of the image used by the child narrator at the beginning of Proust's novel, when, waiting for dinner time to see his mother again, he watched pictures projected by a magic lantern, of Golo advancing towards the castle of Geneviève de Brabant: ' . . . To be sure, I found plenty of charm in these brilliant projections, which seemed to be from a Merovingian past and surrounded me with such old reflections of history.'[3] The romantic nature of France and her history is proclaimed at the outset of both works.

Almost as though on cue, de Gaulle himself goes on to refer to his mother. To be sure, he mentions his father as being 'imbued with the feeling of the dignity of France'.[4] But he goes on to insist that it was his mother who had 'an uncompromising passion for her country, equal to her religious piety'. The words are as strong as they could be. He is clear that his mother's feelings about France were of the same intensity and on the same level – since de Gaulle never wrote anything by accident, least of all the first page of his memoirs – as her feelings about God. It is equally clear, from the context and the subsequent narrative, that it was those feelings that were inherited by, and drove, her second son.

The opening passage of the *Mémoires de Guerre* thus tells much about de Gaulle's own view of his emotional inheritance. But to those emo-

tional foundations were added an intellectual superstructure from outside the family, from his reading during the period of his education.
From his adolescence on, particularly while he was at St Cyr, de Gaulle
was a voracious reader. Literature became, and remained, his absorbing
interest, even to the point where, much later in his life, he could reply
to one of his ministers of the Fifth Republic, who asked him to rank
categories of men – and women – in the order of his admiration: 'First,
great writers; next, great thinkers; third, great statesmen; and fourth,
great generals.'[5] The minister, it need hardly be said, was astonished, but
also deeply impressed.

At the time de Gaulle started his serious reading there was certainly
plenty of heavy material to absorb him. The first decade of the twentieth century saw, in the aftermath of the Dreyfus affair, the rise to
prominence of a remarkable number of writers of great strength and
influence, all of whom were read by, and to a greater or lesser extent
influenced, the young de Gaulle.

There was Maurice Barrès, an advocate of extreme nationalism, tradition and patriotism, and Charles Maurras, who added to those ideals
that of the restoration of the monarchy. Both were founder members of
the Ligue de la Patrie Française in 1898, whose newspaper, *Action
Française* – which by 1908 had become a daily – was required reading in
the circles in which de Gaulle moved. But it was not only the firebrands
who were in intellectual fashion. Charles Péguy★ was widely read, not
just for the beauty of his prose, but because, although at first a socialist
and an atheist, he developed, after his conversion to Catholicism in
1908, a basic view of social reform, paternalistic in nature and mould-
ed by traditionalist concepts. It fitted well with the climate of the times,
and in turn attracted a number of acolytes, such as the novelist and soldier Ernest Psichari, who inspired the generation that went to war in
1914 with patriotic and religious enthusiasm.

But of all the intellectuals of the time who left their mark on the
young de Gaulle, the most persuasive was Henri-Louis Bergson.†
Indeed, in his study at Colombey, de Gaulle had a much treasured set of

---

★ Charles Péguy (1873–1914): Poet, nationalist, Catholic and socialist. Militant supporter of Dreyfus, and subsequently mystical patriot; influential in the nationalist
revival 1910 onwards (e.g. presented Joan of Arc as patriotic Christian).

† Henri Bergson (1859–1941): Philosopher. Professor at several universities, most
notably Collège de France 1900–14; Académie Française 1914; Nobel Prize for
Literature 1927. Major influence on French philosophy of his time, and particularly
on de Gaulle. Still revered, but with diminishing enthusiasm.

Bergson's works, which were read and re-read. In his open lectures at the Collège de France, and in his book *L'Evolution Créatrice*, published in 1907, Bergson had broken away from the dry rationalism that had dominated French philosophy in the nineteenth century by asserting the primacy of the freedom of the human spirit – *l'élan vital*, which inspired all life. The lesson was that it was the individual's intuition that should be relied upon; de Gaulle took it to heart, and applied it in his later political life.

There was also the reading prescribed by, or related to, military studies: Clausewitz and Machiavelli, Lyautey on the social role of the officer, military history from Alexander the Great through to the German strategists of the Franco-Prussian War. As though all this were not enough, de Gaulle revelled in French history, loved to read Chateaubriand and Corneille, took to Shakespeare and, thanks to his prodigious memory, could quote extensively from all that he read.

In short, the adult de Gaulle emerged not just as a man of strong emotion but of formidable education as well. Furthermore, he was by no means a slave to his own learning. He was evolving his own ideas. He rejected the monarchism of Maurras – and of his mother – and the elements of Bergson's philosophy that were anti-Catholic. He accepted the Revolution of 1789 as part of the continuity of French history – indeed in *La France et son Armée* he praised the Committee of Public Safety for organising the defence of the country during the Revolutionary war of 1792. Nor did he ever challenge the legitimacy of the Third Republic, however much he disliked its effects.

Out of this ideological whirlpool came two clear political currents which de Gaulle followed with total consistency all his life. Those currents could lead him in strange tactical directions, and frequently did, but the underlying ideas never varied. The first was the ultimate superiority, over all other political imperatives, of the interests of France. There could be no compromise, no bending of the principle to take account of temporary sentiment or of selfish ambition. The second was that by its very nature leadership, if it were to be effective and serve the overriding interests of France, had to be both aloof and determined. These two ideological currents inform the themes of all four of the inter-war books. Even if, for instance, *Vers l'Armée de Métier* is in appearance a book about armoured warfare, it is in reality a book about defending France at the weakest point of its frontier on the northern European plain. Even if *La France et son Armée* is a book about French military history, it is equally a commentary on French leadership. De Gaulle's experience in the Second World War and its immediate aftermath added a third conviction: to be successful, a leader had to have a direct relationship with the people he governed; they were his source of legitimacy, and therefore the sole support for the strength of the state.

Taken together, these elements form the basis of the political philosophy that is sometimes known as 'Gaullism'. As a concept, it is without a doubt powerful. In the real world, however, that philosophy, when called on to serve as a guide to practical action, was frequently disturbed, sometimes to the point of being disregarded, by the vagaries of the General's own very individual character.

This divergence is shown most clearly in his attitude towards the United States. Theoretically, the interest of France was served by maintaining the closest possible relationship with the United States. The country, after all, had been born out of a colonial revolt against France's traditional enemy, Britain, and the revolt had been helped by the French themselves, in pursuit of their own interests.

In reality, de Gaulle's relationship with America was always prickly and difficult. Roosevelt had treated him with barely disguised scorn; the State Department had pursued a pro-Vichy policy, against all the odds, almost to the end of the war. They had constantly tried to undermine his position in Algiers, preferring François Darlan or Henri Giraud, when he alone had stood out against the armistice, and they had kept him in the dark about the North African and Normandy invasions. Nor had Truman been any more accommodating than Roosevelt.

Quite apart from these official slights, it seems that he simply did not know what to make of America and Americans. In the whole of *Discours et Messages*, the record of de Gaulle's speeches and broadcasts, there is no thumbnail portrait of the United States, as there is of Britain, Russia or Germany. The difficulties were several. For a start, US history went back only 200 years, which in the General's span of time was a relatively short period. Then there was the mixture of peoples, colours, races and languages in the great melting pot; there was no clear social cohesion or state identity. There was also the outright pursuit of profit in a highly aggressive capitalist system, with no pretence of working towards a common goal other than self-enrichment. There was brashness and vulgarity.

America and Americans made for a confused picture in the mind of a Jesuit-educated child of the nineteenth century. But for all that, de Gaulle might have come to a greater understanding of, and sympathy for, America if his personal relations with American leaders had been better. Where Jean Monnet, the internationalist, was liked and respected, de Gaulle, the champion of the nation state, was disliked and distrusted. Roosevelt was hostile from the beginning, not least because he thought that de Gaulle treated him in a condescending way. But even after Roosevelt's death, de Gaulle could not find a friend until Kennedy; and he exasperated even that most European of Presidents. As for Lyndon Johnson, when the General asked him to withdraw all American forces from France before the deadline he had set, the President instructed Dean Rusk, his Secretary of State, to ask bitterly: 'Do you want us to move American cemeteries out of France too?'[6]

The fact is that until Richard Nixon became President in 1968, bringing with him as Secretary of State Henry Kissinger – one of de Gaulle's greatest admirers – official France had few friends in official Washington. At one stage, the General was popular with the American people, but he dissipated that popularity by the determined anti-American campaign of his last few years. Of course, de Gaulle was never one to mind unpopularity if he thought it to be in France's interests. The difficulty with his relations with America was that he seemed too often to be working against France's interests and to an agenda set by his own personal prejudice.

The case of Britain was quite different. She had long been the traditional enemy of France, but at least she fitted into the comprehensible scheme of things in which he was brought up. In that sense, de Gaulle was anglophobe only by inheritance; and when he arrived in England in 1940 and saw how he was welcomed, his attitude softened. To be sure, he would give no quarter when it came to fighting for what he perceived to be French interests, and he made mistakes – through over-sensitivity more than anything else – about the direction of British policy and British motives. But the fact that he was prepared on three occasions, in 1940, 1944 and 1969, to propose a partnership between France and Britain is evidence of a mind that was far from closed.

It was only when Britain leant towards America rather than Europe that the inherited anglophobia revived memories of slights received from clumsy British politicians in the Second World War and of times when the historical ambitions of France had been thwarted by British armies. It was then that de Gaulle came out in fierce anti-British colours; and they were all the fiercer for his conviction that Britain was not acting in its own best interests by taking America's part.

If there was one constant enemy, it was Germany. After all, Germany had invaded France three times in the hundred years after its unification under Prussian leadership and had decisively defeated the French twice. At the end of the Second World War, de Gaulle was in favour of the most extreme measures to dismember Germany so that nothing of the sort could ever happen again. But as time went by that aim changed to one of controlling a resurgent Germany through an advantageous treaty system – hence the Franco-German 'reconciliation' of the late 1950s. De Gaulle had realised that the French economy badly needed the support of a strong German economy. Even if modern Germany had been a powerful and aggressive enemy, the General found it possible to look back along the continuum of history to the Europe of Charlemagne, and ignore the upsets of a mere eighty years.

This sense of historical continuum lay at the heart of de Gaulle's feelings about his country. The first few pages of the *Mémoires de Guerre* make this clear. France was not just a country made up of diverse human beings. It was a totality of history, full of successes and failures, embracing 'all the generations' of the French people. This was the France that de Gaulle conceived of himself as representing, and it followed that France, with all her history, could not be France without greatness.

To the Americans and, to a lesser extent, the British, all this was mysticism carried to absurd lengths, and was the butt of many jokes. At its worst, it was simply the product of an oversized ego. It was no wonder that there was such a chasm between de Gaulle and the 'Anglo-Saxons'. They were looking at each other through different cultural telescopes.

Relations with any country, friend or foe, were complicated by the General's methods of conducting diplomacy. As one who was devoted to de Gaulle has remarked, 'He appeared to me always to be a man of war. He had reversed the principle of Clausewitz which had left such a deep mark on Lenin, Trotsky and Mao – "War is diplomacy by other means" – to make of it: "Diplomacy is war by other means." '[7] He studied carefully the strengths and weaknesses of other countries, and played to their weaknesses. The method he used was first one of surprise, as every good soldier should, and second the careful deployment of verbal fire power. In diplomatic wars, words were his weapons.

Thus his assaults on other countries or governments were delivered with a brutality that was often shocking, particularly if they came at unexpected times. If his language was orotund, and sometimes perhaps archaic, the message that came across in its delivery was, more often than not, particularly wounding. To be sure, as the General grew older, the language became less aggressive. His tirades against Spears, or even Churchill, during the Second World War gave way to the relative calm of his attack, for instance, on the generals in Algiers in 1961. But, even to the end, he was still able to shock, and shock deliberately.

If it was a mystical view of French history that formed the foundation for de Gaulle's view of France's place in the world, it was his own experience of French government that determined his views on the constitution for the France of domestic politics. As he himself writes, he served no fewer than fourteen different governments between 1932 and 1937 in the General Secretariat of National Defence – an experience which enabled him to see, as he put it, the weakness of the state. For example, when he tried in 1934 to explain to Léon Blum the ideas of forward armoured defence contained in *Vers l'Armée de Métier*, Blum, although interested, could not concentrate on what de Gaulle was saying because his telephone kept ringing throughout the conversation. De Gaulle was not impressed.

The collapse of the Third Republic in 1940, and the emergence of Vichy, led de Gaulle to denounce the former as inevitably leading to the latter. He believed that the management of war also required strong central authority – indeed, his authority at times during the Second World War seemed to many far too oppressive – and by 1945 he was already arguing against a return to the errors of 'yesterday'. But that is precisely what happened. The 1946 constitution was worked out in the full light of public scrutiny, day after day in the Constituent Assembly, and in the end made little change to the constitution of the Third Republic. It was, in political terms, the organisation of chaos.

The Bayeux speech of June 1946 took de Gaulle's argument a stage further by advocating a strong presidential system, authoritarian but legitimised by popular approval. It was this concept that formed the basis of the subsequent constitutional programme of the RPF. Critics have called it 'Caesarist' or 'Bonapartist' – not that labels necessarily mean very much. But the Bayeux ideas, before they became reality, had to contend with other ideas put forward by de Gaulle's supporters, notably Michel Debré, who was equally critical of the Third Republic but had a strong preference for a parliamentary regime on the British model.

In the end, the constitution of the Fifth Republic represented something of a compromise between de Gaulle and Debré. It was not reached easily. Learning the lesson from the Constituent Assembly of 1945, de Gaulle decided that the new constitution should be drafted in secret, and appointed Debré to carry out the task. The result embraced a combination of de Gaulle's strong presidency, with ministers outside the legislature, and Debré's rationalisation of the Senate and Assembly, with a body to rule on the constitutionality of laws. The French Empire, meanwhile, would become a community with a federal system of government. De Gaulle had foreshadowed this as far back as July 1944 in the conference at Brazzaville. The difficulty was that the right to independence had to be written into the constitution for the Empire, because of pressure from the African states. The community, unlike the Fifth Republic in metropolitan France, got off to an uncertain start.

It was said that, while Debré was the midwife to the constitution of the Fifth Republic, de Gaulle was its father and mother; and that it could consequently only work while the General himself held the reins as President. As it turned out, that analysis proved to be unfounded during the twenty years that followed de Gaulle's departure from office. His successor, Georges Pompidou, was able to live quite calmly within the same constitution; but, more important, so was a President of political views opposed to those of the majority in the Assembly. In March 1986, a socialist President, François Mitterrand, had no hesitation in inviting the neo-Gaullist Jacques Chirac to form a government as Prime Minister. To be sure, the experiment was not a particularly happy one for Chirac, but it worked, and indeed added a new expression – 'cohabitation' – to the French political vocabulary.

The result of the Assembly elections of March 1993 posed much more severe problems, and has raised again the question whether the constitution is workable in all foreseeable circumstances. First, the Socialist defeat was of a different order of magnitude to the relatively minor setback of 1986. Second, Mitterrand had only two years more to serve as President, and there was no question, on grounds of age and health, of his standing again; his position was consequently weaker. Third, the right had been out of power, apart from the unhappy two years 1986 to 1988, for some twelve years, and were consequently determined to enjoy to the full the fruits of victory. Last, they were themselves fighting off a serious challenge from a more brutal contender, a revived National Front.

But, as a counterweight, the constitutional rights of the President – the power of appointment and dismissal of the Prime Minister, of early dissolution of the Assembly at any moment of his choosing, and, above all, his control of the armed forces as their legal chief – preserved for Mitterrand a position which, if previous form was any guide, he would not be slow to exploit. The impact of the large majority in the Assembly, itself a clear reflection of a democratic decision, could to that extent be deflected, with potentially dangerous consequences to democracy itself. To be sure, in matters of detailed domestic legislation the President's power was limited to the right of veto; and even that powerful weapon could only be used in dire extremity, since under Article 49 of the constitution the Prime Minister could make the refusal of the President to endorse any Bill a matter of confidence, thus provoking a constitutional crisis. Nevertheless, the potential for stalemate between a stubborn presidency and an aggressive Assembly became obvious in a way it had not been before. The Fifth Republic, as a permanent constitution for France rather than a vehicle for de Gaulle's own particular style of government, was again, and is still, on trial.

The overall result is ironic, to say the least. The constitution was essentially the creation of de Gaulle, the most anti-American of French, or indeed of European, politicians; and yet the outcome has been a constitution closer to the American model than any other in Europe. It allows the executive of one political party – directly elected – to live in reasonable harmony with the legislature controlled by a different party (or group of parties) – also directly elected. Such an outcome, again ironically, would be impossible in any other European country. American commentators can hardly resist a quiet chuckle.

But there is no reason to believe that de Gaulle himself would have been shocked by such an outcome. He might not have liked it; indeed, he resented even the idea that anybody but he could lead France to her true destiny. But, once he had left office, he would have been resigned to the view that France should be left to sail freely on. If the ship veered off course from time to time, so be it; but the important point was that France, that proud galleon, should continue to sail in greatness. 'Old France,' he wrote at the end of the *Mémoires de Guerre*, 'weighed down with history, prostrated by wars and revolutions, endlessly vacillating from greatness to decline, but revived, century after century, by the genius of renewal.'[8] It was that mystical and heroic view of his country, shared in Proust's childish recollection, which would have reassured him that, whatever the vacillations, the 'uncompromising passion' which his mother had felt, and which he had inherited from her, had not been pursued in vain.[9]

2

ON PUBLIC AND
PRIVATE LIFE

On oublie trop souvent que je suis un homme comme un autre. Comme je
le dis parfois, les hommes ne sont jamais que les hommes, qu'ils soient
grands ou petits, qu'ils s'appellent de Gaulle ou Dupont.★

'It was the sheer presence of the man that was so compelling,' said one
ambassador's wife. 'When he was in a room it was almost impossible to
look at anybody else. He was not particularly attractive as such; "compelling" is the only word I can use.'[1] Henry Kissinger spoke of him as
possessing a power of personality that he had previously met only in
Mao Tse Tung. Princess Margaret was reported to have said, during his
visit to Britain in April 1960, 'He is so distinguished, so impressive, that
I nearly curtsied to him!'[2]

To be sure, de Gaulle's physique helped to reinforce this impression
of a huge personality. He was tall; not absurdly so – at six foot five inches – but tall enough to stand out. What made his natural height the
more striking was his upright, almost stiff, military bearing and his
long neck. He appeared as someone used to giving commands and seeing them obeyed. In his time in the army and during the war his stance
appeared aggressive and arrogant; and in his earlier days, from his adolescence right up to his middle fifties, de Gaulle's physique and
personality both seemed decidedly menacing. People were frightened of
him; some were even rendered speechless with terror, particularly at his
outbursts of anger. In later years, both his personality and his body
movements became more controlled, and hence less menacing. But by
then, because of worsening sight, he had developed another unnerving

---

★ 'It is too often forgotten that I am a man like any other. As I sometimes say, men are
never anything but men, be they large or small, be they called de Gaulle or Dupont.'
Charles de Gaulle, quoted in Robert Lassus, *Le Mari de Madame de Gaulle,* page 107;
Editions Jean-Claude Lattès, Paris, 1990.

facial expression: a fixed gaze. 'I have never,' wrote one of his aides late in de Gaulle's life, 'felt stripped so naked by a look.'[3] Strangely enough, and in total contrast to the strength of his other features and body movements, his hands were long and slender – musician's hands, 'as though made to hold a bow or caress a keyboard'[4] – and his handshake was surprisingly limp. In a curious way, the contrast made the impact of his personality all the more powerful.

De Gaulle himself was uncomfortable and embarrassed by his physique. He was conscious of its oddities: the gangling walk, large nose, wide ears, small head and receding chin. They made him feel awkward and shy. For a start, he did not like his own face. 'I practically never look at myself in the mirror,' he said, 'unless I have to . . . for instance just before a television appearance. But,' he went on to say – characteristically – 'the advantage of having an unattractive face is that it allows one to hide, and to master, the emotions that one might reveal in public.'[5] Nor was he any happier about his height or figure. As he wrote when describing his triumphal march down the Champs-Elysées in August 1944: 'It was true, finally, that I myself had neither the physique nor the taste for those attitudes and gestures that can charm the public.'[6] Besides, it was always difficult to get in and out of cars and most beds were too small for him. 'We people are never quite at our ease,' he told Joxe one day, and then added with a smile, 'I mean . . . giants. The chairs are always too small, the tables too low, the impression one makes too strong.'[7]

But then de Gaulle was shy by nature, as he himself had admitted. It was not just his physique; his whole childhood and education had left him uneasy. He had been brought up with a very partial, even bizarre, view of the world, and that partial view turned into an egocentric view when he found others with their own differing certainties which clashed with his. It became impossible for him to admit that he was wrong – that would have been to overthrow what his parents and the Jesuit fathers had drilled into him. The only answer was to retreat into himself.

When he came into contact with those outside his family or close acquaintance, he erected barriers. He often seemed solitary and, to outsiders, silent. He rarely used Christian names or allowed others, apart from his wife, to use his. The familiar *tu* was used to address his children, grandchildren and his contemporaries at St Cyr – but only occasionally to address his wife. He disliked being touched, and shrank in horror from the Mediterranean French who wanted to take hold of his arm or elbow to emphasise points in conversation. Even his closest colleagues were treated with dry formality.

The barriers were noted not only by Churchill; Macmillan observed them too. While in Algeria in June 1943 he decided to visit the Roman ruins at Tipasa, a little way along the Mediterranean coast. De Gaulle asked to accompany him, and as they walked through the ruins they talked 'on every conceivable subject – politics, religion, philosophy, the Classics, history (ancient and modern) and so on'. But then, when Macmillan stripped naked and went for a swim in the sea, de Gaulle refused to join him; he 'sat in a dignified manner on a rock, with his military cap, his uniform and belt . . .'. Macmillan went on to describe him as 'this strange – attractive yet impossible – character'.[8]

De Gaulle was also a man of volatile and often unruly temperament. When the volcano erupted, those around him ran for shelter. This in turn added to his own sense of loneliness. Indeed, such was his need to protect himself from public displays of his emotions that he built round it almost a whole philosophy of leadership.

Put simply, the view of leadership that de Gaulle expounded in his lectures at the Ecole Supérieure de Guerre and in the book that followed, *The Edge of the Sword*, elevates what might be thought of as diffidence into a prime virtue of a leader. Authority and prestige, he wrote, need to be promoted by aloofness, by keeping distance and by creating mystery through silence. The original model for the 'leader' may have been Marshal Pétain, but there is little doubt that when he refers to 'aloofness' de Gaulle is talking about himself. Nor is there doubt that he was, even at this stage in the 1920s and early 1930s, envisaging himself in the role of leader, and fiercely ambitious as he always was, self-consciously cultivating the quality that he described. 'The leader . . . must have an inborn propensity which can be strengthened by the exercise of his craft.'[9] In other words, if diffidence is a characteristic by nature, it should be deliberately cultivated by the man who wishes to lead.

Furthermore, the leader, in *The Edge of the Sword*, is obliged to live a life of depression and loneliness owing to the self-discipline that the role imposes. 'What people agree to call happiness' cannot be reconciled with leadership. Again, it is hard not to believe that de Gaulle was taking what he perceived to be his own characteristics and representing them as the necessary requirements of a leader. After all, he himself was given to acute depressions if he thought that he had failed, as at Dakar in 1940, or had been rejected, as in Paris in May 1968. Admittedly, some

of these moods were faked; he quite frequently used the trick of painting a gloomy picture simply in order to hear the expressions of support
and encouragement that inevitably followed.

But most of his introspective depressions were genuine. Furthermore,
never in all his life did he express himself as 'happy'. Indeed, his wife's
comment after his death was that he 'has suffered so much these past
two years'.[10] Nor is it clear that he enjoyed his triumphs, in war or in
peace; and the number of times that he is recorded as laughing outright
– as opposed to smiling drily – are very few in his whole life. His model
of a leader, in this sense, is no more than a description of, and rational
defence of, his own personality.

There are two other features of his model of the leader which give
clues to the personality of de Gaulle himself. The first is the clear statement that the leader is an artist, the player of a role. It was not for
nothing that de Gaulle's admiration for Churchill was not just, indeed
not primarily, for his qualities as a 'great fighter' but for his skills as a
role-player and the consequent ability to carry his followers, those who
are led, along with him. The second is even more remarkable: there is
a passage in *The Edge of the Sword* describing the role of the leader, or
now the 'hero' as he has become, as a 'divine game'. It was all, apparently, a big gamble, a succession of throws of the dice for the highest of
stakes. In itself this is not so remarkable, but, of course, it reads almost
like a script for de Gaulle's own great gamble in June 1940. It was as
though, almost with deliberation, he wrote the script and then acted it
out – and then, perhaps, wrote the critic's approval of the hero's performance of the whole play in the *Mémoires de Guerre*.

Of course, the role of leader that de Gaulle described in *The Edge of
the Sword* does not encompass his least attractive characteristics: a streak
of vindictiveness – witness, for instance, his treatment of Lady Spears's
ambulance unit on VE Day or, later on, of Gaston Monnerville,* the
opponent of the Fifth Republic; lack of generosity, witness his treatment
of former colleagues who offended him, from Muselier to Rémy; sudden and furious anger, of which his life is full of examples; conceit,
which led him to feel contempt for otherwise perfectly worthy public
figures and to lament at the end of his life that he had never had an
intellectual adversary truly of his own stature, as Napoleon had had

* Gaston Monnerville (1897–1992): Lawyer. Son of colonial administrator in Cayenne,
French Guiana. Radical Deputy 1932; junior minister 1936; joined Resistance 1941;
commander all French forces in Massif Central 1944; French delegate to UN 1946;
President of the Council of the Republic 1947–58; President of the Senate 1958–68.

Chateaubriand; and insensitivity to the sufferings of fellow human beings outside his family, for instance his comrades in arms at Dinant Bridge, Montcornet or Abbeville.

In so far as he recognised them in himself, and he certainly recognised his propensity to bouts of rage, they were defects which needed to be mastered. In this, he had at least a measure of success. The roughness of the personality of the wartime de Gaulle became less pronounced as the years went by. For a start, he had learnt to master his uncertain temperament. The volcano erupted less frequently. Age itself made him more relaxed in his dealings with, and more sympathetic towards, his fellow creatures. But, although he mellowed with time, the old Adam was still there, and even in his later years could emerge disconcertingly and without warning; and his pride, the protection of his own dignity and *amour-propre*, stayed with him undiminished throughout his life.

So, for that matter, did his physical and moral courage. He was almost impervious to fear, to the point of refusing even to take the reasonable precautions that were urged on him. Equally, he was never deflected from a chosen course even by the most virulent of attacks. Also, to the end of his life, de Gaulle kept his two other most notable characteristics: his formidable power of will and his speed of perception, both of situations and of people. Of his willpower there are abundant examples – his tenacity of purpose throughout the Second World War being the most obvious. Of his speed in getting the feel of, as opposed to merely analysing, political situations there are, again, numerous instances. Less widely understood, however, is his instinctive perception of people and their character. 'It was in this understanding of others,' wrote an aide, 'that he had in him something feminine.'[11] He could size up complete strangers with uncanny accuracy, and his quick pen portraits of people he had met for the first time always succeeded, in their lapidary fashion, in catching the essence of the new acquaintance.

There is no doubt that there were major turning points in de Gaulle's life, bringing changes which altered his view of himself and, through that, altered his own behaviour. The first came with the collapse of France in 1940. Up until then, he had fretted at his own inability to find a cause in which he could exercise the power of leadership that he saw in himself. June 1940 provided it. But at first it was not at all clear. Although he was supported by Churchill, he was still prepared to serve under any more senior French leader, civil or military, who was prepared to reject the armistice. He had, after all, even appealed to General

Noguès in Morocco. Gradually it appeared that he was alone. The conclusion was that it was he, and only he, who would have to shoulder the burden of France.

It was at this point that his *Mémoires de Guerre* start to reflect the change in self-perception. This is the moment that a character called 'General de Gaulle', or sometimes more simply 'de Gaulle', starts to appear. The author is referring to himself, but he now does so in the third person, and the stylistic change is significant. The first time this new character appears with any force is at the moment at which the British officially decide to support him as Free France. 'Then . . . the London Cabinet found itself once more face to face with General de Gaulle alone and took the decision, on 28 June, to recognise him publicly as "leader of the Free French".' But he goes on: 'It was therefore in this capacity that I opened the necessary conversations . . .' In other words, 'General de Gaulle' at that point became the symbol of the legitimacy of the continuing France, and 'I' was there to serve him.

Over the years this method of expressing his dedication to – even identification with – France became more pronounced and his pursuit of the cause more intense. 'De Gaulle' had been created as an instrument of destiny, as France had created others before him. 'De Gaulle' was the source of French legitimacy, regardless of the rough and frequently unscrupulous methods that 'I' used to assert it. The year 1958 was to be the second turning point. 'I was forced more than ever to be de Gaulle,' he wrote about his return to power in May of that year. '[There is] the fact of de Gaulle. I do not understand it very well myself but I am a prisoner of it.'[12]

How far this separation of the two identities was a rhetorical trick is of little matter. What matters is to understand that it was not merely a rhetorical trick, in other words was not simply a cynical way of cloaking his own personal ambition in respectable guise. For good or ill, Charles de Gaulle undoubtedly felt that he was in the same category as Joan of Arc and Clemenceau – a saviour of France. It was this feeling that provided – conveniently enough – further justification for the aloof reserve that was anyway a part of his own psychological defence.

Yet aside from the public 'de Gaulle', and, indeed, if the rhetoric is followed, the 'I' that served him, there was another Charles de Gaulle. The public persona gave way to the private man when he was with his family. In his childhood and adolescence, well before the public persona developed, he had at least had a stable, if somewhat eccentric, family life.

But as his military career progressed and more of his time was spent out-side France, his closeness to his family started to fade. His father and mother continued to play a role – he consulted his father on his writings right up until his death in May 1932, regularly wrote to his mother and went dangerously out of his way to visit her in June 1940 when she was dying. He also kept close to his sister Marie-Agnès, not least because she and her husband had looked after his father in their home for the last ten years of his life.

But less and less is heard of his three brothers, Xavier, Jacques and Pierre. In their boyhood the others had been led by Charles in their games and in simulated wars with tin soldiers – the second son always insisting on being 'France'. As they grew up, their paths diverged. Charles de Gaulle broke out from his childhood through his reading at St Cyr and afterwards, through his experiences in the First World War and his subsequent military career, and through his education in the broader world of politics with Pétain. Meanwhile Xavier became an engineer in the Department of Mines and subsequently consul-general in Geneva. Jacques also became an engineer, but was struck down by a sleeping sickness virus at the age of thirty, and spent the next twenty years with a badly damaged brain, paralysed, unable to speak and in great pain. Pierre, the youngest, appears from time to time in the General's life, particularly during the period of the RPF, when he was chairman of the Paris City Council, senator for the Seine district and finally deputy for a Paris constituency. But the General's relationship with Pierre never seems to have been close. Of the three, de Gaulle seems to have felt most for Jacques, out of sympathy for his dreadful illness. When his sister and her husband, their son Michel, his brother Pierre and his niece Geneviève, Xavier's daughter, were all deported, the General was adamant in his refusal to make any concessions for their release.

It was after the war, through his marriage and his own children, that de Gaulle found his other, more benign self. Both before and during the war there had been many separations and much travelling. Little Anne was a constant source of worry, from the time she was born in 1928 until her death twenty years later. The de Gaulles took her with them wherever they went – to military postings before the war, to England and Algiers during the war. Although there was always a governess to look after her, de Gaulle felt special pleasure in being with her and Yvonne could never quite relinquish the responsibility in her own mind. It was not until after Anne's death, and the foundation carrying her name had been set up, that the life of a normal bourgeois family from northern France could properly establish itself and contentment set in.

The other two children, Philippe and Elisabeth, were much less of a worry. Philippe was much in awe of his father – he had noticed at an early age that de Gaulle was 'somebody out of the ordinary' – and he said later that his childhood was not much fun, any more than de Gaulle's own had been. Times were hard, he was made to study hard and there were not many jokes in the de Gaulle household. Almost before he had grown to manhood war broke out and he joined the Free French naval forces. From then on, the relationship between father and son was one of sporadic meetings during the war and of a certain emotional distance afterwards. De Gaulle was a conscientious father, but the relationship, although strong, was shy and reserved.

With his daughter Elisabeth the relationship was, as might be expected, much easier. She was a lively girl, and had the same dry sense of humour as her father. Nevertheless, she was high-spirited and, according to 'Roo', her undergraduate contemporary at Lady Margaret Hall, apt to engage in furious rows, particularly when anybody was critical of France or the Free French. She had her father's touchiness (as did Philippe, both of them refusing to attend the celebration of the centenary in 1990 at the Arc de Triomphe because President Mitterrand was to be there). But her bond with her father was strengthened during the 1950s, when she typed the *Mémoires de Guerre*.

La Boisserie was the centre around which all revolved, and as the years went by, the children got married and grandchildren appeared, so the General unwound and relaxed. Here the perfect manners, which in the war he had had deliberately to cultivate, came naturally to him; he was charming and witty to visitors, family and servants alike. True, he was inclined to become overexcited when watching a football match on television – particularly if France were losing, when the referee would suffer severe verbal attack; but otherwise his language was as decorous as could be – unless, of course, he wanted to tease Yvonne.

Yvonne, de Gaulle's wife for little short of half a century, was the focal point of La Boisserie. She had been born and brought up in Calais, and kept a particular place in her affections for her home town. Indeed, some said that she wished she had never left it. She certainly kept to the narrow path along which her upbringing had directed her, and never wished to break out in the way that her husband had. This could, on occasions, be irritating. She used to speak so much about Calais that the General himself used to say that she reminded him of

Mary Tudor, who had said that if her heart were opened the name of Calais would be found written on it.

Her family – the Vendroux – were of the conventional, and very provincial, upper middle class, though not quite as stuffy as some; after all, Yvonne's mother had been the fourth person in the whole of France to acquire a driving licence, and it was in the Vendroux house that the first telephone line in Calais had been installed. Yvonne herself had been educated in the usual way, at a convent, and apart from an occasional outburst of adolescent rebellion – she thought it absurd to be required to wear a shift while bathing – seems to have been a model pupil. Her studies were interrupted during the First World War, when Calais was bombed and she was sent to Canterbury in England while her mother nursed the wounded soldiers from the front, but generally she grew up an accomplished and pretty girl, expecting to settle down to some suitable marriage and rear a family. The one category of man she said she would never marry was a soldier.

It was, of course, a soldier that she did marry; not only that, but it was a soldier of six foot five inches to her five foot two inches. The pretty bride of spring 1921 learnt dutifully to accommodate herself to her husband's difficult character, and it was made easier by their shared northern French background, with its stern values and unbending Catholicism. In truth, as she grew older, Yvonne, already prudish, developed into something of a puritan. She is said to have thought that the novels of Françoise Sagan, much in vogue during the 1960s, and indeed enjoyed by the General – 'for the subjunctives', he said – were the works of the devil. Not only did she disapprove of anything approaching loose morals, but she disliked even the grandeur and show that went with her husband's official position in later years. Her preference was for the quiet life of a housewife, mother and subsequently grandmother. She loathed formal functions; nor was she much good at them, conversation with her being, according to one ambassador's wife, 'sticky, to say the least'.[13] She never consented to be interviewed by a journalist and intensely disliked photographers.

During the war, Yvonne spent her time looking after her children. She was, of course, left to herself for long periods, either because she was too far from de Gaulle's base in London – for example, at Dudleston Heath – or because the General himself was travelling in Africa or the Levant. She never really made friends in England. She was too shy, and her English was not at all good. Besides, the houses in which she lived, Petts Wood, Gadlas Hall, Rodinghead and Frognal were too far from the centres of population – Hampstead was at that time almost a village north of London – to make it easy to travel around, particularly as she herself could not drive. But she was liked by the shopkeepers, by her maids, and indeed by everybody she met. She was always kind and considerate, and her tastes, like her sense of humour, were simple.

These simple tastes remained with her all her life. The little black dresses may have started as a way of sharing the hardships of the Free French during the war, but they continued thereafter, alleviated from time to time, in the summer, by conventional flowered frocks. She usually felt it proper to wear a hat when going out of doors. But her taste in hats was noticeably old-fashioned, and the chic Parisian women tended to laugh at her, which made her even more timid. Her time was taken up with her family, particularly Anne until her death, and afterwards with the foundation created in Anne's name; and of course, with knitting or reading. It was said, probably with truth, that all the babies in Colombey-les-Deux-Eglises wore smocks knitted for them by Mme de Gaulle. She loved her garden at La Boisserie, particularly the roses and the wild flowers, and supervised the gardeners from the village with care and attention – and with the help of a large collection of flower catalogues. Her taste in entertainment was equally conventional: easily absorbed classical music (Vivaldi or Handel), uncomplicated films and television; and, as might be expected, she liked dogs. 'A little woman from the provinces,' they said.[14] It was little wonder that she became known to the French, not without a touch of malice, as 'Tante Yvonne'. It was, after all, symbolic of the position she occupied in France.

She may have had simple tastes which the French sniggered at, but she was a kindly person and held in great affection by her family, particularly her seventeen nephews and nieces in Calais. As one of them said, 'What sums up . . . the character of Yvonne is the wish not to hurt or upset anybody . . . the concern not to cause the least worry to her nearest and dearest.'[15] After her husband's burial, Yvonne stayed on at La Boisserie by herself for another nine years, keeping herself to herself, until, in September 1978, she moved to a religious institution in the Avenue de Bourdonnais in Paris, where she had chosen a small and very simple room. She did not want to be any trouble to anyone. On the walls there were only four photographs: of her husband, of her daughter Anne, of their joint grave, and of a Cross of Lorraine. There she died on 8 November 1979, the day before the ninth anniversary of her husband's death. The National Assembly stood in silence at the news.

Yvonne de Gaulle was in many ways the ideal companion for the General. They shared the view, in which they had both been brought up, that the role of the man was to go out into the world and the role of the wife was to mind the hearth and home and to bring up the children. Whether the General was an ideal companion for her is another matter. To be sure, he recognised that she provided the haven to which he could return from his political forays, and he also recognised that he came to depend on the haven always being there. Yet there was no discussion of politics at the General's home as there had been in his parents' house. Yvonne took little part in her husband's public life, accompanying him only sometimes on his travels or being at his side when duty called her to state occasions. She had no deep involvement, nor in truth did she want any. But there were penalties. 'You know, my little Claude,' she said to one of her nieces in a moment of frankness, 'I am very proud of being the wife of the President of the Republic, but I would so much have liked to stay a simple housewife.' There was a short pause; and then she went on, 'Do you know that sometimes I take a pair of your uncle's shoes and clean them in the bathroom, to prove to myself that I am still a normal woman?'[16]

It has become customary to assume that in the course of a long marriage such as that of Charles and Yvonne de Gaulle there must have been infidelities on one side or the other, or both. In the case of the de Gaulles there is no evidence to justify any such assumption. As far as Yvonne was concerned, strictness of religious discipline allied to her obvious devotion to her husband – it amounted at times almost to worship – makes any breach of fidelity highly unlikely. In the case of the General, the matter is not quite so clear cut. It has been said that during the long periods away from his wife de Gaulle may have formed relationships with other women. It has even been suggested that he had an illegitimate son, and a candidate has come forward. But more thorough investigation has failed to reveal any substance to the claim.

Nevertheless, it is true that de Gaulle was always attracted to 'pretty young ladies'.[17] Before his marriage, he had acquired something of a reputation. He was said to have chased the same women as Pétain when at Arras in 1913; and there was the matter of the Countess Strumilla in Warsaw – it was even rumoured that he had fought a duel to defend her honour. Even after marriage, the General enjoyed mild flirtations; he was much taken with Jackie Kennedy, and wives and daughters of ambassadors to Paris were frequently singled out for special attention.

But it was all harmless enough, and there is no reason to suppose that the General followed many of his ministerial colleagues in their pursuit of extra-marital affairs.

For Yvonne, life at home at La Boisserie, with the occasional visit to Calais to see her family, was all she really asked for. After 1946, the last thing she wanted was for her husband to return to public life. The General, of course, thought differently. But the times were, for the moment, against him, and he had to content himself with his writing and his family. One friendship that became very close during this period, and remained close thereafter, not least because of a shared interest in politics, was with Jacques Vendroux, Yvonne's brother. Indeed, Vendroux may have been a substitute for de Gaulle's real brothers, who were now distant from him. Letters were signed 'Your brother, Charles', and when there were holidays the de Gaulles and the Vendroux went together. Jacques Vendroux was the first person to arrive at La Boisserie after the General's retirement in April 1969.

Apart from holidays with the Vendroux, and the visits of the grand-children, there was not much to entertain the de Gaulles in the mid-1950s. There were occasional trips in the surrounding countryside, and journeys to Calais, but wherever he went de Gaulle was instantly recognisable, and the press had not lost their interest in his movements. The General had to take great care not to be seen. At La Boisserie itself, life was simple. The de Gaulles had local acquaintances but no friends. As would be expected, they were on good, if respect-fully distant, terms with the local dignitaries at Chaumont and Bar-sur-Aube and the *curé* at Colombey. There was little social life of consequence, but then neither de Gaulle nor his wife seemed to miss it. They led the life of a provincial bourgeois family as it had been lived by their parents at the end of the nineteenth century. It was not just the company. It was, as a visitor (whose own background was from the Champagne) remarked, 'just like the life my parents led'. The visitor recognised 'the way of setting out dinner' and 'the way of pouring out the wine'.[18] He might, he reported, have been back in the home of his childhood.

This was, of course, the de Gaulles' own preference. It was how they felt content together. But, quite apart from the style, their finances did not allow anything much grander. There was not much money to spare until the publication of the *Mémoires de Guerre*, since de Gaulle had refused the pension offered by the Government in 1946, preferring to live on the retirement pay of a brigadier-general. He and Yvonne had a farm which provided some income, but de Gaulle was much more interested in the workings of the farm itself – about forty-five acres at Coulogne, a few miles from Calais – than he was in the revenue. Once royalties from the memoirs came in, the financial position became easier, but a large part of them was diverted to the Fondation Anne de Gaulle and only a small part was devoted to cheering up life at La Boisserie.

It was not, however, a life that either of them wanted cheering up very much. There were four long trips that they took together, in the DC4 that the French air force agreed that he should use after he had handed it to them in 1946, but, however enjoyable they were, it was always a relief to come back to Colombey. Once back, work started again. The *Mémoires de Guerre* were not completed until 1957, and the rhythm of Colombey life was undisturbed while de Gaulle continued to work on them. Yvonne went on knitting, while the General wrote, walked and read. In the evenings it was television or, for the General, successive games of patience – at which he seems to have been inclined to cheat, since he did not like being defeated by the cards. There was no music, since their tastes differed. The General could bear to listen only to military marches and traditional jazz (although he occasionally whistled tunes from the operettas of the 1920s) and thought Mozart 'a profoundly unpleasant noise'.[19] Yvonne liked her simple classics.

Neither of them cared much for architecture or painting. When, very late in his life, they visited Spain, de Gaulle said he would spend only half an hour in the Prado ('I want to see the Goyas and the Velasquez, and that will be enough'). Nor did either of them worry about clothes. Yvonne always appeared in her conventional dresses, and the General always wore a collar and tie and a suit of thick worsted. Nobody, least of all their children, ever saw them in anything else, even on the hottest summer afternoons, although on one recorded occasion the General appeared in a dressing gown to say goodbye to a departing guest. It was such a strange event that it was much remarked on.

De Gaulle and his wife both enjoyed robust health. He used to have frequent snuffles, which sometimes developed into colds, putting him into a bad temper. The malaria that had affected him in the war had disappeared, as had the minor trouble with his kidneys. Up until 1947 he was a chain smoker of cigarettes – almost all photographs of those years have him either lighting one, or putting one out, or with one drooping from the side of his mouth. But he gave it up from one day to another, when he heard of Leclerc's death, so it is said. 'I gave it up in one go,' he remarked. 'It was terrible. But since I had told my wife and my ADC, I could not go back to it.'[20] The big problem was his eyesight. In late 1952 he had a cataract operation, which was extremely painful and only partially successful. The lenses in his spectacles became thicker, and he had trouble finding his way up and down stairs.

In all other respects, de Gaulle's health was excellent. He slept well, as he did all his life, unless some major crisis kept him awake, and ate in abundance. The food he most enjoyed was the peasant food of the country – *tripes à la mode de Caen* or *blanquette de veau* – and cheeses, such as a strong *mi-mollette* from the north or ewe's milk cheese from the Pyrenees. He was a good eater but a poor drinker; a glass or two of *vin de pays* was enough for a meal – enough, too, for his guests, as those of his colleagues who came from Paris to visit him used to grumble. Afterwards it was coffee, which he liked very black and very strong.

De Gaulle took no exercise to work off his heavy diet, other than walking. True, when he was not accompanied by Yvonne, he walked at a fast pace and a long stride. But he was not one for shooting or tennis – that was simply not his style. Furthermore, his walks not only served the mundane purpose of exercise but also gave him the psychological space for his reflections. He noted himself that he must have walked thousands of times round his garden at La Boisserie, and that it was on those walks that he puzzled out the problem, whatever it might be, with which at that moment he was confronted.

Even leaving aside particular and identifiable problems, he found much to think about on his walks. His religion, for example, was to all outward appearances that of the conventionally strict Catholicism of French Flanders – Mass every Sunday and on the appropriate feast days, regular confession and absolution, observance of the required rites; indeed, when he moved into the Elysée he had it rearranged to make room for a private chapel. But without a doubt there was alongside that a streak of nihilism and pessimism in him which led at least one of his closest companions in later life to wonder whether he had any real faith at all. Nietzsche, with his contempt for Christianity, and Chateaubriand, its fervent champion, seemed to be in constant warfare in his mind. He was constantly reminded of his religious duty by his res- olutely devout wife. Furthermore, as leader in later life of a Catholic country, he felt that he had to observe the proprieties. On the other hand, it was impossible to forget that the French bishops had been Vichyites to a man – unlike the parish priests. Moreover, Bergson, whom he so much admired, had been declared heretical.

But de Gaulle's religious beliefs, whatever they were in truth, and however he thought about them in his walks around the garden of La Boisserie, are only one of the puzzles in his personality. Perhaps the greatest puzzle of all is the relationship between 'de Gaulle' – the public persona – and 'I' – the private persona, between the highly public, ambitious, tough and often unscrupulous man of action and the sensitive, introspectively intellectual private man. The retreat to Colombey in the 1950s gave him plenty of time to reflect on that.

PART SEVEN

HEAD OF STATE

1

THE GENERAL'S
RESURRECTION

It is the nature of all greatness not to be exact. ★

By the time he celebrated his sixty-seventh birthday on 22 November 1957, at a small family party at La Boisserie, Charles de Gaulle was beginning to look an old man. His figure had become, to use the polite French expression, *arrondi*; in other words, not to put too fine a point on it, he had put on a good deal of weight. His stomach muscles had slackened and, with the years, he had developed a slight stoop. His hair had thinned and greyed, as had his moustache. The angle of his neck was less abruptly vertical, and that, together with a second chin that age had brought with it, made the forward thrust of his small head less pronounced. Even his now seriously short sight, which made him strain forward to see unless he was wearing thick spectacles, seemed to reduce the visual impact of his huge ears.

But the figure was not in any way less impressive than it had been twenty years earlier; indeed, in many ways the changes had given him a more dignified presence, conveying wisdom rather than intransigence. His whole physique, while still gigantic by normal standards, had achieved a much better balance. Nor was it only the shape of his body that had changed with age. His voice, too, had softened, was less harsh. To be sure, he could from time to time summon up the trumpet tone of old, but generally he spoke at a less abrasive pitch.

With these physical changes came also a corresponding softening of his personality. Visitors to La Boisserie remarked that he was more affable, less inclined to hector and, indeed, was – at least from time to time – prepared to listen to what other people were saying. He was more relaxed, witty and, to his intimates, affectionate.

★ Edmund Burke, in a speech on American taxation, 1774.

None of these changes, however, had affected the central core of de Gaulle's character. He was still unremittingly ambitious; and by the beginning of 1958, feeling his life slipping gently towards its final chapter, he appeared almost desperate to get back into power. 'He can't think about anything else,' Pompidou confided to a friend.[1] There were times when he thought that he was starting to scent a shift in the political wind. As he remarked to representatives of ex-servicemen's organisations at the end of March of that year, 'a slight awakening seems to have been occurring over the past two years. If this public awareness develops, if, under the pressure of events and the progressive paralysis of the regime, it becomes irresistible, I would face up to my responsibilities and would again gather up into my hands the national reins.'[2] The thought itself made him cheerful and relaxed.

In spite of these occasional bouts of optimism, he did not rate his prospects very highly, and his mood was correspondingly gloomy. He knew also that Yvonne wanted him to stay quietly at Colombey, resigned to a distinguished old age, partly because she disliked the artificial, indeed boring, life to which wives or husbands of the politically powerful are subjected, but also because she felt that his reputation as the liberator of France was secure and should not be put at risk by a further leap into the ever dangerous political arena. Yvonne's voice, in these latter years, was one which the General was more and more inclined to listen to. Furthermore, all the polling evidence suggested that the French people simply did not want him back. It was depressing, but true.

All in all, his conclusion at the time was that he doubted whether he would ever return. In deep despair, he told Gladwyn Jebb, the British ambassador, in late March 1958 that before the regime collapsed he would be dead. Listening to this gloomy assessment, Jebb noticed with surprise that the General's eyes were brimming with tears. The old man obviously felt that his time had run out.

In fact, at the very moment that the General was having his mournful conversation with Jebb, the Fourth Republic was entering precisely the full-blown political crisis that he had long predicted. Only nine weeks from that time, General Charles de Gaulle, rejuvenated by political adrenalin and recharged by the challenge of power, was installed, with full legitimacy, as sole, and highly personal, ruler of France.

The story of those nine weeks is unquestionably one of the most remarkable in the history of modern politics. The crisis, of course, had its origins in the instabilities of the Fourth Republic, but the final conflagration came in Algeria. To be sure, the 'rebellion', as the French called it, had started at the end of the Second World War. But the situation, indeed the whole dirty war, had been reasonably contained until the mid-1950s. It was the defeat of the French army in Indochina, and the consequent blow to its pride, that gave special impetus to its determination not to lose in Algeria. This determination, and the weakness of successive governments in Paris, led to the army in Algeria, not just becoming more brutal in its methods, which was bad enough, but also taking more responsibility for administration, and hence, inevitably, becoming more overtly political.

This was no minor matter. The army's behaviour in Algeria was eroding the tradition of military obedience to civil authority which had held good throughout most of French history. The stage was set for a bruising struggle for control of France. Like many such struggles, it was in the end to bring down the main protagonists, the army and the Fourth Republic, and produce, to solve the problem, an arbiter who had had no involvement in the initial battles. As the month of May 1958 progressed, the General became ever more convinced that he was that arbiter, the only person who could save France, and that power was his for the taking.

There had, of course, been others who for some time had been working in de Gaulle's interest. The faithful had lunched together most Wednesdays for the past year or two – Debré, Soustelle, Chaban-Delmas, René Capitant,★ and now François Mauriac, Olivier Guichard and others – to discuss how to promote the common cause. The office in the rue de Solférino had been kept going. But, apart from continued opposition inside and outside the Assembly, there was little that most of them could do.

Chaban-Delmas, however, as leader of the Gaullist Social Republicans, the rump of the old RPF, had become Minister of Defence in the Government formed in November 1957 by Félix Gaillard. Strangely enough, he had been allowed to continue his undisguised efforts to secure de Gaulle's return to power. The most open sign of these efforts was his appointment of a fellow Gaullist Deputy, Léon Delbecque, as the Ministry of Defence's adviser on 'psychological warfare' in Algiers. It was in practice no more than a cover for an operation to bring the

★ René Capitant (1901–1970): Politician and academic lawyer. Left-leaning, founder member of Resistance group Combat; sent by Vichy to Algiers University 1941; fomented pro-de Gaulle agitation and imprisoned; National President of RPF; Minister for Justice 1968. Loathed by Pompidou.

army and the white settlers over to de Gaulle's side. Between December 1957 and early May 1958 Delbecque made twenty-eight trips, on Chaban-Delmas's instructions, between Paris and Algiers. They were certainly not to discuss psychological warfare in Algeria.

The General was well aware of a great deal of what was going on, partly through the briefings that he received from the office in the rue de Solférino, partly through visitors to Colombey. 'We did not tell him everything,' recalled Olivier Guichard, one of the newer and younger members of de Gaulle's staff. 'We told him all it was necessary for him to know.'[3] But whatever he did or did not know, the General was careful to distance himself either from any publicly stated view on the Algerian problem – although he had privately held the view for some time that a phased independence was the only practicable solution – and from suggestions that he might assume power by anything other than wholly legal means. He was not going to mount a coup d'état. On the other hand, he was not going to stop those who were prepared to threaten one.

The prelude to the final drama of the Fourth Republic had been played on 8 February 1958 at the Tunisian village of Sakhiet Sidi Youssef. Sakhiet, which was just inside the frontier with Algeria, had certainly served as a refuge for Algerian nationalists, but the reprisal for that role, when it came, was brutal. The French air force bombed and strafed the village without warning. Over seventy people were killed and one hundred injured, including women and children. The village school was destroyed and a Red Cross lorry with a Geneva number-plate was completely wrecked. There was an inquiry, of course. It turned out that the raid had not been authorised from Paris, but had been a decision of the French high command in Algiers itself. Félix Gaillard, the Prime Minister, knew nothing about it until several hours after the event.

Tunisia's reaction was immediate. President Bourguiba of Tunisia withdrew his ambassador in Paris – who returned home, interestingly enough, by way of Colombey-les-Deux-Eglises – and demanded action from the Security Council of the United Nations. Action there was, but of a particularly ineffective kind. An Anglo-American mission was dispatched, charged with using its 'good offices' to resolve the quarrel. There was a row, but in the end the mission accomplished nothing. Yet its very ineffectiveness led to a sense of humiliation in France, which was, after all, one of the permanent members of the Security Council and supposedly a Great Power. By the beginning of April, it was clear that the Gaillard Government would have difficulty in surviving; indeed, Gaillard himself seemed to have lost the will to continue.

On 15 April, after a debate on the result of the mission, the right-wing parties again joined with the Communists in a vote against the Government. Gaillard lost the vote; even though he was defeated by only a simple majority, he felt that his Government was finished, and resigned. France was yet again without a government. The President, René Coty,★ first tried Bidault as a successor; then, when that failed, he tried Pleven. The period of governmental vacuum dragged on into May. It was starting to get ominous. Opinion polls were beginning to show a marked rise in those wanting de Gaulle back in power. But there was total silence in Colombey. The General sat, listened and watched.

In Algiers, the political vacuum was quickly filled. Failing any clear lead from Paris, by the end of April Delbecque had succeeded – with the help of, among others, the sinister-looking Colonel Thomazo, known as 'Leather Nose' because of the strap across his nose that hid war wounds – in setting up a committee of vigilance; and, on 26 April, in organising a demonstration of some 30,000 Algerians of all races demanding military government. At the end of the rally, Delbecque was able to signal to Chaban-Delmas, 'I now have Algiers in my hand.'[4]

With this achieved, Delbecque then went to Colombey to try to persuade de Gaulle that the time had come for him to make a move. But he found the General in a mood of gloom and apparent indecision. He was not, as he pointed out to Delbecque, going to come to power as the prisoner of the army; nor, indeed, without the full endorsement of the French people. Furthermore, he knew that the army in Algiers had, apart from one general, Massu, strong Pétainist roots. He knew, too, that he was not popular with the white settler families there – and anyway he despised them. If he was to return, therefore, it had to be in Paris, with the full legitimacy of France. Algeria was no more than a sideshow. But, it was then pointed out to Delbecque in the severest tones, 'They will create a scorched earth; they will wait until there is nothing left before calling for de Gaulle. I shall never come back to power in my lifetime.'[5]

Nevertheless, the General was careful not to discourage Delbecque in

★René Coty (1882–1962): Lawyer and politician. Norman; plodder but well educated at Caen university. Practised in Le Havre 1902 onwards, also on local council; Deputy for Seine-Inférieure 1923–32, Senator 1935; at Vichy 1940–4; member Constituent Assembly then National Assembly 1945–6; Vice-President 1949; President of Republic 1953–9.

his efforts. 'Delbecque,' he said solemnly, 'I would know how to face up to my responsibilities.'[6] With this ambiguous message Delbecque returned to Algiers, and de Gaulle, perhaps a little too ostentatiously, asked his son-in-law, Alain de Boissieu, to organise his summer holiday – a long trip through the Ardèche, well away from Paris or Colombey.

April dragged on into May, and still there was no government in Paris. The Socialists had voted against joining a Pleven Government, and when the Radicals also made difficulties Pleven gave up. But by now reports were arriving from Delbecque in Algiers – formally to Chaban-Delmas as the caretaker Minister of Defence, and informally to Olivier Guichard at the offices in the rue de Solférino – that Robert Lacoste, nominally the Minister for Algeria, no longer had control, and that an extremist group, led by the student Pierre Lagaillarde, was openly advocating violent revolution, in the hope that the army would be forced to take control. It looked as though Algiers was determined to force Paris's hand.

The army was by no means unsympathetic to Lagaillarde's idea. But only one senior officer, Massu, wanted de Gaulle. The others were preparing to install a 'Government of Public Safety' – the old formula for a revolutionary coup. The commander-in-chief in Algeria, General Raoul Salan,* knew about the plan, but he did not know how far it had gone. Salan passed what news he had on to General Ely, chief of the defence staff in Paris, who, horrified, immediately passed the news on to President Coty.

Coty then started to panic. On 5 May, even while Pleven was still in the middle of his negotiations to form a government, Coty sent his staff officer to see Guichard, Jacques Foccart and Guy de Bonneval, all three of them de Gaulle's men. They were asked to find out what the General's conditions might be if he were invited, instead, presumably, of Pleven, to form a government. Colombey was consulted, and the answer came back: It is too soon to say. An exchange of letters was suggested. But it was now clear to de Gaulle – and nobody was quicker to feel a shift in the wind than the General – that Coty was prepared to move in his direction, and that he obviously had no great confidence in Pleven's laborious efforts. It was at that point that the General started to make his own dispositions.

* Raoul Salan (1899–1984): Soldier. Orthodox military career; C.-in-C. Indo-China 1952, Algeria 1958; Military Governor of Paris 1959–60; retired 1960, but leader of uprising in Algeria 1960; Head of OAS 1961–2; condemned to death 1961; in prison 1966–8, pardoned 1968.

The pace began to quicken. On 8 May, as Robert Lacoste was packing his bags to leave Algiers, he was unwise enough to hint that there would soon be a new government in Paris prepared for another Indo-China – in other words, surrender. The generals in Algiers were so alarmed that on 9 May, led by Salan himself, they wrote a detailed letter to Ely, which Lacoste took back with him. It had a clear message for Coty: the army wanted no surrender in Algeria. For the first time in anybody's memory, the army was trying to dictate policy to the republic.

On 10 May, the spokesman for the ultra-right wing in Algiers, Alain de Sérigny, used his newspaper, *L'Echo d'Alger,* to call for a de Gaulle Government. Then word got about in Algiers that Pierre Pflimlin, who had been asked by Coty to form a government the day after Pleven had thrown in his hand – 'You are my last card,' Coty had said to him, 'If you fail there will be only one way out, to call on de Gaulle'[7] – had succeeded in securing a majority in the Assembly. The news brought Algiers to boiling point.

By 12 May, everybody knew that there would be trouble on the following day. But nobody could quite guess where the trouble would be, what form it would take or what would be the consequences; even a report from Thomazo that Lagaillarde and his supporters had met that evening and were determined to prevent the Gaullist coup that they suspected was only half believed. There was fever in the air, and the fever quickly spread to Paris. There was panic buying in the shops, and arguments and jostling in the streets. But again, the one person who was not going to be drawn was General de Gaulle. When Guichard reported to him on the afternoon of the 12th, to ask whether Soustelle should try to get to Algiers to give a political lead, the General's reply was curt: 'Tell him that I have nothing to say to him.'[8]

The day of 13 May started peacefully in Algiers. The weather was benign. A general strike was planned for later in the day, but that simply meant an afternoon off for a walk in the sunshine. A memorial service was held at 6 p.m. for two French prisoners-of-war executed by Algerian rebels in reprisal for the death of a Tunisian. The ceremony passed off calmly. Appropriate speeches were made and flowers laid on the hideously ugly Monument des Morts. Apart from one or two scuffles in the side streets, it could not have been more dignified.

Delbecque's intention was to capitalise on such a peaceful and orderly demonstration. It was quite simple: there would be the demonstration, after or during which – it was not quite certain – Soustelle, the hero of the French Algerians, would appear suddenly and triumphantly, take over the political leadership in Algeria and, with the support of the army, call for the return of de Gaulle to power in France.

Needless to say, it all went wrong. Soustelle did not arrive because he was still prevented from leaving France. Then the supposedly peaceful demonstration was hijacked by Lagaillarde and his rumbustious students. They stormed the main government building, the Gouvernement-Général, and ransacked it. Papers and files flew all over the place, but such was the confusion that the army made no effort to intervene. Indeed, some of the paratroopers outside had lent the students a lorry with which to force the gates.

The crowd now took over. Massu arrived half an hour later, to find Lagaillarde on the roof of the building, exchanging triumphant songs and slogans with the mob below. Even Massu could not restore order; his troops refused to fire on the students. Delbecque and the other Gaullists arrived on the scene even later. By that time the crowd had demanded a Committee of Public Safety, with Massu at its head. Massu had no option but to agree, and a committee was declared formed. Its members were picked more or less at random from the participants in the riot. Delbecque just managed to get in on it. When the count was taken, the membership of the committee numbered no fewer than seventy-four. It was hardly a recipe for competent government.

Salan himself appeared at about eight o'clock and, horrified and frightened, made an attempt to impose his authority as commander-in-chief. The crowd would have none of it; he was booed and hissed off the balcony. They wanted Massu, and in the end he emerged to announce, in his gruff soldier's voice, that he had formed a Committee of Public Safety in order – and then the dramatic words came out – 'that a Government of Public Safety might be formed in France under General de Gaulle'.

Later in the evening, the Gaullists pursued their advantage. Delbecque persuaded Salan, still smarting at having been upstaged by Massu, that the situation was serious enough for a further message to be sent to President Coty: 'The . . . military authorities esteem it . . . necessary to appeal to a national arbiter with a view to constituting a Government of Public Safety.'[9] There was no need to say who the 'national arbiter' might be. It was now not just Massu and the paratroopers, but the official high command of the army in Algeria, that had committed itself to de Gaulle.

When the news arrived at Colombey, the General's optimism about his prospects moved up another notch. When the news arrived at the Assembly in Paris, however, it was enough to send the Deputies into a state of shock. The republic, they said to one another, was in danger. As his last act as caretaker Prime Minister Gaillard cut all communications with Algiers, including all flights from French mainland airports. He was desperate to stop Soustelle or, even worse, de Gaulle, from flying immediately to assume the leadership in Algiers. The Assembly itself sat into the night and, at 3 a.m. on 14 May, gave an overwhelming vote of confidence to the new Pflimlin Government. France had a legitimate authority again. That, they said, was the reply of legitimate Paris to the rebels in Algiers.

It was a direct challenge. Nobody had expected the Assembly to act so decisively and the effect was immediate. In Algiers, there was disarray. The whole venture, it was said, had been a failure. 'We'll all be shot,' was a typical comment; Delbecque felt 'the sky falling on top of him'. In Paris, the Gaullists were equally depressed. Chaban-Delmas, wandering around by the river at 4 a.m., met Soustelle; he suggested that the best plan might be for Soustelle to be smuggled out to Algiers. 'Go to bed, little Jacques,' came the reply. 'Go back to being Mayor of Bordeaux. It's all finished. The General will not come back.'[10]

The 14th passed tensely but quietly, both Paris and Algiers waiting to see who would be included in Pflimlin's Government. When the announcement came, it turned out to be the same mixture as before. Pierre de Chevigné, an old Resistance stalwart, was the new Minister for Algeria, Jules Moch took the Interior and Guy Mollet became Pflimlin's deputy. Nevertheless, the new Government had a mandate from the Assembly, in particular for its first task: the reassertion of Paris's authority in Algiers. Commander-in-Chief Salan was duly instructed to make sure that this was done.

Salan was now, to say the least, in a most uncomfortable position. He had committed himself to the request for a 'national arbiter', but he was under instruction, from the duly elected Government of the Republic, to enforce the legitimate authority of France. Salan was never a decisive man, and he swung to and fro. But finally, on the morning of 15 May, he crossed his own Rubicon. He cabled de Chevigné that he felt that the only solution was a government led by General de Gaulle. Then, at midday, he appeared on the balcony of the Gouvernement-Général and spoke to a crowd of some 10,000, who appeared by now to be permanently encamped. He almost made a mess of it. He had been carefully briefed by Delbecque but, at the end of his speech requesting order and a return to legality, he forgot to say the magic words. Delbecque pushed him roughly back onto the balcony. 'Shout "*Vive de Gaulle*",' he hissed between his teeth. '*Vive de Gaulle*,' shouted Salan. The deed was done.

Salan's formal and explicit rejection of the instructions of the new Government coincided with another equally dramatic event. The General had decided that it was time for him to move onto the offensive. Almost exactly at the moment when Salan was making his declaration in Algiers, Olivier Guichard, who had been summoned to Colombey for lunch, was handed a statement, drafted that morning, which de Gaulle told him to release through Agence France-Presse that afternoon. Guichard duly did his bidding.

The statement was terse, but no less effective for that. There were only ten lines; but it was the last that counted: 'Today, in face of the difficulties which are again looming in front of [the country], may it know that I hold myself ready to assume the powers of the Republic.'[11]

It was, of course, outrageous, since there was already a legally constituted government. But, as a manoeuvre, it was brilliant. The General had, at a stroke, put himself, at exactly the right time, and in exactly the right manner, at the centre of events. Still pursuing the initiative, he followed his statement up by calling a press conference for 19 May, at the Palais d'Orsay in Paris. The interval was carefully calculated. It allowed two days to observe the fall-out from the bomb that he had dropped.

On 17 and 18 May, while the world was waiting for the General, and digesting Salan's repudiation of the Pflimlin Government, several things happened. Soustelle was indeed smuggled out, and appeared in Algiers to an enthusiastic reception. General Ely, Salan's nominal superior as chief of the general staff, had had enough and resigned. The Communists called for a general strike. The French air force started flying in formations representing the Croix de Lorraine. But, most sinister of all, two officers of Massu's staff flew from Algiers to Toulouse. This was no routine event. Their mission was to find out whether the paratroopers there would support 'Operation Resurrection'.

Operation Resurrection had been conceived by Massu and his staff towards the end of April. The plan was simple. Paratroopers from Algiers and Toulouse would arrive in Paris, together with tank squadrons based just outside Paris, and occupy the Hôtel de Ville, the police headquarters, the post office, the National Assembly, the radio and television centre and the Eiffel Tower. This show of force would have only one object: to persuade the authorities in Paris to accept a government led by General de Gaulle. If that did not happen peacefully, the sequel did not have to be spelled out.

It was, by any other name, a plan for a coup d'état. The details had not been fully worked out, but the outline was there. From all the evidence, there is little doubt that the General was aware of the outline, if not the detail. Indeed, although this is denied now by some of the General's supporters, there is little doubt that even the details of Operation Resurrection were known to de Gaulle's staff in the rue de Solférino – and that the venture was supported by them.

Be all that as it may, the General was quite clear, when he entered the Palais d'Orsay for his press conference at precisely 3 p.m. on 19 May, that the initiative was in his hands. He took it right from the start. He hardly referred to his notes, but used his thick spectacles to great rhetorical effect, taking them off with a flourish of indignation, followed by a shrug of his enormous shoulders, when answering a question about his view of civil liberties: 'Why should I, at the age of sixty-seven, begin a career as a dictator?'[12] He was serious, confident and authoritative, avoiding condemnation of the rebellion in Algiers, being complimentary to the Socialists but caustic about the 'parties' generally. Having come to an end he announced, 'Now I shall return to my village and remain there at the disposal of the country.'

It was great theatre. De Gaulle had learnt that much from Churchill; he had hardly missed a trick. Even those who remained hostile to the General and all that he stood for could not but admire his command and authority. There was no other contemporary French politician who could compete with him on that ground.

The reactions to the press conference were, as might be imagined, mixed. Pflimlin tried hard to be conciliatory, Mendès-France was overtly hostile, muttering about – unnamed – spokesmen for minor interests who exploit patriotic emotions for their own fraudulent schemes. But there was no conclusive government view. For the moment, the General had got away with it.

In the days that followed, the number of visitors at La Boisserie reflected the changing mood. Pinay, the eternal bellwether, came and went, impressed by the General's desire for national unity. Georges Boris, an old friend of Mendès-France, promised support from the old socialist Resistance. Salan sent an emissary with the message that his words had given 'them' enormous hope.

Events moved quickly. On 21 May Pascal Arrighi, a Radical Deputy for Corsica, spoke in favour of extending the principle of a Committee of Public Safety to the island. Then, at dawn on 24 May, Arrighi and a few paratroopers from Algiers landed in Corsica and – with the approval, at least, of Henri Maillot, de Gaulle's cousin and former head of the Resistance in the island – quickly overcame any opposition. It was all done very smoothly, and without incident. When asked whether anybody had been killed in the episode, Arrighi replied, 'Of course not! It was a revolution, not an election!'[13]

De Gaulle felt no need to react to the Corsican coup, in spite of efforts, not least by Mollet, to get him to condemn it. But matters were not yet moving at the speed that the General would have liked. It was time to step up the pace. On 26 May he summoned Marcel Diebolt, the prefect of the department of the Haute-Marne, to say that he had 'learnt' that an operation similar to the Corsican coup was to be launched on Paris during the night of 27/28 May; it was therefore imperative that he see Prime Minister Pflimlin that evening. De Gaulle suggested that they meet at the house of one Colonel Félix Bruneau, the curator of the park at St Cloud, on the western fringe of Paris. The time: 10.30 p.m.

It was a measure of the underlying shift in political power that Pflimlin dutifully turned up. In the event, the meeting was cordial, but no more. De Gaulle said that he was the only person who could avert civil war and that Pflimlin should resign in his favour. Pflimlin was not prepared to go unless de Gaulle straightaway disavowed the Algiers and Corsican rebellions. De Gaulle was not prepared to disavow them unless Pflimlin went; it was no good arguing – that was the end of the matter.

As dawn broke on 27 May, both men went back to their respective homes, Pflimlin to the Prime Minister's residence, the Hôtel Matignon in Paris, and de Gaulle to Colombey. Their accounts of the St Cloud meeting were quite different. Pflimlin's version, supported by those to whom he talked on his return, admittedly totally exhausted, was that he told de Gaulle that the best he could agree to was a round-table conference of all parties to discuss the conditions under which a transfer of power might take place. De Gaulle wrote in his memoirs that he returned home 'convinced that Pierre Pflimlin will soon take the road that I outlined to him during the night'.[14]

Back at Colombey, without pausing for sleep, the General drafted a statement. Delivered to Pflimlin's office just before midday on the same morning, 27 May, and released immediately afterwards, it started, 'I began yesterday the regular process necessary to the establishment of a

Republican government capable of assuring the unity and independence of the country . . .'[15]

It was, even by de Gaulle standards, breathtaking cheek. The meeting with Pflimlin the night before was disregarded. Even the fact that there was already a legally constituted government was ignored. But it was another brilliant manoeuvre, the second of the month. The General had again seized the political high ground. The pressure on Pflimlin was now intense: either he had to bring this unruly private citizen to order or he had to throw in his hand. The pressure on Mollet and the Socialists was stepped up: either they agreed to support de Gaulle or they accepted responsibility for civil war. The message to Algiers was clear: suspend Operation Resurrection until negotiations are completed – or until they fail.

Once again, the General's initiative threw the Government into disarray. Moch, for his part, was prepared to be convinced that the move was meant to be constructive. As Minister for the Interior, he believed that, had it not been for de Gaulle's statement, the 'serious troubles' that were expected for the night of 27/28 May would have occurred – in other words, Operation Resurrection would have been launched on Paris. Mollet took broadly the same view, while resenting the tone of the statement. Pflimlin, on the other hand, felt that de Gaulle had put him in an impossible position, and wanted to repudiate the whole thing; it was only President Coty prevented him from doing so.

The reaction in the Assembly was one of horror at the impertinence. When it met later in the evening, Pflimlin won a vote of confidence by a majority of 240. But in spite of the strength of the vote, the reality was that the Government was now virtually without power. At a ministerial meeting called as soon as the Assembly had risen, at 2 a.m. on the 28th, it was Pleven, normally the mildest of ministers, who pointed out quietly that the Minister for Algeria could not go to Algeria, that the Minister of National Defence was defied by the armed forces, and that the Minister for the Interior could no longer control the police. 'We claim to exert power,' he said, 'but we do not have it.'[16]

That was enough for Pflimlin. He went straight to the Elysée to present his resignation. Somewhat to his surprise, he found Coty and his staff still dressed, and indeed waiting for him. In fact, they had been waiting for him for some time. But Pflimlin's resignation was by no means plain sailing. He insisted that de Gaulle should accede to office, if he were to do so, by legal means – and that meant a confirming vote in the National Assembly. Since the Socialists were obviously opposed, and the Communists would certainly vote against, the majority was simply not there.

At Colombey, de Gaulle had stayed up for news of the Assembly vote. When it came, he saw immediately that, as it stood, he had no chance of winning a majority. He reacted by calling Algiers and asking Salan to send one of his officers to Colombey straightaway. Salan agreed, and on the morning of 28 May, General André Dulac and three junior officers, who had been rudely shaken from their beds, arrived at La Boisserie to wait upon the General. De Gaulle wanted to know what would happen if the Socialists were to vote against him in the Assembly and thus prevent him from assuming power by legal means. Dulac's response was to present in detail the plan for Operation Resurrection. De Gaulle's response was ambiguous: 'It would have been vastly preferable for my return to have been achieved by the normal means . . . Tell General Salan that what he has done, and what he will do, is for the good of France.'[17] Ambiguous or not, Dulac received the message loud and clear. Operation Resurrection had the General's blessing.

On the same morning, there was a demonstration in Paris in support of the Fourth Republic. Only one minister, Albert Gazier, the Minister of Information, took part, but the Parisian intellectual élite was out in force. So too were republican politicians – Mendès-France, Mitterrand, Daladier and André Philip. The Communists mustered their troops, from the Renault works at Billancourt and elsewhere. There were some 150,000 people, marching on the traditional route from the Place de la Nation to the Place de la République. But, unlike previous marches along the same route, it was mild and good-tempered, and 'as disciplined and unexciting as a Sunday school picnic'; and unlike previous marches it impressed nobody. In short, it was a flop.

Coty was by now fully aware of the plans for Operation Resurrection and of the opposition to de Gaulle in the Assembly. He tried to compromise. He invited de Gaulle to a further meeting, at the same house in St Cloud. Gaston Monnerville, President of the Council of the Republic, and therefore second only to the President, and André Le Troquer, President of the National Assembly, were the negotiators for the Government. But again it all came to nothing. Le Troquer was not prepared to negotiate on constitutional changes, and those were an essential part of de Gaulle's conditions. The whole exercise was reported to Coty at around 1 a.m. on 29 May as a failure. The General, for his part, calmly returned to Colombey.

After hearing the result of the St Cloud meeting, Coty stayed up all night. He drafted what he earnestly hoped would be a conclusive message to the Assembly. France, he wrote, was on the verge of civil war. There was only one man who could save the country and the republic: he was therefore sending for General de Gaulle. If the Assembly refused to ratify his appointment, his message continued, he would resign.

By the time Coty's statement was read that afternoon by Le Troquer to a packed Assembly, its members standing in respect for the office of the presidency, the air was thick with rumours of paratroop movements and of armoured units taking up positions around Paris. When Le Troquer had finished, indeed before he had sat down, there was pandemonium. The Communists were furious and hammered on their desks. That set off the others. Fists were brandished; there were chants and counter-chants, and insults were screamed across the chamber. The previous day's march had been nothing politically, but the scene in the National Assembly was so uncontrolled as to be interpreted by most of those present as a clear indication of impending civil war.

Civil war, indeed, was just what was being planned – by the leaders of Operation Resurrection. By the time the Assembly had met to hear Coty's message, the generals in Algiers had been convinced, rightly or wrongly, that they had de Gaulle's explicit approval. The least that can be said is de Gaulle was aware of their plans, and would not stop them until he was firmly on his way to government. Beyond that, recollections differ. But what is beyond doubt is that a telegram was sent at 4.10 p.m. to Algiers stating categorically that de Gaulle was 'in complete agreement' and that landings should start at 2.30 a.m. on the morning of the 30th.

De Gaulle left Colombey at 4.30 p.m., twenty minutes after the telegram to Algiers, for a further discussion with Coty. The meeting went well, and later in the evening of the 29th he issued a statement from his office. Coty and he, it said, had agreed the conditions under which he would form a government: full power, no parliamentary interference for six months and a new constitution. A second telegram went to Algiers: 'President of the Republic receiving Great Charles; operation postponed.' Resurrection was again put on standby in Algiers, and the General again went home to Colombey.

De Gaulle spent 30 May courting the Socialists. Apart from Juin, who came to assure the General of the loyalty of the army, the visitors to Colombey were all politicians: Auriol, Mollet, Maurice Deixonne – they were all treated with the greatest charm and courtesy. The General had certainly learnt the politics of flattery. Mollet went back and told

Moch, 'That meeting was one of the great moments of my life. He is a great man, a great man.'

The next day the General left Colombey, after pausing for a moment to note the end of his period of 'long solitude'. This time, at long last, he was accompanied by his wife. He was now convinced that his accession to power was no more than a formality.

In the event, the drama was played out to the very end. On his arrival in Paris, de Gaulle met the party leaders at the Hôtel La Pérouse and explained his plans in the most affable and persuasive manner. The Socialist leaders were just persuaded – apart from François Mitterrand – and the parliamentary group voted in his favour 77–74. But that was the crucial vote. It determined whether there would or would not be a majority in the Assembly the following day. When the day came, de Gaulle was due to arrive at the Assembly in the morning, but there was a hitch. So tense was the atmosphere that Guichard called Salan, so Salan said later, telling him to stand by to activate Resurrection. By 3 p.m. de Gaulle was ready. He arrived at the Assembly, made a short speech, which was heard in silence, and then left for his hotel to await the result. When it came, the majority was disappointingly small – 320–224 – but a majority it was. The General had won. Operation Resurrection was finally called off.

2

'I HAVE UNDERSTOOD YOU'

*'De Gaulle', Winston said, 'has a great chance. He is on top . . .' I
asked him what the Algerian Committee would do. 'They will bloody
well try to make trouble, but they won't succeed.'*★

On the morning of 2 June 1958 General and Mme de Gaulle moved
house. They left their suite in the Hôtel La Pérouse and transferred to
the Hôtel Matignon. The Matignon was the traditional residence of
French Prime Ministers, but in terms of their domestic life it was not a
happy move. Truth to tell, neither of them liked the place; justifiably so,
since their accommodation was extremely cramped. Out of the sizeable
building only four rooms formed the residential quarters. One of these,
a small salon, served as Mme de Gaulle's drawing-room; but it was next
door to the dining-room, which was from time to time put to official
use. The General spent most of his time in his office, in the more formal part of the building which constituted the Prime Minister's 'official
residence'. It was far from satisfactory.

But the Matignon was a symbol, and the General saw his move as a
necessary symbolic act. He had assumed power and all the world should
know it. Along with him came most of his personal staff from the rue
de Solférino, with Pompidou as his Chef de Cabinet, and the others in
tow. They seemed to move in, rather to the General's surprise, as to the
manner born. Mme de Gaulle, on the other hand, saw the move as an
irritation. She wanted to get back to Colombey. It was spring, the season of flowers, and she missed the garden. There was work to be done
in Paris, however, let alone Algiers, and Yvonne could only escape
when duty did not require her to be present. Fortunately, duty, at least
for her, at that point only lasted three days, until her husband left for
Algiers. In those three days, however, there was not much time to rest.

★ Winston Churchill, in a conversation with his doctor, 19 May 1958. Quoted in
Lord Moran, *Churchill: The Struggle for Survival 1940–65*, page 741; Constable,
London, 1966.

Apart from settling in to the small apartment, she had to support, and cater for, the newly revived General. He was full of enthusiasm and life and wit. Life in the Matignon immediately after the move was nothing if not hectic.

The new Government, of course, had already been announced. It had not been, as de Gaulle was himself to admit later, the Government that he would have liked. He would have liked to include a North African – preferably Moslem – and a trade unionist, but there was no room within the constraints of the time. The result had been a revealing mix. Many of the new ministers were the familiar names of the Fourth Republic: Mollet, Pinay, Pflimlin – as though the General wished to emphasise continuity. Others were civil servants, whose job was faithfully to carry out the General's will. Couve de Murville, for instance, a former Vichy civil servant and currently the Fourth Republic's ambassador to West Germany, was hauled off a golf course in Bonn to become Foreign Minister. Three other civil servants were given the portfolios of defence, interior and French overseas territories. Finally there were some, but not all, of the faithful: Debré, Malraux and Edmond Michelet. But there was no Soustelle, Palewski, Catroux, Chaban-Delmas, Fouchet or Billotte.

The choice of ministers went down badly in Algiers. None of the obvious heroes, Salan, Delbecque or Massu, had been given a job. It was certainly not by accident. General de Gaulle did not do that sort of thing by accident. What was happening was a repeat performance of August 1944, when the General, having been brought to power, at least in some measure, by the Resistance, had immediately repudiated it. He was reaffirming one of his deeply held beliefs. Neither the Resistance then, nor Algiers now, had any claim to be above France. The Government represented France, and he represented the Government.

De Gaulle's most important appointment for the longer term future of his country was that of Michel Debré, possibly his most faithful and able lieutenant, as Minister for Justice and chairman of a committee to prepare the new constitution. It would not be easy to get the enabling bill through the Assembly. Never before had power been given to a government to devise a republican constitution. It had previously always been the responsibility of an elected Constituent Assembly. It was a matter, as was pointed out at great length, of fundamental principle.

On 3 June 1958, the Assembly met to consider three bills to meet the conditions under which de Gaulle had accepted the post of Prime

Minister. Special powers to deal with Algiers were quickly granted – after all, Mollet had been given the same in 1956; government by decree for six months was less easy but nevertheless was grudgingly accepted; the bill on constitutional reform, however, caused endless trouble.

The Assembly's own committee had been looking at the bill, and had proposed whole pages of amendments. De Gaulle would have none of them. 'Circumstances are such,' he told the Deputies late in the evening of 3 June, 'that it would not be possible for my Government to continue in office beyond tonight [if the amendments were accepted].'[1] An old but gifted lawyer of the traditional right, Jean-Louis Tixier-Vignancour, reminded the Assembly of the last occasion when powers to devise a new constitution had been delegated – to Pétain, on 10 July 1940. There was then, needless to say, uproar, and the session was suspended for forty-five minutes. In the end de Gaulle agreed to accept a 'new consultative committee' on the constitution, chosen from members of Parliament. That was enough, and the bill went through the Assembly by 350–161. The Council of the Republic – the second chamber – approved it by 236–30. Both Houses were then prorogued for six months. The General had passed his first test. His authority in Paris was unchallengeable. Parliament would take a prolonged holiday, and the General would govern alone.

De Gaulle's next task was to assert his Government's authority in Algiers. It was certainly not going to he easy. The generals there were firmly of the view that it was they who had brought de Gaulle to power in France; and that they had done so specifically in order that Algeria might be incorporated into France and the rebellion ruthlessly put down. De Gaulle had done nothing to dispel that view while he was conducting his negotiations with Coty and Pflimlin; indeed, he had not hesitated to invoke the threat of Operation Resurrection, and that threat had been a powerful card in his hand.

But having obtained power, by whatever means, the General, as before in 1944, was not one to recognise debts to those who had put him there. The first sign to the generals in Algiers that all was not going the way they wanted came with de Gaulle's ministerial appointments. Delbecque immediately flew to Paris to protest, but de Gaulle hardly bothered to listen to him. It was not a question of those ridiculous Committees of Public Safety, he said, but of the army of the republic.

As though to make his point, de Gaulle summoned instead General Salan and two of his main associates, Esmond Jouhaud and André Dulac

– not, significantly, Massu. Salan was interviewed first. It was not a happy occasion. De Gaulle was at his most frigid. He was surprised, he said, that General Salan had not thought it proper to wear uniform on his first visit to his new Prime Minister. There followed a long silence. Salan obviously did not know what to say. He had expected de Gaulle simply to give him instructions. Jouhaud was then called in. He was less nervous and explained to the General the proposal for the integration of Algeria into France. 'But,' he went on in a rather rambling manner, 'this solution is perhaps not definitive since everything in life evolves.' 'I agree,' replied the General drily.[2] The meeting ended with de Gaulle, as Minister for Algeria, appointing Salan his delegate-general and saying that he would be arriving in Algiers himself the next day. Salan and his colleagues returned to Algiers in the evening, aware that they had been out-manoeuvred but not quite sure how.

In fact, the position was quite simple. In August 1944 de Gaulle had refused to allow the Resistance a political role, and effectively dissolved it. This time the army in Algiers was playing the role of the Resistance. Whatever had been their responsibility for bringing de Gaulle to power, they were not going to be allowed to set up or maintain any political power structure which might rival the Government. There was only one Government, and that was his. The General was being perfectly consistent. He was also certainly right. A system of Committees of Public Safety, of which there were already 120 in being, according to Delbecque, would have led to chaos. The General, as so often, had seen matters much more clearly than either his allies or his opponents.

On the morning of 4 June, de Gaulle arrived, as promised, in Algiers, accompanied by Soustelle, three junior ministers and General Ely, now reinstated as chief of staff. They landed at Maison Blanche airport, from where he had taken off just after D-Day in June 1944 to assume control of the liberation of Paris. The welcome was delirious. There was a reception at the Summer Palace with speeches from the Mayor, greet-ings from the diplomatic corps and the heads of the Church and the university. Then, and only then, was Massu allowed to speak on behalf of the Committee of Public Safety. There was a visit to the Admiralty and more speeches; de Gaulle finally arrived at Government House at about seven o'clock. As he came out on to the balcony, the huge crowd below him erupted. 'Then, in a speech of a few minutes,' he wrote, 'I tossed them the words, seemingly spontaneous but in reality carefully calculated . . . "I have understood you",' and he went on to speak of 'renewal and brotherhood'.[3]

The ambiguity was masterly. The cheers which followed that one sentence lasted several minutes. Of course, what they thought they were cheering had nothing to do with de Gaulle's real intentions. But his purpose had been achieved, and he proceeded to speak of the 'magnificent work of understanding and pacification', secure in the knowledge that he had gained the sympathy of the crowd without committing himself to anything.

The speech in Algiers was followed by a tour of the country, made at almost manic speed, with stops of only a few hours – and sometimes less – in each place. Wherever he went, he insisted that the army was the servant of the state and the Committees of Public Safety mere passing phenomena. But the army, he said time and time again, must not only control Algeria on behalf of the state but also guarantee that all its inhabitants, of whatever ethnic origin, could really feel themselves to be French. At Mostaganem he made his only slip, shouting, in his enthusiasm, quite clearly and specifically '*Vive Algérie Française*' – a phrase which until then he had always avoided and which was to return, again and again, as the battlecry of his opponents. De Gaulle tried to explain it away by a dubious analogy, saying that Algeria would 'in many respects' remain French, just as France, which had originally been Gaul, remained 'in some measure' Roman. It can hardly be said to have sounded very convincing.

On 8 June the General was back in Paris. To be truthful, his first visit to Algiers had not been more than a holding operation. But he had made one or two discoveries. For a start, he had discovered that the whole structure of the Committees of Public Safety was, in political terms, founded on unreality. The people in charge seemed to be unaware of the simple political fact that there were only a million Europeans to nine million Moslems. Although his view remained that 'we cannot keep Algeria', as he told Pierre Lefranc at lunch the next day,[4] it was obvious to him, having seen the problems on the spot, that the way forward would be either quick and sudden, or would be long, wearisome and dangerous. The 'Ultras', the white settler families who made their life there, were openly hostile, the junior officers in the army were uncertain and, most significant of all, poster portraits of him, put up only a week or two earlier, were now being torn down. Nobody tried to stop it. It was a depressing augury for the future.

But there was business to be done in Paris. As soon as he arrived back, de Gaulle called a meeting of the Council of Ministers. It was his first since January 1946. 'Gentlemen, let us resume,' he started, as though there had been only a brief interval. Coty presided. Reports were received from different ministers and commented on by the Prime Minister. The procedure had not changed. But it was noted that the discussion was more relaxed than it had been twelve years earlier; the General was more inclined to listen to opinions.

Within the confines of his own group of ministers and his secretariat in the Matignon, the arguments were extremely lively. Georges Pompidou in particular made his presence felt. Indeed, at times it looked as though Pompidou was running large areas of domestic policy. He certainly seemed to be in charge of financial policy, and was the decisive voice in pushing through the programme of the monetarist economist Jacques Rueff – against the counter-arguments of Pinay, the Minister of Finance, himself. A loan, whose value was linked to the price of gold, was announced by the General in a broadcast on 13 June. Ironically, it was dubbed the 'Pinay loan'. Given the traditional French habit of buying gold in times of uncertainty, it was an immediate success – although it was extremely expensive to redeem when it matured. Then, in July, there were cuts in public expenditure and a year's wage and salary freeze in the public sector. It was crude and unfair, but it had the effect of demonstrating that the Government was in charge of events, and financial confidence, badly shaken by the Algerian crisis, started to return. It may have been good politics at the time, but the financial price that had to be paid later was to be heavy.

If the General's style of governing had altered since 1946, so too had the circumstances of the de Gaulles' life. Now that Anne was dead there was no central point around which family life revolved. The houses they had lived in before had been specifically chosen for the facilities available for looking after their handicapped daughter. Even if she had always had a governess, she had been the main preoccupation of Yvonne de Gaulle's private life. Now the choice of homes, apart from Colombey, was to be a matter of official convenience. It was a far cry from the household that it had been where the binding link was little Anne.

That summer, that particular summer, it was not just that the Matignon was uncomfortable – full of false marble and Second Empire furniture, the apartment reserved for the Prime Minister and his wife small and inconvenient. It was the first summer that they had spent away from Colombey in twelve years, and Yvonne was for ever wanting to go back there. She missed the early mornings, the late evenings and, above all, the flowers. But the General did not try to improve matters, even for his wife. After all, President Coty was still in the Elysée, and once the new constitution was passed it was generally assumed that the lease, as it were, would fall in and the de Gaulles would move house. The rest could wait.

The General's new mood was clearly perceived at the end of June 1958 by one of the first foreign politicians to visit him in his new position, his old friend and opponent from the days in wartime Algiers, Harold Macmillan, now British Prime Minister. 'It was astonishing to me to see de Gaulle in his present mood,' Macmillan recorded in his diary. 'His manner is calm, affable and rather paternal. But underneath this new exterior, I should judge that he is just as obstinate as ever.'[5] Macmillan tried to engage de Gaulle in conversations about the European Free Trade Area and its relations with the European Economic Community, but failed to spark any interest. All de Gaulle wanted to talk about was Algeria and French constitutional reform.

Macmillan had failed to understand the true nature of de Gaulle's agenda, and the stakes for which the General was playing. During June the situation in North Africa – and arguably the situation in France, but that, for the moment, was less important, although still tense – had moved forward. By the time of Macmillan's visit, French troops had mostly been withdrawn from Tunisia and Morocco, as the General had promised. De Gaulle had given a press conference, his first as Prime Minister, on 13 June, at which he had hinted at a federal solution for France and French North Africa. There was nothing specific, of course, but there was just the thought of a possible break in the North African deadlock.

The General made a further visit to Algeria at the beginning of July. This time he took Mollet with him. But instead of trying to woo the big crowds in the cities, he set himself the task of speaking to the army on its own ground. He visited units in garrison towns, talked to junior officers in their own down-to-earth language, praised the paratroopers and the Foreign Legion – and ignored the high command. It was only on the last day of his visit that Massu managed to lodge a request, on behalf of the Committee of Public Safety, to see him. The request was refused, and a similar request from the trade unions referred to Mollet.

The pattern was now emerging. De Gaulle was out to secure the firm support of the army as servants of the republic, and no more. As part of this campaign, on 7 July he appointed Soustelle Minister of Information in place of Malraux, who had scared the army with his high-sounding advocacy of civil rights. The General went on to make a very special occasion of the 14 July celebrations in Paris. There was the usual Bastille

Day parade, but on this occasion there was a march down the Champs-Elysées led by the 'heroes' of 13 May in Algiers. For the occasion, many medals were awarded: Salan was given the Military Medal, Massu – now a full general – was on the list of lesser awards, as were Dulac, Jouhaud and a new general of the air force, Maurice Challe. The parade itself was of particular magnificence. Alongside the generals and the paratroopers from Algeria, units of Moslem troops marched in colourful display. The good old days, the message was, were here again.

It was as though there had been a victory in Algeria, and it was being celebrated in the time-honoured manner. The crowds cheered. But they, indeed least of all they, were not to know that the General was even then preparing his ground for the future divorce. The ground that had to be prepared, of course, was a change in a way that France was governed. Until that change occurred, barring a miracle, the Algerian problem would remain insoluble.

The key to the future of France, in de Gaulle's long-held view, was a new constitution. To be sure, he had explained his ideas at Bayeux in 1946, but they still needed drafting into a text. That would be Debré's main function, supported by the formidable team under Pompidou in the Hôtel Matignon. Debré himself was as contemptuous as anybody of the constitution of the Fourth Republic. He had been senator for the department of Indre-et-Loire since 1948, and had seen it working at close quarters. He had long been hoping, and at times planning with his own brand of explosive enthusiasm, the downfall of the Fourth Republic. He had demonstrated this in his 1957 pamphlet *Ces princes qui nous gouvernent* and the political review which followed its publication, the *Courrier de la colère*. He had so infuriated the government of the day that his home was kept permanently under surveillance by plain-clothes police.

But Debré was a great admirer of the British parliamentary tradition, and introduced into the new constitution some of its features, not least the balance between the presidency, which de Gaulle wanted to be all-powerful, and the Assembly, which was to be able to bring down the Government that the President had appointed. Debré, always a hard worker, did not spare himself. He went through 120 drafts – 'What cheek' was the comment of the General, who had thought it had all been decided years earlier. By the time the final text was published, it owed almost as much to Debré as it did to its originator, de Gaulle. In fact, de Gaulle, having set out the principles, only appeared once in person before the committee responsible for the drafting.

It was then a question of selling the new constitution to the French

people and, since it was not only for France but for a new 'Community'
of overseas territories, to their inhabitants as well. De Gaulle himself led
the campaign. He started in Africa even before the text was published,
and in ten days at the end of August, in the searing heat, covered all the
French territories of the continent.

In Paris there was a rally in the Place de la République on the date of
the publication of the text itself – 4 September, the anniversary of the
proclamation of the Third Republic. The police were nervous about the
choice of place, since the Communist leader, Waldeck Rochet, had an
apartment overlooking the square; there were endless opportunities for
disruption, ranging from clouds of red balloons released at the crucial
moment to tear-gas grenades. But in spite of the police nerves, de
Gaulle decided to go ahead.

On the day, it was almost impossible to get near the Place de la
République. Armed police were out in force, 3000 of them, sitting
threateningly in dark blue security vehicles or marshalling the crowds in
the surrounding streets. There were scuffles, and police truncheons
were used without hesitation. The Communists led a demonstration,
but the Place de la République was so carefully sealed off – and Waldeck
Rochet's flat was under such a strong armed guard – that they were easily prevented from doing much more than making a great deal of noise,
which, quite understandably, they proceeded to do.

On that 4th of September, the Place de la République was decorated in the manner of the old rallies of the RPF. Malraux had personally
supervised the whole affair. There were flags, streamers, flowers and,
above all, huge placards in the form of a capital V. As the event drew to
its climax, Malraux himself made a speech reminding the crowd of
1940 and what had happened since. As a piece of oratory it was hopelessly overdone. 'Here is Paris,' he shouted ecstatically into an already
strained loudspeaker system. 'Honour and fatherland. One more time,
at the meeting point of the republic and at the meeting with history,
you are going to listen to General de Gaulle!'[6] Right on cue, a black
Citröen drove into the square, came to a halt in front of the platform,
and out stepped the General. He walked with ceremonial deliberation
up the steps to the platform, stood in front of the microphones, paused
and then raised his huge arms above his head in his celebrated V sign.
It was no doubt magnificent, but there were some foreign journalists
there who, while admiring, were unable to keep completely straight
faces.

What the General said was quite brief. There was a relatively restrained summary of the events that had brought him to power, followed by a description of the methods used to draft the new constitution. There was much emphasis on the legitimacy of the whole procedure. He then went on to describe the main elements of what the Government was proposing, on which the accompanying official text was much more specific. The central point concerned the position of the President. He was to be 'above political battles . . . a national arbiter . . . elected by the citizens . . . with the right to have recourse to the judgement of the sovereign people . . . responsible for the integrity of France and the safety of the republic'.[7] There was to be, in addition to a President, a government whose function was to govern and a legislature which would 'pass laws' and 'control' the executive.

All this sounded very comforting. But the text of the draft constitution spelt it out in detail, and it looked much less attractive in published form. The President was to be elected, not by 'the citizens' as such, but by an electoral college drawn from the Assemblies in France and overseas and from departmental and municipal councils. So far from being a 'national arbiter', the President would appoint his ministers and would preside over the Council of Ministers. Furthermore, he would appoint all civil and military officials and would be commander-in-chief of the armed forces. The Assembly would control the budget, but if the budget were rejected the President had the right to rule by decree. In a national emergency the President could suspend the constitution altogether. All in all, it was hardly a model of pluralist democracy. But there it was, for what it was worth, and it was to be put to a referendum in just over three weeks, on 28 September.

There was, of course, a riot. All around the Place de la République, the Communists made their noise and, as the details of the proposals became clearer, their physical protest. Again the police used their truncheons liberally, and tear-gas canisters were thrown about randomly, like confetti. Ten demonstrators were taken to hospital, along with six riot policemen, and there were eighty-seven arrests.

The campaign had started. It was, as might be imagined, one of extreme bitterness. The opposition was grouped around the Communists, with Mendès-France, Mitterrand and the intellectual left in support. Jean-Paul Sartre denounced those Frenchmen who supported de Gaulle as 'frogs who demand a king'.[8] Mitterrand wrote that the new constitution combined the faults 'of Louis Philippe and Louis Napoléon at the same time'.[9] The press was full of the old accusations of Bonapartism.

Up to a point, there was some justice in the criticism of the new pro-posals. They did give extraordinary powers to the President – much greater, for instance, than those granted to the President of the United States. On the other hand, Debré had managed to introduce a number of powers for the Prime Minister, and hence the Assembly, which had not been referred to in the Bayeux speech of 1946. The Prime Minister was to be responsible to the Assembly. He could not be dismissed by the President. Furthermore, the exercise of presidential power was to be constrained by possible appeal to a constitutional council, whose inter-pretation of the constitution was to be final. It may not have been pluralist, but it certainly was not wholly Bonapartist.

The General threw himself into the campaign with vigour. There were meetings, broadcasts on radio and television and any number of press interviews. The message was always the same: 'With all my heart and in the name of France, I call upon you to answer "Yes" on 28 September. If you do not do so, we shall, on that very same day, revert to the errors that you know so well.'[10]

There were meetings in Rennes and Bordeaux on 20 September, and in Strasbourg and Lille on the 21st, all to huge crowds. After the speeches the barriers were let down and de Gaulle carried out what the Gaullists call a '*bain de foule*'. The procedure was always the same. The General was seen wading in among the crowd, towering over them in height while acknowledging their enthusiasm by frequent handshakes. Needless to say, the whole exercise was covered in detailed close-up by the official news agencies, and the resulting footage screened at length. It was technically very impressive for its time. It looked as if the General were genuinely enjoying this contact with the 'people', and it looked also as though the 'people' were hero-worshipping him.

Whatever the truth, if indeed in these matters there is ever a truth, the 'Yes' campaign was handled with great professionalism by Malraux and his associates. Of course, they also benefited from almost total gov-ernmental control of the broadcasting media, which they did not hesitate to exploit. Furthermore de Gaulle could point to internation-al events where France had been ignored to support his own case as a strong French leader. King Faisal had been assassinated, American and British troops had been sent for by the Lebanon and Jordan without France being consulted, and de Gaulle himself had been assailed by the Soviet General Secretary, Nikita Khrushchev, as another Hindenburg, conspiring with French big business to set up a new Hitlerite dicta-torship, this time in France. It all helped enormously.

Finally, and perhaps decisively, the Algerian freedom fighters entered the campaign. Four policemen in Paris were murdered; plastic explosive was distributed everywhere – it destroyed oil tanks, transformer stations and even post offices. But the greatest insult was their attempt to blow up the ladies' lavatory on the top floor of the Eiffel Tower – by planting explosive under the seat.

That was altogether too much. It was almost as significant as the alleged assassination attempt of 15 September on Soustelle, which he described to a press conference hastily convened within the hour, with sticking plaster all over his face. An attack on a ladies' convenience could not, under any circumstances, be considered fair play, and from then on the 'Yes' majority was never in doubt.

Nevertheless, the result, when it came, surpassed the expectations even of the optimists. In metropolitan France, there was an 85 per cent turn-out, and 80 per cent of those voted 'Yes'. Algeria had an even higher 'Yes' vote, although some of the methods to obtain it were not above suspicion. Guinea voted 'No'. All aid to Guinea was stopped forthwith; even its telephone system was dismantled.

After the referendum result, the next step was a general election. The new constitution specified that it should be a two-stage process, based on constituencies and held on two successive Sundays. On the first Sunday all candidates could stand, but on the second Sunday only the two leading contenders could stand again, unless there had been an overall majority in the first round or subsequent withdrawals. In that way one candidate would be bound to win a majority of votes cast in a constituency.

The dates were fixed for 23 and 30 November. Soustelle had already picked up the threads of the old RPF and founded a new Gaullist party, which was to campaign under the name of Union for the New Republic (UNR). But before the elections, and perhaps to bolster his chances, de Gaulle made one bold, almost foolhardy, effort to achieve a miracle by solving at one stroke the whole North African problem. On 4 October, in a speech at Constantine in Algeria, he proposed a deal to the Moslems. Salaries were gradually to be brought up to French levels; half a million acres of land owned by the government would be distributed to Moslem farmers; two-thirds of all children in Algeria would have proper schooling as a prelude to universal education.

That was bad enough for the Ultras, the white settler families, but worse was to come. 'In two months from now,' the General went on, 'Algeria will elect its representatives in the same conditions as France. It is essential that at least two-thirds of these should be Moslems.'[11] He followed this up with an instruction to Salan to the effect that all candidates, whatever their religion or colour, must be able to compete on equal terms. Finally, on 23 October, he offered the rebels, who as the Front de Libération Nationale (FLN) had set up a government-in-exile, what he called a 'peace of the brave'. He guaranteed safe conduct to any Algerian leader who wished to come to France to negotiate.

It was bold, and it nearly worked. If it had been left to the FLN government-in-exile it might well have done, but the commanders in the field had been through too much simply to lay down their arms on the mere invitation of the General. On 25 October the FLN turned him down. De Gaulle was deeply depressed. There was now no doubt, he knew, that a settlement in Algeria would take years to achieve. He had perhaps thought it a little too easy – he had, after all, said all along that only he could solve the problem. He may have been over-confident after the referendum result; or possibly he had not yet appreciated the bitterness and hostility that had accumulated during the years when he was sitting peacefully at Colombey. Maybe he simply thought that he could not lose much by trying. As it turned out, he did indeed lose nothing in electoral terms. But the penalty he paid was the rift created by the sudden and – from the point of view of the French in Algiers – unexpected revelation of his true intentions. In attempting to achieve a quick miracle he had made a bad long-term mistake. He could, and should, have waited for his own election, and for the process of time.

But none of that was to harm him in the short term. When the elections came, the left, in all its forms, was trounced. Only 10 Communists out of 138 were re-elected, 44 Socialists out of 88, 23 Radicals out of 56. Distinguished heads rolled: Mendès-France, Mitterrand, Moch, Pineau, Duclos, Le Troquer. On the other side, the UNR took 196 seats and the pro-Gaullist independents 132.

The final brick in the edifice of the Fifth Republic was the election of a President. There was not much doubt who it would be, but it was still necessary to go through the motions. The date was set for 21 December. It was a walk-over. De Gaulle won 78.5 per cent of the votes of the electoral college, with Marrane, the old communist trusty, polling 13.1 per cent and Albert Chatelet, for the 'democratic left', 8.4 per cent.

But, whatever the celebrations that followed de Gaulle's election as President, there was a shock in store for the French voters. The new President-elect made a broadcast to the nation on television and radio on 28 December. The message was, to say the least, extremely unpleasant. Taxes would be increased, social security payments cut, farm subsidies reduced. Trade quotas with the other countries of the Common Market would be substantially dismantled, the franc was to be devalued – it was left to Pinay to say that the devaluation would be by 17.5 per cent – and pensions to First World War veterans were to be partially suspended.

It must be rare, in any democratic system, for an election to have been fought and won on an economic prospectus that was so misleading. It was not that an incoming government found a situation that required immediate and unexpected action. Rueff and his group had been working on the programme for months, with the knowledge and cooperation of de Gaulle's team in the Matignon, and the help of the economists at the Ministry of Finance in the rue de Rivoli. They all believed, rightly or wrongly, that the French economy needed electric-shock therapy to allow it to face up to the new Common Market. But it had been wise not to tell the voters.

The formal decision to proceed with the programme was only taken in the Cabinet meeting of 26 December, but nobody was fooled by that. Certainly Mollet was not, and he and his fellow Socialists resigned on the spot. They were just persuaded, but only just, to stay in office for Inauguration Day.

On 8 January 1959 General Charles de Gaulle was installed as the first President of the Fifth Republic. He lunched with President Coty at the Elysée, the traditional home of Presidents of France, and they drove together up the Champs-Elysées to lay a wreath on the Tomb of the Unknown Soldier. Protocol had it that the incoming President should escort the outgoing President to his car. But, when the ceremony had been completed, President de Gaulle turned away towards a group of veterans who were in the crowd. As he turned, he said over his shoulder, '*Au revoir, M. Coty*,' got into his own car and drove off. Coty was left stranded, forlorn and alone. It was a brutal, and deliberate, assertion of the transfer of power to the new order.

The Fifth Republic was now well and truly in place. The electoral system ensured, barring some unnatural shock, a period of political tranquillity. The change in the constitution had been achieved in a curious, almost off-hand, way. There had been no revolution, as in 1789, or general violence, as in 1848, or defeat in war, as in 1871 and 1940. There was no particular economic discontent. In fact the 1950s in France had been a decade of steady and balanced growth – much less good than in West Germany but still twice as good as in the United Kingdom. There had been difficulties over the migration of workers from the land to the industrial towns, but on the whole the post-war French economy had enjoyed reasonable success. Moreover the mass of the French people had shown little interest in what was going on. To be sure, there had been panic buying at times, but that was a regular reaction to any disturbance, however inconsequential. But the holiday season of 1958 was generally agreed to have been successful, and away from Paris and Algiers the tempo of life had not changed.

The truth was that it had been above all a crisis of politics; as Mendès-France said, it was a failure of men rather than of institutions. As such, it had been a crisis confined to a relatively small number of actors. De Gaulle had seen his chance and played his hand skilfully. In a time of alarm and bewilderment about the Algerian problem, France had been content to turn to a figure whose prestige was beyond question, as she had turned to Thiers in 1871, Clemenceau in 1917, Poincaré in 1926 and – although the Gaullists would have spurned the analogy – Pétain in 1940. The surprising, and paradoxical, similarity between Pétain and de Gaulle was that both brought with them new constitutional proposals which involved a high degree of personal rule. But then the two men were never quite such opposites as many have supposed.

3

ALGERIA IS NOT FRENCH

*Certains veulent la République sans le Général de Gaulle et
d'autres le Général sans la République; la France, elle, veut la
République avec le Général de Gaulle.* ★

There was a sniper, so it is said, stationed in a window of an apartment
block just opposite the balcony of the Gouvernement-Général in
Algiers when General de Gaulle started his speech on the evening of 4
June 1958. The sniper was under instruction from a group of diehard
white settlers, who were convinced of the General's ultimate intention
to betray them. His orders were to have done with de Gaulle once and
for all. When the rifleman heard the famous words 'I have understood
you', as the story goes, he removed the telescopic sight which he had
carefully focused on the General's head, put down his rifle and listened
to what followed. Having heard the rest of the speech, he dismantled his
rifle and abandoned his mission.

The story may be true, or it may be an invention. If it is true, and if
the sniper had obeyed his instructions, it would have been the first of
perhaps as many as thirty attempts over the next four years to assassinate
the General. It is hard to think of any modern political figure who has
been subjected to such an intensive campaign of attempted murder. It is
a mark of the bitterness and hatred engendered by the Algerian War and
its aftermath that the campaign was so persistently waged, and a mark of
the General's courage, and that of his wife Yvonne, that they accepted
the risks so phlegmatically.

Had the General been assassinated that day, there would, of course,
have been mourning at the murder of a Prime Minister, and one, at
that, with such a heroic personal history. The events of May 1958

★ 'Some want the Republic without General de Gaulle and some others want the
General without the Republic; France herself wants the Republic with General de
Gaulle.' André Malraux, in a speech at the Hôtel de Ville, 14 July 1958.

would have had a different sequel. Perhaps there would have been some form of military takeover; or perhaps, under the shock of the tragedy, the Fourth Republic might have pulled itself together and produced a leader worthy of the name. The General's passing would have been regretted, but no more.

If, on the other hand, a similar sniper had completed his work on inauguration day, 8 January 1959, the obituaries would have carried a quite different message. De Gaulle's war record would have been written up in full, as would the post-war political history of Europe and France, and the rise and fall of the RPF. But they would certainly have recorded, and perhaps highlighted, his period as Prime Minister and the astonishing outburst of activity in France in the months from May to December 1958. It was one of those periods, which have occurred from time to time in French history, when a new government seemed to unlock all the national reserves of talent and hard work. Life, for no obviously apparent reason, seemed worth living again.

It was not just a question of devising a new constitution, or of the intense and impassioned debates that surrounded the process. It was not even a question of the work being done to prepare the country for the Common Market, or of the new initiatives that France was taking in Europe and the world. It was as though, in every walk of life, France had moved up a gear. By no means the least impressive feature was the amount of sheer intellectual and physical effort that the sixty-seven-year-old General put into his job.

Quite apart from the trips to Algeria in the height of the North African summer, he had made an immediate start on his foreign policy objectives. The first was 'to detach France, not from the Atlantic Alliance but from its integration under American command'.[1] To that purpose he had, on 4 and 5 July, held talks in Paris with the US Secretary of State John Foster Dulles. The General had explained that France must play her proper role at the summit of world affairs, which in his view, meant the reform of the NATO command structure to include her. 'There is no France which is of any value, particularly in the eyes of Frenchmen, without a world responsibility,' he said.[2] The United States could no longer intervene at will without proper consultation and joint decision, as had recently happened in the Lebanon. Dulles was, as might be imagined, indignant at being told what the United States could or could not do, and the visit was an abysmal failure. But the General had made his point – and set down a marker for the future.

Equally difficult, although in a different way, had been Harold Macmillan's visit in June. In the General's view, the European Economic Community – comprising France, West Germany, Belgium, Italy, Luxembourg and the Netherlands – was only a stepping stone to the establishment of close trading links with the states of the eastern bloc, and first of all with Russia. Macmillan's preoccupations with a European Free Trade Area were, by that standard, petty and irrelevant.

On 14 and 15 September, the General's diplomatic activity in his period as Prime Minister reached its climax. The question, as it always was with France, was Germany. Clearly, there could be no advance in France's position in Europe and the world without an understanding with the new West German Federal Republic, however painful it might be to reach such an understanding. The General decided to invite the Federal Chancellor, Konrad Adenauer, to discuss what are known in diplomatic language as 'outstanding issues'.

Adenauer was invited to the General's own home. That was surprising enough. But the West German diplomatic staff planning the visit soon learnt that Mme de Gaulle was not entirely pleased with this proposed invasion of her privacy. She was not prepared to call on the official catering service, or any other service, from the Matignon. If her husband were going to invite guests to her home, she said, they should come as her guests and receive the same treatment as any other guest. She might borrow a servant or two from her brother Jacques Vendroux, at that time Mayor of Calais, but there would be no silver, porcelain, chefs or anything else from Paris. Furthermore, there was no room at La Boisserie for the customary diplomatic retinue. The two Foreign Ministers and the two ambassadors would have to stay at the Préfecture at Chaumont. Adenauer himself would have to leave behind his three daughters, who normally looked after him on his journeys. He would have to sleep in the one guest-room, which had no separate bathroom. The West German diplomats must have been horrified.

As it turned out, the whole event was a tremendous success. Adenauer was immensely flattered to have been asked to the General's home. According to the traditions of the Catholic Rhineland from which he came, it was the ultimate compliment. He was all the more pleased when de Gaulle told him that he thought the time had come for an historic reconciliation between France and Germany.

The proposal, and its presentation, was made with great subtlety. Adenauer arrived to find the General at his most charming. In those simple, almost Spartan, surroundings de Gaulle won the old man's heart.

By dinner time on the 14th, when the ministers and ambassadors arrived for what was by their standards something of a frugal country meal, the atmosphere was relaxed and cordial. There was a further advantage: Adenauer was having no difficulty in hearing what was being said – which made the official record of discussions that much easier.

In essence, the deal that the General proposed was simple. France would allow the European Economic Community to proceed on schedule on 1 January 1959, which was what the Germans wanted, but its terms would have to embrace agriculture. Furthermore, Germany would have to accept her present frontiers to the east; reunification was off the agenda; and under no circumstances whatsoever would Germany be allowed to develop a nuclear bomb.

Adenauer was greatly impressed, to the point where he was prepared to agree to all the General's propositions. 'De Gaulle was nothing like the press accounts of the last few months,' he wrote in his own memoirs. 'He had . . . the energy of youth . . . [his] nationalism [was] much less aggressive . . . [he was] well informed on world affairs. . . . I was surprised by his simplicity and naturalness.'[3] It was hardly a picture that would have been painted by others at the time, but it reflected the effort that de Gaulle had made to charm his guest. Moreover, he knew that the charm had worked.

The memorandum that de Gaulle addressed to Eisenhower and Macmillan on 17 September 1958, only two days after Adenauer's departure, revealed his confidence. It was aggressive and direct. There were complaints about American and British action in the Far East. NATO was now, the General claimed, obsolete in its command structure. In short, what the General was suggesting was a tripartite body, of the United States, Britain and France, which would be responsible for all security decisions in the non-Communist world.

As a proposal, it was, in the context of the time, quite unrealistic. France could not yet deliver a nuclear bomb, but was now apparently trying to exercise a veto over the use of the American nuclear strike force. There could be no question of the Americans accepting it, as President Eisenhower made clear in his reply on 20 October. All he could offer was a forum for continuing discussions on world matters between ambassadors in Washington, which would anyway have been normal practice.

It was doubtful whether the General's initiative was meant to be taken seriously. Couve de Murville, always a devious – and, it is said, frequently bad-tempered – civil servant, was clearly doing his master's bidding when he wrote subsequently of his conviction that the whole exercise had been intended simply to pave the way for future negotiations. Given the General's ambitions for France, it seems more likely that he was reverting to the demand made so often during the war to Roosevelt and Churchill that France should be treated as an equal power with them. Whatever the current realities, that was where France should be.

There was, after all, only one rational argument in support of the General's position. If American nuclear weapons were positioned in France, then France, he argued, should have a say in how they were used. Unfortunately for the General, the same argument could be used by the Turks, Greeks, Italians and, of course, the Germans. But in spite of his new understanding with Chancellor Adenauer, the idea of the Germans participating in a NATO directorate did not fill the General with any enthusiasm at all. In de Gaulle's view, France was to be the leader of Europe, and that leadership could not possibly be shared.

Fortunately, in a way, the whole simmering dispute, which in reality was no more than the revival of the dispute with the Allies in 1945, was overtaken by Nikita Khrushchev's attempt to assert Soviet authority over Berlin in November 1958. Thanks to Churchill's efforts at Yalta, France was one of the three guarantor powers in Berlin. There was no doubt that, on this issue, the Western response had to be concerted. Dulles returned to Paris on 15 December. The General was firm: the Soviets must be resisted. In practice, they could only be resisted by NATO troops and – be it said – by American nuclear weapons. Since almost all the French army was tied down in Algeria, and since France had no nuclear weapons to contribute, the General seemed again to be playing his cards too strongly – at least, that was Dulles's conclusion. To his surprise, Dulles found himself having to restrain the General's belligerence.

The Berlin crisis, which was only one manifestation of the general crisis of relations between the Soviet Union and the West given the name of the 'Cold War', rumbled on. In the end it merged into the Cuban crisis of 1962 and the subsequent fall of Khrushchev. There were moments of great heat and moments of calm, but while it was unresolved, the General felt obliged to adhere to the alliance that was in place and of which France was a member. In other words, he was unable to move forward with what he really wanted to do – rearrange France's role both in Europe and in the world. But it was fortunate for him in that the crisis had given him, perhaps against his own volition, a period of time and a degree of political space. He badly needed it, since there was one domestic matter still unresolved, but which needed resolving quickly and conclusively, and which only he could resolve.

That matter was, of course, Algeria. It was messy, nasty and dangerous. It had all the characteristics that politicians most fear: there was no obviously popular solution; the passions aroused were intense; violence had become commonplace; and positions were so entrenched that there was no identifiable room to manoeuvre. But it was a matter that had to be dealt with. Quite apart from the drain on France's resources, both material and human, it was to be the test of survival for de Gaulle's Fifth Republic. Algeria had been the Fifth Republic's midwife – and could just as easily turn into its executioner. The General would far rather have being doing other things, but this was the problem of the moment and it had to be solved. Furthermore, until it had been solved, no grand project for France could conceivably be successful. The sore festered too obviously.

As it turned out, de Gaulle's extrication of France from Algeria was the making of his reputation as a statesman. Over a four-year period, from 1959 to 1962, he played his cards with a mixture of strength and calculated deception that his opponents were never able to match. He was adept at changing direction when the circumstances demanded it. No politician was quicker than de Gaulle to recognise a brick wall when he met it, and he had to face many such walls over Algeria. But the whole affair cost him dearly. He worried, lost weight, became more bad-tempered and tetchy. The confident, relaxed de Gaulle of June 1958 had already disappeared by the following year.

His first move, after the rejection by the FLN of his overtures in October 1958, was to order a change of personnel in Algeria. In other words, he and Ely conducted a purge of those officers in the army in Algeria whom they considered 'unreliable'. Salan became military governor of Paris, where he could be watched carefully. Jouhaud went to early retirement. Only Massu was allowed to stay, provided he gave up the nonsense of the Committee of Public Safety, which he was only too happy to do. But a further 1500 officers of lower rank were inconspicuously transferred or retired.

Salan's former job was split into two. The civil administration was put into the hands of a personal friend of Debré, a young civil servant of already proven ability, Paul Delouvrier. The military command was given to an old Resistance veteran, the air force general Maurice Challe.

Delouvrier and Challe took up their posts in Algiers on 19 December 1958. On appointing Challe as commander-in-chief, de Gaulle expected operations to take a 'dynamic' turn which would result in undisputed mastery of the field. This was exactly what happened. Throughout the spring and summer of 1959 Challe conducted a campaign of terrifying efficiency and brutality against the Algerian Army of National Liberation. Overwhelming ground and air forces were deployed. The techniques of psychological warfare were perfected. More than a million Moslems were transferred from their homes to 'regroupment' camps – in other words, concentration camps. The guerrillas were chased into the hills by day and by night, their villages bombarded, their families taken away and tortured.

It was appalling, but militarily it was successful. Politically, on the other hand, it did not work. The Algerian troops refused to give up. Moreover, as the pictures of the horrors leaked out, they increased concern among leaders of world opinion – which the Algerian Provisional Government, formed in September 1958 and by then resident in Tunis, was not slow to exploit.

The General visited the army camps in Algeria at the end of August 1959. He then took a holiday – the first since his accession to power in May 1958. But it was a holiday with a difference. Armed with a memorandum from Bernard Tricot, his newly appointed special adviser on Algeria, he thought long and hard about the Algerian problem. As he paced around the garden at Colombey, he came to two conclusions. First, the cost of the war was politically and economically too great and in the end would pull down France herself. Second, the only solution that made any sense was Algerian independence.

On 16 September the General announced on radio and television the result of his deliberations. There were only three possible solutions to the Algerian problem: total secession, integration with France or some form of association. But it would be for the Algerians themselves to decide. 'Self-determination' had found its way at last, onto the agenda. '*Algérie Française*', words which the white settlers lived by – and to which the General himself had been unwise enough to refer a year earlier – was now forgotten.

The broadcast pleased the French in France but nobody in Algeria. The Algerian Provisional Government welcomed the idea of self-determination but nothing else. The extreme white settlers were so disillusioned that they formed their own paramilitary force, the Front

National Français (FNF), and the army no longer knew what it was fighting for. Even the elderly, and only surviving, Marshal of France, Alphonse Juin, went on the record in mild criticism, but was promptly told to keep quiet. Finally it was Massu, until then the most steadfast of Gaullists, who blew things apart.

Massu's interview with the German journalist Hans Kempski, himself a former paratrooper, appeared in the *Suddeutsche Zeitung* of 18 January 1960. Massu was reported as saying that the army no longer understood de Gaulle's policies, had perhaps made a mistake in bringing him back to power and, as far as he and the majority of officers in positions of command were concerned, would 'not execute unconditionally the orders of the head of state'.[4]

That was the final blow; it could hardly have been worse. Recalled to Paris, Massu was given a furious dressing-down, not, significantly, by de Gaulle himself – old military loyalties were too strong for that – but by Pierre Guillaumat, the Minister of Defence, on de Gaulle's instructions; and then posted to be garrison commander of Metz. He would not reappear in Algiers. The General's colleagues, from Debré, his Prime Minister, to Challe and Delouvrier, tried to persuade him that Massu's sacking would lead to bloodshed in Algiers. De Gaulle would have none of it. A soldier had broken the first rule of his profession; unquestioning allegiance to the civil power. That was all there was to be said.

It says much that the General was prepared to stick so firmly to that fundamental principle at such a tense time. He knew perfectly well what the likely result would be in Algiers. Frenchmen would start killing Frenchmen. But he believed that it would have been even worse to allow the armed forces to dictate political decisions. France would have been relegated to the status of a minor Latin American republic, and the General was not going to allow his whole career, all he had stood for, to be thrown away like that.

Frenchmen did indeed start killing Frenchmen, a week later, in what became known as 'Barricades Week'. The FNF, led by the café-owner Ortiz, tore up the paving stones in the streets and made them into barricades. Lagaillarde, the 'student' leader of May 1958, assembled a different group, but to the same purpose, occupying the main university building. The gendarmerie tried to intervene but, as they walked in orderly fashion towards Ortiz's positions, the FNF opened up with rifle and automatic fire. The gendarmes did not have a chance. It became a massacre. Not only were gendarmes shot down in cold blood, but the wounded were finished off mercilessly as they tried to crawl to safety in the nearby buildings. The paratroopers arrived late – deliberately so, it was said. By that time, fourteen gendarmes had died and 123 had been wounded.

De Gaulle, looking tired but calm, went again on television with the simple message: the rioters must lay down their arms. There was no response from the barricades. Not only that, but the paratroopers surrounding Ortiz and his fellow insurgents started to fraternise with them. De Gaulle's broadcast had seemed weak. They all thought that the matter would be settled soon, and that de Gaulle was bound to agree to the formula of integration with France. '*Algérie Française*', in their view, had won.

The crisis lasted a full week. The army unit commanders in Algiers shilly-shallied. They refused to use the only weapon against the barricades that would have been effective – tanks. There was even a risk of their joining Ortiz and the rebels. Delouvrier and Challe had both started to crack. They left Algiers on 28 January to avoid being kidnapped, but Delouvrier left behind his wife and baby son, together with the text of a hysterical speech which was to be broadcast after he left. It looked as though it was all breaking up.

De Gaulle went on television yet again at 8 p.m. on 29 January. This time, he seemed to realise that the Fifth Republic, his own creation, was on the brink of disintegration, and that the speech that he had to make was to be one of the most important of his whole long life. He did not look well: he seemed tired, as though he had not been sleeping. But he had deliberately put on his uniform of brigadier-general, and when he spoke his voice was determined, each point being emphasised by a raised finger in what was otherwise a clenched fist. It was not simply the head of state who was speaking; it was General de Gaulle. He refused to waver from his decision of September: 'The Algerians shall have free choice of their destiny.' In the most measured tones, he ordered the army not to associate itself with insurgence in any manner whatsoever, and to re-establish law and order.

Finally he spoke to France, and as he did so his voice softened. '*Eh bien, mon cher et vieux pays, nous voici donc ensemble, encore une fois, face à une lourde épreuve.*' ('Well, my dear and old country, here we are together, once again, facing a harsh test.') There could be no concessions to those 'who dream of being usurpers'. If there were, France would become a 'poor broken plaything adrift on a sea of chance'.[5] He was speaking straight from the heart.

It was de Gaulle at his very best, and the response from the French people was electric. Within minutes, thousands of messages of support were received at the Elysée, and within a quarter of an hour forty army units in Algeria had declared their loyalty. As though to underline the gravity of what the General said, the insurgents in Algiers had had to listen to the broadcast in a crashing thunderstorm. It seemed, as de Gaulle himself wrote, 'symbolic'. Bernard Tricot, sitting next to the General, said to himself, 'We have won.'[6]

Indeed they had. It took a little time, but by 1 February Ortiz had fled Algiers and Lagaillarde had surrendered. It was all over – for the moment. But the political fall-out was serious. Debré offered to resign as Prime Minister, but de Gaulle refused to accept it. Soustelle, on the other hand, was finished. De Gaulle had lost trust in him, and ever since he had declared himself, in May 1958, openly in favour of an '*Algérie Française*', had been looking for a way to sever connections. 'Barricades Week' had taken its toll in Paris as well as Algiers.

For three months there was relative calm in both cities. But in May 1960 news came through of another surprising event: one of the Algerian military leaders, Si Salah, wanted to talk. It was thought that this might be the breakthrough that de Gaulle had hoped for since launching the Challe offensive. Perhaps the FLN were preparing to admit defeat. If so, it was certainly a straw worth grasping at, not least because the French army itself – by then largely conscript – was getting bored and irritated when it was not frightened.

It was hopeful enough for the General to send Tricot to see Si Salah. Those preliminary discussions were in turn promising enough for de Gaulle to invite Si Salah to Paris, for personal talks, and subsequently for the French Government to invite the Algerian Provisional Government to negotiations, to be held at Melun at the end of the month. The Algerians arrived, heard what the French had to say – lay down your arms and we will then start to negotiate an honourable settlement – and promptly left. Si Salah was never seen or heard of again.

By September 1960 the impasse seemed total. The FLN had survived the military onslaught of Challe – who had by then been posted to Germany – and had started to reassert its strength under a new leader, Houari Boumédienne. Politically, the anti-war movement in France was gaining ground. An anti-war manifesto was issued by a group of 121 intellectuals, including Jean-Paul Sartre, Simone de Beauvoir, Françoise Sagan and Simone Signoret; it was followed by demonstrations on the Paris streets. On a visit to Algiers in October, Tricot noted a 'rapid deterioration' in relations between the two communities. It looked again as though there would be a serious blow-up.

Again, de Gaulle timed his move carefully. On 4 November he announced that he had chosen the path of an 'Algerian Algeria'; later in the month he formally gave up the post of Minister for Algeria, appointing Louis Joxe in his stead and accepting the resignation of Delouvrier as delegate-general – he had had enough and more than enough. On 9 December, de Gaulle went again to Algeria; in the two days of his visit there were four assassination attempts and a universally hostile reception from the white community. But on the day he left the Moslems demonstrated in force. FLN flags appeared everywhere, and the cry was '*Vive de Gaulle!*' The General left Algeria, never, as it happened, to return.

It was time to take the matter direct to the French people. On 20 December the General announced a referendum to decide whether or not independence should be granted to Algeria once peace had been restored. The vote, on 8 January 1961, went decisively in de Gaulle's favour. The way was now open for formal negotiations between the French Government and the Algerian Provisional Government, and on 30 March a joint announcement was published to the effect that the two Governments would meet at Evian on 7 April 1961.

The referendum also opened the way to the formation of a last-ditch group wholly wedded to '*Algérie Française*'. It was called Organisation Armée Secrète (OAS), and meant what its title said: a secret army, using terrorism to resist Algerian independence. At first, it was regarded as little more than comic, but when bombs exploded almost at random in Paris it became a serious threat. For the moment, however, the much more serious threat was from the army in Algiers.

There was now widespread talk of a *putsch*. Challe had shocked his colleagues by announcing early retirement at the age of only fifty-six. He was known to be fed up with de Gaulle's manoeuvring. Salan was in Madrid, also in retirement. But Jouhaud and André Zeller, the two other generals spoken of as possible leaders of a coup, were in Algiers. Strangely, in spite of the gossip, the French authorities took no particular precautions.

The *putsch* came on the night of 21 April. For a while, it looked as though it might be a success. On the morning of the 22nd, it was announced in Algiers that the army had assumed control of Algeria and the Sahara. Immediately, cars appeared on the streets blowing their horns in celebration and Tricolor flags were raised everywhere. Challe announced that he was in Algiers and would move into his old head-quarters.

As it turned out, events followed much the same pattern as before, although this time de Gaulle was worried enough to declare a state of emergency. There was talk of paratroopers from Algeria landing on the mainland and surrounding Paris. France seemed on the verge of panic. Even the British were frightened, and a Cabinet meeting was held to assess the possibility of sending British troops to help de Gaulle in the event of an invasion from Algeria.

Yet again, the General broadcast, and yet again he broadcast in his uniform. He was obviously depressed and angry, and indeed genuinely pained by the sight of the army, to which he belonged and in whose traditions he himself had been educated, quite clearly in revolt. Yet again, the performance was compelling. Banging his fist on the desk, he forbad every Frenchman, and above all every soldier, to 'execute any of their orders'. He finished with an almost desperate appeal: '*Françaises, Français, aidez-moi!*' ('Frenchwomen, Frenchmen, help me!')

Yet again, the speech had its effect. De Gaulle had appealed over the heads of the generals to the ordinary soldiers of the army and they had listened. The generals found that they had no support. In the end, on 27 April, Challe gave himself up, as did Zeller a few days later, while Salan and Jouhaud slid secretly out of Algiers. The *putsch* was over. France breathed a sigh of relief.

The Evian negotiations finally opened on 20 May. It was a dreary process. The FLN knew the strength of their negotiating position, and the French team, under Joxe, knew the weakness of theirs. The discussions were long and tedious, punctuated by violence both in Algeria and from the OAS in France. In September there was another assassination attempt on de Gaulle, this time on the road to Colombey, at Nogent-sur-Seine, about 100 miles out of Paris. The OAS had laid down a path of petrol and explosive in front of the General's car and ignited the petrol as the car approached. But de Gaulle's driver was brave and skilful, and the explosive failed to detonate.

It was obvious now that there was only one solution, and in his 1962 New Year message the General made it clear: one way or another he was determined that France should free herself from her ties with Algeria. By 18 March agreement had been reached in Evian, and a ceasefire came into effect the following day.

As might be imagined, the withdrawal of French troops and support services from Algeria was full of danger and difficulty. Although the

OAS had by then collapsed as an effective organisation, individual groups were still able to create difficulties. Furthermore, there was a mass exodus of white settlers from Algeria to mainland France. In May 1962 alone 300,000 left their North African homes.

By the time the referendum was held in Algeria to ratify the Evian agreements, no more than 100,000 whites had stayed behind. But the OAS, if defeated in their main campaign to keep Algeria French, were still out for revenge, and their principal target was still the General. There were many botched assassination attempts; and the security services did their job well. But there was one that came within a hair's breadth of success.

The OAS were well organised. A commando group, set up under Colonel Jean-Marie Bastien-Thiry, had been tracking de Gaulle's movements for some time. On 22 August 1962 the General's son-in-law de Boissieu had taken the place of his usual ADC for the journey from Colombey to Paris for the usual Wednesday meeting of the Council of Ministers. The General and Mme de Gaulle were travelling together, and they had flown to the airport at Villacoublay, to be met by a car to take them into Paris by way of Clamart.

On the return journey, Boissieu again sat next to Francis Marroux, the General's driver. They left at 7.30 p.m. It was only at that point that the route back to Villacoublay was decided upon. But somehow the assassins were ready, tracing the General's convoy as it crossed the Seine on its way out of Paris. There were twelve of them, armed with automatic weapons, and four cars.

At 8.08 p.m. the General's car and its one escort arrived at Clamart. They were approaching the crossroads at Petit-Clamart, as it was known, when Bastien-Thiry gave the signal to open fire. Marroux put his foot down. But just as the General's party thought that they had escaped, de Boissieu saw two more cars in front of them. It was the second wave. De Boissieu shouted to his father-in-law to get down, which he did, dragging his wife with him.

Their car was riddled with bullets, some fourteen hitting the car direct, one going through the rear window passing just over de Gaulle's bowed head. Two of the car's tyres were hit and its gearbox was severely damaged. Fortunately, in the twilight, Marroux, driving on one gear, managed to lose his pursuers, and they made the airport at Villacoublay – with difficulty, but without serious casualty. The General and Mme de Gaulle were covered in glass, but there was nothing worse than that, apart from shock.

It had been a matter of luck only. The General, on the surface, shrugged the whole thing off – 'They shot like pigs,' he told Pompidou that evening on the telephone[7] – and he presented himself to the press the following day quite unharmed, and indeed in good spirits.

Nevertheless it had shaken him, and had shaken everybody. There had been too many assassination attempts, too much killing. That was the price that France, and the General personally, had had to pay for the resolution of the Algerian problem. But he had done it. There may have been no sniper taking aim at him on 4 June 1958 when he spoke from the balcony of the Gouvernement-Général in Algiers, when he first came to power, but there had been many since; and the last, over four years later, had nearly succeeded.

4

THE NEW AGENDA

*Au fond, c'est au Louvre que j'aurais dû
m'installer. . . . On ne fait pas l'Histoire dans
le huitième arrondissement.* ★

The domestic life of the de Gaulles hardly changed with the move
from the Matignon to the Elysée after his installation as President in
January 1959. In fact, the move itself was little more than the exchange
of one official apartment for another – more comfortable and spacious,
to be sure, but still remote and impersonal. The General's style of life
did not change, nor did that of his wife. Neither of them liked their
new home any better than the old. Mme de Gaulle was particularly critical. She spoke of the Elysée, her husband was to say to those who
asked, as she would speak of a concentration camp. The General himself was no more enthusiastic, although he was never one to bother
much about his surroundings – he simply did not notice them. He had,
it is true, asked whether there was any reasonable alternative on offer.
The Invalides was suggested, or the Louvre, or even Versailles – 'that
would be a bit too much' the General thought. In the end, the Elysée
seemed to be the sensible, if reluctant, choice. The Elysée it was, then,
that was to be their Paris residence for the next ten years.

The historical omens, of course, were not favourable. The Palais de
l'Elysée, although built in the early eighteenth century for the perfectly respectable Comte d'Evreux, had been subsequently acquired by
Mme de Pompadour. During her tenure a number of ceilings had been
painted with frescoes depicting scenes illustrating the gallantry of her
times, of which Mme de Gaulle certainly did not approve. The cherubs
in the General's office were particularly fetching – and much surprised

★ 'Really, I should have set myself up at the Louvre . . . The 8th arrondissement is not
a place for making History.' Charles de Gaulle, quoted in Claude Dulong, *La vie quotidienne au temps de Charles de Gaulle*, page 10; Hachette, Paris, 1974.

his visitors. Furthermore, the place had been turned into a popular dance-hall during the Revolution – another indication of its somewhat disreputable past.

In the General's mind the place was equally objectionable, though for different reasons. Napoleon had signed his second abdication there on 22 June 1815 after his defeat at Waterloo. The Duke of Wellington had then quartered his troops there – English troops, with their boots on the table, so it was said – until the Congress of Vienna had restored a sense of order and decency to post-Napoleonic Europe.

But there it was – the seat of Presidents of France since 1873. General de Gaulle could not lightly abandon it. This being so, as he was to write himself, they made the best of it. They moved the private apartments from the ground to the first floor. There at least there were five rooms available – overlooking the street admittedly, but comfortable if kept curtained. At the back, the apartments looked on to an agreeable garden, with an attractive little duck pond, but it was difficult to go for a walk without being seen by onlookers in the apartments in the rue de l'Elysée. Also it was spoilt by the incessant traffic noise which came from the town around, and particularly from the neighbouring Champs-Elysées. The real disadvantage, which nobody could work out how to avoid or even mitigate, was the distance between the apartments and the kitchens; for ten years the de Gaulles ate tepid meals.

It is little wonder that Mme de Gaulle preferred her home at Colombey to life at the Elysée. Equally, it is little wonder that the General was quite prepared to embark on numerous travels, both to the provinces of France and abroad. Apart from his firmly held belief that his authority would be increased if he showed himself to the people in the style of a medieval monarch, and apart from domestic discomfort, he tended to get bored with day-to-day problems of the management of government. Those were more properly left to his Elysée staff of some forty-five trusties – Courcel, Foccart, Guichard, Lefranc and other veterans of Fighting France and the RPF.

When the General travelled, his programme was, as might be imagined, hectic. The pace left other, much younger men breathless in his wake. Almost every month he visited one or other region of France. These visits caused extreme difficulties both of security and of organisation; the first because his figure was unmistakeable to any potential assassin, the second because wherever he slept a 7½-foot bed had to be found to accommodate him, a whole communications system had to be set up, his medical team had to be accommodated and room found for his substantial retinue. Furthermore, the General did not like flying, and although he had his own special airplane, the inside tailored for his large frame, he was never in the best of moods after an air journey.

The result of this peripatetic activity, in terms of the conduct of the de Gaulle Government, was a slow but steady loss of the collective sense of cohesion, and consequently of the excitement, that had characterised the General's days at the Matignon. De Gaulle was never good at delegating – it was not his style – and he wished to be kept in touch at all moments. He insisted on seeing the morning Paris newspapers wherever he was, a requirement which stretched the resources of the provincial gendarmeries to the limit, since they were ordered to provide the courier service. The General would then relay complaints arising from his reading of the newspapers to his office. Even on his journeys, he wished his presence to be felt in Paris.

The consequence was inevitable: the Elysée staff became progressively more powerful and collective government gradually turned into collective administration of the Elysée's decisions. Nor was it just a matter of style. Even the personnel changed. In his first Council of Ministers, for instance, there had been eleven professional politicians out of twenty-one members. But by the end of 1959 all but two ministers were civil servants or experts brought in from outside politics. Unlike the professional politicians – who could, and did, live to fight another day if they were sacked or resigned – the new appointees lived entirely at the General's pleasure. If they were forced out, it was the end of their career.

By this process, deliberate or not, de Gaulle's hold on his Government was steadily reinforced. Ministers would no longer argue about his decisions. Failing counter-argument, the General stopped bothering about them; even in 1958, as Prime Minister, he had tended to disregard the full Council of Ministers and act on his own in foreign affairs. For instance, his offer in October 1958 to the FLN of a 'peace of the brave' was shown to the Council only an hour or so before it was broadcast. The aggressive memorandum to Eisenhower and Macmillan demanding a tripartite command structure for NATO was never put to the Council at all; and one of his ministers, who was actually with the General in Africa when Guinea refused the constitution and was given immediate independence, noted the fact only from headlines in the local newspapers.

The process had continued and accelerated after de Gaulle became President. In the end, it was all too much for the politicians in his

Government. In January 1960 even Pinay went. He had been the most revered survivor of the Fourth Republic – and, apart from Mendès-France, its most successful politician – and had been the only minister in the Council of the Fifth Republic to stand up to de Gaulle's sarcastic sallies. He had even insisted on a doctrine of 'collective responsibility'. When de Gaulle reproved him for airing his views in Council meetings on matters which were outside his departmental responsibility, Pinay protested that there was no other forum in which to air them. It was a fair point, but it was not one that impressed the General. Although one or two others clung on, it was said by a former colleague that after Pinay's resignation the Council of Ministers became a mortuary in which from time to time the dead spoke. It was a depressing picture of the bright new republic.

De Gaulle's defenders claimed that those ministers who had left the Government were plainly not up to the measure of the General's vision. De Gaulle's detractors on the other hand claimed that the General was no longer respecting the spirit of his own constitution and was reverting to the Bonapartism that was his true political nature.

In fact, as is often the case in disputes of this kind, both sides had a point. But the General's defenders would have had stronger arguments had they been able to explain precisely what the General's vision was that departing ministers had failed to live up to. There was, of course, the overriding principle of enhancing the 'greatness' of France, but it was difficult to translate that principle into more specific and precise tactical action which could be approved or disapproved, other than by the mere assertion that whatever the General did was for the good of France. The only clear policy commitment which they could latch on to was the express instruction, made at a meeting of the Council on 17 March 1959, to make the development and production of a French nuclear bomb an absolute priority. There was no particular defence strategy behind the commitment. One of his later ministers put the General's view thus: 'France is a great power; all great powers have nuclear weapons; therefore France must have them.'[1] At least it was simple and clear. But beyond that the General's overall intentions were far from precisely stated. Indeed at this time his speeches, and there were many as he travelled up and down the country, seem more than usually Delphic.

De Gaulle's detractors, who by mid-1960 were growing in number, could at least point to specific items for complaint. Certainly they supported the General on Algeria, as did a large majority in the country, but there was a limit. Quite apart from the progressively more author-itarian nature of his government, the limit was drawn by the General's own constitution, which he himself was, in their view, now violating. For instance, in March 1960 the General had refused to recall the Assembly for a debate on agricultural prices, in spite of a motion with the correct number of signatures; and in May he had forced a constitu-tional change to facilitate independence of African members of the French 'Community' by the simple but constitutionally dubious device of taking a bill and all amendments through the Assembly en bloc. The opposition was vocal and effective. For the first time since May 1958 de Gaulle was starting to get a bad press.

The clue to his current constraints, and to his ultimate intentions, was let slip by the General in a talk with Macmillan in March 1960. The Prime Minister had come to Paris to prepare for the planned state visit by the President of the Republic to Britain. After dinner, when the conversation became more expansive, Macmillan asked de Gaulle why he kept harping in his memoirs on the 'Anglo-Saxons'. The only response, inadequate as it was since the question raised much deeper questions about de Gaulle himself, was that the General 'believed in NATO' but that its 'set-up' was absurd. When the French army was free of Algeria, he told Macmillan, 'he would raise the whole issue'.[2] In other words, his hands were tied until the Algerian problem was out of the way. In the meantime all he could do was to keep open as many options as possible, at the risk, of course, of confusing his allies and sup-porters. Once Algeria was out of the way, his reasoning seems to have been, he would be free to pursue the option that appeared to him at the time to be most promising.

In his memoirs, de Gaulle claimed that his design was clear. American domination of NATO had to be resisted, but the alliance must be kept intact as an 'ultimate precaution'.[3] Relations with eastern bloc countries, particularly, were to be cultivated. France could only be properly independent if she were a nuclear power.

Even allowing for the hindsight that so frequently colours de Gaulle's memoirs, his claim is probably a reasonably accurate summary of his views at the time. Only one point is missing: his view of Europe. But the visit of Chancellor Adenauer to Colombey in mid-1958 had already provided a good indication of that.

Although all major initiatives were stalled until Algeria was settled, preparatory work could be done. In March 1960 the French Medi-terranean fleet was withdrawn from the NATO command structure.

The move could perhaps be justified in the context of the war in Algeria, and the fleet consisted of only twelve ships, but, as was widely remarked, it was the principle of withdrawal itself that was important.

The General then set about establishing better relations with the Soviet Union. His reasoning was simple. Either 'Russia' – the expression he always used – would return to her traditional alliances, of which France was the foremost, or she would continue down her current path of communist imperialism accompanied by a pursuit of the Cold War. In his reflections, influenced, no doubt, by his historical perspective, the General thought that Russia's current path was not sustainable in the long run. It was this belief that gave rise to the expression that he used rather loftily from time to time of 'Europe from the Atlantic to the Urals'.

But in the meantime 'Russia' was the Soviet Union. De Gaulle saw no harm at all in dealing with the Soviet leaders. He knew perfectly well that both Russia and China, under whatever regime they lived from time to time, respected their old friendships. It would be to France's benefit with any future 'Russia', if there was a change of regime in the way he expected, to have been seen to deal with the Soviets.

The tangible expression of this view was an invitation, gladly accepted, to President Khrushchev to a ten-day state visit to France, starting in late March 1960. During such a long visit there was, of course, plenty of time for discussion, and de Gaulle managed to convey the impression that he did not agree with the United States on all issues, and that he wished his guest to know it. Khrushchev, although irritated at what he thought was too close a relationship between France and Germany, took the point. The General, on his side, believed that 'the centuries-old relations between Russia and France' had been cemented by Khrushchev's visit. Nobody quite knew what this meant, but it sounded impressive.

Nevertheless, the General was realistic about his 'Russian' option, particularly when Khrushchev broke up the four-power summit in Paris six weeks later by angry demands for an apology from Eisenhower for the flight over Russian territory of an American U-2 spy plane, which had been spotted and shot down. Without an apology, Khrushchev said, there could be no discussion. The summit collapsed in confusion. The General was calm and philosophical, but behind the scenes he urged the British and American governments to show maximum firmness towards the Soviets. 'Khrushchev makes a lot of noise,' he said on one occasion, 'but he does not do anything. If you want to be a Hitler, you must make war. Khrushchev won't make war, and everybody knows it, beginning with Khrushchev.'

De Gaulle's second initiative was a revival of his idea for a tripartite directorate for the West, of the United States, Britain and France. It was not a new idea; indeed, it had been rumbling around the diplomatic foothills ever since 1944 without ever developing into a full-scale storm. In early March 1960 de Gaulle raised with Macmillan the possibility of Franco-British nuclear cooperation following the successful testing of the first French nuclear device in the Sahara in February. The British did not take the hint; nor was there any reason for them to do so, since the French nuclear strike force was at that time a weak and uncertain fledgeling. Then, during the summer of 1960, there was a series of letters between de Gaulle and Eisenhower suggesting a number of expedients and further meetings, but no satisfactory formula could be agreed, and the whole scheme seemed yet again to lose whatever small momentum it still had.

It was a difference of views on Africa that finished it, at least for the time being. The difference erupted over the Belgian Congo, then fighting for independence. The Americans had openly encouraged the colonial revolt. De Gaulle, on the other hand, had been dismayed throughout the summer of 1960 by the succession of French African dependencies which had left, or were leaving, the 'Community' of which he was President. Dahomey, Niger, Upper Volta, Ivory Coast, Chad, Gabon, Mali: one after the other they peeled off. He wanted to stop the Congo doing the same to Belgium. On that issue, neither France nor the United States could, in the light of their respective histories, give any ground. The tripartite directorate never seriously re-emerged from the darkness of the Congolese rain forest.

There remained the General's view of Europe: a Europe dominated by France, with Germany as the politically subservient but economically powerful partner. The difficulty here, in mid-1960, was that France was too weak, its energies too wasted in the sands of Algeria to sustain the role of political leader. De Gaulle's Europe would have to wait.

But there was one option that was definitely not on the General's agenda: it was known, in shorthand, as the 'United States of Europe'. As long ago as October 1955, Jean Monnet, the inspiration behind, and then the President of, the European Coal and Steel Community of the early 1950s, had set himself the task of building on its supra-nationalism. 'Mere cooperation between Governments will not suffice,' he had written in that October to leaders of political parties, trade unions and employer organisations throughout Europe. 'It is indispensable for States to delegate certain of their powers to European federal institutions mandated by all the participating countries as a whole.'[4] Since then the movement had grown in strength. An 'action committee' had been set up. Subcommittees had regular meetings. Seminars were held, papers produced.

In the light of de Gaulle's accession to power in France, Monnet had been wise enough to declare in October 1958 that the prime necessity was to 'make the economic union effective'. For the moment, perhaps for the duration of de Gaulle's tenure of office in France, political union was not on the agenda. But even then there was no doubt that the purpose of 'making economic union effective' was to promote 'the political union of tomorrow'.

It was, of course, anathema to the General, and whenever he had the chance he was scathing about Monnet and his principles. Power rested with nation states. States might make agreements one with another, but there was no question of compromising their individual sovereignty. No organisation other than the nation state could coherently exercise power. That was the end of the matter.

Uncomfortably for de Gaulle, as 1961 was to show, he had not heard the end of the matter. For the moment, however, it was something that could be left on the shelf; and, for the moment, the pursuit of the 'greatness' of France lay not in foreign policy initiatives but in ceremonial. The General, by virtue of his own temperament and his physical characteristics, was well suited to the role that he was about to play – that of President of the French Republic. His travels in France – together with the 'bains de foule' that he so much enjoyed – became even more frequent. Nor was there any doubting the success of his ceremonial role abroad. Wherever he went, his large figure was regarded with awe. Crowds turned out to see him, and he responded by putting on the sort of performance that he felt they expected from a President of France.

His visits abroad started with Britain in early April 1960, in a visit carefully orchestrated by Macmillan. The General, with all the wartime memories, was fulsomely received. He called on the Queen Mother, dined at Buckingham Palace and the Mansion House, went to see the old warrior Winston Churchill; and delivered a majestic address to both Houses of Parliament in Westminster Hall. One witness reported its effect, recalling that not only was the address itself majestic but the delivery was superb. Moreover, members of both the Lords and the Commons were astonished not just to find on their chairs, as they filed in, a complete script of the General's speech, but to hear the entire text delivered from memory without a downward glance or a single error. When he had finished, this 'exalted and a rather mystical figure' descended the stone steps, marched down the red carpet and out of the great doors.[5]

It was the same story in the United States and Canada. 'I have seen General de Gaulle reduce the Americans to the size of dwarfs,' wrote a journalist following the French cavalcade. 'Beside him Eisenhower, in spite of his charm . . . seemed ponderous and prosaic . . . At Washington, at Gettysburg, I felt the force of this man.'[6] He received a prolonged standing ovation from Congress when he addressed a joint session. The reception in New York was ecstatic: 'Eight hundred kilos of confetti were showered on the President of the Republic,' reported *France-Soir*, adding rather nastily, 'as opposed to the mere four hundred that Mr Khrushchev received.'[7]

But however well the General played his ceremonial role, time was moving on; by November 1960 he was already seventy, and had in his own mind hardly begun his real task. At least he could see an end to the Algerian crisis; but it was becoming abundantly clear that the end would be both tense and dangerous. In the very solution to the crisis, prolonged and painful as it had been, he had forfeited the coalition of interests that had brought him to power, and he knew that it could only be reassembled in a similar national emergency. On 31 December, when he broadcast a New Year message to the French people, exhorting them to vote 'Yes' in the referendum on Algerian self-determination, as well, of course, as wishing them the usual banalities of the season, he knew perfectly well that 1961 would bring risks and dangers; but he must have hoped that it would also unlock some of the options for France that he had been considering; and he must equally have hoped that, if all went well, 1962 would unlock the remainder.

January 1961 brought, among other things, a decisive change of the guard in Washington. The new President, John F. Kennedy, had brought with him a new team to the White House – and a new effort to try to understand the direction of the General's international policy. To be sure, the questions that were asked were the same as those that had been asked in France and the rest of Europe for some time. Why was the General so fiercely opposed to Khrushchev and at the same time so destructive in his attitude to the NATO command structure? Why was he so determined to persevere with an expensive and ineffective nuclear force while at the same time trying to exercise influence over how the Americans would use their strategic deterrent? It made no sense to the new American leaders, any more than it had to their predecessors.

The American understanding of de Gaulle's intentions – or of the options that were in his mind – was not advanced in any great measure by the visit of President and Mrs Kennedy to Paris from 31 May to 2 June 1961, important though it was cosmetically. In any case, the main centre of attraction was the glittering Jackie Kennedy. Paris was at its springtime best, and the reception in the Hall of Mirrors at Versailles was remembered long afterwards by those present. But politically there was little movement. The General regarded the whole thing as simply an elaborate ceremony, in which the appropriate noises and gestures had to be made.

In fact, the time given to serious discussion was surprisingly limited, and then only served to emphasise the age difference between the old General and the young President. The one political point on which Kennedy was adamant was that there would be no United States help on the delivery system for a French nuclear weapon. Of course, that was the only thing the General really wanted, and once that was denied him the rest of the period of the visit was given over to the exchange of compliments, sincerely meant at the time, but of no practical effect.

The inability of the early Kennedy administration to understand de Gaulle's frame of mind might not have mattered very much had it not been for the determination of the British Government, and of Macmillan himself, to join the European Economic Community – an aim which the United States supported and which Kennedy pressed during his Paris visit. The reasons were simple: Britain could no longer prosper either politically or economically outside the Community, even as a satellite of the United States. Having missed the initial opportunity to join the Coal and Steel Community conceived by Monnet in the early 1950s and then the full Economic Community, its natural successor in the late 1950s, Britain now found herself uncomfortably perched between a resurgent Europe led by West Germany's economic strength, and the United States. It was not a happy position, and Macmillan knew it. So did Kennedy.

For de Gaulle, the British approach, which was made formally in July 1961, came at a particularly inconvenient time. The OAS had launched a brutally destructive wave of bombing attacks in Paris following the failure of the Generals' *putsch* in Algiers in April. Paris was nervous, intensifying the nervous state of the whole country after the scare over suspected plans for an invasion by paratroopers from Algeria.

Furthermore, the controversy over a possible 'United States of Europe', in other words the political nature of the European Community of the Six, was starting to take off at precisely the same moment. At preparatory meetings with Adenauer during 1960 and then at formal meetings of heads of Government of the European Community in February and July 1961, de Gaulle had expounded his views on the future of political Europe. There should be, he had said, a solution based on the sovereignty of nation states: regular meetings between heads of Government and other subordinate national ministers, with the current apparatus of three communities – Euratom, the European Coal and Steel Community and the European Economic community – brought together under a new 'Cabinet' of European heads of Government.

At the Bonn summit on 18 July 1961, after much suspicious argument, de Gaulle had agreed to the creation of a committee of officials under Christian Fouchet, the French ambassador to Denmark (and, be it said, a hard-line Gaullist), 'to present proposals on the means which will as soon as possible enable statutory character to be given to the union of their peoples'. But as far as de Gaulle's own proposal was concerned, there was one important and essential feature which had not gone unnoticed by the other five: the capital of the new Europe, whatever form it might take, was to be Paris.

As for the British application, the only thing to do was to play for time, and this de Gaulle did. From the time the opening negotiating sessions took place in October to the end of the year there were many speeches, position papers and the usual paraphernalia of international negotiations; but nothing of any consequence was decided.

The Fouchet committee produced its report in mid-November 1961. It was for the most part a reflection of the ideas that the General had put forward previously – Fouchet himself was not a Gaullist for nothing – with one significant difference: the plan was now for a 'Union of States' rather than for a 'Union of Peoples'. In themselves, those ideas were given a reasonable, if guarded, welcome by five out of the six members of the Community. But the Dutch would have none of it until and unless the British were involved in the negotiations – which meant dealing with the British application first. The two sets of negotiations were becoming inextricably muddled – precisely the situation the General had been so anxious to avoid.

It was all becoming a dreadful mess. Negotiations on the Fouchet plan were more and more bad-tempered, and the British application was bogged down in arguments about the price of butter. Macmillan tried his best to move things forward. He invited de Gaulle to his home at Birch Grove at the end of November. Oddly enough, the choice of Birch Grove was at the General's suggestion; he let it be known that he would like to talk as '*vieux copains*'.[8] Whether the General intended it as a friendly gesture or as just a diversion is unclear, but there were many complications. For a start, there were logistical difficulties: a special refrigerator had to be set up – in the squash court, as it happened – for the stock of de Gaulle's blood that he took with him everywhere in case of an assassination attempt. They had tried to put it in the cook's fridge, but she had complained that it was 'full of haddock and all sorts of things for tomorrow'.[9] Then Macmillan's gamekeeper complained that the security service were tramping around and disturbing the pheasants. It was turning into a disaster.

Disaster indeed it was. The difference between the two men on the future of Europe was set out with complete clarity. France, said the General, did 'not want to change the character of their Europe. . . . they would lose themselves; Europe would have been drowned in the Atlantic'.[10]

It could not have been clearer. But the British persisted, with the support of the other five member countries. When the Fouchet committee was wound up and negotiations about political union came to an end – de Gaulle rejected a 'supra-national' Europe in favour of a 'Europe of States' at his press conference in May 1962 – the British thought that perhaps then their chance had come. After all, on the future political structure of Europe they were at one with the General, and would support him.

Again Macmillan suggested a meeting, and again the General agreed, suggesting it took place in the Château de Champs – another of Mme de Pompadour's residences, just outside Paris – which it did in early June 1962. Both sides seemed content with the meeting, and the atmosphere was good. At one point even Couve de Murville thought that 'we were nearly there'. But there does not appear to have been anything said that was not said at Birch Grove, and the real difficulties, of the Commonwealth and British agriculture, had not by that time been addressed.

If ever there was a time at which the General seemed that he might become reconciled to British entry it was at the Château de Champs. To be sure, he repeated his preference that Britain should stay outside, not least because there could be no nuclear collaboration between the two countries – which Macmillan may have hinted at – without American consent. But at least there was discussion of a common policy on Berlin, and the General himself brought up the issue of defence.

The atmosphere was again soured, however, this time conclusively, by speeches, first from the US Defense Secretary, Robert McNamara, and then from Kennedy himself, describing French nuclear policy as 'unfriendly' and proclaiming the interdependence of the NATO allies. The General was reinforced in his view that Britain could not detach herself from America, and therefore had no place in his Europe.

It was soon after this, in August, that the sticking points came in the negotiations, and even an all-night session did nothing to remove them. On 5 August 1962, the meeting broke up and everyone went on holiday. As Pierson Dixon, the head of the official British team, who had been so optimistic after the Champs meeting, realised, it was really the end of the Brussels negotiations.

It had been the referendum of 8 April 1962 on the Evian settlement with the Algerians that had marked the decisive point of change. The Algerian problem was now to all intents and purposes resolved, and the General could feel free to mount a concentrated assault on the fortified bastions of international politics at which he had been only sniping during the past four years, the best defended of which was NATO. Furthermore, France now had the beginnings of a nuclear strike force. The West Germans had agreed to a Common Agricultural Policy at the beginning of the year, and had convinced the other four Community members – Belgium, the Netherlands, Luxembourg and Italy. The world was beginning to look a much rosier place. The General had regained his confidence; he looked much fitter. Others would say that he became even more arrogant, even more convinced of his own infallibility.

De Gaulle immediately started to assert himself in a much more aggressive manner. He sacked Debré, who had disagreed with his Algerian policy, and put Georges Pompidou in his place as Prime Minister. Pompidou had never held elective office, and had spent the last seven years as a banker; but he had been one of de Gaulle's chief advisers during those years. Indeed, he had looked after the setting up, and running, of the Fondation Anne de Gaulle, and had acted as de Gaulle's literary agent in placing the *Mémoires de Guerre* for publication.

It was quite clear that Pompidou, like Couve de Murville, had been put there simply to carry out his master's wishes; and the General now wished to pursue his third foreign policy option, a French-dominated Europe. The Fouchet plan was dead. Russia would take years, if not decades, to reach the point where a sensible alliance with France could even be envisaged. The North Atlantic directorate was not acceptable to the 'Anglo-Saxons'. There remained the European option. It was to be the consummation of the marriage between the reborn France and the resurgent Germany. The Empire of Charlemagne was to be recreated. The time to do it was then, in July 1962; the occasion, the state visit of the West German Chancellor Konrad Adenauer; the place, quite obviously, Rheims Cathedral.

Adenauer's visit had taken him to Bordeaux on 8 July. The hospitality had been lavish, particularly at Château Margaux. Looking slightly bemused, the old Chancellor flew out of Bordeaux an hour behind schedule. The following day French and German troops paraded side by side on the plain of Mourmelon just outside Rheims. It was the first time, it was remarked, that French and German troops had been on the same side since the battle of Leipzig in 1813 – although even that hardly counted, since the soldiers from Saxony and Württemberg had run away before the battle. This time there were no fewer than 500 tanks from both armies, performing manoeuvres in front of the admiring Adenauer and de Gaulle. It was also remarked that the most senior French general present was none other than General Massu, and that he and de Gaulle exchanged greetings of great cordiality.

From there it was on to the cathedral itself. The two leaders, both in suitably dark suits, arrived at the steps to be greeted by the Archbishop of Rheims, Monsignor Marty, and numerous minor clergy. A silver crucifix led the procession into the church and up the long nave. The General and the Chancellor were ushered to their places, two priesdieu, their kneelers and the seats behind them covered in red velvet, set in the sanctuary to the right of a high altar sumptuously decorated with banks of white roses and lilies. The Mass proceeded with the greatest solemnity. Immediately after the gospel reading, Monsignor Marty welcomed the two men to the cathedral which 'remained the sign of joyous and lasting hope',[11] and went on to preach a sermon on the theme of reconciliation. De Gaulle and Adenauer both knelt for the elevation of the host, Adenauer staying for a long time on his knees.

A crowd of several thousand had been listening to the service in the bright sunlight in the Place du Parvis outside the cathedral, and when the Chancellor and the President emerged they cheered and waved flags. The whole event had gone as well as could be expected. The only cloud in the sky was that the relations between the French and the Germans in the crowd were not nearly as cordial as relations between the two leaders. Indeed, there were some reports of scuffles, and the police had to intervene.

The formal act of reconciliation had been completed, and the General set an informal seal on it by a visit to West Germany in September. He was welcomed wherever he went – at Ingolstadt, where they reminded him affectionately that he had been a prisoner there in the First World War; at the Thyssen steelworks in the Rhineland, where he spoke to the workforce in his fluent German; and in the streets of the towns and villages through which he sped. Couve de Murville intoned on West German television, 'The unity and cooperation of France and Germany shall be today and tomorrow the basis for the unity of Europe.'[12] The voice was that of the Foreign Minister, but the sentiments were those of the President of the Republic.

Between Adenauer's visit to France and de Gaulle's visit to Germany, the General had nearly lost his life at Petit-Clamart, but there was no sign in his behaviour in Germany that anything untoward had happened. In fact, as it turned out, the General was able to use the assassination attempt to his advantage. It allowed him to do what he had wanted to do now for some time: ensure his own direct election by the French people. It would be the final response to the old political parties.

His method of achieving his objective, it must be admitted, was devious almost to the point of deception. First, he announced an interpretation of the constitution which allowed him to do what he wanted. He then broadcast his intentions, on 20 September, to the French people. When, on 1 October, the Council of State declared his interpretation of the constitution illegal, he ignored it and bullied the Constitutional Council into agreeing with him. A bill to provide for direct elections to the Presidency was submitted to the Assembly, which promptly voted it down. Pompidou offered his resignation; de Gaulle rejected it, dissolved the Assembly and announced a referendum on the same bill for 28 October, with general elections to follow three weeks later.

The referendum produced a 62 per cent vote in favour of de Gaulle's bill, although nearly a quarter of the electorate had abstained. The Parliamentarians tried one last throw. Monnerville, the President of the Senate, who had previously called the bill 'a deliberate, thought-out, planned and outrageous violation of the Constitution'[13] referred it again to the Constitutional Council on grounds of illegality. The Council met, but decided that it had no power to declare against laws passed by referendum. The bill was promulgated as law on 7 November.

That evening de Gaulle made his campaign broadcast. He asked for a majority for the loyalist Union pour la Nouvelle République (UNR), and threatened resignation if he failed to achieve it. It was no longer a question of his being in some mysterious way above politics. As with the RPF, circumstances had obliged him to descend into the arena. He needed a majority, and had to say so openly. The electorate responded to his appeal, and returned an Assembly with a clear majority of UNR and Gaullist independents. The General was now securely in power, with an Assembly that had a five-year life ahead of it.

The result, declared at the end of the second round on 18 November 1962, was one of the General's greatest political triumphs. Not only was his administration secure in power but most of the General's bitterest critics had lost their seats. Only Mitterrand had survived. As a consequence, de Gaulle felt that he had come into his kingdom. He was, at last, able to show his true colours.

He proceeded to do so. He had chosen the option of a French-led Europe. It was time to follow the logic of his choice. On 15 December Macmillan made another visit to France, this time to the Château of Rambouillet. The visit started off pleasantly enough with a pheasant shoot. The General did not himself take part, contenting himself with standing behind those who did, remarking with irritating interest on each bird that was missed. When the two men got down to business it became clear that de Gaulle was discouraging. The details of the meeting are even now disputed, but the message was beyond doubt. France was saying 'non'. At the meeting of the Council of Ministers on 19 December, de Gaulle read the funeral notice: 'The poor man [Macmillan] to whom I could give nothing was so sad, so cast down, that I wanted to put my hand on his shoulder and say, as Edith Piaf in her song, "Do not cry, milord".'[14]

In his press conference of 14 January 1963 de Gaulle delivered the final blow. There was, of course, a handsome eulogy of the England that had stood out against the forces of evil in 1940. But the consequent rejection of Britain as a partner in Europe was not just brutal – it was savage.

To be sure, there were sensible and logical reasons why a British entry into the Community was not timely. There were many in Britain, including the Labour leader Hugh Gaitskell, who had told de Gaulle so to his face. But above all, what came across to those present at the

General's press conference was that his whole expression changed, became even wolfish, when the time came for him to shut the door on Britain. The effect was one of politically high-voltage shock. De Gaulle was quite unrepentant. When the old Paul Reynaud, de Gaulle's champion in 1940, wrote to him protesting at de Gaulle's treatment of the old ally and friend, he received after two weeks an envelope addressed to him personally in the General's hand. The envelope was empty. But on the back there was a message, in the same hand: 'In case of absence, please forward to Agincourt (Somme) or to Waterloo (Belgium).'[15] The message was clear. The long shadow of Fashoda was still present, adding an emotional darkness to de Gaulle's intellectual judgement. When England acted against France, as in her close friendship with America, she reverted to her historical role of an enemy. It would ever be thus.

5

A PROFESSIONAL AT WORK

*Talking with de Gaulle was like crawling up a mountainside on
your knees, opening a little portal at the top, and waiting for the
oracle to speak.* ★

General de Gaulle was now at the height of his power. Aged seventy-
three, he was still full of vigour. His Government was firmly in place,
with a secure majority. The second Pompidou administration, formed
after the November 1962 elections, was proving to be smoothly competent in the management of domestic affairs. The 1959 devaluation,
and the accompanying freeze on wages and salaries, had given the
French economy the dynamic boost needed to allow France to cope
successfully with the rigours of the Common Market. As the General
himself said at the time, the Algerian problem had been solved, the
army had returned to its customary discipline under the civil authority,
the franc was strong, and the prestige of France in the world was high.
All in all, it looked as though he would be able to celebrate his fifth
anniversary in office with a large measure of self-congratulation.

Life at the Elysée had also settled into a comfortable rhythm. Always
a martinet in domestic as in other matters, the General had established
a detailed and unvarying routine. He was woken each morning at half-
past seven, made a light breakfast of tea and rusks, shaved and dressed,
and then settled down to an hour or so reading the morning Parisian
press. He went through to his office usually just after half-past nine, and
sat down at the large table at which he worked. On his arrival he found
by his left hand a pile of papers which had been prepared by his private
secretariat – a digest of the morning's press, telegrams of importance and
his diary for the day, together with notes on any visitors that the day
might be bringing and the agenda for discussion.

By 10.30 a.m. the pile had been cleared, annotated in the General's

★ Dean Rusk, *As I Saw It,* page 240; I.B. Tauris, London, 1991.

own hand and removed by the duty secretary. There was no question of dictation; he was not familiar with modern office technology and did not want to be. He even disliked the telephone, particularly when it was used in an emergency which caught him unawares. For instance, in the middle of an Algerian crisis, Delouvrier made an urgent call to the Elysée. De Gaulle came to the telephone, and said impatiently into the machine, 'Hello! Hello! Delouvrier, I can hardly hear you at all.' The poor Delouvrier made the mistake of replying: 'I can hardly hear you either, *Mon Général*.' The retort was quick and decisive: 'Then why are you calling me?' asked the General and promptly put down the receiver.[1] Apart from his instinctive abhorrence of the machine itself, it had broken into what was otherwise a well-ordered day.

By mid-morning the General was ready to receive visitors, the Prime Minister twice a week, the Ministers of Foreign Affairs and Armed Forces at least once a week and the Minister of Finance once a week. In addition, there were other visitors such as ambassadors or foreign dignitaries. At one o'clock, three times a week, there were luncheons, not large – six or seven guests at most. The menu was generally light, but elaborate enough to do justice to his position as head of state. Mme de Gaulle determined what was on offer; indeed sometimes she used to do the shopping herself at Fauchon in the Place de la Madeleine just around the corner. She was particularly concerned that her husband should not overeat, which he was apt to do unless kept on a tight rein.

By three o'clock the General was back in his office reading the first edition of *Le Monde*, which he did from the first to the last page, expostulating from time to time at some particular inanity that he had discovered. After that, the afternoons were occupied either by drafting speeches, which he did on his own, or reading memoranda prepared by his secretariat. Once a week, he allocated an afternoon to receiving letters of accreditation and, twice a week, to receiving visitors.

By six o'clock the formal business of the day was over, and the General discussed outstanding matters with his secretariat, in particular the secretary-general of the Elysée and his principal private secretary. That was a daily event, followed by the retreat to the television room to see the eight o'clock news. This was never missed, unless the General was away on his travels or unavoidably held up by official business. It was, unless exceptional circumstances intervened, a clockwork day and a clockwork week

After the television news it was time to retire, generally to spend the evening with his wife. Both of them liked watching television, even the banal quiz shows of the time. Then there was the cinema, and films were brought in for their entertainment. Yvonne's particular favourite was Jules Verne's *Around the World in Eighty Days*. The General, on the other hand, preferred something more meaty. James Bond films, for instance, were his special choice. Failing a good movie, they liked the popular soap series of the day, and failing all of those, Yvonne would settle down to her knitting and her husband to a good book. Again, it was not all Chateaubriand; the General was an avid reader of thrillers.

Every Wednesday morning there was the meeting of the Council of Ministers. Ministers assembled at a quarter to ten in a waiting-room and, when all were present, moved into the old dining-room on the ground floor. The General joined them at 10 a.m. precisely, followed one pace behind by the Prime Minister. He shook hands all round, and then sat down in the middle – rather than at the end – of the large oval dining table. The Prime Minister sat opposite him.

The business of the day, drawn up by the Prime Minister with the two secretary-generals, the one of the Elysée and the other of the Government, then began. There was little discussion; simply reports from various ministers as and when called for by the General. A long-serving minister, Pierre Messmer, could recall only three occasions in nine years on which there had been a genuine debate. Soustelle, who fell from grace over Algeria and subsequently preferred exile in Switzerland to prosecution for treason in France, believed that the quality of minister was so poor that nobody dared speak – and that furthermore de Gaulle liked it that way.

Decisions were announced by the General, when he had heard enough. 'It is true of course', he wrote later, 'that, having heard [the Government's] views, it was for me to determine the overall direction which it must follow.'[2] As it stands, it is an accurate enough summary of the proceedings of the Council of Ministers. But, as though scenting possible criticism, de Gaulle went on to write, in self-justification, that no one becomes a minister unless he wants, and he can always cease to be one of his own free will.

It was fair comment in one way, but it ignored the reality that ministers were expected to defend Government decisions on whatever subject without question or hesitation. Collective responsibility was imposed without collective discussion. De Gaulle the soldier was at ease with this method of government, although he would have been the first to admit that when he was a serving soldier he was adept at finding ways of expressing disagreement with his superiors. From his subordinates, however – and he regarded his ministers as subordinates – he demanded unquestioning loyalty.

His ministers were one thing, but the French people were another. De Gaulle recognised the need for, indeed drew his strength from, direct communication with those whom he felt to be his primary constituency. In the early years, in 1958 and 1959, repeating his experience of 1944 and 1945, his main method of communication with his compatriots was through his travels in France, with the '*bains de foule*' and speeches from the balconies of the Hôtel de Ville of all the towns that he visited.

As television spread and the number of television sets multiplied, not just in homes but in cafés and bars, he developed the technique of the televised press conferences. Television became a natural medium for his type of oratory. Of course, he broke all the conventional rules. Instead of keeping his head still, he threw it back when he wanted to emphasise a particularly scornful point. Instead of speaking direct to camera without moving, he threw his arms forward, waved them about like a semaphore, with mighty shrugs of his shoulders. Instead of taking his audience into his confidence, he lectured them like an oversize headmaster. He stunned the viewers into attention and, that achieved, bullied them with the force of the personality that came right through the screen and straight at their watching eyes. It almost no longer mattered what he said; the effect was mesmeric. More than Kennedy, more than Macmillan – much more than Macmillan – de Gaulle was the first political star of the television age.

The back-up was elaborate and minutely planned. Twice a year, the General held formal press conferences. He soon stopped answering questions that were actually put to him, making sure that questions were grouped in advance, and then delivering himself of a prepared speech covering those topics on which he wished to pronounce. The stage management was carefully planned. His platform – behind which hung long red velvet curtains through which the General would emerge at the appointed hour – was set up on one side of the huge salon in the Elysée. Ministers were seated in rows to his right and junior ministers in rows to his left, like cathedral choirboys in their best turnout. In front were a thousand journalists, carefully interspersed with trusted supporters, sweating under the vast chandeliers and the television lights. Only when everything was completely ready – and the audience, as one irreverent journalist recalls, fully cooked – did the General stride into his place.

The performance, as he well knew, was that of a virtuoso. He would speak for an hour or more. The text had been minutely prepared in advance, and de Gaulle had learnt it by heart – he had not been to a Jesuit rhetoric class for nothing. He refused to use notes, not just because he considered it beneath him but, more prosaically, because he could not read them without his spectacles, and he was far too vain to appear with them. But there were almost no slips. Of course, he always asked his aides after the event whether it had gone well. He need hardly have asked – partly because he would never have received an honest answer, but principally because he was fully conscious of his own virtuosity. He often remarked that he had fought the war against the Germans with the radio, but that he could beat the French politicians with the television. He was even confident enough on one occasion to make a joke about a comedian, Henri Tisot, who not only looked like de Gaulle but was able to imitate his voice and gestures almost to perfection. Just before his entrance on that occasion, the General muttered, half self-mockingly, 'I must try to match up to the national parrot.'[3]

If the technique was effective, and it was, it was at least in part because events had moved in favour of the General. His later press conferences were less impressive. But in early 1963 it seemed that he could do no wrong. Yet even then, almost exactly halfway through his long period in office, the political tide had started to turn against the General. His success until then had been to create the impression that he stood for a France that was proud, stable and united. He *was* France. Even the words that he used – '*rassemblement*', '*grandeur*', '*indépendence*', '*ordre*' – conveyed a sense of national cohesion. Anybody who was against these concepts was 'factional', 'divisive', 'mediocre', 'decadent'. The tactic had undoubtedly worked. Opposition to de Gaulle had to struggle against the all-pervading sense of a de Gaulle that was the incarnation of France herself.

Furthermore, the General had succeeded by his constitutional reforms, and the long consensus over Algeria, in neutering his political opposition. Social disputes could no longer be successfully argued out in the Assembly, since debates there no longer mattered. Since they did not matter, the Assembly itself had ceased to perform its primary role. It had ceased to be a political safety-valve. But if there was no safety-valve within the political process, there was only one place to go: on to the streets. It was when the General's opponents took to the streets that they found, somewhat to their surprise, a good deal of sympathy from the public around them. The miners were the first, in March 1963. After

the miners, it was the turn of the electricity workers, the railway workers, rubbish collectors and even government clerks. France had again
become a country in which the political process reasserted itself, but in
a violent and extra-parliamentary manner.

This change in the tide was to take several years to work itself out,
and it was certainly not appreciated by commentators at the time. As for
de Gaulle, it is doubtful whether he ever fully understood it. He
believed that he had set France on a course of political and economic
stability which was permanent. To be sure, the idea that the Fifth
Republic might be in danger was a theme that he used on a number of
occasions, but it became less persuasive as time went on, and he was
adamant that there was no danger as long as he was at the helm. Later
events were to demonstrate the fragility of that view, but in the meantime it was, so to speak, business as usual.

6

BAITING UNCLE SAM

*Sir, I am willing to love all mankind, except an American.**

It was not only the British – indeed, some would say it was not primarily the British – who were the object of the General's attack at his press conference of 14 January 1963. The United States was put in its place as well. President Kennedy had tried to 'throw the French a bridge back into NATO'[1] by offering to supply Polaris missiles for French submarines – the same offer as he had made to the British. The condition was that France would assign to NATO command the units that carried those missiles. The General was not even grateful for the offer. 'Putting our forces into one multilateral force, under foreign command, would be to go against the [main] principle of our defence and our policy.'[2] In return he accepted 'cooperation' with the Americans, just as he had offered 'association' with Europe to the British. In neither formula would France's policy aims be compromised. But he knew perfectly well that neither the United States nor Britain could or would be satisfied with his proposals. If the truth were told, they were probably little more than a tactic to deflect criticism.

The General's underlying assumption was that the United States would in the course of time withdraw from the defence of Europe, as it had done after the First World War. France would then have to assume the role of nuclear protector. Nothing could have been better calculated to irritate the Americans, who were well aware that the French nuclear strike force was primitive by their – and Soviet – standards; and who suspected that the General was preaching 'independence' in a particularly self-indulgent manner, knowing full well that

* Dr Samuel Johnson, in James Boswell's *Life of Johnson*.

the United States was essential to the defence of Europe but not wishing to acknowledge the fact openly.

The American response was immediate. Kennedy held a press conference of his own. 'There may be reasons,' he said in a carefully controlled voice, 'for a country to wish a nuclear force of its own, and France has put forward its reasons, but in my judgement it is inaccurate and not really in the interests of the Alliance for it to justify itself on the grounds that the United States would fail to defend Europe with whatever means necessary.'[3]

Macmillan was equally angry about the General's rejection of Britain's efforts to join the Common Market. He went on television, looking bleak and depressed. 'France and her government', he said, 'are looking backwards. They seem to think that one nation can dominate Europe and, equally wrong, that Europe can stand alone.'[4] In private, he was even more bitter. He said on the telephone to Kennedy that de Gaulle was 'simply inventing any means to knock us out and the real simple thing is he wants to be the cock on a small dunghill instead of having two cocks on a larger one'.[5] Couve de Murville, he wrote, had 'behaved with a rudeness which was unbelievable'.[6]

It was not the sort of response that had ever impressed the General, nor did it now. Besides, he was about to produce his second ace. On 22 January 1963 Adenauer and de Gaulle signed in Paris a Franco-German treaty. To be sure, it was at Adenauer's request that it was a formal treaty rather than a memorandum; but that suited the General's purposes perfectly. The treaty in many respects was uncontroversial. It provided for exchanges of pupils in the two educational systems, for the teaching of French in German schools and vice versa, and so on. But most controversially, it also provided for consultations between the two Governments 'before any decision, on all important questions of foreign policy . . . with a view to reaching, as far as possible, analogous decisions'. The spider had woven his web well. It is no wonder that the pro-American German Foreign Minister, Gerhard Schroeder, was seething with anger on the way back to Bonn.

It nearly worked. The General's solution for Europe, in default of the Fouchet plan, seemed now to have been put in place. It was quite simple, as Macmillan had written as long ago as November 1961: 'He talks of Europe and means France.' The new Franco-German treaty, of 'friendship and cooperation' as it was called, was the cornerstone of the recreation of the Empire of Charlemagne – in other words, a French-led Europe.

It nearly worked, but in the end it failed. Neither the declaration of independence from the United States nor the Franco-German treaty went at all according to the General's plan. Kennedy's riposte to the Franco-German treaty was quick and decisive. He made a flying visit to Europe in June, a visit whose political highlight was his speech in Berlin – 'Ich bin ein Berliner' – assuring West Germany of US support. He then reiterated his proposal for an Atlantic community based on equality between the North American and European pillars.

This was enough to encourage de Gaulle's pro-American opponents in Bonn. The West German parliament watered down the treaty. In its final version it included a preamble that required the German Government to implement it in such a way as to encourage the general aims of the Federal Republic – in particular, to maintain close relations with the United States and to preserve the integration of western forces within NATO. Jean Monnet, it was said, had been working behind the scenes.

For the General, it was more than simply a great disappointment. He had worked hard for five years to achieve the Franco-German understanding of which the treaty was the culmination, and had relied upon his common heritage with Adenauer to bring it to fruition. In fact, it was the first serious diplomatic reverse that he had suffered. But he was philosophical in defeat. By the time he visited Bonn in early July, de Gaulle seemed to be resigned to the failure of the treaty to live up to his hopes. He was even able to manage an elegant quip: 'Treaties, you see, are like young girls and roses; they last as long as they last.'[7]

The General's declaration of independence from Washington had provoked annoyance elsewhere. The Dutch and Belgians particularly, and to a lesser extent the Italians, supported Kennedy's proposal for an Atlantic community. They depended on NATO for their defence, and did not in the least want that relationship to wither. Even the Soviet Union, when approached through its ambassador in Paris, refused to be drawn into a more accommodating relationship with France. It, too, had an unspoken understanding with the United States which, after Cuba, it did not wish to disturb.

The General aggravated diplomatic tensions by withdrawing French naval units in the Atlantic from NATO command in June and by refusing to sign the Moscow nuclear-test-ban treaty in August. Neither of those moves impressed his European partners, while causing, it need hardly be said, much irritation in Washington. But they were all now getting used to that. As Kennedy said of a meeting he had with Couve de Murville. '[We] had to admit that we were not in agreement on any-thing.'[8] It was no more and no less than the truth. The stalemate was complete.

By early 1964 much had changed – and none of it to de Gaulle's advan-tage. Adenauer had given way in August 1963 as Chancellor of West Germany to Ludwig Erhard, the architect of the revived West German capitalism, who was intensely pro-American. Furthermore, United States influence in the world had markedly increased, and the Soviet Union's had correspondingly declined, as a result of Kennedy's handling of the Cuban missile crisis in October 1962 and the consequent weak-ening of Khrushchev's internal position.

Worst of all, from the General's point of view, Kennedy's assassination in November 1963 had brought to the presidency Lyndon Johnson – a Texan politician known as 'Landslide Lyndon' after he had won election to the Senate for the first time by the margin of a handful of dubious votes stuffed into the ballot box in a remote small town in southern Texas. De Gaulle, the product of a northern France and a Jesuit educa-tion, might have hoped to get on with a Roman Catholic Irishman from Massachusetts such as Kennedy, but he could never hope to get on with Johnson, the rough product of Texan politics. It was all too pre-dictable. In the event the two men met only twice – once at Kennedy's funeral and once at Adenauer's. The best that de Gaulle could say about the new President was that he had a curious face that reminded him sometimes of Popeye.

If the international climate for the General was becoming more stormy, there was no comfort for him domestically. To be sure, with the devaluation and wage freeze of early 1959, which had itself followed a devaluation by the Gaillard Government two years previously, the French economy had caught the upswing of world trade and the dis-mantling of tariff barriers in Europe at the right moment. At the time it had all seemed very simple. Growth was averaging over 5 per cent per annum; trade was in surplus; inflation was under control; foreign exchange reserves were greater than they had ever been; and the reor-ganisation of the French industrial base, under the Planning Commission, commanded universal praise. De Gaulle was convinced that he and his Government had discovered the golden touch – the way to sustained growth and simultaneous modernisation of the industrial base. It was a mistake that many governments, before and since, have made.

There certainly had been an economic transformation, but it was at great social cost. Older industries had been left to die without ceremony. Unemployment was rising; the benefits of modernisation were unevenly spread. Sooner or later there was bound to be a volcanic eruption. It came in the early spring of 1963. The first seismic shock occurred in the mines of the northern coalfield. The pits in the Lille basin were old-fashioned and mined poor quality coal. Markets were weak and production was declining. Besides, the textile industry in the north was moribund; there was no other work if the pits closed.

The confrontation with the northern miners in March 1963 was almost a rebellion. Tens of thousands of miners marched on Paris after calling an all-out pay strike on 1 March. De Gaulle was appalled. These, after all, were his people – men from the north, with whom he had fought in the 33rd Infantry in the First World War. Not only that, but by their action they were casting doubt on the General's conviction that the peaceful economic miracle had arrived. Above all, they were defying the legitimate authority, and that had to be stopped.

On the unanimous advice of Pompidou and his ministers, de Gaulle signed a decree declaring the strike illegal and ordering the miners to resume work. It was a dreadful tactical mistake; the miners simply refused to budge. Furthermore, they found themselves, as miners frequently do on occasions of this kind, widely supported by the public. It was the end of winter, and supplies of coal to the home were getting short. Besides, for the first time for four years there was something that looked like a political crisis, and many felt that the Government had grown too smug. By April 1963, the General's approval rating in the polls was down to 42 per cent – the lowest it had been since his return to power.

The Government took the only way out. To save face, Pompidou appointed a committee of 'three wise men', who duly recommended a settlement very close to the miners' original claim. That crisis was over, but others had learnt the lesson, and they were going to use their new knowledge. De Gaulle could no longer be sure of his own people, and the opposition parties saw a new life in front of them

After four years in the Elysée, surrounded by ministers and officials who were naturally reluctant to tell him the full truth, it is hardly surprising that the General failed to understand the underlying nature of the social discontent. He thought that it was yet again a case of his compatriots becoming bored and fractious, and he therefore continued regardless with his international campaign.

In January 1964 the French Government formally recognised communist China. It was, as *Le Monde* reported, 'a double coup, since Washington cannot disguise its anger or the French Left its embarrassment'[9]. It was as though the General seemed determined to give offence. His state visit to Mexico in March, during which he called repeatedly for closer relations between France and Mexico, might have been specifically designed to irritate the Americans. On 16 April he broadcast on French radio and television, officially a summing-up of his first four and a half years as President, but in fact an assertion of France's international role in Latin America, Africa and Asia, and a denunciation of the 'two hegemonies'. On 6 June he refused to attend the Normandy ceremonies marking the twentieth anniversary of the American and British landings in 1944.

Of course, the logic in all these moves is quite clear. It was de Gaulle's continuing and consistent ambition, of which he never made any secret, to promote what he perceived as the greatness of France. But if the logic is clear there is no doubt that the method was unnecessarily abrupt. It was certainly part of the campaign to spring surprises, to catch the headlines; but even so, some of the General's attacks at this time seem to show a persistent hostility to the United States – now aggravated by personal dislike of President Johnson. True, throughout his Mexican trip he had been in considerable pain from an enlarged prostate – and had to be cared for by a medical retinue of considerable size – but by June he was well again, and the boycott of the Normandy ceremonies was reminiscent, for those with long memories, of his vindictive treatment of Lady Spears's ambulance unit at the VE Day parade in June 1945. It now seemed to be the Americans' turn.

On de Gaulle's return from Mexico, his doctors told him that surgery to remove his prostate could no longer be avoided or delayed. On 16 April 1964, immediately after his broadcast, he was admitted to the Cochin hospital for the operation, which was to take place the following morning at eight o'clock. He had by then drafted two texts. One, handed in a sealed envelope to Etienne Burin des Roziers, the secretary-general at the Elysée, was marked 'Only to be opened after my death; but you will return this to me the day after tomorrow if, as I believe, everything has gone well.' The other was the text of the announcement to be issued following the success of his operation.

The secret was kept from everybody except his immediate family, intimates such as Malraux and Palewski, and Prime Minister Pompidou.

Gaston Monnerville, who, as President of the Senate, would become head of state in the event of de Gaulle's death, was not informed. He and the rest of the world learnt of the operation, and its success, only when de Gaulle's own draft had been officially released – and Burin des Roziers had given back the envelope with which he had been entrusted.

The announcement, when it was made, had an effect as dramatic as that of the announcement of the attack at Petit Clamart in August 1962. Suddenly the General seemed mortal, a thought which had hitherto seemed absurd. There was talk, of course, as there always is on such occasions, of the succession. For a very brief twenty-four hours, Pompidou had had a taste of the supreme power – he had received express delegation, as the constitution allowed and the situation dictated, to take the chair at the Council of Ministers and, if necessary, to order France's nuclear strike force into action. Even after the announcement that the operation had been successful, there were still a few days of relative glory while de Gaulle was convalescing. Pompidou made good use of them. In a debate in the Assembly on 24 April, he set out his view of the role of the Prime Minister: 'I could not continue if I were not in agreement with the head of state . . . [but] I consider it an elementary duty of a Prime Minister never to reveal in public differences which might occur between him and the head of state.'[10] It was a bold move. Up to that point nobody had imagined that the function of the Prime Minister was anything other than carrying out the General's instructions. The Dauphin was growing up.

The impact on the General himself was more subtle. Certainly, he himself had intimations of mortality, witness the letter for Pompidou – written in spite of the assurances of his surgeon that the operation was virtually risk-free. Equally, the 'shipwreck of old age' was suddenly much closer. On the other hand, Pompidou's behaviour while he was out of action irked him sufficiently to spark off some lively reprisals. The result was that when the General came out of hospital on 27 April, he came close – but not too close – to recognising Pompidou as his heir apparent. He told him to get out more, travel in France and abroad, to get himself known. Yet, at he same time, he made it clear that nothing was assured; the position of Prime Minister was in the gift of the head of state, and everyone should remember it. Pompidou was left not quite knowing where he stood – which was precisely how the General wanted it.

De Gaulle now seemed to feel a sense of urgency. He was nearing seventy-five, had survived a serious operation, and was having trouble with worsening eyesight. His campaign for international recognition of France's true stature moved up several gears. By the end of May 1964 he was fit enough to go to Metz and Trier; by mid-June he was off on another tour of northern France, and on 2 July he paid an official visit to Bonn. On 20 September he set off on a tour of ten countries in Latin America.

The General's Latin American pilgrimage in the autumn, like his trip to Mexico in the spring, seemed to be another deliberate affront to the United States. At the time of Kennedy's funeral there had been a diplomatic muddle with the new President, ending in an apparent refusal by de Gaulle to call on Johnson – although it was not clear that a formal invitation had ever been received. The incident had not been forgotten either in the Elysée or in Washington, and de Gaulle's Latin American visits only served to reopen a particularly unpleasant wound. 'Gaullist policy towards the Third World,' wrote the *New York Times*, 'irritates the Allies and baffles the French . . . President de Gaulle's second visit in six months to Latin America, while he refuses to come to Washington, draws attention once again to the continuing deterioration in Franco-American relations.'[11]

Worse was to come. De Gaulle knew that the one constant factor in Latin American politics was an intense and abiding dislike of the powerful neighbour to the north. By emphasising France's role in the world and the historic ties between French and Hispano-American culture, and adding to the cocktail a thinly disguised hostility towards the United States, the General knew that his reception would be ecstatic – and it was. But, as the temperature soared in Latin America, it sank to freezing-point in Washington.

In reality, the Americans need not have worried as much as they did. For all the uncomfortable rhetoric, delivered in the General's very respectable Spanish, there was nothing much that France could do in practice to help the countries of Latin America, even if she had wanted to. De Gaulle's hosts, too, knew that perfectly well. But it was irritating. For more than a century the United States had regarded South and Central America as its own 'backyard', and did not want any unwelcome intrusions. 'De Gaulle,' wrote *Paris-Presse* rather gloomily on his return, 'has just poached on private and protected hunting ground.'[12]

The General was unabashed. He seemed to thrive on American criticism. 'You know,' he said to Malraux, 'my only real international rival is Tintin. We are the small people who do not allow themselves to be taken for a ride by the big ones. Nobody sees the likeness, because of my height.'[13]

De Gaulle's seventy-fourth birthday on 22 November 1964 passed, as always, without public attention but with a family party – of growing numbers as grandchildren appeared – at Colombey. But this did not stop the General from going to Strasbourg the same day to speak at the ceremony which marked the anniversary of the city's liberation in 1944. Life at home had to take second place to official engagements. He was in a hurry.

The next major move against the United States – apart from a final and successful assault in October 1964 on the American proposal for a multilateral nuclear force – was on the economic front. Since the end of the Second World War, the western world had operated with fixed exchange rates based on the US dollar and the commitment of the US Treasury to buy gold, whenever and wherever presented to it, at $35 an ounce. At his press conference on 4 February 1965 – after France had bought $150 million worth of gold the previous month – the General demanded a return to the pure gold standard of the 1920s and 1930s, in other words an end to both fixed exchange rates and the 'hegemony of the dollar'.

It was a strange press conference. The General was obviously on uncertain ground – monetary economics was by no means his long suit – and his method of overcoming the difficulty was to speak of gold in a romantic manner, as 'eternal . . . which does not change in its nature, which can be shaped equally into bars, ingots or coins, which has no nationality . . .' and to point nostalgically to the gold standard that operated 'before the great misfortunes of our century'. He had been carefully coached by Jacques Rueff, but his language and demeanour were less confident than usual.

The attack, however clumsy, had its effect. The Americans were again furious – there were even anti-French demonstrations in the streets, with bottles of French wine broken open and the contents poured into the gutters. As if this attack on American monetary pre-eminence was not enough, there was also a widely leaked letter to the North Vietnamese President, Ho Chi Minh, disapproving of 'foreign' – that is, American – intervention in Vietnam. Johnson was by now resigned to the situation. 'When General de Gaulle winds up to pitch,' he remarked in baseball language, 'I step out of the batter's box.'[14]

On 9 September 1965, de Gaulle announced that France would cease to accept 'integration' within NATO after 1969 and that he

attached great importance to 'the new trend taken by our relations
with Russia'. Three weeks later Couve de Murville told the United
Nations that France would sponsor communist China as one of the five
permanent members of the Security Council.

Even the Europeans were not spared. On 30 June, after the failure of
negotiations on the future of the Community agricultural policy –
France objecting that the European Commission's proposals were too
'integrationist' – the General ordered all French participation in
Community institutions to cease. The 'empty chair' policy was in place.
The Common Market came to a full stop.

It was all very high-handed, as all diplomats – of whatever nationality other than French – hurried to agree. But the truth is that in the
latter half of 1965 particularly, but even before then, de Gaulle's joke
that Tintin was his only international rival was a reasonable reflection of
reality. There was no serious competitor. Johnson, after demolishing his
opponent in the Presidential elections of November 1964, had become
embroiled in the Vietnam War and racial violence in the United States.
Khrushchev had been overthrown by the uncertainly balanced trio of
Brezhnev, Kosygin and Podgorny in October 1964. Harold Wilson, the
new British Prime Minister, was skating on an almost invisible majority in Parliament; and the leaders of France's Common Market partners,
Chancellor Erhard included, were scuttling about like frightened chick-
ens with no clear idea of the direction in which they should go.

Nowhere was this situation more openly demonstrated than at the
funeral of Winston Churchill on 30 January 1965. Among all the statesmen who had come to pay their final respects in St Paul's Cathedral on
that morning, the tall figure of the General stood out. On hearing of
Churchill's death, he had written to the Queen, 'In the great drama he
was the greatest of all.' His message to the British Government had
been: 'I see in the passing away of this very great man the death of my
war companion and friend.'[15] But looking round the cathedral, de
Gaulle was bound to think that there was nobody of Churchill's stature
in the modern world, apart, that is – and de Gaulle would not have
been de Gaulle if the thought had not occurred to him – from the
General himself.

Yet domestic politics were starting to press in on him. The first
Presidential elections to be held under universal suffrage were due to be
held in December 1965. The General had to decide whether or not he
was prepared to fight. There was no doubt that there would be a fight.
Ever since the miners' strike, opposition parties, with a new heart, had

been organising themselves. An opinion poll at the end of June of that year showed de Gaulle at 50 per cent, a Socialist/Centrist candidate at 29 per cent and a Communist candidate at 11 per cent. It was promising without being overwhelming. What was clear, however, was that the General's ideal – de Gaulle remaining over and above the rough and tumble of electoral fistfights – was no longer sustainable.

The decision was by no means easy. Yvonne was all in favour of his retiring to Colombey, and was heard to express her view openly – a rare event – to his advisers. Besides, his eyes were bad. Some thought that he was afraid of becoming another aged Pétain. But the decision, one way or the other, had to be made. On 29 June de Gaulle called a meeting at the Elysée of his closest supporters: Malraux, Palewski, Debré and Pompidou. They set out their views in turn. Pompidou was guarded – de Gaulle later said that he had advocated retirement. Malraux took Yvonne de Gaulle's line – that a further seven years would destroy the image of what had been achieved, and it was better to leave it at that. Palewski was in favour of continuing – he spoke in adulatory tones of the General's health and wisdom. Debré was the most enthusiastic. The General, he pointed out, should not be dictated to by a mere electoral calendar. He should continue to guide France until he himself felt it was appropriate for him to retire. None of their remarks was free from the taint of personal ambition, as the General realised, and he concluded the meeting by saying only that he would bear what they had said in mind and would let them know his decision in due course.

It was – probably – all in the balance, since his wife's voice was a powerful one. But it so happened that the Elysée meeting had coincided with the Brussels meeting at which Couve de Murville had broken off negotiations with the other members of the Community over the agricultural problem. It was obvious that there would be a crisis in Europe, and there was nothing like a crisis to breathe fresh life into the General. It seems almost certain that at that point the decision was taken to fight.

Nonetheless, it was not de Gaulle's habit to show his hand too soon, even to his Prime Minister. Pompidou was kept guessing until early September 1965, when he was informed privately that the General had decided to stand – but he was also told to keep it to himself. De Gaulle continued to tease the press at his conference of 9 September, in spite of their evident and growing irritation, particularly since Mitterrand had announced his candidature that very day.

Mitterrand had, to be fair, chosen his ground well. He had made sure of the support of his own Socialist Party, and of the Communists, who had realised that Mitterrand was the only prospect if de Gaulle was to be beaten. He had also been endorsed by Pierre Mendès-France. Admittedly, there had been a late effort by the socialist Mayor of Marseille, Gaston Defferre, to launch a non-communist federation of the left, but, although at first blush exciting, in the end it came to nothing.

It was Mitterrand's candidature that is said to have provoked the General. Although he did not give him a chance – polls at the time were showing 70 per cent against him – he had noted Mitterrand's consistent and bitter opposition over the years, and decided to let it be known that he considered a personal challenge had been issued which he could not refuse. That was what was given out by the General's friends, but perhaps the more likely truth is that de Gaulle, like most ageing public figures, was reluctant to give up office, and any excuse to stay on would do.

On 4 November 1965, the General finally announced that he would present himself as a candidate at the approaching Presidential elections. In fact, it was the first time in his long life that de Gaulle had ever presented himself as a candidate for popular election to anything. On all previous occasions, his advance had been by simple assertion – as in the war – or by election by a committee or electoral college. This was the first time that he had had to woo the people – and, if the truth be told, he was not sure quite how to do it.

It showed in his campaigning. After his opening, somewhat lugubrious, television broadcast announcing that either he was elected or the country would descend irretrievably into chaos, he declined to participate. He was almost drawn into the battle against his wishes by a bizarre intrigue of international espionage, which in the end became something of a scandal, known as the Ben Barka affair; Ben Barka being an unfortunate left-wing Moroccan who had been tortured and then whisked out of France under the noses of, or perhaps with the connivance of, the French police. Roger Frey, de Gaulle's Minister of the Interior, seemed to be in some way implicated – although nobody was quite certain how. Mitterrand spoke darkly of the 'unhealthy' activities of a certain number of political police who did the Government's dirty work.

But de Gaulle was not to be drawn. He wished to remain above the battle. It was a mistake. His Minister for Information, Alain Peyrefitte, seeing the polls starting to slide away, pleaded with him to speak, to make his appeal less lofty and more personal, as the other candidates were doing. He did not get very far. 'Really, Peyrefitte,' replied the General, 'do you want me to sit myself down in front of a television camera and say: my name is Charles de Gaulle and I am seventy-five years old?'[16]

Peyrefitte, of course, had been right. He knew the campaign was going badly, but he could do nothing without the General's approval. He managed to secure agreement for Debré to engage in a debate on television with Mendès–France, but no more. De Gaulle's last appeal, on 30 November, was a flop. He attacked his opponents but put forward no constructive ideas of his own. He looked neither well nor confident. 'It was either sabotage or incompetence,' was the general response of those professionals who watched – the majority inclining to the second view.

On Saturday 4 December, de Gaulle left Paris for Colombey to await the result of the first round, which would take place the following day. The final opinion polls had been discouraging: 43 per cent de Gaulle, 27 per cent Mitterrand, 20 per cent Jean Lecanuet, the centre candidate. On the Sunday, the General shut himself up in his study until teatime. The tension was obvious: he did not go for his usual afternoon walk; he took no telephone calls. He was waiting, with his wife, for the verdict of the people of France. At 8 p.m. that verdict started to come through. De Gaulle was polling around 43–44 per cent, Mitterrand around 32–33 per cent, Lecanuet less than 16 per cent. There was no doubt; it was going to a second round.

The General was depressed and angry. He knew that he had made a mistake in treating a Presidential election as though it were a single-issue referendum. When Pompidou, Joxe and Peyrefitte called from the Matignon in Paris, they heard nothing but criticism, particularly of himself, fury about Mitterrand and doubt about the future. They insist-ed that he should fight the second round. Peyrefitte took him through the electoral arithmetic, concluding that the margin between him and Mitterrand was too great for Mitterrand to bridge. Most of Lecanuet's votes were anti-Mitterrand rather than anti-de Gaulle. The telephone went silent. The General said he would think about it. But when Pompidou rang again an hour later he seemed to have made up his mind. He would fight Mitterrand.

On Wednesday de Gaulle took the chair at the Council of Ministers as usual. What was not usual was his opening remark. 'I was mistaken,' he said to his ministers, who could hardly believe their ears. 'It was I, and I alone,' he went on, 'who mistook an election for a referendum. Of course, I will persevere.'[17]

That was the signal. The General was going to fight. All his supporting staff moved into battle positions. Malraux, Maurice Schumann, François Mauriac were all brought into action. The General himself agreed to be interviewed, albeit by a friendly interviewer. Again, he insisted that the 'parties of yesterday' were trying, by using the mechanism of direct elections to the presidency, to restore the old discredited regime. The air started to thicken with insults. Mitterrand responded in kind, with a series of calculated verbal assaults.

Peyrefitte had done his sums well. When the results came in on that Sunday evening, they were just all right, but far too close for the General's comfort: de Gaulle 54.6 per cent, Mitterrand 45.4 per cent, on an 85 per cent poll. De Gaulle carried the over-forties, especially women, and did well in the north, west and east. Mitterrand was an easy victor among the young and carried the areas south of the Loire.

The General had won, but it had not been the victory that he had been hoping for. As one respected commentator of the day remarked, 'De Gaulle will never be the same. He has had to behave as a candidate, to take part again in a party political battle . . . he has abandoned sainthood, and come down from the level of mysticism to the level of ordinary politics.'[18] It was true. De Gaulle would never be the same; but just how far his authority had been eroded, just how far he had ceased to be the father of his country and had become a party politician like any other, remained to be shown. In the aftermath of the election, the General greeted his new Council of Ministers, headed again by Pompidou, and shook each of them by the hand in his usual manner. But it was noted that the head was less confidently poised, the hair whiter, the stoop more pronounced. The General seemed suddenly to look, and perhaps to feel, very much older.

7

ALL THE WORLD'S A STAGE

Il nous reste beaucoup, beaucoup, beaucoup à faire. ★

Old soldiers never die, it used to be said – or rather sung. They only
fade away. As much can be said of old politicians, even of the greatest
among them. General de Gaulle was by now one of the greatest of old
politicians. He was certainly not ready to die. To be sure, he had
thought of fading away, of giving up the presidency after what he had
considered to be a humiliating election result – had, indeed, been
encouraged to do so by his wife – but in the event the thought of relinquishing power had been too unpalatable. Old soldier that he was, he
decided to soldier on.

But, as is so often the case, the decision led in the end to disappointment and eventual defeat. Even before the convulsions of May 1968,
events were leaving him behind; the world was moving into an era
beyond his time. The years 1966 and 1967 seemed to pass without great
achievement or great events that could have roused the General to his
former energy and enthusiasm. There was, of course, intense activity,
but with hindsight the activity seems to have been little more than that,
an old soldier's longing for the noise of battle, while the modern world
was passing him by, feeling only that, whatever disturbances the General
might create, it was enough to wait for his successor.

Disturbances, of course, there were in plenty. There was grand theatre in both 1966 and 1967, and it was played on a wide international
stage. Domestic matters hardly concerned the General during these
two years. To be sure, the Ben Barka affair erupted again at the beginning of 1966, but de Gaulle was able to dismiss it as 'vulgar and

★ 'A great, great, great deal remains for us to do.' Charles de Gaulle, on the eve of the
1967 local elections, *Discours et Messages*, vol.5, page 148; Plon, Paris, 1970.

second-rate'.[1] But for the rest, the domestic scene was suitably calm. Furthermore, 1966 saw a resumption, and 1967 an acceleration, of economic growth, with the consequent decline in industrial unrest. Pompidou was in charge of domestic policy, with Debré at finance. The country was looking, and feeling, prosperous.

In January 1966, France settled with the other five Common Market members at Luxembourg with an agreement – which came to be known as the 'Luxembourg compromise' – that no measure, even if it was within the ambit of the Treaty of Rome, would be pressed by the other five members if it was against the 'vital national interest' of one. Another French objective was achieved – the adoption of a common agricultural policy, clearly favouring France's own farmers – which could not have been achieved by the usual negotiating procedures. There were, as always, those who resented de Gaulle's negotiating techniques. As Monnet later wrote, 'If [de Gaulle's] aim had been to freeze the Community's institutional development and prevent any further transfers of sovereignty, he had gained nothing but a little time, which for the Europeans was wasted time. What de Gaulle denied them in 1965 they have since acquired as a matter of course.'[2] But it is not clear which 'Europeans' Monnet was speaking for, or by what right he was speaking for them.

The fact was that there had to be a settlement. The Common Market had ceased to function without France, and the French electorate had felt embarrassed – the issue had damaged de Gaulle in the Presidential elections. But, that settlement concluded, the General's agenda could now be extended: there was still NATO to be dealt with. He knew perfectly well that he could not manage two crises at the same time. One had to be settled before the other broke. The Five had therefore to be placated before the General struck at NATO.

That done, de Gaulle was ready to move forward. He was careful to disguise his true intentions, even going so far as to tell one of the western ambassadors at the annual dinner for the diplomatic corps on 10 February that France did not intend anything dramatic. He followed this up at his press conference of 21 February with hints referring to NATO as an 'American protectorate' – but he said nothing specific. Immediately after that, however, he astonished his ministers by instructing them, as a matter of urgency, to prepare briefs not only on the implications for France of withdrawal from the NATO command structure, but also of more momentous withdrawal from the alliance itself.

This, of course, was quite new. The General had always accepted the need for alliances between sovereign states and rejected supra-national command structures. He now seemed to be prepared to go much further, rejecting all alliances. There was panic in the French Foreign Office, where officials saw the prospect of a France friendless and alone. They thought the General was going much too far – perhaps (dare they say it?) he was even a bit past it. In the end, they managed to find the conclusive argument which brought de Gaulle back from the brink: France would be, they pointed out, a much more attractive prospect for the Soviet Union if she stayed within the North Atlantic alliance, able to create mayhem when she wanted, than if she left.

In the event, their argument won the day. But this did not prevent the General from acting with typical abruptness. On 7 March 1966 de Gaulle wrote messages in his own hand to Johnson, Wilson, Erhard and Giuseppe Saragat, the Italian President. They were almost identical, but with some subtle variations. The message to Wilson expressed fears that France would be pulled, against her wishes, into the Vietnam War; the message to Johnson made no mention of that. On the other hand, the General told the US President that France would remain in the alliance, and 'plans as of now to remain, when the time comes, a party to the Treaty'.[3] That part was not in his letter to the others. In his message to Chancellor Erhard, the General referred to the Franco-German treaty, but by a slip of the pen mentioned 1869 as the year of the treaty rather than 1969. The Germans were worried that the General believed himself to be poised for the Franco-Prussian War of 1870.

It was, as all admitted, very disconcerting. Both Dean Rusk, Johnson's Secretary of State, and McGeorge Bundy, the Secretary of Defence, went before a congressional committee and confessed that they were flabbergasted by the turn in French policy. Bundy was particularly critical. Even the Soviets were doubtful. If the French withdrew from NATO, they thought, the Germans would fill the vacuum and that, with the memories of the Great Patriotic War still uppermost in their minds, was far from a happy thought. Nevertheless, the message to France's NATO allies, whatever the differences between one version and another, was simple. French forces would no longer be assigned to NATO command – although French troops would remain in Germany under French command; all French officers and staff would be removed from their NATO functions; Supreme Allied Headquarters in Europe would move from French territory; and in future no units or installations would be allowed to remain in France unless they were under French control. Furthermore, on 29 March 1966, the General set deadlines: 1 July for French staff to leave allied commands, and 1 April 1967 for foreign troops to leave France.

It was all very dramatic, and much resented by his supposed allies. But the General, by now hardly bothering to tell his ministers what he was doing, continued on his course. He insisted, however, that his ministers defended his decisions even though they had not been party to them, and Pompidou duly did so in three successive speeches on 13, 14 and 20 April.

This done, the time had come for the General's next move: the counterpart to his detachment from the NATO military command. It was to be reconciliation with 'Russia'. France in future was to be placed firmly between the two great power blocs, belonging in military terms to neither and able to mediate between both where appropriate. De Gaulle did not believe – indeed, he had never believed – that the Soviet empire would last. In truth, he had hardly ever, in his mature years, believed in empires as such, as his opening speech to the Brazzaville conference in January 1944 had hinted. Nation states – yes; empires – no. The Soviet empire would therefore break up in the course of time. It was at that time that France, the quintessential nation state, would play a pivotal role.

These thoughts – and many would say this vision – were the basis for the article by General Ailleret in the *Revue de la Défense Nationale* later in the year. The theme of the article, which had previously been read and endorsed by the General, was that France's nuclear shield should offer protection from whatever quarter a threat could arise. In the West this was interpreted as yet another example of Gaullist arrogance; and so, to some extent, it was. But the General, in foreseeing the break-up of the Soviet empire, accurately as it has turned out, had also foreseen the possibility of new threats to France, from wholly unsuspected directions.

In immediate reality, of course, the General was fully aware that in the shorter term, if there were serious conflict between the West and the East, France's place would be with the West. He had demonstrated as much in the support he had given Kennedy over the Cuban missile crisis of 1962. But, the perception among the western allies of France's policy was of virtual neutrality between the United States and the Soviet Union and, in the longer run, as the aspiring leader of a 'Europe' that would include 'Russia', at least as far as the Urals. That was to be the grand, if somewhat hazy, design. Nor was the perception wholly wrong. It was to set the stage for that position of virtual neutrality that

Couve de Murville was sent on official visits in May 1966 to Poland and Czechoslovakia. They were but the prelude to the General's own state visit to the Soviet Union in June.

The General himself arrived in Moscow on 21 June 1966. It was a grand occasion. His departure from Paris had been accompanied by the familiar ceremonial. Ministers were lined up to see him off. The police escort and cavalcade arrived with lights flashing and sirens blaring to deposit the General – and a clutch of accompanying ministers and offi-cials – on the tarmac in front of the carpet leading to the steps into the aircraft. Mme de Gaulle was one step behind him. His doctor, with medical equipment, particularly for emergency blood transfusion, which seemed to have become heavier as the years went by, was already on board. So were his personal bodyguards, armed with automatic pis-tols. The General shook hands solemnly with each of the waiting ministers, climbed slowly, with his party behind him, up the steps, and out of sight – or, at least, out of television coverage.

The reception ceremony at Moscow airport was equally impressive. As a head of state, he was greeted with a broad red carpet and a line of Soviet dignitaries, each of whom he shook by the hand. A cavalcade of cars, accompanied by a motorcycle escort with flashing lights and blar-ing sirens, set off on the journey from the airport to the Great Palace in the Kremlin and thence, after a brief meeting of welcome, to the French embassy.

The Soviet leadership ensured a tumultuous reception for the General. A million people, it was said, turned out to greet him when, the day after his arrival, he spoke from the balcony of Moscow City Hall. His theme was Franco-Russian friendship, and he celebrated it, in his usual manner on such occasions, with a few carefully rehearsed sen-tences in Russian. He was then taken on a long tour, just as he had taken Khrushchev on a long tour of France in March 1960. He was taken to Novosibirsk, to Academgorod in Siberia, Zezdograd in Kazakhstan, back to Leningrad, on to Kiev in the Ukraine, from there to Volgograd and finally back to Moscow. The General seemed to take it all in his stride. He particularly enjoyed a banquet in his honour in Leningrad, at which he is said to have attacked the food with a solid *coup de fourchette*. Mme de Gaulle, on the other hand, was reported as being slightly intimidated by the surrounding company of 'Bolsheviks'.[4]

It was all quite exhausting, and it was perfectly understandable that the General slipped in his language at the University of Moscow, when he spoke of the 'new alliance of Russia and France'.[5] His aides were quick to correct the slip, reminding the accompanying press that it was not an official occasion. Their reminders were the less convincing in that in private, and indeed in public, the General seemed consistently to refer to the Soviet Union as 'Russia' and to Leningrad – although this only in private – as 'St Petersburg'. Nevertheless, in his formal speeches, he stuck to his official line: that 'détente' should continue until it became 'entente'; and that 'entente' was, and should remain, a purely European matter.

Even while the General was in Moscow his next move was leaked. He would go to the Far East in August to visit Cambodia, travelling by way of French Somaliland and Ethiopia. It seemed that he could never stay still. Even on his return from the Soviet Union, when he might have been expected to take a few weeks' rest, there was no let-up. Between 1 July and 25 August, when he left for his Far Eastern trip, the General fitted in a series of receptions for heads of state of former French territories in Africa, a state visit from the King of Laos, attendance at the customary 14 July ceremonies at the Arc de Triomphe, and a further journey to Bonn to see Chancellor Erhard and to call on Adenauer.

When it came, the General's journey to the Far East was just as long and tiring as had been his journey to Russia. It took him through East Africa, to Cambodia, to New Caledonia and the New Hebrides, to French Polynesia and finally to Guadeloupe in the West Indies – all in the space of eighteen days, three of which were spent on board the cruiser *De Grasse* watching a French nuclear test at Muraroa in the Pacific.

The nuclear test was much publicised in the French press, and provoked corresponding irritation in Washington and throughout the whole Pacific. But if continued French nuclear testing was an irritation, it was nothing to the seismic effect of his speech in the Phnom Penh stadium in Cambodia. The Cambodian Government had made sure that his reception was all that he could want. 80,000 people were in the stadium, many with placards which, when they were raised simultaneously on a signal, spelt out '*Vive Général de Gaulle*' in huge characters along the whole of one side of the stadium. The General could not have been more delighted, and in his turn he gave the Cambodians exactly the message that they had hoped to hear.

It was openly hostile to the United States. Conveniently forgetting France's imperial past – and his own devotion to it – he condemned American intervention in South-East Asia root and branch. 'There is', he pronounced, 'no chance that the peoples of Asia will subject themselves to the law of the foreigner who comes from the other shores of the Pacific, whatever his intentions, however powerful his weapons.'[6] The crowd roared its approval.

Not so Washington, as might be imagined. Some thought the General was no longer to be taken seriously, that he was simply an old man making mischief; others were furious that he seemed intent on making as much capital as possible from American discomfort over Vietnam – 'cynical anti-Americanism', they called it. Whatever the opinions, it was clear to everybody that the United States could no longer regard de Gaulle even as somebody to be placated; the Phnom Penh speech had finally ensured that the General would in future have no influence on United States policy. He had moved beyond the area of possible compromise.

But the General was, as always, undeterred. At his press conference of 28 October 1966 he described events in Vietnam as 'the bombing of a small people by a very large one'; and he was even rougher at the turn of the year, describing the war as an 'unjust war, since it results from the armed intervention of the United States on the territory of Vietnam, a detestable war, since it leads a great nation to ravage a small one.'[7] It sounded strong, and was reported as such in the French press. The difficulty was that his anti-American position had by now become so extreme that anything he said was heavily discounted outside France. Nobody in Washington was any longer listening to him.

The General fared little better in his attempts to woo the Kremlin. Prime Minister Alexei Kosygin reciprocated de Gaulle's visit to the Soviet Union with an official visit to France from 1 to 9 December 1966. But the discussion was conducted at cross-purposes. The Soviets wanted France to recognise East Germany – their continued preoccupation being a resurgent and possibly revanchist West Germany, against which they needed secure defence. The General, on the other hand, was seeking something different: a new structure for Europe within which 'Russia', Germany and France would be reconciled and Europe would once again belong to the Europeans, without American intervention and under French leadership. The Soviets thought that he was talking nonsense, and as a result the Kosygin visit produced nothing beyond polite expressions of goodwill.

1967 opened with the usual ceremonial good wishes from the President of the Republic to the armed forces and to the citizens of France, but it was difficult not to notice an atmosphere of increasing boredom, at least in Paris. The first half of the year passed calmly enough for the General, although there were some irritating distractions. There were, for instance the Assembly elections of 5 and 12 March, which saw a drop in Gaullist support and produced a majority of only one seat for the Gaullists and their, by now uncertain, allies – and the formation of the third Pompidou administration.

Most irritating of all was the decision of the British Government to renew its application to join the Common Market. Prime Minister Wilson had become a late convert, and his journeys around the capitals of Europe with his Foreign Minister, George Brown, had convinced him that the door could now be forced.

The problem was by now familiar. De Gaulle regarded Britain as an American dependency – 'Trojan Horse' was the expression used in Gaullist circles – and as such not a 'true' European. At his press conference on 16 May 1967, he raised the customary objections, together with new objections about the role of sterling as a reserve currency. It was now almost a matter of routine. France's five partners in the Community supported the British application. De Gaulle opposed it. 'In what kind of society are we living,' Jean Monnet expostulated, 'if the Six are to reject without debate the request of a great democratic country, massively backed by its elected representatives, to join in the building of Europe?' Monnet's problem was, of course, that there were many in Britain who did not share his idea of Europe, and who were more in sympathy with the General's view. The argument was by no means clearly in one direction only.

Although de Gaulle did not manage finally to bury the second British application until November, it was obvious to everybody that the roadblocks he had raised were impassable. As it happened, the whole matter was driven off the front pages by a much more interesting event – a new crisis in the Middle East. The General had been attending a football match on 21 May at the Parc des Princes stadium – the final of the Coupe de France – at which he had surprised those around him by his knowledge of the game, referring frequently to his youthful career as full-back in the college team at Antoing. No sooner had he returned than he learnt of the blockade of the Gulf of Akaba ordered by the Egyptian leader, Colonel Gamal Abdel Nasser. It was immediately clear that the world was facing a full-scale and dangerous crisis.

The General, of course saw his chance to play the world role that he had always coveted. He met Abba Eban, the Israeli Foreign Minister, on

24 May, and warned him against launching offensive action. At the same time, he invited the United States, the Soviet Union and Britain to a conference at which the whole Middle Eastern matter could be resolved. Oddly enough, under the circumstances, the Americans and the British agreed but the Soviets – again oddly enough – turned the project down. On 2 June the General issued a statement warning that 'the state that would be the first . . . to take up arms will not have [France's] approval or, even less, her support'.[8] In fact, nobody took much notice – least of all the Israelis, who promptly launched what became known as the Six Day War. The Egyptian air force and armour was taken out by surprise raids, the Syrian infantry was forced off the Golan Heights and the Jordanians were ejected from east Jerusalem.

The aftermath of the war was a time of international confusion. Nobody knew what to do next. Kosygin arrived in Paris on 16 June to canvas French support for the Soviet view that there should be an emergency meeting of the United Nations General Assembly. Kosygin's argument was that the Six Day War had seriously disturbed the East–West balance in America's favour, and that Soviet interests were thereby threatened. True to form, the General surprised his allies, and his ministers, by giving his unqualified support to the Soviet position. Not only did the General give Kosygin his support, but, after dealing with an official visit by Prime Minister Wilson – at which, it need hardly be said, no progress was made on the British application – he went on to deliver a homily to the meeting of the Council of Ministers in the fiercest terms. The text of his homily was subsequently published – 'a violent text', one commentator described it[9] – blaming the United States' intervention in Vietnam for the situation in the Middle East. This was followed up by the General's comments at a reception at the Elysée on 22 June 1967, where he remarked that France had been led to take a position similar to that of the Soviets, for different reasons. The Americans thought that he had taken leave of his senses.

But more was to come. The next theatrical event was de Gaulle's visit to Canada. It started quietly, with a stop at St Pierre et Miquelon. From there his ship, the cruiser *Colbert*, took him to Quebec City, at the mouth of the St Lawrence river and the scene of the defeat of the French General Montcalm in 1759. Quebec province was, at the time, agitating for independence from Canada, and it came as a shock to the outside world to hear the General salute Quebec City as 'the capital of French Canada'.[10] The shock was the greater when he spoke, at a dinner in his honour, of Quebec as 'a part of our people . . . after . . . French sovereignty had been wrested from its territory two hundred years ago', and of the wish of the French part of Canada to organise 'in conjunction with the other Canadians means of safeguarding . . . their independence in contacts with the colossal state which is their neighbour'.[11] In other words, the General had turned the whole thing – yet again – into an attack on the United States.

The melodrama continued. De Gaulle drove the last forty miles into Montreal standing upright in his car. It was said that up to half a million people were waiting for him in the centre of the city. When he spoke from the balcony of City Hall the excitement was almost uncontrollable; and the General did nothing to calm it. On the contrary, he raised the level a further notch. 'This evening', he said in his most sonorous tones, 'and all along my route, I found myself in an atmosphere like that of the Liberation.' As if that was not enough, he went on to finish: '*Vive Montréal! Vive le Québec!*' There was a pause, and then came: '*Vive le Québec libre!*'[12] It was, of course, intolerable; but the crowd enjoyed it enormously. The noise of cheering could be heard halfway across Montreal, and it went on as though it would never stop. The General stood quite still. He knew perfectly well the effect that his words would have.

The effect was indeed explosive. Lester Pearson, pushed into action by Jean Marchand and Pierre Trudeau, the two French-speaking federalists in his Cabinet, issued a statement that what de Gaulle had said was 'unacceptable'. Somewhat oddly, however, the statement went on to say, as did Pearson himself when he went on television, that discussions with the General would continue in Ottawa later in the week.

De Gaulle ignored the olive branch. He had no wish to go to Ottawa and rang Pompidou in the middle of the Parisian night to tell him so. He had decided to return to Paris. After a day spent touring Montreal – 'It's the first time since 1936 that I have taken the Métro'[13] – there was another speech at City Hall, only slightly less inflammatory than the previous one; then the General and his entourage, followed by a crowd of journalists, drove out to the airport and took off for home.

Mme de Gaulle, undoubtedly sensing trouble, immediately immersed herself in a book. But the General was obviously still in a state of high excitement. He interrogated his fellow travellers one by one in the forward cabin, which had been arranged as a small sitting-room for himself and his wife. 'What do you think?' he asked. It was a difficult question to answer in a way that would satisfy the General. Only one civil servant was apparently obsequious enough. '*Mon Général,*' he said, 'you have paid the debt of Louis XV.' It was said without a blush. 'I knew I had to do something,' the General replied. 'I would no longer have been de Gaulle if I had not done it.'[14] It was the clearest possible statement of the view, already set out in his memoirs, that there were in his mind almost two separate people: 'I' and 'de Gaulle'. If 'de Gaulle' demanded a particular course of action, 'I' could not possibly refuse to follow it, whatever the immediate cost. The alternative was to abandon the mission which the General, at least by now, felt was his by destiny.

The reaction in the foreign press was predictable, but this time the French press turned against the General. *Le Monde* was very critical, *Le Figaro* scathing. The provincial newspapers worried that France was not strong enough financially to assume the burden of supporting an independent Quebec. Even his ministers, assembled dutifully to welcome the General back at Orly airport at 4 a.m., were starting to complain. 'This time he has gone too far,' said one. 'He's mad,' said another.[15]

On 10 August de Gaulle made a defiant broadcast. He referred to the unanimous and indescribable desire for emancipation that the French of Canada had shown the President of the French Republic. This in turn provoked a reaction from Valéry Giscard d'Estaing, the leader of a bloc of forty or so Deputies in the Assembly, who openly talked about preparing 'France for her future'. The agenda of 'après de Gaulle' now became, for the first time, the subject of intense and widespread discussion in Paris.

Again, none of this deterred the General, who seemed by now to be listening only to himself and those advisers who told him what he wanted to hear. His visit to Poland, from 6 to 12 September 1967, simply confirmed this. There was little to be gained politically from the trip. The old Franco-Polish friendship was toasted and memories of 1920 evoked. For the General, of course, it was a sentimental journey. The journalists who accompanied him still speak of de Gaulle's deeply felt emotion when he spoke of Poland. 'It was as though he was speaking of a woman,' said one,[16] and there were those who recalled the stories of the young Captain de Gaulle, the Countess Strumilla and pastries from Chez Blikle. On his tour of Warsaw Cathedral, the General stopped deliberately for a moment at the tomb of Marshal Pilsudski – 'I knew that man,' he remarked to those around him. He had made his point.

There were, of course, the formal occasions. A speech calling for joint efforts to build a new European order from the Atlantic to the Urals fell on deaf ears, President Gomulka replying that Poland was quite happy with her alliance with the Soviet Union. The General did manage to please his hosts when he confirmed his support for the western frontier of Poland along the line of the rivers Oder and Neisse. That did not offend the West Germans, who had known in advance what he was going to say.

What did upset them, however, was his speech in a small cinema in Zabrze, which the Germans claimed as theirs and still called by the German name of Hindenburg. The General seemed to go out of his way to refer to the town as 'the most Silesian of all Silesia, and that means the most Polish of all Poland'. It was, to say the least, an unfortunate slip of the tongue, if that indeed was what it was. The German journalists were furious as they congregated outside the cinema. Kempski, the doyen of them all, declared formally, 'De Gaulle is finished.'[17] Another could not stop laughing, helplessly sliding to the ground in mirth. Other journalists gathered round – there were two bus loads of them – but could make no sense of it all other than that the General had succeeded in making the maximum amount of mischief, and drawing the maximum attention to himself – which, if the truth be told, was probably the object of the exercise.

The General returned to what was beginning to seem like an attack on the whole of the rest of the world at his press conference on 27 November 1967. His line was even harder, confirming the opinion of one diplomat that age was hardening his prejudices without blurring his style. He was again in favour of the gold standard; he called the Jews 'an élite people, self-confident and dominating'; he proclaimed the arrival of Quebec to 'the rank of a sovereign state, master of its national existence'; he dismissed the British application as the 'fifth act of a play during which Britain's very diverse attitudes with regard to the Common Market come one after another without seeming to be alike';[18] and finally he criticised the French press for its hostility over his visit to Canada. All in all, the General was in his most robust form, and all his targets were duly offended.

But de Gaulle was now seventy-seven. He had been in power for nearly ten years. The last two years had seen him become progressively more isolated in his own quasi-royal court. In Poland there had been stories of meetings cancelled, of an erratic timetable due to periodic 'indispositions'. He had lost touch, too, with his fellow countrymen. Furthermore, he himself was becoming rather bored. In April 1968, the

General was to say to one of his closest aides, Captain Flohic, 'This no longer amuses me much; there is nothing any longer to do which is difficult or heroic.'[19] In view of what was to happen the following month there is more than a touch of irony about the message he had delivered at the New Year: 'One does not see how France could be paralysed by crises like those from which we suffered in the past. . . . In the midst of so many countries shaken by so many jolts, ours will continue to set the example of efficiency in the conduct of its affairs.'[20] It was a bold statement, and it could not have been more wrong.

8

THE IDES OF MAY

Dix ans – c'est assez!★

1968 could easily be described, by those given to such fancies, as the year of the General's Waterloo. To be sure, it was not a defeat at the hand of foreign enemies, as in 1815, but it was a defeat nonetheless. The events of May, in their ferocious explosion of French youth, fatally undermined his domestic position; and the Soviet invasion of Czechoslovakia in August, with its cynical and unconcealed brutality, finally destroyed his hopes that France could achieve independence through neutrality in the struggle between the two great power blocs.

Unlike Napoleon, however, the General lived in freedom, albeit with grievous political wounds, to fight another day. Admittedly, even in 1966 and 1967 living was becoming more and more burdensome unless there was the stimulus of foreign travel. It was becoming more and more difficult to make the Monday morning journey from Colombey to Paris, and the working day at the Elysée had been cut down to a maximum of six hours. The General's eyesight was failing badly – a television broadcast had to be retaken because the General had addressed the French people staring blindly at the wrong camera – and the difficulty of wearing spectacles with an ever thicker lens made the hazards of travel more threatening. After his '*Québec libre*' speech from the balcony of the Montreal City Hall, for instance, he had stumbled, and almost fallen, on the staircase leading down, missing a step as he quickly took off his spectacles before facing the crowd outside. Since mid-1966, too, he had lost the taste for tours of the French provinces, with the accompanying '*bains de foule*'. The fact was that without his spectacles he simply could not see and, sensitive always to his physical

★ 'Ten years – that's enough!' Students' slogan during the riots of May 1968.

appearance, he refused to go into a crowd with horn-rimmed glasses perched on his large nose. It looked ridiculous, and simply would not do.

But no prospect of defeat was on the horizon at the beginning of 1968, or in the sunny months of the early Parisian spring. Certainly, there was some minor unease in the economy, with unemployment on the increase and wages moving up more slowly than inflation. Higher education was also a problem, with the universities physically unable to cope with the growing number of students, which had more than doubled in ten years. There was the matter of women students, and the official policy of segregation in student residences, which needed to be addressed. If there was a new spirit of student protest abroad, from a generation which had not known the Second World War and was shocked by the cynicism of Vietnam, it was, or seemed to be, no more than youth letting off its usual steam. 'France is bored,' commented *Le Monde* on 15 March; but if that was all it was, there was no cause for great concern. Life, therefore, after the hectic travels of 1966 and 1967, started to take on a relatively leisurely tempo – at the Elysée during the week and at Colombey during the weekends. But it was not to last. Indeed, it was all too quickly to be shown to be an illusion by the earthquake of May.

Even in February the first tremors had been felt – in the University of Nanterre, a bleak enough place in the western suburbs of Paris. Built in the 1950s with prefabricated slabs of concrete and plaster into anonymous tower blocks which housed dreary students' halls and lecture rooms, it was, and is, an environment enough to depress any young and idealistic student. In 1968 it was a nursery for all the characteristics of French youth that the Gaullist culture detested: rock and roll, hamburgers, and the sexual revolution of the Pill.

In mid-February, François Missoffe, Minister of Youth and Sport, went to open an indoor swimming pool at Nanterre. His speech was rudely interrupted by a red-haired German student by the name of Daniel Cohn-Bendit, demanding, with vociferous support from his friends, an end to separate accommodation for male and female students. Missoffe managed to avoid argument by diving into the new swimming pool, but Cohn-Bendit and his friends were not to be so easily deflected. On 22 March they not only invaded the girls' hostels – with some encouragement, it should be said, from the residents themselves – but also burnt an American flag. That was altogether too much. The police were called by the university authorities and duly made a number of arrests, thinking that the whole matter would thereby be calmed down. The response from the students, far from being calm, was to raise the level of protest. Led by Cohn-Bendit, they occupied the whole university – and followed the occupation with a sit-in. The subsequent negotiations were long and acrimonious, and the students were finally persuaded to return to normal life only on the understanding that their grievances would be heard in the highest places.

The General himself duly heard a report at the meeting of the Council of Ministers on 3 April 1968. There was to be no question, he said, of student cohabitation – even if the General himself had been inclined to accept that proposal Mme de Gaulle would have had her say – but it was decided to reform the process of university entry, by removing the automatic right for anyone who had passed the baccalauréat and instituting a selection procedure. It was a bad tactical error. The students at Nanterre now had two grievances: first, that nobody had paid any attention to their demands; and, second, that the Government had introduced a new measure directly hostile to their interests.

Throughout April the situation at Nanterre was little short of anarchic. By 1 May it had become so bad that the General had to tell Christian Fouchet, the Interior Minister, to put a stop once and for all to the whole Nanterre incident; and on the following day the university was closed. It was another tactical error. The student response was to evacuate Nanterre and, still under the leadership of Cohn-Bendit, to march the twelve miles into the centre of Paris and occupy the Sorbonne.

By the morning of 3 May the students were encamped in the main courtyard of the university, and had started to tear up paving stones for barricades behind which to defend themselves. At this, Fouchet made the third tactical mistake. Encouraged by Peyrefitte, who assured him – probably rightly – that he was following de Gaulle's own line, Fouchet ordered the police in to clear the Sorbonne.

It was the first time since the Revolution that the civil power had broken into the precincts of the University of Paris. Not only that, but they did so with wholly unnecessary force. Four students were arrested and locked up in the Santé prison. Ejected from the Sorbonne, the students, by now commanding a great deal of public sympathy, occupied the Odéon and a large section of the Latin Quarter. 'Free our comrades!' they shouted – the revolutionary slogan of all time. So far from being freed, their comrades were sentenced to two months' imprisonment

At that point the Boulevard St Michel and the surrounding streets became a battlefield. On the night of 6 May barricades were thrown up, made of grilles torn up from the streets and doors wrenched from neighbouring shops. Cars were overturned and set on fire. More riot police were drafted in – many from Corsica, so it was said, just in case the Parisians were too sympathetic to the students. Clouds of tear-gas enveloped the students and police alike. It was a shambles. By midnight there were some 400 student injuries, and 200 police had to be taken to hospital.

It went from bad to worse. By now, the Parisian public, horrified by the police violence, were siding openly with the students. The next day 20,000 students and sympathisers assembled at the Arc de Triomphe, waving red flags and singing songs before returning to the Latin Quarter. All sense of order appeared to have broken down. The Government, from the General downwards, seemed paralysed. Pompidou was in the middle of an official visit to Iran and Afghanistan, leaving Joxe, as deputy Prime Minister, to do the best he could. The General kept on muttering that the situation was '*insaisissable**', while insisting, as he did to a group of Deputies on the afternoon of 8 May, that 'violence in the street cannot be tolerated'.[1] Quite so, but nobody in the Government had any clear idea how to stop it.

The worst night was that of 10/11 May. There was an all-night running street battle of unrelenting ferocity between the students and their supporters, now growing in number, and the riot police. The General went to bed before 11 p.m. Nobody dared to disturb him. But, while he slept, the fights raged on. It was not until 2 a.m. that Joxe finally gave the order to the riot police to storm the barricades. It was not until 5.30 a.m., after a fierce battle, that Cohn-Bendit told his troops to disperse.

De Gaulle was woken at 6 a.m. by Joxe, who reported that order had once more been established on the streets of Paris. But the cost had been heavy: 370 injured, nearly 500 arrests, more than 100 cars burnt. The mess would take days to clear up, and relations between the police and the people of Paris had been seriously – perhaps permanently – damaged. Joxe suggested reopening Nanterre and releasing the four imprisoned students; but the General would have none of it. The only thing to do was to await the return of Pompidou that afternoon.

But the students' revolt now took on a whole new dimension. The brutal police tactics of the night before had been described in detail by radio reporters, with running commentary from the scene throughout

---

* Literally, 'ungraspable'.

the night, and public opinion, as Joxe had told the General, had been deeply affronted. The trade unions, particularly the communist Confédération Générale de Travail (CGT), could no longer keep out of it. Their members simply would not let them. Besides, if ever there was a chance to attack a Government in disarray and secure large wage increases, this was it. The CGT therefore called a one-day general strike for the following Monday, 13 May. It was now not just a confrontation between the forces of order and some wild students but a confrontation between the Government and the whole labour movement.

Pompidou tried to defuse the crisis over the weekend. In spite of de Gaulle's initial objections, he persuaded both his ministerial colleagues and the General that the Sorbonne should be reopened. But the peace lasted only 24 hours. The next collision came with a Communist-led demonstration on the Monday, coinciding with the general strike. It started, as all good revolutionary marches in Paris start, from the Place de la République. By the time it reached the Place de la Concorde, over 250,000 marchers were shouting slogans which, for the first time for ten years, included demands for de Gaulle's resignation: 'Ten years – that's enough!' 'De Gaulle to the museum!' At one point, the major threat was that the students would cross the river from the Left Bank, join the demonstration and, together, with the marchers, storm the Elysée. The General's naval ADC, François Flohic, prepared the evacuation. 'Don't worry, Flohic,' the General said, 'the Communists will keep them in order.'[2]

Indeed, the Communists, either as a party or as a trade union, had not the slightest wish to stage a coup d'état; de Gaulle was too valuable to Moscow, they believed. If they jumped on the revolutionary bandwagon, which they were forced by circumstance to do, it was only to slam on the brakes. The General understood their aims as well as anyone, and it was in the expectation that they would succeed that on 14 May, leaving Pompidou in charge with complete authority, he set off on a long-planned state visit to Romania.

It was an extraordinary time to go, and the visit turned out to be nothing if not bizarre. The General and his party were welcomed at Bucharest by President Ceausescu, to whom he conveyed France's warmest friendship. He embarked on a heavy schedule of visits and speeches. Mme de Gaulle, knowing how tired he was, asked for his programme to be light, but the General wanted all his time to be occupied. It was as though his energy came flooding back when he escaped from

France. On 17 May, for instance, he returned to Bucharest from Craiova – some 200 miles – standing upright all the way, his car travelling slowly so that the crowds could get a good view of him. The journey itself took four hours, and there were stops – and improvised speeches – at Stalina, Pitesti, Tirgoviste and Ploesti, all in a temperature in the mid-eighties. On his arrival at Bucharest, the General thanked his exhausted staff and went off to dine alone with his wife. He seemed to take it all as a light day's work.

Nevertheless, the news from France was getting worse. The trade unions had lost control of the strikes that they had encouraged and the students were still on the rampage. The General was forced to cut short his stay in Romania by a day. By the time he arrived back in Paris on 18 May, ten million workers were on strike and the country was at a standstill. He was furious, and treated the sheepish ministers lined up to meet him at Orly airport to an hour-long tirade in the language of the barrack room. Then he took Pompidou with him in his car and continued the barrage. Pompidou offered his resignation, which was curtly refused. 'One does not abandon one's post in the middle of the battle. First of all, the war must be won. After that, we will see.'[3]

It was the same story the following morning. Pompidou was summoned again, this time with the men whom the General called 'those responsible for order', Fouchet, Pierre Messmer, Georges Gorse and Maurice Grimaud, the chief of police in Paris. 'In five days,' he told them, 'ten years of struggle against idiocy have been lost.'[4] He wanted the Odéon evacuated by the next day, even if it meant using force. He wanted news broadcasts on radio and television brought under proper control and the police to take a tougher line. Finally, he told Gorse to let it be known that his views could be summed up simply: '*La réforme, oui; le chienlit,* * *non.*' After that, he virtually shut himself up in the Elysée to prepare the text of a broadcast he was to make on 24 May. There is no doubt that, after the exhilaration of Romania, the General had been badly shaken by what he had found on his return to France. During the ensuing three days, he seemed to at least one visitor, who had not seen him for some time, to be old and indecisive, his stoop accentuated. It seemed as though it was all getting too much for him.

The broadcast of 24 May, when it came, was a complete flop. The General looked, and sounded, shifty and scared. True, he announced a referendum on 'participation', but it was not clear what the precise

---

* The meaning has been much disputed, but the favoured translation is 'mess in the bed'.

terms of the question would be, and it seemed to those who heard him to be suspiciously like a device. He said that it was the duty of the state to ensure public order, but his voice lacked its old resonance, and the phrases, although still in the same solemn language, somehow no longer carried conviction. He came across as an old man, tired and wounded. He knew it himself. 'I missed the target,' he said that evening.[5] The best that Pompidou could say was: 'It could have been worse.'[6]

But in fact it could hardly have been worse. As though encouraged by the failure of de Gaulle's broadcast, the students that night burst out of the Latin Quarter, crossed the Seine and headed for the business sector of the city – the Bourse and the Banque de France. They sang as they went, and shouted their slogans: '*L'imagination au pouvoir!*' and '*Le chienlit, c'est lui*'. They went on to try to burn down the Stock Exchange – ineffectively as it turned out – and rampaged through the Right Bank as though the new Revolution had come.

All the old memories of the Paris Commune of 1871 were revived. The city was again self-destructing. The lawful authority seemed powerless. The General was holed up in the Elysée, alone but for his closest staff and military ADCs. The police set up barricades in every main boulevard, and on every corner there were armoured vans with police in riot gear. Nobody else ventured out.

The crisis gradually passed as the night wore on. The students drifted raggedly back across the river. The police presence became more discreet. Best of all, it seemed as though the trade unions were prepared to negotiate a return to work. They had had enough of youthful irresponsibility. It was time for men to take charge.

But de Gaulle's mood, on the morning of the 25th, had turned for the worse. He was, in the words of one of his ministers, 'prostrate – stooped and aged'.[7] He kept on repeating, 'It's a mess.' Another minister found an old man who 'had no "feel" for the future'.[8] The General sent for his son Philippe, who found his father 'tired' and noted that he had hardly slept. Philippe suggested that his father might make for the Atlantic port of Brest – shadows of 1940 – but was told that he would not give up.

From 25 to 28 May de Gaulle remained in a state of profound gloom. Pompidou's negotiations with the trade unions had been a farce. He had simply given them all they asked for: sweeping increases in pay and social benefits, and an increase in the minimum wage of 35 per cent. The only snag was that, even after the deal had been signed, the CGT had insisted that it would have to be ratified by their membership.

Georges Séguy, the CGT leader, hurried off to the Paris suburb of Billancourt, where 12,000 Renault workers were on strike. When the agreement was put to them, they humiliated Séguy by turning it down flat. The accords of Grenelle, as they were called, were stillborn.

The Council of Ministers met at 3 p.m. on 27 May, soon after the Renault workers' rejection of the Grenelle accords. The General presided, but it was noted that his heart and mind were elsewhere. He stared at his ministers without seeing them, his arms flat on the table in front of him, his shoulders hunched, seemingly 'totally indifferent' to what was going on around him.[9] There was a discussion about the referendum; the General apparently heard only bits of it.

The students were cock-a-hoop, believing that the natural alliance between students and workers was now poised to take power. Their union called a meeting at the Charléty stadium on the evening of 27 May to celebrate their triumph. Scenting blood, Mitterrand called a press conference on 28 May to announce his candidature if de Gaulle stepped down and to demand Pompidou's resignation and the formation of an interim government. The Communist Party called for mass demonstrations for the next day, and word got about that they were preparing a coup d'état.

It was time for a show of force, but the General seemed incapable of rousing himself. The troops were there. A brigade of 'armoured police', with light tanks at their disposal, was waiting just to the south of Paris. The 2nd Armoured Brigade was on alert at Rambouillet, ready to move. There were motorised brigades at Montlhéry and Maisons-Lafitte, within easy reach of Paris, and parachute units at Castres and Carcassone ready to fly in. Yet no sign came from the Elysée.

Constitutionally, of course, it was clear that it was the Prime Minister who had the right to call on the armed forces to maintain public order. In practice, Pompidou could not act without the General's approval. In the light of what promised to be a Communist insurrection the following day, he met de Gaulle after dinner on the 28th to seek that approval. It was likely, he told the General, that the demonstration would be peaceful. The Communists had, after all, sent a message through one of their Deputies that they were not trying to dislodge the General, and indeed would support him, on the understanding that, as after the Liberation, he would bring Communist ministers into his government. On the other hand, since the demonstration would pass within 800 yards of the Elysée, it was as well to be prepared for the worst.

De Gaulle thought that Pompidou was underestimating the danger, but in fact the analysis was right. It was not, as he interpreted a 'revolutionary situation' in the classic Marxist–Leninist sense. The Communists wished to hold a demonstration simply 'to let everybody know that the Party is the only one to command the big battalions, and, as a consequence, the only possible alternative if the State collapses'. That was what Moscow had – almost certainly – instructed, and that is what they would do. In that case, Pompidou went on to point out, it was the end of the crisis. The Communist Party was determined to stop the stampede to revolution, and that meant, in his own words, that 'we will win'.[10] 'You are optimistic,' replied the General gloomily. 'Besides,' he went on, 'you have been too optimistic since the beginning.' Pompidou left without any clear guidance. Fouchet arrived next, to be told by Bernard Tricot as he went in, 'He is not at his best.' Again the General was depressed, but less so than earlier. It seemed, Fouchet reported to Pompidou afterwards, that 'he had something in mind'.[11]

What neither of them knew was that there had been an incident involving Yvonne de Gaulle that afternoon in the Place de la Madeleine while she was on her shopping expedition. She had been recognised by a passing motorist, and had been stopped and then shouted at by a group of shop assistants, who told her that she had 'slandered' them. It was the first time that anything like that had happened to her. At dinner that evening she broke down, and the meal had to be abandoned. She complained bitterly, not only about the incident, nor just about the Elysée itself, which she hated, but also about the situation faced by her son and grandchildren, who had to cross a hostile picket line every time they went in or out of their house. It was all too much, and she had had enough.

The General knew that he had to get her away from Paris. He himself also needed a rest. 'He was tired and depressed,' said one of his aides. 'He spoke continually of resigning.'[12] Pompidou came to see him after dinner, when he had started to take decisions again – but they were family decisions, not to be divulged to his political associates, however close, particularly Pompidou. He told his son that he had instructed General Lalande, his principal military adviser, to arrange for transport for the whole of his son's family, including Philippe himself, to the headquarters of General Massu, now commander-in-chief of French forces in West Germany, at Baden-Baden. He recalled his son-in-law, Alain de Boissieu, away from his command of the 7th Division at Mulhouse on the Rhine and back to Paris. Mme de Gaulle telephoned her brother, Jacques Vendroux, to pick up her maid the next day and

take her back to her home near Calais. In the meantime, the maid had
to do a lot of packing – 'much more than usual', she said.[13]

Early in the morning, after another night of fitful sleep, the General
summoned Xavier de la Chevalerie, his principal private secretary, and
told him that he was tired and was going to Colombey to rest. He
instructed Lalande to go personally to Generals Beauvallet at Metz,
Hublot at Nancy and Massu at Baden-Baden, to find out their views
and assess the state of their troops. Lalande was also to tell Massu that he
was being entrusted with the safekeeping of Philippe and his family. An
hour later Tricot was told by the General to put off the normal
Wednesday meeting of the Council of Ministers until the following day.
When he heard the news, Pompidou tried desperately to talk to de
Gaulle, but was fended off. Just before eleven o'clock, he was put
through to the General, who promised his Prime Minister that he
would be back early the next afternoon for the meeting. But he added,
'I am old. You are young. It is you who are the future. You would be
the one to hold the fort. But I am telling you: I will come back.' There
was then a short pause, and the General added: '*Je vous embrasse.*'[14] It
was, as Pompidou said straightaway, quite out of character, and nobody
knew what was going to happen next.

Indeed, what happened next was that the General simply vanished.
The de Gaulles, accompanied by the ADC Flohic, a bodyguard, a doctor and a good deal of luggage, set off in two helicopters from an
airport just outside Paris at around noon. Earlier that morning, Boissieu
had, on de Gaulle's instructions, flown by helicopter to La Boisserie,
from where he was supposed to telephone Massu in Baden-Baden and
tell him to meet the General later that day in Strasbourg; he was then to
fly the short distance to St Dizier, meet the de Gaulles there and report.
On arrival at La Boisserie – where there was a secure telephone line –
Boissieu had tried to get through to Massu, but was told by the opera-
tor that she was on strike and would put through no calls. After
Boissieu's furious explanation that he was calling on behalf of the
President, she agreed to refer the matter to her superintendent. He,
when it was put to him, turned the request down flat. There was no
contact possible with Massu; not only that, but there was trouble with
the rotor blades of Boissieu's helicopter, and he was delayed when trying to take off to meet the General's party at St Dizier airport. The
result was that the de Gaulles arrived at St Dizier to find no Boissieu and
no message about the rendezvous with Massu.

The plan, such as it was, had fallen to pieces. De Gaulle and Boissieu were out of contact, and there was total confusion about who was where. The General ordered the two helicopters to take off again and to try to make contact with Massu from the air. But the pilots were unable to speak to Massu's headquarters at Baden-Baden since they did not have the right radio frequencies. Furthermore, they were fast approaching the German frontier, without any clear destination and with only Michelin road maps to guide them. The General's decision, when it came, was written on the back of an envelope and passed to Flohic; they were to make immediately and directly for Baden-Baden – and in secret. The two helicopters altered course, dropped to tree-top height to escape radar detection and crossed the Rhine just north of Strasbourg. Still flying low and reduced to spotting landmarks to see where they were, the two helicopters managed to reach the small airfield at Baden-Oos.

Flohic immediately called Massu from the airfield. Massu was in the middle of his siesta, but was woken abruptly to be told that the President and Mme de Gaulle were about to arrive on his front lawn. He leapt out of bed and managed to dress himself just in time to organise a reception party. The de Gaulles landed a few minutes later. The journey from the airport had been short, but at least, as they took off, they had seen two Beechcraft aircraft landing at Baden-Oos – carrying Philippe de Gaulle, his family and General Lalande. Fortunately that part had gone according to plan.

'*Tout est foutu, Massu*' were de Gaulle's first words.[15] 'Everything has gone wrong.' France had had enough of him. He was going to give up. The French ambassador must be told to inform the West German President, Kurt Kiesinger, that he was on German soil and might be there for some time. His family was safe. There was no more to be said.

It was Dakar in September 1940 all over again. In his despair the General's spirit seemed to have broken. There followed nearly an hour and a half of discussion between the two men, first on the lawn, then in Massu's office, and then over a light meal. Mme de Gaulle was taken in charge by Mme Massu, and given something to eat, while the men talked. Massu urged de Gaulle not to give up, speaking of the chaos that would ensue and recalling the crises that he had faced successfully in the past. In the end he won, and the General's spirits revived as suddenly as they had collapsed. Mme de Gaulle was summoned again, the helicopters were repacked, and the General announced that they were going back to France – to Colombey.

On arrival at La Boisserie, the General called Bernard Tricot at the

Elysée. His voice was quite different. Instead of sounding tired and depressed, he was confident and full of fight. He would return to Paris, he said, the following morning. He slept well, and was up early to draft a broadcast to be made later that day. By lunchtime on 30 May he was back at the Elysée and saw Pompidou early in the afternoon before the meeting of the Council of Ministers fixed for 3 p.m.

Meanwhile, during the period of confusion when the General had disappeared without leaving any indication of his future movements, or indeed his future intentions, the lieutenants had been loyally at work. The Communist-led demonstration of 29 May, when the General had broken contact with Paris, had been both a success and a threat: a success in that the Party had succeeded in restraining the wilder elements, and in doing so lowering the temperature of the crisis; a threat in that, failing a response from the Government, the feeling was strong enough to push the Communists beyond where they wanted to go – and into a full-scale attempt to seize power.

The Communist dilemma had provided the Gaullists with their opportunity. They had organised a counter-demonstration for the next afternoon – 30 May – and it was manna from heaven to them that the General himself had reappeared in time to stamp the authority of legitimacy on their efforts.

This he did with his old voice of authority. He broadcast on the radio at 4.30 p.m. – nobody in those days watched television at that hour but everybody was within reach of a radio. It was a performance up to the standard of the wartime years. He accused the Communists of trying to establish a totalitarian dictatorship; he said he would not resign, nor would he change the Prime Minister. He announced – after prompting from Pompidou – the postponement of the referendum, the dissolution of the National Assembly and a general election. Finally, in face of what he called the Communist 'threat', he declared, in theatrical tones, that the republic would not abdicate, and that he, de Gaulle, would not go.

That was all that was needed. Not more than an hour after the General's broadcast, the Place de la Concorde was full. By 6.30 p.m. more than half a million Parisians were on the streets to march for the preservation of the Fifth Republic. The battle was over; the General had won his victory. But, in the event, it was to be his last.

9

ENDGAME

Il n'est point d'exemple qu'un plébiscite n'ait pas réussi à celui qui l'avait provoqué, fût-ce pour ratifier un coup d'état. Le plébiscite est la loi du nombre. Le nombre, c'est la bêtise. ★

The General's rallying call of 30 May had done the trick. But it was a measure of the political damage sustained that he had had to concede to his Prime Minister not just the postponement of the referendum but, more seriously, the dissolution of the Assembly and the calling of a general election. Indeed, the crucial words 'I am today dissolving the National Assembly' were written into the text only on Pompidou's insistence.[1] It was not at all what the General wanted. He was perfectly well aware that a successful election campaign would strengthen Pompidou's own position at his expense. Needless to say, that was not something that he was prepared to accept.

Relations between the two men were by now very fragile. From the outset in the early 1950s when Pompidou had become de Gaulle's right-hand man at the RPF, they had made an odd pair: de Gaulle, the unbending man of the north, the soldier of France and of Jesus; and Pompidou, the teacher from the Auvergne, the social climber from the south, who never lost his peasant accent. But, while the General had been cruising in high diplomatic waters and Pompidou had been looking after the French hearth and home, the relationship had worked almost to perfection. It was when their roles crossed, when de Gaulle was faced with the domestic crisis of May 1968 and trampled on Pompidou's turf, that ill temper succeeded disciplined respect. Then the relationship had virtually broken down when de Gaulle had vanished to

★ 'There is no example of a plebiscite where the instigator did not get the result he wanted, even the ratification of a coup d'état. A plebiscite is mob law, and mob law is folly.' Henri de Gaulle (the General's father), quoted in J.-R. Tournoux, *Pétain et de Gaulle*; Plon, Paris, 1964.

Baden-Baden leaving his Prime Minister without any clue where he had gone.

To retrieve his position, the General had first of all to offer some explanation for his apparently eccentric behaviour of 29 and 30 May. 'Yes,' he said in a television interview with his favourite journalist, Michel Droit, on 7 June, 'on 29 May I was tempted to resign. And then, at the same time, I thought that, if I went, the subversion that was threatening would erupt and sweep away the Republic.'[2] It was not a very convincing explanation, but it would have to do.

His second task was to bring Pompidou down to earth. Much to the General's irritation, but not altogether unreasonably, the Prime Minister was putting it about that it was he and Massu who had saved the republic in May. De Gaulle's response was typically abrupt. He imposed on his Government a ministerial reshuffle. Debré switched places with Couve de Murville and took over Foreign Affairs, but much more important, and insultingly, the General forced on his reluctant Prime Minister a senior minister in the shape of the one man Pompidou could not abide – René Capitant.

It was not just a question of personal dislike. Capitant was the most enthusiastic supporter of 'participation', which would be the General's main political theme over the next year, but which Pompidou thought was 'dreaming'. Furthermore, Capitant was a de Gaulle trusty from Algiers in 1942, where he had formed, together with Louis Joxe, a group of academics, lawyers and Vichy dissidents in support of the General's leadership of Fighting France. His relationship with de Gaulle not only went back further than Pompidou's but had been forged in the heat of war.

The reshuffle inevitably gave rise to intense and widespread speculation about the future of the Prime Minister himself. Obviously, there could be no change before the general elections, fixed for 23 and 30 June, but the polls already showed that there would be a Gaullist landslide, and the only question that the press asked was who would be the real winner: de Gaulle or Pompidou. True to form, the General kept aloof from the campaign, but nevertheless invited the country, before the first round, to unite 'around the President'. He was more forthright on the eve of the second round, asking on television for a strong majority, and adding that 'participation [would be] the rule and the strength of a renewed France'.[3] To say the least, it was not at all what his Prime Minister had in mind.

The strong majority was achieved. The Union pour la Défense de la

République (UDR), as the UNR had now become, swamped the opposition, winning 360 seats out of 485 in the National Assembly. It was undoubtedly a great triumph, but it was not a particularly happy outcome for the General. He dismissed the new Assembly as the 'chamber of panic' (his precise wording was more vulgar), and he was irritated that his message of 'participation' had not been appreciated by, or even explained to, the voters.

He was quite right. But the result only served to emphasise the division between de Gaulle and Pompidou. The General wished to have one, possibly last, chance to change France in his image. As always, through whatever compromises circumstances forced him to make, the General was nothing if not consistent. In his post-war Government, he had stressed the need for the middle way between pre-war capitalism and the command economies of the eastern bloc. In his old age, he now returned to that theme. Nobody quite knew what the word 'participation' meant in practice – least of all, perhaps, the General, who was not one for economic and social detail – but he had an instinctive, paternalistic, Catholic and perhaps military feeling that a more collaborative, less antagonistic society was the proper way forward for what he still regarded as his country – the country that still looked to him as her father.

Pompidou, on the other hand, thought that this was little short of sentimental rubbish. After the RPF days, he had worked in Rothschild's bank, and had come to believe that what France needed was more competition and a greater entrepreneurial spirit in her industries. He thought of 'participation', at least on the Capitant model, as either 'sovietisation' or 'running firms by popular assembly'.[4] Neither of the two ideas found any response either from him or from any of his banking friends.

After the success of the elections, there therefore followed a curious and dangerous minuet between the General and his Prime Minister. Pompidou met de Gaulle on 1 July to report on the election results, which he did with an air of open self-congratulation. The General in turn wanted to know how Pompidou intended to proceed, particularly with 'participation'. Pompidou's reply was ambiguous, but seemed to suggest that the burdens of office, and the election campaign, had made him tired – perhaps too tired to continue as Prime Minister.

That same afternoon Pompidou told a gathering of victorious UDR candidates that they should organise themselves as a coherent force to present government policy. To the General, this seemed to be an attempt to arrogate to the majority in the Assembly a role that challenged the presidency. De Gaulle riposted indirectly by informing the Council of Ministers that he regarded the result as 'a great movement which is bringing the country towards participation'.[5]

The minuet continued. Pompidou let the secretary-general at the Elysée, Bernard Tricot, know that he had had enough and was looking to the time when he would become President. The news leaked out, raising the political temperature. Pompidou, under pressure from his family and supporters, decided after all that it was in his best interests to carry on as Prime Minister. But he had left it too late. Tricot had told de Gaulle that Pompidou had again said that he was tired, and that was enough. Once was possible; twice was too much. In the General's life there was no room for tiredness. The job was offered to Couve de Murville. He accepted. Both Pompidou and de Gaulle were left feeling aggrieved.

The inheritance left to the new government by the old was dismal. The country was still demoralised by the turbulence of May and the sudden realisation that it had been near the abyss of revolution and perhaps civil war. There had been a damaging flight of capital – the gold and foreign exchange reserves had been savaged in defence of the parity of the franc and stood at no more than 20 per cent of their pre-May level. Strikes, even after the highly inflationary settlement finally agreed with the unions, were still badly damaging the productive potential of industry, and management was still in a state of shock. The whole matter of the reform of higher education had to be resolved quickly, for fear of another outbreak of student violence. Political uncertainty had returned. After his sudden burst of energy on 30 May, the General himself seemed to the outside world again to be fading into old age. The press talked openly about a future without de Gaulle.

The uncertainty was hardly surprising. After all, not only had the General's domestic position been badly weakened by the events of May. His standing abroad had also been damaged. Furthermore, his foreign policy was showing no rewards. West Germany had been a sad disappointment, courteously but firmly insisting that she preferred American to French leadership. The other members of the Common Market remained determined to have Britain inside, and were biding their time until the end of 1969, when the agricultural support arrangements were due to be renewed. The message would be quite simple: no Britain, no money for French farmers.

If the General's dream of a French-led Europe was fading rapidly, so were his wider international ambitions. The Soviets, with whom he had been carefully cultivating a relationship which, he hoped, would bear long-term fruit, sent their tanks into Czechoslovakia on 21 August to suppress an attempt at liberalisation by a new Czech Government. Apart from the brutality of the Soviet army, which was universally condemned in the West, the action itself removed at a stroke all possibility of progress on the General's international 'grand design'. It was no longer possible for France to claim a position of independence from the two power blocs, because it was no longer possible to persist with any serious dialogue with 'Russia' while the Soviets remained in power. His policy had, in other words, collapsed.

The General admitted as much at his press conference of 9 September 1968 – which was, as it turned out, to he the last of his career. His condemnation of the Soviet action was, it was noted, not as severe as it might have been, but he recognised that French policy appeared 'set back for the moment'; and he insisted, albeit somewhat plaintively, that it was still 'in accordance with the deep realities of Europe'.[6] The policy of detente was frozen for the foreseeable future, but the General seemed to be unwilling to admit that he had been wrong to commit so much of his, and France's, authority to the policy in the first place.

De Gaulle's attitude was in part due to his disappointment at the failure of a carefully constructed policy. Nevertheless, there was a resentful undertone, unstated but reported by Tricot, of criticism of West Germany. The Germans, in the General's view, had been far too aggressive in their attempts to take commercial advantage of the new liberalism of the 'Prague Spring'. They had seen a market for their products opening up on their very doorstep and had moved too swiftly to exploit it. German salesmen had advanced into Czechoslovakia with the same aggressiveness as the German troops had shown in 1939. No wonder, the General argued, that the Soviets had acted as they had; given time, and patience, they might have accepted a degree of liberalisation, but the German commercial assault had forced their hand.

But the facts were the facts, and the General, as always, was prepared to face them. At the same time, however, domestic policy was undergoing a similar reversal, and it was that reversal which the General spent most of his press conference announcing. To the astonishment of his audience, he endorsed the radical proposals of the Education Minister Edgar Faure, under which faculties at universities would be abolished, the universities themselves would be run by elected committees of students and lecturers, selection for entry would be abolished, and political and trade union activity would be allowed on campus. The underlying principle of the reforms was, as one commentator remarked, 'to turn everything upside down'.[7]

The surprise that greeted this announcement turned to shock when, continuing his press conference, the General expanded on the theme of 'participation', of which the Faure proposals were, to his mind, only one element. As far as industry was concerned, he said, there must be a proper sharing of rewards, adequate information for the workers about the activities of their firms and the opportunity to make known their views and to have their practical suggestions accepted. 'It is a matter of acting in the way shareholders act,' he went on. 'The management must from time to time receive and act on suggestions from the workers, whose representatives must be elected by secret ballot . . . The control of what such a law lays down would be with a court.'[8]

Whatever the merits of the General's proposals, they were greeted with consternation by the French business community. 'The man is dangerous' was the immediate comment of Paul Huvelin, the head of the Employers' Federation, and it summed up the reaction of the French business community as a whole. Such ideas were revolutionary, it was said, and could not be countenanced. A renewed flight of capital followed in the next few days and weeks. There was a widespread feeling that the General had taken leave of his senses; if his proposals were to be put into effect, investment in France would be in no sensible person's interest. The Swiss frontier at Geneva was the scene of hectic activity, as suitcases bulging with their load of French francs passed across, often with the connivance, if the truth be told, of French customs officials.

Of course, nobody who recalled the direction of the General's post-war Government should have been particularly surprised at his proposals. After all, in 1945 he had presided over a Government which proposed the nationalisation of a large section of French commercial and industrial activity; not only that, but he had set up works councils in the same year – Capitant had even then been at work.

But a knowledge of history was not the long suit of the new generation of French entrepreneurs. What had or had not happened two decades earlier was of no interest to them. They were worried about the problems of the day. Nor were those worries confined to the General's proposals on 'participation'. They raised the whole question of the direction of economic policy. After the shambles of May, they said, the Government had pursued an almost reckless policy of monetary expansion to try to relaunch what seemed to be a broken economy. This policy had in October suddenly been replaced by one of extreme fiscal rigour. Income tax was raised, and a large increase in inheritance tax was proposed. The second measure was so unpopular that the proposal had been thrown out by the Assembly later in the month. The Government showed every sign of having lost control. The only question was not whether the franc would have to be devalued – that was regarded as a certainty – but by how much.

That question was at the head of the agenda of the meeting of the Group of Ten, the 'Ten' being the most powerful financial countries of the West, dominant among them, of course, being the United States. The meeting was held in Bonn, starting on 20 November 1968. The French Government was asking for a $2 billion line of credit in support of the franc. By the evening of the 22nd there was general agreement to grant the request – subject only to a French devaluation. Even that condition was left uncertain, and de Gaulle was able to assure himself – through Raymond Barre, who had attended the meeting as an observer from the European Commission, and leaked the necessary information to the General – that the condition would, in the last resort, be dropped.

The devaluation never came. At a meeting of the Council of Ministers in the following afternoon, Couve de Murville and his Finance Minister, François Ortoli, reported the assurances that they had given at Bonn. The General told them of his decision that deep cuts in public expenditure would suffice – with the line of credit – to defend the franc's existing parity. Therefore there would be no devaluation.

The announcement caused astonishment and fury in the business community. But they should have known. The decision was entirely consistent with the General's character. The parity of the franc had become a matter of the prestige of France, and in that case there was only one answer. There was no more to be said. At least, all that was to be said was said by the General himself, who explained his decision in a television broadcast on the following day by blaming the whole crisis on the 'shock' of May and 'odious speculation'.

The decision to maintain the franc's parity was immediately popular with the French public, however much resented by business; but the accompanying cuts in public expenditure had a longer term effect. By the end of 1968 not only business had been offended, but popular opinion was once more turning against the General and his Government.

Matters were made worse by the decision, taken personally by the General at the end of December – without any consultation with his ministers – to ban all French arms sales to Israel. The Israeli offence had been to send a commando force to Beirut airport to destroy the greater part of the Lebanon's civil airline, as a reprisal for an attack on an El Al aircraft at Athens airport. The General's punishment had been immediately meted out. But whatever the merits of the decision, French opinion was badly shocked by both its content and the manner in which it was made. The press contrasted his heavy-handed reaction to the Lebanese raid with his mild reaction to the Soviet attack on Prague. They were not impressed. Opinion polls, too, registered strong public disapproval.

It was at that point that Pompidou threw down his first challenge. Since he had left office, Pompidou had continually sniped in private at the new Government. De Gaulle on his side had seemed to be trying to patch things up. He had, after all, made some favourable remarks about his former Prime Minister at his press conference of the previous September. 'He is . . . at the reserve of the Republic [and] should prepare himself for whatever mandate that one day the nation could grant him.'[9]

As an interlude, there had been an unpleasant moment in late 1968, when Pompidou had had to extricate himself from a damaging scandal over the death of a certain Markovitch, a former bodyguard of the film star Alain Delon. It was the sort of scandal that Paris enjoyed. Nor had some ministers been exactly displeased, and it became clear that Capitant in particular had been in no hurry to pass on to his colleagues information that he had uncovered, still less to alert Pompidou himself.

The scandal gradually blew itself out, but not before Pompidou had complained to de Gaulle about the behaviour of the Government – the underlying and unspoken complaint, of course, being about the inaction of the General himself. The General tried to deflect Pompidou's anger by a friendly letter and an official invitation to the Elysée. It would be good, he thought, if Pompidou were to travel a bit. Perhaps, the General suggested, it might be good for him to go to Rome, to see the Italian Prime Minister and make himself known to the Pope.

So it was to Rome that Pompidou went, on 14 January 1969. He did indeed make himself known, partly by the methods that the General had recommended – an audience at the Vatican, and so on – but mostly by a meeting with a small group of French journalists at his hotel. When asked the by now almost routine question about whether he would be a candidate for the presidency of France, he gave the routine answer: 'The question is not one that needs to be addressed at this time.' But he went on to say, unprompted, 'If General de Gaulle were to retire, it goes without saying that I would be a candidate.'[10]

Pompidou was no fool. He could have stopped himself before the second – crucial – sentence. As it was, the story made the headlines in the Paris press the following day. It also forced a statement from the General. 'To accomplish the national task with which I am charged,' came the announcement from the Elysée on 22 January 1969, 'I was re-elected President of the Republic on 19 December 1965 for seven years. I have the duty, and the intent, to fulfil that mandate until its final date.'[11] Pompidou's reply was delivered in Geneva in mid-February. Interviewed on Swiss television, and asked how he saw his political future, he replied, 'I have no political future in the sense in which you use the term. I will have, perhaps and if God wills, a national destiny.'[12]

Even the Rome interview had irritated de Gaulle, but Geneva had been worse. Everybody knew what 'national destiny' meant, and it was clear that Pompidou thought that his chance would come sooner rather than later. The General was furious. His ministers could no longer dissuade him from holding his referendum. He had long seen it as the only way to reassert his ageing authority against the self-proclaimed Dauphin. Challenge must be met by challenge. It was at Quimper in Brittany on 2 February he announced that the referendum on 'participation', postponed on the hectic day of 30 May 1968, would now be held in the spring. Battle had now been decisively engaged.

Before the final campaign, however, de Gaulle wanted to have one more attempt at reasserting France's international prestige. If foreign policy had to be reversed, so be it. One policy had collapsed; another had to take its place. As with his domestic policy, so with his foreign policy the General turned back to his ideas of the immediate post-war period, when he had offered Churchill a solution for Europe which could encompass Britain and accommodate her particular problems. He had also tried to build whatever bridges he could with the United

States, after the contemptuous hostility of Roosevelt's presidency. It was time now, failing the alternative, to return to these themes.

In these objectives, the General was helped by events. The United States had just elected President Richard Nixon to replace Lyndon Johnson, and Britain was still anxious to force the door of the Common Market – to the point where a Labour Government appointed Christopher Soames, Churchill's son-in-law, as its ambassador to Paris. De Gaulle was delighted by the appointment. 'You know,' he said to Tricot, 'he is married to Mary.' 'Who is Mary?' Tricot was unwise enough to ask. 'You don't know who Mary is?' came the irritated reply. 'She is Churchill's daughter.'[13]

At first all went well. At last there was an opportunity to reopen dialogue with Britain – as though he were again talking to Churchill himself. The occasion was carefully planned and advance warning carefully given. Finally it arrived: an invitation to Soames and his wife Mary to an informal lunch at the Elysée with the General and his wife Yvonne on 4 February 1969.

The meal was simple, and the conversation at first about generalities. At the start, de Gaulle and Soames talked mainly to each other, in the most courteous terms, while the ladies remained silent. After a while the General turned to Lady Soames and, obviously in some difficulty to know what to say, asked, 'Well, madame, what do you do in Paris?' Nonplussed, Lady Soames replied, 'What do I do? Well, *Monsieur le Président*, I . . . take my dogs for walks.' 'And where do you take your dogs for walks?' pursued the General. 'Generally along the quais by the river,' was the reply. At this point the General seized on the matter as one of extreme interest, no longer a matter of idle small talk but a topic that needed careful study. After a pause, he said to Lady Soames: 'Do you know the Allée des Cygnes? That is an excellent place for dogs';[14] and he went on to describe the island, its history and how it should be approached. He managed to turn it into an intellectual adventure. Needless to say, Lady Soames was so struck by what the General was saying, and the way he was applying his mind to what was, after all, a minor problem, that thereafter she took to walking her dogs on the Allée des Cygnes for the rest of her stay in Paris.

After lunch the ladies retired and the General and the ambassador sat down to a long discussion. De Gaulle spoke freely, outlining ideas for far-reaching future Franco-British cooperation. The wheel had come full circle. In essence de Gaulle's proposals followed, with allowance for changes that had occurred in the interim, the proposals he had made to

Churchill nearly twenty-five years earlier, in November 1944. Instead of the Treaty of Rome, there should be a much looser arrangement, with the four major European powers – there had only been two in 1944 – Britain, France, Germany and Italy coordinating their foreign and defence policies. Obviously, he went on, France could not not make such proposals, but if the British Government were attracted to the idea it had only to suggest talks with the French Government, and the suggestion would be well received.

It was clearly an important initiative, and Soames sat down that afternoon to draft a full account for dispatch to London. Furthermore, he checked his text, first with Tricot and then, on Tricot's recommendation, with Debré. The dispatch, suitably checked, was studied with care in London. At first, the ideas contained in it were considered promising, but Michael Stewart, the Foreign Secretary, took the view that Britain should settle for no less than full membership of the Common Market, and that nothing less was acceptable. Furthermore, he was adamant that the General's propositions should be communicated to the other members of the Common Market without telling the French in advance. Wilson himself was doubtful – indeed, was anxious to take the General at face value, or at least have a fuller analysis from Soames – and went on a long-planned visit to Chancellor Kiesinger in Bonn without having made up his mind whether or not he would tell Kiesinger about de Gaulle's proposals. When he arrived in Bonn, a Foreign Office briefing awaited him detailing all the circumstances of the affair.

However he might try to dissemble, Wilson could not keep from the Germans the fact that something was up. He therefore told them as shortly and as factually as possible what was happening. Unsurprisingly, the Germans asked their embassy in Paris whether there was any substance to the matter. The whole business then leaked out to the press, with, as might be imagined, disastrous results.

It was the end of any constructive discussion between the two countries while the General retained office. Even after his retirement, he spoke of the British behaviour as another instance of 'English' perfidy; and even then he could not understand the extent to which he himself had alienated the British by what they regarded as 'French' perfidy. It was now clear, once and for all, that relations between the two countries would never improve while the General was in power. The bitterness and suspicion, accumulated over ten years, was too great an obstacle. Better relations would have to await de Gaulle's successor.

With the Americans it was all rather easier. The Johnson era was over, and the new President, Nixon, was an admirer of the General. The admiration was reciprocated. It was not just the new President but the new Secretary of State, Henry Kissinger, who felt that it was time relations with France took a turn for the better. Nixon and Kissinger came, with this intention, on an official visit at the end of February. It was only five weeks after Nixon had formally become President, and the timing marked the enthusiasm with which the President approached his task.

The visit went well. The two Presidents talked about China, and the need to bring her into the comity of nations; they talked about Vietnam, and the need, which Nixon recognised, for American disengagement; and they talked about Europe and the emergence of West Germany as a major European power. De Gaulle was in his element, discussing with ease and authority the international problems of the moment.

But it was the domestic problem of the moment that was in the end to defeat the General. He had insisted on a referendum to reassert his authority after the débâcle of May 1968 and Pompidou's challenge, and he was stuck with it. The problem now was to decide what the referendum was to be about.

It was supposed to be about 'participation', but nobody knew what that really meant. In March 1968, in a speech at Lyons, de Gaulle had proclaimed that it was the devolution of power to the regions that would constitute the future strength of France: that was 'participation'. But this had been followed, in July, by his Prime Minister, who had hinted at the reform of the Senate based on regional representation: that was 'participation' too. At his press conference of 9 September 1968, on the other hand, the General had defined it as the middle way between capitalism and socialism, designed to abolish the class war by bringing workers into the management of institutions and companies. By December, 'participation' was spoken of, according to one of de Gaulle's ministers, as simply tinkering with a few institutions. It was difficult to know what to make of it all.

In early January 1969 de Gaulle told a group of journalists that the referendum on 'participation' would deal both with reform of the Senate and with joint decision-making in companies. His ministers had pointed out, and were still pointing out, that a combination of the two themes was absurd. One of them, Jeanneney, was quite explicit on the matter. Changing the relationship between capital and labour, he said – on legal advice – was not a proper matter for a referendum. Others muttered that the Senate did not want to be reformed and would not pass the necessary resolutions to allow the referendum to go ahead.

None of this weighed with de Gaulle. The referendum was essential to re-establish his personal and direct relationship with the French people, and referendum there would be. He dispelled all doubt right at the end of a speech he made at Quimper in Brittany on 2 February 1969. For the most part, the speech was a rambling affair. He spoke of Brittany, '. . . a peninsula . . . naturally distanced from the centre', of Breton history ' . . . du Guesclin . . . the two Breton Queens of France, Anne and Claude . . . Chateaubriand', and of his uncle Charles de Gaulle, the author of the history of the Celts. Finally, he came to the point. 'Since it is now a matter of opening the way to new hope, we will do it in the spring,' he declared.[15] The die was well and truly cast.

The General had locked himself on to a course to disaster. On 19 February the Council of Ministers fixed the date for the referendum – 27 April; and the two questions, institutional reform and worker participation, would be linked. Almost every minister tried to persuade the General to backtrack, and there was at least a moment when one, Debré, thought that he had succeeded. But de Gaulle would not be moved. It was not only a question of pride; either the French people wished to renew their special and direct relations with him, to follow him along the path that he had chosen, or they did not. If they did not, he was resigned to going.

The General's broadcasts – a 10 April interview with Michel Droit, and direct to camera on 25 April – were not impressive. He looked, and sounded, old and tired. By the 25th he had known that Valéry Giscard d'Estaing's party was advising its followers to vote against him in the referendum, and the polls were telling him that he would lose. The meeting of the Council of Ministers on 23 April was valedictory. That evening the General instructed his private secretary to make arrangements for his files to be removed from the Elysée. At lunchtime on the 25th, after recording his broadcast announcing his resignation in the event of defeat, he left for Colombey.

On Sunday 27 April 1969 France returned its verdict. The day had passed quite calmly at La Boisserie – Mass in the morning, a stroll down to the village (accompanied by half the world's press) to vote, lunch, a walk in the garden; and then seclusion. Soon after 8 p.m. word came through from Tricot at the Elysée that the first returns were bad.

By 10 p.m. it was confirmed: the referendum had been lost 53 per cent against 47 per cent.

There was no more to say. At ten minutes past midnight Agence France-Presse carried the following statement from de Gaulle: 'I am ceasing to exercise my functions as President of the Republic. This decision takes effect at midday today.'[16] There was no need to ask who was the 'I' in the statement. The General had left office, this time for good.

EPILOGUE

Return to Colombey

RETURN TO COLOMBEY

Ô quel farouche bruit font dans le crépuscule
*Les chênes qu'on abat pour le bûcher d'Hercule.**

All in all, it was a dignified enough retreat. Charles de Gaulle realised, and had realised for some time, that his contract with France was broken. He had expected defeat in the referendum, but when it finally came he was bruised and depressed. Perhaps he still kept alive the hope that he might be recalled – his son Philippe has said so many times – but, if so, he had only to give the idea a moment's thought to see that it would not work. He was too old, too tired, and his time had passed.

Once the exhilaration of resignation, of creating a stir, had died away, it was a question of re-ordering life. There were, of course, the letters that had to be answered; thousands of them, the first coming from General Franco, the most moving from Lady Churchill. In his reply to her, the General said so, and went on, 'When I received it from you, it seemed that it came to me, at the same time, in the name of the great and dear Winston Churchill. I thank you with all my heart.'[1]

That done, he settled down to the preparation and writing of his last memoirs. It was not easy. Although the spirit was clearly willing, the flesh was starting to betray him. His eyesight was still worsening – a visiting cleric wearing a cassock was addressed as 'Madame' – and he was again putting on weight. His meals were once more large and fattening, and he had taken to sucking sweets while writing. But he was sleeping

---

* 'Oh what a fearsome noise the oaks make in the twilight as they are cut down for Hercules's funeral pyre!' Victor Hugo. The first words of the second line form the title of André Malraux's book on his 'conversation' with Charles de Gaulle on 11 December 1969.

well and still walking well. His light-infantry pace had slowed, but he was capable of a two- or three-mile walk without difficulty. The main problem was an abdomen which was slowly enlarging; his intestine was becoming displaced, forward and downward, within the abdominal cavity. There was nothing to worry about, as there was no suggestion of malignancy, but it was uncomfortable, and made him look fatter than he really was. 'If God lends me life,' he used to say, there was no reason why he should not complete the two volumes of *Mémoires d'Espoir* in the time that he had in mind, for delivery to his publisher in early 1972.

Before he could settle down to his writing, however, there was one political loose end to be tied up. Pompidou wanted approval for his candidature as President, and sought it in a letter to the General on 28 April. The reply was cool, and only just stopped short of refusal. 'It would certainly have been better,' he wrote, 'if you had not announced [your candidature] several weeks too early,' and he ended by telling Pompidou that he would have nothing to do with the campaign. 'In particular,' he went on, 'your letter of 28 April and my reply of today will remain private between us.'[2] The clear message was that Pompidou could not even make public the General's endorsement. Furthermore, when Capitant threatened to stand as a 'left-wing Gaullist', the General refused point blank to try to dissuade him.

One thing was certain: if he remained in France during the Presidential campaign, it would be virtually impossible for him to remain silent. The sensible thing to do was to go abroad, and this is what he decided to do. His choice fell on Ireland, partly because it was a neutral country – and Roman Catholic – and he probably had as good a chance there as anywhere of staying out of the limelight, partly because, as he explained to Flohic, he had Irish ancestors on his mother's side – who seemed to belong to a family known generically as the 'MacCartans' – and he was interested to see where they came from.

The de Gaulles' departure was kept strictly secret. Even the pilot of the fighter aircraft that Couve de Murville had put at his disposal knew neither the identity of the passengers nor their destination. The small twelve-room Heron Cove hotel at Sneem on the Irish south-west coast had been mysteriously booked in its entirety for a month – nobody knew for whom. It was only when a lorry arrived from the Irish Department for External Affairs to deliver an eight-foot-long bed on the morning of 10 May that the hotel owner had any clue about his guests. Later that morning the de Gaulles arrived at Cork airport. 'Sneem', the local newspaper *The Kerryman* proudly announced, 'makes the world headlines.'[3]

The boast was justified. The press had quickly got wind of his whereabouts, and a corps of sixty or so proceeded to occupy the larger Great Southern hotel at neighbouring Parknasilla. Mr Mangan at the Sneem post office reported that they had never had so many calls, and Bridie, his daughter, had had to have help at the switchboard. Nor were the press particularly scrupulous. Photographers hid behind the dunes when the General and his wife, with Flohic delicately a few paces behind them, went for a walk. Hundreds of shots were taken of the huge, ungainly old man and his plump wife. Journalists enjoyed themselves, writing about them, at length and with developing fantasy. They even reached a comparison of the General with King Lear.

It was good copy, but the truth was that the de Gaulles were quite happy – even, to use Flohic's word, 'serene'.[4] They spent most of their time in the blue and white suite reserved for important guests, or walking in the spacious garden, well protected by the Irish Gardai from press intrusions. Father Flavin came in to say Mass for them on Ascension Day, and on Sunday they went to Sneem parish church.

It was a relaxing time. The General was able to start drafting his memoirs, and Mme de Gaulle found plenty of time for her knitting. Indeed, he completed the first draft of an opening chapter, dealing with his return to power in May 1958, within a few days. But the Irish Government had plans for their distinguished visitor. De Gaulle grumbled. 'I am enjoying it here,' he said.[5] Nevertheless, before the fortnight was up, the whole party moved northwards – leaving at 8 a.m. with the police blocking a press car which tried to follow – to a more comfortable hotel at Cashel Bay in Connemara. The landscape was even more wild and beautiful than in County Kerry.

The first day of the two-round Presidential election fell on 1 June. When the results began to come in, it was clear that Pompidou was in the lead, and would probably win the second round, but it was far from decisive. De Gaulle refused any comment. Then, on 3 June, he and his party moved again, back to County Kerry, to a cottage in the grounds of the Kenmare estate. *The Kerryman* regarded the move as a minor triumph for Kerry over Connemara. But by that time the magic of Ireland was beginning to wear thin for the General and his wife. It was beautiful and tranquil, but it was cold and wet. Besides, the whole point of the exercise, to be absent from France during the election, was now lost.

On 14 June 1969 the final result came through. Pompidou had won, but abstentions had been high, and de Gaulle was able to remark, with some satisfaction, that the 37 per cent of the total electorate that had put the Dauphin in office was way below the 47 per cent that he, de Gaulle, had achieved in the referendum. His congratulatory message to Pompidou, telephoned from Ireland to Xavier de la Chevalerie, was far from enthusiastic: 'For all national and personal reasons, I send you my very cordial congratulations.'[6]

It was time to go home – but not before the official part of his visit had been accomplished. His hosts were not going to let him off that easily; but they were acutely sensitive about the Northern Ireland issue, and were anxious that he should say nothing that could damage the already difficult relations with Britain. Great care was taken with the programme. On 17 June the General and his wife stayed as official guests with the Irish hero of the 1920s, now President of the Republic, Eamon de Valera, at eighty-five old and blind. From there they went to the French embassy, where a dinner was held in his honour.

By that time, however, the 'MacCartans' had caught up with him. The following morning, no fewer than thirty MacCartans turned up to claim the General as one of their own, and one at least recounted the episode of his ancestor who had died fighting William of Orange at the Battle of the Boyne in 1698. This was quite enough to prompt the General, with his usual – somewhat mischievous – sense of occasion, to propose a toast at the farewell lunch given for him the next day by Prime Minister Jack Lynch at Dublin Castle: 'To a united Ireland.'[7] It could have provoked a sensation but, surprisingly, it passed almost unnoticed – perhaps because the General's microphone, it is said, failed at the appropriate moment.

After lunch the General and his party returned to Colombey. Once there, the routine of writing was re-established. A small team had been provided for him: a private secretary, three military ADCs and four secretaries. An office had been set up in the Avenue de Breteuil in Paris to accommodate the team, to handle the tens of thousands of letters which came in, and to sort out the files which had been left behind in the old office in the rue de Solférino. The Government was being generous; but in fact de Gaulle never visited the new office, preferring to stay in

Colombey and send packages to and fro, and waiting for the weekly
visit – on Tuesday – of one or other of the team from Paris. Indeed,
during his retirement he only revisited Paris once, for the First
Communion of his granddaughter Anne, and then it was in secret and
for the shortest possible time.

At Colombey itself, the pattern of life hardly varied. The General
would come downstairs at about 9 a.m. and write until about midday.
Then came lunch, a walk, and more writing from 4 to 6 p.m. It was
about as much as he could manage, not least because he wrote slowly,
with innumerable crossings out and amendments. He refused to be disturbed while he was writing – nor was there any incentive to do so,
since while he was writing he kept his study at the temperature of a
tropical greenhouse. It was said that he could write only in an over-
heated room.

Once outside, however, the General was impervious to climate. True,
he wore an overcoat in the winter when he went walking and his suits
were of heavy cloth, but he refused to put up an umbrella if it rained.
Nor did he like wearing a hat, unlike Mme de Gaulle who, in winter,
would insist on a hat for herself – not elegant, to be sure, but comfort-
ably functional. Both of them by now felt more at ease with a walking
stick; the General's with a silver ring just below the handle, and both
with a silver tip and spike to dig into the mud to forestall unnecessary
accidents.

It was a dull life. There were few excursions, and not much social
activity. De Gaulle wrote, Yvonne knitted and they both watched the
television. The General went to Verdun on 11 November 1969,
Armistice Day, but the visit was kept quiet, and there was no speech.
Occasionally, the de Gaulles would make expeditions in their car, but it
seemed to be more by way of diversion from the daily chore of writing
than for any serious sightseeing. As for visitors, apart from the weekly
call from the Avenue de Breteuil, there were few. Malraux came on 11
December, and there was a long conversation – elaborated and much
lengthened by artistic licence in the book that Malraux subsequently
published.

Family visitors were frequent and welcome, particularly those of the
grandchildren. Like any grandfather, de Gaulle spoilt his grandchildren, although he was always careful to comment diligently on their
performances at school. Nevertheless, family parties at La Boisserie
were moments of rare joy, and the old man could be seen, from time to

time, throwing back his head and laughing out loud at the antics of the children. It was not a liberty that he had permitted himself during his long years in office.

The New Year of 1970 came and went. The writing continued, but more laboriously and without the fire that burns through the *Mémoires de Guerre*. True to form, the old General decided in January that their next trip should take them outside France for the anniversary of 18 June of that year. This time it was to be Spain. The planning took time. Mme de Gaulle insisted on going to Santiago de Compostela and Roncevalles; the General wanted to go to Madrid, the Escorial and a quiet place in southern Spain for ten days' rest.

The negotiations were completed to the satisfaction of both, and on 3 June they left Colombey, again in total secrecy, to drive to the Spanish frontier. Stopping twice on the way, they crossed the Spanish border and headed for Santiago. Then it was on to Avila and Madrid, where they were entertained by General Franco. The meeting was not altogether to de Gaulle's liking. 'I had to say to him,' the General subsequently reported, ' "At the end of the day, you have been good for Spain," and you understand exactly what underlay my expression "at the end of the day" . . . Yes, good for Spain, in spite of all the repressions and all the crimes. Stalin too committed crimes – in fact, many more.'[8]

From Madrid they went south: through Toledo and down to Andalusia. They stayed near Jaén and visited the mosque at Cordoba. Then came the longer stay that the General had insisted on, ten days in a hunting lodge at Ojén, just above Marbella in the Sierra Blanca. After that it was all movement – Seville, the wide plains of Extremadura (with a pause at the monastery of Yuste, where the Emperor Charles V had spent his last months), and then across Old Castile to Burgos. It was hard travelling; the long stretches of road were bare and hot; there had to be roadside picnics – in some parts inns had never been heard of, except to shelter the animals of passing drovers; the sun was fierce. Yet the very harshness of the country and its climate seems to have appealed to the General. He saw how the Spanish character had been formed over the centuries by the physical environment; and there was something in its brutality that attracted him. It had not the peace of western Ireland, but it was none the less moving.

The de Gaulles returned to France by way of Roncevalles – Mme de Gaulle's request – and reached Colombey on 27 June. Once back at home, the General settled down again to his writing, to his games of patience and to the television. Mme de Gaulle settled down again to her domestic life. They were neither of them to know that they had made their last voyage together.

The General's last months were not happy ones. True, he sent the typescript of the first volume of *Mémoires d'Espoir* to his publisher in the middle of July, and it was published on 23 October. It was an immediate success, and that cheered him up. There was also the celebration of his name day, the feast of St Charles, on 4 November. But these were only islands in a sea of depression. His son spent two days at Colombey at the end of September and found his father 'even more sad and melancholy than usual.'[9] Many of his old colleagues – Georges Catroux, René Capitant, François Mauriac – were dead or dying, and he himself felt that his time was running out.

Nor was he at all content with the direction that France was taking under his successor. Pompidou was no romantic, and had no idealised view of France. In December 1969, at a summit meeting of the European Community, he had agreed to a plan for European economic and monetary union put forward by Willy Brandt, the newly elected Chancellor of West Germany, and decided that negotiations with Britain on entry into the European Community should be resumed. As Jean Monnet remarked, 'The French Government . . . was ready to drop its long-standing opposition, in which ill-humour had overruled reason and even self-interest.'[10] In an opinion poll at the time, more than 60 per cent of those questioned in France said that they would be in favour of a European Government, even if it were headed by a non-French statesman. In the end Monnet's arguments had prevailed. The era of the General was over.

Charles de Gaulle was finally struck down by death on 9 November 1970. The long life that had begun in the middle of the night at his grandparents' home in Lille had ended in the early evening, nearly eighty years later, in his own home at Colombey-les-Deux-Eglises.

But the General was not to be left to rest easily in peace. His death, as he would have expected, was an important political event. The authorities, not least President Pompidou, would have to be involved, and they were. There was an immediate news blackout to allow his family to assemble at La Boisserie to pay their last respects. But by the following morning it was clear that the story was too big to be contained. On the other hand, there was political advantage to be gained in being the first to break it.

Pompidou wished personally to announce the event, and also to read the General's instructions on his own funeral arrangements, a copy of which he had had since 1952, to the Council of Ministers that morning. The family wished to publish the will themselves. There was a great deal of agitation; but in the end Pompidou won. At 9.40 a.m. on 10 November, Agence France-Presse carried a 'flash': General de Gaulle was dead. At 11 a.m. there was a release from the Elysée containing the text of the General's funeral instructions, issued – as might be imagined – without the authority of the de Gaulle family. At one o'clock Pompidou himself appeared on television to announce, 'Frenchmen, Frenchwomen; General de Gaulle is dead; France is a widow.'[11] By using the General's death, and declaring that he would preside over the national mourning, the new head of state had finally established himself as the Dauphin who had succeeded.

Of course, none of this would have surprised the General. He was well aware that his death would be a public event, however much he might try to prevent it. He of all people appreciated the contrast between the public reality of his life as a statesman and the private reality of his life as a husband, father and grandfather. He had, after all, lectured about the public persona of a leader and written about it in *The Edge of the Sword*. But modern democratic politics cannot separate the private from the public. Voters want to know about their leaders; and de Gaulle's efforts to raise an impenetrable curtain between his private life and the public role he assumed as the personification of France were out of tune with the world he had just left.

The unseemly squabble that followed the General's death over the timing of the announcement and the funeral arrangements has echoed down the years, and has spilled over into a wider dispute about how his life should be assessed. At the time of his death, his family wished to maintain privacy for their own grief; the French public wished to breach the wall of privacy, to know more about the man, in order to express their own sense of loss. The argument has shifted. The grief is over. France and her friends now need to be able to place the General in history. Of course, there will be continuing reappraisal from generation to generation; but the essence of Charles de Gaulle remains clear. Colombey, his home, was the home of a very affectionate, emotional and private man; France was the home of a very cold, ruthless and proud public man. The contradiction between the two sides of his character has yet to be resolved. Perhaps it never will be. If so, and if indeed he was the last great Frenchman, he went to his private grave in Colombey – beside his little daughter Anne, as he had instructed – taking with him the enigma of his own extraordinary personality. France, in his own words, has shrouded them both 'in her kind and holy earth'.

NOTES

Part One: CHILD

1: A Parisian Boy from Lille (pages 13–22)

[1] Quoted in J. Lacouture, *De Gaulle*, page 8 (tr. Price; Hutchinson, London, 1970).

[2] Quoted in J.-R. Tournoux, *Pétain and de Gaulle*, page 4 (tr. Coburn; Heinemann, London, 1966).

[3] *Espoir*, no. 39, June 1982, page 66.

[4] *Lacouture*, op. cit., page 8.

[5] *Espoir*, loc. cit.

2: The Steps of St Ignatius (pages 23–9)

[1] J.W. Padberg, SJ, *Colleges in Controversy*, page 279; Harvard University Press, Cambridge, Massachusetts, 1969.

[2] Padberg, op. cit., page 241.

[3] Joseph Burnichon, SJ, *La Compagnie de Jésus en France 1814–1914*, vol. 3, page 484. Quoted in Padberg, op. cit., page 222.

Part Two: SOLDIER

1: The Army of the Republic (pages 33–40)

[1] Rémy de Gourmont in *Mercure de France*. Quoted in Douglas Porch,

The March to the Marne, page 55; Cambridge University Press, Cambridge, 1981.

[2] Charles de Gaulle, *Mémoires de Guerre*, vol. 1, page 2; Plon, Paris, 1954.

[3] Jean Pouget, *Un certain Capitaine de Gaulle*, page 51; Fayard, Paris, 1973.

[4] Pouget, op. cit., page 45.

[5] D.B. Ralston, *The Army of the Republic*, page 329; MIT Press, Cambridge, Massachusetts, 1967.

[6] J.-R. Tournoux, *Pétain and de Gaulle*, page 21 (tr. Coburn; Heinemann, London, 1966).

2: A War to End Wars (pages 41–50)

[1] Charles de Gaulle, *Lettres, Notes et Carnets*, vol. 1, page 78; Plon, Paris, 1980–86.

[2] De Gaulle, op. cit., page 88.

[3] De Gaulle, op. cit., pages 106–7.

[4] De Gaulle, op. cit., page 273.

[5] Ferdinand Plessy, *'J'ai connu de Gaulle captif'*, in *Revue de la France Libre*, January 1981. Quoted in J. Lacouture, *De Gaulle*, vol. 1, page 94; Seuil, Paris, 1984.

3: Polish Interlude (pages 51–61)

[1] Charles de Gaulle, *Lettres, Notes et Carnets*, vol. 2, page 17; Plon, Paris, 1980–86.

[2] Norman Davies, *White Eagle, Red Star, The Polish–Soviet War 1919–20*, page 105; Orbis, London, 1983.

[3] Davies, op. cit., page 131.

[4] Davies, op. cit., page 148.

[5] Jean Pouget, *Un certain Capitaine de Gaulle*, page 143; Fayard, Paris, 1973.

[6] Pouget, op. cit., page 143.

[7] *Revue Historique des Armées*, no. 2, 1990, page 25.

4: Pétain's Chicken (pages 62–71)

[1] 'The preferred foal [i.e., the favourite]'. Jean Pouget, *Un certain*

Capitaine de Gaulle, page 161; Fayard, Paris, 1973.

[2] Quoted by J.-R. Tournoux, *Pétain and de Gaulle*, page 46 (tr. Coburn; Heinemann, London, 1966).

[3] A. Laffargue, *Fantassin de Gascogne*, page 122; Flammarion, Paris, 1962.

[4] Pouget, op. cit., page 168.

[5] Pouget, op. cit., page 187.

[6] Tournoux, op. cit., page 55.

[7] Tournoux, op. cit., page 58.

[8] Tournoux, op. cit., page 61.

[9] Charles de Gaulle, *The Edge of the Sword*, dedicatory note (tr. Gerard Hopkins; Faber and Faber, London, 1960).

[10] Lieutenant Rupp. Quoted by A. Frossard in *En ce temps-là . . . de Gaulle*, no. 26.

[11] Tournoux, op. cit., page 69.

5: A Toe in Political Waters (pages 72–81)

[1] Quoted in R.A. Doughty, *The Seeds of Disaster*, page 9; The Shoe String Press, Hamden, Connecticut, 1985.

[2] Jean Pouget, *Un certain Capitaine de Gaulle*, page 221; Fayard, Paris, 1973.

[3] Declaration by Jean Barthou, Foreign Minister, 17 April 1934.

[4] J.-R. Tournoux, *Pétain and de Gaulle*, page 83 (tr. Coburn; Heinemann, London, 1966).

[5] Tournoux, op. cit., page 88.

[6] Tournoux, op. cit., page 88.

6: The Cut of the Sickle (pages 82–93)

[1] Quoted in Alistair Horne, *To Lose a Battle*, page 102; Macmillan, London, 1969.

[2] V. Bartlett MP, House of Commons official report, vol. 400, cols. 780–81, 24 May 1944.

[3] Quoted in J. Marin, *De Gaulle*, page 53; Hachette, Paris, 1973.

[4] Charles de Gaulle, *Mémoires de Guerre*, vol. 1, page 24; Plon, Paris, 1954.

[5] De Gaulle, op. cit., page 31.

[6] Quoted in Horne, op. cit., page 482.

[7] Quoted in Horne, op. cit., page 482.

[8] Telegram from Winston Churchill to Maurice Gamelin, 19 May 1940. Quoted in Horne, op. cit., page 540.

7: Is He a New Napoleon? (pages 94–106)

[1] Clare Booth. Quoted in Alistair Horne, *To Lose a Battle*, page 212; Macmillan, London, 1969.

[2] Horne, op. cit., page 212.

[3] Edward Spears, *Assignment to Catastrophe*, vol. 2, page 195; Heinemann, London, 1954.

[4] Martin Gilbert, *Finest Hour* (vol. 6 of *The Churchill Biography*), pages 486–7; Heinemann, London, 1983.

[5] John Colville, *The Fringes of Power*, page 151; Hodder and Stoughton, London, 1985.

[6] Cabinet papers 99/3. Quoted in Martin Gilbert, op. cit., page 507.

[7] Quoted in Horne, op. cit., page 213.

[8] Quoted in François Kersaudy, *Churchill and de Gaulle*, page 62; Fontana, London, 1990.

[9] Charles de Gaulle, *Mémoires de Guerre*, vol. 1, page 57; Plon, Paris, 1954.

[10] Canadian Public Archives: William Mackenzie King diaries 1944, page 653. Quoted in Kersaudy, op. cit., page 65.

[11] Colville, op. cit., page 155.

[12] Winston Churchill, *The Second World War*, vol. 2, page 162; Cassell, London, 1947.

[13] De Gaulle, op. cit., page 58.

[14] Colville, op. cit., page 159.

[15] Colville, op. cit., page 160.

[16] Churchill, op. cit., page 189.

[17] Quoted in Jean Monnet, *Memoirs*, page 24 (tr. Richard Mayne, Collins, London, 1978).

[18] Spears, op. cit., page 323.

[19] Kersaudy, op. cit., page 68.

[20] J.-R. Tournoux, *Pétain and de Gaulle*, page 85 (tr. Coburn; Heinemann, London, 1966).

Part Three: EXILE

1: Laying the Corner Stone (pages 109–21)

[1] Edward Spears, *Assignment to Catastrophe*, vol. 2, page 323; Heinemann, London, 1954.

[2] Text of Philippe Pétain broadcast, monitored by the BBC, 17 June 1940.

[3] John Colville, *The Fringes of Power*, page 164; Hodder and Stoughton, London, 1985.

[4] Charles de Gaulle, *Discours et Messages*, vol. 1, page 3; Plon, Paris, 1970.

[5] H. Amouroux in *Paris–Match*, 15 November 1970.

[6] De Gaulle, op. cit., page 5.

[7] British Cabinet Paper 65/8, 28 June 1940.

[8] Jean Monnet, *Memoirs*, page 144 (tr. Richard Mayne; Collins, London, 1978).

[9] Warren Tute, *The Reluctant Enemies*, page 58; Collins, London, 1990.

2: Afric's Sunny Fountains (pages 122–36)

[1] Mary Borden, *Journey down a Blind Alley*, page 113; Hutchinson, London, 1946.

[2] Borden, op. cit., page 113.

[3] Quoted in J. Lacouture, *De Gaulle*, vol. 1, page 416; Seuil, Paris, 1984.

[4] Emile Muselier, *De Gaulle contre le Gaullisme*, page 13; Editions du Chêne, Paris, 1946.

[5] Foreign Office papers (France): signal from Halifax to Henderson, 21 July 1940. Quoted in P.M.H. Bell, *A Certain Eventuality*, page 196; Saxon House, London, 1974.

[6] John Colville, *The Fringes of Power*, page 210; Hodder and Stoughton, London, 1985.

[7] Charles de Gaulle, *Mémoires de Guerre*, vol. 1, page 97; Plon, Paris, 1954.

[8] Foreign Office circular, 6 September 1940 (intelligence summary on French African colonies).

[9] Letter from Inter-Services Security Board to chiefs of staff. Quoted in P.M.H. Bell, op. cit., page 208.

[10] Quoted in Warren Tute, *The Reluctant Enemies*, page 107; Collins, London, 1990.

[11] Georges Catroux, *Dans la bataille de la Méditerranée*, page 23; Juillard, Paris, 1949.

[12] Naval assistant to the vice-chiefs of the naval staff. Quoted in Tute, op. cit., page 109.

[13] Edward Spears to Winston Churchill. Quoted in Tute, op. cit., page 111.

[14] British commanders' ultimatum to the Governor-General of Dakar, broadcast on radio, 23 September 1940.

[15] Tute, op. cit., page 123.

[16] *Daily Mirror*, Cassandra column, 28 September 1940.

[17] Colville, op. cit., page 250.

[18] Charles de Gaulle, *Discours et Messages*, vol. 1, page 39; Plon, Paris, 1970.

3: Who is Fighting Whom? (pages 137–50)

[1] Edward Spears, *Two Men who Saved France*, page 218; Eyre and Spottiswoode, London, 1966.

[2] Warren Tute, *The Reluctant Enemies*, page 22; Collins, London, 1990. And du Moulin de Labarthete, *Le Temps des Illusions* – quoted in Alexander Werth, *France 1940–55*, page 81; Hale, London 1956.

[3] Alain Darlan, *Darlan Parle*. Quoted in Werth, op. cit., page 81.

[4] Alistair Horne, *To Lose a Battle*, page 543; Macmillan, London, 1969.

[5] Werth, op. cit., page 117.

[6] Charles de Gaulle, *Mémoires de Guerre*, vol. 1, page 126; Plon, Paris, 1954.

[7] Edward Spears, *Fulfilment of a Mission*, page 28; Leo Cooper, London, 1977.

[8] Anthony Eden, *The Eden Memoirs: The Reckoning*, page 245; Cassell, London, 1965.

[9] Parr (Consul-General in Brazzaville) to the Foreign Office, 14 May 1941. Quoted in François Kersaudy, *Churchill and de Gaulle*, page 130; Fontana, London, 1990.

[10] Winston Churchill. *The Second World War*, vol. 3, page 289; Cassell, London, 1947.

[11] Churchill, op. cit., page 290.

[12] Kersaudy, op. cit., page 135.

[13] Spears, *Fulfilment of a Mission*, page 89.

[14] Spears, *Fulfilment of a Mission*, page 93.

[15] De Gaulle, op. cit., page 164.

[16] De Gaulle, op. cit., page 165.

[17] Spears, *Fulfilment of a Mission*, page 127.

[18] Oliver Lyttelton, *Memoirs*, page 248; quoted in Kersaudy, op. cit., page 143.

4: The Eagle and the Bear Join the Party (pages 151–65)

[1] René Cassin, *Les hommes partis de rien*, page 358; Plon, Paris, 1975.

[2] Edward Spears, *Fulfilment of a Mission*, page 142; Leo Cooper, London, 1977.

[3] Spears, op. cit., page 121.

[4] Georges Catroux, *Dans la bataille de la Méditerranée*, pages 160 and 200; Juillard, Paris, 1949. And Charles de Gaulle, *Mémoires de Guerre*, vol. 1, page 175; Plon, Paris, 1954.

[5] De Gaulle, op. cit., page 173.

[6] Note from Charles de Gaulle to General Wilson. Quoted in J. Lacouture, *De Gaulle*, vol. 1, page 484; Seuil, Paris, 1984.

[7] *Chicago Daily News*, 27 August 1941.

[8] Prime Minister's papers, 27 August 1941. Quoted in François Kersaudy, *Churchill and de Gaulle*, page 153; Fontana, London, 1990.

[9] Kersaudy, op. cit., page 153.

[10] Foreign Office minute, 30 August 1941. Quoted in Kersaudy, op. cit., page 153.

[11] Minute by Desmond Morton, 1 September 1941. Quoted in Kersaudy, op. cit., page 153.

[12] Note on Charles de Gaulle by Anthony Eden, 1 September 1941. Quoted in Kersaudy, op. cit., page 153.

[13] Prime Minister's papers, 2 September 1941. Quoted in Kersaudy, op. cit., page 155.

[14] John Colville, *Footprints in Time*, pages 113–14; Collins, London, 1976

[15] Prime Minister's papers: meeting between Winston Churchill and Charles de Gaulle, 12 September 1941. Quoted in Kersaudy, op. cit., page 158.

[16] Colville, op. cit., page 114.

[17] Prime Minister's papers, 1 September 1941. Quoted in Kersaudy, op. cit., page 164.

[18] Edward Spears's papers. Quoted in Kersaudy, op. cit., page 165.

[19] Kersaudy, op. cit., page 165.

[20] Prime Minister's papers: Winston Churchill to Anthony Eden, 26 September 1941. Quoted in Kersaudy, op. cit., page 169.

[21] De Gaulle, op. cit., vol. 1, page 193.

[22] J.G. Hurstfield, *America and the French Nation 1939–45*, page 8; University of North Carolina Press, 1986.

[23] Hurstfield, op. cit., page 67.

[24] Hurstfield, op. cit., page 68.

5: Resistance on All Fronts (pages 166–79)

[1] Franklin D. Roosevelt papers on St Pierre–Miquelon (in FDR Library, Washington DC). Quoted in François Kersaudy, *Churchill and de Gaulle*, page 173; Fontana, London, 1990.

[2] Foreign Office papers: St Pierre et Miquelon – diary of events. Quoted in Kersaudy, op. cit., page 173.

[3] Charles de Gaulle, *Mémoires de Guerre*, vol. 1, page 185; Plon, Paris, 1954.

[4] De Gaulle's order to Emile Muselier, 18 December 1941. Quoted in Kersaudy, op. cit., page 174.

[5] Roosevelt papers on St Pierre–Miquelon. Quoted in Kersaudy, op. cit., page 174.

[6] Cordell Hull, *Memoirs*, vol. 2, page 1130; Hodder and Stoughton, London 1948. Quoted in Kersaudy, op. cit., page 175.

[7] J.G. Hurstfield, *America and the French Nation 1939–45*, page 122; University of North Carolina Press, 1986.

[8] Telegram from de Gaulle to Winston Churchill 27 December 1941. Quoted in de Gaulle, op. cit., page 503.

[9] Quoted in Kersaudy, op. cit., page 176.

[10] Churchill to Anthony Eden, 13 January 1942, in the Canadian Public Archives. Quoted in Kersaudy, op. cit., page 178.

[11] Kersaudy, op. cit., page 178.

[12] From *De Gaulle vu d'ailleurs*, part 1 (video of contemporary newsreel; LMK Images).

[13] Quoted in Kersaudy, op. cit., page 183.

[14] Charles de Gaulle, *Discours et Messages*, vol. 1, page 183; Plon, Paris, 1970.

[15] Churchill to chiefs of staff committee no. 29 of 1942, 24 April 1942. Quoted in Martin Gilbert, *Road to Victory*, page 96; Heinemann, London, 1986.

[16] Prime Minister's papers: Roosevelt to Churchill, 29 April 1942 – draft of speech. Quoted in Gilbert, op. cit., page 96.

[17] L. Grafftey-Smith, *Hands to Play*, page 38; Routledge, London, 1975. Quoted in Kersaudy, op. cit., page 187.

[18] French Foreign Ministry papers: *Entretiens Eden–de Gaulle*, 11 May 1942. Quoted in Kersaudy, op. cit., page 188.

6: Mediterranean Storms (pages 180–94)

[1] Pierre Billotte, *Le Temps des Armes*, page 224; Plon, Paris, 1972.

[2] Foreign Office papers: meeting between Churchill and de Gaulle, 10 June 1942. Quoted in François Kersaudy, *Churchill and de Gaulle*, page 189; Fontana, London, 1990.

[3] Charles Peake to the Foreign Office, 17 June 1942. Quoted in Kersaudy, op. cit., page 193.

[4] Minister of State in Cairo to the Foreign Office, 24 June 1942. Quoted in Kersaudy, op. cit., page 193.

[5] US foreign relations papers. Quoted in Milton Viorst, *Hostile Allies*, page 73; Macmillan, New York, 1965.

[6] Edward Spears, *Fulfilment of a Mission*, pages 182–3; Leo Cooper, London, 1977.

[7] R.G. Casey. Quoted in Kersaudy, op. cit., page 201.

[8] Georges Catroux, *Dans la bataille de la Méditerranée*, page 282; Juillard, Paris, 1949.

[9] Edward Spears diary, 25 August 1942. Quoted in Kersaudy, op. cit., page 202.

[10] Charles de Gaulle, *Lettres, Notes et Carnets*, vol. 4, page 369; Plon, Paris, 1980–6.

[11] Charles de Gaulle, *Mémoires de Guerre*, vol. 2, page 32; Plon, Paris, 1956.

[12] De Gaulle, *Mémoires de Guerre*, vol. 2, page 33.

[13] J. Harvey (ed.), *War Diaries of Oliver Harvey 1941–45*, page 164; Collins. London, 1978. Quoted in Kersaudy, op cit., page 211.

[14]De Gaulle, *Mémoires de Guerre*, vol. 2, page 34.

[15] De Gaulle, *Mémoires de Guerre*, vol. 2, page 35.

[16] De Gaulle, *Mémoires de Guerre*, vol. 2, page 9.

[17] Telegram from Winston Churchill to Franklin D. Roosevelt, 29 April 1942. Quoted in Martin Gilbert, *Road to Victory*, pages 248–9; Heinemann, London, 1986.

[18] Quoted in Warren Tute, *The Reluctant Enemies*, page 227; Collins, London, 1990.

[19] Tute, op. cit., page 236.

[20] Mark Clark, *Calculated Risk,* page 91; Harper, New York, 1950.

7: The Darlan Deal (pages 195–206)

[1] Pierre Billotte, *Le Temps des Armes*, page 239; Plon, Paris, 1972.

[2] Foreign Office papers 371: memorandum to the Secretary of State, 8 November 1942. Quoted in François Kersaudy, *Churchill and de Gaulle*, page 220; Fontana, London, 1990.

[3] Jacques Soustelle, *Envers et contre tout*, vol. 1, page 452; Laffont, Paris, 1947. Quoted in Kersaudy, op. cit., page 223.

[4] Charles de Gaulle, *Discours et Messages*, vol. 1, page 250; Plon, Paris, 1970.

[5] Cordell Hull, *Memoirs*, vol. 2, page 1198; Hodder and Stoughton, London, 1948. Quoted in Kersaudy, op. cit., page 224.

[6] Kersaudy, op. cit., page 229.

[7] J.G. Hurstfield, *America and the French Nation 1939–45*, page 172; University of North Carolina Press, 1986.

[8] Charles de Gaulle, *Mémoires de Guerre*, vol. 2, page 51; Plon, Paris, 1956.

[9] De Gaulle, *Mémoires de Guerre*, vol. 2, page 52.

[10] François Darlan to Mark Clark. Quoted in Warren Tute, *The Reluctant Enemies*, page 285; Collins, London, 1990.

[11] De Gaulle, *Discours et Messages*, vol. 1, page 263.

[12] Sumner Welles's account of a meeting between Franklin D. Roosevelt, Adrien Tixier and André Philip, 20 November 1942. Quoted in Milton Viorst, *Hostile Allies*, page 129; Macmillan, New York, 1965.

[13] Aidan Crawley, *De Gaulle*, page 192; Collins, London, 1969.

[14] Quoted in Tute, op. cit., page 301.

[15] Tute, op. cit., page 301.

[16] Alain de Boissieu, *Pour combattre avec de Gaulle*, page 171; Plon, Paris, 1981.

[17] De Gaulle, *Mémoires de Guerre*, vol. 2, page 67.

[18] *Hampstead and Highgate Express*, 30 May 1958.

[19] *Hampstead and Highgate Express*, 30 May 1958.

8: From Anfa to Algiers (pages 207–22)

[1] *Les Dossiers de l'Histoire*, no. 73, page 69.

[2] Harold Macmillan diaries, 26 April 1942. Quoted in Alistair Horne, *Macmillan*, vol. 1, page 181; Macmillan, London, 1988.

[3] Charles de Gaulle, *Lettres, Notes et Carnets*, vol. 4, page 453; Plon, Paris, 1980–6.

[4] Letter from Macmillan to his wife. Quoted in Horne, op. cit., page 165.

[5] Horne, op. cit., page 165.

[6] *Public Papers and Addresses of Franklin D. Roosevelt*, page 83; Rosenmann, 1943. Quoted in François Kersaudy, *Churchill and de Gaulle*, page 241; Fontana, London, 1990.

[7] Elliott Roosevelt, *A Rendezvous with Destiny*, page 330; quoted in Kersaudy, op. cit., page 242.

[8] Telegram from de Gaulle to Winston Churchill, 17 January 1943: US foreign relations papers (Casablanca). Quoted in Kersaudy, op. cit., page 245.

[9] Roosevelt to the Secretary of State. Quoted in Kersaudy, op. cit., page 246.

[10] Winston Churchill, *The Second World War*, vol. 4, page 610; Cassell, London, 1947.

[11] Churchill, op. cit., page 611.

[12] Charles de Gaulle, *Mémoires de Guerre*, vol. 2, page 78; Plon, Paris, 1956. And Kersaudy, op. cit., page 252.

[13] Lord Moran, *Churchill – The Struggle for Survival 1940–65*, page 81; Constable, London, 1966.

[14] Elliott Roosevelt. Quoted in Kersaudy, op. cit., page 252.

[15] Robert Sherwood, *Roosevelt and Hopkins*, page 685; Harper, New York, 1948.

[16] Henri Hettier de Boislambert, *Les Fers de l'Espoir*, page 383; Plon, Paris, 1973. And Kersaudy, op. cit., page 254.

[17] De Gaulle, *Mémoires de Guerre*, vol. 2, page 84.

[18] De Gaulle, *Mémoires de Guerre*, vol. 2, page 84.

[19] Sherwood, op. cit., page 693.

[20] Robert Murphy, *Diplomat among Warriors*, page 219; Collins, London, 1964.

[21] J. Lacouture, *De Gaulle*, vol. 1, page 644; Seuil, Paris, 1984. And De Gaulle, *Mémoires de Guerre*, vol. 2, page 86.

[22] Cordell Hull, *Memoirs*, vol. 2, page 1208; Hodder and Stoughton, London, 1948. Quoted in Milton Viorst, *Hostile Allies*, page 147; Macmillan, New York, 1965.

[23] Anthony Eden, *The Eden Memoirs: The Reckoning*, page 373; Cassell, London, 1965.

[24] J. Harvey (ed.), *War Diaries of Oliver Harvey 1941–45*, 28 February 1943; Collins, London, 1978. Quoted in Kersaudy, op. cit., page 265.

[25] Harold Nicolson, *Diaries and Letters*, vol. 2,12 March 1943; quoted in Kersaudy, op. cit., page 265.

[26] Foreign Office papers 371: note for Churchill, 8 May 1943. Quoted in Kersaudy, op. cit., page 275.

[27] Foreign Office papers 371: Churchill to the Deputy Prime Minister and Foreign Secretary, 24 May 1943. Quoted in Kersaudy, op. cit., page 275.

[28] Eden, op. cit., page 386.

[29] Churchill, op. cit., page 729.

[30] De Gaulle, *Mémoires de Guerre*, vol. 2, page 102.

9: Checkmate for 'Kingpin' (pages 223–38)

[1] Alistair Horne, *Macmillan 1894–1956*, page 185; Macmillan, London, 1988.

[2] Charles de Gaulle, *Mémoires de Guerre*, vol. 2, page 103; Plon, Paris, 1956.

[3] J. Harvey (ed.) *War Diaries of Oliver Harvey 1941–45*, 5 June 1943; Collins, London, 1978. Quoted in Martin Gilbert, *Road to Victory, Winston S. Churchill 1941–45*, page 421; Heinemann, London, 1986.

[4] Harold Macmillan diaries. Quoted in Horne, op. cit., page 186.

[5] Macmillan diaries. Quoted in Horne, op. cit., page 187.

[6] De Gaulle, op. cit., page 110.

[7] Jean Monnet, *Memoirs*, page 203 (tr. Richard Mayne; Collins, London, 1978).

[8] Prime Minister's papers: Franklin D. Roosevelt to Winston Churchill, 17 June 1943. Quoted in J.G. Hurstfield, *America and the French Nation 1939–45*, page 197; University of North Carolina Press, 1986.

[9] Roosevelt's papers (secret file): Roosevelt to Dwight D. Eisenhower, 17 June 1943. Quoted in François Kersaudy, *Churchill and de Gaulle*, page 292; Fontana, London, 1990.

[10] Charles de Gaulle, *Discours et Messages*, vol. 1, page 335; Plon, Paris, 1970.

[11] Pierre Viénot to René Massigli, 2 September 1943. Quoted in Kersaudy, op. cit., page 298.

[12] US foreign relations papers (Quebec 1943). Quoted in Kersaudy, op. cit., page 300.

[13] US foreign relations papers (Quebec 1943). Quoted in Kersaudy, op. cit., page 300.

[14] Dutch archives (Algiers). Quoted in Kersaudy, op. cit., page 300.

[15] Edward Spears, *Fulfilment of a Mission*, pages 235–6; Leo Cooper, London, 1977.

[16] French foreign affairs papers. Quoted in Kersaudy, op. cit., page 303.

[17] French foreign affairs papers. Quoted in Kersaudy, op. cit., page 304.

[18] Spears, op. cit., page 263.

[19] François Coulet, *Vertu des Temps Difficiles*, page 215; Plon, Paris, 1966. Quoted in Kersaudy, op. cit, page 310.

10: Waiting for Overlord (pages 239–50)

[1] Quoted in Milton Viorst, *Hostile Allies*, page 189; Macmillan, New York, 1965.

[2] Letter from Roger Makins (Lord Sherfield) to his wife from Algiers (unpublished).

[3] Letter from Makins to his wife from Algiers (unpublished).

[4] State Department papers: memorandum from Franklin D. Roosevelt to Cordell Hull, Cairo, 27 November 1943. Quoted in Viorst, op. cit., page 184.

[5] Emmanuel d'Astier de la Vigerie, *Les Dieux et les Hommes,* page 28; Juillard, Paris, 1952. Quoted in François Kersaudy, *Churchill and de Gaulle*, page 311; Fontana, London, 1990.

[6] Mary Soames in an interview with the author, 4 March 1992.

[7] Prime Minister's papers: report of British consul in Marrakesh on a conversation with the head of the local branch of the Front National de la Libération, 15 January 1944. Quoted in Kersaudy, op. cit., page 317.

[8] Charles de Gaulle, *Discours et Messages,* vol. 1, page 401; Plon, Paris, 1970.

[9] Draft US directive, 15 March 1944. Kersaudy, op. cit., page 323.

[10] Louis Joxe, *Victoires sur la Nuit*, page 136; Flammarion, Paris, 1981.

[11] Cordell Hull, *Memoirs*, vol. 2, page 1429; Hodder and Stoughton, London, 1948. Quoted in Kersaudy, op. cit., page 326.

[12] Foreign Office papers: Winston Churchill to Roosevelt, 24 April 1944. Quoted in Kersaudy, op. cit., 327.

[13] Charles de Gaulle, *Lettres, Notes et Carnets*, vol. 4, page 138; Plon, Paris, 1980–6.

[14] De Gaulle, *Discours et Messages*, vol. 1, page 436.

[15] Joxe, op. cit., pages 179–80.

[16] De Gaulle, *Mémoires de Guerre*, vol. 2, page 221.

[17] House of Commons official report, 24 May 1944, col. 790.

[18] De Gaulle, *Mémoires de Guerre*, vol. 2, page 637.

[19] De Gaulle, *Mémoires de Guerre*, vol. 2, page 222.

11: Who Won the Battle for France? (pages 251–8)

[1] Charles de Gaulle, *Mémoires de Guerre*, vol. 2, page 640; Plon, Paris, 1956.

[2] De Gaulle, op. cit., page 222.

[3] Anthony Eden, *The Eden Memoirs: The Reckoning*, page 452; Cassell, London, 1965.

[4] Eden, op. cit., page 453.

[5] De Gaulle, op. cit., page 223.

[6] E. Béthouart, *Cinq Années d'Espérance*, page 243; Plon, Paris, 1968. Quoted in François Kersaudy, *Churchill and de Gaulle*, page 344; Fontana, London, 1990.

[7] De Gaulle, op. cit., page 223.

[8] De Gaulle, op. cit., page 224.

[9] Béthouart, op. cit., page 243. Quoted in Kersaudy, op. cit., page 346.

[10] De Gaulle, op. cit., pages 225–6.

[11] Winston Churchill, *The Second World War*, vol. 5, page 556; Cassell, London, 1947.

[12] Charles de Gaulle, *Lettres, Notes et Carnets*, vol. 4, page 229; Plon, Paris, 1980–6.

[13] D. Dilks (ed.), *Cadogan Diaries*, page 634; Cassell, London, 1971. Quoted in Kersaudy, op. cit., page 349.

[14] Pierre Viénot in *Le Monde*, 6 July 1974. Quoted in J. Lacouture, *De Gaulle*, vol. 1, pages 772–3; Seuil, Paris, 1984.

[15] A. Gillois, *Histoire secrète des Français à Londres 1940–44*, page 24; Hachette, Paris, 1973. Quoted in Kersaudy, op. cit., page 350.

[16] B. Lockhart, *Comes the Reckoning*, page 301; Puttnam, London, 1947. Quoted in Kersaudy, op. cit., page 350.

[17] *Cadogan Diaries*, page 635. Quoted in Kersaudy, op. cit., page 351.

[18] Charles de Gaulle, *Discours et Messages*, vol. 1, page 442; Plon, Paris, 1970.

[19] Foreign Office papers: Churchill to Eden, 13 June 1944. Quoted in Kersaudy, op. cit., page 335.

[20] Foreign Office papers: Churchill to Eden, 13 June 1944. Quoted in Kersaudy, op. cit., page 335.

[21] De Gaulle, *Mémoires de Guerre*, vol. 2, page 230.

Part Four: HERO

1: A Parisian Summer (pages 261–75)

[1] From *De Gaulle vu d'ailleurs*, part 1 (video of contemporary newsreel; LMK Images).

[2] Anthony Eden, *The Eden Memoirs: The Reckoning*, page 457; Cassell, London, 1965.

[3] Alfred Duff Cooper, *Old Men Forget,* page 334; Rupert Hart-Davis, London, 1953.

[4] Henry Stimson, *On Active Service in Peace and War*, page 456; Hutchinson, London, 1949. Quoted in François Kersaudy, *Churchill and de Gaulle*, page 364; Fontana, London, 1990.

[5] W. D. Hassett, *Off the Record with F.D.R., 1942–1945,* page 257; Allen & Unwin, London, 1960. Quoted in Kersaudy, op. cit., page 364.

[6] Franklin D. Roosevelt's press conference, 11 July 1944. Quoted in J.G. Hurstfield, *America and the French Nation 1939–40*, page 215; University of North Carolina Press, 1986.

[7] Morgenthau diaries, 15 July 1944. Quoted in Hurstfield, op. cit., page 218.

[8] J. Harvey (ed.), *War Diaries of Oliver Harvey 1941–45*, 15 July 1944; Collins, London, 1978. Quoted in Kersaudy, op. cit., page 365.

[9] *War Diaries of Oliver Harvey*, 15 July 1944. Quoted in Kersaudy, op. cit., page 365.

[10] Duff Cooper, op. cit., pages 335–6. And Kersaudy, op. cit., page 367.

[11] Winston Churchill to Eden, 12 August 1944. Quoted in Kersaudy, op. cit., page 368.

[12] Diana Cooper, *Trumpets from the Steep*, page 212 (quoting from her diary for 20 August 1944); Rupert Hart-Davis, London, 1960.

[13] Editorial in *Combat*, 20 August 1945. Quoted in Alexander Werth, *France 1940–55*, page 218; Hale, London, 1956.

[14] Charles de Gaulle, *Mémoires de Guerre*, vol. 2, page 705; Plon, Paris, 1956.

[15] De Gaulle, op. cit., page 305.

[16] J. Lacouture, *De Gaulle*, vol. 1, pages 834 and 835; Seuil, Paris, 1984.

2: Government must Govern (pages 276–88)

[1] Charles de Gaulle, *Lettres, Notes et Carnets,* vol. 5, page 297; Plon, Paris, 1980–6.

[2] Philippe Viannay ('Indomitus'), *Nous sommes les rebelles*. Quoted in J. Lacouture, *De Gaulle*. vol. 2, page 29; Seuil, Paris, 1985.

[3] Quoted in Don Cook, *Charles de Gaulle*, page 251; Secker and Warburg, London, 1984.

[4] Pierre Villon, *Résistant de la première heure*, pages 193–4; Editions Sociales, Paris, 1983. Quoted in Lacouture, op. cit., page 37.

[5] Charles de Gaulle, *Discours et Messages,* vol. 1, page 488; Plon, Paris, 1970.

[6] Claude Mauriac, *Aimer de Gaulle*, pages 48–9; Grasset, Paris, 1978. And Lacouture, op. cit., page 16.

[7] Henri Noguères, *Histoire de la Résistance en France*, vol. 5, page 780; Laffont, Paris, 1967. And 'Ravenel' in *De Gaulle vu d'ailleurs*, part 1 (video of contemporary newsreel; LMK Images). And Lacouture, op. cit., page 49.

[8] Alexander Werth, *France 1940–55*, page 228; Hale, London, 1956.

[9] Werth, op. cit., page 237.

[10] Charles de Gaulle, *Mémoires de Guerre*, vol. 3, page 107; Plon, Paris, 1959.

[11] Editorial in *Franc-Tireur,* 20 November 1944. Quoted in Werth, op. cit., page 241.

[12] Werth, op. cit., page 246.

3: The End of the General's War (pages 289–301)

[1] Anthony Eden, *The Eden Memoirs: The Reckoning,* page 477 (quoting his diary for 15 September 1944); Cassell, London, 1965.

[2] Franklin D. Roosevelt to Cordell Hull, 19 September 1944. Quoted in François Kersaudy, *Churchill and de Gaulle,* page 370; Fontana, London, 1990.

[3] Kersaudy, op. cit., page 371n.

[4] Eden, op. cit., page 485 (quoting his diary for 12 October 1944).

[5] Cadogan to the Foreign Secretary, 20 October 1944. Quoted in Kersaudy, op. cit., page 373.

[6] D. Dilks (ed.), *Cadogan Diaries.* pages 674–5; Cassell, London, 1971. Quoted in Kersaudy, op. cit., pages 373–4.

[7] Alfred Duff Cooper, *Old Men Forget,* pages 340–1; Rupert Hart Davis, London, 1953.

[8] Charles de Gaulle, *Mémoires de Guerre,* vol. 3, page 49; Plon, Paris, 1959.

[9] Winston Churchill, *The Second World War,* vol. 6, page 218. Cassell, London, 1954.

[10] De Gaulle, op. cit., page 50.

[11] De Gaulle, op. cit., page 50.

[12] De Gaulle, op. cit., page 52.

[13] De Gaulle, op. cit., page 52.

[14] De Gaulle, op. cit., page 56.

[15] De Gaulle, op. cit., page 61.

[16] De Gaulle, op. cit., page 75.

[17] De Gaulle, op. cit., page 79.

[18] De Gaulle, op. cit., page 146.

[19] Alphonse Juin, *Mémoires,* vol. 2, pages 85–6. Quoted in Kersaudy, op. cit., page 394.

[20] Duff Cooper, op. cit., page 348.

[21] Foreign Office papers: Churchill to Eden, 19 January 1945. Quoted in Kersaudy, op. cit., page 345.

[22] Don Cook, *Charles de Gaulle,* page 277; Secker and Warburg, London, 1984.

[23] De Gaulle, op. cit., page 155.

[24] Mary Borden, *Journey down a Blind Alley*, page 295; Hutchinson, London, 1946.

Part Five: POLITICIAN

1: With Peace Comes Politics (pages 305–16)

[1] Letter from Philippe Pétain to Adolf Hitler, 5 April 1945. Quoted in Don Cook, *Charles de Gaulle*, page 286; Secker and Warburg, London, 1984.

[2] Interview in *De Gaulle vu d'ailleurs,* part 2 (video of contemporary newsreel; LMK Images).

[3] Charles de Gaulle, *Mémoires de Guerre*, vol. 3, page 112; Plon, Paris 1959.

[4] H.G. Nicholas (ed.), *Washington Despatches 1941–45*, page 613; Weidenfeld and Nicolson, 1981.

[5] De Gaulle, op. cit., page 214.

[6] J.-M. Royer, *Les petites malices du Général,* pages 132–3; Balland, Paris, 1990.

[7] De Gaulle, op. cit., page 220.

[8] Lacouture, *De Gaulle*, vol. 2, page 151; Seuil, Paris, 1985.

[9] F. Kupferman, *Les Procès de Vichy*, page 152; Editions Complexe, Paris, 1980. Quoted in Lacouture, op. cit., page 152.

[10] De Gaulle, op. cit., page 204.

[11] Alain de Boissieu, *Pour combattre avec de Gaulle*, page 337. Quoted in Lacouture, op. cit., page 230.

[12] Interview between Francisque Gay and Georgette Elgey. Quoted in Lacouture, op. cit., page 238.

2: The Gamble that Failed (pages 317–31)

[1] Charles de Gaulle, *Mémoires de Guerre*, vol. 3, page 647; Plon, Paris, 1959.

[2] Charles de Gaulle, *Discours et Messages*, vol. 1, page 720; Plon, Paris, 1970.

[3] Quoted in J. Lacouture, *De Gaulle,* vol. 2, page 266; Seuil, Paris, 1985.

[4] De Gaulle, *Discours et Messages*, vol. 1, page 723.

[5] Claude Mauriac, *Aimer de Gaulle*, page 335; Grasset, Paris, 1978. Quoted in Lacouture, op. cit., page 276.

[6] De Gaulle, *Discours et Messages*, vol. 1, page 743.

[7] De Gaulle, *Discours et Messages*, vol. 1, page 746.

[8] Quoted in Lacouture, op. cit., page 281.

[9] Quoted in Lacouture, op. cit., page 285.

[10] Quoted in Lacouture, op. cit., page 292.

[11] Quoted in Lacouture, op. cit., page 296.

[12] Quoted in Lacouture, op. cit., page 296.

[13] Quoted in Lacouture, op. cit., page 299.

[14] Quoted in Lacouture, op. cit., page 301.

[15] Both quoted in Lacouture, op. cit., page 303.

[16] Quoted in Lacouture, op. cit., page 302.

[17] Quoted in Frank Giles, *The Locust Years,* pages 78–9; Secker and Warburg, London, 1991.

[18] Quoted in Lacouture, op. cit., page 322.

[19] Charles de Gaulle, *Lettres, Notes et Carnets*, vol. 6, page 247; Plon, Paris, 1980–6.

[20] Quoted in Bernard Ledwidge, *De Gaulle,* page 220; Weidenfeld and Nicolson, London, 1982.

Part Six: PHILOSOPHER

1: A Certain Idea of France (pages 335–44)

[1] Pierre-Louis Blanc, *Charles de Gaulle au soir de sa vie*, page 265; Fayard, Paris, 1990.

[2] Charles de Gaulle, *Mémoires de Guerre*, vol. 1, page 1; Plon, Paris, 1954.

[3] Marcel Proust, *À la recherche du temps perdu,* page 10; Gallimard, Paris, 1954.

[4] De Gaulle, op. cit., page 1.

[5] Pierre Messmer in an interview with the author, 3 April 1992.

[6] Dean Rusk, *As I Saw It*, page 243; I.B. Tauris, London, 1991.

[7] Blanc, op. cit., page 152.

[8] De Gaulle, op. cit., vol. 3, page 290.

[9] De Gaulle, op. cit., vol. 1, page 1.

2: On Public and Private Life (pages 345–59)

[1] Mary Soames in an interview with the author, 4 March 1992.

[2] Robert Lassus, *Le Mari de Madame de Gaulle,* page 167; Editions Jean-Claude Lattès, Paris, 1990.

[3] Pierre-Louis Blanc, *Charles de Gaulle au soir de sa vie*, page 50; Fayard, Paris, 1990.

[4] Blanc, op. cit., page 94.

[5] Lassus, op. cit., page 108.

[6] Charles de Gaulle, *Mémoires de Guerre*, vol. 2, page 311; Plon, Paris, 1956.

[7] Louis Joxe, *Victoires sur la nuit*, page 144; Flammarion, Paris, 1981.

[8] Harold Macmillan diaries. Quoted in Alistair Horne, *Macmillan 1894–1956*, page 189; Macmillan, London, 1988.

[9] Charles de Gaulle, *Le Fil de l'Epée*, page 6; Plon, Paris, 1932.

[10] Jean Mauriac, *Le Mort du Général de Gaulle,* page 162; Grasset, Paris, 1972.

[11] Blanc, op. cit., page 95.

[12] J. Jackson, *Charles de Gaulle*, page 100; Macdonald, London, 1990.

[13] Mary Soames in an interview with the author, 4 March 1992.

[14] For example, the French ambassador in London, Vicomte Luc de la Barre de Nanteuil, in conversation with the author, 25 June 1990.

[15] Lassus, op. cit., page 84.

[16] Lassus, op. cit., page 82.

[17] Piers Dixon, *Double Diploma, The Life of Sir Pierson Dixon,* page 313; Hutchinson, London, 1968.

[18] Bernard Tricot in an interview with the author, 3 April 1992.

[19] Possibly apocryphal, but reported in Lassus, op. cit., page 141.

[20] Blanc, op. cit., page 139.

Part Seven: HEAD OF STATE

1: The General's Resurrection (pages 363–78)

[1] Quoted in J. Lacouture, *De Gaulle*, vol. 2, page 454; Seuil, Paris, 1985.

[2] J.-R. Tournoux. Quoted in Frank Giles, *The Locust Years*, page 312; Secker and Warburg, London, 1991.

[3] Olivier Guichard. Quoted in Giles, op. cit., page 311.

[4] Quoted in Alistair Horne, *A Savage War of Peace*, page 277; Macmillan, London, 1977.

[5] Horne, op. cit., page 280.

[6] Quoted in Paul-Marie de la Gorce, *De Gaulle entre Deux Mondes*, page 535; Fayard, Paris, 1964.

[7] Jean Ferniot, *De Gaulle et le 13 Mai,* page 244; Plon, Paris, 1965.

[8] Quoted in Lacouture, op. cit., page 462.

[9] Horne, op. cit., page 287.

[10] Quoted in Lacouture, op. cit., page 464.

[11] Charles de Gaulle, *Mémoires d'Espoir*, vol. 1, page 25; Plon, Paris, 1970. Agence France-Presse, 15 May 1958.

[12] From *De Gaulle vu d'ailleurs* (video of contemporary newsreel; LMK Images).

[13] Horne, op. cit., page 294.

[14] De Gaulle, op. cit., page 29.

[15] De Gaulle, op. cit., page 29.

[16] Quoted in Ferniot, op. cit., page 448.

[17] André Dulac, *Nos Guerres Perdues,* pages 87–8; Fayard, Paris, 1969. Quoted in Lacouture, op. cit., pages 480–1.

2: 'I Have Understood You' (pages 379–93)

[1] Quoted in J. Lacouture, *De Gaulle*, vol. 2, page 498; Seuil, Paris, 1985.

[2] Edmond Jouhard, *Serons-nous enfin compris?*, page 69; Albin Michel, Paris, 1984. And Lacouture, op. cit., page 505.

[3] Charles de Gaulle, *Mémoires d'Espoir*, vol. 1, pages 51–2; Plon, Paris, 1970.

[4] Pierre Lefranc in an interview with the author, 3 April 1992.

[5] Harold Macmillan diaries. Quoted in Alistair Horne, *Macmillan 1957–86*, page 108; Macmillan, London, 1989.

[6] Lacouture, op. cit., page 561.

[7] Official text of Charles de Gaulle speech, 4 September 1958.

[8] From *Temps modernes*. Quoted in Lacouture, op. cit., page 563.

[9] Quoted in Lacouture, op. cit., page 563.

[10] For example, official text of de Gaulle speech, 4 September 1958.

[11] Quoted in Aidan Crawley, *De Gaulle*, pages 364–5; Collins, London, 1969.

3: Algeria is Not French (pages 394–407)

[1] Charles de Gaulle, *Mémoires d'Espoir*, vol. 1, page 214; Plon, Paris, 1970.
[2] De Gaulle, op. cit., page 221.
[3] Konrad Adenauer, *Erinnerungen*. Quoted in J. Lacouture, *De Gaulle*, vol. 2, pages 637–8; Seuil, Paris, 1985.
[4] *Süd-Deutsche Zeitung*, 18 January 1960.
[5] From *De Gaulle vu d'ailleurs* (video of contemporary newsreel; LMK Images).
[6] Bernard Tricot in an interview with the author, 3 April 1992.
[7] Quoted in Lacouture, op. cit., vol. 3, page 278.

4: The New Agenda (pages 408–24)

[1] Pierre Messmer in an interview with the author, 3 April 1992.
[2] Harold Macmillan diaries. Quoted in Alistair Horne, *Macmillan 1957–86,* page 222; Macmillan, London, 1989.
[3] Quoted in J.-R. Tournoux *La Tragédie du Général*, pages 364–5; Plon, Paris, 1967.
[4] Jean Monnet, *Memoirs*, page 413 (tr. Richard Mayne, Collins, 1978).
[5] Mary Wilson in an interview with the author, 19 July 1991.
[6] *Daily Mail*, 27 April 1960.
[7] *France–Soir* 27 April 1960.
[8] Horne, op. cit., page 314.
[9] Horne, op. cit., page 315.
[10] Horne, op. cit., page 318.
[11] *Le Figaro,* 9 July 1962.
[12] *Le Monde*, 5 July 1962.
[13] At a conference of the Radical Party, 30 September 1962. Quoted in J. Lacouture, *De Gaulle*, vol. 3, page 581; Seuil, Paris, 1986.
[14] Quoted in Lacouture, op. cit., page 335.
[15] Recounted to the author by Gladwyn Jebb (Lord Gladwyn), 10 October 1991; see also *Espoir*, no. 12.

5: A Professional at Work (pages 425–30)

[1] From Ernest Mignon, *Les Mots du Général;* Fayard, Paris, 1962. Quoted in Olivier Germain-Thomas and Philippe Barthelet, *Charles de Gaulle jour après jour*, page 194; Nathan, Paris, 1990.

² Charles de Gaulle, *Mémoires d'Espoir,* vol. 1, page 287; Plon, Paris, 1970.

³ Quoted from '*L'Evénement du jeudi, 18 January 1990*', by Jean-Michel Royer, *Les Petites Malices du Général,* page 194; Balland, Paris, 1990.

6: Baiting Uncle Sam (pages 431–44)

¹ A.M. Schlesinger, Jr. Quoted in Don Cook, *Charles de Gaulle,* page 360; Secker and Warburg, London, 1984.

² Text of Charles de Gaulle press conference, 14 January 1963.

³ Quoted in Cook, op. cit., page 362.

⁴ Alistair Horne, *Macmillan 1957–86,* page 449; Macmillan, London, 1989.

⁵ Horne, op. cit., page 446.

⁶ Horne, op. cit., page 448.

⁷ Quoted in John Newhouse, *De Gaulle and the Anglo-Saxons,* page 243; Deutsch, London, 1970.

⁸ Cook, op. cit., page 366.

⁹ *Le Monde,* 3 February 1964.

¹⁰ Debate in National Assembly. Quoted in J. Lacouture, *De Gaulle,* vol. 3, page 616; Seuil, Paris, 1986.

¹¹ *New York Times,* 21 September 1964.

¹² *Paris-Presse,* 24 September 1964.

¹³ André Malraux, *Les Chênes qu'on abat. . .,* page 52; Gallimard, Paris, 1971.

¹⁴ Quoted in Cook, op. cit., page 368.

¹⁵ Quoted in François Kersaudy, *Churchill and de Gaulle,* page 432; Fontana, London, 1990.

¹⁶ Quoted in Lacouture, op. cit., page 633.

¹⁷ Quoted in Lacouture, op. cit., page 637.

¹⁸ Pierre Viansson-Ponté. Quoted in Lacouture, op. cit., page 640.

7: All the World's a Stage (pages 445–57)

¹ Charles de Gaulle press conference, 21 February 1966. John Newhouse, *De Gaulle and the Anglo-Saxons,* page 285; Deutsch, London, 1970.

² Jean Monnet, *Memoirs,* page 484 (tr. Richard Mayne; Collins, 1978).

[3] Newhouse, op. cit., page 286.

[4] René Andrieu, *Du bonheur et rien d'autre*. Quoted in Olivier Germain-Thomas and Philippe Bartelet, *Charles de Gaulle jour après jour*, page 292; Nathan, Paris, 1990.

[5] Charles de Gaulle, *Discours et Messages*, vol. 5, page 46; Plon, Paris, 1970.

[6] Charles de Gaulle speech, 1 September 1966, from *De Gaulle vu d'ailleurs*, part 3 (video of contemporary newsreel; LMK Images).

[7] De Gaulle press conference 28 October 1966 and broadcast 31 December 1966; Newhouse, op. cit., pages 293–4.

[8] Newhouse, op. cit., page 299.

[9] Marc Ullmann, 'De Gaulle's Secret Diplomacy', in *Interplay*, Aug.–Sept. 1967. Quoted in Newhouse, op. cit., page 300.

[10] Quoted in J. Lacouture, *De Gaulle*, vol. 3, page 516; Seuil, Paris, 1986.

[11] Lacouture, op. cit., pages 517–18.

[12] Lacouture, op. cit., page 521.

[13] Lacouture, op. cit., page 527.

[14] Lacouture, op. cit., pages 529–60.

[15] Hervé Alphand, *L'Etonnement d'être*. Quoted in Germain-Thomas and Barthelet, op. cit., page 307.

[16] Neal Ascherson in an interview with the author, 27 November 1991.

[17] Neal Ascherson in an interview with the author, 27 November 1991.

[18] Charles de Gaulle, *Discours et Messages*, vol. 5, pages 232–5; Plon, Paris, 1970.

[19] François Flohic, *Souvenirs d'outre-Gaulle*, page 172; Plon, Paris, 1979.

[20] De Gaulle, op. cit., page 252.

8: The Ides of May (pages 458–69)

[1] Quoted in J. Lacouture, *De Gaulle*, vol. 3, page 671; Seuil, Paris, 1986.

[2] Philippe Alexandre, *L'Elysée en péril*, page 299; Fayard, Paris, 1969. Quoted in Lacouture, op. cit., page 678.

[3] Pierre Viansson-Ponté, *Histoire de la République gaullienne*, vol. 2, page 613; Fayard, Paris, 1971. Quoted in Lacouture, op. cit., page 681.

[4] Quoted in Lacouture, op. cit., page 681.

[5] François Flohic, *Souvenirs d'Outre-Gaulle*, page 175; Plon, Paris, 1979. Quoted in *L'Espoir*, no. 46, March 1984, page 4.

[6] Quoted in Lacouture, op. cit., page 686.

[7] Lacouture, op. cit., page 688.

[8] Pierre Messmer in an interview with the author, 3 April 1992.

[9] Alexandre, op. cit., page 316. Quoted in Lacouture, op. cit., page 690.

[10] Georges Pompidou, *Pour rétablir une vérité*, pages 190–1; Flammarion, Paris, 1982.

[11] Anne and Pierre Rouanet, *Les Trois Derniers Chagrins du Général de Gaulle*, page 287; Grasset, Paris, 1980. Quoted in Lacouture, op. cit., page 696.

[12] Pierre Lefrance in an interview with the author, 3 April 1992.

[13] Jacques Vendroux, *Ces grandes années que j'ai vécues*, page 319; Plon, Paris, 1975.

[14] Bernard Tricot in an interview with the author, 3 April 1992.

[15] Lacouture, op. cit., page 705 (quoting Jacques Massu, *Baden 68*; Plon, Paris, 1983).

9: Endgame (pages 470–83)

[1] Charles de Gaulle, *Discours et Messages*, vol. 5, page 292; Plon, Paris, 1970.

[2] De Gaulle television broadcast, 7 June 1968.

[3] De Gaulle television broadcast, 29 June 1968.

[4] Georges Pompidou, *Pour rétablir une vérité*, page 204; Flammarion, Paris, 1982.

[5] Quoted in J. Lacouture, *De Gaulle*, vol. 3, page 728; Seuil, Paris, 1986.

[6] De Gaulle, op. cit., pages 334–5.

[7] Pierre Viansson-Ponté, *Histoire de la République gaullienne*, vol. 2, page 665; Fayard, Paris, 1971.

[8] De Gaulle, op. cit., pages 327–38.

[9] De Gaulle op. cit., pages 327–38.

[10] Agence France-Presse: Rome dispatch, 17 January 1969.

[11] Ministry of Information press statement, 20 January 1969.

[12] Pompidou, op. cit., page 270.

[13] Bernard Tricot in an interview with the author, 3 April 1992.

[14] Mary Soames in an interview with the author, 4 March 1992.

[15] Olivier Guichard, *Mon Général*, page 441; Grasset, Paris, 1980.

[16] Agence France-Presse communiqué, 28 April 1969.

Epilogue: Return to Colombey (pages 487–95)

[1] Mary Soames, *Clementine Churchill*, page 514; Cassell, London, 1979.

[2] Georges Pompidou, *Pour rétablir une vérité*, page 287; Flammarion, Paris, 1982.

[3] *The Kerryman*, 17 May 1969.

[4] Quoted in J. Lacouture, *De Gaulle*, vol. 3, page 765; Seuil, Paris, 1986.

[5] Lacouture, op. cit., page 765.

[6] Lacouture, op. cit., page 764.

[7] Bernard Ledwidge, *De Gaulle*, page 374; Weidenfeld and Nicolson, London, 1982.

[8] Charles de Gaulle in an interview with Michel Droit, 28 July 1970. Quoted in Lacouture, op. cit., page 777.

[9] Jean Mauriac, *La Mort du Général de Gaulle*; Grasset, Paris, 1972.

[10] Jean Monnet, *Memoirs*, page 496 (tr. Richard Mayne; Collins, 1978).

[11] Georges Pompidou broadcast, 10 November 1970. From *De Gaulle vu d'ailleurs* part 3 (video of contemporary newsreel; LMK Images).

SELECT BIBLIOGRAPHY

This bibliography is not meant to be comprehensive. It lists those works which have been particularly helpful in the research for this book. The fullest bibliography available is that published by the Institut Charles de Gaulle, 5 rue de Solférino, 75007 Paris, entitled *Nouvelle Bibliographie Internationale sur Charles de Gaulle* (Plon, Paris, 1990). But one warning: although it has an almost complete record of books published in France, it has not been able to rely on an equally systematic non-French coverage. For convenience, this bibliography has been divided into four parts:
1. de Gaulle's own major works;
2. biographies and partial biographies;
3. general;
4. journals and other.

1. *De Gaulle's major works*

La Discorde chez l'Ennemi; Berger-Levrault, Paris, 1924.
Le Fil de l'Epée; Berger-Levrault, Paris, 1932.
Vers l'Armée de Métier; Berger-Levrault, Paris, 1938.
La France et son Armée; Plon, Paris, 1938.
Mémoires de Guerre (3 vols.); Plon, Paris, 1954, 1956, 1959.
Discours et Messages (5 vols.); Plon, Paris, 1970.
Mémoires d'Espoir (2 vols., one incomplete); Plon, Paris, 1970–71.
P. de Gaulle (ed.), *Lettres, Notes et Carnets* (9 vols); Plon, Paris, 1980–6.

English translations:

The Army of the Future (Vers l'Armée de Métier); Hutchinson, London, 1940.

France and her Army (La France et son Armée); Hutchinson, London, 1945.

War Memoirs (Mémoires de Guerre); Weidenfeld and Nicolson, London, 1955, 1959 and 1960.

The Edge of the Sword (Le Fil de l'Epée); Faber and Faber, London, 1960.

Memoirs of Hope (Mémoires d'Espoir); Weidenfeld and Nicolson, London, 1971.

2. Biographies and partial biographies

Aglion, Raoul: De Gaulle et Roosevelt; Plon, Paris, 1984.

Aron, Robert: Charles de Gaulle; Perrin, Paris, 1964.

Blanc, Pierre-Louis: De Gaulle au soir de sa vie; Fayard, Paris, 1990.

Cattaui, Georges: Charles de Gaulle, l'homme et son destin; Fayard, Paris, 1960.

Chaban-Delmas, Jacques: Charles de Gaulle; Editions Paris-Match, Paris, 1980.

Cook, Don: Charles de Gaulle; Secker and Warburg, London, 1984.

Crawley, Aidan: De Gaulle; Collins, London, 1969.

Crozier, Brian: De Gaulle (2 vols.); Eyre Methuen, London, 1973.

Debray, Régis: A demain de Gaulle; Gallimard, Paris, 1990.

Ferniot, Jean: De Gaulle et le 13 mai; Plon, Paris, 1965.

Gaulle, Philippe de: De Gaulle; Plon, Paris, 1989.

Germain-Thomas, Olivier, and Barthelet, Philippe: Charles de Gaulle jour après jour; Nathan, Paris, 1990.

Gorce, Paul-Marie de la: De Gaulle entre deux mondes; Fayard, Paris, 1964.

Guichard, Olivier: Mon Général; Grasset, Paris, 1980.

Jackson, Julian: De Gaulle; Macdonald, London, 1990.

Kersaudy, François: Churchill and de Gaulle; Fontana, London, 1990.

Lacouture, Jean (tr. Price): De Gaulle; Hutchinson, London, 1970.

Lacouture, Jean: De Gaulle (3 vols.); Seuil, Paris, 1984, 1985, 1986.

Lacouture, Jean: De Gaulle, vol. 1 (tr. O'Brian); Collins Harvill, London, 1990.

Lacouture, Jean: De Gaulle, vol. 2 (tr. Sheridan); Collins Harvill, London 1991.

Ledwidge, Bernard: *De Gaulle*; Weidenfeld and Nicolson, London, 1982.

Lefranc, Pierre: *Avec de Gaulle*; Plon, Paris, 1979.

Lefranc, Pierre: *De Gaulle, un portrait*; Flammarion, Paris, 1989.

Maillard, Pierre: *De Gaulle et l'Allemagne*; Plon, Paris, 1990.

Mauriac, Claude: *Aimer de Gaulle*; Grasset, Paris, 1978.

Mauriac, François: *De Gaulle*; Grasset, Paris, 1964.

Mauriac, Jean: *La Mort du Général de Gaulle*; Grasset, Paris, 1972.

Nachin, Lucien: *Charles de Gaulle, général de France*; Plon, Paris, 1945.

Pouget, Jean: *Un certain Capitaine de Gaulle*; Fayard, Paris, 1973.

Rémy (Colonel, pseudonym of Renault Gilbert): *De Gaulle, cet inconnu*; Solar, Monaco, 1947.

Terrenoire, Louis: *De Gaulle 1947–54*; Plon, Paris, 1981.

Tournoux, J.-R.: *Pétain et de Gaulle*; Plon, Paris, 1964 (tr. Coburn; Heinemann, London, 1966).

Tournoux, J.-R.: *La Tragédie du Général*; Plon, Paris, 1967.

Vendroux, Jacques: *Cette chance que j'ai eue . . .*; Plon, Paris, 1974.

Vendroux, Jacques: *Ces grandes années que j'ai vécues . . .*; Plon, Paris, 1975.

Wailly, Henri de: *De Gaulle sous le casque*; Perrin, Paris, 1990.

Weisenfeld, Ernst: *Charles de Gaulle, der Magier im Elysée*; Beck, Munich, 1990.

Werth, Alexander: *De Gaulle, a political biography*; Penguin, London, 1965.

Willis, F. Roy (ed.): *De Gaulle*; European Problem Studies; Holt, Rinehart and Winston, New York, 1967.

3. General

Alphand, Hervé: *L'Etonnement d'être*; Fayard, Paris, 1977.

Aron, Robert (tr. Hare): *The Vichy Régime, 1940–44*; Macmillan, London, 1958.

Aron, Robert: *An Explanation of de Gaulle*; Harper and Row, New York, 1966.

Aron, Raymond: *Mémoires*; Juillard, 1983.

Astier de la Vigerie, Emmanuel d': *Les Grands*; Gallimard, Paris, 1961.

Bell, Philip M.H.: *A Certain Eventuality*; London, Saxon House, 1974.

Beloff, Nora: *The General Says No*; Penguin, London, 1962.

Bessborough, Eric (Earl of): *Return to the Forest*; Weidenfeld and Nicolson, London, 1962.

Bidault, Georges: *D'une Résistance à l'autre*; Presses du Siècle, Paris, 1965.

Billotte, Pierre: *Le Temps des Armes*; Plon, Paris, 1972.

Bohlen, Charles: *Witness to History*; Norton, New York, 1973.

Boissieu, Alain de: *Pour combattre avec de Gaulle*; Plon, Paris, 1982.

Boissieu, Alain de: *Pour servir le Général*; Plon, Paris, 1982.

Borden, Mary: *Journey down a Blind Alley*; Hutchinson, London, 1946.

Cassin, René: *Les hommes partis de rien*; Plon, Paris, 1975.

Charmley, John: *Duff Cooper*; Weidenfeld and Nicholson, London, 1986.

Churchill, Randolph S., and Gilbert, Martin: *The Churchill Biography* (8 vols.); Heinemann, London (final vol. 1988).

Colville, Sir John: *Footprints in Time*; London, Collins, 1976.

Colville, Sir John: *The Fringes of Power*; Hodder and Stoughton, London, 1985.

Cooper, Alfred Duff: *Old Men Forget*; Rupert Hart-Davis, London, 1953.

Couve de Murville, Maurice: *Une Politique Etrangère 1958–59*; Plon, Paris, 1971.

Daniel, Jean: *De Gaulle et L'Algérie*; Seuil, Paris, 1986.

Davies, Norman: *White Eagle, Red Star, The Polish–Soviet War, 1919–20*; Orbis, London, 1983.

Debré, Michel: *Mémoires* (3 vols.): Albin Michel, Paris, 1985–89.

Dixon, Piers: *Double Diploma, The Life of Sir Pierson Dixon*; Hutchinson, London, 1968.

Doughty, Robert A.: *The Seeds of Disaster*; Archon, Hamden, Connecticut, 1985.

Dulac, André: *Nos Guerres Perdues*; Paris, Fayard, 1969.

Dulong, Claude: *La Vie Quotidienne à l'Elysée au temps de Charles de Gaulle*; Hachette, Paris, 1974.

Eden, Anthony (Earl of Avon): *The Eden Memoirs*; Cassell, London, 1965.

Eisenhower, Dwight D.: *Crusade in Europe*; Heinemann, London, 1949.

Elgey, Georgette: *Histoire de la IVe. République* (2 vols.); Fayard, Paris, 1965–68.

Evans, Alfred J.: *The Escaping Club*; Penguin, Harmondsworth, 1943.

Farrell, Allan, SJ: *Jesuit Code of Liberal Education*; Milwaukee, Bruce Publishing, 1938.

Flohic, François: *Souvenirs d'outre-Gaulle*; Plon, Paris, 1979.

Footitt, Hilary and Simmonds, John: *France 1943–45*; Leicester University Press, Leicester, 1988.

Fouchet, Christian: *Mémoires d'hier et de demain* (2 vols.); Plon, Paris, 1971 and 1973.

Gaunson, A.B.: *The Anglo-French Clash in Lebanon and Syria, 1940–45*: Macmillan, London, 1987.

Gilbert, Martin: *Churchill, A Life*; Heinemann, London, 1991.

Gilbert, Martin: *The Churchill War Papers*, vol. 1; Heinemann, London, 1993.

Giles, Frank: *The Locust Years, 1946–58*; Secker and Warburg, London, 1991.

Greenhill, Denis: *More by Accident*; Wilton, London, 1992.

Griffiths, Richard: *The Reactionary Revolution, The Catholic Revival in French Literature, 1870–1914*; Constable, London, 1966.

Hettier de Boislambert, Claude: *Les fers de l'espoir*; Plon, Paris, 1978.

Horne, Alistair: *A Savage War of Peace*; Macmillan, London, 1977.

Horne, Alistair: *Macmillan, 1894–1956* and *Macmillan, 1957–86*; Macmillan, London, 1988 and 1989.

Horne, Alistair: *To Lose a Battle, France, 1940*; Macmillan, London, 1969.

Hurstfield, Julian: *America and the French Nation, 1939–45;* University of North Carolina Press, 1986.

Jebb, Gladwyn (Lord Gladwyn): *De Gaulle's Europe, or Why the General Says No*; Secker and Warburg, London, 1969.

Jebb, Gladwyn (Lord Gladwyn): *The Memoirs of Lord Gladwyn*; Weidenfeld and Nicolson, London, 1972.

Jouhaud, Edmond: *Serons-nous enfin compris?*; Albin Michel, Paris, 1984.

Jouhaud, Edmond: *La Vie est un Combat*; Fayard, Paris, 1975.

Joxe, Louis: *Victoires sur la Nuit*; Flammarion, Paris, 1981.

Kettle, Michael: *De Gaulle and Algeria 1940–1960*; Quartet, London, 1993.

Kissinger, Henry: *The Troubled Partnership*; McGraw Hill, New York, 1965.

Kitzinger, Uwe: *Diplomacy and Persuasion*: Thames and Hudson, London, 1973.

Krumeich, Gerd: *Armaments and Politics in France on the Eve of the First World War* (tr. Conn); Berg, Leamington Spa, 1984.

Lassus, Robert: *Le Mari de Madame de Gaulle*; Editions Jean-Claude Lattès, Paris, 1990.

Leahy, William: *I Was There*; Gollancz, London, 1950.

Malraux, André: *Les Chênes qu'on abat . . .*; Gallimard, Paris, 1971.

Massu, Jacques: *Baden 1968*; Plon, Paris, 1983.

Meribel, Elisabeth de: *La Liberté souffre violence*; Plon, Paris, 1981.

Monnet, Jean: *Mémoires*: Fayard, Paris, 1976.

Moran, Lord: *Churchill*; Constable, London, 1966.

Murphy, Robert: *Diplomat among Warriors*; Collins, London, 1964.

Newhouse, John: *De Gaulle and the Anglo-Saxons*; Deutsch, London, 1970.

Nicholas, H.G. (ed.): *Washington Despatches, 1941–45*; Weidenfeld and Nicolson, London, 1981.

Noguères, Henri: *Histoire de la Résistance* (5 vols.); Laffont, Paris, 1967–81.

Padberg, John, SJ: *Colleges in Controversy, The Jesuit Schools in France, 1815–80;* Harvard University Press, Cambridge, Massachusetts, 1968.

Pakenham, Thomas: *The Scramble for Africa*; Weidenfeld and Nicolson, London, 1991.

Palewski, Gaston: *Hier et aujourd'hui*; Plon, Paris, 1974.

Parodi, Jean-Luc: *Les rapports entre le Légistlatif et l'Exécutif sous la Ve. République*; Armand Colin, Paris, 1972.

Pickles, Dorothy, *The Fifth French Republic, Institutions and Politics*; Praeger, New York, 1966.

Pompidou, Georges: *Pour rétablir une vérité*; Flammarion, Paris, 1982.

Porch, Douglas: *The March to the Marne, The French Army 1871–1914*; Cambridge University Press, Cambridge, 1981.

Ralston, David: *The Army of the Republic, 1871–1914*; MIT, Cambridge, Massachusetts, 1967.

Reynaud, Paul: *La politique étrangère du gaullisme*; Juillard, Paris, 1964.

Roberts, Andrew: *The Holy Fox: A Life of Lord Halifax*; Weidenfeld and Nicolson, London, 1991.

Royer, Jean-Michel: *Les Petites Malices du Général*; Balland, Paris, 1990.

Rusk, Dean: *As I Saw It*; I.B. Tauris, London, 1990.

Sedgwick, Alexander: *The Ralliement in French Politics 1890–90*; Oxford University Press, Oxford, 1965.

Sherwood, Robert: *Roosevelt and Hopkins*; Harper, New York, 1948.

Soames, Mary: *Clementine Churchill*; Cassell, London, 1979.

Soustelle, Jacques: *Vingt-huit ans de gaullisme*; Tables Rondes, Paris, 1968.

Spaak, Paul-Henri: *Combats inachevés* (2 vols.); Fayard, Paris, 1969.

Spears, Edward: *Assignment to Catastrophe* (2 vols.); Heinemann, London, 1954.

Spears, Edward: *Two Men who Saved France*; Eyre and Spottiswoode, London, 1966.

Spears, Edward: *Fulfilment of a Mission*; Leo Cooper, London, 1977.

Thomas, R.T.: *Britain and Vichy, The Dilemma of Anglo-French Relations 1940–42*; Macmillan, London, 1979.

Thomson, David: *Democracy in France since 1880*; Cassell, London, 1989.

Tricot, Bernard: *Les Sentiers de la Paix, Algérie 1958–62*; Plon, Paris, 1972.

Tute, Warren: *The Reluctant Enemies*; Collins, London, 1990.

Vendroux, Jacques: *Yvonne de Gaulle, ma soeur*; Plon, Paris, 1980.

Verrier, Anthony: *Assassination in Algiers*; Macmillan, London, 1990.

Viansson-Ponté, Pierre: *Histoire de la République gaullienne* (2 vols.); Fayard, Paris, 1970–71.

Viansson-Ponté, Pierre: *Après de Gaulle, qui?*; Seuil, Paris, 1966.

Viorst, Milton: *Hostile Allies*; Macmillan, New York, 1965.

Werth, Alexander: *France, 1940–55*; Robert hale, London, 1956.

Wheeler-Bennett, John: *King George VI, his life and reign*; Macmillan, London, 1958.

Williams, Philip, and Harrison, Martin: *Politics and Society in de Gaulle's Republic*; Longman, London, 1971.

4. *Journals and other*

Periodicals:

Espoir: Institut Charles de Gaulle (quarterly).

En ce temps-là . . . de Gaulle: Hennin.

Historia: Editions Tallandier.

Franco-British Studies: British Institute in Paris (twice yearly).

The Salisbury Review (only vol. 8, no. 3, March 1990).

Paris-Match (particularly Nov. 1970; Henri Amouroux interview with de Gaulle).

TV:

LMK Images: *De Gaulle vu d'ailleurs* (3 parts); first broadcast in Nov. 1990.

Papers submitted to the seminar '*De Gaulle en son siècle*' held at UNESCO in Paris, 19–24 November 1990 (7 vols.); Institut Charles de Gaulle/Plon/Documentation Française, Paris, 1991.

ACKNOWLEDGEMENTS

The author and publisher have made every effort to trace all copyright holders to obtain permission for various excerpts quoted in the book which require such permission. The author also wishes to make it clear that he is the translator of all French texts except where indicated. The translation of de Gaulle's speech at Tunis on 27 June 1943, which appears in the front matter, is by Helen Waddell and quoted in D. Felicitas Corrigan, *Helen Waddell: A Biography* (page 325); Victor Gollancz Ltd, London, 1986.

The author and publisher are grateful for the following permissions: Cassell plc, for quotations from Winston S. Churchill, *The Second World War*; HarperCollins (Fontana) for material from François Kersaudy, *Churchill and de Gaulle*; HarperCollins for material from Warren Tute, *The Reluctant Enemies*; Harvill for material from Jean Lacouture, *De Gaulle*, vols. 1–3; Hodder & Stoughton Ltd for quotations from Sir John Colville, *The Fringes of Power*; Librairie Arthème Fayard for quotations from Pierre-Louis Blanc, *Charles de Gaulle au soir de sa vie*; Librairie Ernest Flammarion for quotations from Louis Joxe, *Victoires sur la nuit*; Mrs David Bowes-Lyon for quotations from Sir John Colville, *Footprints in Time*; Viscount Norwich for quotations from Alfred Duff Cooper, *Old Men Forget*; Lord Sherfield and Mr George Ball for quotations from unpublished letters; Random House UK Ltd (Hutchinson) and the Estate of Mary Borden for quotations from Mary Borden, *Journey Down a Blind Alley*.

For pictures reproduced in the book, the following sources are acknowledged: Archives de Gaulle – Giraudon (1, 2, 3, 4, 5, 8, 9, 13,

23, 24 & 30); Frank Spooner Pictures (12, 16, 29, 34 & 35); the Centre for the Study of Cartoons and Caricature, University of Kent at Canterbury, and John Appleton (31); Keystone (10, 15, 20, 21 & 22); Keystone/Sygma (7); Imapress (17); Magnum/Cartier-Bresson (18); Roger Viollet (19); André Lefebvre (33); and Philippe de Gaulle, *De Gaulle* (Plon, Paris, 1989) for photos from the private collection of Philippe de Gaulle (25, 26, 27, 28 & 32).

INDEX

N.B. A family relationship to General de Gaulle is indicated in bracket.